T0331826

China's Healthcare System and Reform

This volume provides a comprehensive review of China's healthcare system and policy reforms in the context of the global economy. Following a value-chain framework, the 16 chapters cover the payers, the providers, and the producers (manufacturers) in China's system. It also provides a detailed analysis of the historical development of China's healthcare system, the current state of its broad reforms, and the uneasy balance between China's market-driven approach and governmental regulation. Most importantly, it devotes considerable attention to the major problems confronting China, including chronic illness, public health, and long-term care and economic security for the elderly. Burns and Liu have assembled the latest research from leading health economists and political scientists, as well as senior public health officials and corporate executives, making this book an essential read for industry professionals, policy-makers, researchers, and students studying comparative health systems across the world.

LAWTON ROBERT BURNS is James Joo-Jin Kim Professor in the Health Care Management Department at the Wharton School, Co-Director of the Roy & Diana Vagelos Program in Life Sciences and Management at the University of Pennsylvania, and Programme Leader for Healthcare Management at the Indian School of Business. He is co-editor of the popular textbook *Health Care Management: Organization Design and Behavior* (2012) and the author of *India's Healthcare Industry* (Cambridge, 2014), *The Business of Healthcare Innovation* (Cambridge, 2012), and *The Health Care Value Chain* (2002).

GORDON G. LIU is a PKU Yangtze River Scholar Professor of Economics at Peking University National School of Development and Director of PKU China Center for Health Economic Research (CCHER). He sits on China's State Council Health Reform Expert

Advisory Committee and the UN Leadership Council of Sustainable Development Solution Network (SDSN). He was the president of Chinese Economists Society (CES) for 2004–2005. He has served as associate editor for academic journals including *Health Economics, China Economic Quarterly*, and *Value in Health*.

China's Healthcare System and Reform

Edited by

LAWTON ROBERT BURNS
The Wharton School, University of Pennsylvania

GORDON G. LIU
Peking University National School of Development, Beijing

CAMBRIDGE
UNIVERSITY PRESS

University Printing House, Cambridge CB2 8BS, United Kingdom

One Liberty Plaza, 20th Floor, New York, NY 10006, USA

477 Williamstown Road, Port Melbourne, VIC 3207, Australia

4843/24, 2nd Floor, Ansari Road, Daryaganj, Delhi – 110002, India

79 Anson Road, #06–04/06, Singapore 079906

Cambridge University Press is part of the University of Cambridge.

It furthers the University's mission by disseminating knowledge in the pursuit of
education, learning and research at the highest international levels of excellence.

www.cambridge.org
Information on this title: www.cambridge.org/9781107164598
DOI: 10.1017/9781316691113

First published 2017

A catalogue record for this publication is available from the British Library

Library of Congress Cataloging-in-Publication Data
Burns, Lawton Robert, editor | Liu, Gordon G., editor
China's healthcare system and reform / edited by Lawton Robert Burns, Gordon G. Liu.
Cambridge, United Kingdom : New York : Cambridge University Press, 2017. | Includes
bibliographical references and index.
LCCN 2016031778 | ISBN 9781107164598 (hardback) | ISBN 9781316616468 (pbk.)
MESH: Health Care Reform | Health Policy | China
LCC RA395.C53 | NLM WA 540 JC6 | DDC 362.10951–dc23
LC record available at https://lccn.loc.gov/2016031778

ISBN 978-1-107-16459-8 Hardback
ISBN 978-1-316-61646-8 Paperback

Additional resources for this publication at www.cambridge.org/burns

Contents

Figures

Tables

Contributors

M. Kate Bundorf is Associate Professor of Health Research and Policy at the Stanford University School of Medicine; Associate Professor, by courtesy, at the Stanford Graduate School of Business; and a Stanford Health Policy Fellow. She is also Faculty Research Fellow at the National Bureau of Economic Research. She received her MBA and MPH from the University of California at Berkeley and her PhD from the Wharton School. She was a Fulbright lecturer and visiting professor at Fudan School of Public Health in Shanghai, China, in 2009 and 2010. Her research, which focuses on health insurance markets, has been published in leading economics and health policy journals and has received funding from the US National Institutes of Health, the Agency for Health Care Research and Quality, and the Robert Wood Johnson Foundation. Specific research topics include the determinants and effects of individual and purchaser choices, the effects of regulation in insurance markets, the interaction of public and private systems of health insurance, and incentives for insurers to improve healthcare quality. Bundorf received the 13th Annual Health Care Research Award from the National Institute for Health Care Management in 2007.

Lawton Robert Burns is the James Joo-Jin Kim Professor, Professor of Health Care Management, and Professor of Management in the Wharton School at the University of Pennsylvania. He is also Director of the Wharton Center for Health Management & Economics and Co-Director of the Roy & Diana Vagelos Program in Life Sciences and Management. He received his doctorate in Sociology and his MBA in Health Administration from the University of Chicago. Dr. Burns taught previously in the Graduate School of Business at the University of Chicago and in

the College of Business Administration at the University of Arizona.

Dr. Burns has analyzed physician–hospital integration and integrated delivery networks over the past 30 years. In recognition of this research, Dr. Burns recently received the 2015 Distinguished Research Scholar Award from the Academy of Management and its Health Care Administration Division. He was named the Edwin L. Crosby Memorial Fellow by the Hospital Research and Educational Trust in 1992. Dr. Burns has also published several papers on hospital systems, physician group practices, accountable care organizations (ACOs), managed care, and price transparency. He spent the last 15 years studying the healthcare supply chain. He completed a book on supply chain management in the healthcare industry, The Health Care Value Chain (Jossey-Bass, 2002), and a recent analysis of alliances between imaging equipment makers and hospital systems. These studies focus on the strategic alliances and partnerships developing between pharmaceutical firms/distributors, disposable manufacturers, medical device manufacturers, group purchasing organizations, and organized delivery systems. He has also edited The Business of Healthcare Innovation (Cambridge University Press, 2012), which analyzes the healthcare technology sectors globally: pharmaceuticals, biotechnology, medical devices, and information technology. Most recently, he has served as lead editor of the sixth edition of the major text Healthcare Management: Organization Design & Behavior (Delmar, 2011). His latest book is India's Healthcare Industry (Cambridge University Press, 2014).

Tsung-Mei Cheng, JD, MA, is Health Policy Research Analyst at the Woodrow Wilson School of Public and International Affairs, Princeton

University, USA. Cheng's current research focuses on cross-national comparisons of health systems in East Asia, health reforms in China and Taiwan, health technology assessment and comparative effectiveness research, healthcare quality, financing, payment reform, including evidence-based clinical guidelines and clinical pathways, and pay for performance (P4P) in East Asian health systems.

Cheng is an advisor to the National Institute for Health and Care Excellence International (NICE International) of the United Kingdom, which advises governments and agencies overseas on capacity-building for evidence base to inform national health policy as well as knowledge transfer among decision makers across national borders. She is also an advisor to the China National Health Development Research Center (CNHDRC), the official Chinese government think tank for health policy under China's National Health and Family Planning Commission (formerly the Ministry of Health). In addition, Cheng serves as a special advisor to the Center for the Study of Major Policies (CSMP), Tsinghua University, China. Cheng is a member of the editorial board of Health Affairs, the leading US health policy journal. Cheng is also a member of the Emerging Market Symposium (EMS) Steering Committee – an Oxford University–based initiative that addresses pressing sectoral issues facing emerging market countries.

James Deng is one of the most influential healthcare industry leaders in China with over 25 years' management experience in multinational companies. He was the first healthcare MNC China CEO with Chinese nationality when he was appointed as the president and CEO for Novartis Pharma China back in 2006. He is now Vice President, General Manager for Becton, Dickinson and Company Greater China, and also the elected Chairman of AdvaMed China Council Board for two consecutive terms. James has lectured on healthcare strategy in emerging markets in Wharton School MBA classes. James is a physician by training and also a graduate from China Europe International Business School (CEIBS) MBA class and Harvard General Management Program (GMP).

Karen Eggleston is Senior Fellow at the Freeman Spogli Institute for International Studies (FSI) at Stanford University and Director of the Stanford Asia Health Policy Program at the Walter H. Shorenstein Asia-Pacific Research Center at FSI. She is also Senior Fellow with the Center for Innovation in Global Health at the Stanford University School of Medicine and Faculty Research Fellow of the National Bureau of Economic Research. Eggleston earned her PhD in Public Policy from Harvard University in 1999. She has an MA in Economics and Asian Studies from the University of Hawaii and a BA in Asian Studies summa cum laude (valedictorian) from Dartmouth College. Eggleston studied in China for two years and was a Fulbright scholar in Korea. Her research focuses on comparative healthcare systems and health reform in Asia, especially China; government and market roles in the health sector; payment incentives; healthcare productivity; and the economics of the demographic transition. She was a consultant to the World Bank on their project on health service delivery in rural China in 2004, to China's Ministry of Finance and the Asian Development Bank from 2010 to 2011 for an evaluation of China's health reforms, and to the World Bank/WHO/Government of China 2015 study on China's health service delivery system. She is a member of the Strategic Technical Advisory Committee for the Asia Pacific Observatory on Health Systems and Policies.

Vanessa Folkerts is Senior Manager for External Partnerships and Initiatives at United Family Healthcare (UFH, 和睦家医疗). UFH, the healthcare services division of Chindex International Inc., operates an expanding network of hospitals and clinics throughout mainland China, and is the only Joint Commission International–accredited healthcare system in Asia. She has been leading transactions ranging from the partial acquisition of Mongolia's first high-end private hospital in 2014 to the development of international referral networks for medical tourism and the opening of one of China's largest surgical training centers in 2015. She is currently managing a public–private partnership to establish China's first US-accredited medical school. Prior to working at UFH, Vanessa worked at Cedars-Sinai Medical Center in the Center for Neurosurgical Outcomes Research. She graduated from Princeton University with a BA in East Asian Studies.

Yanzhong Huang is Senior Fellow for Global Health at the Council on Foreign Relations and Professor and Director of the Center for Global Health Studies at Seton Hall University's School of Diplomacy and International Relations. He is the founding editor of *Global Health Governance: The Scholarly Journal for the New Health Security Paradigm*. Huang has written extensively on global health governance and public health in China. He has published numerous reports, journal articles, and book chapters, including articles in *Survival, Foreign Affairs*, *Journal of Health Politics*, *Policy and Law*, as well as op-ed pieces in the *New York Times*, *International Herald Tribune*, and the *Lancet*, among others. He is author of *Governing Health in Contemporary China* (Routledge 2013). He is frequently consulted by major media outlets, the private sector, and governmental and nongovernmental organizations on global health issues and China. He has taught at Barnard College and Columbia University. He received his BA and MA from Fudan University and PhD from the University of Chicago.

Sam Krumholz is currently in the PhD program in Economics at the University of California, San Diego, where he is focusing on labor, environmental, and development economics. Sam has worked with the PKU China Center for Health Economic Research (PKU CCHER) on several projects relating to the economic and health effects of China's recent healthcare reform. Prior to beginning his PhD, Sam received a master's in Public Policy from the University of California, Los Angeles, where he worked on domestic health policy issues.

Ambar La Forgia is a doctoral student at the Department of Health Care Management and in the Wharton School, University of Pennsylvania. Ambar's research focuses on the industrial organization of healthcare, particularly, integrated healthcare, physician networks, physician practice management, and the role of competition on hospital and physician cost and quality. To further these interests, Ambar worked as a summer associate with the Congressional Budget Office to study competition on the healthcare exchanges. She is funded by the National Science Foundation graduate research fellowship in Economics.

Prior to her doctoral studies, Ambar worked in Washington DC as a policy analyst for the Quantitative Economics and Statistics (QUEST) group of Ernst and Young. At QUEST, she worked exclusively on health industry topics, including company compliance with the Medical Device Excise Tax and nonprofit hospital compliance with uncompensated care requirements. Ambar holds a BA from Swarthmore College, where she graduated in 2011 from the honors program in Economics and Mathematics.

Gerard M. La Forgia is Lead Health Specialist at the World Bank, currently working out of Washington for the East Asia Region with primary responsibility for China. He was formerly the bank's lead health specialist in India, Brazil, and Central America. He has published books on service delivery reform in China (2016), health insurance in India (2012), hospital performance in Brazil (2008), and health systems reforms in Central America (2005). He is also the author of a number of articles and technical reports on health systems in developing countries. Before joining the World Bank, he was a research associate at the Urban Institute and a senior health specialist at the Inter-American Development Bank. He has a ScD in Health Service Administration from the University of Pittsburgh.

Rachel Lee has been advising companies on their China strategy for over a decade. She was a partner and managing director of the Boston Consulting Group in its Shanghai office. In this capacity, she co-led the healthcare practice, published viewpoints, and spoke at industry conferences. She also briefly served as the country manager for Shire Pharmaceuticals prior to returning to the United States. Rachel holds an MBA from the Wharton School. She is a native of Nanjing, China and currently lives in San Diego, California.

Xiaofeng Liang is Deputy Director of the Chinese Center for Disease Control and Prevention (China CDC) and Director of the Tobacco Control Office of China CDC since 2011. Dr. Liang earned his medical degree at Shanxi Medical University in 1984 and then went to Gansu Province and served as a staff member of Gansu Health Bureau (1984–1992). Between 1993–1995, he obtained his Master's in Public Health from the College of Public Health of Peking University of Medicine. After that, he was an exchange scholar at the Department of Psychiatry and Behavioral Sciences, College of Medicine, University of Miami, Florida, USA (1996–1998).

He returned to China in 1998 and was the vice-director of Epidemic Prevention Station of Gansu Province (1999–2000), vice-director of the Institute of Epidemiology and Microbiology, Chinese Academy of Preventive Medicine (2000–2001), and the director of National Immunization Program, the subcenter of China CDC (2001–2011).

He was a member of the Global Strategic Advisory Group of Experts on Immunization from 2008 to 2013. He was also a member of the Chinese Committee Advisory of Immunization Practice, Chinese Association of Community Health, and Chinese Association of Prevention Medicine (Branch of Biological Products).

As the deputy director of China CDC, his research in public health led to advances in immunization, vaccination, and vaccine-preventable disease control in China. Currently, he has switched to non-communicable diseases control, nutrition, and tobacco control. He is the author of more than 30 articles in national and international journals, such as the *Lancet* and the *New England Journal of Medicine*.

Roberta Lipson is Chief Executive Officer and President of United Family Heathcare (UFH), Chindex International, Inc. Roberta co-founded Chindex in 1981 and launched the United Family Healthcare hospital brand in 1997. Under her direction, UFH has become the market leader in high-end private healthcare in China. In 2015, Lipson secured financing for the expansion of the healthcare system in a buyout that valued the company at $463 million. Lipson is an active member of the business community in Beijing. She is a governor of the American Chamber of Commerce – China, a director of the US–China Business Council, and chairwoman of the United Foundation for China's Health, the charitable arm of Chindex. Lipson holds a BA from Brandeis University and an MBA from Columbia University.

Gordon G. Liu is a PKU Yangtze River Scholar Professor of Economics at Peking University (PKU) National School of Development, Vice-Chairman of PKU Faculty of Economics and Management, and Director of PKU China Center for Health Economic Research (PKU CCHER). His research interests include health and development economics, health reform, and pharmaceutical economics. Prior to PKU National School of Development, he was a full professor at PKU Guanghua School of Management (2006–2013); associate professor at the University of North Carolina at Chapel Hill (2000–2006); and assistant professor at the University of Southern California (1994–2000). He was the 2004–2005 President of the Chinese Economists Society and the founding chair of Asian Consortium for the International Society for Pharmacoeconomics and Outcomes Research (ISPOR). Dr. Liu has served as associate editor for academic journals including *Health Economics, Value in Health* (The ISPOR official journal), and *China Economic Quarterly*. Dr. Liu sits on China's State Council Health Reform Expert Advisory Committee and the UN SDSN Leadership Council, where he co-chairs the Health Thematic Group.

Nan Luo is Assistant Professor in Saw Swee Hock School of Public Health at the National University of Singapore (NUS). Before joining NUS, Dr. Nan Luo was a research fellow at the University of Alberta and Institute of Health Economics (Alberta, Canada). As a health services researcher, Nan Luo's research interests are measurement of patient-reported outcomes and economic evaluation of health technologies. His main expertise is developing and validating measures of patient-reported outcomes and health-state utilities. Nan Luo has authored and co-authored more than 100 original research papers in peer-reviewed journals.

Steven M. Sammut currently holds an appointment as Senior Fellow, Health Care Management, and Lecturer, Entrepreneurship, at the Wharton School of the University of Pennsylvania, and visiting faculty at the healthcare programs at the Indian School of Business, the Strathmore Business School, and the Recanati School of Tel Aviv University. He teaches and lectures extensively on the biotechnology industry, its growth prospects, and its responsibilities for serving global needs. His research focuses on human resource capacity building in healthcare and life sciences in the emerging markets.

His 40-year career has included numerous roles as a founder and CEO of biotechnology companies, as well as a partner in biotechnology venture capital funds. He holds graduate and undergraduate degrees from Villanova University in biological sciences and ethics, holds an MBA from the Wharton School, and is a DBA candidate at the Fox School of Business at Temple University.

Claudia Süssmuth-Dyckerhoff has been Senior Partner at McKinsey's Greater China Office and has been with McKinsey for more than 20 years – the last 11 years in China/Asia. She led McKinsey's Asia Health Systems and Services Practice and co-led McKinsey's Greater China Healthcare Practice. She joined McKinsey in 1995 in Switzerland. Since then, she has focused on working for healthcare companies – pharmaceutical/medical device companies, payor, provider and health systems in Europe, the United States, and, since January 2006, in Greater China and across Asia. In 1998, she joined the New Jersey Office for a 15-month period.

Most of her recent work focuses on market entry or market growth strategies, business development, assessment of potential privatization assets in the health services arena, commercial excellence, organizational redesign and capability building, post-merger integration, and operational performance improvement in hospitals.

In March 2016, she got elected as Board Member of Roche and in April 2016 she got elected as Board Member of Clariant. For McKinsey, she now acts as Senior Advisor.

Claudia holds a PhD in Business Administration from the University of St. Gallen/University of Michigan, Ann Arbor, focusing on strategy and organization, and she holds an MBA from ESADE in Barcelona. She publishes regularly on consumer and healthcare trends in China and is the proud mother of four boys and a little girl.

Florian Then is Partner at McKinsey's Shanghai office where he is a co-leader of McKinsey's Greater China Healthcare Practice. He joined McKinsey in 2007 and has since worked extensively with health systems, healthcare providers, and in the health insurance field. He has spent seven years in China. Florian is a physician by background, trained in Munich, Boston, and Nanjing. He completed his doctoral thesis in tumor immunology. After working in clinical medicine for some time, he moved on to pursue postdoctoral studies at Institute for Neurodegenerative Disease at Massachusetts General Hospital.

Margaret Triyana is currently Assistant Professor at the Division of Economics at Nanyang Technological University, Singapore. She holds a PhD and a BS from the University of Chicago, and was previously the Asia Health Policy Postdoctoral Fellow at the Shorenstein Asia-Pacific Research Center at Stanford University. Triyana's main research interest lies at the intersection of development and health economics, particularly regarding how social policies affect health outcomes for the poor, early health investments, and health-seeking behavior in limited resource settings. Her recent work includes measuring the effects of a conditional cash transfer on healthcare prices and the long-run effects of a community-based midwife program.

Yan Wang (王燕) is Deputy Director of the Division of Disease Control and Prevention, Health and Family Planning Commission of Shandong Province. She earned her PhD from Shandong University in 2007 and was a visiting scholar with the Asia Health Policy Program at the Shorenstein Asia-Pacific Research Center, FSI, Stanford University, in 2009–2010.

John Whitman has been active in the field of aging and long-term care for over 30 years. For the past 29 years, he has taught at the University of Pennsylvania's Wharton MBA Healthcare

Management Program and has twice received the coveted Excellence in Teaching Award. John is on the Board of the Philadelphia Corporation for Aging (PCA), the third largest Area Agency for Aging in the nation, and recently completed a term on the Dean's Advisory Board of Drexel University's School of Public Health.

John is a graduate of the Wharton MBA Healthcare Management Program and an active member in the Alumni Association, where he served as president and received the Alumni Achievement Award. He has also taught at LaSalle University, Villanova University, and the University of Pennsylvania's School of Nursing. In addition, John has presented at over 400 national, state, and local professional organizations on a wide array of topics related to care of seniors.

Winnie Yip is Professor of Health Policy and Economics at the Blavatnik School of Government, University of Oxford, and Senior Research Fellow of Green Templeton College, Oxford, where she directs the Global Health Policy Program. She is also Adjunct Professor of International Health Policy and Economics at Harvard School of Public Health, where she was a faculty member before moving to Oxford. Winnie received her PhD in Economics from the Massachusetts Institute of Technology and BA in Economics from the University of California, Berkeley.

Winnie's primary research interests include: (1) the design, implementation, and evaluation of health system interventions for improving affordable and equitable access and delivery of quality healthcare, especially for those most in need and (2) modeling and evaluating the effects of incentives on the behavior of providers (organization and individual) and patients. In addition, she is an expert on China's healthcare system. Her works have been funded, among others, by the Bill and Melinda Gates Foundation, the Health Result Innovation Trust Fund (HRITF) of the World Bank, the National Science Foundation (US), the European Union Commission and the Economics and Social Science Research Council (UK).

Winnie is a member of the Institute of Medicine (US) Standing Committee to Support USAID's Engagement in Health Systems Strengthening, the United Nations Sustainable Development Solutions Network's Health for All Thematic Group on the post-2015 sustainable development goals and strategies, and the Lancet Global Surgery Commission to promote affordable access and delivery of effective and safe surgical care worldwide. She has served as consultant to the World Bank and the World Health Organization and has extensive executive training experience in Asia, especially China. In addition, she is Associate Editor of *Health Economics*, *The Journal of the Economics of Ageing*, and *Health Systems and Reform*, and an editorial board member of *Health Policy, Health Economics, Policy and Law* (Cambridge University Press).

Zhongyun Zhao is Director of Global Health Economics at Amgen. Before joining Amgen, Dr. Zhao worked for Merck-Medco, Eli Lilly, and Johnson & Johnson in the United States and China National Commission of Development and Reform in Beijing, China. He received his PhD in Economics from the University of Southern California. His research interests include health economics, outcomes research, market access, and health policy, primarily in therapeutic areas of oncology, neuroscience, and cardiovascular disease. Dr. Zhao has authored and co-authored more than 250 manuscript, poster, and abstract publications.

Sen Zhou is a doctoral student in Economics of Education and International Comparative Education program at the Stanford Graduate School of Education. She holds a BA in Law from Beijing International Studies University and an MA in Economics of Education from Peking University. Her interests include higher education, educational choices, health economics, and literacy development. Her dissertation is on the distribution of higher education opportunities in China.

Foreword

A national healthcare system has many interconnected sectors composed of public and private organizations. These sectors, circumscribed by the governance structure and the dynamics of the marketplace, interact with each other. China, a nation with a vast landmass and 1.38 billion people, has a complex bifurcated healthcare system that affects the sectors. The financing and delivery systems are different for urban and rural residents. There is no comprehensive book that informs interested people and students about the intricate and multifaceted Chinese healthcare system. The editors of this volume, Lawton Robert Burns and Gordon G. Liu, have undertaken an ambitious endeavor in giving a comprehensive coverage of the sectors in China's healthcare system. They have assembled a group of experts to write on these different sectors. The editors' ambitious coverage also extends to the recent Chinese health system reforms since 2009.

In order to understand China's current healthcare system, its various sectors with their behavior and performance, the reader must grasp the history of Chinese health policies that molded the system. The traumatic shift from central planning to a market-driven healthcare after the liberalization of the Chinese economy in 1978 caused China's healthcare system to become convoluted with contradictory goals and incentives for healthcare providers and health-product producers such as pharmaceutical companies. The health reforms introduced since 2009 have tried to correct some of the previous haphazard policies and the resulting discordant governance and incentive structures that impacted the various sectors.

China's health policy that governs the health system vacillates between the public sector goal of equity and the efficiency that a free market with its driving force of profit motive can bring. Equity was the hallmark of China under the Chinese Communist government prior to 1978. The economic liberalization in 1978 sharply reduced government revenues and prompted the switch to private household financing. Nevertheless, the government wanted to assure that most people had access to affordable basic healthcare by regulating health service prices, setting them below the actual costs. At the same time, the government allowed profit margins on drugs and new diagnostic and laboratory tests so that providers could earn income and profits to sustain themselves. Under this policy, the government induced its public providers (i.e., hospitals and clinics) to become for-profit public organizations to garner their income in an unregulated (other than prices) marketplace. To generate income and profits, providers resorted to vast over-treatment, over-prescribing, and over-testing. Meanwhile, the producers (i.e., pharmaceuticals and medical devices), who supplied the technological inputs to the providers operating in this distorted marketplace, responded accordingly. The production and distribution of pharmaceuticals became the key Chinese sector to drive up the cost of healthcare. In short, the development of China's healthcare system since 1978 can best be understood by viewing it through the lens of China's attempts to balance equity and capricious market forces.

The bifurcation of the Chinese healthcare system between urban and rural was largely due to the financial survival of providers, who mainly depended on what their patients were able and willing to pay (until the 2009 reform). With the huge income disparity between China's rural and urban residents, partly a result of the residency (*hukou*) system, the providers in urban and rural communities offer vastly different healthcare in terms of quality and sophistication. When the demand and supply of healthcare depends largely on patients' income, the affluent and the poor also access vastly different healthcare. In sum, China has third-world as well as first-world healthcare, coexisting side by side, as the cover of this book suggests.

This book organizes the sectors in the healthcare system in three categories: the *providers* (physicians, hospitals, and long-term care facilities), *payers* (public and private insurance, drug approval, and reimbursement), and *producers* (pharmaceuticals, medical technology, and biotechnology). The editors and authors break new ground by bringing the producers into the picture, offering analysis and new information about the less-documented side of China's healthcare system. The editors also address the critical sector of human resources and medical education.

In sum, *China's Healthcare System and Reform* is a groundbreaking book that gives a more holistic understanding of China's healthcare system by organizing the information into sectors. It will stimulate policy analysts to think about how to design policy to create the "best" governance and incentives for interactions among the sectors. It will stimulate the managers in each sector about how to strategize the future of their businesses in dealing with the other sectors. Lastly, this book paves the way for researchers to examine the dynamic interactions between the sectors, a desired effort in deepening our knowledge of healthcare systems globally.

William C. Hsiao, PhD
K.T. Li Research Professor of Economics
T.H. Chan School of Public Health
Harvard University
January 2016

Preface

It is a daunting task to analyze the entire healthcare system of any country. One reason is that there is no real "system" of healthcare. Rather, there are multiple firms that (a) span multiple industry sectors, such as hospitals, physicians, insurers/insurance funds, and pharmaceutical companies (b) transact with one another and (c) respond to a complex web of regulatory and reimbursement regimes (d) developed by multiple government ministries/agencies at various geographic levels. In other words, the healthcare system is a confusing mess. This is true of every country. The two editors have taught for years on the structure and functioning of their native systems (the United States and China). The lead editor has also published an analysis of India's healthcare system that consumed 600 pages of print.

Although challenging, the task is important. One cannot understand any particular segment of one's own healthcare system without knowing (a) how it impacts, and is impacted by, developments in other adjacent segments, and (b) how it is shaped by government regulation and policy. With regard to the first assertion, the editors discovered long ago that both the quality and cost of care are inextricably tied to the behavior of physicians practicing inside and outside the walls of hospitals, as well as to the methods used by insurers to reimburse both sets of providers. With regard to the second assertion, the second editor has long been engaged in policy formation in China with an end to changing provider behavior, making healthcare services more accessible and affordable, and increasing the capacity of the delivery system to provide higher quality care and satisfy unmet demand.

Moreover, the task is particularly important for China as the country invests heavily in improving the capacity and skill levels of its delivery system, the breadth and depth of its insurance schemes, and the quality and accessibility of new medical technologies. The country is so large, both in terms of population and geographic size, that these investments will likely fuel rising public expectations and costs of care.

The opportunity to pursue this task and prepare this volume arose serendipitously from the initial meeting of the two editors in August 2009. Professor Burns traveled with a small contingent of Wharton faculty members to China to learn about the Chinese context and incorporate more global lessons into both their research and classrooms. During this trip, he spent a day with Professor Liu and his health economics research team. At the time, Gordon was on the faculty of the Guanghua School of Management, Peking University's business school, and was already centrally involved in the ongoing state health reforms in China. The two editors exchanged perspectives on the US and Chinese healthcare systems and the impending reforms in both countries.

At the same time, the Wharton School developed a strategy of "global modular courses" (GMCs) to teach global subject matter in countries around the world. GMCs were MBA courses taken for credit by Wharton students who (along with the professor) would fly to distant sites for one to two weeks. Professor Burns taught the first such GMC on "India's Healthcare System" at the Indian School of Business in 2010 and then again in 2011. In 2012, professors Burns and Liu collaborated on a second healthcare GMC, a joint MBA course on "The Chinese Healthcare System and Reform," hosted at Guanghua and attended by both Wharton and Guanghua students. They repeated the course in 2013. The instructors invited Chinese executives and consultants from the healthcare industry to teach several of the class sessions. They, along with professors Liu and Burns, author many of the chapters in this volume. The editors also asked several leading scholars on China from around the world to contribute additional chapters that nicely round out the book's content.

The book has thus been six years in the making. The rough outline of chapters has evolved in an iterative fashion to become this text. This evolution has occurred as China's healthcare reforms have unfolded and the country's healthcare issues have become more striking. The book has also evolved as the editors developed a collegial network of researchers all focused on the same issues. We are very thankful that they have joined us in this endeavor. They are all first-rate scholars who are well known in their own right. Working together and with them has been perhaps one of the most gratifying experiences the editors have ever had. We trust you will enjoy reading this as much as we enjoyed writing it.

Acknowledgments

Lawton Robert Burns

I first wish to thank Wharton's Vice Dean for Wharton Global Initiatives, Professor Harbir Singh. Harbir not only encouraged me to travel to China in August 2009 as part of a Wharton Faculty immersion but also arranged the site visit to the Guanghua School of Management and my first meeting with Professor Gordon G. Liu. Harbir subsequently encouraged me to teach Wharton's first GMC on "India's Healthcare Industry" (2010) and a subsequent GMC on "China's Healthcare Industry and Reform" (2012). When asked to do the latter, I immediately reached out to Gordon to assist me with the course and stage it at the Guanghua School of Management.

I cannot thank Gordon enough for his willingness to co-teach the class with someone he barely knew and who was a relative newcomer to both global health and the Chinese context. Gordon shared a lot of research and invaluable insight into China's healthcare system to help me get up to speed. Based on my experience at Wharton and other business schools, it is unusual for economists like Gordon to teach and write with management professors like myself. We are trained very differently, think very differently, and conduct research very differently. After six years of dialogue and collaboration, Gordon and I have found it very easy to work together in compiling this volume.

I also thank Professor Ziv Katalan, Managing Director for Wharton Global Initiatives, who steadfastly supported and encouraged me in teaching both GMCs. Ziv actually flew to one of the sites and attended class in order to assist me. I am also grateful to Wharton's Dean, Geoffrey Garrett, who graciously attended a "master class" on China's healthcare system that I taught in Beijing during the summer of 2014.

In fashioning the course curriculum and lecture material, I necessarily relied on a lot of people who have studied the topic for some time. These included, first of all, Professor Liu, a distinguished scholar of China's healthcare system. I also relied heavily on several Wharton and Guanghua teaching assistants, all of whom were Chinese and had worked in the industry, or had studied various sectors in China. They include (in alphabetical order): Di Cai, Cang Fu, Vivian Hsu, Jennifer Lee, Tianyue Ruan, Yonghui Shi, Xi Xie, Ying Zhang, and Yanan Zhu. I have also learned a considerable amount from the healthcare industry executives who came to speak to our Guanghua class or sent me background reading material (again, in alphabetical order): Chuan Chen, James Deng, James Huang, Rachel Lee, Xiaofeng Liang, Roberta Lipson, Katherine Lu, Li Ma, Jeff Towson, Jian Wang, Xiaobin Wu, and Xin Zhang. Finally, I wish to thank some of my friends in the consulting community who shared with me presentations on China's healthcare industry: Claudia Suessmuth-Dyckerhoff and Jonathan Wang.

Every author knows the singular importance of a good editor and editorial help. Many thanks to Chris Harrison and Paula Parish at Cambridge University Press for adroitly seeing the potential of a volume like this. My administrative assistant, Tina Horowitz, did excellent work in editing this entire volume. I hired her exclusively for this task and she did not disappoint.

Finally, I want to thank my wife, Alexandra, who initially suggested to me that I ought to get more "global" in my research and consider countries like China. She has patiently endured the last nine months as Gordon and I prepared this volume.

Gordon G. Liu

First of all, my greatest thanks go to Professor Robert Burns for inviting me to join in this great effort to prepare this volume. It has been an honor and a wonderful opportunity to co-teach the joint Wharton–Guanghua MBA course on China's healthcare system and reform held four years ago at PKU's Guanghua School of Management. It was really his idea, courage, and leadership to develop such a comprehensive syllabus for the class, followed by his highly professional and patient guidance in editing the book. I have enjoyed greatly and learned so much from Robert throughout the class and the editorial work.

Second, I wish to thank our teaching assistants for the class and my research assistants for assisting me in editing some of the chapters. In particular, I want to thank Mr. Sam Krumholz for his major contribution to a chapter we have co-authored in this volume, and also for his extremely helpful assistance in my other related research. Sam is currently pursuing his PhD in Economics at UCSD. I am also very grateful to the students from both Wharton and Guanghua, who took the class in 2012 and 2013, for their contribution through active participation, discussion, and feedback. Their contribution was crucial to making this volume more comprehensive and interesting.

Finally, I want to join Robert again in thanking all the chapter contributors for their input to this volume. I trust we will find more opportunities in the future to conduct collaborative work.

PART I

Introduction

Analytic Framework, History, and Public Health

China's Healthcare Industry

A System Perspective

LAWTON ROBERT BURNS AND GORDON G. LIU

Introduction

To western readers, analyzing a new healthcare system in the East might seem daunting. Indeed, it takes some of us decades to master an understanding of the healthcare system of our origin country. Nevertheless, there are several methods for approaching an analysis of another country's healthcare system. These include exposition of some (hopefully) invariant principles regarding healthcare that apply across contexts: analysis of what a system of health might look like; comparison with the US system (with which many are already familiar); comparison with other emerging systems such as India; application of existing frameworks for healthcare system analysis; and an appraisal of the major transitions under way in the country's socioeconomic, epidemiologic, and economic profile. This chapter analyzes China's healthcare system using each of these methods.

Some Invariant Principles of Healthcare Systems

The Iron Triangle

One way to analyze a healthcare system is in terms of a set of principles that are (or at least seem to be) invariant across cultural contexts. One principle is that every system aspires to achieve both efficiency and effectiveness. "Efficiency" encompasses three intermediate ends: ensuring access to healthcare, promoting the quality of healthcare, and controlling the cost of healthcare. "Effectiveness" encompasses three corresponding ultimate ends: public satisfaction, positive health outcomes, and financial protection.

A related principle is the "iron triangle" depicted in Figure 1.1. The logic of this triangle is that there

are inevitable societal trade-offs in pursuing any of the goals (vertices) in the triangle.[1] If the triangle is an equilateral triangle, and thus each angle is 60 degrees, policy initiatives that expand one angle beyond 60 degrees force one or both of the other two angles to contract below 60 degrees. Thus, efforts to promote access to care (e.g., via insurance coverage) will lead to higher demand for care, rising utilization, and higher costs. Similarly, efforts to promote quality by virtue of enabling access to modern technologies (drugs, medical devices, and equipment) will also likely raise costs. Determining the right thrust and mix among the three angles constitutes the balancing act in resource allocation faced by most countries.

Perhaps no country allocates equal attention to all three goals in the manner of an equilateral triangle. Indeed, healthcare policy in the United States has alternated its focus and attention between these three angles since the late 1920s. In the 1960s, policy makers focused on expanding access to healthcare services via broader insurance coverage by enacting the Medicare and Medicaid programs (to cover the elderly and poor, respectively). In subsequent decades, the policy focus shifted to cost containment to deal with the rising utilization and cost of services that naturally followed from expanding access to insurance for population segments with greater need for healthcare services. During the past decade, policy makers have devoted more attention to quality via such initiatives as pay-for-performance (P4P), value-based purchasing (VBP), accountable care organizations (ACOs), and "never events" (reimbursement withheld for controllable adverse events in hospital episodes).

China faces challenges in pursuing each of these three goals. With regard to *cost*, national health expenditures in China have risen exponentially since the start of the new millennium (see Figure 1.2). Indeed, China seems poised to emulate the trajectory of spending in other western countries. Moreover, a large percentage of all healthcare is financed out of pocket by the population. Until recently, there has been little health insurance or other forms of risk pooling. The new health insurance schemes enacted in the new millennium now cover most of the population for basic hospital benefits and have only recently begun to implement (or call for) supplemental insurance protection against catastrophic costs. There is also little accountability of providers and a predominance of fee-for-service payment, all of which are associated with high costs. Finally, there is questionable efficiency of the roughly 50–60 percent of the healthcare system financed directly or indirectly (via social insurance) by government sources, with little measurement of inpatient utilization and appropriateness of care.

With regard to *quality*, there is little effective regulation of providers, treatments, and medical products (often from spurious sources), considerable variation in the training and education of providers, and enforcement of laws and regulations at the national or provincial levels. There is considerable overuse of pharmaceuticals and IV solutions. There is also mixed evidence regarding the health of the Chinese population. On the one hand, China's rates of infant mortality, mortality of children under five years old, and life expectancy are all average compared to the region; on the other hand, China

Figure 1.1 The iron triangle of healthcare: balancing act

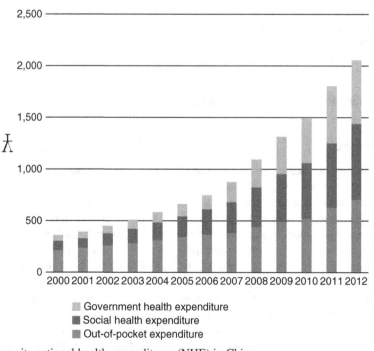

Figure 1.2 Per capita national health expenditures (NHE) in China

exhibits some of the highest declines in mortality rates and increases in life expectancy (covered below).

With regard to *access*, a substantial majority of the population still dwells outside of the cities where most (modern) healthcare facilities exist. Government spending on healthcare is disproportionately allocated to the urban areas rather than rural areas. Rural residents pay higher healthcare costs out of pocket as a percentage of household income. Access is also particularly problematic for the poor and migrant workers. Large variations also exist in the population's access to healthcare across China's provinces.

Countries like the United States and China face similar "iron triangle" trade-offs in sectors other than healthcare. For example, in the policy domain of energy, countries must balance their need for low-cost and efficient energy (cost angle) with low-emission and green energy (quality angle), and with rising demand and sustainable energy (access angle).

The balancing acts here seem formidable. Most economists believe it is impossible to achieve all three goals simultaneously and, thus, that trade-offs must be made.[2] After all, marketing executives believe that in order to position their product against the offerings of competitors, they must excel on one dimension (product cost, quality, or service) and seek parity on the other two. Optimization on all three is rarely considered (and is more rarely observed).[3] Nevertheless, there have been periodic efforts in the United States to pursue all three goals, usually in the context of national healthcare reform. The Health Security Plan (better known as the Clinton Health Plan) sought to do all three; more recently, the Patient Protection and Affordable Care Act (PPACA, better known as Obama Care) is likewise seeking to achieve all three. Underlying the new reform is "the triple aim": improved experience of care, reduced per capita cost, and improved health of the population (accomplished partly by enabling access to preventive services).[4] The jury is out regarding whether the triple aim is achievable, although there are organizations (e.g., Institute for Healthcare Improvement) actively involved in training providers on how to do so. Even its proponents recognize, however, that while the three goals

are interdependent, sometimes they are negatively associated with one another (i.e., trade-offs are required).[5]

This discussion is pertinent to China's healthcare system and subsequent chapters in this volume because the country has historically undertaken a series of initiatives that seek to solve the iron triangle in the delivery of healthcare services. Nearly every healthcare reform undertaken by the Chinese government has espoused the goal to make healthcare more affordable, higher in quality, and more accessible to its population. The 2009 reform's goal is "to establish a basic, universal health system that can provide safe, effective, convenient, and low-cost health services to all of China's 1.38 billion citizens."[6]

Market Failure

Other principles observed in the US healthcare system also likely apply to China and elsewhere. These include the principle of market failure: i.e., non-competitive market conditions in the healthcare industry that inhibit the efficient operation of supply and demand. These features include lack of price information and pricing transparency; lack of data on product quality; the resulting inability to assess the comparative value (defined as quality divided by cost) of products and services; asymmetric information between providers and consumers; imperfect agency relationships between physicians and their patients; the heavy role of government as both a buyer and regulator; and moral hazard flowing from insurance coverage. Such features lead to distortions in market efficiency.

Principles Inherent in Healthcare Reform

Several principles emanating from healthcare reform efforts around the world may comprise an additional set of invariant principles. These include the reality of ever-rising healthcare costs (driven by population demographics and technological improvements, among other factors); rising public expectations from healthcare (driven by economic growth and rising national incomes, as well as increased global travel and immigration); the limited capacity of nations to afford the growing demand of their populace for increasingly expensive healthcare; and increased skepticism regarding traditional methods of organizing and managing healthcare finance and delivery (e.g., the breakdown of centrally planned systems, as well as the recognition of market failures).[7]

Healthcare System Defined

A second way to study another country's healthcare system is through formal definitions. The phrase "health system" is widely used in discourse on global health (e.g., health systems strengthening) but enjoys no agreed-upon definition.[8] "Health system" actually combines two nebulous terms. The first is "health." According to the World Health Organization (WHO), "health" is "a state of complete physical, mental, and social well-being, and not merely the absence of disease and infirmity."[9] "Health" has also been defined as an important capability "that enables individuals to pursue things they might value."[10] There are as many indicators of health as there are definitions. These include life expectancy at birth, infant mortality rates, the percentage of children underweight, the percentage of women with body mass index (BMI) below 18.5, quality-adjusted life years (QALYs), and disability-adjusted life years (DALYs). Comparative historical data suggest that China has outpaced other developing countries on many of these indicators (see Table 1.1). Getting a comprehensive picture of a country across lots of indicators is impossible and probably futile. The United States, for example, is commonly lambasted for ranking relatively poorly among developed countries on infant mortality; on other indicators, however, such as cancer survival, the United States ranks quite highly.

The concept of a "system" is also rather elusive. Piecing together definitions from several dictionaries, we might define a system as a whole comprised of several interdependent parts that have differentiated roles, are interconnected by three processes (input, throughput, output), and thus are integrated in a holistic fashion. Such a comprehensive definition begs the question: does any country have a "system" of healthcare? The payer, provider, and producer components found in any country's healthcare industry are surely interdependent and interconnected (in the sense of serving one another as buyers and suppliers). But are they really integrated? And do they commonly focus on the provision of "health" as defined above?

The answer to both questions is likely "no." There are few collaborative partnerships between these sectors in the United States.[11] As noted earlier, there are huge disconnects between them in terms of their goals and incentives. Moreover, these sectors are commonly oriented to funding and delivering acute *care*, rather than promoting the *health* of the population. The latter would require greater emphasis and funding of prevention, healthcare promotion, and public health activities. Health, as defined in this section, is typically left to the public health system in most countries. What, then, does the United States have if not a system that delivers health? The reality more closely resembles a collection of public and private sector entities (e.g., firms, individuals, governmental bodies, professional associations) that pursue their individual interests, pursue one or more of the goals in the iron triangle, and may or may not interact with the patient.

Harvard University researchers define a healthcare system in a similar fashion as the collection of institutions and actors who provide healthcare (e.g., doctors, nurses, hospitals, pharmacies, and traditional healers); the organizations that supply specialized inputs to the providers (e.g., training schools, manufacturers of products); the financial intermediaries, planners, and regulators who control, fund, and influence the providers (e.g., insurers, government agencies, regulatory bodies); the organizations that offer preventive services; and the financial flows that finance the provision of healthcare.[12]

The World Health Organization defines a healthcare system more simply but more broadly as "all of the activities whose primary purpose is to promote, restore or maintain health."[13] In addition to the list of actors and institutions mentioned throughout this section, this definition of a healthcare system also includes health-enhancing interventions such as road improvements and environmental safety efforts. It also includes the efforts of informal healthcare givers in the home, behavioral change interventions conducted by employers or governments, and efforts

Table 1.1 China's health improvements relative to other countries

Age-standardized death rates, YLL rates, YLD rates, and life expectancy at birth and health-adjusted life expectancy at birth for 1990 and 2010, both sexes combined

Country	Age-standardized death rate (per 100,000) 1990 Rate	Rank	2010 Rate	Rank	Age-standardized YLL rate (per 100,000) 1990 Rate	Rank	2010 Rate	Rank	Age-standardized YLD rate (per 100,000) 1990 Rate	Rank	2010 Rate	Rank	Life expectancy at birth 1990 LE	Rank	2010 LE	Rank	Health-adjusted life expectancy at birth 1990 HALE	Rank	2010 HALE	Rank
Algeria	762	2	584	1	23,346	5	15,484	4	12,395	6	12,215	11	70.9	3	75.5	2	60.3	6	64.2	3
El Salvador	809	4	661	5	26,931	8	18,474	6	12,585	10	11,781	7	69.6	7	74.2	5	59.5	8	63.9	5
Albania	666	1	653	4	19,166	1	15,110	3	11,609	3	11,628	5	73.1	1	74.9	4	63	1	64.6	2
Ukraine	913	7	917	11	22,976	4	23,559	10	11,316	2	11,159	2	70	6	69.7	11	60.9	4	60.8	10
Marshall Islands	1,270	14	1,309	15	36,253	12	36,337	14	14,368	15	13,968	15	63.9	12	63.9	14	54	12	54.4	14
Tonga	914	8	882	10	22,822	3	22,195	9	12,546	9	11,940	9	70	5	70.4	10	60.1	7	61	9
Turkmenistan	1,144	12	919	12	39,780	14	24,522	12	11,911	5	11,933	8	62.8	13	69.3	12	54.4	11	60	11
China	**896**	**6**	**607**	**2**	**24,989**	**7**	**14,024**	**1**	**9,639**	**1**	**8,782**	**1**	**69.3**	**8**	**75.7**	**1**	**61.7**	**2**	**67.8**	**1**
Namibia	1,259	13	1,298	14	39,681	13	42,112	15	13,774	14	13,809	14	62.4	14	61.6	15	53.2	14	52.5	15
Samoa	1,088	11	863	9	28,245	9	21,441	7	12,397	7	11,587	3	67.2	9	70.8	7	58	9	61.5	7
Egypt	1,065	10	844	8	35,058	10	22,148	8	12,868	12	11,979	10	64.6	10	70.6	8	53.6	13	59.1	12
Guatemala	1,061	9	787	7	36,242	11	24,337	11	12,800	11	11,705	6	64.5	11	70.5	9	55.3	10	61	8
Armenia	809	5	674	6	24,125	6	17,197	5	11,778	4	11,588	4	70.3	4	73.9	6	60.6	5	63.7	6
Jordan	792	3	619	3	21,127	2	14,448	2	12,452	8	12,527	12	71.5	2	75.4	3	60.9	3	64	4
Vanuatu	1,507	15	1,291	13	41,590	15	34,595	13	13,346	13	12,657	13	61.6	15	64.3	13	53	15	55.7	13

Notes:

YLL = years of life lost to premature mortality

YLD = years lost to disability

HALE = health-adjusted life expectancy

to promote female education. The WHO explicitly acknowledges that their system definition does not imply any degree of integration among the activities and services performed.

United States versus China: Convergences and Divergences

A third method to approach another country's healthcare system is by way of comparisons and contrasts with one's own. There are a few commonalities worth noting at the national level. The United States is one of the world's oldest democracies, while China is one of the world's oldest countries. Both are distinguished by pluralistic systems of healthcare financing; both are currently seeking to simultaneously reform their financing and delivery systems and to reach nearly universal insurance coverage of their populations; and both need a concerted effort by their federal/central and state/provincial governments, along with considerable help from the private healthcare sector, in order to accomplish this reform. Both systems focus on the treatment of disease rather than the promotion of health. Finally, both offer a mix of allopathic and more traditional medicine (complementary and alternative medicine in the United States, traditional Chinese medicine in China) that formed the roots of their earlier healthcare delivery.

As noted in the Preface, healthcare systems in rapidly developing countries like China bear a number of remarkable similarities with the US context (see Table 1.2). Both countries (indeed, most countries around the world) worry about managing the iron triangle of healthcare: i.e., the difficulty in simultaneously pursuing the three goals of controlling healthcare costs while also expanding health insurance access to the population and improving the quality of care – for example, by ensuring access to new technologies and medicines. The affordability of healthcare is a common concern, especially with high and rising costs of hospitalization being a cause of impoverishment and personal bankruptcy in both countries.

There is also a common concern with geographic variations in healthcare spending, whereby more money is spent in some regions than in others (e.g., rich vs. poor states/provinces, urban vs. rural areas); there is the parallel concern with geographic disparities in health status (which may or may not result from spending variations). Another common concern is that the population's lifestyle and personal behaviors contribute to chronic illness and increase healthcare spending. There is a common concern with supplier-induced demand – i.e., that providers over-prescribe and over-treat as one means to increase their incomes – and the conflicts of interest that providers have with one another

Table 1.2 Convergence between China and the United States

• Concern with iron triangle	• Hospital waste and inefficiency
• Affordability of healthcare	• Fee-for-service payment system
• Seeking universal coverage via healthcare reform	• Falling out-of-pocket spend as percent of health costs
• Concern with hospital costs as cause of impoverishment/ bankruptcy	• Mixture of financing mechanism: government, employer, individual
• Concern with high costs of technology as percentage of healthcare costs	• Fragmentation between federal and state government funding
• Hospital competition via technology wars	• Effort to balance market approach with regulatory approach
• Concern with chronic illness	
• Concern with geographic variations in spending and health status	• Low consumer literacy and information
• Concern with conflicts of interest and supplier-induced demand	• Local government competing priorities: education, services, health
• Concern with lifestyle issues and behaviors	• Experimentation with new payment models
• Need to develop primary care delivery system	• Integrate allopathic with complementary and alternative medicine

Table 1.3 Divergences between China and the United States

System Dimension	China	United States
• Spend per capita on healthcare	Low	High
• Government spend as percent of NHE	Low	High
• Private health insurance	Low	High
• Depth and breadth of insurance coverage	Low	High
• Role of public sector hospitals	High	Low
• Preference for private providers	Low	High
• Centralized purchasers	Low	High
• Role of central government in healthcare	Low	High
• Governance mechanisms to monitor providers	Low	High
• Measures of utilization, appropriateness	Low	High
• System of outpatient care/primary care	Low	High
• Amount of money spent on pharmaceuticals	High	Low
• Integration of hospitals and pharmacies	High	Low
• Integration of physicians and hospitals	High	Low
• Role of hospitals in public health	High	Low
• Locus of conflict	Doctor–patient	Doctor–hospital
• Physician payment	Salary	FFS
• Standardized doctor training	Low	High
• Role of medical profession	Low	High
• Hospital length of stays	Long	Short
• Smoking viewed as major problem	No	Yes

(e.g., incentives and kickbacks for referrals) and with product manufacturers whose products they may be incented to (over) use.

There are numerous other similarities between the United States and China. Both operate a fee-for-service system combined with other payment approaches to reimburse providers. Both also include a mix of financing mechanisms that include payments from the federal/central government, state/provincial governments, employers, and individuals. As a result, both feature fragmentation between federal and provincial government efforts, and contend with the reality that provincial governments have many competing priorities for their limited budgets (e.g., education, social services, healthcare). Both desperately need to develop and invest in a broader capacity for primary care delivery (in terms of numbers and accessibility of providers), and both must confront a low degree of consumerism in getting their populations to take better care of themselves.

Despite the evident similarities, there are important differences in the details between the two countries (see Table 1.3).

The US spends roughly 18% of GDP on healthcare, with wide spending variations across geographic regions. Concerns over geographic variations in the US stem from parallel concerns with over-utilization and wasted resources. China spends only 5–6% of its GDP on healthcare. In China, geographic variations are framed as issues of societal inequities, especially between rural and urban populations, in resource allocation and access to healthcare.

In the US, the primary care movement argues for patient-centered medical homes (PCMH) that augment the solo physician's office with information technology (e.g., an electronic medical record) and physician extenders (e.g., nurse practitioners). In China, by contrast, the concern is with both rural and urban populations bypassing lower acuity providers to seek outpatient care services at tertiary hospitals. Another issue is the low level and variable (and sometimes nonexistent) training of primary care practitioners outside of major cities.

In the US, consumerism is focused heavily on getting people to respond to financial incentives (e.g., through cost-sharing), to utilize information on provider costs and quality in their provider search and purchasing decisions, and to change their lifestyles. In China, by contrast, consumerism is much more basic: the government wants its population to be more active consumers of healthcare by increasing their domestic consumption and save less. The country also wants to address the lack of information among the population regarding the availability of healthcare services (as well as the effects of unhealthy behaviors like smoking).

The hospital and insurance sectors in the US have suffered stagnating growth for the past decade; in China, by contrast, these two sectors have been booming, due to heavy government investments as part of current healthcare reforms. China is witnessing an explosion in hospital capacity and insurance coverage, and is encouraging entry by the private sector into both.

Finally, hospitals and physicians in the US have been seeking to integrate over the past 20–25 years; in China, by contrast, most physicians are fully employed by public hospitals due to their common government ownership and sponsorship. In China, all hospitals also operate pharmacies for outpatient drug sales, drawing huge criticism as the central cause of the over-prescribing problems in China.

Beyond these differences in institutional details, there are several divergences dealing with financing, delivery, and regulation. In contrast to the United States: (a) China has spent relatively *little* per capita on healthcare; (b) its government accounts for a smaller share of national spending on healthcare, while out-of-pocket costs represent a greater proportion of total healthcare spending; (c) the government plays a strong role in healthcare provision (e.g., hospitals, physicians); (d) there are no powerful, centralized purchasers of healthcare services (outside of drugs) dealing with providers, such as large insurance companies; (e) there has been little private health insurance coverage; (f) there are only weakly developed governance mechanisms overseeing providers' behavior, with resulting concerns dealing with overutilization; (g) there are few mechanisms and incentives in the system to promote outpatient care in non-hospital clinics; and (h) the population

favors treatment by public sector providers over the private sector.

China, India, and Other Emerging Countries

A fourth approach to understanding the healthcare system in China is by comparison with other emerging countries. In many of these countries, government lacks the infrastructure to levy taxes on workers in the large informal sector of the economy. This limits the tax base (which is relatively low compared to GDP) and thus the public funds available for healthcare investments. Cultural issues, divisions within government, the lack of political will, competing political jurisdictions, and competing investment needs all prevent efforts to redistribute what is collected. To the degree that public funds are invested in healthcare, they tend to go toward large public hospitals in urban areas rather than smaller primary care–oriented clinics in rural areas. The latter are poorly capitalized, poorly staffed and equipped, and offer poor access with long waiting times. Patients often bypass local facilities to seek care in large cities. Most patients pay for healthcare out of pocket, and often pay providers "informal payments" for better treatment and greater access.

We can draw these analyses more sharply by comparing China and its neighbor, India. Both countries have historically had large rural populations, while China has experienced rapid urbanization. Both countries also have rapidly growing economies, dramatic declines in poverty, and rising demand for healthcare services.[14] Until recently, both countries have lacked widespread insurance coverage: the Chinese central government has implemented broad coverage in the last two decades, while in India state governments and voluntary schemes have helped to increase insurance coverage to roughly one-quarter of the population. Both countries are concerned about access to affordable primary and specialty care, are increasingly concerned with the rising costs of healthcare, and are witnessing rising healthcare costs as a significant cause of impoverishment. Nevertheless, both countries spend a small percentage of their gross domestic product (GDP) on healthcare.

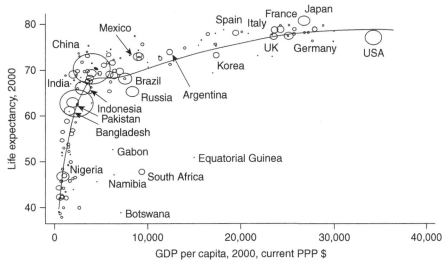

Figure 1.3 The Millennium Preston curve
Source: http://www.thelancet.com/journals/lancet/article/PIIS0140-6736(06)69746-8/abstract.

In addition, both countries are located on the upward sloping portion of the Millennium Preston curve, which depicts the association between GDP per capita and life expectancy (see Figure 1.3). Both China and India can be expected to move up this curve as their GDP grows; the United States is an outlier. China's provinces can be arrayed along a similar curve: provinces with higher per capita incomes also exhibit higher life expectancy at birth.

The logic behind the association depicted in the curve is straightforward. Increased societal wealth can be channeled to greater investments in education, literacy, and public health, as well as purchases of health insurance and healthcare services that improve health status and longevity. The curve suggests that further improvements in health status (i.e., reduced mortality) may be achieved in these developing countries by greater societal spending on healthcare as a percentage of GDP. Not all economists agree, however, that the relationship in the curve is causal (i.e., that increasing income leads to longer life expectancy).[15] Indeed, improvements in health can come without any increase in societal wealth, and vice versa. In some developing countries like India and China, the dramatic improvements in health occurred prior to periods of great economic growth or during only small intervals of those growth periods. Moreover, it may be the case that to the degree there is any causality, it may be more that increasing health leads to increased societal wealth (an issue addressed empirically later on).

Why does the Millennium Preston curve quickly bend and begin to flatten out?

Not all spending is productive toward the end of greater longevity. Recent research suggests that greater spending on "home run" technologies and treatments – i.e., those that are cost-effective and useful for nearly all patients in the population, such as antibiotics for bacterial infections, aspirin and beta-blockers for heart attack patients, antiretroviral drugs for patients with HIV/AIDS, improved health behaviors – contributes the most to improved health outcomes and survival. Greater spending on potentially cost-effective technologies with heterogeneous benefits across patients (e.g., angioplasties with stents, imaging tests, antidepressants, Cesarean sections) can also improve productivity and health but with rapidly diminishing returns as more of the population uses these treatments. Finally, greater spending on technologies with modest or uncertain effectiveness (e.g., arthroscopic surgery for knee osteoarthritis, referrals to specialist physicians, vertebroplasty, intensity-modulated radiation therapy for prostate cancer) is likely to result in only marginal health improvements while substantially increasing costs.[1]

A related explanation for the flattening portion of the curve in Figure 1.3 is that much of the increased spending is devoted to treating the chronically ill population.[2] Such spending does not cure chronic illness but only helps to manage their conditions. Research from the United States documents that 46 percent of the population with one or more chronic conditions account for 84 percent of all healthcare spending.[3]

A third perspective on the flattening curve is historical. Research suggests that declines in mortality (and thus increases in life expectancy) have traversed three phases: improved nutrition and economic growth (mid-1700s to mid-1800s), investments in public health (mid-1800s to early 1900s), and then investments in medical interventions such as antibiotics and vaccines and medical technology (1930s to the present).[4] In the poorer countries of the world, recent improvements in life expectancy have occurred as a result of the rapid introduction of public health measures and basic medical interventions, as well as broader social factors such as rising incomes, literacy, and nutrition. Once these rapid gains have been achieved, further progress proves more difficult.

A final explanation for the flattening curve is that increased spending on healthcare is not always associated with increased quality or other health outcomes. Figure 1.4 depicts the likely association between cost and quality of healthcare. Some portion of the population does not receive the healthcare that is appropriate (underuse); here, improved cost results in improved quality. Another portion receives healthcare that is unnecessary but not necessarily harmful (misuse); here, improved cost has no effect on quality. Another portion receives healthcare that is both unnecessary and harmful (overuse); here, higher cost leads to lower quality.

1. Amitabh Chandra and Jonathan Skinner. 2011. "Technology Growth and Expenditure Growth in Health Care," NBER Working Paper 16953 (Cambridge, MA: National Bureau of Economic Research).
2. Gordon Liu, Yao Yao, Nianyu Du et al. 2015. *Health and Economic Prosperity* (Beijing: Peking University National School of Development).
3. Hamilton Moses, David Matheson, Ray Dorsey et al. 2013. "The Anatomy of Health Care in the United States," *Journal of American Medical Association* 310(18): 1947–1964.
4. Cutler et al. 2006. "The Determinants of Mortality."

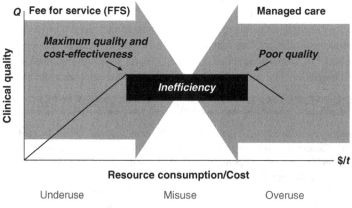

Figure 1.4 Issues behind cost–quality relationship

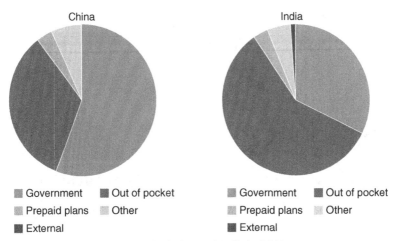

Figure 1.5 Healthcare financing structures in China and India in 2013
Source: WHO Global Health Observatory (2015).

Following the chaos of the World War II era, both China and India defined healthcare as the responsibility of their provinces/states, which have many other duties and inadequate funds to perform them. Both countries have divided public responsibility for healthcare between the federal/central government (regulation and a relatively low level of financing) and state/provincial governments (financing and provision of care). Both governments assume a small share of total healthcare spending and require their populations to bear a large percentage of total healthcare costs by paying out of pocket for services (see Figure 1.5). The bulk of public funding goes for wages and salaries of employees in public facilities, in lieu of the financing of technologies or advanced services. There is thus little money available to actually target health conditions. Both countries also feature a three-tiered structure of healthcare delivery to a largely rural population (e.g., barefoot doctors in the villages, primary health centers at the local level, and community health centers and hospitals at the district and small city level). In both countries providers are paid primarily on the basis of fee for service, have incentives for over-utilization and problems of induced demand, receive informal payments from patients, and face issues of corruption in the management of public hospitals. And in both countries there is the "double disease burden" of communicable and non-communicable (i.e., chronic) diseases to tackle among the increasingly affluent urban population.

There are several important institutional differences between the two countries, however. China has placed greater emphasis on the public sector provision of healthcare services, as evidenced by the much higher percentage of beds found in public hospitals; by contrast, India has a more developed private sector of delivery and more private investment in public hospitals. China's government has also pursued more public financing of healthcare and wider population coverage via public insurance schemes, has set prices that private sector providers can charge, and has a more developed regulatory apparatus (although with weak enforcement). In contrast to India, China has also increased its healthcare spending as a percentage of GDP at a faster rate since the middle of the 1990s. China's system also features a more developed system of hospital care and a tiny private sector in the provision of services. China, unlike India, has also made a sustained commitment to disease eradication among the young and pursued policies backed by resources and social mobilization.[16] Finally, China embarked on economic reforms a full decade earlier than India (1980s vs. 1990s), giving China a head start on economic growth and attraction of foreign direct investment. As a result of these investments,

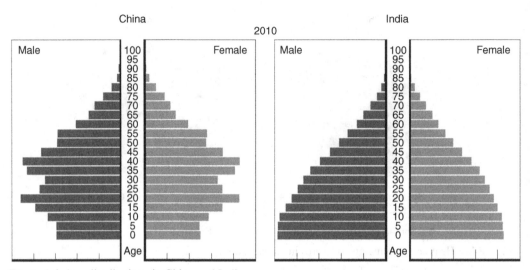

Figure 1.6 Age distributions in China and India
Source: RAND, *China and India: The Asian Giants Are Heading Down Different Demographic Paths* (2011).

China has two-thirds more nurses and midwives per 1,000 population, and 160 percent more physicians per 1,000 population compared to India. By contrast, India has benefitted from greater involvement of international donors (e.g., World Bank, International Monetary Fund, Gates Foundation, Clinton Foundation) in the direct financing of services and in supporting healthcare reforms (e.g., encouragement of partnerships with the private sector).

All of these differences manifest themselves in divergences in the health statistics of the two countries, according to the World Bank. India's infant mortality rate (41 per 1,000 live births; 2013 data) is more than three times the rate in China (11 per 1,000 live births). The mortality rate for children under five years of age (53 per 1,000 live births; 2013 data) in India is quadruple than in China (13 per 1,000 live births). Likewise, the percentage of births by skilled attendants in India (estimates ranging from 43 percent to 58 percent) is roughly half of the percentage achieved in China (97–100 percent).

There are also important demographic differences between the two nations. Unlike China, India did not impose family planning restrictions on its population. China thus has an older population than India, whose young citizens represent a quickly increasing

proportion of the population (see Figure 1.6): 28 percent of India's population is 0–14 years old, while only 8.1 percent are 60+ years old (2011 data).[17] For its part, China has a lower "dependency ratio" – defined as the percentage of non-working population to working population (42 percent vs. 60 percent in India).[18] China has a more literate population (due to its focus on primary education vs. India's focus on advanced education) that allows healthcare promotion to be more effective. These factors among others contribute to China's lower mortality rates and higher life expectancy.

Frameworks for Analyzing Healthcare Systems

A fifth way to approach a new healthcare system is through analytical frameworks. There are multiple frameworks one can use to analyze a country's healthcare system.[19] An early framework is the "actors" framework which classifies four major actors in a health system: providers, payers, regulators, and the population served. Another is the "funds flow and payment" framework that identifies seven major subsystems of financing (out of pocket, private reimbursement, public reimbursement, etc.).[20]

National Health Accounts

One widely used framework is the analysis of a country's "national health accounts" (NHA). These accounts rigorously classify the types and purposes of all expenditures made by/to all the actors in a healthcare system. Stated more simply, the accounts depict the sources and destinations of all healthcare spending in that country. Sources include government (both federal and provincial, and by public program) and non-government (employers, community insurance schemes, individual payments out of pocket); destinations include hospitals, physicians, dentists, retail pharmaceuticals and other products, public health, construction, etc. An NHA scheme allows for ongoing analysis of time trends in these money flows, which can serve as the basis for performance appraisal and stewardship. The Centers for Medicare and Medicaid Services (CMS) maintains these data for the United States over time. The Organisation for Economic Co-operation and Development (OECD) has developed an International Classification for Health Accounts to facilitate international comparisons.[21] The Chinese government has historically tracked the sources of healthcare spending coming from the government, social insurance, and out-of-pocket payments (see Figure 1.2).

Health Systems Strengthening

The NHA scheme itemizes investments at the country level and typically focuses on the investments undertaken by that country. By contrast, developing countries often are also the recipient of investments and income transfers from outside organizations and donors to tackle specific problems. The "health systems strengthening" framework tracks the activities and investments undertaken by different donors/funders to strengthen specific system components.[22] These investments are typically designed to make changes in the healthcare system and accomplish certain system goals. The components targeted include "health services" (staffing infrastructure, operational support systems), the "financing system" (e.g., health financing policies and legislation, resource generation, fund pooling, provider reimbursement system), "monitoring/evaluation and information system" (data analysis and reporting, disease surveillance), and "stewardship and governance" (e.g., planning, priority setting, management).

Functions, Objectives, and Priorities

Another method to analyze healthcare systems is to examine what they do: i.e., what functions they perform and what objectives they pursue. Functions include the creation of resources and inputs (investments, training), stewardship (oversight) of these resources, financing (pooling and purchasing), and the provision (delivery) of services. Objectives served include the production of health, fairness, and responsiveness to societal expectations.[23] Thus, for example, one framework analyzes the interplay between four functions (regulation, financing, resource allocation, and service provision) and four key actors (government, providers, payers, and patients).[24]

A complementary approach is to categorize the country's healthcare priorities (e.g., the various initiatives and interventions to reduce the disease burden in the population), the types of provider organizations and incentives given them to deliver the interventions, the other resource inputs required to achieve these initiatives (budgets, manpower, technology), and the specific financing mechanisms (e.g., revenue collection, pooling, purchasing).[25]

Building Blocks

The World Health Organization has described the framework of a healthcare system in terms of its basic building blocks. These include service delivery of effective, safe, quality personal and non-personal interventions; a health workforce that is adequate in numbers, competently trained, and fairly distributed; a health information system that produces, analyzes, and disseminates reliable and timely information; medical products and technologies that are safe, efficacious, cost-effective, and accessible; a financing system that raises adequate funds to ensure the population can use needed services and is protected from financial catastrophe; and governance and oversight of the above.[26] All six building blocks are viewed as essential for improving health outcomes.

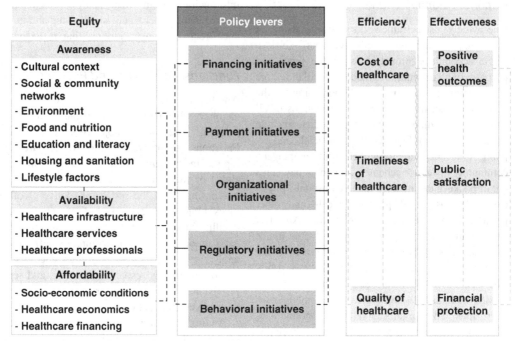

Figure 1.7 "Control knobs" framework
Source: Hsiao (2003).

Control Knobs

Researchers at the World Bank and the WHO have developed another framework ("control knobs") that analyzes the policy levers that can be used to impact the intermediate ends of cost, access, and quality (the vertices of the iron triangle) and hopefully the ultimate ends of improved health status, protection from the financial risks of illness, and consumer satisfaction.[27] These policy levers – the financing, payment, organizational, regulatory, and behavioral initiatives – are themselves conditioned by the country's economic, social, and cultural context (see Figure 1.7). Such a framework is helpful for understanding the broader societal and regulatory constraints within which a healthcare system operates.

As an illustration, we can apply a portion of Figure 1.7 to explicate some of the issues facing China's healthcare system. Looking at the left-hand column, the historical context that both directs and constrains policy initiatives includes the emphasis on public health; a dichotomous system that favors the urban population with access to more providers with higher technology over the (poorer) rural population; restricted access by China's migrant population; and the "proletarianization" of the medical profession under Mao. The cultural context includes health as the responsibility of the individual, stemming from Confucianism. This has resulted in higher out-of-pocket payments and a lower depth of insurance coverage. The system is further shaped by environmental factors, such as the prevalence of infectious diseases which led governmental health policy following the revolution to orient around "vertical health programs" to deal with such diseases on an individual basis rather than develop a comprehensive public health approach, but also to tackle problems of unclean water and sanitation.

Looking at the next column in Figure 1.7, we see that China is also hampered in terms of the "policy levers" at its disposal to change the system. With regard to *financing*, China spends roughly 5–6 percent of its GDP on healthcare, or about $400 per capita (2014 data, current US dollars). A large percentage of healthcare expenditures (ranging from

35 percent to 60 percent over the last 15 years) are paid out of pocket by the population, whereas the government (all levels) accounts for only about 25–35 percent. While there is an emergent private insurance sector, there is little means to finance broader access to healthcare.

With regard to *payment*, as noted above, China has a fee-for-service system that is poorly regulated and monitored less closely than in the United States. Providers typically have strong incentive to over-prescribe medicine, especially expensive drugs and devices, in the absence of alternative payment models (e.g., capitation, diagnosis-related groups (DRGs)). Among physicians, there is price regulation and transparency but little quantity transparency, few medical audits, and meager standard setting. With regard to *organization*, most providers work in the public sector and are employed by hospitals. Despite a growing number of private hospitals and government efforts to promote more hospital competition, the majority of hospital beds are publicly provided. The public also distrusts the private sector due to perceived pecuniary motives.

With regard to *regulation*, there has been little effective regulatory oversight and even less enforcement. Regulatory structures are relatively underdeveloped and diffused across central and provincial governments. For example, there are few efforts at mandatory registration, accreditation, and credentialing of providers, little in the way of regular service evaluations, and substandard quality control. There is also wide variation among hospitals regarding availability of equipment, record keeping, and staffing. Finally, with regard to *behaviors*, there is little consumerism, little professional self-control and monitoring, and few effective educational campaigns targeted at the population.

Of course, the model depicted in Figure 1.7 suggests a one-way causation that is likely inaccurate. Not only are the intermediate and ultimate ends of a healthcare system impacted by macroeconomic conditions, they can also determine them. There is growing evidence that societal health shapes societal wealth, as well as vice versa. For example, poor health is positively associated with absence from work, job loss, higher out-of-pocket spending, debt levels, and loan defaults – all of which contribute to lower income. In addition, poor health

among pregnant mothers and children is negatively associated with education and long-term cognitive development. There is also evidence that societal health shapes nation state security that, in turn, fosters economic growth.[28] Economists argue that a country's health status, incidence of illness, and likelihood of catastrophic illness heavily influence the country's labor force participation rates, labor productivity, savings and poverty rates, and healthcare demand and consumption. These latter forces influence, in turn, inflation rates, wage rates, exchange rates, and the country's fiscal health.[29] A later section explicates these relationships.

Value Chain

Another complementary framework is the healthcare value chain outlined in the Preface. According to this framework, a healthcare system can be studied in terms of the buyers and suppliers of products and services that make up this chain, who engage in the important market exchanges that comprise this system, and whose activities add value to system outputs as they move along the chain. The value chain of the US healthcare system is presented in Figure 1.8.

This framework highlights the upstream (supplier) and downstream (buyer) trading partners of any firm operating in a healthcare industry, the parties that may mediate these transactions, and the possible competitors and substitutes for the firm's product/service.

China has not yet developed all of the value-chain players depicted in Figure 1.8, but the nation's trajectory suggests continued expansion and eventual development of these stages. One depiction of China's healthcare system as a value chain is presented in Figure 1.9 covered in subsequent chapters.

OECD Data on Outcomes

Another framework analyzes the dynamics of healthcare system development by examining trends in the iron triangle dimensions of cost, access, and quality/outcomes across nations.[30] The analysis here examines health expenditures per capita, percent of GDP spent on healthcare, insurance coverage, hospital utilization and

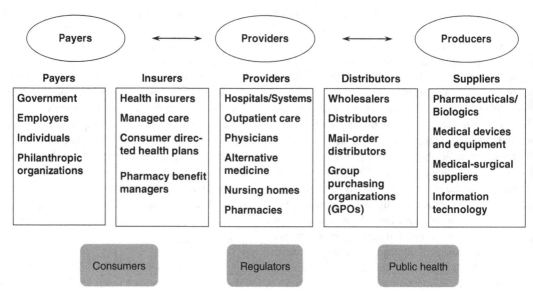

Figure 1.8 The healthcare value chain
Source: Lawton R. Burns, *The Health Care Value Chain* (2002).

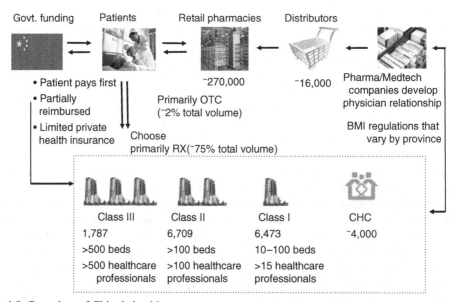

Figure 1.9 Overview of China's healthcare system

expenditures per capita, physician visits per capita, and such outcomes as life expectancy at birth, infant mortality, and disability days. Inferences in healthcare system development are derived from cross-national comparisons among these trends. One limitation of this framework for our purposes is that nearly all of the data (e.g., statistics assembled by the OECD) are drawn from western and fully

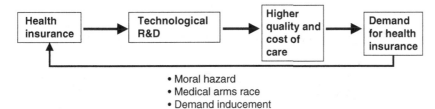

Figure 1.10 The healthcare quadrilemma
Source: Weisbrod, *Journal of Economic Literature* (1991).

developed nations, with little data from the developing countries in Asia.

The Healthcare Quadrilemma

A final framework shows the interplay of cost, access, and quality. The "healthcare quadrilemma" model suggests that efforts to address problems in access to healthcare by extending insurance coverage to previously uncovered segments of the population have multiple downstream effects (see Figure 1.10).[31] These include financial incentives to manufacturers and producers to invest more in technological research and development (R&D) since the costs of innovation are more likely to be covered. The resultant innovation appeals to both providers and patients and thus leads to widespread adoption; the innovation carries a higher price tag as well, leading to simultaneously higher costs and higher quality. As costs rise and care improves, there is subsequent demand for greater insurance coverage. This cycle offers one plausible explanation for the iron triangle dilemma noted above.

This model is quite germane to China today. Since the late 1990s, China has expanded insurance coverage to several segments of its population in a series of reform measures. An estimated over 95 percent of the population now has some level of (mostly inpatient) coverage. This rising coverage allows the population to access expensive hospital facilities and the technologies they offer; providers rely on the utilization of these services to cover their operating costs and generate their operating margins. Not surprisingly, medical suppliers and device companies are targeting these hospitals as customers for their expensive technologies and products.

Expanded insurance coverage also serves as a spur to the formation of domestic suppliers of these products who increasingly will compete with multinational companies to serve the higher-end market. The result will be more innovation and product proliferation. These developments will inexorably lead to higher utilization of hospitals and their services, which in turn will lead to higher quality of healthcare offered in these settings and the higher cost of services. All of this will lead to higher costs of providing healthcare and the need for greater insurance coverage to finance it.

Application of Frameworks to Major Transitions Under Way in China

China's healthcare system can thus be studied from the vantage point of each of the frameworks above. These frameworks are mostly static, however. We can also develop a dynamic model that draws on many of these frameworks to illustrate the dramatic changes under way in China's socioeconomic and epidemiologic characteristics using the systems perspective presented in Figure 1.11. These changes have been recently chronicled by a research team at Peking University, led by one of the co-editors of this volume.[32]

The logic of the left side of the figure is that changes in several pieces of a country's environmental context – such as public health, healthy lifestyles, and government spending on healthcare – can impact the health outcomes of the population. The figure draws on research in the United States that suggests there are four major determinants of the health of a population: lifestyle, environmental

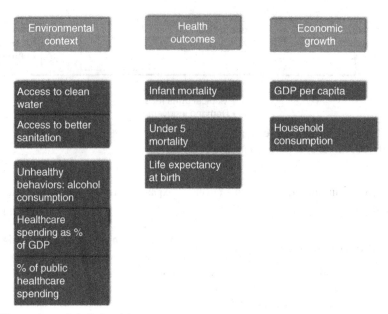

Figure 1.11 Dynamic model of transitions

conditions, genetics, and access to healthcare resources (see Figure 1.12). All but genetics are potentially mutable in the short term and thus amenable to policy interventions.

The logic of the right side of Figure 1.11 is that health outcomes promote economic growth.[33] A healthier population translates into several societal benefits that promote growth, including higher educational attainment, improved worker productivity, increased size of the labor pool, higher income, higher consumption and savings patterns, and higher foreign direct investment.[34] These trends and the hypothesized relationships between them are explored below.

Environmental Transitions

Environmental Hazards

China is currently plagued by several environmental hazards, as outlined later in Chapter 3. As a result, the country ranks fairly low among its neighbors – the members of the Asia-Pacific Economic Cooperation (APEC) – on several of these measures. For example, in 2012, China ranked 15th out of 17 countries on the percentage of the population with access to improved

sanitation; China also ranked 14th out of 18 countries in terms of the percent of its population with access to improved water. China has made enormous strides in the past two decades to clean up these particular elements in its environment. Between 2002 and 2012, China ranked second among APEC members in the percentage improvement in the population's access to improved sanitation and access to improved water. Figures 1.13 and 1.14 show the improvements between 1990 and 2012 on both dimensions in China have been quite dramatic. Such improvements are important because they help to reduce the population's exposure to pathogens and waterborne diseases (e.g., diarrhea).

Lifestyle Behaviors

According to a report issued by the World Health Organization on global health risks, the three top drivers of disease burden are three behaviors. They are undernourishment (underweight children), unsafe sex, and alcoholism. Alcohol consumption has become an enormous public health problem in China over the past decade. Between 2000 and 2010, China exhibited the highest increase in per

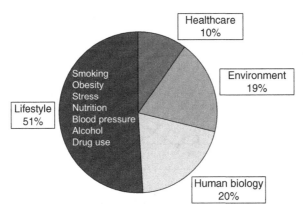

Figure 1.12 Health and healthcare
Source: McGinnis, J.M. Foege, W.H. "Actual Causes of Deaths in the US," *JAMA* 270(18): 2207–2212 (1993).

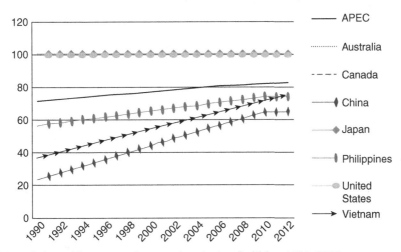

Figure 1.13 Population with access to improved sanitation facilities, 1990–2012

capita alcohol consumption among APEC members (see Figure 1.15). Much of this increase is attributed to the country's rapid economic growth and rise in average per capita incomes.

Healthcare Spending

Healthcare spending per capita in China has historically been among the lowest among APEC members and globally. In 2012, China spent only $322 per capita, ranking the country 14th out of 19 APEC members (with an average spend of $2,012). Between 2002 and 2012, healthcare spending per capita in China increased by only $268, compared to the APEC average of $1,146. Similarly, China's level of healthcare spending as a percentage of GDP ranked the country only 11th out of 19 APEC members (5.4 percent vs. an average of 6.8 percent). Between 2002 and 2012, China's spending as a percent of GDP rose by only 0.6 percent (compared to the APEC average of 1.0 percent).

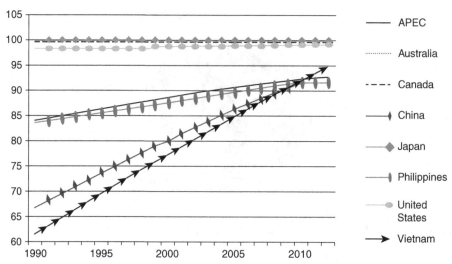

Figure 1.14 Population with access to improved water sources, 1990–2012

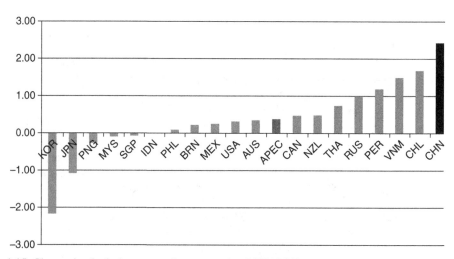

Figure 1.15 Change in alcohol consumption per capita, 2000–2010

The story is slightly different, however, for the government's share of this healthcare spending. In 2012, China ranked 10th out of 19 APEC members with 56 percent of national health expenditures contributed by government (compared to the APEC average of 60.1 percent). Between 2002 and 2012, China exhibited the highest increase in the government's share of spending, rising 20 percent versus the APEC average of 4 percent (see Figure 1.16).

Health Outcome Transitions

Mortality Rates

China has historically exhibited high rates of infant mortality per 1,000 live births and mortality for children under age 5. In 2012, the country ranked 13th out of 19 APEC members on both measures. China's infant mortality rate was 12.1 and under-5 mortality rate was 14.0 (versus the APEC average of

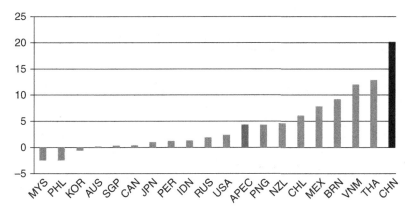

Figure 1.16 Percentage change in public health spending, 2002–2012

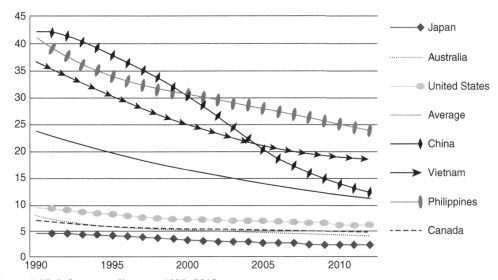

Figure 1.17 Infant mortality rate, 1990–2012

11.9 and 14.6, respectively). However, China has made astonishing progress in reducing its mortality rates: between 2002 and 2012, the country ranked first among APEC members in the percentage improvement achieved on both measures. This progress is even more apparent over a longer time period from 1990 to 2012 (see Figure 1.17 for infant mortality).

What explains these improvements? Falling infant mortality has resulted from government efforts to reduce famine and poverty, as well as to improve the living conditions of its population and increase public access to healthcare facilities. Falling rates of under-5 mortality have been impacted by reduced malnutrition, improved access to primary care, and improved access to medical treatment and technologies by children.

Life Expectancy

In 2012, life expectancy in China was 75.2 years, compared to the APEC average of 76.4. This put

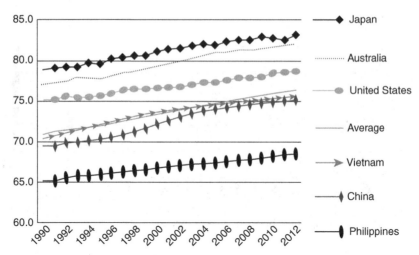

Figure 1.18 Life expectancy at birth, 1990–2012

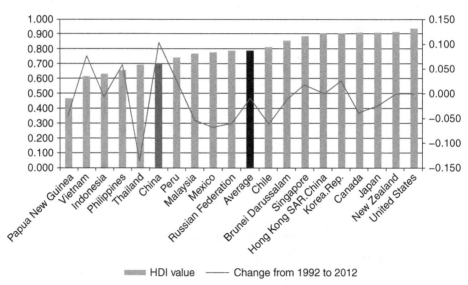

Figure 1.19 Human Development Index, 2012, and change from 1992 to 2012

China 12th out of 19 APEC members. Between 2002 and 2012, the country saw only modest gains in life expectancy; China ranked 11th out of 19 APEC members in terms of this improvement. Over a longer time period (1990–2012), China witnessed the greatest increase in life expectancy around the turn of the century, only to see improvement level off thereafter (see Figure 1.18). The observed improvement in life expectancy has been attributed to government efforts to reduce poverty, increase access to health insurance coverage, and improve general socioeconomic conditions. Such improvement is reflected in the enormous gains China has made in terms of its "Human Development Index" (HDI), which encompasses education and income along with population longevity (see Figure 1.19).[35]

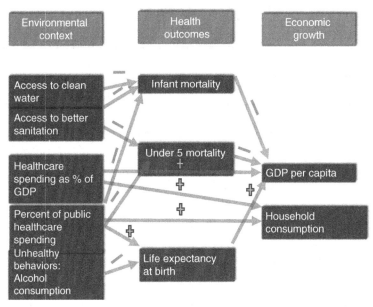

Figure 1.20 Empirical relationships between transitions

Economic Transitions

Despite the country's economic growth following liberalization in the late 1970s, China still has a low level of GDP per capita. The country ranked 14th out of 19 APEC members in 2012, and 12th out of 19 members in terms of the increase in GDP per capita between 2002 and 2012. Similar figures describe the change over the longer time period from 1990 to 2012. However, China stands out from the others in terms of its GDP per capita growth rate (i.e., increase over the prior year). In 2012, China had the highest rate among APEC members (more than 7 percent); between 2002 and 2012, China also exhibited the highest average growth rate (more than 10 percent). Similar data are observed over the longer 1990–2012 period.

In addition to the increase in GDP per capita growth, China has also attempted to increase household consumption as an internal driver of economic growth and rely less on investment and trade. To date, the country has been less successful here. In 2012, China ranked 17th out of 18 APEC members in terms of household consumption as a percentage of GDP (34.7 percent vs. the average of 54.8 percent). Over the time interval from 2002 to 2012, the country

again ranked 17th in terms of the increase/decrease in household consumption as a percent of GDP. Indeed, since 1990, the contribution of household spending to GDP has fallen in China.

Systemic Effects among Transitions

Researchers at Peking University recently examined panel data across APEC members and over time to assess the strength of the causal linkages between the environmental, health outcomes and economic trends discussed above and depicted in Figure 1.11. Their empirical findings are summarized in Figure 1.20. The results show that environmental factors such as access to clean water and sanitation reduce mortality rates, which in turn leads to increases in GDP per capita. Conversely, unhealthy behaviors such as alcohol use reduce life expectancy that in turn reduces GDP per capita. Increased national spending on healthcare (as a percentage of GDP) leads to higher GDP per capita and higher household consumption. Finally, an increase in government's share of this spending reduces mortality rates, improves life expectancy, and increases household consumption.

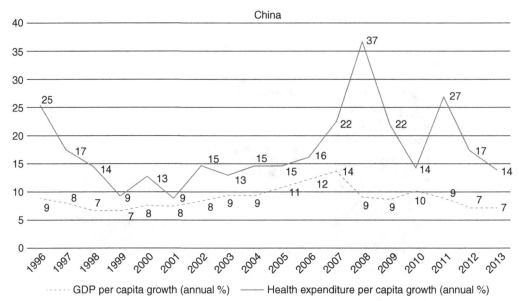

Figure 1.21 Annual per capita growth of GDP and total health expenditures (THE)

Supplemental analyses (not depicted in the figure) further show that greater investments in infrastructure such as construction of hospital beds per 1,000 population lead to falling maternal mortality rates. The latter, in turn, are associated with higher GDP per capita growth rates at the provincial level. This further suggests that public sector interventions to improve capacity can foster economic growth.

The Peking University study also shows there is a positive relationship between GDP per capita and healthcare spending per capita, replicating evidence found in other countries that healthcare is a luxury good: national spending on healthcare increases as a country increases in wealth. The relationship is reciprocal: higher spending on healthcare promotes economic growth. This latter relationship is quadratic, however: after reaching a certain point, rising spending on healthcare can negatively impact the economy. The study also finds a positive relationship between increased household consumption and both economic and employment growth. The study authors surmise that (a) higher consumption leads to higher demand for products, which stimulates the economy, and (b) the spread of health insurance coverage spurs consumption and reduced savings.

Finally, the study shows that growth in China's per capita healthcare spending has consistently outstripped growth in the country's per capita GDP since 1996 (see Figure 1.21). The gap between the two lines means that healthcare spending accounts for an increasing share of the country's economic growth. Moreover, the growth in healthcare spending has continued to accelerate even as China's economic growth cools off. This means that healthcare will account for an even greater share of GDP going forward. Lessons from the United States show that such growth raises the visibility of healthcare spending and increases calls for healthcare cost containment measures to deal with it.

Implications for China's Healthcare System

Several of these transitions will increase demand for healthcare services and insurance coverage to pay for them. In particular, unhealthy behaviors will foster more disability and chronic illness; increased government spending will foster more investment in expensive healthcare infrastructure (facilities and manpower) that will increase access and utilization. Government investment has now extended to healthcare technology sectors (e.g., biotechnology, medical devices) that will spur more innovation and innovative products that will, in turn, increase costs and utilization.

These transitions are reinforced by a series of parallel transitions enabling this demand to be realized, such as the growth of the Chinese economy, the enormous decline in China's poverty rate, the rise of private sector employment, rising urbanization, and rising income levels. Over the past three decades, China's economy grew at an average annual rate of 9–10 percent, largely due to the high rate of investment (35–45 percent) as a percentage of GDP. Another historical factor promoting growth has been the shift of the workforce from primary (e.g., agriculture) to secondary (e.g., manufacturing, construction) and tertiary (e.g., service) sectors: the share of these three sectors changed dramatically between 1975 (77 percent vs. 14 percent vs. 9 percent) and 2005 (45 percent vs. 24 percent vs. 31 percent). Additional historical factors include the shift from agricultural communes to private control over farmland, the rise in agricultural prices and productivity, the formation of township and village enterprises (TVEs), the huge migration of rural populations to the larger cities, and the subsequent increase in the urbanization rate from 18 percent to 45 percent between 1978 and 2007. All of these factors have contributed to a decline in the number of people living in poverty ($1.25/day) by 678 million between 1981 and 2010. Officially, only 4 percent of China's population now lives in poverty. The growth of industry and the country's cities has led to rising non-agricultural and formal corporate employment – often in jobs that offer higher wages and health insurance – and growing income disparity between urban and rural dwellers.

This growth has led to the co-presence of "Two Chinas": an urban and increasingly middle and upper-middle class which accesses allopathic medicine from modern tertiary facilities, and a large poor and rural population who face both greater physical and financial barriers to access care in the urban centers. The two Chinas have very different income levels, life expectancies (75.2 years vs. 69.6 year in 2005), and infant mortality rates (10.7 vs. 25.7 per 1,000 live births).[36]

Summary and Overview of the Volume

This chapter has described a variety of lenses and frameworks through which one can begin to analyze China's developing healthcare system. None are inherently superior or inferior. Instead, they alternatively highlight goals and tensions, structures, functions, corporate and individual actors, flows and exchanges, and dynamic transitions. One might wisely employ multiple approaches to develop a comprehensive understanding of China or any other healthcare system in an emerging economy.

In analyses of the US healthcare system, we typically rely on a value-chain framework that focuses on the major actors and the economic exchanges (as buyers and sellers) between them. We loosely adopt that framework (see Figures 1.8 and 1.9) in this volume to focus on several of the key actors in China's healthcare system: hospitals, physicians, public and private insurers, pharmaceutical firms, biotechnology firms, and medical device firms. Consistent with the "control knobs" approach depicted in Figure 1.7, we also spend considerable time describing the wider societal context underpinning China's healthcare system and the policy levers used in the past to achieve its desired intermediate and ultimate ends.

There are two additional introductory chapters in this first section of the book. Chapter 2, by Lawton Robert Burns and Yanzhong Huang, expands upon some of the issues dealt with in this chapter. The chapter describes the history of China's healthcare system and succession of reforms undertaken since the Maoist era. It also discusses some of the key historical events in the evolution of China's healthcare system and the wider Chinese economy. Chapter 3, by Xiaofeng Liang and Lawton Robert Burns, provides an in-depth overview of China's public health system and the manifold challenges it faces in dealing with non-communicable diseases (NCDs).

The second section of the book describes the healthcare reforms under way in China and the challenges such reforms face. Chapter 4, by Gordon G. Liu and Sam Krumholz, describes the prior impact of healthcare reform on China's epidemiological transition. Chapter 5, by Claudia

Suessmuth-Dyckerhoff and Florian Then, examines the current state of reform efforts. Chapter 6, by Tsung-Mei Cheng, assesses the challenge facing reform efforts going forward to deal with China's chronic disease burden.

The third section of the book focuses on healthcare provision. Chapters 7 and 8 provide an introduction to the two main providers in China's healthcare system: physicians and hospitals. Chapter 7, by Lawton Robert Burns, describes the different systems of medicine in China and focuses on the training and organization of allopathic physicians. Chapter 8, by Gerard La Forgia and Winnie Yip, focuses on China's public hospital system and efforts to reform it. Chapter 9, by Vanessa Folkerts and Roberta Lipson, presents a case study of one of the most prominent examples of a private hospital chain: United Family Hospitals. Chapter 10, by John Whitman and Lawton Robert Burns, describes the market for eldercare and long-term care services in China.

The fourth section of the book focuses on healthcare finance issues. Chapter 11, by Ambar La Forgia and Lawton Robert Burns, describes China's healthcare insurance sector, stemming from its roots in the public sphere and its nascent expansion into the private sphere over the past decade. Chapter 12, by Karen Eggleston, Kate Bundorf, and colleagues, describes experiments under way in rural China to provide insurance coverage that tackle chronic disease. Chapter 13, by Gordon G. Liu, Nan Luo, and Zhongyun Zhao, discusses the technology assessment and reimbursement policies in China and Southeast Asia.

The final section of the book focuses on three sectors of producers in China's healthcare system: pharmaceutical manufacturers (Chapter 14 by Rachel Lee and Lawton Robert Burns), medical device manufacturers (Chapter 15 by James Deng and Lawton Robert Burns), and life sciences investment and biotechnology (Chapter 16 by Stephen M. Sammut and Lawton Robert Burns). Due to their historical prominence, multinational corporations are a major topic of discussion when considering these sectors; we endeavor to counterbalance that discussion with a description of the domestic players developing within each of these sectors.

Notes

1. Oftentimes these trade-offs are described as the tension between promoting access to care for everyone and using price as a rationing tool to healthcare services, or the tension between balancing equitable access and efficiency in the provision of services.
2. David Dranove. 2008. *Code Red* (Princeton, NJ: Princeton University Press). William Kissick. 1994. *Medicine's Dilemmas: Infinite Needs versus Finite Resources* (New Haven, CT: Yale University Press).
3. One global firm that came close to achieving all three simultaneously (at least in past decades) was the Swedish furniture maker Ikea. In the health care industry, Becton Dickinson also achieved strong performance on all three dimensions in prior decades.
4. Donald Berwick, Thomas Nolan, and John Whittington. 2008. "The Triple Aim: Care, Health, and Cost," *Health Affairs* 27(3): 759–769.
5. Berwick et al. 2008. "The Triple Aim."
6. Claudia Süssmuth-Dyckerhoff and Jin Wang. 2010. "China's Health Care Reforms," *Health International* 10: 54–67.
7. Marc Roberts, William Hsiao, Peter Berman et al. 2008. *Getting Health Reform Right* (New York, NY: Oxford University Press): Chapter 1.
8. Richard Smith and Kara Hanson. 2011. "What Is a 'Health System'?" in Richard Smith and Kara Hanson (Eds.), *Health Systems in Low and Middle Income Countries* (Oxford, UK: Oxford University Press): Chapter 1: pp. 3–19.
9. Daniel Callahan. 1973. "The WHO Definition of 'Health,'" *The Hastings Center Studies* 1(3): 77–87.
10. Amartya Sen. 1999. *Development as Freedom* (New York, NY: Alfred A. Knopf).
11. Lawton R. Burns. 2002. *The Health Care Value Chain: Producers, Purchasers, and Providers* (San Francisco, CA: Jossey-Bass).
12. Roberts et al. 2008. *Getting Health Reform Right*.
13. World Health Organization. 2000. *The World Health Report 2000 – Health Systems:*

Improving Performance (Geneva, Switzerland: WHO).

14. Jayati Ghosh. 2010. "Poverty Reduction in China and India: Policy Implications of Recent Trends," DESA Working Paper No. 92. New York: Department of Economic and Social Affairs, United Nations.

15. David Cutler, Angus Deaton, and Adriana Lleras-Muney. 2006. "The Determinants of Mortality," *Journal of Economic Perspectives* 20(3): 97–120.

16. R. Srinivisan, "Healthcare in India – Vision 2020: Issues and Prospects." Available online at: http://planningcommission.nic.in/reports/genrep/bkpap2020/26_bg2020.doc. Accessed on October 21, 2016.

17. Registrar General of India provides data for 2011. For 2010 data, see Central Bureau of Health Intelligence. 2010. *National Health Profile 2010* (New Delhi, India: Government of India). According to the 2001 Census data, the percentage of the population 0–14 was 35.5%; the percentage 60+ years old was 6.9%.

18. A second definition of the dependency ratio is the "age dependency ratio": the number of people aged 0–14 plus the number of people aged 65+ divided by the number of people aged 15–64. Using 2007–2011 data from the World Bank, China's age dependency ratio is .38 compared to India's ratio of .54. A third definition of the "dependency ratio" is the number of people aged 65+ divided by the number of people aged 15–64. This ratio reached roughly 7.5% in 2005 and will rise to 20% by 2050. Ajay Mahal and Victoria Fan. 2010. "The Case for Improving Health in India," in Ajay Mahal, Bibek Debroy, and Laveesh Bhandari (Eds.), *India Health Report* (New Delhi: Business Standard Books): 1–20.

19. George Shakarishvili. 2009. "Building on Health Systems Frameworks for Developing a Common Approach to Health Systems Strengthening," Paper prepared for the World Bank, the Global Fund, and the GAVI Alliance Technical Workshop on Health Systems Strengthening (Washington, DC: June 25–27).

20. J. W. Hurst. 1991. "Reforming Health Care in Seven European Nations," *Health Affairs* 10 (3): 7–21.

21. World Health Organization. 2003. *Guide to Producing National Health Accounts* (Geneva, Switzerland: WHO).

22. George Shakarishvili, Mary Ann Lansang, Vinod Mitta et al. 2011. "Health Systems Strengthening: A Common Classification and Framework for Investment Analysis," *Health Policy and Planning* 26: 316–326.

23. World Health Organization. 2000. *The World Health Report 2000.*

24. Anne J. Mills and M. Kent Ranson. 2001. "The Design of Health Systems," in Michael H. Merson, Robert E. Black, and Anne J. Mills (Eds.), *International Public Health: Diseases, Programs, Systems, and Policies* (Gaithersburg, MD: Aspen Publishers): Chapter 11.

25. World Health Organization. 2000. *The World Health Report 2000*; Jane Menken and M. Omar Rahman. 2001. "Reproductive Health," in Merson, Black, and Mills (Eds.), *International Public Health: Diseases, Programs, Systems, and Policies.* Chapter 3; Arthur L. Reingold and Christina R. Phares. 2001. "Infectious Diseases," in Merson, Black, and Mills (Eds.), *International Public Health: Diseases, Programs, Systems, and Policies.* Chapter 4.

26. World Health Organization. 2007. *Strengthening Health Systems to Improve Health Outcomes* (Geneva, Switzerland: WHO).

27. William Hsiao. 2003. *What Is a Health System? Why Should We Care?* (Cambridge, MA: Harvard School of Public Health, August).

28. D.C. Esty et al. 1999. "State Failure Task Force Report: Phase II Findings," *Environmental Change and Security Project Report*, no. 5 (Washington, DC: Woodrow Wilson Center, Summer): 49–72.

29. Hsiao. 2003. *What Is a Health System?*

30. Gerard Anderson and Peter S. Hussey. 2001. "Trends in Expenditures, Access, and Outcomes Among Industrialized Countries," in Walter Wieners (Ed.), *Global Health Care*

Markets (San Francisco, CA: Jossey-Bass): 24–40.

31. Burton Weisbrod. 1991. "The Healthcare Quadrilemma: An Essay on Technological Change, Insurance, Quality of Care, and Cost Containment," *Journal of Economic Literature* 29(2): 523–552.

32. Liu et al. 2015. *Health and Economic Prosperity*.

33. David Bloom, David Canning, and Dean Jamison. 2004. "Health, Wealth, and Welfare," *Finance and Development* (March): 10–15.

34. M. Suhrcke and M. McKee. 2005. *The Contribution of Health to the Economy in the European Union*. Luxembourg: Office for Official Publications of the European Commission.

35. United Nations Development Programme. "Human Development Index." Available online at: http://hdr.undp.org/en/content/human-development-index-hdi. Accessed on October 21, 2016.

36. Ghosh. 2010. "Poverty Reduction in China and India."

History of China's Healthcare System

LAWTON ROBERT BURNS AND YANZHONG HUANG

Pre-revolutionary China

Chinese healthcare has existed for nearly 3,000 years, but China's healthcare "system" is more recent in origin (in the mid-twentieth century). To the extent there was healthcare in Imperial China, it was primarily oriented around traditional Chinese medicine (TCM). TCM encompassed a range of practices and therapies including locally available herbal remedies, acupuncture, massage, exercise, diet, and other techniques to promote wellness and healing. TCM was codified in the *Yellow Emperor's Canon of Internal Medicine* sometime between the late Warring States period (475–221 BC) and the early Han period (206 BCE–220 CE). The *Canon* included a discussion between the emperor and his physicians of diagnosis and clinical reasoning. The emperor's interest spurred research and advances in healthcare by his court physicians. The published writings of the latter might disseminate to civilian physicians, similar to the "town and gown" pattern of influence in western academic medicine.[1]

Healthcare was organized around private practices and clinics, as well as in specific cultural institutions (e.g., in temples and charitable societies). There was no public health system; healthcare was a purely private sector activity.

Chinese medicine considered illness the result of incorrect action or thought and thus emphasized the importance of "bringing order" (*zhi*), eliminating disturbance and restoring balance, and the similarity between governing and curing.[2] Centuries later, Mao would invoke this theme in the early establishment of the People's Republic of China (PRC).

This chapter draws extensively on the work of one of the co-authors for many of the statistics and historical details. See Yanzhong Huang. 2013. *Governing Health in Contemporary China* (Routledge: New York).

Chinese medicine emphasized the importance of preventive healthcare. According to a saying from the Han period, "The sage does not cure the sick, but prevents illness from arising."[3] There was also a strong dose of self-reliance. According to the Confucian system, every gentleman should possess sufficient medical knowledge to take care of his own family.[4] This did not accord much room for or reliance on a medical profession that was superordinate to the patient, but rather placed responsibility for health on the individual and the household.

The arrival of western missionaries in the early nineteenth century introduced allopathic medicine and rudimentary western medical education. The weakening of the monarchy in the late nineteenth century in tandem with western exposure and intervention led to a rejection of all things "Chinese" by the populace, including healthcare. TCM was supplemented by a smattering of western healthcare institutions (hospitals, medical schools) and practices (public health, vaccinations, sanitation) introduced by western missionaries. Both systems of medicine now existed side by side.

China transitioned to a republic after the monarchy ended in 1912. The country's first president, Sun Yat-sen, was a western-trained allopathic physician. He pushed China to adopt western-style medical institutions and practices (noted above). One of the country's first teaching hospitals, Peking Union Medical College (PUMC), was constructed in 1917 with funding from the Rockefeller Foundation.

Over the next three decades, these efforts were interrupted by (a) conflicts between the Nationalist government and the regional warlords during 1912–1927; (b) war with Japan during 1937–1945; and (c) civil war between the Nationalist government and the Communists during 1927–1949. The tumult of these decades – including the spread of contagious diseases such as cholera, plague, smallpox, malaria, and tuberculosis (TB) – weakened the country and its existing healthcare system. By the time the Communists prevailed, the Chinese population suffered from low life expectancy and high morbidity. The low health status reflected not only the spread of infectious disease, but also problems in environmental hygiene, malnutrition, low education, and inadequate healthcare infrastructure (e.g., beds, physicians).

At the end of the civil war, the vast majority of healthcare was delivered by an estimated 500,000 private medical providers, most of them practitioners of TCM; Western-style medicine had gained a foothold but was still uncommon. The number of allopathic physicians with college training may have been as few as 40,000–85,000; this represented less than 15 percent of the workforce and yielded a physician/population ratio as low as 1:14,000. Nearly two-thirds of these college-trained physicians practiced in urban areas. By 1957, the country still had only 79,000 college-trained practitioners, three-quarters of whom now practiced in urban settings. As a consequence, the largely rural population was totally reliant on TCM.

China also had 768 hospitals: 520 private hospitals (mostly administered by missionaries and their churches) and 248 public hospitals run by the government.[5] The small number of hospitals meant a limited capacity of only 80,000 hospital beds, or one bed per 6,667 population. As with China's medical manpower, most of this limited capacity (75 percent of hospital beds) was confined to China's urban areas.[6]

Healthcare Following the Revolution: 1949–1978

Central Planning

In 1949, following the revolution, the People's Republic of China formed under the leadership of Mao Tse-tung. The government bureaucracy, the Chinese Communist Party (CCP), and the rural communes directed the Chinese economy. The bureaucracy and party served as parallel hierarchies of control over economic life. The government employed most workers; the party's network influenced management decision making at most levels of government, and party members occupied all important administrative positions at every level/branch of government and in every work unit.[7]

Soviet Model

Under Mao, China pursued economic development patterned after a Soviet-style planned economy: land was gradually appropriated, agriculture was gradually collectivized, and industry was nationalized. State enterprises became the major employers; college graduates (including those from medical schools) were "allocated" to fill managerial, technical, and provider posts in the growing public sector.

As another feature of the Soviet model, the government moved to restrict the geographic (as well as occupational) mobility of the population. The government classified its citizens according to their geographical location (using a registration system known as *hukou*) and tied housing registration to food rationing.

In this primarily rural country, the vast majority of the population was engaged in agriculture, supplemented by a small number of government employees (or cadres) and party members. The government favored the small cohort of managers and technical professionals who comprised the urban population by extending them health insurance in the early 1950s. The Labor Insurance Regulations of 1951 offered free medical care, lifetime pensions, and disability pay to full-time employees of the state industrial firms. In 1955, they also received housing subsidies and access to the educational system for their children. The *hukou* system blocked rural dwellers' access to these government jobs and benefits. Indeed, banishment to the rural areas was a severe punishment meted out by the government to disobedient urban workers. The *hukou* system acquired greater teeth after the debacle of the Great Leap Forward and resulting famine, when the government distinguished the rural population (those who raised grain, fed themselves, and lived in rural collectives) from the urban population (those who ate "state grain" and worked in state enterprises). In later years, rural residents would travel to larger cities seeking employment but their *hukou* status remained unchanged.

The cornerstone of everyday life was the rural People's Communes, established in 1958. The CCP developed the local work unit as the main vehicle for assigning administrative responsibilities and maintaining social order. The communes represented the reach of the CCP and state into local life, as well as the merger of political and economic life. Communes owned the land and organized farming production and distribution. Commune responsibilities extended to social services such as healthcare (see below). There were 23,630 communes, each containing roughly 5,443 households; communes were subdivided into production brigades and production teams.[8] Communes were later called "townships"; production brigades were later called "villages."[9]

Healthcare Strategy with Limited Resources: Mass Campaigns

In addition to the local rural communes, China extended central planning to healthcare. Unlike his successors, Mao believed that social issues such as disease and illness were the purview of the CCP. In order to gain the political support of the population as well as exert control over them, the state needed to tend to their welfare needs. At the First National Health Conference held in August 1950, the government identified four guiding principles for healthcare services: serve workers, farmers, and soldiers; prioritize preventive medicine over curative medicine; foster unity between TCM and allopathic medicine; and combine health efforts with mass mobilization.[10] A three-pronged healthcare system was also conceptualized that included "public medicine" (insurance coverage for public servants), "collective medicine" (insurance for workers in state-owned enterprises), and "cooperative medicine" (insurance for rural residents).

Mao's regime placed great emphasis on the organization and staffing of rural healthcare, including preventive services. He initiated public health campaigns, organized under the newly formed Ministry of Health (1949) and the leadership of the CCP. These campaigns mobilized the local population and trained them in basic public health activities. This marked the beginning of Mao's emphasis on prevention, egalitarianism, and mass participation –

all of which countered the prior concentration of healthcare infrastructure in urban areas.

Mass mobilization efforts absorbed abundant "surplus labor" in rural areas and utilized them directly in public health projects that were patriotic in fervor and community development in nature. A key element here was the "mass campaign": the mass of ordinary people capable of tackling complex problems. The Red Army had employed prevention campaigns to deal with epidemics during the civil war with the nationalists. Mao now initiated mass campaigns to eradicate specific infectious diseases (e.g., schistosomiasis). The mass campaign was employed again during the Korean War to combat the perceived (not real) threat of germ warfare used by US soldiers, then again during the Great Leap Forward to combat pests (see below), and then again in prevention programs to improve sanitation, personal hygiene, health education, and combat specific vector-borne diseases.[11]

The impact of mass campaigns was profound. They reinforced the tradition of self-reliance and the belief that financing activities to promote public health should be borne by those who directly benefit from them. They also spawned the idea that public health problems could be addressed by using and deploying available human resources that were inexpensive and abundant. Effective public health initiatives could thus be quickly fielded at low cost. This was important, as central government funding of healthcare during the 1950–1957 period was a meager 1.2 percent. Finally, the campaigns not only supported the legitimacy of state and party domination of social life, but also that health was a matter of national security.

Great Leap Forward

Ironically, the state's intervention using mass campaigns sometimes weakened the country and its already limited healthcare infrastructure. During 1959–1961, Mao launched the Great Leap Forward to simultaneously increase agricultural and industrial production. The effort ushered in collectivization of the land, prohibition of private property, and the shift of agricultural workers to heavy industry. To offset the loss of manpower and spur agricultural production, China launched a patriotic hygiene campaign to combat the "four pests" (initially rats, flies, mosquitoes, and sparrows). Mao targeted the sparrows due to peasant complaints they ate their grain and grain seed, even though there was no good evidence for this. However, efforts to kill off the sparrow population fomented a plague of locusts, large crop failures, an enormous famine, and the deaths of anywhere from 30 million to 45 million Chinese.[12] In March 1960, Mao dropped the sparrows from the list of pests and replaced them with bedbugs.

China's health system was supported by local agricultural output; as long as the latter was robust, healthcare financing was stable. The dependency between agricultural success and healthcare became problematic during the Great Leap Forward. As agriculture collapsed and famine spread, the rural populace suffered illnesses that could not be treated locally. Commune health centers referred their members to county and urban hospitals, increasing their utilization and costs but not paying their bills. County hospital finances thus also suffered. The central government did not intervene to shore up rural health financing, choosing instead to funnel investments into heavy industry. All of this led to a collapse of the free medical system in rural areas. Between 1958 and 1960, the number of commune hospitals dropped from 43,600 to 26,200.

Three Tiers of Rural Healthcare

As part of the quid pro quo for collectivization, healthcare became a right to which Chinese citizens were entitled. The healthcare system now emphasized the egalitarianism promoted by Mao via the goal of equal access for all. This was now manifested in public financing of a public delivery system, public employment of physicians (what some have called the "proletarianization" of the medical profession – see Chapter 7), and the organization of a three-tiered system of delivery in rural areas:

• paramedics (later known as barefoot doctors) operating out of village (earlier known as production brigade) clinics that were set up to handle minor illnesses;
• commune (later called township) health centers offering curative services with 10–30 beds and

a small staff of physicians or assistant physicians; and
• county hospitals with up to 300 beds and staffed by physicians.

Public hospitals and clinics received their annual budgets from the government; they were not allowed to accept other payments. With meager financing from the Ministry of Health (MOH), however, most financing and staffing of this system was decentralized to the appropriate level – and remained so until rural health insurance was developed.

To deal with constrained government financing, the MOH sought to promote more cost-efficient delivery methods, including secondary medical schools that produced physician assistants and group practices ("united clinics" that aggregated formerly independent private physicians) as primary healthcare delivery. Some infrastructure (midwives, health aides) also existed at the production team level below the villages to even further extend prevention and delivery. During the interval 1947–1957, China witnessed a 50 percent rise in the number of county hospitals from 1,437 to 2,193 – or roughly one per county.

Rural healthcare gradually became funded through agricultural communes and the country's new Cooperative Medical Scheme (CMS). An early version of this scheme had been developed during the war with Japan in the Shanxi-Gansu-Ningxia region where the Chinese Communists operated; otherwise, the rural agricultural population paid for medical care out of pocket. The CMS was first developed in Henan Province in 1955, spread after the formation of the communes to cover about 20 percent of the production brigades by 1958, and received further impetus from the Central Committee of the CCP in the early 1960s. Around 1965, Mao urged communes to adopt the CMS to stabilize the country's socialist economy and strengthen "the proletarian class dictatorship."[13] By the end of the 1960s, nearly 80 percent of the rural population was covered by the CMS; by the end of the 1970s, it reached its zenith of 90 percent.[14]

The CMS was organized at the production brigade (village) level and overseen by a management committee that included representatives from the village administration and the village clinic. The brigade would sell the output of its agricultural and non-agricultural enterprises and set a portion of the proceeds aside as a welfare fund. The village administration transferred financial subsidies from its welfare fund to run the clinic, pay the salaries of the clinic worker(s), and cover roughly half of the member's premium. As part of their responsibility, village members paid an additional monthly premium (roughly 0.5–2.0 percent of income) to receive clinic services (visits, drugs). Service benefits might also include partial subsidies for visits and admissions to township and county hospitals to which the villager was referred.

Rise of Urban Health Insurance Schemes

The majority of China's farming population were commune members covered by the CMS during the 1950s and 1960s. By contrast, the state employees in both rural and urban areas were covered by different insurance schemes developed in the early 1950s and overseen by the Ministry of Labor. As in rural areas, urban healthcare was funded through work units (*danwei*) for employees in state-owned enterprises (SOEs) and government. Those not employed or not covered by these two schemes received public assistance from poverty aid programs.[15]

Government employees (both rural and urban), college teachers, and students received health insurance coverage through the mandatory Government Insurance Scheme (GIS). Created in 1952, the GIS covered inpatient and outpatient care at public hospitals located in national and provincial capitals, and was financed by public appropriations from general revenues. In 1952, GIS covered 4 million workers; by 1957, GIS covered 7.4 million government workers.

Employees of state-owned enterprises, commune, and brigade enterprises received health coverage through the Labor Insurance Scheme (LIS, also known as the Labor Medical Service), established in 1951. This scheme was financed by the enterprises welfare funds, a portion of which was designated for medical services. The LIS was a voluntary scheme that covered primarily inpatient expenses only. By 1953, the LIS covered 4.8 million workers.

Both schemes increased demand for curative healthcare and, as a result, demand for infrastructure

in urban areas. As in rural China, urban healthcare now consisted of three tiers of public providers:

- street health clinics and workplace clinics (prevention, primary care), again staffed by paramedics;
- district and enterprise hospitals and specialist clinics; and
- provincial and city hospitals.

Constrained central government resources meant that the meager spending was concentrated in urban areas where the insured population (and thus demand) was also concentrated. The urban bias was reinforced by the state socialist welfare regime, which explicitly linked production with entitlement. The planned Soviet-style economy focused on heavy industry; this focus led to an emphasis on urban health insurance coverage and thus urban healthcare infrastructure.

Rise of Public Health

In addition to equal access to healthcare, Mao also emphasized the provision of public health and the development of healthcare infrastructure.[16] With meager funding and a primarily urban-based infrastructure, the emphasis on prevention became the hallmark of the Maoist era healthcare system. The MOH established a Bureau of Contagious Diseases and the Epidemic Prevention General Team with several brigades at the regional level; these were later replaced by epidemic prevention health stations at the provincial, prefecture/city, and county levels in the 1960s. However, insufficient central government funding meant the MOH had to rely on other ministries and local government to control epidemics. Moreover, as noted above, two episodes disrupted China's progress in public health: the Great Leap Forward and the Cultural Revolution.

Threats to CMS and Commune Health Centers

The rural health system was briefly undermined by the famine of 1959–1961 and new regulations stipulating that the basic accounting unit be changed from the commune to first the production brigade and then to the production team – with a devolution of authority and resources for healthcare. In 1962, the MOH stated that the united clinics (group practices) should serve as the basic form of local healthcare delivery. This led to the downsizing or demise of the commune health centers: from a total of 43,600 centers in 1958, the number dropped precipitously to 32,100 (1961) and to 27,500 (1963). It also led the transfer of control over personnel, management, and financing back to the practitioners – effectively reversing what had happened in 1958. These clinics were responsible for their own bottom lines. Some doctors returned to private practice. Rural healthcare became a mosaic of a dwindling number of commune health centers, united clinics (groups), brigade health stations, and private practitioners.[17]

More importantly, these lower levels of administration were too small in population to serve as adequately sized entities to pool insurance risk. The percent of brigades adopting the CMS dropped from 46 percent in 1962 to 30 percent in 1964. The drop in local communal financing was accompanied by fiscal pressures on each level of government above. Constrained finances meant little investment in training of physicians and non-physician personnel, as well as a diminution of effort in patriotic hygiene campaigns to promote public health. It did not help that the raging famine of 1959–1961 had weakened the population and its physical capability to participate in such campaigns. Effort was instead focused on rejuvenating agricultural production, not public health.

The Cultural Revolution

A second disruptive campaign waged during this period was the Cultural Revolution from 1966 to 1976. Like the Great Leap Forward, the revolution caused a further deviation in China's socioeconomic trajectory. The seeds of the revolution may have been planted during the Great Leap Forward, when the rural population suffered heavily from famine, reduced access to healthcare, and high mortality rates. During this period, there was also a policy shift from agricultural development to development of heavy industry, which favored investment in urban areas. There was a concomitant shift in urban-based and industrial-based employment, which meant greater investment in the two urban-based insurance schemes (GIS, LIS), and thus greater investment in the urban healthcare infrastructure to serve the urban working population at the expense of the suffering rural population. An estimated 30 percent of government spending on healthcare was directed to financing just the care for 7–8 million workers covered by one of these schemes (GIS), while only 16 percent went to pay for care for 500 million rural dwellers.

The growing disparity between urban and rural areas in terms of investment and healthcare spending (see Table 2.1),[18] as well as the failure of the Great Leap, led to growing alienation in the rural population. Moreover, the failure of the Great Leap and the shift to industry and urban development increased the role of the government bureaucracy

Table 2.1 Comparison of resources and service use between rural and urban areas

	Rural	Urban	Urban/Rural
Population (%)	85	15	
Health Service Fund per capita (yuan)	2.26	9.8	4.34
Number of beds per 1,000 population	1.57	4.23	2.69
Number of doctors per 1,000 population	0.98	3.01	3.07
Annual number of visits per person	3	4	1.33
Number of hospital days per person	0.48	1.34	2.79
Health service expenses per person (yuan)	18.62	52.13	2.8

Sources:
1. Hospital Administration Department of Ministry of Public Health, *National Health Service Research in the Rural Areas* (1986).
2. Hospital Administration Department of Ministry of Public Health, *China's Medical Service Research in the Urban Areas* (1987).

in policy making, the size of the bureaucracy and its insured GIS constituents, as well as its focus on the urban elite. The MOH focused on building a more westernized healthcare system (that was capital-intensive, physician-centric, urban-based) to cater to the urban population – all of which ran counter to Mao's emphasis on egalitarianism, public health, and rural care. These developments irked Mao and threatened his political standing.

In 1965, Mao criticized the MOH for abandoning the rural population. To counter the growing power of the government bureaucracy, Mao mobilized support from below in a manner reminiscent of the mass campaigns (described earlier). Mao used the July 1966 Plenum of the Central Committee to launch his Cultural Revolution – much of which was targeted at the elitism of the health bureaucracy. Within two years, the MOH bureaucracy had been gutted and replaced with army officers with little or no medical training. For the next five years, the MOH ceased to conduct health policy making, a function now assumed by the CCP.

The revolution represented a political comeback for Mao after the disaster of the Great Leap Forward, as well as an attack of the Red Guard on China's urban intelligentsia, including its cadre of senior physicians. It also marked a renewed emphasis on rural healthcare. In October 1968, Mao once again emphasized the unmet health needs of rural communities. To address the lack of physician manpower, Mao resorted to mass mobilization strategies. Initially these included efforts to relocate western-trained, urban practitioners to the country, as well as dispatch mobile medical teams from urban hospitals to circulate in rural areas.[19] Medical schools and universities were closed down until the mid-1970s, with their students and faculty sent to the country-side. The country's production of physicians came to an abrupt halt. By 1973, 100,000 medical personnel were relocated, while another 800,000 medical workers joined mobile medical teams to serve rural needs. China then embarked on an experiment. The government sought to recruit and rapidly train medical personnel from the rural areas themselves as paramedics that became better known as barefoot doctors.[20] These practitioners possessed a high school diploma at best. Their medical training consisted of a three-month course taken at the commune

or a county hospital, followed by one to three months of additional training provided by the mobile health teams. Their responsibilities covered sanitation (human waste management), immunizations and basic prevention, health education, and primary care for common illnesses. They might continue to do agricultural work or even escape it – one motivation for becoming a barefoot doctor. Rural residents did not complain about the peasant doctors, despite their low level of training, perhaps because the residents were more consumed with scratching out a living.[21]

Rural Health Delivery and Financing

In addition to the barefoot doctors, the rural multi-level delivery system also enjoyed a revival. The hierarchy included (from bottom to top) a health aide at the production team level, a barefoot doctor at the brigade level, a health center at the commune level, and a hospital at the county level. The brigade health station offered preventive services and treated whatever diseases it could; the commune clinic trained the barefoot doctors and supplied basic inpatient and all outpatient care; the county hospital served as the tertiary referral center and the training site for rural healthcare providers.

As part of this revival, Mao ordered the construction of rural healthcare facilities and expansion of hospital beds at different governmental levels. The number of commune (township) health centers grew from 28,656 (1962) to 36,965 (1965) and then to 55,000 (1981). By contrast, the number of county hospitals barely increased during the comparable period from 2,123 (1952) to 2,276 (1965) to 2,367 (1981).[22] In terms of manpower, China had roughly 1.5 million barefoot doctors and another 2.36 million health workers.

To supplement the medical manpower, Mao reinstated traditional Chinese medicine (TCM) as a backbone of China's system of primary care. TCM already enjoyed a solid institutional footing in the Peking-based Academy of Traditional Chinese Medicine founded in 1955. Mao's interest was partly ideological, resting on TCM's roots in Chinese culture (see Chapter 7); it was also pragmatic, due to the cost of allopathic medicine and shortage of allopathic providers. Mao also sought to shorten medical education to three years of training to speed up production and supply rural areas with physicians with basic training. In tandem with TCM, the goal was to maximize therapeutic success at the lowest possible cost. By the next millennium, TCM accounted for an estimated 10–20 percent of the healthcare provided in China.

China also sought to integrate TCM and allopathic medicine. Some integration took place at the practitioner level: some physicians practiced both allopathic medicine and TCM, and might prescribe a mix of pharmaceuticals and TCM products. More typically, TCM and allopathic medicine coexisted as parallel systems of training and practice: hospitalized patients could choose which type of practitioner they wanted, and hospital pharmacies stocked both types of products.

Emphasis on the CMS was likewise renewed during the revolution. Three different versions developed, each with a different risk pooling mechanism: one financed by the brigade, one financed by the commune supported by brigade contributions, and one jointly administered and financed by both. By 1971, 70 percent of the brigades had implemented the new CMS, encompassing 350,000 plans and 500 million covered people. At the provincial level, CMS coverage was more uneven and only partly explained by variations in agricultural productivity. While CMS coverage spread broadly across the rural population, the degree of insurance coverage was shallow. By the 1980s, CMS covered only a portion (38–54 percent) of the cost of providers' services.[23]

Demise of Private Sector Healthcare

Prior to CMS, the largely rural and agricultural population paid for all care out of pocket to private practitioners. The advent of CMS rendered private practice incompatible with the new socialist scheme. As the rollout of CMS proceeded, private sector healthcare was quickly replaced as the dominant mode of governance: by 1958, the percentage of physicians in private practice plummeted from 78.3 percent to 2.7 percent. By the time of the Cultural Revolution, private practice had been eliminated. All hospitals were made public and all providers became salaried, government employees. Private practitioners and united clinics (nascent group practices) were converted to public ownership and/or merged into public facilities. The ruling egalitarian slogan was "doctors and medicine should be available wherever human beings exist." In addition to financing insurance, Mao also focused on price controls to reduce the costs of care, with most services priced well below cost.

Legacy of Maoist Era

Much of Mao's legacy lies in public health improvements. Between 1949 and 1978, China witnessed a major change in the disease profile among its population. The leading causes of death in the 1950s included infectious diseases affecting the respiratory, pulmonary (TB), and gastrointestinal systems of the body. By the end of the Maoist era, the leading causes of death had begun to switch to cardiovascular, cerebrovascular, and cancer conditions. Overall, the health status of the population improved dramatically:

- the infant mortality rate dropped sixfold from 250 per 1,000 live births in 1952 to 40 in 1982;[24]
- the mortality rate declined 63 percent from 20/1,000 to 7.3/1,000 between 1949 and 1975; and
- life expectancy at birth rose 88 percent from 35 years to 66 years.

Such improvements were due not only to Mao's public health campaigns but also to increases in educational attainment.[25] The Maoist era also introduced into China two key elements of infrastructure supporting demand for and supply of healthcare: health insurance and medical practitioners. By 1975, 90 percent of the brigades and 85 percent of rural dwellers were covered by CMS; 1.8 million barefoot doctors had also been trained.

However, the shift in disease patterns led to a mismatch with the shift in physician training. Communicable diseases were more amenable to treatment by the relatively untrained barefoot doctors; by contrast, treatment of chronic conditions required trained primary care physicians (PCPs) to detect these conditions as well as highly trained specialists and more technologically intensive inpatient facilities to care for them. As the period came to a close, China had a large supply of barefoot doctors but an undersupply of PCPs and specialists.

Another legacy of the Maoist era was the emphasis on access to affordable healthcare. Providers were not allowed to bill patients or accept other forms of payment, but instead were required to operate with the meager funds allocated to them as lump-sum global budgets by the state. Communes, local government bodies, and the central government supported insurance schemes (to stimulate demand) and provider budgets (to stimulate supply) out of tax revenues. Input prices and provider salaries were regulated and kept low to keep healthcare affordable. As a result, healthcare incomes and services remained low cost for years to come, and access to healthcare was extended to a large percentage of the working population.

The creation of the rural infrastructure of healthcare delivery did not ensure quality, however, given the lack of government funding and shortages of trained manpower. The rural system rested heavily on the cohort of untrained barefoot doctors and was plagued by variations in local economic and agricultural productivity. The infrastructure was also developed in accordance with local political jurisdictions, rather than population bases and referral regions that lent themselves to adequate risk pooling. This resulted in a shortage of financial and managerial means to efficiently manage the rural system, particularly at the lowest levels. Finally, the Cultural Revolution diminished the role of the government healthcare bureaucracy in policy and planning for several years. The MOH was gradually restored to its former role in the early 1980s.

From 1949 to 1978, China served as an experimental laboratory for healthcare reform at both the macro and micro levels. At the macro level, China developed a collectively planned and managed system in rural areas patterned after the Soviet model. This model was later supplanted by a socialist market model that decentralized both fiscal and administrative responsibility (see below). This sequence was opposite the trajectory of healthcare in the United States, where a private sector system was gradually accompanied by the emergence and growth of the public sector. At the micro level, China's goal was to serve the people via an egalitarian, non-hierarchical system that relied on prevention and public health, erasing China's image as "the sick man of East Asia." This model was also succeeded by an acute care model that relied on fee-for-service (FFS) payment, private practice, and financing based on the individual's ability to pay.

Ironically, the net long-term effect of the Great Leap Forward and the Cultural Revolution was to diminish the legitimacy of central government control and to promote the future policy of economic liberalism pursued by Deng Xiaoping. This led to a marginalization of public health, other health issues such as insurance and rural healthcare, and the egalitarian agenda pursued by Mao.

Economic Reform: 1978–2000

Reverse Gear: Decentralization and Market Orientation

China underwent another momentous transition following Mao's death in 1976 and the ascendance of Deng Xiaoping. In 1978, the 11th Communist Party's Central Committee's 3rd Plenum adopted several resolutions that initiated a series of important experiments. China's agricultural and healthcare systems underwent market-oriented reforms that accelerated economic development and decentralized both political and economic power (e.g., responsibility for finance and management). This created incentives for local economic growth and entrepreneurship. Such incentives were supported by a new tax system whereby local authorities collected certain taxes to support local spending (with a reduced role for income transfers across regions).

Prior to the market reforms, governments at all levels collected roughly 90 percent of their revenues from taxes (industrial and commercial) and the profits earned by SOEs; the central government collected these revenues and allocated them to lower levels of government. In 1979, the Law on Local Organization restructured China's legislative system. The law empowered People's Provincial Congresses to draft local rules and regulations. Subsequent amendments to the constitution (1982) and to the Law on Local Organization (1982, 1986) extended powers even further down to local government bodies. The revised constitution in 1993 called for a "socialist market economy" in which the CCP retained political power but encouraged a free-market model.

Household Production and Local Government Financing

The command and control economy developed under Mao and rooted in the agricultural communes gave way to a system of household production, profit-making enterprises at village and township levels, and increasing autonomy, self-reliance, and profit and loss (P&L) responsibility by the SOEs. Local level enterprise became the engine of China's growth. Local governments appropriated farmlands to develop into commercial enterprises, which led to a continuing migration of rural labor to the urban areas in search of employment.

While not officially abandoning Mao's health policies, party leaders indicated that health goals would not be achieved through central government financing. Instead, social policy was now pursued through the market and relaxation of government policy. In the new division of labor, the central government would formulate policy and reform programs; the provincial government would collect its own tax revenues and administer policy; and the provincial and city governments would implement policy and deliver services. The various taxes (income, transfer, sales) were re-allocated across governmental levels. As the central government tax base declined, so did government revenue as a percent of GDP and central government support of healthcare. Government revenues could not keep pace with economic growth (or the rising cost of healthcare). Local government now became the major public financier of healthcare. Like their industrial counterparts, government service units were to have their own P&L responsibility and pursue economic solutions to their constituents' needs. As a result, "economic efficiency replaced social efficacy as the primary objective."

Tax Reform, Retained Surpluses, P&L Responsibility, Dispersion of Power

The 1994 tax reform centralized fiscal power by allowing central and provincial governments to appropriate most of the lucrative taxes. Revenues collected by and directed to the central government were transferred to provincial governments in proportion to the shares of revenue they generated, but also allowed for limited transfers from richer to poorer provinces. Such transfers were insufficient to correct inequities across provinces in their healthcare resources.[26]

Tax reform also delegated fiscal and budgetary responsibility to local governments but left them with only low-revenue-bearing taxes that were difficult to collect. This left counties and the political jurisdictions below them with insufficient revenue to cover their spending, including subsidies for the provision of most healthcare services. After 1980, governments at each level collected and retained taxes and profits only from enterprises at their respective levels, and spent those monies on institutions at their respective levels. By 2004, the central government was responsible for only a small fraction of public health spending; government bodies at or below the provincial level (e.g., counties) financed much of the remainder (see Table 2.2).

Given the low degree of government financing at the central, provincial, and local levels, it is not surprising that the higher levels exerted only narrow and limited control over resource allocation at lower levels. Central government financial support was limited to block grants. Such grants did not fully cover operating costs and thus served as a budget constraint on local authorities; the latter therefore sought to generate revenues via their own SOEs. The central government also allowed local governments to retain any surplus they generated. Central government scrutiny was also limited by the growing political and administrative federalism in the structure of the Chinese government. Multiple centers of power developed across geographic levels of government; multiple bases of authority developed within each level of government; greater functional differentiation of departments and personnel occurred within ministries; and several new regulatory agencies were established.

Changes in the Ministry of Health's Sphere of Influence

Following the reforms, China's health policy was more directed by the health bureaucracy and less directed by the CCP, its political leadership, and its ideology. In the early 1980s, the MOH regained

Table 2.2 Central government versus subnational government spending on healthcare

Year	Total	Central Government	Subnational Government	Central Government (%)	Subnational Government (%)
	100 million	100 million	100 million		
2002	908.51	24.68	883.83	2.716	97.284
2003	1,116.94	31.68	1,085.26	2.837	97.163
2004	1,293.58	33.89	1,259.69	2.620	97.380
2005	1,552.53	31.83	1,520.70	2.051	97.949
2006	1,778.86	32.65	1,746.21	1.835	98.165
2007	2,581.58	44.38	2,537.20	1.719	98.281
2008	3,593.94	60.98	3,532.96	1.697	98.303
2009	4,816.26	76.57	4,739.69	1.590	98.410
2010	5,732.49	87.77	5,644.72	1.531	98.469
2011	7,464.18	82.80	7,381.38	1.109	98.891
2012	8,431.98	86.46	8,345.52	1.025	98.975
2013	9,545.81	88.43	9,457.38	0.926	99.074

operating control over health policy making from the State Council. Other parallel changes occurred that changed the relationships between the government and the CCP. In 1979, the new MOH minister expanded the MOH bureaucracy, reduced the impact of party leaders on ministry decisions and appointments, and initiated the dismantling of Mao's healthcare system.

At the same time, however, decentralization of bureaucratic and fiscal responsibility reduced the power of MOH officials to implement health policy. Policy-setting was already constrained by the large number of other ministries and agencies that had a voice in health policy, requiring more time and effort for consensus building and policy coordination. At this time, as many as ten ministries and agencies had input into the policy process for healthcare, reducing the MOH's ability to pursue its goals independently. This resulted in a policy structure where, according to Deng Xiaoping, "no one is responsible" and cooperation between many political actors was required to implement policy changes. This created a disjunction between government policy set on high and execution of that policy far below at the local level.[27] The situation was further fueled by the delegation of decision-making authority and control over local financial resources, as well as the emphasis on achieving economic growth targets. The tangible nature of such targets, and the incentives to achieve them, made it easier for local officials to ignore or de-emphasize achievement of more subjective policies such as prevention, public health, and population health that did not lend themselves to easy measurement and oversight.

The weak stature of the MOH was also fostered by the prevalent government view that healthcare spending was more akin to welfare than entitlement. According to this view, healthcare spending did not promote economic growth (the country's primary objective) or impact worker productivity – contrary to the analysis in Chapter 1. As a result, other ministries and government departments had little to gain from cooperation with the MOH.

Disjunction between Central and Local Government

The 1982 constitution made local control official and vested budgetary decision making in local governing bodies. Public health bureaus were replicated across the various levels of Chinese government (see Figure 2.1).[28] Policy implementation was now constrained by the reality that health bureaus at the provincial and local levels were more likely to take their staffing, funding, and cues from provincial and

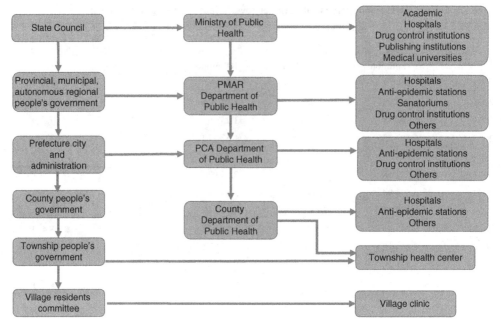

Figure 2.1 China's healthcare structure

local government than the central MOH. Historically, local government rather than central government has financed most of the public funding of healthcare (see Table 2.2).

The reliance of local governments on locally derived revenues put pressure on health budgets to cover operating deficits in their hospitals and public health activities. To make up for the shortfalls, local governments resorted to collecting extra-budgetary revenues in the form of charges levied on individuals and local enterprises outside of traditional taxes. Such revenues were not part of the formal taxes passed on to higher levels and were kept out of the purview of central government which had little control over them. While collected, they might not even be used to finance healthcare services, but instead might be earmarked for other infrastructure improvements. Poorer local governments did not have the ability to collect these extra revenues; in those areas, healthcare costs may have outpaced the average income of the population.

Top government efforts to monitor and control policy at the lower levels were further thwarted by variations in the managerial and administrative capacity of lower level officials, by limited

resources to implement centrally developed policies, by local protectionism exerted by local regulatory authorities working with local party officials, by incentives to show progress on economic goals and budget targets for which officials were rewarded, and by a historical tradition of local autonomy.[29] As a result, local governments lacked the incentive to accurately report information on the economic and clinical performance of the healthcare institutions under their jurisdiction to higher-level authorities. Instead, some have characterized such information as a bargaining chip in intergovernmental relations.[30]

Demise of the Communes and Rise of Household Production

To boost agricultural production, China shifted away from collectively organized farming to a household production responsibility system, and from a government system of administered pricing to a free market. The former happened more rapidly than the latter. De-collectivization of land occurred between 1979 and 1983, by which time production teams no longer existed.[31] Management of the land was contracted out to households. The state purchased the output at a fixed price based on a certain crop quota; crop levels beyond the quota were sold at a higher price, with the farmer retaining the surplus. By 1990, roughly 80 percent of agricultural products were bought and sold in competitive markets, compared to only 8 percent in 1978. The household system also allowed farmers to diversify away from agricultural crops to dairy, poultry, and pig production. Such a production focus weakened the collectivist orientation of the communes, the motivation of barefoot doctors to provide their communal services in public health, and the motivation of local communities to engage in mass campaigns.

The People's Communes were transformed into townships, while the production brigades dissolved back into the villages. The collective welfare funds in many brigades disappeared, taking with it the financial base of the CMS and their brigade (village) clinics, and the will to pool funds and collectively finance healthcare. Healthcare transformed from a prepaid capitated basis to a fee-for-service basis. Individual villagers were now self-employed and earning household incomes; such incomes transformed them into paying patients who now had discretion to bypass local health stations and seek care elsewhere.

Impact on Healthcare and Social Services

These changes affected the provision of social services such as healthcare. China's collectivized, public, communal, and prevention-oriented healthcare system gave way to an individually based, privately owned, fee-for-service based, and acute care–oriented system. At the same time, the government also reduced its outlays on healthcare services, due to the rising healthcare costs and the burden that such costs imposed on the budgets of government and its state-owned enterprises.

This posed a threefold problem for healthcare providers. First, China experienced rising costs of healthcare following economic liberalization. Between 1980 and 1989, national health expenditures (NHEs) more than quadrupled from RMB 10.7 billion to 56.74 billion. Between 1978 and 1990, NHE as a percentage of GDP rose from

2.96 percent to 3.59 percent.[32] Between 1990 and 1999, the cost of healthcare rose nearly 600 percent; between 1980 and 2002, the rise was 4,000 percent.[33] Not surprisingly, the 2006 National Survey on Social Harmony and Stability identified the top social concern in China as "high medical expenses."[34]

Part of the rise was due to the extension of insurance to large segments of the population, which led to higher utilization of services. Part was due to the heavy government subsidies and lack of efficiency incentives in the GIS and LIS, which led to rapidly rising utilization and costs in urban areas. Part was due to the aging of the working populations that they covered; part was due to the shortage of healthcare providers in rural areas (partly a result of barefoot doctors leaving the communes for private practice or leaving medicine altogether) which, combined with the withdrawal of government financial support for CMS[35] and the rise of fee-for-service payment, led to higher out-of-pocket costs by rural residents. Finally, part was due to the increased autonomy ceded to healthcare providers.[36]

Second, to deal with rising costs of care, the government continued the use of administered prices for basic services (per diem rates, office visits, surgical procedures) to keep them affordable for the population.[37] Pricing was set to achieve political and social objectives, not to sustain provider operations or provide a margin. Low, stipulated prices for hospital stays further meant that patients had an economic incentive to remain in the hospital for long periods (e.g., 30 days), which reduced bed turnover and impeded other patients getting access to hospital beds.

Third, the government directed most of its funding of healthcare to worker salaries and major capital investments (e.g., facilities, beds, equipment), perhaps accounting for only 25–30 percent of hospital spending in the 1990s. This left the funding of most operating expenses (which were rising along with healthcare costs) to the health facilities themselves. As government employees, physicians were thus poorly paid and their hospitals insufficiently financed. As one analyst described the situation, "the hospitals relied on the government to get built, but had to rely on themselves to eat."[38]

The economic changes presented providers with several opportunities to deal with these problems.

Like SOEs, public hospitals were expected to generate profits by selling extra services to cover their operating costs and responsibilities for basic service provision. They were given more autonomy to moonlight, open supplemental sites of care, and charge higher fees to paying patients for specialty services not subject to price regulation. This helped public hospitals to improve their financial condition and provide the technical and professional services that patients now demanded.

To keep solvent, providers charged 15 percent markups on the cost of drugs and high-technology diagnostic tests not covered in the administered pricing scheme. Providers also induced utilization for such services to increase volumes (e.g., more drugs or tests per patient). Such fees grew in importance in hospital funding – from perhaps half in 1981 to three-quarters by 1992 according to one study, or 50–90 percent of profits according to another.[39] Of course, to reap these markups, hospitals had to invest in the adoption of the new equipment, leading to expensive technology wars. Hospitals used the profits from these markups to pay higher salaries and bonuses to their staffs in order to retain/attract labor. Physicians also accepted bribes ("red envelopes") from patients (particularly those undergoing procedures) who wanted to assure themselves good service and favorable outcomes. The profit-making activities of providers attracted a lot of new entry. Between 1980 and 2000, the number of healthcare units delivering services rose from 180,000 to 320,000. This served to diminish some of the access barriers to higher quality care that patients wanted.

Healthcare institutions' operating costs and margins were increasingly funded by such care: unit revenues from pharmaceutical sales increased 600 percent between 1985 and 1994. As a percent of China's total healthcare spending in 1989, drug spending represented 45 percent, followed by hospital personnel salaries (17 percent), and supplies and maintenance (15 percent). By contrast, drug spending as a percentage of national health expenditures was less than 10 percent in the United States and only 15–40 percent in other developing countries. Drug sales were an even more important source of the bottom line of rural health institutions, where surgical procedures and diagnostic testing

were less available. Hospital pharmacies became important revenue-generating centers, retaining non-taxable revenue from the sale of drugs at government-stipulated prices, as well as revenues from markups on drugs sold at unregulated prices and kickbacks from manufacturers for selling their products. Since roughly 80 percent of drugs were dispensed out of their pharmacies, hospitals did not face much retail competition and could capture the spread between wholesale and retail prices.[40] Not to be left behind, public health institutions leased out their facilities to private organizations to conduct lucrative procedures and testing.

The growing supply of drugs, procedures, technologies, and sophisticated facilities helped to fuel rising utilization of these services due to their perception as high quality. Demand for quality healthcare was further fueled by rising farmer and household incomes and higher expectations for services beyond what traditional rural providers offered.[41] Facilities at the local levels in rural areas had difficulties keeping up with the income expectations of providers and thus relied on less qualified personnel. Rural residents recognized the substandard quality of their local doctors and suspected they were engaged in fraudulent practices to boost their incomes. Dissatisfied with the training of the barefoot doctors in the village clinics and the assistant doctors at the township health centers, many patients began bypassing the traditional referral system and went directly to the hospitals located at the county level or even higher. Between 1985 and 2000, hospitals at these geographic levels saw an increase in their share of both inpatient visits (from 58.6 percent to 66.9 percent) and outpatient visits (from 51.4 percent to 58.4 percent). By doing so, the rural population effectively reversed Mao's solution of sending practitioners to the rural communities.

The pattern of rural-to-urban care seeking accelerated, despite government efforts to increase the quality and attractiveness of services at the local level. The MOH raised the skill levels of rural medical personnel by tightening screening criteria and regulatory oversight (e.g., certification and credentialing) of private physicians and barefoot doctors. Indeed, by 1985–1986 the "barefoot doctor" program was abandoned as the MOH phased out support. That same year, roughly 40 percent of barefoot doctors had attained the same level of training as physician assistants (vocational school graduates); after passing an examination, they became retitled as village or rural doctors. Those that failed to pass the examination were retitled as health workers or medical aids.[42]

Even further left behind in all of these changes were prevention and public health. Such activities constituted only 5 percent of the amount spent, mostly paid by government. Half of the amount contributed by government went toward public health, prevention, medical education, and research institutes; the other half was spent on medical services at national hospitals.[43] Competition among provinces and rural areas to make these investments and garner these revenues was plagued by an uneven playing field. Richer regions resisted transfers of tax revenues to regions less well-off, exacerbating income and infrastructure disparities in the country and leading to diversions of limited funds in these regions to non-operating spending.[44] This also meant a de-emphasis on public health and prevention activities, even in the public health departments responsible for hosting these activities. The shift was abetted by inadequate government funding and the focus of most government officials on meeting concrete and measurable fiscal targets rather than less observable performance metrics. The retreat from public health activities was made easier by the fact that such activities generated no demand and no patient fees.

Unintended Consequences

The shift to a market approach engendered several unintended consequences. First, the primacy of economic growth and the relaxation of government policy subordinated healthcare goals to economic goals at every level of government. The 1994 tax reforms forced each governmental level to fund its own healthcare services – a problem particularly manifested in local rural areas. This situation left local government no choice but to cut health spending, shirk their responsibility to implement health policies from above, levy additional fees on farmers, and/or assume sizable debt burdens. Local governments also turned to privatization and industrial/commercial development, both of which diminished the amount of farmland available to agriculture.

The loss of agricultural work (and the lure of higher pay) helped to initiate an enormous population migration to the cities. This had important health consequences for the migrant workers (see Chapter 4), who did not have access to health insurance in the cities (due to the *hukou* system) until the 2009 healthcare reform. It also had consequences for health and welfare of their children (the "left behind children," or *liushiou ertung*), estimated at 61 million as of 2013.[45]

Limited government funds available for healthcare were disproportionately directed to larger urban areas. The urban healthcare infrastructure was modernized to satisfy the rising demand of the growing urban population as well as the swelling numbers of farmers and peasants from rural areas that bypassed local facilities to seek care in the cities. According to the 2004 National Health Accounts data, 50 percent of 2002 provincial supply-side subsidies went to city hospitals, compared to only 9 percent for county hospitals and 7 percent for township health centers.[46] Local healthcare infrastructure deteriorated, fostering even greater demand for services at the county level and higher. The urban focus did not immediately threaten the CMS, however, which retained official MOH support. However, in 1983 a change in MOH leadership combined with a new Chinese premier and a new government document[47] led to a more rapid government retrenchment from rural healthcare responsibility. The entire sector was now expected to run like the market-based institutions outside of healthcare and be "tubs on their own bottom" rather than welfare organizations. This established the pattern of under-use of local level and rural facilities, the over-use of larger and urban facilities, and the positive impact of both on the level of health spending in China – a pattern that continues to this day.

These shortcomings – in tandem with local officials' appropriation of lands to support economic development and neglect of the life quality issues engendered by that development – also served to build villagers' resentment toward the Chinese government and the CCP, thereby undermining social harmony. These and similar factors set the stage for the series of health reforms undertaken by the central government starting in the late 1990s.

Second, the withdrawal of government spending and the emergence of paying patients meant that hospitals and other health institutions began to rely on the sale of profit-making services. This meant an emphasis on paying higher salaries and bonuses to retain staff, and generating surpluses to pay for new technologies to attract both staff and paying patients. Hospitals and health facilities at different governmental levels began competing for paying patients, leading to duplication of expensive equipment and bed capacity, and under-utilization of capacity at lower governmental levels. Despite the lower levels of use, local government was constrained by government standards that mandated staffing levels based on population catchment areas, as well as by work rules that prevented making workers redundant. These constraints meant idle staff (who still had to be paid out of the facilities' limited budgets) as well as idle equipment. This situation also led to the over-provision of high-technology products and services such as surgical procedures and pharmaceuticals. Such induced demand by providers proceeded unchecked due to the absence of any governmental scrutiny and regulation, as well as the inability of patients to gauge whether the services were necessary or appropriate. The result was a lot of unnecessary care, estimated by some as high as one-fifth of all healthcare spending.

This technological imperative received further impetus after 1989 when the MOH categorized hospitals into three classes (I, II, III) and by gradations within classes (A, B, C). For example, Peking University People's Hospital was categorized as a Class IIIA facility. The three levels reflected a hierarchical ranking according to administrative level (patient referral status: source vs. destination), bed size, and technological capabilities. To a certain degree, this ranking paralleled the three-tier structure of government – with top hospitals overseen and financed by the MOH, middle hospitals administered by provincial government, and lower-level hospitals administered by city government.[48] The MOH's goal was to strengthen the referral linkages between facilities with increasing levels of care (e.g., primary, secondary, tertiary). However, the classification

system was based on the presence of sophisticated technologies, which motivated lower-level hospitals to acquire medical devices and equipment to upgrade their ranking. This led to a proliferation of expensive facilities, with quality problems of inappropriate overuse and economic problems of rising utilization of expensive services and duplication. For example, in 2006, the average cost of admission to a Class IIIA tertiary hospital was 12,650 yuan, or 90 percent of China's GDP per capita.[49] This also undermined the intended referral patterns, as smaller and lower-level institutions sought to retain patients and treat them in their own facilities rather than refer them upwards.

Third, efforts to improve the supply of healthcare facilities and services increased the attractiveness of healthcare as a good, and thus the demand for this good, by an urban population that had insurance coverage and/or rising incomes. This led to rising utilization of care, especially among the GIS and LIS enrollees, who disregarded the referral structure and sought treatment in the large tertiary hospitals since they had free choice of provider. During the 1990s, these two groups of beneficiaries accounted for only 19.6 percent of the population (230 million) but 42.5 percent of total medical spending. Between 1978 and 1994, the two programs' spending rose from 3.16 billion RMB to 56 billion RMB. This represented an annual growth of 11.5 percent net of inflation, compared to the growth in total government spending of only 3.2 percent. Their generous insurance coverage encouraged not only moral hazard on their part, but also induced demand on the part of providers. An estimated 20–30 percent of GIS spending was considered to be inappropriate and wasteful utilization. Efforts to reform this spending excess paralleled efforts to reform Medicare spending in the United States: both groups viewed their insurance coverage as an entitlement that government dare not cut.

Fourth, the promotion of market and profit-making approaches to healthcare supply and the proliferation of institutions offering health services led to a sprawling and diverse provider sector no longer controlled or closely scrutinized by the government. Only half of Chinese hospitals were overseen by health administrative departments; even then, these departments lacked the personnel to oversee them. An estimated one-third of hospital beds were owned by state enterprises, which did not operate under the authority of the health ministry or provincial health bureaus. Still, other providers did not have licenses from the local health bureaus to operate their clinics. Pluralistic ownership and control resulted in service duplication and widely varying occupancy levels.[50]

Pressures on Urban Health Insurance Coverage

Urban health insurance had been financed by the SOEs and their LIS. Under market reforms, however, the SOEs saw their governmental support drastically reduced. This prompted a collapse of the urban work units. They found it difficult to insure their employees and cover their medical expenses. In prior years, Chinese firms also used to provide their workers with a host of social services such as maternity care, day care, housing, kindergartens, health clinics, and canteens. Under reforms, firms needed to be more self-sufficient and generate profits; social services could no longer be subsidized by state allocations.

This began a slowly building pressure to abandon coverage and outsource all health insurance costs to centralized insurance providers – a move that came to fruition in the late 1990s (see below). In 1993, nearly three-quarters of the urban population had insurance coverage (LIS, GIS); by the late 1990s, barely half of the urban population retained such coverage. The GIS covered about 7–9 percent of this urban population, while the LIS covered another 40 percent. By 2002, only 29 percent of the Chinese population had any health insurance coverage. The situation was much better for the urban population (49 percent covered) than it was for rural residents (only 7 percent covered). The situation was even worse in the poorest provinces in western China (3 percent covered).[51]

Pressures on Rural Health Insurance Coverage: Demise of the CMS

The demise of the communes and the government's withdrawal from financing healthcare led to a precipitous collapse of CMS. The latter half of the century witnessed the meteoric rise and fall of villages with the CMS scheme. From an early base of 10 percent villages with CMS in 1958, the percentage increased sharply to 32 percent by 1960, 46 percent by 1962, 80 percent by 1968, and 90 percent by 1976. The percentage of villages with the CMS scheme fell precipitously thereafter to 82 percent in 1978, 58 percent in 1981, 11 percent in 1983, 9.5 percent in 1986, and then 4.8 percent by 1989.[52] The situation was exacerbated as MOH officials pressed to cut CMS subsidies, which fell three-quarters by 1987 and then terminated thereafter.

To be sure, there were other causes of the CMS demise, including the failure of the Great Leap Forward (1958–1961) and the Cultural Revolution. CMS was ideologically linked to these two (now discredited) approaches and viewed as expendable. Moreover, the reaction against the intense political mobilization during the Cultural Revolution, coupled with the demise of communal agriculture and mandatory participation in CMS, meant that mass mobilization campaigns to improve public health were not as likely to occur. Instead, local government officials and residents gave priority to economic growth, revenue generation, and increasing income levels.[53]

CMS was also strapped financially during the era of market forces in the 1980s due to rising prices for scarce medical supplies and rising premiums to pay for the now unsubsidized clinic services. CMS schemes had already been challenged by a lack of technical acumen in assessing the proper premiums to charge villagers and controlling costs, as well as the small enrollment base over which to spread risk, avoid unfavorable selection, and mitigate moral hazard.[54] As villagers disenrolled from CMS, the system became insolvent.[55] Public subsidies for rural health dropped from RMB 39 billion to RMB 22 billion during the period 1978–1988. The vast majority of China's (heavily rural) population now once again lacked health insurance coverage. This loss in coverage helped reverse the public health gains achieved under Mao's regime and the CMS. The country witnessed an increase in the mortality rate and the incidence of infectious diseases. Table 2.3 depicts the change in quality and access indicators between the CMS era and the emerging fee-for-service era.[56]

Table 2.3 Comparison of cooperative medical system and fee-for-service system

Indicators	CMS	FFS
1. Percentage of patients seeking medical care when ill	89.17	81.8
2. Percentage of patients not seeking medical care because of economic difficulty	27.3	53.4
3. Percentage hospitalized of the patients needing hospitalization	95.42	52.96
4. Percentage non-hospitalized because of economic difficulty	6.32	19.33
5. Percentage using advanced birth delivery method	92.7	85.63
6. Percentage with antenatal examination	54.81	40.58
7. Percentage with postpartum examination	79.38	69.18
8. Infant mortality (per 1,000)	25.09	27.6
9. Morbidity from diseases preventable by immunization (per 100,000)	90.76	175.16
10. Life expectancy (years)	73.51	72.21
11. Percentage of poverty resulting from diseases	9.36	25.7

Sources: 1. G.L. Cao, "The Development and Changes of Our Country's Medical System," *Chinese Primary Health Care* 7 (1990): 5–10.
2. D.S. Wu, "The Comparison of the Cooperative Medical System and the Fee-For-Service System," *Chinese Rural Health Administration* 9 (1987): 33–35.

The CMS system that survived now rested on a fee-for-service model, which hampered access to care (for those unable to afford it) and reduced health status levels (since prevention and public health activities that promote health status were non-revenue-generating services). The handful of villages that still retained a collective fund were also financed more by village factory production than agricultural production.

Along with CMS, there was a total collapse of the Mao-era infrastructure at the ground level, including barefoot doctors, brigade/village health clinics, and commune/township health centers. The cohort of barefoot doctors declined rapidly from 1.8 million to 1.2 million between 1978 and 1982;[57] the number of CMS village clinics likewise fell quickly from 390,000 in 1983 to 305,000 in 1985. Between 1982 and 1992, the volume of patients treated at the township centers dropped from 1.467 billion to 1.015 billion.[58] The number of township center beds likewise dropped from 775,413 to 726,124 between 1978 and 1988 as did the number of personnel working in them (from 1.038 million to 0.870 million). By the 1990s, the bulk of the population (80 percent) still resided in rural areas, but much of the healthcare infrastructure (exceeding 50 percent of hospital beds and professionals) operated in urban areas.[59] As each

level decayed, so did the referral linkages between the three tiers of the rural healthcare system and active government involvement in rural healthcare and financial support for the operating costs of facilities. Patients now self-referred themselves to facilities at higher governmental levels, such as county hospitals, which saw their annual visits soar from 1.223 billion in 1982 to 1.439 billion in 1992.

Return of Private Practice and Fee-for-Service Medicine

Prior to the 1980s, the government tolerated private practice among four types of individuals: private practitioners granted private practice licenses prior to the Cultural Revolution, providers released from public employers and made redundant, TCM providers, and retired doctors (mostly TCM practitioners). Such practitioners were not supervised by the government and essentially operated in an illegal private market (partly filled with quacks). To boost the supply of practitioners, the MOH lobbied for private practitioners to supplement the public market; the government gradually relaxed its restrictions on private medical practice during the decade of the 1980s.[60]

• In 1980, the MOH issued its *Report on the Granting of Permission for Solo Private Medical*

Practice (sent to the State Council) which recommended the legalization of private medical practice;[61]

- By 1984, private practice was allowed on a trial basis in several provinces;
- In 1985, the State Council encouraged private medical practice;
- In 1987, the State Bureau of Industry and Commerce Administration granted permission to public sector health professionals to own and operate private medical clinics after their retirement from public service;
- In 1988, the MOH and the State Bureau of Traditional Medicine Administration jointly issued a set of regulations spelling out the criteria for the establishment of private medical practices. Included in these regulations were details of the licensing process (to be handled by municipal and county authorities), the accreditation process (to be handled by the MOH and provincial health authorities), and the penalties for non-compliance; and
- In 1989, the MOH allowed part-time private medical practice in public healthcare facilities.

The government also allowed local collectives to operate for-profit medical businesses. Barefoot doctors and others who had retired from the public sector migrated to existing settings, as well as set up their own clinics and hospitals. They were joined by doctors currently in the public sector who resigned or moonlighted. While only 5 percent of village clinics were privately owned in 1982, they were a majority by 1985; by 1989 nearly 60 percent of the village clinics featured private practice models charging patients a fee for service. Of this 60 percent, 48–49 percent were organized as solo offices, while another 11–12 percent were group (unified) clinics.

Private practice remained at the periphery of China's delivery system for at least four reasons. First, all individual private practitioners and most private hospitals were excluded from the public insurance schemes enacted over time. Second, elite physicians were attracted more to the public hospitals since they offered some semblance of a career track with occupational and academic titles – something that private hospitals could not offer. Third, the public distrusted the private

delivery system. Fourth, private hospitals tend to be ranked lower in China's hospital accreditation system (which was controlled by local government), thus limiting their attractiveness to patients and thus to physicians. Private hospitals thus found themselves limited to retired physicians (see Chapter 7), which likely undermined their quality and service reputation.[62]

The country had 1.88 million doctors working in county level (and higher) facilities, another 0.41 million doctors working in township facilities, and roughly 1 million barefoot doctors working in villages. The total Chinese labor force engaged in healthcare at that time was 5 million.[63] By 1998, the country had 126,068 private healthcare institutions in China that accounted for 40 percent of the total; however, they employed only 3.7 percent of the country's total healthcare personnel.

Like physicians and clinics, hospital financing was now based on fees rather than funding pools at the commune level. However, the prices for their services (routine drugs, routine visits, standard diagnostic tests, surgeries) had been set in the late 1950s at levels well below costs. Moreover, public sector financial support to hospitals was limited to salaries and perhaps only 10 percent of operating budgets; the remainder of hospital costs now had to be covered by patient fees, higher prices on services and products not covered by price controls, and greater clinical volumes. Public hospitals were encouraged to generate surpluses that could be used to finance equipment purchases (e.g., high-end diagnostic imaging), facility upgrades, and bonuses paid to physicians to help them generate these surpluses (known as the "responsibility system"). The government allowed hospitals to supplement low physician salaries (e.g., anywhere from 3,000 to 4,200 yuan a month in urban areas, and perhaps as low as 800 yuan a month in rural areas) with bonuses based on the hospital revenues that doctors generated. Hospitals charged user fees and high markups (15–20 percent) on new technologies and drugs, as well as induced patients to utilize these services (price and quantity). Recovery of operating costs from these charges and services constituted two-thirds of total revenues in the early 1980s and four-fifths by the mid-1990s.

The percentage of total drug sales through institutional outlets rose from 37 percent in 1978 to 57 percent by 1988.[64] Hospitals also competed for patients by recruiting well-known physicians that could attract paying patients. This engendered China's own version of the "medical arms race" among hospitals.[65]

Diminished Emphasis on Public Health

Government funding of prevention and public health suffered heavily. Such activities did not generate patient revenues and were thus not heavily promoted by public health departments (which also needed to be more self-reliant). Government funding of disease control and prevention was cut from 0.11 percent of GDP in 1978 to 0.04 percent of GDP by 1994. Local public health officials neglected health education, maternal and child health, and contagion control efforts. Physicians were likewise not rewarded for offering such services as health promotion and disease prevention. They thus de-emphasized physical examinations, health screenings, and the reduction of risk factors. Such retrenchment in public health activities served to slow the country's progress in improving population health and actually led to a resurgence of some infectious diseases.

This retrenchment was abetted by a marked shift in China's government from "bandwagoning" – which entailed the concentration of power under Mao and the Communist Party, the marginalization of the health bureaucracy, and coordination of policy in pursuit of public health goals – to "buckpassing" whereby each stakeholder shirked their public health responsibility, pursued their own agendas (e.g., the MOH's effort to modernize the country's healthcare system), and focused instead on economic growth.[66] Government funding of healthcare shrunk during the era from 39 percent of national health spending (1986) to 16 percent (2002).[67]

More significantly, reduced government funding laid the foundation for the emergence of chronic illness in the Chinese population that now serves as the country's most significant health threat. The economic miracle that China underwent was thus accompanied by a public health disaster, a ticking population health time bomb, and a growing crisis of rising cost and utilization. According to an official report, between 2000 and 2025 China will experience a 70 percent rise in the number of patients, a 43 percent rise in inpatient hospitalization, a 37 percent increase in outpatient visits, and a 50 percent rise in total medical expenditures.[68]

With regard to social changes, perhaps the most important reform was China's one-child policy. The policy was introduced in 1979 and enforced in urban areas through a system of rewards and penalties (e.g., fines, loss of employment), but slightly relaxed in rural areas due to the need for labor in an agricultural economy and the elderly's dependence on children.[69] This contributed to the falling fertility rate in China from 6 during 1950–1955 to 2 by 1990–1995; the most rapid decline occurred in the 1970s prior to the policy's implementation, however.[70] This policy, combined with a low rate of in-migration from other countries, accelerated the aging of China's population. It fostered a social structure of 4-2-1: four grandparents supported by two parents supported by one child. The one-child policy increased the "dependency ratio" and meant that the one child played an important role in the social security of his/her parents and grandparents. This led the country to put greater emphasis on child health as part of its de facto social security system. The one-child policy was reinforced by China's push to modernize the country, contain population size, and increase the standard of living; this resulted in more government investment in education and growing personal incomes, both of which contributed to a lower birth rate.

Trends in Health Spending, Government Spending, and Out-of-Pocket Financing

The period 1978–2000 saw rising healthcare spending. Annual per capita spending on personal health services rose 32-fold during this period, from 11 RMB to 352 RMB. National health expenditures rose from 3.07 percent of GDP to 4.62 percent of GDP – half of this paying for pharmaceutical products (see Table 2.4). Drugs with high price mark-ups and intravenous (IVs) injections became

Table 2.4 National health expenditures by source

| Year | Total Health Expenditure (100 million yuan) | Government Health Expenditure | | Social Health Expenditure | | Out-of-pocket Health Expenditure | | Per Capita Health Expenditure (yuan) | | | Health Expenditure as Percentage of GDP (%) |
		Level (100 million yuan)	As Percentage of Health Expenditure	Level (100 million yuan)	As Percentage of Health Expenditure	Level (100 million yuan)	As Percentage of Health Expenditure	Total	Urban	Rural	
1978	110.21	35.44	32.16	52.25	47.41	22.52	20.43	11.50			3.02
1979	126.19	40.64	32.21	59.88	47.45	25.67	20.34	12.90			3.11
1980	143.23	51.91	36.24	60.97	42.57	30.35	21.19	14.50			3.15
1981	160.12	59.67	37.27	62.43	38.99	38.02	23.74	16.00			3.27
1982	177.53	68.99	38.86	70.11	39.49	38.43	21.65	17.50			3.33
1983	207.42	77.63	37.43	64.55	31.12	65.24	31.45	20.10			3.48
1984	242.07	89.46	36.96	73.61	30.41	79.00	32.64	23.20			3.36
1985	279.00	107.65	38.58	91.96	32.96	79.39	28.46	26.40			3.09
1986	315.90	122.23	38.69	110.35	34.93	83.32	26.38	29.40			3.07
1987	379.58	127.28	33.53	137.25	36.16	115.05	30.31	34.70			3.15
1988	488.04	145.39	29.79	189.99	38.93	152.66	31.28	44.00			3.24
1989	615.50	167.83	27.27	237.84	38.64	209.83	34.09	54.60			3.62
1990	747.39	187.28	25.06	293.10	39.22	267.01	35.73	65.40	158.80	38.80	4.00
1991	893.49	204.05	22.84	354.41	39.67	335.03	37.50	77.10	187.60	45.10	4.10
1992	1096.86	228.61	20.84	431.55	39.34	436.70	39.81	93.60	222.00	54.70	4.07
1993	1377.78	272.06	19.75	524.75	38.09	580.97	42.17	116.30	268.60	67.60	3.90
1994	1761.24	342.28	19.43	644.91	36.62	774.05	43.95	146.90	332.60	86.30	3.65
1995	2155.13	387.34	17.97	767.81	35.63	999.98	46.40	177.90	401.30	112.90	3.54
1996	2709.42	461.61	17.04	875.66	32.32	1372.15	50.64	221.40	467.40	150.70	3.81
1997	3196.71	523.56	16.38	984.06	30.78	1689.09	52.84	258.60	537.80	177.90	4.05
1998	3678.72	590.06	16.04	1071.03	29.11	2017.63	54.85	294.90	625.90	194.60	4.36
1999	4047.50	640.96	15.84	1145.99	28.31	2260.55	55.85	321.80	702.00	203.20	4.51
2000	4586.63	709.52	15.47	1171.94	25.55	2705.17	58.98	361.90	813.74	214.65	4.62

Table 2.4 (cont.)

Year	Total Health Expenditure (100 million yuan)	Government Health Expenditure		Social Health Expenditure		Out-of-pocket Health Expenditure		Per Capita Health Expenditure (yuan)			Health Expenditure as Percentage of GDP (%)
		Level (100 million yuan)	As Percentage of Health Expenditure	Level (100 million yuan)	As Percentage of Health Expenditure	Level (100 million yuan)	As Percentage of Health Expenditure	Total	Urban	Rural	
2001	5025.93	800.61	15.93	1211.43	24.10	3013.89	59.97	393.80	841.20	244.77	4.58
2002	5790.03	908.51	15.69	1539.38	26.59	3342.14	57.72	450.70	987.07	259.33	4.81
2003	6584.10	1116.94	16.96	1788.50	27.16	3678.66	55.87	509.50	1108.91	274.67	4.85
2004	7590.29	1293.58	17.04	2225.35	29.32	4071.35	53.64	583.90	1261.93	301.61	4.75
2005	8659.91	1552.53	17.93	2586.41	29.87	4520.98	52.21	662.30	1126.36	315.83	4.68
2006	9843.34	1778.86	18.07	3210.92	32.62	4853.56	49.31	748.80	1248.30	361.89	4.55
2007	11573.97	2581.58	22.31	3893.72	33.64	5098.66	44.05	875.96	1516.29	358.11	4.35
2008	14535.40	3593.94	24.73	5065.60	34.85	5875.86	40.42	1094.52	1861.76	455.19	4.63
2009	17541.92	4816.26	27.46	6154.49	35.08	6571.16	37.46	1314.26	2176.63	561.99	5.15
2010	19980.39	5732.49	28.69	7196.61	36.02	7051.29	35.29	1490.06	2315.48	666.30	4.98
2011	24345.91	7464.18	30.66	8416.45	34.57	8465.28	34.77	1806.95	2697.48	879.44	5.15
2012	27846.84	8365.98	30.04	9916.31	35.61	9564.55	34.35	2056.57	2969.01	1055.89	5.36

(a) Data in this table are at current prices. Data of 2011 are preliminary data.
(b) Since 2011, total health expenditure does not include that of educational expenditure of higher education. Since 2006, it includes medical aid expenditure in urban and rural areas.

a mainstay of therapy in hospitals: in 2011, they still accounted for 40–45 percent of hospital revenues.[71] In rural China, the village doctors made their living prescribing and selling drugs and IV infusions to patients; some suspect that as much as one-third of these rural drugs were counterfeit products that allowed sellers to make even higher profits at patients' expense (financial and clinical).[72]

By far, the largest financier of care was the individual citizen. Out-of-pocket payments as a percentage of national health expenditures rose from 20 percent in 1978 to 59 percent by 2000. As a percentage of rural household income, out-of-pocket payments slowly crept higher during the period from 2.41 percent (1985) to 3.15 percent (1994). Such payments were higher than those borne by urban residents, due to the higher benefit levels offered by insurance in urban areas and their higher income levels.[73]

By contrast, the government's role in financing healthcare dropped from 32 percent in 1978 to 15 percent in 2000, as did contributions to social insurance (which fell from 47 percent to 26 percent) (see Table 2.4).[74] Central government funding was heavily targeted at the GIS and subsidies to poorer regions of the country. In 1989, direct support from the central government accounted for only 1 percent of national health expenditures, while GIS outlays accounted for an additional 7 percent. State-owned firms and the LIS scheme accounted for a larger share (32 percent), followed by provincial and local governments (19 percent) and the CMS (5 percent).

As the central government's share of public spending fell, the remaining government share was left to provincial and local governments, who had to support the funding of healthcare through taxation. This situation meant that richer provinces and coastal regions with greater tax bases could and did finance more healthcare development than poorer and rural provinces.

Pro-rich, Top-heavy, Urban-centric System

Government spending during this period was "pro-rich." Between 1980 and 1989, government expenditures for city hospitals (as a percentage of total public investments in curative services) rose from 38.5 percent to 48.2 percent; spending on county hospitals dropped from 26.3 percent to 21.3 percent; and spending on township health centers fell from 32.3 percent to 26.8 percent.[75] At the provincial level, government spending on health was heavily directed to subsidies to support health insurance coverage for urban dwellers who were more economically advantaged than rural residents.[76] These same subsidies also favored urban healthcare facilities utilized by the urban insured population. According to the 2004 National Health Accounts data, urban hospitals captured 50 percent of the supply-side subsidies in 2002, while county hospitals captured another 9 percent. By contrast, township health centers captured only 7 percent of these monies.

In addition to these funding levels, China's healthcare infrastructure has been, and still is, "top-heavy" – resting on a large population of hospitals. In 1994, there were 14,762 urban hospitals at the county level or higher, another 51,929 township hospitals and health centers,

and another 300 or so hospitals operated by the military. In total, they accounted for one-third of all health facilities, 90 percent of all beds, and 74 percent of the healthcare workforce. Roughly 90 percent of China's healthcare is delivered in hospitals, with little rendered in community health centers (CHCs) or village clinics, which have lost most of their qualified physicians.[77] Utilization of this urban-focused infrastructure intensified in the period from 1980 to 2011 when the urban population swelled from 19 percent to 50 percent.

Roughly half of all public spending is generated by hospitals. Moreover, most of the growth in inpatient volume occurred in Class III tertiary hospitals; one-third of all outpatient visits take place in Class II and III hospitals. The heavy concentration of spending (80 percent of government spending on urban institutions) and facilities (80 percent of urban healthcare resources in large hospitals) in the urban areas is perhaps only partly explained by the higher incomes of urban residents and the larger tax base of the cities. Government officials promoted the modernization of China (including increased government spending on education) and China's healthcare infrastructure, particularly the Class III hospitals found in the large cities. Such hospitals were closely tied to the burgeoning medical research facilities in Chinese universities and enjoyed higher status and prestige. Also closely allied with government officials and researchers was a coalition of CPC members, city officials, and the growing number of urban residents who felt they should receive more attention in the country's healthcare system.

Legacy of Market Reforms

The market reform era was not just about economics; it was also about government. Just as Mao had subordinated the government bureaucracy to his will and the CCP, so did Deng Xiaoping delegate fiscal and managerial autonomy to lower levels of government and promote the role of the bureaucracy in carrying out the new economic agenda. More of a balance thus developed between the party and the bureaucracy.

The net consequence of the market reforms begun in the late 1970s was a dismantling of the system of healthcare insurance, delivery, and public health promotion developed under Mao. According to some economists, China exhibited "regression to the mean" following its public health gains under Mao. Utilizing the framework described in Chapter 1, these health gains contributed to the economic and wealth gains during the period of economic reform.[78]

Starting in 1981, official statistics suggest a slowdown in improvements in population health compared to the Maoist era. For example, life expectancy rose only 6.9 years from 1981 to 2010, compared to an increase of nearly 33 years between 1949 and 1980.[79] China's stagnating rate of improvement paled in comparison to the improvements observed in other East Asian and other emerging nations despite their lower levels of economic growth. National health surveys conducted by the MOH revealed an increase in the percentage of the population – from 14 percent (1993) to 19 percent (2008) – who said they had suffered illness during the past two weeks. Much of this illness burden was due to the rise in chronic illness such as diabetes (see Chapter 3) and the changing lifestyle and diet of the population.

The iron triangle solution developed by Mao also disintegrated. Rising costs led to access problems. Access to care plummeted for the 70–76 percent of the rural population without insurance coverage, largely due to the demise of the CMS and the collapse of the rural delivery system. Access problems were reflected by the fact that nearly half of the Chinese population refused to see a physician when sick, mostly due to affordability. Access further suffered due to income and spending variations across China's provinces and regions; such variations bred huge and growing inequities in the availability of healthcare services. Urban areas received disproportionately more investment in hospital beds and medical professionals. The vast majority of the government's health budget was devoted to funding health coverage and utilization for 8.5 million government employees, who accounted for only 1 percent of the population.

Quality issues exacerbated access problems. The least of the quality issues was the nascent state of hospital accreditation, which only began in 1989 and which focused on structural indicators. Quality of care fell due to incentives to over-treat (e.g., tests, procedures) and over-prescribe (e.g., IVs, antibiotics), as well as the removal of incentives and funding to conduct health promotion and prevention. In one audit of the prescribing behavior of Chinese hospital-based physicians, 62 percent of patients received antibiotics; 39 percent were still prescribed antibiotics even when they expressed concern over their inappropriateness. Excessive prescribing of antibiotics also contributed to growing drug resistance among the population and the rise of superbugs. Over-prescribing may also foster greater patient distrust of physician motives, leading to downstream problems of under-compliance and under-diagnosis of chronic disease.[80]

Even though economic growth increased the wealth of the population, healthcare costs outpaced growth in GDP, leaving the population to finance the majority of healthcare spending out of pocket. The out-of-pocket share of health spending reached 60 percent by 2001.[81] Between 1980 and 2005, disposable income rose 21-fold for urban residents and 16-fold for rural residents, and GDP per capita rose 27-fold; by contrast, national health spending per capita rose 40-fold and out-of-pocket spend rose 102-fold. [82] A hospitalization could thus cost an individual their entire annual income. Not only was healthcare less affordable to individuals, it was also less affordable for the country. During the 1980–2003 period, healthcare spending rose 45-fold, while government spending on healthcare rose only 20-fold (see Table 2.4). This meant greater cost shifting to the private sector and, especially, individuals: out-of-pocket spending as a percentage of total spending rose from 21 percent to 56 percent during this period. This all occurred as the percentage of the population not covered by health insurance remained stationary. Not surprisingly, high healthcare costs became the top concern of patients queried in national health surveys.

Patients thus grew increasingly dissatisfied with the cost of care, their low access to care, and the quality of facilities and personnel in rural areas. According to one analyst, "by the mid-2000s, medical care, education, and social security became the 'three new mountains' that burdened the Chinese people, reminiscent of the old 'three mountains' (imperialism, feudalism, and bureaucrat-capitalism) that were used by the Communist Party to justify its social revolution that led to the founding of the People's Republic in 1949."[83] This set the stage for the reforms to come in the new millennium.

At the same time, government subsidies to hospitals dropped from 30 percent of revenues in the 1980s to less than 8 percent by 2000. Hospitals, clinics, and doctors were required to support themselves through the provision of expensive medicines, tests, and services – inaugurating China's own "technological imperative."[84] As in the West, this imperative was favored by the providers and patients alike; unlike the West, it was financed on the backs of patients in the form of rising out-of-pocket costs, not via health insurance.

Various cities and provinces devised efforts to curb rising health costs, but on a scattered, piecemeal, and experimental basis. There was no concerted, national effort to "bend the trend." There was also no successful effort to develop primary care and more community-based (rather than hospital-based) services. Such endeavors were thwarted by China's own version of the "military-industrial complex" in healthcare: public hospitals and the pharmaceutical companies whose products supported them. In poorer and more rural areas, these endeavors were impeded by the lack of resources to implement central government policies.

Reforms Since 2000

Capital Expansion

Capital expansion within China's healthcare industry accelerated during the new millennium. A 1999 trade agreement with the United States led to China's membership in the World Trade Organization (WTO) in 2001. The country's compliance with WTO regulations in 2003 allowed for foreign direct investment (FDI) in healthcare products and services and foreign ownership of hospitals (including joint ventures and partnerships). In 2004, one-quarter of the world's FDI ($268 billion) went to Asia, with China gleaning $60 billion of this total. The country's high and rising gross savings rate (roughly one-third in the 1980s, rising to roughly 40 percent in the 1990s, and

then rising above 50 percent in the first decade of the 2000s) made additional capital available to finance infrastructure growth.[85]

Between 1950 and 2000, China built an average of 250 hospitals per year; between 2000 and 2004, that number swelled to 519 hospitals per year. In addition to more hospitals, the country saw an expansion of its private hospital sector. By 2004, roughly 14 percent of hospitals (2,545) were privately owned. By 2008, 27 percent of hospitals were privately owned, but accounted for only 9.5 percent of total beds. These figures crept up slightly by 2011 to 38 percent of hospitals and 12.5 percent of beds. 72 percent of clinics (145,375) were likewise privately owned.[86] The expansion of the hospital sector meant a concomitant expansion in the country's medical equipment and medical device sectors – products that accounted for 25–35 percent of healthcare facility spending.

SARS and Renewed Emphasis on Public Health

The SARS crisis in late 2002 and 2003 was a pivotal moment in the history of China's healthcare system. The epidemic was first unreported and then subsequently under-reported. The government responded quickly to the crisis thereafter, leading to some re-invigoration of the country's faltering public health and disease control systems. China established a national network for reporting infectious diseases and public health emergencies. It also launched thousands of projects to prevent and control disease, including free health screenings, child vaccinations, and antiretrovirals for people infected with HIV-AIDS. The crisis may also have contributed to the recognition that the entire public health system (including hospitals, clinics, personnel) had deteriorated and needed substantial investment – an initiative put into operation in 2009 (see below).

Just as importantly, the SARS crisis exposed other problems with China's health system, including the imbalances between economic versus social investment and urban versus rural investment. This new realization coincided with a new government in 2002 under the leadership of Hu Jintao. His vision of healthcare called for a renewed effort to tackle the iron triangle: "safe, effective, convenient and low-cost healthcare services available to everyone in China."[87] This vision and the central government's newly found political will to address two decades of growing problems may have been prompted by several considerations: rising social discontent with the inequities in China's economic progress, the realization that China's economic growth had been achieved by sacrificing investments in social welfare and well-being, growing distrust of healthcare providers, rising out-of-pocket costs of care, growth of the individual's share in financing national health expenditures, and growing fears that healthcare costs could bankrupt households.

The Beginnings of Insurance Reforms (1998)

Reforms in 1998 targeted health insurance in an effort to deal with the pressure on urban coverage, as well as control rising costs and overutilization of services. A national medical insurance scheme – known as the Urban Employee Basic Medical Insurance (UEBMI) – combined and supplanted the old GIS and LIS plans, covering up to 70 percent of the health expenditures for roughly 100 million urban workers. The UEBMI marked a three-pronged effort by the central government to provide demand-side subsidies in the form of health insurance to make healthcare more accessible and affordable, to address inequities in the population, and improve the public's satisfaction with healthcare and the government. The government continued this effort in the new millennium with additional insurance schemes (see below).

Selected cities (Zhenjiang, Jiujiang) conducted a series of pilot experiments as the forerunner to the UEBMI. The experiments followed a 1993 State Council decision to establish a pooled health insurance fund that combined employer premium contributions with local government-administered funds and individual premium contributions. While the local experiments failed to reduce costs, the central government expanded the model to more than 40 cities in 1996 and then went nationwide as the UEBMI.

The UEBMI was devised to overhaul the shaky finances of the SOEs by putting all of their workers into a citywide insurance risk pool. All SOEs and private employers were required to offer their workers coverage that included medical savings accounts (MSAs) coupled with catastrophic insurance. Funding of the scheme consisted of payroll taxes (6 percent from employers, 2 percent from employees) as well as individual medical savings accounts (funded through the employee contribution and a portion of the employer contribution). The MSAs, modeled after those in Singapore, placed the onus on employees to save their own money to pay a portion of their personal medical costs. The MSAs covered the initial costs up to 10 percent of the worker's annual wage, after which the catastrophic plan covered costs incurred that amounted to 10–400 percent of wages.

One goal of the MSAs and the risk sharing with beneficiaries was to induce patients to seek care at community hospitals and have physicians at those hospitals serve as de facto general practitioners. The MSA provided a subsidy of 300 RMB for medical consults and another subsidy of 400–1,600 RMB for hospitalization (depending on the type of hospital utilized); the higher subsidy was for Class III hospitals. Similarly, the payment by the individual MSA was higher for Class III hospitals. The net effect of the MSA subsidies, combined with fixed hospital prices, was to incentivize beneficiaries to seek care from the expensive tertiary hospitals, further widening the gap in utilization between Class III and community hospitals, as well as increasing the workload on physicians practicing in Class III facilities.

Not surprisingly, the costs of care borne by UEBMI began to grow. The enrollees in these plans were the remnant of a now aging and retiring workforce that populated the SOEs. Their higher healthcare costs were not offset by lower costs for younger employees; the latter sought employment outside of the struggling SOEs in the private sector that now fueled the country's growth and served as the source of entrepreneurship. Although mandatory, by 2007 only 180 million (53 percent) of the target urban population of 340 million was enrolled in UEBMI. Part of the problem was the high geographic mobility of the population; the UEBMI also relied on self-identification of firms and employee tracking.[88]

New Rural Health Insurance Scheme (2003)

A new government initiative increased subsidies for less wealthy areas and spread the country's growing economic surplus. In 2003, the central government established the New Cooperative Medical Scheme (NCMS),[89] overseen by the MOH, to replicate the original CMS scheme and cover all of the rural population. By 2007, 86 percent of China's counties had enrolled in NCMS, covering 730 million people.

There were several differences between the old and new schemes. CMS was mandatory and focused on prevention, while NCMS was voluntary and focused on acute care. Moreover, the NCMS pooled risk at the county level (200, 000–300,000), whereas the CMS pooled risk lower down at the commune level. The central thrust of NCMS was to cover catastrophic (hospital) expenditures. Initial government subsidies amounted to 40 RMB per capita annually but then rose to 200 RMB by 2011; the government subsidy was supplemented by an individual contribution (initially 10 RMB per capita, but then increasing to 250 RMB by 2011). Such subsidies permitted only low reimbursement to providers, which then had to be supplemented by high patient copayments. The central government intended to support the new program in tandem with matching investments by local governments and households; however, all three parties have struggled to keep up with rising costs of care.

New Urban Health Insurance Scheme (2007)

Unlike its rural counterpart, the tiered system established in urban areas had not broken down. Now the government sought to develop community health centers to promote primary care and reserve district hospitals for inpatient care. The government faced a huge challenge here, since the country's training programs produced specialists but no primary care doctors. In the eyes of patients "the only good care is from a specialist in a hospital."[90]

In 2007, the country developed a third insurance scheme, this time for urban residents who were unemployed or were employed in the informal sector of the economy. This population included students, children, the elderly, poor, and disabled. This scheme was called the Urban Resident Basic Medical Insurance (URBMI). Like the UEBMI, the URBMI was overseen by the Ministry of Human Resources and Social Security; unlike the UEBMI, the URBMI was voluntary. And like the NCMS, it covered only hospitalization expenses and catastrophic care. The government has increasingly subsidized the URBMI scheme and now accounts for 80 percent of its funding, supplemented by household contributions. The growth in enrollment by the three insurance schemes in the new millennium is depicted in Figure 2.2.

National Healthcare Reform (2009)

The new political will to reform China's health system found real expression in a 2005 report by the State Council Development Research Center. The report criticized the market-based reforms undertaken in 1980 and concluded they had failed. Two competing remedies surfaced, one favoring greater government funding of both the supply and demand side, the other also favoring more government investment but relying more on demand-side reform using insurers to purchase healthcare. The following year the central government set up a small group to consider these approaches. In 2007, the small group solicited health reform proposals from six organizations: a government think tank, two Chinese universities, the WHO, the World Bank, and McKinsey. Debate continued over supply-side approaches (e.g., government funding of hospitals) versus demand-side approaches (provide insurance coverage to the population), eventually leading to a compromise between the two.

The new reform approach was announced in January 2009. As before, the government's goal was a basic healthcare system that could provide care that was "safe, effective, convenient and affordable" by 2020. The implementation plan focused on the issues of access and affordability, and emphasized five initiatives: expanded insurance coverage (90 percent coverage by 2011), increased funding of public health, expansion of local level infrastructure to deliver services, the formation of an Essential Drugs List, and reforms of public hospital operations.

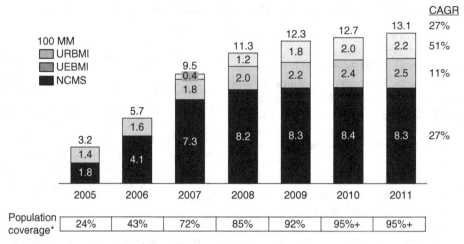

Figure 2.2 Expansion of insurance coverage, 2005–2011

* Calculated by dividing the enrolled population by total population in China; 2010 and 2011 data triangulated with MOH stat yearbook.

Source: MOH, MOHRSS, National Statistic Bureau, JJMC CS&P Team Analysis.

The reform called for massive government funding – initially $124 billion for the years 2009–2011, with the central government picking up 40 percent of the bill (or roughly $50 billion). By 2011, the central government had in fact contributed nearly $71 billion, leading to a growing share of national health expenditures picked up by the government (from 15.7 percent in 2002 to 28.7 percent by 2010). In 2015, researchers reported the government had spent an additional $230 billion beyond the $124 billion originally projected.[91] Half of the spending financed insurance reforms; the other half supported building of the delivery system and public health system.

The first initiative focused on expanded insurance coverage. The annual government subsidy for insurance increased from 80 RMB per capita in 2008 to 200 RMB per capita by 2011. By the close of 2011, 95 percent of the population was covered by UEBMI, URBMI, or NCMS: 45.8 million through UEBMI, 221 million through URBMI, and 832 million through NCMS.[92] This translated into urban insurance coverage of 89 percent and rural insurance coverage of 97 percent. The oft-quoted insurance coverage rate of 95 percent or more may be an overstatement, however; according to one researcher, the rate included 200 million migrant workers who have coverage in their rural residence but lack coverage in the cities where they work due to the *hukou* system. The effective level of insurance coverage may thus be about 87 percent.[93]

The insurance coverage was now more broadly spread across the population, but was still rather shallow in what it covered. Both inpatient and outpatient reimbursement rates still left more than half of the bill (52–56 percent of inpatient charges depending on urban–rural location, 70 percent of outpatient charges) up to the responsibility of the individual. Moreover, the changes in coverage were not accompanied by any changes in provider payment, which left intact fee-for-service payment and incentives to over-utilize. This meant the problem of rising utilization and costs would likely persist and continue to pose affordability challenges. This was particularly true as healthcare costs rose faster than China's GDP and per capita income. As a percentage of consumption spending, urban healthcare spending rose from 2 percent to 7 percent between 1990 and 2008, while rural healthcare spending rose from 5 percent to 6.7 percent.

Moreover, the patchwork insurance coverage offered through UEBMI and URBMI (overseen by the Ministry of Human Resources and Social Security) and the NCMS (overseen by the MOH until recently) led to several predictable problems: dual coverage, government overpayment of subsidies, duplicate information systems and staffing, and lack of portability across geographic settings.[94] The latter posed a particularly difficult problem for China's migrant worker population. The patchwork system thus failed to reduce the gaps in access to healthcare providers between urban and rural areas.

A second initiative promised to increase public health funding per capita from 15 RMB to 25 RMB. Health records were developed for both urban and rural residents, although there was greater penetration in urban areas. Efforts were also undertaken (e.g., screening, management protocols) to tackle the rising problem of non-communicable diseases (NCDs), with uncertain success (see Chapter 3).

A third initiative sought to develop local infrastructure and delivery using 63 billion RMB of central government investment. The plan called for (a) rebuilding thousands of community health centers and community health stations (CHSs); (b) construction of thousands of new health centers (CHCs, CHSs), county hospitals, and village clinics; (c) financing equipment purchases; and (d) improving manpower levels via on-the-job training of clinicians and managers in township and village clinics, hiring physicians to serve in central and western provinces, and subsidizing medical school tuition for those willing to serve in these areas.[95] One goal was to build and replenish the supply side of the country's long-absent primary care system by placing two family physicians in each township health center (THC). To stimulate demand for local treatment and reduce self-referrals to urban hospitals, the government also raised the rate of reimbursement to these health centers to 70 percent while also reducing the reimbursement rate for urban health centers. The functions of the THCs were also redefined to include public health as well as primary care. Increased reimbursement for THC services did not lead to increased utilization, however. Rural residents favored the village clinics over the THCs due to their proximity and lower price. They also favored the county hospitals over the THCs due to the perceived higher quality and easier access due to transportation improvements.

A fourth initiative to develop an Essential Drugs List (EDL) was designed to reduce the cost patients had to pay for prescription medications in primary healthcare institutions. The EDL consisted initially of a catalogue of 307 drugs considered to be cost-effective; a later version issued in March 2013 contained 520 drugs. Drugs on the EDL were covered by the public insurance schemes. Drugs included on the EDL were also permitted to participate in centralized tenders, organized by the provinces, employing a competitive bidding process to reduce drug prices. Roughly half of EDL drugs experienced an average 12 percent drop in price; prices on 49 percent of EDL drugs remained the same, while prices on 6 percent of EDL drugs rose to correct shortages.[96]

Township facilities were initially required to prescribe drugs from the EDL and sell them at cost instead of the 15 percent markup previously charged. The removal of the markup was to be phased in among 50 percent of county hospitals in 2014, and then among the remaining 50 percent in 2015. Lost revenues from the markups were to be compensated through an earmark of 15 percent of drug sales paid by local government to hospitals. However, neither government officials nor hospitals necessarily complied with this arrangement. Local officials could retain the funds to cover their own operating budgets. For hospitals and clinics, the markups that funded much of their operations far exceeded this compensation level, thus giving them the incentive to accept kickbacks from manufacturers as well as purchase and prescribe higher-price drugs not on the EDL; indeed, evidence suggests that public and private community health centers used an average of only two-thirds to three-quarters of the 307 drugs on the EDL.[97] Research also suggests local facilities induced demand for inpatient services to offset the lost revenue.[98]

The final initiative to reform the system of public hospitals targeted seven areas:[99]

1. Improve the capacity of public hospitals and healthcare delivery in geographic areas (rural areas, newly urbanized areas, suburban areas) and in clinical areas (pediatrics, obstetrics, mental health, elderly nursing, rehabilitation), and enhance access to health services.
2. Establish cooperative linkages and referral mechanisms between public hospitals and primary care. Encourage urban hospitals to assist

rural hospitals and community health service centers, and encourage county hospitals to assist township hospitals.

3. Prioritize the development of needed infrastructure at the county level, including the building of county hospitals.

4. Extend alternative models of payment to hospitals to incentivize lower-cost care. Channel direct reimbursement to hospitals.

5. Improve the quality of healthcare to promote patient satisfaction; improve standardization of care in patient treatment, including promoting electronic clinical pathways; and control the costs of diagnosis and treatment.

6. Standardize training for resident physicians in order to ensure quality of care.

7. Improve hospital information systems, establish telemedicine systems, and set up hospital information networks using electronic medical records.

These reforms have been slow to materialize. MOH officials and hospital executives naturally resisted these efforts. The MOH was reportedly pressured to hire hospital executives with ties to the CCP. Such executives were typically senior physicians with no managerial training; they also had short tenures in their executive roles, giving them little ability or motivation to pursue reforms.[100] Efforts to separate government operation from hospital management have not progressed much (see below); nor have efforts to change the revenue models of public hospitals.

Since the reform effort in 2009, the government has allowed greater private sector investment (up to 20 percent of hospitals by 2015) to expand capacity and serve as a competitive spur to the public sector. As noted above, there were more private hospitals by 2011, but they accounted for a tiny portion of China's bed capacity. Public facilities still accounted for 89–92 percent of all inpatient and outpatient utilization, while comprising only 55 percent of hospital capacity; at local levels, government facilities dominate the provision of services rendered by CHCs (90 percent of visits) and THCs (99 percent of visits).[101] Part of the problem is the lengthy and byzantine process of getting approvals

to construct new hospitals by private entities (see Chapter 9). There is also considerable evidence from the United States that the entrance of private hospitals spurs nonprofit hospitals to become more efficient; however, privatization and ownership conversions alone are insufficient to rectify the problems in hospital management and operations.[102]

Did Anything Really Change?

Despite the reform, some things did not change. Roughly one-third to one-half of reform spending was directed to demand-side health insurance coverage and subsidies. Half or more of the money went to the providers of healthcare: the major destination of healthcare spending, the major cause of the problem of rising costs, and now the recipients of the new insurance payments. The higher revenues flowing to hospitals were thus borne by payments from the newly insured populations and citizens. Moreover, in the face of these large transfers, the government still contributed less than one-tenth of public hospitals' revenues. There was no real national reform of the governance of public hospitals or the incentives under which they worked; government subsidies to fund the operating costs of public hospitals remained low. As described in Chapter 8, several local governments initiated pilot projects to reform provider payment to separate drug sales from hospital financing ("selling drugs to feed medicine").[103]

The central government also directed only 2 percent of reform spending to implementation of the EDL, which could in no way offset the losses hospitals (estimated as high as 20 times the government investment) would incur if they complied with it.[104] Several problems complicated the EDL reform.

First, the government may have underestimated the mark-up rates that hospitals charged (illegally) for drugs; larger hospitals with political power may also have been successful in continuing their mark-up practices.

Second, hospitals would need to compensate for lower drug revenues with higher revenues from medical services, but such services (e.g., dialysis, cancer care) may be in short supply.

Third, the sale of drugs accounted for at least 40% of hospital revenues, while medical services (a broad category including examinations, treatments, nursing, beds) accounted for only 29%, and sales of medical consumables accounted for only 7–8%.[105]

Fourth, the county hospitals affected accounted for only 10% of total drug sales;[106] the national impact of drug spending would thus be low.

Fifth, there was slow and uneven rollout of the provincial tenders to price the drugs on the EDL: as of December 2014, 8 of 31 provinces had not completed this task.

Sixth, the brunt of the EDL reform fell on the local level county hospitals and providers who responded to the no mark-up policy by reducing drug prescribing, thereby incentivizing patients to go to the large urban hospitals entailing higher spending.[107] Patients might also bypass local providers and seek care from urban providers if they perceived the EDL drugs to be of inferior quality – further exacerbating the dual problems of underuse of local facilities and over-crowding in urban facilities.[108]

There was unlikely to be any immediate impact on the quality and efficiency of the care provided, and little impact on the population's health status. Instead, the spending was likely to further fuel healthcare inflation: between 2010 and 2020, China's healthcare spending is predicted to triple to $1 trillion and account for 7 percent of GDP.[109] Moreover, there is some evidence that healthcare costs are higher among China's chronically ill population (e.g., those with diabetes), suggesting that the growing burden of non-communicable diseases will further fuel this inflationary trend.[110] This explains why the economic burden of healthcare on the Chinese population has continued to increase despite the reform. In a 2013 survey, 87 percent of the population reported the cost of healthcare was higher compared to four years earlier; 57 percent reported it was more difficult to meet with a physician.[111] Over a quarter of the respondents stated they had opted to forego hospitalization, partly because of high cost and partly because of unavailability of beds.

The government announced in 2009 that $123 billion would be spent over the next three years on five initiatives; however, only 25 percent was to be financed by the central government, with 75 percent coming from provincial and local governments. It was not clear that lower governmental levels had the capacity (especially in poorer provinces) or the incentive to make such large investments. Local governments developed a habit of generating a large share of their revenues from land transfers (roughly 45 percent in 2009). However, between 2009 and 2011 a decline in land transfer revenues threatened these governments' financial base. In addition, any monies contributed by local government could be diverted by the hospitals toward the purchase of expensive equipment and staffing of specialized services to compete in the medical arms race.

Moreover, reform implementation again hinged on cooperation across the 20 or so ministries, departments, and agencies within the central government that now had some responsibility for healthcare. The total set of government stakeholders depicted in Figure 2.3 adds further complexity to the layers of public health and healthcare providers shown in Figure 2.1. For example, the Ministry of Finance oversaw the financial support and investment in healthcare, as well as the insurance subsidies; the Ministry of Health (renamed the National Health and Family Planning Commission) oversaw the public hospitals, public health, and policy dealing with essential medicines; the Ministry of Human Resources and Social Security oversaw the two urban insurance schemes; the Ministry of Civil Affairs oversaw medical aid for the poor; the National Development and Reform Commission set the prices for healthcare services and drugs; and the Ministry of Commerce oversaw drug wholesaling and distribution.[112] The need for multi-sectoral cooperation was evident from the large number of actors participating in the "small group" that developed the reform (see box on the next page). Competition among the ministries, departments, and agencies, combined with the perceived low value-added of the MOH's contribution to attaining economic growth targets and managing provincial health bureaucracy, limited this cooperation and the long-term prospects for reform implementation.[113] In 2012, then minister of health Chen Zhu referred to the situation as "nine dragons regulating the waterways."[114]

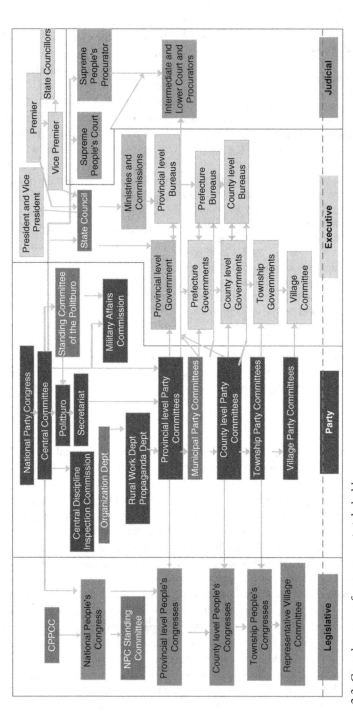

Figure 2.3 Complex map of government stakeholders

Government ministries and agencies involved in healthcare reform

To illustrate the challenge of inter-sectoral cooperation, it is useful to describe the government agencies that participated in the reform discussions of 2007. The "small group" was actually composed of 16 different bodies – each with different responsibilities:[1]

- National Development and Reform Commission
  Set economic policy, including prices for drugs and services
  Generate five-year plan and budget
- National Health and Family Planning Commission
  (Formerly the Ministry of Health and the State Population and Family Planning Commission)
  Manage healthcare system – oversee hospitals and clinics
  Provide universal access to basic health services
  Maintain public health
  Oversee reproductive health of women
- Ministry of Finance
  Produce annual budget
  Monitor financial performance in accord with five-year plan
- Ministry of Labor (now Human Resources) and Social Security
  Manage state medical insurance programs
  Set prices for essential medicines
  Manage civil servants, including those in healthcare sector
- State Commission Office for Public Sector Reform
  Oversee management of government departments at national and provincial levels
  Establish division of labor between State Council-level ministries and provincial bureaus

Supervise reforms at national and provincial levels
- Ministry of Education
  Oversee medical schools
- Ministry of Civil Affairs
  Maintain safety net (e.g., healthcare access) for the poor in rural areas
- Legislative Affairs Office of the State Council
  Draft the rules established by the reform small group
  Coordinate activities of departments and ministries
  Narrow discrepancies and resolve disputes
- State Council Development Research Center
  Government think tank that initiated the reform process
- China Insurance Regulatory Commission
  Supervise and manage the private health insurance market
- China Food and Drug Administration
  Ensure drug safety
  Incorporated into the MOH in 2008
- State Traditional Chinese Medicine Administration
  Oversee TCM practitioners and TCM research
- State-Owned Assets Supervision and Administration Commission of the State Council
  Oversee and manage SOEs
- All-China Federation of Trade Unions
  Represent the Chinese labor force

[1] Drew Thompson. 2009. "China's Health Care Reform Redux," in Charles Freeman (Ed.), *China's Capacity to Manage Infectious Diseases: Global Implications* (Washington, DC: Center for Strategic & International Studies): 59–80.

More problematic, different ministries and agencies were assigned responsibility by the small group for different elements of the reform's implementation.[115] There was no central government body with overall responsibility for administering the various initiatives. Government bodies and officials had been accountable for some time to only their immediate superiors. Moreover, there was no countervailing outside pressure exerted by the press or the public to hold bureaucrats accountable. Problems in healthcare implementation were easily blamed on others.

Reform Not Radical Change

In many ways, the 2009 healthcare reform was not a radical departure. The reform was likely intended to support the ongoing economic reforms begun in 1978. China's economy had developed over nearly three decades since the post-1978 reforms as an export-focused model, financed largely by foreign trade and the country's high savings rate (ranging from 30 to more than 50 percent).[116] Now, following the worldwide economic downturn in 2008, the country faced falling demand for its products and the need for a new vehicle to sustain a high rate of economic growth to support the growing expectations of its population. The country turned to a series of healthcare initiatives that were congruent with the emerging and broader economic goal of rebalancing the economy and spurring domestic consumption. As a proportion of the economy, total consumption has steadily increased since 2010. The government's intent may have been to provide a greater social security net (e.g., in the form of demand subsidies for health insurance, greater access to providers) that would induce households to spend more of their savings on domestic goods and services.

In a related light, scholars have suggested the entire period of insurance reform was a double-edged instrument used by government leaders to maintain the market approach begun in the 1980s.[117] On the one hand, the insurance extensions were partly a "political instrument" to maintain social stability among urban workers (from state and collective enterprises) who were laid off during the period of economic liberalization in the late 1990s and early 2000s, subject to a more competitive labor market due to the influx of rural migrants, faced higher unemployment (1999–2004) and/or lower-wage jobs, and experienced difficulties in getting employer reimbursement for their rising medical expenses. The rural migrants were concentrated in the private sector, which usually did not provide health coverage. In the early 2000s,

government officials estimated that 45 percent of the urban population and 80 percent of rural residents lacked health insurance; economists estimate that 73 percent of the urban population lacked insurance coverage under the new UEBMI scheme for workers in the formal sector.[118] In 2005, the government initiated its discussions of broader healthcare reform.

On the other hand, some of the insurance extensions (URBMI) were also partly an "economic instrument" used by the government to satisfy the country's new entrepreneurial class by not intervening to stem growing unemployment. Instead, the government offered some insurance coverage to urban workers to "smooth out the deregulation process." The less generous NCMS and URBMI schemes (fewer services covered required contributions only from beneficiaries and as much as 30–40 percent copays) and the voluntary nature of enrollment provided economic relief and political cover for the government and the new class of employers: if individuals remained uninsured or employers did not contribute, the lack of insurance coverage could be ascribed to personal choice. It also maintained the government's long-held view that health insurance was not a right but a privilege that was proportional to the individual's contribution. This suggested that the more generous coverage and lower cost-sharing of the UEBMI scheme reflected the higher contribution of urban civil servants.[119]

Overall, the 2009 reform did not produce a national insurance system that might promote a "harmonious society." Instead, as in the United States, it solidified a patchwork system of different insurance plans with unequal levels of coverage and reimbursement.[120]

Limits on the Healthcare Reform's Prospects

To be sure, expanded insurance coverage helped to ameliorate the cost of care burden on the population. As one illustration, the average cost of an inpatient hospitalization consumed roughly 60 percent of annual per capita income (according to a 2008 estimate).[121] Between 2007 and 2011, average spending on a hospital admission rose 40 percent; however, as a percentage of average income, that hospitalization decreased from 32 percent to

28 percent in urban areas and from 82 percent to 67 percent in rural areas.[122]

Despite this, the Chinese citizen faced a sizeable risk in paying for healthcare. Recent research suggests that China's reforms failed to achieve two reform goals: (a) reduce the ratio of out-of-pocket payments to national health expenditures to below 30 percent, and (b) reduce the ratio of out-of-pocket payments to disposable personal income over a five-year period. Out-of-pocket payments accounted for 40.4 percent of national spending in 2008 and 34 percent in 2012; moreover, the 64 percent increase in total health spending swamped the small decrease in out-of-pocket payments. Between 2005 and 2011, out-of-pocket payments grew at an annual rate of 8.8 percent and nearly doubled overall; growth in out-of-pocket payments roughly doubled the growth of disposable personal income.[123] In addition, the percentage of households experiencing catastrophic spending on healthcare rose from 12.2 percent in 2003 to 12.9 percent in 2011, suggesting that the new and expanding health insurance schemes had not protected the population from this risk.

The failure to achieve these goals resulted from several forces. First, it reflected the reality that greater financing through social insurance was not an option: URBMI and NCMS beneficiaries could perhaps not bear any increase in cost sharing, while UEBMI beneficiaries (and their employers) were already paying high levels of contribution. Second, it reflected the inability or reluctance of local governments to invest more in healthcare by assuming a higher share of national health expenditures. Third, the failure reflected rising and uncontrolled medical inflation.[124] In 2009, the real growth rate in national health expenditures (20.7 percent) and in out-of-pocket spending (12 percent) both exceeded growth in China's GDP (10 percent). Moreover, government spending on the five-year reform during 2009–2013 was not the $124 billion as originally intended, but actually $371 billion (and then $480 billion and then $640 billion).[125]

To the extent that healthcare costs continue to skyrocket and outpace economic growth and per capita incomes, and to the extent that insurance coverage remains shallow, the Chinese population may continue to rely on their savings to prepare for anticipated future healthcare outlays.[126]

The inflationary incentives put in place by insurance extensions, which follow the logic of the "healthcare quadrilemma" discussed in Chapter 1, have induced greater (and perhaps excessive) amounts of inpatient care which fuel the problem.

In tandem with the aging of the Chinese population (more retirees, longer life expectancy among those aged 60 and over) and a peak in the workforce (fewer workers paying for more dependents), the Chinese economy may not be able to finance these rising costs. Alternatively, the government may have to divert spending on other social services or infrastructure projects to healthcare.[127] This has been the experience of the Commonwealth of Massachusetts (United States) in dealing with the rising cost of healthcare following insurance expansions in 2004–2005. Moreover, a growing population of chronically ill patients will further challenge the country's ability to maintain economic growth without some form of "demographic dividend" (e.g., increase in the size of the working population).[128]

The reforms also failed to address the problematic revenue model of the public hospitals. Because there was no increase in their operating cost subsidy, hospitals continued with "business as usual" practices of generating fees and margins from the use of expensive drugs, tests, services, and equipment. Hospital managers have directed their limited subsidies to capital investments rather than personnel salaries. Reforms in the public hospitals will be key and will have ramifications for other sectors of China's healthcare industry. Recent data suggest that the public hospitals house 47 percent of the country's physicians, 65 percent of nurses, 54 percent of pharmacists, 50–60 percent of drug sales, and more than 70 percent of device/consumable sales.[129]

A hallmark of hospital efficiency is patient "throughput" (i.e., timely processing of patients during their visits). Western hospitals have experimented with lean techniques borrowed from the Toyota Production System to increase patient flow through their facilities and decrease patient waiting times. Chinese hospitals, particularly urban and Class IIIA facilities, have enjoyed tremendous growth in patient volumes and flows through their institutions, but with increased patient waiting times – both to register at the hospital and then again to see the physician once inside. After such long waits, patients then enjoy little time that may not even be private or confidential (owing to doctor visits with groups of patients present).

Recent testimony suggests that China's hospitals suffer from low rates of staff productivity and morale, and high rates of inefficiency in terms of the time and cost resources expended to treat illness (e.g., low occupancy rates in smaller hospitals, widespread adoption of expensive equipment like MRIs).[130] Data from the National Health and Family Planning Commission in 2012 indicate the average public hospital generated net income of 5.1 million RMB; without the average government subsidy of 8.9 million RMB, most hospitals would be running a deficit.[131] The 27 percent of public hospitals run by state-owned enterprises incurred a net loss of 50,000 RMB in 2012. The situation is not much better for the physician, who may see 20 patients an hour, be treated like a public servant, and be paid a salary only 20 percent higher than the national average for all laborers.[132]

Iron Triangle Revisited

In the end, delivering on all three angles of the iron triangle remains an elusive goal for China's government. The widespread slogan *kan bing nan, kan bing gui* (getting healthcare is difficult and expensive) remains a real concern among the Chinese population. As in the United States and its recent healthcare reform efforts, China has only recently (2009–2011) developed a dashboard of health system performance metrics that span the areas of access, coverage, equity, efficiency, and quality.[133] These metrics assess China's progress on many of the issues discussed above. However, quality measurement, management, and improvement are even more recent goals in China than they are in the United States, where minor progress has been made since the 1990s when greater attention was focused on quality. Over the past few decades, China's providers have clearly emphasized quantity over quality. Given the documented rise in costs and the questionable quality, it is reasonable to conclude that China has yet to deliver "value" (i.e., quality divided by cost) in its healthcare system.

Iron triangle problems have been exacerbated by an imbalance between rising demand and sluggish improvements in supply. Between 1980 and 2010, healthcare spending per capita grew 140-fold, but the number of healthcare organizations grew only 4.6-fold, the number of hospital beds grew only 1.3-fold, the number of nurses per capita grew only 2.9-fold, and the total personnel per capita and physicians per capita grew less than 1-fold (73 percent and 66 percent, respectively).

Calling for Local Healthcare Reform

The Chinese central government spent 127.7 billion RMB on health in 2007. Of this amount, the central government spent 6.35 billion RMB directly; the remainder consisted of transfers to local governments.[134] In a similar vein, between 2009 and 2011, the government projected to spend a total of 850 billion RMB on healthcare reform; only 332 billion RMB was to be spent by the central government. This suggests that local government – in particular, its allocation of resources and prioritization of economic versus social goals – must play a critical role in any reform's success. Thus, national healthcare reform will require a concomitant local healthcare reform.[135] Reform success thus hinges on a series of issues such as local government commitment to healthcare, local government resource allocation to the reform, local government resources available to allocate to healthcare, local government ability to steward the resources placed at its discretion, and local government's ability to coordinate the other sectors and government bureaus with a stake and responsibility for healthcare.

One huge complication is the fact that many local governments labor under significant debt burdens. According to China's National Audit Office, as of March 2014 nine provinces needed to raise new debt to pay off their older debt due to problems in generating cash flows. Even after financing, the local governments still had 821 million RMB in overdue debt.[136]

Recent Developments

Additional government reforms are in the air that may address several of the issues discussed previously. These include market pricing, an expanded role for the private sector, promotion of ethical practice among physicians, addressing problems of chronic illness, changing patient referral patterns, changes in hospital governance, and a relaxation of the one-child policy.

Market Pricing

In May 2015, the government indicated it would remove price controls on most pharmaceuticals and institute a new system relying partly on market pricing (along with some government guidance). This may or may not impact cost inflation in China, depending on the response of the urban public hospitals.

Expanded Role for Private Sector

In 2015, the government announced it would encourage greater involvement of the private sector in the delivery of healthcare services. In June 2015, the State Council announced it would allow patients with public insurance to receive reimbursement for services rendered in private hospitals. In January 2015, the government announced it would encourage physicians to practice at multiple institutions.

Encourage Ethical Practices

The government has also moved to extend its anti-corruption campaign into the healthcare sector, beginning with payments by drug manufacturers to physicians, public hospitals, and officials. The campaign was marked by a highly publicized investigation of GlaxoSmithKline in 2013. While initially focused on the western manufacturers, the government crackdown also targeted some domestic drug manufacturers. The National Health and Family Planning Commission has also issued a "Prohibition on 9 unethical conducts to strengthen the moral[s] in healthcare industry" in 2013:[137]

- Relating medical staff's income to drug sales/revenue from examinations
- Medical staff taking a portion of medical service fee as their own income
- Charging patients at will or not in accordance with government standards

- Accepting illegal donations from other organizations
- Participating in marketing and promotion activities
- Medical staff generating statistics about their own organization for commercial purposes
- Procuring drugs/devices at will or not in accordance with legal procedure
- Receiving rebates from sales of drugs/devices
- Receiving extra money/reward from patients

Adherence to this policy is supposed to be included in the performance appraisal of physicians working in public hospitals, which can influence their promotion and career track.

Address Chronic Illness

At the same time, the government will increase spending to tackle the country's growing burden of non-communicable diseases (see Chapters 3, 4, and 6). In August 2012, the MOH released its *Healthy China 2020 Strategic Research Report* as part of a long-term plan to improve China's metrics in population health. According to the *Report*, the government will increase healthcare spending to 6.5–7.0 percent of GDP by 2020 to achieve 10 metrics (e.g., life expectancy, infant mortality, maternal mortality).[138]

Change Referral Patterns

In October 2014, the National Health and Family Planning Commission announced it would pilot a new "patient classification system" to redirect patient movement across the different levels of Chinese healthcare facilities. Using economic incentives, the government would encourage patients to seek care initially at the local community level to relieve congestion in the large urban hospitals, and thereby develop a pyramidal structure with a large primary care base feeding more specialized centers above them.

Hospital Governance

One of the most significant objectives in the 2009 reforms was the designation of 745 hospitals in 17 counties and 37 pilot provinces and cities to experiment with new governance and operating practices. In particular, there is now an ongoing effort in some cities (e.g., Shanghai) to separate the ownership from the management of public hospitals, place them under the control of hospital management organizations separate from the local department of health, allow the units to contract with the local health bureau for hospital services, and cede greater control to local government.[139] The goal is to move hospital control away from local health departments and possible interference from bureaucrats that resist reform and allow local governments to adapt reforms to local level needs, develop more business acumen (e.g., internal accounting and auditing, asset management, command and control), and foster more professional hospital management personnel.

As one illustration, 70 percent of respondents to a survey of hospital middle management in Wuhan stated that the failure to separate ownership from management was the biggest impediment to the professionalization of Chinese hospital administration. Analysts suggest that governance reforms require hospital managers to have control over hiring of administrators, disposal of assets and residual funds, investment decisions, and strategic decision making.[140] Whether such reforms will reshape hospital incentives, provide new revenue models, and improve management remains to be seen.

One-Child Policy

In late 2015, the Chinese government announced it would relax the one-child policy instituted in 1979 and allow two children for couples in urban areas (already permitted in rural China). The change is intended to address future labor shortages in the country, the high dependency ratio, the 4:2:1 pyramid in China's social structure, and the imbalance in the country's "sex ratio at birth" (currently 116 males vs. 100 females).[141]

The policy change comes at a time of slowing growth in China's economy and is intended to boost economic growth going forward. Its success is not assured. The current Chinese generation of

child rearing age has grown up in a one child environment and may find larger family size to be totally unfamiliar. Larger family size also means greater effort and expense that they may not want or be able to afford. Finally, nearby cities such as Macau and Hong Kong still have low fertility rates in the absence of any population restrictions.[142]

Other Changes

The government also announced its intention to correct a myriad of other system deficiencies, as follows:

- an effort announced in September 2012 to expand insurance coverage to include treatment of critical illnesses (catastrophic care)
- a pilot project announced in December 2013 to improve the delivery of healthcare to migrant workers in 40 cities in 27 provinces
- the government's intention announced in 2014 to increase annual per capita spending on basic public health services
- an effort to increase government subsidies for the rural insurance scheme and reimbursement rates for both inpatient hospitalizations (to 75 percent) and outpatient services (to 50 percent)
- a plan to implement a system of general practitioners (primary care physicians) across the country by 2020, including two to three PCPs for every 10,000 residents.

Notes

1. Brittany Carr. 2011. *Government and Medicine: The Evolution of the Chinese Health Care System* (Greenville, NC: East Carolina University).
2. Carr. 2011. *Government and Medicine.*
3. S. Griffiths. 2008. "One Country, Two Systems: Public Health in China," *Public Health* 122: 754–761.
4. Christopher Beam. 2014. "Under the Knife: Why Chinese Patients are Turning against Their Doctors," *The New Yorker* (August 25).
5. John Dudovsky. "Historical Evolution of Chinese Healthcare System: A Brief Overview," Available

online at: http://research-methodology.net/his
torical-evolution-of-chinese-healthcare-sys
tem-a-brief-overview/. Accessed on October
21, 2016.

6. P. G. K. Panikar. 1986. "Financing Health Care
in China: Implications of Some Recent
Developments," *Economic and Political
Weekly* 21(16): 706–710.

7. Ryan Leonard. 2010. "Working Lives of
Chinese Physicians," 2009–2010 Penn
Humanities Forum on Connections (April).

8. Communes held an average of 16,000 people;
production brigades contained 1,000 people;
production teams contained 100–200 people.
William Hsiao. 1984. "Transformation of
Health Care in China," *New England Journal
of Medicine* 310(14): 932–936.

9. In terms of population size, villages ranged
from 100 to 1,000 people; an average of 14–16
villages comprised a township, which had
roughly 16,000 population; an average of 25
townships made up a county, with an average
population of 400,000; an average of 10 counties
subsumed under each of the country's prefecture
cities/administrations (PCAs), and an average of
8 PCAs (71 counties) subsumed under the 27
provinces and autonomous regions (there are no
PCAs in the national municipalities).

10. Victor Wong and Sammy Chiu. 1998. "Health-
Care Reforms in the People's Republic of
China," *Journal of Management in Medicine*
12(4/5): 270–286.

11. Panikar. 1986. "Financing Health Care in
China."

12. Frank Dikotter. 2010. "Mao's Great Leap to
Famine," *New York Times* (December 15).
Available online at: www.nytimes.com/2010/
12/16/opinion/16iht-eddikotter16.html?_r=0.
Accessed on June 6, 2014.

13. Yuanli Liu, William Hsiao, Qing Li et al. 1995.
"Transformation of China's Rural Health Care
Financing," *Social Science and Medicine* 41(8):
1085–1093.

14. Xingzhu Liu and Huaijie Cao. 1992. "China's
Cooperative Medical System: Its Historical
Transformations and the Trend of
Development," *Journal of Public Health Policy*
13(4): 501–511.

15. Jin Ma, Mingshan Lu, and Hude Quan. 2008.
"From a National, Centrally Planned Health
System to a System Based on the Market:
Lessons from China," *Health Affairs* 27(4):
937–948.

16. According to the World Health Organization,

> Public health refers to all organized measures
> (whether public or private) to prevent disease,
> promote health, and prolong life among the
> population as a whole. Its activities aim to
> provide conditions in which people can be
> healthy and focus on entire populations, not
> on individual patients or diseases. Thus, public
> health is concerned with the total system and
> not only the eradication of a particular disease.

Available online at: www.who.int/trade/glossary/
story076/en/. Accessed on October 9, 2015.

17. Commune health centers rebounded by 1965,
rising in number to 36,965, and then mushroomed to 55,000 by 1981.

18. Xingzhu Liu and Junle Wang. 1991.
"An Introduction to China's Health Care
System," *Journal of Public Health Policy* 12(1):
104–116.

19. Panikar. 1986. "Financing Health Care in
China."

20. This volume's co-editor, Gordon G. Liu, served
as a barefoot doctor himself. His story has been
chronicled by Christopher Beam. 2014. "Under
the Knife."

21. Beam. 2014. "Under the Knife."

22. Panikar. 1986. "Financing Health Care in
China."

23. Liu and Cao. 1992. "China's Cooperative
Medical System."

24. William Hsiao. 1995. "The Chinese Health Care
System: Lessons for Other Nations," *Social
Science and Medicine* 41(8): 1047–1055.

25. Karen Eggleston. 2014. "Testimony, Hearing on
China's Healthcare Sector, Drug Safety, and
the U.S.–China Trade in Medical Products."
U.S.-China Economic and Security Review
Commission (April 3). Available online at:
origin.www.uscc.gov/sites/default/files/tran
scripts/USCC%20Hearing%20Transcript_April
%203%2C%202014_0.pdf. Accessed on July
15, 2015.

26. Adam Wagstaff, Winnie Yip, Magnus Lindelow et al. 2009. "China's Health System and Its Reform: A Review of Recent Studies," *Health Economics* 18(S2): S7–S23.

27. Some observers have labeled the resurgence of provincial power as "economic warlord-ism" which often ignores orders from the central government; others have labeled the process as "buck passing" whereby local authorities subvert central initiatives to pursue their own interests.

28. Liu and Wang. 1991. "An Introduction to China's Health Care System."

29. Thomas Hou. 2009. "The Chinese Primary Care System: Its Evolution, Challenges and Legal Aspects of Reform," University of Pennsylvania. Available online at: http://repository.upenn.edu/curej/96.

30. Gerald Bloom and Gu Xingyuan. 1997. "Health Sector Reform: Lessons from China," *Social Science and Medicine* 45(3): 351–360.

31. Liu et al. 1995. "Transformation of China's Rural Health Care Financing."

32. Lok Sang Ho. 1995. "Market Reforms and China's Health Care System," *Social Science and Medicine* 41(8): 1065–1072.

33. Griffiths. 2008. "One Country, Two Systems.".

34. Ma et al. 2008. "From a National, Centrally Planned Health System to a System Based on the Market."

35. Liu et al. 1995. "Transformation of China's Rural Health Care Financing."

36. Sang Ho. 1995. "Market Reforms and China's Health Care System."

37. State pricing was promulgated through the "Yellow Book."

38. Gabe Collins and Andrew Erickson. 2015. "China's Public Hospital Governance Reforms are Setting the Stage for Corporatization," *China SignPost* (January 26).

39. Bloom and Xingyuan. 1997. "Health Sector Reform." Arthur Daemmrich. 2013. "The Political Economy of Healthcare Reform in China: Negotiating Public and Private," *SpringerPlus*.

40. Daemmrich. 2013. "The Political Economy of Healthcare Reform in China."

41. In developing countries, rising per capita income can serve as the shock that sets in motion the "health care quadrilemma" – just as health insurance does.

42. Daemmrich. 2013. "The Political Economy of Healthcare Reform in China."

43. Hsiao. 1995. "The Chinese Health Care System."

44. Bloom and Xingyuan. 1997. "Health Sector Reform."

45. No author. 2015. "Little Match Children," *The Economist* (October 17): 26–28. For a different view, see Chengchao Zhou, Sean Sylvia, Linxiu Zhang et al. 2015. "China's Left-Behind Children: Impact of Parental Migration on Health, Nutrition, and Educational Outcomes," *Health Affairs* 34 (11): 1964–1971.

46. Wagstaff et al. 2009. "China's Health System and Its Reform."

47. Central Document Number 1.

48. Jens Leth Hougaard, Lars Peter Osterdal, and Yi Yu. 2008. "The Chinese Health Care System: Structure, Problems and Challenges." Discussion Paper No. 08–01. Department of Economics, University of Copenhagen.

49. Gordon Liu. 2009. "Beijing's Perspective: The Internal Debate on Health Care Reform," in Charles Freeman (Ed.), *China's Capacity to Manage Infectious Diseases: Global Implications* (Washington, DC: Center for Strategic & International Studies): 51–58.

50. Hsiao. 1995. "The Chinese Health Care System."

51. David Blumenthal and William Hsiao. 2015. "Lessons from the East – China's Rapidly Evolving Health Care System," *New England Journal of Medicine* 372(14): 1281–1285.

52. Liu et al. 1995. "Transformation of China's Rural Health Care Financing."

53. Bloom and Xingyuan. 1997. "Health Sector Reform."

54. Liu et al. 1995. "Transformation of China's Rural Health Care Financing."

55. Liu and Cao. 1992. "China's Cooperative Medical System."

56. Ibid.

57. Hsiao. 1984. "Transformation of Health Care in China."

58. Liu et al. 1995. "Transformation of China's Rural Health Care Financing."
59. Yanzhong Huang. 2014. "Health-care Provision and Health-care Reform in Post-Mao China," Prepared Statement, Hearing on China's Healthcare Sector, Drug Safety, and the U.S.–China Trade in Medical Products. U.S.-China Economic and Security Review Commission (April 3).
60. Lim Meng Kin, Yang Hui, Zhang Tuohong et al. 2002. "The Role and Scope of Private Medical Practice in China" (March). Available online at: www.wbginvestmentclimate.org/toolkits/public-policy-toolkit/upload/China-Health-Assessment.pdf. Accessed on July 8, 2015.
61. The report is also known as "Report of Requesting Instructions on the Issue of Permitting Individuals' Practicing Medicine." Jingqing Yang. 2008. "Medical Practice in the Non-public Sector in China," Journal of Asian Public Policy 1(3): 346–351.
62. United States – China Economic and Security Review Commission. "China's Healthcare Industry, Drug Safety, and Market Access for U.S. Medical Goods and Services." Hearing on April 3, 2014. Available online at: origin.www.uscc.gov/sites/default/files/transcripts/USCC%20Hearing%20Transcript_April%203%2C%202014_0.pdf. Accessed on July 15, 2015.
63. Yanrui Wu. 1997. "China's Health Care Sector in Transition: Resources, Demand and Reforms," Health Policy 39: 137–152.
64. Liu et al. 1995. "Transformation of China's Rural Health Care Financing."
65. Ma et al. 2008. "From a National, Centrally Planned Health System to a System Based on the Market."
66. Huang. 2013. Governing Health in Contemporary China.
67. Huang. 2014. "Health-care Provision and Health-care Reform in Post-Mao China."
68. Chinese Center for Market Investigation and Research. 2011. Cited in Huang. 2013. Governing Health in Contemporary China.
69. Therese Hesketh, Xudong Zhou, and Yun Wang. 2015. "The End of the One-Child Policy: Lasting Implications for China," Journal of the American Medical Association (November 6). Available online at: http://jama.jamanetwork.com/article.aspx?articleid=2469505. Accessed on December 7, 2015.
70. Eggleston. 2014. "Testimony, Hearing on China's Healthcare Sector, Drug Safety, and the U.S.–China Trade in Medical Products."
71. Swedish Agency for Growth Policy Analysis. 2013. China's Healthcare System – Overview and Quality Improvements (Ostersund, Sweden: Swedish Agency for Growth Policy Analysis). United States–China Economic and Security Review Commission. 2014. "China's Healthcare Industry, Drug Safety, and Market Access for U.S. Medical Goods and Services."
72. David Blumenthal and William Hsiao. 2005. "Privatization and Its Discontents – The Evolving Chinese Health Care System," New England Journal of Medicine 353: 1165–1170.
73. Wu. 1997. "China's Health Care Sector in Transition."
74. Despite the retrenchment, the Chinese government increased its spending on health care in real terms. Between 1978 and 2003, government spending rose 8.7 percent annually, just 0.3 percent less than growth in GDP. Much of this spending was targeted on public health institutions such as maternal and child health centers, epidemic centers, and supply-side subsidies to operate hospitals and township health centers. Such support was enabled by the country's new economic growth, allowing an increase in real government spending even though government funding fell as a proportion of the total funding of health care.
75. Hsiao. 1995. "The Chinese Health Care System."
76. Owen O'Donnell, Eddy van Doorslaer, R. P. Rannan-Eliya et al. 2007. "The Incidence of Public Spending on Health Care: Comparative Evidence from Asia," World Bank Economic Review 21(1): 93–123.
77. Soeren Mattke, Hangsheng Liu, Lauren Hunter et al. 2014. The Role of Health Care Transformation for the Chinese Dream (Santa Monica, CA: Rand Corporation).

78. Eggleston. 2014. "Testimony, Hearing on China's Healthcare Sector, Drug Safety, and the U.S.–China Trade in Medical Products."

79. Huang. 2014. "Health-care Provision and Health-care Reform in Post-Mao China."

80. Eggleston. 2014. "Testimony, Hearing on China's Healthcare Sector, Drug Safety, and the U.S.–China Trade in Medical Products."

81. Between 1980 and 2005, the average medical fee for an outpatient visit rose from $0.20 to $15.65 (a 78-fold increase); the average medical fee for inpatient care rose from $4.90 to $575.00 (a 11-fold increase).

82. Nominal GDP per capita exhibited a 5 percent compound annual growth rate (CAGR) from 1949 to 1978, a 17 percent CAGR from 1979 to 1996, a 11 percent CAGR from 1997 to 2004, and a 16 percent CAGR from 2005 to 2009. Liu. 2009. "Beijing's Perspective." Similar statistics are presented in Griffiths. 2008. "One Country, Two Systems."

83. Huang. 2013. *Governing Health in Contemporary China.*

84. In 2011, medical services rendered to patients accounted for 55.8 percent of hospital expenditures, but only 48.7 percent of hospital revenues. Swedish Agency for Growth Policy Analysis. 2013. *China's Healthcare System – Overview and Quality Improvements.*

85. United States – China Economic and Security Review Commission. 2014. *China's Healthcare Industry, Drug Safety, and Market Access for U.S. Medical Goods and Services.*

86. Yuanli Liu. 2009. "The Anatomy of China's Public Health System," in Charles Freeman (Ed.), *China's Capacity to Manage Infectious Diseases: Global Implications* (Washington, DC: Center for Strategic & International Studies): 33–47.

87. The vision was also consonant with the World Health Organization's call for "health for all by the year 2000."

88. Liu. 2009. "Beijing's Perspective."

89. NCMS is alternatively referred to as the New Rural Cooperative Medical Insurance (NRCMI) or New Rural Cooperative Medical Scheme (NRCMS). For purposes of consistency, the chapters throughout this volume will use NCMS.

90. Susan Brink. 2015. "What China Can Teach the World about Successful Health Care," *NPR Blog* (April 3).

91. Winnie Yip and William Hsiao. 2015. "What Drove the Cycles of Chinese Health System Reforms?," *Health Systems and Reform* 1(1): 52–61.

92. Swedish Agency for Growth Policy Analysis. 2013. *China's Healthcare System – Overview and Quality Improvements.*

93. Yanzhong Huang. 2014. Testimony. United States – China Economic and Security Review Commission. *China's Healthcare Industry, Drug Safety, and Market Access for U.S. Medical Goods and Services.* Hearing on April 3, 2014. Available online at: origin.www.uscc.gov/sites/default/files/transcripts/USCC%20Hearing%20Transcript_April%203%2C%202014_0.pdf. Accessed on July 15, 2015.

94. Swedish Agency for Growth Policy Analysis. 2013. *China's Healthcare System – Overview and Quality Improvements.*

95. Tsung-Mei Cheng. 2012. "Early Results of China's Historic Health Reforms: The View from Minister Chen Zhu," *Health Affairs* 31 (11): 2536–2544. According to Cheng, the reform rebuilt many of the 2,200 county hospitals and 33,000 primary health care facilities; it also built nearly 2,400 urban CHCs and CHSs. By the end of 2011, the number of urban CHCs had increased 93 percent to reach 7,776; the number of CHS had increased 24 percent to reach 25,036.

96. Cheng. 2012. "Early Results of China's Historic Health Reforms."

97. Xiaoxv Yin, Yanhong Gong, Chen Yang et al. 2015. "A Comparison of Quality of Community Health Services Between Public and Private Community Health Centers in Urban China," *Medical Care* 53(10): 888–893.

98. Hongmei Yi, Grant Miller, Linxiu Zhang et al. 2015. "Intended and Unintended Consequences of China's Zero Markup Drug Policy," *Health Affairs* 34(8): 1391–1398.

99. Yan Guo. 2011. "A Mid-Term Assessment of China's Health Care Reform," in Charles W. Freeman III and Xiaoqing Lu Boynton (Eds.), *Implementing Health Care Reform Policies in China: Challenges and Opportunities* (Washington, DC: Center for Strategic and International Studies, December): 7–11.

100. Carr. 2011. *Government and Medicine.*

101. Half of all visits at local levels occurred in village clinics, most of which are privately owned. Eggleston. 2014. "Testimony, Hearing on China's Healthcare Sector, Drug Safety, and the U.S.–China Trade in Medical Products."

102. Lawton R. Burns, Rajiv Shah, Frank Sloan et al. 2009. "The Impact of Hospital Ownership Conversions: Results from a Comparative Field Study," *Biennial Review of Health Care Management: Meso Perspectives* 8: 171–229.

103. Cheng. 2012. "Early Results of China's Historic Health Reforms."

104. Yanzhong Huang. 2014. "What Money Failed to Buy: The Limits of China's Healthcare Reform," *Forbes* (March 4).

105. Mark Kong. 2015. *China Healthcare Sector* (Hong Kong: DBS Vickers Securities, February 16).

106. Kong. 2015. *China Healthcare Sector.*

107. United States – China Economic and Security Review Commission. 2014. *China's Healthcare Industry, Drug Safety, and Market Access for U.S. Medical Goods and Services.*

108. Eggleston. 2014. "Testimony, Hearing on China's Healthcare Sector, Drug Safety, and the U.S.–China Trade in Medical Products."

109. Daemmrich. 2013. "The Political Economy of Healthcare Reform in China."

110. Yanzhong Huang. 2015. "China's Healthcare Reform: Calling for Top-Level Design." Unpublished essay.

111. Huang. 2014. "What Money Failed to Buy."

112. Swedish Agency for Growth Policy Analysis. 2013. *China's Healthcare System – Overview and Quality Improvements.*

113. Winnie Yip and William Hsiao. 2008. "The Chinese Health System as a Crossroads," *Health Affairs* 27(2): 460–468. As one illustration, the inefficiency of the MOH has been the target of criticism by the Ministry of Finance, which sets the MOH's budget. As another illustration, growing problems in China's public health system encompassed HIV, TB, and STDs – diseases that were managed by different agencies and government infrastructures (see Chapters 3 and 6).

114. Cheng. 2012. "Early Results of China's Historic Health Reforms."

115. Christine Kahler. 2011. "China's Healthcare Reform: How Far Has It Come?" *China Business Review* (January 1).

116. The 30 percent statistic comes from Mattke, Liu, Hunter, et al. 2014. *The Role of Health Care Transformation for the Chinese Dream.* The 50 percent statistic comes from Beam. 2014. "Under the Knife." According to the World Bank, the gross savings rate rose from roughly one-third in the 1980s to over one-half during 2000–2010. See United States – China Economic and Security Review Commission. 2014. *China's Healthcare Industry, Drug Safety, and Market Access for U.S. Medical Goods and Services.*

117. Wei Zhang and Vicente Navarro. 2014. "Why Hasn't China's High-Profile Health Reform (2003–2012) Delivered? An Analysis of Its Neoliberal Roots," *Critical Social Policy* 34(2): 175–198.

118. Eggleston. 2014. "Testimony, Hearing on China's Healthcare Sector, Drug Safety, and the U.S.–China Trade in Medical Products."

119. According to Zhang and Navarro, "the official mentality of the last ten years is that the welfare state is, firstly, unaffordable, and secondly, harmful" (p. 188).

120. Cheng. 2012. "Early Results of China's Historic Health Reforms."

121. United States – China Economic and Security Review Commission. 2014. *China's Healthcare Industry, Drug Safety, and Market Access for U.S. Medical Goods and Services.*

122. Eggleston. 2014. "Testimony, Hearing on China's Healthcare Sector, Drug Safety, and the U.S.–China Trade in Medical Products."

123. Zhang and Navarro. 2014. "Why Hasn't China's High-Profile Health Reform (2003–2012) Delivered?"

124. Lufa Zhang and Nan Liu. 2013. "Health Reform and Out-of-Pocket Payments: Lessons from China," Unpublished manuscript (January 13).

125. Huang. 2015. "China's Healthcare Reform." Yanzhong Huang. 2015. "Road to Reform Filled with Obstacles," *Insight* (July 1). Available online at: http://insight.amcham-shanghai.org/road-to-reform-filled-with-obstacles/. Accessed on July 9, 2015.

126. Beam. 2014. "Under the Knife."

127. United States – China Economic and Security Review Commission. 2014. *China's Healthcare Industry, Drug Safety, and Market Access for U.S. Medical Goods and Services.*

128. Eggleston. 2014. "Testimony, Hearing on China's Healthcare Sector, Drug Safety, and the U.S.–China Trade in Medical Products."

129. Kong. 2015. *China Healthcare Sector.*

130. United States – China Economic and Security Review Commission. 2014. *China's Healthcare Industry, Drug Safety, and Market Access for U.S. Medical Goods and Services.* Cheng. 2012. "Early Results of China's Historic Health Reforms."

131. Kong. 2015. *China Healthcare Sector.*

132. Daemmrich. 2013. "The Political Economy of Healthcare Reform in China."

133. Swedish Agency for Growth Policy Analysis. 2013. *China's Healthcare System – Overview and Quality Improvements.*

134. Zhang and Liu. 2013. "Health Reform and Out-of-Pocket Payments."

135. Wei Zhang. Personal communication.

136. Kong. 2015. *China Healthcare Sector.*

137. Kong. 2015. *China Healthcare Sector.*

138. BMI Research. 2015. *Industry Trends and Developments – China – Q3 2015* (London, UK: Business Monitor International).

139. Collins and Erickson. 2015. "China's Public Hospital Governance Reforms are Setting the Stage for Corporatization."

140. Eggleston. 2014. "Testimony, Hearing on China's Healthcare Sector, Drug Safety, and the U.S.–China Trade in Medical Products."

141. Hesketh et al. 2015. "The End of the One-Child Policy."

142. Hesketh et al. 2015. "The End of the One-Child Policy." Knowledge@Wharton. "From One Child to Two: Will China's Five-year Plan Deliver?" (November 3, 2015). Available online at: http://knowledge.wharton.upenn.edu/article/from-one-child-to-two-will-chinas-five-year-plan-deliver/. Accessed on December 7, 2015.

China's Public Health System and Infrastructure

XIAOFENG LIANG AND LAWTON ROBERT BURNS

Context of Healthcare Reform

Since 1980, China has enjoyed economic growth of roughly 10 percent annually. Such progress has helped nearly half a billion of its population to escape poverty, which is a major contributor to poor health status. Yet, China's economic progress has not been matched by comparable improvements in health status. Indeed, improvements in life expectancy have slowed down since the time of economic reforms, rising only five years from 68 (1981) to 73.5 (2010) (see Figure 1.18). In other countries (e.g., Mexico, South Korea) with similar life expectancy levels in 1981, life expectancy rose 7–14 years despite lower economic growth.[1]

On March 14, 2011, the National People's Congress of China approved a new national development strategy for the five-year period 2011–2015. One of the guiding principles of the 12th Five-Year Plan is "inclusive growth": i.e., ensure that the benefits of the country's economic growth spread to a large proportion of the population. As part of this plan, the healthcare sector is expected to receive a major boost. The 2011–2015 Five-Year Plan on Health takes aim at three targets:

- increase average life expectancy to 74.5 years
- reduce the infant mortality rate (IMR) to 12 percent
- reduce the maternal mortality rate (MMR) to 22/ 100,000

The main tasks include reforms in the country's health security (insurance) sector, public hospital sector, the pharmaceutical and medical equipment sectors, the delivery of public health and medical services, equitable access to an essential package of public health services, traditional Chinese medicine (TCM), elderly care, and healthcare management.

The government's long-term policy goal continues to be the development of an affordable and accessible healthcare system, with an insurance system covering the entire population. The development of the public health system is consistent with the country's emphasis on higher-quality growth over the next five years.

Achievement and Challenge of Public Health in China

According to a 2012 Chinese government white paper, the public health service system covers disease prevention and control, health education, maternity and child care, mental health, health emergency response, blood collection and supply, health supervision, family planning services, and other specialized public health services. This system has achieved some remarkable progress over time; it is also confronted by a host of formidable challenges in many of the same areas.

Overall Challenges

China faces a complex and diverse array of public health issues. These issues begin with the size of the country and the growth of its population. China has been one of the world's most populated countries since the second century A.D., with rapid change during the past 40–50 years. The Chinese population grew from 900 million (1975) to 1.13 billion (1990) to 1.24 billion (2000) and then to 1.38 billion (today). Moreover, this population is spread across a huge territorial landscape of 9.6 million square kilometers characterized by geographic and economic diversity. Part of this diversity is the disparity in healthcare service delivery and public health infrastructure, particularly in western China.

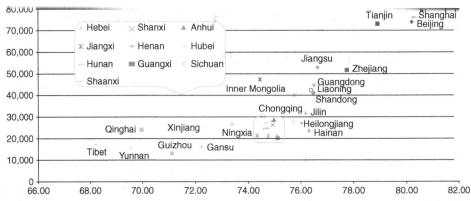

Figure 3.1 Disparity and diversity in life expectancy and per capita GDP across China's provinces, 2010
Source: *China Statistical Yearbook* (2013).

The society is also aging: between 1990 and 2030, the number of people 60 years and older will grow from less than 100 million to nearly 300 million. China has a population (a) that is on the move, with a huge migration from rural to large urban areas and from West to East, and (b) that now enjoys greater economic prosperity. Such prosperity has involved concomitant changes in diet and behaviors that have fostered chronic diseases. Finally, all of these transitions have occurred rapidly and simultaneously, interacting with and reinforcing one another. The systemic nature of these transitions begs for a systemic response from the government – a response that is coordinated, integrated, and long term in focus. These issues are described below.

Public Health Accomplishments

The Chinese government has labored to increase access to public health. The country now provides all residents access to ten categories of public health services: health record, health education, preventive inoculation, child health (under six years), maternity care, elderly care, hypertension and diabetes care, severe psychosis care, reporting and treatment of infectious disease and public health emergency, and healthcare supervision and coordination. In addition, the government has developed public health programs to target specific diseases (cataracts, fluorosis, AIDS) and increase immunizations

under the National Immunization Program (NIP). The NIP now covers Hepatitis B for newborns, an expanded list of 14 vaccines for 15 infectious diseases, and the inclusion of adults as well as children.[2]

Life Expectancy

While average life expectancy has increased from 35 to nearly 74 during 1949–2010, the gains have not been evenly shared across China's provinces. Figure 3.1 shows that life expectancy is correlated with the provincial GDP, much like the Millennium curve discussed in Chapter 1. Shanghai is in the upper right portion of the graph; western China and Tibet are heavily represented in the lower left portion.

Disability

A country's burden of disease is reflected in statistics on disability adjusted life years (DALYs).[3] Between 1990 and 2010, the contribution of communicable, maternal, neonatal, and nutritional disorders to DALYs declined from nearly 27 percent to 10 percent; at the same time, the total DALYs rose by 21 percent. This suggests that communicable diseases are being supplanted by non-communicable diseases as China's major health problem. This has been the result of government efforts to reduce the problem of communicable disease, the legacy of the country's one-child policy, and the growing problem of unhealthy individual behaviors.

A recent report provides an overall view of China's health problems.[4] In 2010, the top 11 causes of DALYs were stroke (30,139), heart disease (17,886), COPD (16,724), low back pain (15,132), road injuries (14,962), lung cancer (11,318), liver cancer (10,088), major depression (9,318), diabetes (7,835), falls (7,058), and self-harm (5,970). The leading risk factors are dietary, which account for 16.3 percent of DALYs and 30.6 percent of deaths. Among the dietary factors at work are high sodium intake, heavy smoking and alcohol consumption, and low intake of fruits and whole grains. The second leading risk factor is high blood pressure (12.0 percent of DALYs, 24.6 percent of deaths), followed by tobacco (9.5 percent of DALYs, 16.4 percent of deaths), ambient air pollution (e.g., burning of solid fuels), and household air pollution (e.g., burning of coal in homes).

Infant and Maternal Mortality

The IMR decreased from 200 percent prior to 1949 to 12.1 percent by 2011 and down to 10.3 percent in 2012 (see Figure 1.17). The largest drop occurred during the Maoist era. The MMR decreased from 88.9/100,000 in 1990 to 31.9/100,000 in 2009, and down to 24.5/100,000 in 2012 (see Figure 3.2).

The urban–rural differential in MMR has also narrowed considerably.

Infectious Disease

There has been a major epidemiological transition under way in China since the 1950s. Back in 1957, vital statistics drawn from 13 cities revealed that the major causes of death were respiratory (16.9 percent), acute infection (7.9 percent), tuberculosis (7.5 percent), digestive (7.3 percent), cardiovascular (6.6 percent), stroke (5.5 percent), cancer (5.2 percent), and neuropsychiatric disorders (4.1 percent). By contrast, data from the period 1991–2000 suggest the top three causes of death were cardiovascular (22.5 percent), cancer (22.3 percent), stroke (21.3 percent) – followed at a distance by pneumonia/influenza (3.2 percent), infectious disease (3.1 percent), accidents (2.8 percent), COPD (1.8 percent), chronic liver disease (1.5 percent), and diabetes (1.5 percent).[5] These rates were higher in rural areas and in northern China. Much of the accomplishment here is attributable to effective and large-scale public health programs and vaccination efforts. Indeed, by the 1960s, China had eradicated 11 infectious diseases (e.g., smallpox); 11 more (e.g., polio) were eliminated more recently.[6]

China currently keeps records on 39 infectious ("notifiable") diseases (see Figure 3.3). They are

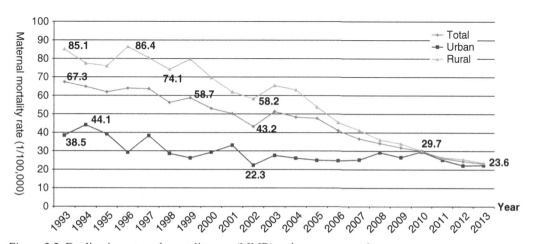

Figure 3.2 Decline in maternal mortality rate (MMR): urban versus rural areas

divided into three categories based on their infectiousness and fatality, social and economic impact, and vulnerability of being contained. Categories A and B (28 diseases) have a high risk of outbreak or spread once an outbreak occurs; they are reported by the Ministry of Health (MOH) on a monthly basis. Category C diseases are less infectious and have fewer epidemiological consequences; they are reported only when outbreaks occur.

- Category A (2):
  - Plague, cholera
- Category B (26):
  - SARS, human infection of HPAI, AIDS, hepatitis, poliomyelitis, measles, epidemic hemorrhagic fever, rabies, Japanese encephalitis, dengue, anthrax, bacillary and amebic dysentery, TB, typhoid fever, meningococcal meningitis, pertussis, diphtheria, neonatal tetanus, scarlet fever, brucellosis, gonorrhea, syphilis, leptospirosis, schistosomiasis, malaria, human infection of avian influenza A(H7N9) (November 1, 2013)
- Category C (11):
  - Influenza (influenza H1N1, modified on November 1, 2013), mumps, rubella, acute hemorrhagic conjunctivitis, leprosy, typhus, kala-azar, echinococcosis, filariasis, infectious diarrhea, hand-foot-mouth diseases (May 5, 2008)

Figure 3.3 List of notifiable diseases

Since 1970, the incidence and mortality rate of infectious diseases have both declined (see Figures 3.4 and 3.5). Morbidity and mortality rates for specific infectious diseases are reported elsewhere.[7] In 2012, China recorded 6.95 million cases and over 17,000 deaths from these 39 diseases. The overall incidence rate was 515.9/100,000, while the overall mortality rate was 1.29/100,000. The diseases with the highest mortality are respiratory infections (195 thousand deaths in 2010), TB (44.7 thousand deaths), hepatitis (43.8 thousands deaths), and HIV/AIDS (36.2 thousand deaths).[8]

Hepatitis B has been an epidemic in China. In the early 2000s, China accounted for nearly one-third of all patients worldwide with the virus (130 million). With the introduction of pediatric vaccination programs starting in 1992, the country reduced the number of hepatitis B-infected pediatric patients (under five years of age) from roughly 100 million to 19 million; the prevalence rate of children under five years old with positive HBsAg (the surface antigen of the virus) fell to 0.96 percent. Among the total population, however, the results have been more modest. The prevalence of HBsAg dropped from 9.75 percent to 7.18 percent. This decline was facilitated by a 2002 gift from Merck, which

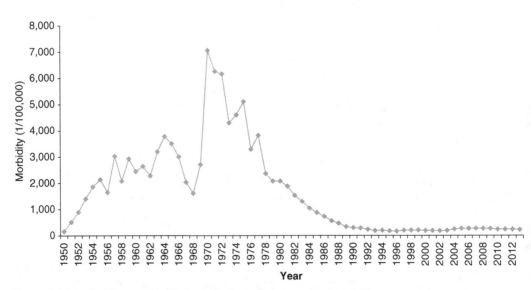

Figure 3.4 The incidence rate of infectious diseases (categories A and B)
Source: *Data from the Health Statistical Yearbook.*

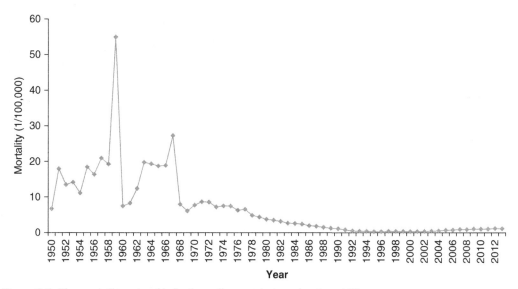

Figure 3.5 The mortality rate of infectious diseases (categories A and B)
Source: *Data from Incidence and Death Annual Report of Notifiable Infectious Diseases in China.*

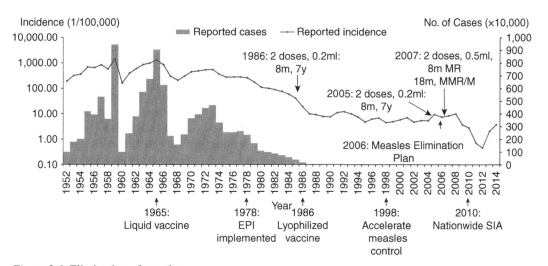

Figure 3.6 Elimination of measles

provided the vaccine to China with the assistance of the GAVI Alliance. The vaccine was made available at a cost of $0.50 for three doses, compared to the normal cost elsewhere of $100 per dose.

Likewise, there have been sharp declines in morbidity from hepatitis A, meningococcal meningitis, and Japanese encephalitis. Between 2009 and 2010, there was a 19 percent decrease in hepatitis A cases,

a 49 percent decrease in meningococcal meningitis cases, and a 35 percent decrease in Japanese encephalitis cases. Measles had been virtually eradicated after the mid-1980s, but increased again in 2013 after the 2010 measles vaccine campaign (see Figure 3.6). Finally, China had been free of polio since 2000, along with other Western Pacific region members of the World Health Organization

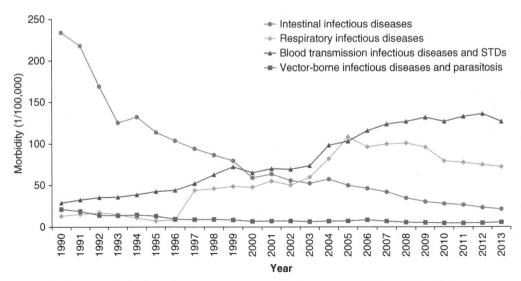

Figure 3.7 Number of infectious disease cases by transmission routes in China, 1990–2013

(WHO); after responding to the 2011 importation outbreak in Xinjiang, China became polio-free again by 2012.

Nevertheless, China still faces several challenges here. The number of cases of infectious diseases varies according to the different routes by which the diseases are transmitted (see Figure 3.7). Hepatitis and AIDS, for example, are transmitted via blood and sexual contact; they have been rising over time. By contrast, intestinal and vector-borne infectious diseases have been falling. Respiratory diseases rose up until the middle of the past decade and have begun to recede.

In addition, China has faced a continuing series of emerging and re-emerging infections over time (see Table 3.1). Infectious diseases constituted the vast majority of public health emergencies in 2011. Since 2005, the emergence of new infectious diseases and the re-emergence of those infectious diseases that were previously prevalent (sexually transmitted infections or STIs, HIV, viral hepatitis, zoonoses) account for the majority of deaths associated with infectious disease. Zoonotic infections (e.g., rabies) have been rising since the 1950s, with epidemics in the 1970s and the 2000s – most recently fueled by the rise in pet dogs (80–200 million), which have a rabies prevalence of

6.4 percent. However, only 30 percent of dog owners register their pets, with an even smaller percentage (2–8 percent) vaccinated against rabies.[9] Rabies was among the top five causes of mortality in 2007 among infectious diseases.

Another source of such infections is the markets serving the growing consumption of game meat, especially in southern China with its dense backyard farms and crowded animal conditions. Animals live in close proximity to humans in the south, which serves as a breeding ground for viral infections. This has been further promoted by the rise in China's animal population: between 1968 and 2005, there has been an increase from 5.2 million to 508 million pigs and from 12.3 billion to 13 billion chickens.[10] Pigs were the source of the H5N1 virus (avian influenza) in 2003. There is no systematic surveillance of these live markets and farms. This suggests that any decrease in prevention efforts will have negative consequences for public health. This threat is not only domestic but also global: China plays a sizable role in the global poultry industry, 70–80 percent of which are raised in backyards.[11] There are a host of reasons why diseases among these animals do not get reported, either by farmers or by local officials. These include the economic loss to the farmer (lack of compensation), the low level of care

Table 3.1 Emerging and re-emerging infections

Year	Place	Epidemic	Number of Patients
1985	Tibet	Measles	15,000
1986	Xinjiang	Hepatitis E	600,000
1988	Shanghai	Hepatitis A	300,000
	Beijing	Acute hemorrhagic conjunctivitis	200,000
1995	Jiangsu	O157:H7	95
2000	Guangxi	Plague	130
2003	Guangdong/Beijing	SARS	5,327
2004	Anhui	Meningococcal meningitis C	201
	Anhui/Fujian	Human-avian influenza	7
2005	Fujian/Zhejiang	Cholera	400
	Sichuan	Streptococcus suis infection	204
2007	Henan	Human granulocytic anaplasmosis	56
	Shandong	Hand-foot-mouth disease	83,000
2008	Anhui	Hand-foot-mouth disease	489,000
	17 provinces	Imported falciparum malaria	780
2009	Shandong/Henan	Hand-foot-mouth disease	78,000
	Guangdong/Fujian	H1N1	2,090
2013	Zhejiang/Shanghai	Human infection of avian influenza A(H7N9)	155
2014	Guangdong/Guangxi	Dengue fever	46,864
2015	Guangdong	Imported MERS	1

seeking by the rural population, and the threat of economic losses suffered by local governments and communities.

To combat this threat, China developed internet connectivity between the Ministry of Agriculture's system to monitor avian influenza and all 2,800 counties by 2005. In addition, 93 percent of hospitals in counties and higher geographic levels and 43 percent of township hospitals had direct access to the Center for Disease Control and Prevention's (CDC) system for disease reporting and control.

HIV/AIDS

Over the past years, international health policies have focused on fighting HIV/AIDS, tuberculosis (TB), and those diseases that cause maternal and child health problems. Since 2007, the top two causes of reported deaths by infectious disease in China were AIDS and TB (see Table 3.2). Between

1990 and 2010, the number of HIV/AIDS deaths mushroomed from 200 to 36,000.[12]

The HIV infection was first reported in 1985 in one city but has since spread across China. Figure 3.8 depicts the increase in annually reported HIV positive and AIDS cases between 1985 and 2011. Figure 3.9 shows the breakdown of newly reported HIV cases in recent years by transmission source. The large increase in prevalence among heterosexuals suggests the infection is spreading quickly due to growing use of drugs and sexual contact. Table 3.3 provides current estimates of the HIV/AIDS burden in China, including persons living with HIV (PLHIV), AIDS, number of deaths from AIDS, the number of new HIV infections, and HIV prevalence. The 0.058 percent HIV prevalence rate suggests they number roughly 1 million in the population.

In 2003, immediately after the SARS crisis, the country established the Comprehensive AIDS

Table 3.2 Top 10 reported deaths by infectious diseases, 2004–2013

Order	2004	2005	2006	2007	2008	2009	2010	2011	2012	2013
1	Rabies	TB	TB	AIDS	AIDS	AIDS	AIDS	AIDS	AIDS	AIDS
2	TB	Rabies	Rabies	TB	TB	TB	TB	TB	TB	TB
3	Hepatitis B	AIDS	AIDS	Rabies	Rabies	Rabies	Rabies	Rabies	Rabies	Rabies
4	AIDS	Hepatitis B	Hepatitis B	Hepatitis B	Hepatitis B	Hepatitis B	HFMD	Hepatitis B	Hepatitis B	Hepatitis B
5	Neonatal tetanus	Japanese encephalitis	Japanese encephalitis	Japanese encephalitis	Neonatal tetanus	Influenza A (H1N1)	Hepatitis B	HFMD	HFMD	HFMD
6	Epidemic hemorrhagic fever	Neonatal tetanus	Neonatal tetanus	Neonatal tetanus	Japanese encephalitis	HFMD	Influenza A (H1N1)	Hepatitis C	Hepatitis C	Hepatitis C
7	Japanese encephalitis	Epidemic hemorrhagic fever	Epidemic hemorrhagic fever	HFMD	Japanese encephalitis	Japanese encephalitis	Hepatitis C	Epidemic hemorrhagic fever	Epidemic hemorrhagic fever	Epidemic hemorrhagic fever
8	Meningococcal meningitis	Hepatitis C (HCV)	Meningococcal meningitis	Hepatitis C (HCV)	Hepatitis C (HCV)	Hepatitis C (HCV)	Epidemic hemorrhagic fever	Syphilis	Syphilis	Syphilis
9	Dysentery	Meningococcal meningitis	Meningococcal meningitis	Hepatitis C	Meningococcal meningitis	Neonatal tetanus	Japanese encephalitis	Influenza A (H1N1)	Japanese encephalitis	Japanese encephalitis
10	Hepatitis C	Dysentery	Dysentery	Dysentery	Epidemic hemorrhagic fever	Epidemic hemorrhagic fever	Neonatal tetanus	Japanese encephalitis	Neonatal tetanus	Neonatal tetanus

Response (CARE) project to address the humanitarian issues facing AIDS victims as well as to partner with the Global Fund to Fight AIDS, Tuberculosis, and Malaria. That same year, China also created a free national AIDS treatment program. The new AIDS policy was labeled "Four Frees, One Care." Free antiretroviral drugs were provided to people in rural areas and the poor in urban areas. Screening/ voluntary counseling and testing (VCT) services were also provided free of charge, as was PMTCT (preventing mother-to-child transmission)/baby testing and schooling for children orphaned due to AIDS. Free care and life support were provided for people who are HIV positive and living with AIDS. One problem with the program is the disjunction between money, information, and treatment.

Table 3.3 HIV/AIDS estimates in China

Year	2005	2007	2009	2011	2013
PLHIV	650,000	700,000	740,000	780,000	810,000
AIDS	75,000	85,000	105,000	154,000	NA
AIDS death	25,000	20,000	26,000	28,000	30,000
Newly infected	70,000	50,000	48,000	48,000	45,000
HIV prevalence	0.050%	0.054%	0.057%	0.058%	0.060%

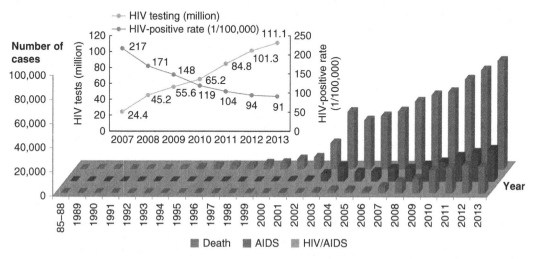

Reported PLHA was 436, 817 by the end of 2013, reported HIV rate was about 0.03% nationally.

Figure 3.8 Annual reported HIV-positive and AIDS cases by transmission source, 1985–2013

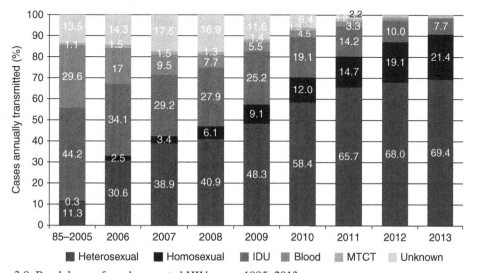

Figure 3.9 Breakdown of newly reported HIV cases, 1985–2013

The treatment program is financed by central and provincial governments along with the help of international donors, while preventive services are administered by the CDC that operates outside of the local healthcare delivery system.

AIDS prevention has received additional support in China's five-year action plan (2006–2010), State Council decrees, and greater latitude for non-governmental organizations to help the country fight AIDS. Despite this, the central government has recognized it needs the support of the population and the private sector to combat the problem.[13]

Other Sexually Transmitted Diseases

Syphilis infected 5 percent of the country at the time of the 1949 revolution, but was virtually eradicated by the 1960s. Besides AIDS, syphilis and other sexually transmitted diseases (STDs) like gonorrhea have resurfaced in China, particularly in the country's largest cities, coastal areas, and the southern provinces. Such diseases are once again among the top five most common notifiable diseases. In 2007, syphilis increased 24 percent, while STDs in general increased 7 percent.[14] Such diseases may promote the further spread of HIV.

China established a network of 16 sites in 1987 as national sentinel surveillance of STDs and expanded it to 23 sites in 1993. A National Center for STD Control was then established in 1996. The center has responsibility for managing these issues but must rely on the system for notifiable disease reporting by government health facilities. Those cases of infected people who receive care in the private sector or outside of the public health system are not likely to be reported. In one province, over 75 percent of those infected were not reported.

Tuberculosis

China accounts for a large portion of the global burden of TB, with 1.3 million cases annually by 2006, second only to India.[15] By 2008, there were 1.5 million new cases and 4.5 million active cases.

These statistics have enormous implications for China's economic growth. TB affects that portion of the population with the highest level of productivity. The typical TB patient (64 percent) is between 15 and 59 years old; males outnumber females, rural residents outnumber urban residents, and western/central province residents outnumber eastern province residents by a two-to-one margin. The economic loss due to the disease exceeds $1 billion, with a cost of $83 for each case detected and $537 for each smear-positive case cured. Since the majority of infected people live in rural areas, deficiencies in the rural delivery system will impede the country's ability to address the problem.

The TB epidemic now includes both multidrug resistant (MDR-TB) and extensively drug resistant (XDR-TB) strains, which require expensive second-line treatment. The WHO estimates that 62 percent of the global burden of MDR-TB (424,000 cases in 2006) are in three countries: China, India, and the Russian Federation; China is the leading contributor. A recent statement by China CDC indicates there are 120,000 MDR-TB cases in China, one-quarter of the global total. Of the 39 notifiable communicable diseases in China, TB has been number one in the past in terms of notified cases and deaths. This is despite the fact that TB control had been the subject of two five-year national plans in the 1980s. As a result of these efforts, TB prevalence fell 3.3 percent annually during the 1980s, but still remained high.[16] In 1990, 360,000 deaths occurred due to TB.

The situation improved markedly during the ten-year national plan in the 1990s. The Chinese government embarked on a TB control program in 1991, with the assistance of a $58 million grant from the World Bank. The program, known as the Infectious and Endemic Disease Control Project (EDC), was the largest TB control project in the world at the time. The program utilized the five-point "directly observed treatment short-course" (DOTS) strategy developed and recommended by the WHO to achieve at least a 70 percent detection rate and 85 percent cure rate. The program included free diagnostic testing (chest fluoroscopy) to all presenting patients at county or district TB dispensaries, followed by sputum samples and chest X-rays for those meeting symptom criteria, and then followed by drug therapy overseen by barefoot doctors paid a case management fee for each case identified and for each patient cured. Patient reports were transmitted from the county to the prefecture to the province and up to the central government.[17] The program also trained a cadre of healthcare workers in DOTS methodology.

The program spread quickly between 1991 and 1995 to cover over 90 percent of the target population and counties (573 million in 12 provinces, roughly half of the country's citizens). Ten of the provinces achieved 100 percent DOTS coverage by the end of 1995. Overall, the project maintained a high cure rate (85–90 percent) due to several factors: broad access to treatment in TB dispensaries without regard to ability to pay, provision of a stable drug supply, and a reporting system that enabled the monitoring of treatments. An estimated 30,000 deaths were prevented annually. There was also a 36 percent reduction in the incidence of TB between 1990 and 2000 in the provinces targeted for change.[18]

Case finding proceeded more slowly, however, and stagnated around 30 percent (compared to the WHO target of 70 percent). The 30 percent represent those individuals with TB that showed up in the CDC systems where the DOTS strategy was implemented. Part of the problem reflects the two-step process to identify cases: hospitals diagnose potential cases of TB using only X-rays, which then must be followed up by sputum exams and confirmation by the CDC. However, hospitals were often reluctant to refer patients to the TB dispensary for sputum testing in order to treat patients themselves. In one study of 40,000 rural households in 2003, 37 percent with suspected TB failed to seek out medical care; of those who did, only 35 percent received recommended testing to confirm the diagnosis; and of those with confirmed diagnoses, only 57 percent received the recommended therapy. If one multiplies these percentages, only 37 percent × 35 percent × 57 percent = 7.4 percent were successfully identified and treated.[19] Another study conducted in Chongqing reported that only 16 percent of TB patients were observed during treatment, and fewer than 5 percent were observed by staff.[20]

The shortcomings in rural detection and treatment likely reflect the high cost of seeking care in rural areas (as a percentage of income) from a rural delivery system that has been privatized over a series of decades (see Chapters 2 and 7). In the early 2000s, an estimated 70 percent of all healthcare visits that did take place occurred in clinics at the village level with village level practitioners (e.g., barefoot doctors) and providers of traditional medicine. Such providers may lack the capacity to identify and then respond to outbreaks of infectious diseases.

In 1996, the MOH required hospitals to report and refer TB patients to the CDC system; such regulations were hard to enforce due to the lack of information on hospital case finding and referral practices.[21] Roughly 90 percent of patients confirmed to have the disease began their TB diagnosis and treatment in hospitals and non-governmental institutions, where they received medication therapy as long as they could afford to pay for it. Patients without the financial means typically discontinued treatment, leading to the development of drug-resistant strains of TB.[22] Moreover, many Chinese patients preferred to be treated in hospitals and therefore did not report to the CDC sites, where TB prevention and control facilities are based.

Case finding was also likely hindered by the low percentage (41 percent in 2002) of CDC funding from the government. With such low funding, the center focused on activities that could generate revenues (e.g., provide drugs and ancillary tests) rather than TB diagnosis and treatment. TB prevalence did not decrease in the provinces not targeted by the CDC. Moreover, the 2000 national survey revealed that 10 percent of affected patients had MDR-TB.

The project demonstrated that rapid implementation of large-scale public health programs was possible. Fast rollout was facilitated by the political will of governmental leaders at all levels down to the county level, which in turn was matched by financial commitments made by finance bureaus to borrow and repay project loans and contribute some matching funds. Rollout was also made possible by the country's system of TB institutions at various governmental levels which enabled implementation of a standard set of TB control guidelines, as well as information and resource flows between levels.

In the new millennium before the severe acute respiratory syndrome (SARS) epidemic, the Chinese government began to increase its political and financial commitment to fighting TB. This resulted in a second ten-year plan to control TB (2001–2010) along with increased annual funding for TB examination and treatment from $300,000 to $4.8 million and then $5.4 million. In 2005, the government provided $70 million on an annual basis for a comprehensive TB containment program that offered free TB screening and drug therapy in both urban and rural areas.[23] The government also obtained increased grant support from outside agencies including the World Bank and the Global Fund to Fight AIDS, Tuberculosis and Malaria.

The SARS epidemic led to a short-term cessation in all TB control and other public health efforts. Following the SARS epidemic, the Chinese government increased its commitment to deal with public health problems, including a public health emergency strategy, increased spending on public health (from $835 million in 2002 to $1.44 billion by 2004), and enhanced CDC funding (whose share of funding from the government increased from 41 percent to 47 percent between 2002 and 2004). TB-specific government funding likewise increased to $36 million in 2005, accounting for one-quarter of all funding for the national TB control program.

In 2004, the MOH implemented a web-based reporting system for communicable diseases to correct delays in reporting as well as inaccurate reporting experienced during the SARS crisis. Using this system, CDC personnel could contact patients diagnosed with TB at hospitals who failed to be referred or show up post-referral. Some mixed success was achieved: of the 562,788 confirmed TB cases reported in 2005, 22.6 percent were reported by hospitals via the web-based system. Of the larger 686,742 confirmed or suspected cases reported by hospitals, 44 percent of patients self-referred to the CDC system, while 56 percent did not. The CDC attempted to contact nearly three-quarters of the latter but in fact contacted only half sought for follow-up. By the end of 2005, 93 percent of 19,716 health facilities located at the county level or higher, along with 66 percent of 38,518 township level health facilities, utilized this system to report communicable diseases. Hospital reports of suspected cases increased from 448,000 in 2004 to 687,000 in 2005; two-thirds of these patients were successfully followed up.

In tandem with these public health initiatives, the government also increased TB control efforts. The DOTS strategy was implemented in all counties within three years following the epidemic. By 2005, the case detection rate had increased to roughly 80 percent of the estimated new cases. Government efforts have helped the country to achieve the target TB prevalence rate ahead of schedule: the prevalence dropped to 0.66 per thousand, 61 percent lower than the corresponding figure for 2000. This target was included in the Millennium Development Goals and formed part of China's 2006–2010 National Action Plan. Detection rates have remained high, along with cure rates (93.8 percent in 2012) and the DOTS coverage rate.

Average TB notifications vary geographically. The highest notification rates are observed in northwest and northeast China, suggesting TB is a disease of the poor. The challenges confronting efforts to control TB are portrayed in Figure 3.10.

Between 1990 and 2010, the number of TB deaths fell dramatically from 169,000 to 47,000.[24] China's Law on the Prevention and Treatment of Infectious Diseases, revised in 2004, categorized TB (along with HIV/AIDS) as a Class B disease, thereby mandating the reporting of all such cases. Nevertheless, the problem of diagnosing and treating TB continues to challenge the country. Mandatory reporting is thwarted by concealment and underreporting by local authorities fearing censure.[25] Local authorities have also placed more emphasis on economic growth, which is a major criterion used by the Chinese Communist Party for political appointments, and less emphasis on public health problems and reporting of crises that might undermine local economic growth.[26]

Moreover, 100 percent DOTS coverage may be less important than the rigor of implementation, as evidenced by the slowdown in TB detection after 2006. The country still has the second largest number of TB patients, now numbering 4.99 million, with 1 million new cases emerging annually. Rising caseloads will place a greater strain on a system where one-third of TB prevention and control agencies are understaffed, and where most local prevention centers have difficulty meeting national biological safety standards. TB cases that remain

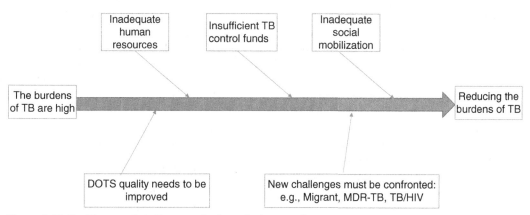

Figure 3.10 Problems and challenges of tuberculosis control

undetected and untreated are rampant; such patients can infect 10–15 others per year and develop the more drug-resistant strain.[27]

Floating Population

Part of the problem is due to the large "floating population" – people who relocate for at least six months without obtaining local household registration status (*hukou*). According to the 2000 census, they numbered 144 million, with 60 percent of them relocating across counties (usually to urban areas) and the remainder typically relocating within the same county – many to the urban county seat. Currently, their numbers are estimated at 170 million, or roughly 9 percent of the population. The floating population is thus quite heterogeneous, not only in terms of their migratory patterns but also in terms of their healthcare needs.

One important constituent group is the population of migrant (or "peasant") workers relocating to cities in search of employment who constitute up to 40 percent of the urban labor force. They are often poor and uneducated adult males, who are at risk of workplace injuries and morbidities: in 2003, adult migrants represented 80 percent of deaths in mining, construction, and chemical factories.[28] According to one study, 40 percent of TB cases in Beijing and 50 percent of such cases in Shanghai were reported among migrants; an even higher proportion (80 percent) has been reported in Shenzhen.[29] They are also at risk for STDs by

sometimes engaging in unprotected sex (frequently with female immigrants recruited for commercial sex work). Some studies suggest that roughly equal percentages of migrants and non-migrants patronize sex workers; other studies suggest the problem is the heavy predominance of migrants among sex workers.[30] Some came from Henan Province, whose population was infected with HIV as a result of questionable blood donation practices in the 1990s.

The migrant worker problem is compounded by the crowded and squalid living conditions in the cities that may promote disease transmission and (due to poverty and laws preventing use of urban services by non-permanent residents) impede their care seeking, diagnosis, and treatment. Migrant workers have to return home to their place of registration to seek treatment, but may be confronted by inadequate facilities, services, and staff in rural areas. Only 19–45 percent of Chinese migrant workers have access to health insurance (due to the separation of their insurance providers from place of residency/registration); those with insurance coverage face variable reimbursement coverage for healthcare services received and limited by the local pooling of funds.[31] As a result, half of migrant patients lack access to physician services when they become ill. The number of urban-based migrants is expected to grow to more than 250 million by 2030.

Migrants infected with TB have lower DOTS therapy levels (<60 percent vs. 84 percent of residents in one study), lower cure rates (37 percent vs. 90 percent of Beijing residents), higher attrition in follow-up care, and lower levels of treatment success (55 percent vs. 89 percent of Shanghai residents). Similarly, children of migrants have lower rates of vaccination than children of the resident population.[32] To address the poor health status of migrants will require efforts to (a) raise their income level (such that they do not need to migrate for employment) and (b) improve their ability to access the urban healthcare system in the absence of low insurance coverage (10–23 percent), which typically reflects the absence of residence permits, employment contracts, and the high cost of urban healthcare. Other initiatives will require improved living conditions for migrant workers that impede disease transmission and closer proximity to healthcare services.[33]

The central government may need to not only take direct responsibility for funding the prevention and treatment of communicable diseases but also ensure funding and implementation of public health programs at lower administrative levels and across government hierarchies. For example, government services to prevent and cure TB require greater coordination to ensure timely referrals and greater emphasis on community health clinics linked to the CDC.

Drug-resistant TB

A second problem is the high prevalence of MDR-TB: China has an estimated one-third of all cases globally. MDR-TB results from inconsistent therapy, low detection rates, supply chain issues with drug availability, and lack of patient follow-up. MDR-TB is more dangerous than TB, is difficult to cure, and is often fatal. The second-line drugs needed to combat MDR-TB cost 20 times more than conventional therapies, involve more side effects, and have longer regimens of treatment. MDR-TB is treated outside the national program at cost to the patient, which further complicates patient adherence and compliance.[34] This is particularly worrisome for treating the large number of cases among the rural poor. Surprisingly, the rate of MDR-TB is high in some provinces that have successfully launched DOTS programs. DOTS may thus be

insufficient; access barriers to health among the poor and rural populations may deter follow-through on TB therapy that fosters the drug-resistant strain. Another complication is that Chinese physicians inconsistently follow TB treatment regimens and tend to overprescribe antibiotics, which further fosters the emergence of drug-resistant bacterial strains.[35]

Absence of Financing Mechanisms

A third problem is the lack of a solid financing mechanism to tackle TB, particularly with the decline of outside grant monies and the financial division of labor between governmental levels. In 2005, the MOH estimated there was a 23 percent funding gap. The country also faces a shortage of trained public health employees, particularly those trained in TB control.

A new five-year program was announced for 2009–2014 to improve case detection and treatment in five provinces and one municipality. The program included new diagnostic tests, new drug regimens, and new drug compliance methods (e.g., mobile phone texting reminders). The country will need to integrate TB control efforts with other public health programs such as HIV/AIDS, immunization, STDs, and maternal and child health. It will also need to consider changes in financing care for urban migrant workers to increase their access to care.

Coinfections

The need for vigilance here is heightened by the growing prevalence of "coinfections" – TB/HIV, HBV/HIV, HCV/HIV – that will increase without public intervention and joint screening programs. It is perhaps not surprising that TB levels have risen in China as has the level of STDs and HIV, particularly in the coastal areas, large cities, and southern provinces. HIV is a leading cause of the global spread of TB: roughly half of the former contract the TB infection. This poses a serious threat because while HIV is spread through sexual contact and needle sharing, TB is an airborne disease that can be easily transmitted to those without HIV. Moreover, as HIV spreads from the high-risk to other segments of the Chinese population, the level of coinfection has risen, resulting in provinces reporting high levels of both diseases. Given the high percentage of the Chinese population with the TB bacilli,[36] the spread of HIV is bound to increase the rates of morbidity and mortality resulting from both.[37]

These three disease threats are managed by different government agencies with different infrastructures, fragmented financing, and limited coordination of effort. The country's hierarchical and bureaucratic healthcare system exhibits many boundaries – segmented financing and personnel at provincial, county, and township levels – which may impede concerted action to deal with emergent infectious disease outbreaks among an increasingly mobile population. Coinfection of people with HIV and TB requires more concerted action than separate vertical disease eradication efforts.

Non-communicable Disease

In addition, due to China's ongoing, rapid socioeconomic and demographic transition, the country is witnessing an epidemic of chronic, noncommunicable diseases (NCDs) that now account for a much greater proportion of the disease burden.[38] This epidemic is part of the "epidemiological transition" from infectious to chronic disease (described above). The two disease classes are not entirely separable, however. Some infectious bacteria (*Helicobacter pylori*) are agents in gastric cancer; other parasitic infections (the fluke worm that infests rivers in rural China) can lead to liver cancer.

The Chinese government began to focus on this transition in 1986, when it established its National Office for Cancer Prevention and Control and developed the first National Cancer Control Plan (1986–2000). The plan sought to reduce cancer incidence and mortality rates, improve survival and patient quality of life, and highlight the need for research on prevention and control. The MOH concluded that comprehensive strategies were required, culminating in 2003 in a second National Control Plan (2004–2010) as well as a Hepatitis B Prevention and Control Plan (2006–2010). In 1997, the government launched the Disease Prevention Project in collaboration with the World Bank. This project inaugurated survey surveillance of behavioral risk factors and health promotion efforts to prevent and control NCDs.

To combat tobacco-bred diseases, the government initiated anti-smoking campaigns along several fronts, including the 2006 implementation of the WHO Framework Convention on Tobacco Control and the 2007 effort, "Towards a Smoke-Free China." The observed 1 percent reduction in the prevalence of smoking among males suggests these programs exerted some positive effect. In addition, China has undertaken a series of vaccination programs (Hepatitis B shots for children in 1992) as well as screening programs for breast, cervical, and digestive tract cancers.[39]

China has developed the first medium-term and long-term national plan to control and prevent NCDs for the 2005–2015 period. The plan mandates an integrated and comprehensive approach that encompasses cancer.[40] Despite some initial gains in reducing smoking prevalence (see below), success was not sustained and required renewed emphasis in China's current set of healthcare reforms. In 2009, the MOH initiated six public health programs to supplement the earlier efforts in Hepatitis B vaccinations and cancer screening. The country's current Five-Year Plan (2011–2015) seeks to address some issues relating to NCDs, in particular environmental protection, social services, social safety nets, and increased provision of health insurance.

Between 1990 and 2010, there was a 21 percent rise in DALYs. This reflects the decline in risks of communicable diseases among children and the rise in NCD risk among adults. These risks are associated with a rise in mental and behavioral disorders, musculoskeletal problems, and impairments due to diabetes and other chronic problems.[41] The prevalence of NCD risk factors in the Chinese population over the age of 18 is portrayed in Figure 3.11; the prevalence of biological risk factors is presented in Figure 3.12.

Key issues here include (1) the high level of salt intake, which is associated with hypertension and; (2) the high level of oil intake and low amount of fruit and vegetable consumption, which are associated with being overweight and having heart disease. Both have steadily increased in the Chinese

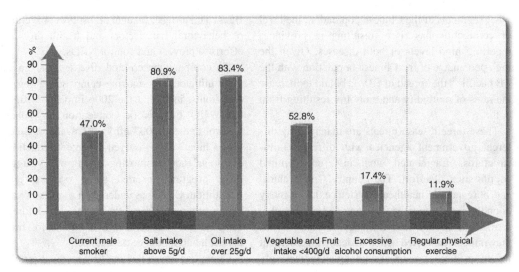

Figure 3.11 Prevalence of NCD risk factors in adults aged >18 in 2010
Source: 2010 PRC BRFSS.

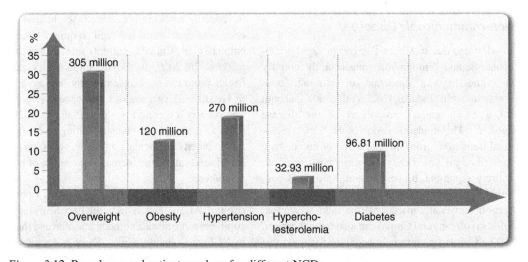

Figure 3.12 Prevalence and patient numbers for different NCDs
Sources: 1. Report on Cardiovascular Diseases in China, 2013 (hypertension).
2. Report on Chronic Disease Risk Factor Surveillance in China, 2010 (Overweight, Obesity,
Hypercholesterolemia, Diabetes).

population since 2000. The prevalence of hypertension has been steadily growing in the country since 1959 and has recently increased during 2004–2010 among all age classes in China. Diabetes has likewise increased in prevalence since 1980 (0.8 percent) to nearly 10 percent of the population by 2010, while oil intake levels have risen from 1982 to 2010 and now exceed the WHO recommended level. Part of this prevalence stems from the large number of people over the age of 60 (170+ million), who are more likely to be afflicted with chronic illness.

During the 1990–2010 time interval, there was an 18.7 percent increase in the percentage of deaths in China caused by NCDs: by 2010, NCDs accounted for 85 percent of all deaths, compared to 60 percent worldwide. As China's one-child policy continues and as the country ages, this shift will continue to intensify the NCD problem.[42] As a result, China needs to develop and promote policies supporting the healthy aging of its populace.

Among those diagnosed (roughly 269 million), NCDs currently account for 68.6 percent of the overall disease burden in China. The number of cases of cardiovascular disease, COPD, diabetes, and lung cancer among the Chinese population over 40 will double or triple over the next two decades – with most of the growth taking place in the next ten years. By 2030, diabetes will be the most prevalent NCD with 64 million cases, followed by COPD (55 million), stroke (31 million), and myocardial infarction (22 million). Lung cancer cases will grow fivefold to more than 7 million. The burden of four NCDs (MI, stroke, COPD, diabetes) will grow by nearly 50 percent between 2010 and 2030. More than half of the country's disease burden will be caused by MI and stroke; deaths from just these two conditions will grow by 80 percent.[43] China's NCD problem will be exacerbated by societal aging, leading to a 40 percent rise in the disease burden due to NCDs by 2030, a decline in the workforce aged 15–64 years which will have to financially (and potentially physically) support the chronically ill, and a fall in economic growth and productivity to financially support the needed care.

According to the GLOBOCAN 2012 data, the WHO Western Pacific region accounts for one-third of new cancer cases globally, with two-thirds of this in China.[44] Compared to the United States, China has a lower cancer incidence rate standardized by age (174 vs. 318) and a lower risk of getting cancer prior to age 75 (16.8 percent vs. 31.1 percent), but an equivalent risk of dying from cancer prior to age 75 (11.5 percent vs. 11.2 percent) and a higher age-standardized cancer mortality rate (122 vs. 106) and higher mortality to incidence ratio (0.70 vs. 0.33).[45] China also has much fewer cancer clinical trials in progress (979 vs. 10,420). Compared to its neighbor India, China has a higher incidence rate, mortality rate, risk of getting cancer, and dying from cancer before age 75.

NCD mortality rates are higher in China than in other G-20 countries. Such diseases cause huge economic loss: unless addressed by government reforms, NCDs such as cardiovascular, stroke, and diabetes could cost China $550 billion during 2005–2015. The World Bank estimated that the economic benefit of reducing cardiovascular deaths by 1.0 percent per year between 2010 and 2040 could generate an economic value equal to 68 percent of the country's GDP in 2010 ($10.7 trillion PPP). If not addressed, such conditions will be exacerbated by an aging population, reduced fertility, smaller workforce, and higher ratio of dependents to healthy workers.[46]

In 2010, NCDs accounted for 7.017 million of the total 8.304 million deaths; this represents an increase from 1990 where NCDs accounted for 5.938 million among the total 7.997 million deaths.[47] The three leading causes of death are now cardiovascular, cancer, and chronic obstructive pulmonary disease (COPD). In 2010, there were 3.136 million cardiovascular deaths, as follows: stroke accounted for 1.727 million deaths, followed by ischemic heart disease (949,000 deaths) and hypertensive heart disease (173,000 deaths).[48] There were also 2.133 million deaths from neoplasms, as follows: lung cancer (513,000 deaths), liver cancer (370,000 deaths), and stomach cancer (297,000 deaths). COPD deaths numbered 934,000.

China has conducted three national surveys on the causes of death in the 1970s, 1990s, and 2004–2005. Cancer deaths have been rising over this period from 74.2 per 100,000 population (1970s) to 108.3 (1990s) to 135.9 (2004–2005). Lung cancer mortality rates increased 465 percent during this time period to become the leading cause of death; liver cancer has also increased markedly, with China accounting for half of all deaths worldwide.[49] There is some disparity in cancer mortality rates between urban areas (150.2 per 100,000) and rural areas (128.6 per 100,000), although cancer mortality rates have been rising sharply in rural China. Lung cancer is the leading cause of death in urban areas, while liver cancer is the leading cause in rural China. The leading causes of cancer death have also shifted over time. In the

1970s, stomach and esophageal cancers were the leading causes; by the 2000s, lung and liver cancer were the leading causes.[50]

The annual mortality rate from cancer now stands at 167.6 per 100,000 population. This constitutes 20 percent of all deaths in China and 25 percent of all cancer deaths worldwide. There are now 2.82 million new cases and 1.96 million deaths annually.[51]

Cancer mortality rates are higher among the elderly Chinese population.[52] This is particularly true for lung, liver, colorectal, stomach, and esophageal cancers. Age-standardized mortality rates among the elderly are five to eight times that of the entire population. In 2008, the "mortality to incidence" (M/I) ratio for all cancers was 0.62 for all age groups, with an increasing gradient of 0.31 (under age 40), 0.46 (40–59 years), and 0.74 (over age 60). These figures are disturbing given the rising number of elderly in the Chinese population (177 million in 2011), an increase of nearly 3 percent since 2000 and the expected increase to 182 million by 2020. The number of cancer deaths among the elderly will rise to 1.44 million, while the number of cancer cases will rise to 1.82 million. China also has more than 20 percent of the world's elderly population over 60 years old, and half of this age group in Asia.

According to the 2003 National Health Service survey, cancer accounted for the highest economic costs among China's disease profile (7.23 percent). Total costs of cancer amounted to 86.85 billion RMB, with 28.45 billion RMB in direct costs and another 58.40 billion RMB in indirect costs.[53] On a per capita basis, the financial burden for cancer patients is $2,202 – much lower than the US burden ($86,759) but much higher than India ($641).[54]

We should note, however, that China currently has no national cancer incidence data and somewhat limited data on cancer mortality. The China National Central Cancer Registry (NCCR) was first established in 2002; the National Cancer Registration Network covers only 200 million or 13 percent of the total population, with data emanating from over 200 registries across China's provinces. Most registries are found in the larger cities in eastern China or in high-risk cancer regions. They thus provide incomplete estimates that may over-reflect cancer rates in rural areas.

Figure 3.13 shows the increasing prevalence of cancer among Chinese males and females. Rates

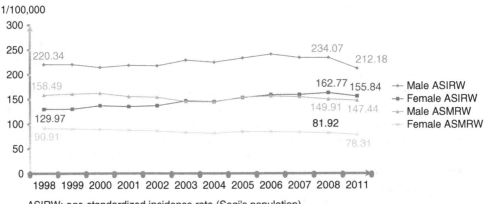

ASIRW: age-standardized incidence rate (Segi's population)
ASMRW: age-standardized mortality rate (Segi's population)

Figure 3.13 Trend of cancer age-standardized incidence and mortality rate, 1998–2011
Sources: 1. ZENG Hong-mei, ZHENG Rong-shou, and ZHANG Si-wei, et al., "Trend Analysis of Cancer Mortality in China between 1989 and 2008." *China J Oncol.* 34(7), (July 2012): 525–531.
2. CHEN Wang-qing, ZHENG Rong-shou, and ZENG Hong-mei, et al., "Trend Analysis and Projection of Cancer Incidence in China between 1989 and 2008." *China J Oncol.* 34(7), (July 2012): 517–524.
3. CHEN Wang-qing, ZHENG Rong-shou, and ZENG Hong-mei, et al., "Annual Report on Status of Cancer in China, 2011." *Chin J Cancer Res.* 27(1), (2015):2–12.

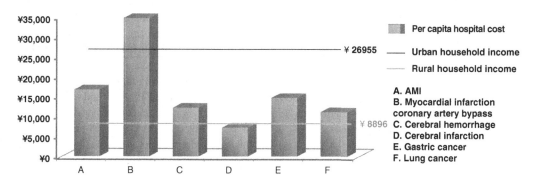

1. Once hospital cost of main chronic diseases occupied *50%* and *110%* of urban and rural capital income generally.
2. The population spent the most money in myocardial infarction coronary artery bypass, which was *120%* and *350%* of urban and rural household income, respectively.
3. Private expenditure on health (out-of-pocket money and private prepaid plans) in China was *45.7%* of total expenditure on health in 2010 and *61.7%* in 2000.

Figure 3.14   Economic burden of NCDs: comparison of average hospital cost and household income, 2012

have been steadily increasing for breast, lung, and liver cancer. Figure 3.14 shows that the economic burden of NCDs on the Chinese population is high relative to household income (particularly for the rural dwellers). This has been a major cause of personal bankruptcy. Nevertheless, NCDs remain very low on the nation's disease control priorities, attracting marginal investment from central and local governments.

Cancer registry data show an increase in both the prevalence and mortality rates from 1998 to 2008 across different cancers (lung, liver, breast). The country's tumor incidence rate is 285.91 per 100,000 population. The greatest spread of tumors has occurred in the population over the age of 40, while people over the age of 80 have the highest rate. Incidence levels are much higher in urban than rural areas for both males and females.

The country's tumor mortality rate is 180.54 per 100,000 population. There are about 2.7 million cancer deaths every year. Mortality is higher among males than females (1.68:1). Lung cancer has the highest incidence rate, followed by gastric cancer, colorectal cancer, liver cancer, and esophageal cancer. The top ten malignant tumors account for 76 percent of the total tumors by incidence. Lung cancer still exhibits the highest mortality rate among the malignant tumors, followed by liver, gastric, esophageal, and colorectal cancers. The top ten malignant tumors account for 84 percent

of all cancer mortalities. Among males, the main sources of cancer deaths include liver, gastric, esophageal, and colorectal cancers; among females, deaths are concentrated in gastric, liver, colorectal, and breast cancers.

The rapid rise in NCDs in China has been occasioned by a host of societal transitions, including urbanization (currently 52.6 percent of the population, but with government policy accelerating the transition this is expected to rise 2.3 percent annually and account for 900 million, or 60 percent of the total population by 2030), rising incomes, population aging due to the one-child policy, growing life expectancy (especially in rural China, and with little of a social security system), environmental pollution, and unhealthy habits (eating, smoking, drinking, stress, etc.). To effectively combat these issues will require a concerted response on the part of multiple government ministries to promote awareness, reduce risks, and promote access to primary care.

As of 2010, at least 580 million Chinese are believed to have at least one modifiable NCD-related risk factor.[55] These risk factors are both behavioral and dietary in nature. If not controlled, they could lead to a 50 percent rise in China's NCD burden. China may need to elevate its efforts here. Relative to other countries, China has higher rates of mortality for major NCDs such as cardiovascular disease, COPD, and cancers, as well as higher admission rates for acute complications of diabetes. Moreover, China lacks the institutional capacity at the local level to deal with the problem. A CDC survey found that 55 percent of counties had no specialized institutions to treat NCDs and 15 percent had no staff. Less than 45 percent of county-level CDCs conducted any NCD surveillance activities, and only 30 percent had implemented any NCD interventions in the prior year.[56]

Smoking and Tobacco

The high rate of lung cancer reflects the widespread prevalence of smoking. There are 300 million adult smokers, including 52.9 percent of adult males (and over 50 percent of male doctors!), as well as 780 million secondhand smokers. One in every three smokers in the world lives in China, giving China the dubious distinction as the number one consumer of tobacco. The smoking rate is 28.1 percent overall, with a very low rate among women (2.4 percent). There are fears that the smoking take-up rate among females, which has historically been low, may increase. This is actually an improvement, however. Viewed historically, the smoking rate used to be higher (60.2 percent among males, 6.9 percent among females, and 34.3 percent overall) in 2000–2001.[57]

Smoking rates are higher in younger-age populations among men, but higher in older-age populations among women. One troubling trend is the decrease in the average age to start smoking, which fell from age 22 in 1984 to 19 in 1996 and again to 18 in 2002.[58] This is despite the issuance of a law in 1999 prohibiting the sale of cigarettes to those under age 18.

About 1 million Chinese die prematurely every year from smoking-related diseases, along with 100,000 household deaths caused by second-hand smoke. Women and children are most vulnerable to these risks, particularly in the home. Respiratory illness, in general, is a major problem in the country. Roughly one in every five deaths in China is due to a lung-related illness; four of the top ten conditions contributing to the country's illness burden are respiratory ailments. The single greatest risk for these ailments is tobacco, which contributes to 9.5 percent of the country's disease burden.

There has been some modest effort by the government to discourage smoking via labeling. In 2005, the country ratified the WHO Framework Convention on Tobacco Control (FCTC), which obligates China to (a) reduce tobacco use by 30 percent for people aged 15 years and older by the year 2025, (b) impose a comprehensive ban on all tobacco advertising and promotion, and (c) ensure that all indoor places are safe from secondhand smoke by 2011.[59] However, recent efforts to add pictorial warnings and impose "sin taxes" (e.g., taxes on harmful products such as tobacco and alcohol) have stalled.

The Chinese government is conflicted here by virtue of tobacco being one of the country's largest state-owned enterprises (SOEs) – the China National Tobacco Corporation. The corporation has a virtual monopoly, is the largest tobacco manufacturer globally (in terms of revenues), and thus serves as a large source (7–10 percent) of government revenue. Tobacco is also a key support to the economy of several provinces. China is not only the number one consumer of tobacco, but also the number one producer of tobacco products worldwide. Cigarette production has also been increasing steeply over the past 15 years: between 2005 and 2012, cigarette manufacturing industry revenues increased from 285 billion RMB to 757 billion RMB. Tobacco is also a large source of income for farmers and a big source of employment. Not surprisingly, tobacco production has steadily increased over time (see Figure 3.15). Moreover, tobacco control has been allocated a tiny portion (0.5 percent) of the total budget for disease control and prevention.[60]

There is evidence that one of the most effective ways to promote wellness and healthy behaviors is to increase sin taxes.[61] The government has resisted any urging to raise prices on cigarettes not only because of its SOE but also because the price of other goods (such as food) has also been rising. The large population of smokers might also likely oppose (and perhaps protest) price hikes on cigarettes. The price of cigarettes can sometimes be so low (2 RMB in rural areas, 5 RMB in urban areas) that taxes might not exert much effect. Moreover, because the price of cigarettes varies enormously across brands, taxes might simply lead to

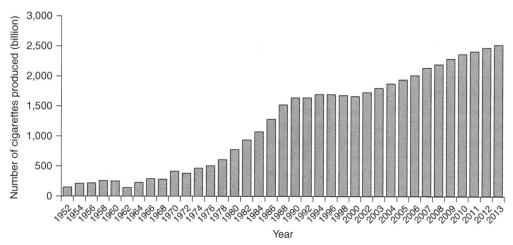

Figure 3.15 Cigarette production in China, 1952–2013
Source: Yang et al., *Lancet* (2015).

substitution of lower-cost for higher-cost brands, without effectively cutting consumption.

Another measure is a national smoke-free law to cut down on secondhand smoke. At the end of 2013, the State Council imposed a partial smoking ban in some public places like hospitals, schools, and public transport. Some cities have passed their own ordinances for smoke-free places, but enforcement has been weak. Smoking is less common than in the past in some venues such as restaurants and urban offices and is discouraged by China's First Lady.[62]

Wellness efforts are further hampered by the absence of smoking cessation clinics. There is also a low level of awareness among the Chinese population regarding the dangers of smoking. Less than half believe smoking causes coronary heart disease; less than one-quarter of the smoking population believes there is a link to lung cancer or lung disease; less than 20 percent believe there is a link to strokes; and only one in six has recently thought about quitting smoking.[63] According to the WHO, an effective anti-tobacco campaign requires six elements:

• reliable data on tobacco use and prevention
• wide imposition of smoking bans
• education of smokers on the hazards of tobacco
• heavy taxation

• smoking cessation assistance with well-funded, accessible schemes
• complete ban on marketing of tobacco

Mental Illness

As noted above, mental and behavioral disorders have become a major issue in China. Data from the 2004 World Mental Health Survey suggested a prevalence rate for major mental disorders ranging from 7 percent to 17 percent. Such disorders were much more prevalent in urban areas and among the younger and educated populations. These disorders are also projected to account for one-quarter of the disease burden by 2020. By 2010, they accounted for 9.5 percent of all DALYs. Between 2003 and 2008, mental disorders increased by more than 50 percent in the population, according to the Ministry of Health.

Public awareness of these disorders and their place in the public health agenda has also increased over the past two decades, beginning with the initial Global Burden of Diseases, Injuries, and Risk Factors Study in 1996. This growing awareness culminated in China's first national mental health legislation that passed in 2012 and went into effect in 2013.

One goal of this legislation is to expand the public's access to mental health services by shifting the site of care from specialized psychiatric hospitals to general hospitals and community health clinics in both urban and rural areas.[64] Legislative success hinges on a host of implementation issues, some already described above, that confront other public health initiatives. These include the shortage of rural healthcare workers, limited training of personnel in psychiatric disorders, resistance among hospitals and their specialists to transfer patients to community settings, urban patient preference for hospital-based care, inadequate medications in local clinics, migrant populations, the reluctance of healthcare professionals to provide psychological counseling, and lack of coordination between inpatient and outpatient care. An even larger issue is the general reluctance of those people with these disorders to engage in care-seeking behavior: 92 percent of those with mental disorders do not seek professional aid, largely due to the stigma associated with their condition.[65] Likewise, the overwhelming majority of alcoholics (98 percent) never seek treatment.

To date, the major method to promote wellness and prevention has been community education. Such programs rest on the untested (and perhaps faulty) hypothesis that mental disorders have social determinants and thus are amenable to education.[66]

Dementia and Neurological Disorders

According to the World Alzheimer Report 2010, of all of the non-communicable diseases, dementia is predicted to have the greatest economic and social impact – greater than the combined effect of stroke, cancer, and heart disease.[67] Such patients need considerable care. One problem is the low priority placed on addressing these problems in low- and middle-income countries. Part of this may reflect the mistaken perception that such problems are not widespread, are just part of the normal aging process, or are not treatable. The problem will be aggravated by China's one-child policy which limits the number of working age adults to care for their elderly parents with dementia, particularly in rural areas. The prevalence of these conditions varies by gender (higher for women) but not by urban versus rural location. Because women live much longer

than men, the urban migration of rural workers will leave many elderly females in rural China without family assistance and, thus, in need of community and government support.

The number of people with dementia has increased from 3.68 million in 1990 to 5.62 million in 2000 and to 9.19 million by 2010 (with an incidence rate of 9.87 cases per 1,000 person-years).[68] The number with Alzheimer's has increased from 1.93 million in 1990 to 3.71 million in 2000 and to 5.69 million by 2010 (with an incidence of 6.25 cases per 1,000 person-years). China has more cases of Alzheimer's than any other country in the world. Between 1990 and 2010, the DALYs due to neurological disorders increased 22 percent from 5,482 to 6,711. The DALYs for Alzheimer's skyrocketed 62 percent from 957 to 1593.[69]

Safety Issues

Further compounding the epidemic of chronic disease, China faces challenges and problems with food supply and safety, injuries and road safety, occupational safety, air quality and environmental health, and water quality. These are highlighted in the following subsections.

Food Supply

The production and consumption of food is a vast enterprise in China, particularly in light of the country's demographic changes and economic growth. There are an estimated 450,000 companies engaged in food production and processing, the majority of which are small firms (fewer than ten employees). It is also a major policy issue, given that the country has 20 percent or more of the global population but less than 10 percent of the arable land. Moreover, the available land is dwindling. More rural people are migrating to the cities to work, cities are swelling in population (and encroaching on adjacent farmlands), dietary habits are shifting rapidly (to animal products such as meat, milk, eggs), the country has shifted to more of a manufacturing base (and the appropriation of arable land for such purposes), and demand for food is rising due to population growth. Food production from the land must also compete with other agricultural uses, such as the growth of cotton and tobacco, which provide economic value to the country.

The arable land available varies in suitability for food production. The most arable land lies along China's east coast where urbanization has been most pronounced. The remaining land is subject to environmental conditions (water supply, salt content, temperature) that occasionally stress output. Water supply is perhaps the most important variable; scarcity and drought frequently limit agricultural productivity. Over-farming of the available arable land has also led to depletion of soil nutrients, which in turn are transmitted to the crops and the Chinese diet in the form of malnutrition. According to survey estimates, 208 million Chinese (mostly rural) suffered from iron-deficiency anemia, while 86 million suffered from zinc-deficiency stunting in 2002.[70]

To keep up with demand, the country has had to increase per-person production using various means such as breeding programs of high-yield grains and use of agrochemicals. Use of the latter poses an additional threat to the deterioration of the soil. The growing use of animal products in the Chinese diet has also fostered an increased need for animal feed and thus greater agricultural output of corn to feed the animals. To offset some of the pressure to produce food for the populace, China has turned to fish farming and marine fisheries.

Food is core to the Chinese culture: "to people food is heaven." Food supply is thus core to social stability.[71] There is a great emphasis on keeping food prices low as well to manage the growing income inequality in the population (e.g., between urban and rural residents). Unfortunately, this has created disincentives for farming in the rural regions. Countering these negative effects, rural agriculture has undergone mechanization to boost productivity and farmer incomes. At the same time, food consumes an increasingly lower percentage of income as income rises (a law known as Engel's Coefficient). The percentage has fallen from 57.5 percent in 1978 to 36.3 percent in 2011 in urban areas; in rural areas, the percentage fell from 67.7 percent to 40.4 percent. As it has become more of a basic commodity good, food is now also another product fit for profiteering, with several

notable scandals involving food manufacturers taking shortcuts (the 2008 episode of using melamine in milk formula).

Food Safety

Soil and water contamination pose risks for China's food supply. According to a 2011 study, a tenth of the country's rice production might be contaminated by heavy metal cadmium, discharged by mines in industrial wastewater. Grain production can be contaminated by aflatoxins generated by fungi and spurred on by high temperatures, humidity, and insect damage. Other sources of contamination include:

- the introduction (and over-use) of fertilizers, pesticides, insecticides, chemicals, and additives in food production.
- the introduction of microbial and chemical contaminants and illegal preservatives and additives in food transportation, processing, and retailing.

Poor sanitation and water pollution can also lead to food contamination, due to the need to use water in food processing and production. The country's infrastructure for water and sanitation needs greater development, particularly in rural areas where much of the food production takes place. Chemical pollution from the country's growing manufacturing base – again often located in rural areas and adjacent to farmland – is an additional hazard. Chemical contamination of soil and water can manifest itself in the food that is produced and consumed, leading to greater risks of cancer.

Safeguarding China's food supply has been the subject of several legislative acts over time. The 1979 Food Hygiene Ordinance introduced the notion of food standards; this was formalized in the 1988 Standardization Law of China and later in the 1995 Food Hygiene Law. In 2006, the country directly regulated farm products via the Agricultural Product Quality Safety Law, followed by the Food Safety Law of 2009 to coincide with international standards that would enable Chinese exports.[72] The government also committed $88 million during the 11th Five-Year Plan (2006–2010) to develop regulatory and enforcement systems for food safety monitoring. The most recent 12th Five-Year Plan calls for a national plan for food safety regulatory systems that include national food safety standards. China has passed a new Food Safety Law that promulgates 187 new national standards covering dairy products, mycotoxins, pesticide and animal medicine residues, food additives, and nutrition labeling.[73]

Of course, legislation does not necessarily translate into practice. Implementation faces the major administrative challenge of ministry cooperation, coordination among the various levels of government, and common standards. To help deal with this, the government established the State Council Leading Group on Product Quality and Food Safety (2007) and the State Council Food Security Committee (2009). In 2013, the country established a new China Food and Drug Administration to serve as a central, unified authority. Given the large number of small firms spread across the vast geography, these councils and bodies face a steep regulatory challenge – particularly given the high cost to small firms of compliance. Small food processors are not closely regulated and follow substandard environmental protection policies.

The government is also carrying out surveillance of food-borne diseases and food contaminants, as well as risk monitoring and risk assessment in food safety. It is conducting the China Nutrition and Health Survey and has recently set up a new Center for Food Safety Risk Evaluation, which parallels the Center for Disease Control (described below).

Injuries and Road Safety

Deaths by injury represent the fourth highest rank among all causes for the population at large (796,000 in 2010) – a ranking that has been stable since 1985. China has nevertheless made remarkable progress here, as injury mortalities decreased 9.9 percent since 1990. However, most of these gains have occurred among drowning and poisoning victims; there has been a 90 percent rise in the number of mortalities resulting from road injuries (rising from 155,000 to 283,000). There has also been a 55 percent increase in DALYs from road injuries. Injuries are the number one cause of death among the population below the age of 18.

Injuries are also a major source of morbidity, with a large increase in injury incidence since 1998. Injuries now account for 3.5 million hospitalizations every year. The problem is particularly acute in urban areas, where China's rate exceeds that in other developed countries.

In 2004–2005, standardized death rates were highest for transportation (14 per 100,000), followed by suicide (7 per 100,000), falls (6 per 100,000), drowning (4 per 100,000), and poisoning (3 per 100,000).[74] One major cause of such fatal injuries is road safety. Another is the low use of front seat belts, even though they are mandatory. A third problem is the lack of auto regulations such as child restraint, rear seat belts, and hands-free mobile usage. Past efforts to address this problem included (a) the Multi-Sectoral Forum on Road Safety in China (2007) sponsored by the Ministry of Health and the WHO, and organized by the CDC; (b) the national launch of the Global Road Safety Week in China (2007) sponsored by several ministries; and (c) the Injury Prevention Division within the CDC (2002) and a National Injury Surveillance System (2006).

Nevertheless, the problem is not stated as one of the major health issues to be addressed in the National Mid- and Long-term Science and Technology Development Planning Outline (2006–2020).[75] Provincial CDC funding varies considerably and is particularly low in western China. Moreover, only two of 31 provincial CDCs have established units for injury prevention and control, and only a third of injury prevention staff work on a full-time basis.

Occupational Safety

Occupational hazards – for example, factory and mine safety – constitute a major problem. This is due to the large number of small plants in China, the large number of workers exposed, and the difficulties of regulatory enforcement.[76] The government has established an Institute of Occupational Health and Poisoning Control (IOHPC). It has also established an institute for radiological protection to promote scientific standards, respond to nuclear and radiation accidents, monitor and assess the effects of nuclear contamination on human health as well as advise on protective measures, and collect, exchange, and disseminate information related to radiation health protection and radiological medicine.

Globally, injury mortality exhibits an inverted U-shaped relationship with GDP. China's injury rate has not surprisingly increased as its economy has grown. Growth in income, labor-heavy manu-facturing, and urbanization are correlated with exposure to injury risk factors. These include popu-lation density, the motorization rate, the percentage of the urban populace exposed to road traffic acci-dents, the number of urban migrant workers in high-risk occupations (and thus more workers exposed to hazardous work conditions), and the rise of the construction industry and exposure to high-rise buildings.

The low level of education among manufacturing workers may also promote injuries due to low safety awareness, equipment, and safety training. According to one study, 60 percent of the overall mortality rate among migrant workers aged 15–39 between 2000 and 2005 were due to injuries, com-pared to 40 percent for local residents.[77] Due to the fact that national mortality statistics reflect house-hold registration rather than residence (and that urban migrant workers are non-resident), these data likely underestimate the true extent of the injury problem.

Air Quality and Environmental Health

Environmental pollution exhibits an inverse U-shaped association with economic development – what some call an environmental Kuznets curve.[78] China's economic development over the past dec-ades has come at the expense of its environmental quality – what some label "growth at all costs." The negative environmental effects include the emission of chemical toxins by industrial plants and the burning of coal and biomass fuels on open indoor fires and stoves in both urban and rural homes. Roughly 60 percent of China's 264 million rural households use wood, while another 58 million use coal for cooking; such emissions place women and children at particular risk. These emissions have seriously eroded the quality of China's air, soil, and water. They are directly

implicated in the cancer rates observed in China's population (see above).[79] Researchers suggest that nearly 60 percent of cancer deaths in the country are due to modifiable environmental risk factors (carci-nogenic chemicals, biological carcinogens, radia-tion levels), with 29 percent due to chronic infections and 23 percent due to tobacco.[80] They may also be implicated in the rising infertility rates among Chinese couples.

In many of these cases, the problem is water pollution leading to high incidence of cancer. A survey of 40,000 chemical and petrochemical plants found that 23 percent of hazardous plants were located within 5 kilometers upstream of sources of drinking water. The Chinese government reportedly plans to spend $850 billion to clean up the country's water; however, despite spending $112 billion on similar efforts during 2005–2010, 43 percent of the water monitored is still hazardous to human health.[81]

Air pollution in China is egalitarian in nature: it affects everyone, rich or poor. It is also difficult to deny its existence. It is widespread across many of China's major cities: according to the WHO, 16 of the 20 most polluted cities in the world are in China. Short-term air pollution inhibits physical activity. Long-term exposure to particulate matters (fine par-ticles smaller than 2.5 μm [$PM_{2.5}$] such as sulfate, nitrates, ammonia, sodium chloride, carbon) are linked to heart disease, stroke, cancer, respiratory infection, and COPD. Higher ozone levels are linked to asthma and lung disease; nitrogen dioxide is linked to bronchitis and reduced lung function; and sulfur dioxide affects the respiratory system. Lung cancer accounts for 21 percent of all cancers in China and 27 percent of cancer-related deaths; these rates are higher in eastern China due to higher smoking levels and worse air pollution, as well as in some rural areas.[82] Researchers estimate that ambi-ent air pollution was responsible for 1.2 million premature deaths in China in 2010 – roughly 40 per-cent of the global total.[83] These deaths imposed heavy welfare costs on the country (estimated by economists at anywhere from $25–112 billion).[84] In January 2013, $PM_{2.5}$ levels in Beijing shot up to 886 μg/m^3 per 24 hours, 35 times the acceptable daily exposure of 25 set by the WHO; in October the levels in Harbin reached 1,000.

These high PM_{25} levels have several sources. They include not only auto exhaust but also the combustion of fossil fuels by power plants and other industries, as well as the complex interactions between PM_{25} and other pollutants (nitrogen oxide, sulfur dioxide) in the air. These pollutants combine with sunlight and the weather (humidity, temperature, wind) to form a complex mixture. Higher temperatures and humidity levels foster more chemical interactions in the skies; the absence of wind means they linger. The major role played by the temperature means the government lacks full control over pollution. The complex interaction with other pollutants suggests the need to coordinate the regulation of auto emissions with the emissions from power stations and manufacturers (e.g., steel mills).

To promote environmental health, the government established the State Environmental Protection Agency (SEPA) – which was then elevated to ministry status (Ministry of Environmental Protection) – as well as the Institute for Environmental Health and Related Product Safety (IEHS). These efforts were supplemented in 2002 by the establishment of a Center for Health Inspection and Supervision and in 2004 by the establishment of the Department of Health Policy and Legislation inside the MOH to strengthen laws and tighten law enforcement. The Ministry of Environmental Protection began reporting PM_{25} levels only in December 2011. Chinese citizens blame the government for environmental hazards; daily papers began to criticize the conditions in January 2013 as well.

Some helpful steps taken to date include new standards for vehicle emissions (announced by the State Council in February 2013), the installation of desulphurization and denitrification equipment in power stations, and the release of real-time data on PM_{25} to boost public awareness. Focus is also needed on other pollutants that interact with one another and the weather to ensure they do not increase while others decline. In Beijing, the government issued 69 measures (reducing vehicle emissions, raising fuel quality, raising vehicle standards, planting new trees) as part of its 2013 Clean Air Action Plan, which are expected to reduce air pollution by 2 percent in the coming years.

The country's new Five-Year Plan (2011–2015) for environmental protection includes the following four initiatives: total pollution control, environmental quality improvement, risk control, and balanced development. The plan seeks to improve the quality level for 60 percent of China's major water systems and the air quality in 80 percent of the cities above the prefecture level. China's Ministry of Environmental Protection has an additional strategy to improve air quality in 13 of the most polluted areas by focusing on several contaminants simultaneously, as well as by increased transparency (results reported to the public).[85]

Water Quality

The Chinese government began development of public water systems in the 1950s. By the 1980s, all major cities possessed water treatment facilities to guarantee the quality of drinking water. By contrast, the rural areas where the vast majority of the population lived still faced difficulties in accessing potable water. Indeed, in 1989, the China Health and Nutrition Survey reported that nearly three-quarters of rural households were using untreated water, 68 percent used open pits as toilets, and 64 percent raised livestock. This contributed to high rates of diarrhea and diarrheal mortality among children compared to the cities.[86] According to 2009 estimates, 26 percent of urban residents and 44 percent of rural dwellers lived without access to basic sanitation.[87]

An estimated 90 percent of China's rivers near its large cities are seriously polluted. Only half of 200 major rivers and less than a quarter of 28 major lakes/reservoirs have water suitable for drinking. Municipal sewage treatment facilities currently have the capacity to treat only 52 percent of urban city wastewater.[88] The situation is worse in rural China: only 3 percent of villages have wastewater management systems, and less than 30 percent of the population can access modern sanitation.

China's drinking water has been at risk for contamination by both naturally occurring chemical impurities such as fluoride and arsenic, as well as human-generated impurities such as fertilizers, insecticides, industrial waste disposal (toxic metals), household wastewater disposal, and livestock breeding. In 2007, the World Bank estimated that 66,000 rural Chinese died due to water pollution every year.

Over the past 15 years, industrial water demand has fallen 30 percent while household water demand has doubled. This means that the sources of environmental pollution have decentralized from large industrial plants to "non-point sources" that are less easily identifiable and targetable. The supply of water available to meet this growing demand is also threatened. China has less than a quarter of the global average water supply per capita. In addition to the problem of supply, there is also the issue of maldistribution of water: 13 percent of the available domestic water supply (found in the northern river basins) serves 44 percent of the populace and 65 percent of the cultivated land.[89]

During the 1980s, the Chinese government initiated a program to improve the drinking water of rural areas. The program included the construction of water plants to provide the water and pipeline systems to route water to residents. The program is a work in progress; construction is still ongoing. As of 2012, 300 million rural residents still use untreated drinking water. Only 41–42 percent access their water from water plants. Between 1985 and 2007, the proportion of the population with access to running water increased from 30 percent to 77 percent (94 percent among urban dwellers). Part of this resulted from a $54 billion investment in water supply and wastewater management in China's 661 designated cities.[90]

Part of the issue is the fragmented financing for this initiative. Between 1981 and 2002, sources of the $8.8 billion invested included central government and local government (25.7 percent), villages (26.9 percent), local households/beneficiaries (42.5 percent), and a host of international grant and lending agencies (4.9 percent: WHO, World Bank, UNICEF, etc.). The ratio of monies from these financing sources varies by region, with poor areas more reliant on government and outside agencies, while rich areas rely more on households and private capital.

Since then, government investment has substantially increased. Between 2006 and 2010, the government spent $112.4 billion on water infrastructure and $489 billion on prevention and treatment for contaminated air and water. Such investments have led to environmental improvements documented in the 2011 Report on the State of the Environment in China, including 2,587 monitoring stations nationwide.[91]

Introduction to China's Public Health System

Countries have available to them two strategies to improve the health of their populations and control disease: develop vertical programs to fight specific diseases and focus on health systems. Most countries have followed the former path; the latter strategy has been promoted by such organizations as the WHO from time to time. Like India, China has developed vertical disease programs. What is needed is a coordinated approach that spans multiple diseases and addresses the rise of coinfections (discussed above).

A systemic approach is also required to successfully control diseases by linking together prevention, detection, and treatment. Such functions are performed separately by a public health system and a healthcare delivery system – one with a public service mentality, the other with a market-driven mission and private sector mentality. This problem manifests itself in hospitals having little incentive (and being unwilling) to provide free antiretroviral drugs to HIV-positive patients (who are often poor); such drugs are distributed by the CDC system, typically with little coordination with the hospital sites of care. Indeed, many infectious diseases like TB, malaria, and HIV/AIDS likely fall outside of the hospitals' responsibility, but are squarely within the charge of the CDC system and are well-defined line items in its budget.[92]

Further, any country of China's size requires a multi-level approach that can span policy-making and funding at the top along with implementation and co-funding at middle and lower levels. Finally, any value-chain model of healthcare requires the coordination of three flows of resources: money, supplies, and information. Some of this requires sustained funding and attention from the government, as well as involvement of the private sector; some of this involves the development of sophisticated supply chains; some of this involves information systems.

Public Health System History

In the decades leading up to the Communist victory in the 1949 revolution, China was referred to as "the sick man of Asia" as a result of high rates of mortality from infectious disease. Such preventable diseases as cholera, plague, measles, polio, parasitic worms, vector-borne illnesses, and STDs were widespread. This situation became the immediate target of the Mao regime, which employed propaganda and mass mobilization campaigns to improve public health.[93]

China's public health system began in the 1950s through 1970s, partially by copying the Soviet model. This included efforts to fight epidemics (plague, cholera, malaria), a network of epidemic prevention stations set up by the MOH, establishment of schools of public health separate from clinical training institutes, a system of barefoot doctors in rural villages as frontline providers, a network of Red Cross clinics in urban areas, and the Patriotic Health Campaign Committee to mobilize political and social support to launch efforts to combat specific vector-borne diseases.[94] The government placed great emphasis on preventing acute infectious diseases, combating pests (the "four devils": flies, mice, mosquitoes, sparrows), providing some basic immunizations, and improving sanitation.

During the last two decades of the millennium, the government developed a three-tier network of rural public health (county hospitals, township health centers, village clinics), strengthened maternal and child health, and expanded its immunization efforts. In 1989, the country passed the Law on the Prevention and Treatment of Infectious Diseases, which mandated reporting for many infectious diseases classified into the three categories described earlier.

Tremendous strides were made over this time period in the incidence of certain parasitic diseases. The number of malaria cases shrank from 30 million annually in the 1940s to a mere 30,000 by the 1990s. Similarly, the number of schistosomiasis cases fell from 12 million annually to only 750,000. With regard to prevention of epidemics, the number of

health agencies grew from 500 in 1952 to 5,900 by 1999, while the number of workers rose from 2,500 to 283,000.[95]

The SARS crisis of 2003 served as a wake-up call to China's leaders to revitalize the public health system. The crisis originated in Guangzhou in Guangdong Province in November 2002 and then spread across the province to Hong Kong and to the rest of the world (ending in August 2003). However, the epidemic was first reported in February 2003 by the Hong Kong Global Outbreak Alert and Response Network and the Global Public Health Intelligence Network. The delay in public reporting had several causes: information flows in the MOH's bureaucratic hierarchy; bureaucratic regulations regarding disclosure of information on infectious disease outbreaks to the public; and the fact that SARS began as atypical pneumonia, which is not included among the notifiable diseases that must be reported. The government responded by allocating about $250 million in emergency financing for SARS control, including the building of a SARS hospital and training of public health personnel in control of infectious diseases.[96]

The SARS crisis also signaled the global impact that China's public health problems could have. That same year, the Institute of Medicine published a report highlighting the interconnectedness of countries around the world due to global travel.[97] China's population was now mobile as worldwide travelers; they were also exposed to new strains of diseases that could affect populations in other countries. SARS was not the only issue, however. China faced a resurgence of TB, AIDS/HIV, and STDs – all in the presence of a public health system that had been systematically weakened by privatization of healthcare and decentralization of funding.

In October 2007, Hu Jintao promised to "establish a basic medical and healthcare system and improve the health of the whole nation" – in effect, pledging to improve both the infrastructure of healthcare and the population's health. This promise reflected the perceived need to match the prior decades' economic progress with concomitant progress in public health. It also reflected the urgency in reversing the downward trend in the public health system (which had collapsed after

Mao) and ensuring the legitimacy of the Communist Party and its political authority.[98]

The 2009 Health System Reform Plan launched by the central government sought to revitalize public health service provision. Key aspects of the reform included improved disease control and health promotion by the three-tiered system, and the provision of a package of 41 basic public health services. Included here are health records for all citizens; screening for major diseases among the elderly, women, and children; expansion of vaccine coverage for 15 vaccine-preventable diseases; hospital-based births, prevention and control for infectious diseases; NCD management; and health education.[99]

Center for Disease Control and Prevention

China CDC is a government-funded national public health institution working in the fields of disease control and prevention, public health management and services, scientific research, and workforce development. The mission is to create a healthy environment, as well as to promote health and quality of life by controlling and preventing disease, injury, and disability so as to ensure the country's economic development, social development, and national security.

China's public health system has four tiers: national, provincial, prefecture, and county level. Its structure originated around 1950 at the county level in the form of the epidemic prevention stations. Below the county level, public health is rendered by community health service centers, village clinics, and township hospitals/health centers. In 2002, these stations were renamed local Centers for Disease Control and Prevention, which reported to the new national level Center for Disease Control and Prevention (CDC), which itself is overseen by the Bureau of Disease Control inside the MOH. At provincial and local levels, CDC offices are similarly housed in bureaus of disease control within the health bureaus of provincial, prefecture/city, and county government. CDC offices at lower levels are supposed to report to (and receive technical guidance from) their counterparts above, but this system of influence and control is described as "weak."[100] Instead, the government health bureau is the primary source of control at each level. The CDC is a key pillar in the country's infrastructure for promoting public health (see Figure 3.16).

The CDC has three main groupings: infectious disease control, public health safety, and NCD control. Roughly 60 percent of the staff is in infectious disease control; another 30 percent are in public health safety. NCD control is a new group; it has a very small staff to deal with arguably China's largest problem. There are a total of 3,534 CDCs at all levels (data from 2012), among which there are 31 provincial CDCs, 403 prefecture CDCs, and 2,822 CDCs at the county level (see Figure 2.3). The CDC's organizational structure is given in Figure 3.17.

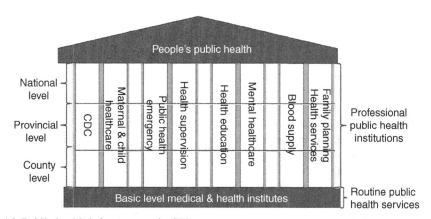

Figure 3.16 Public health infrastructure in China
Source: Xiaofeng Liang: China's Public Health System and Infrastructure.

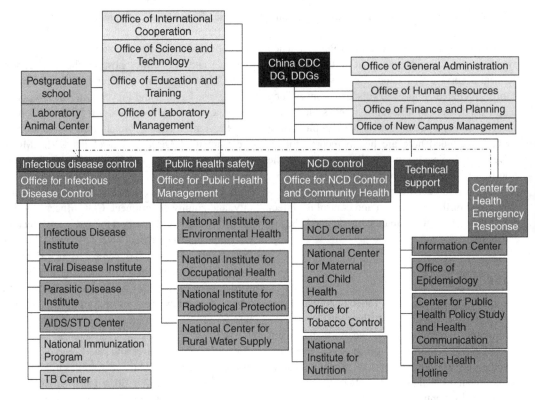

Figure 3.17 China CDC's organizational structure, 2011
Source: Xiaofeng Liang: China's Public Health System and Infrastructure.

A more detailed view of the NCD control portion of the CDC is given in Figure 3.18. Surveillance of NCDs is undertaken using a three-pronged strategy: a Death Cause Registry (2002), an NCD Risk Factor System (since 2004), and a Cardiovascular Disease Registry (under way). Risk factor surveillance itself has been a work in progress. The system relies on participants in the population to provide survey information on tobacco use, alcohol consumption, physical activity, diet, and treatment for NCDs. It also uses physical measurements of weight and blood pressure, as well as laboratory test measurements of glucose levels, lipids, insulin, and HbA1c. In 2004, it included 79 surveillance points in 31 provinces covering 30,000 or more participants; by 2012, it covered more than 162 surveillance points in 170 counties/districts and covering more than 50,000 participants.

The core functions of the CDC, depicted in Figure 3.19, are modeled after the CDC in the United States. Other activities include:

• Advocate and recommend sound public health policies and plans
• Implement major public health services nationwide
• Prevent and control leading and emerging diseases
• Establish and manage a public health surveillance information system
• Support preparedness and responses to disease outbreaks and public health emergencies nationwide and worldwide
• Establish and strengthen a national public health laboratory network: diagnostic techniques, services, quality control, and biosafety.

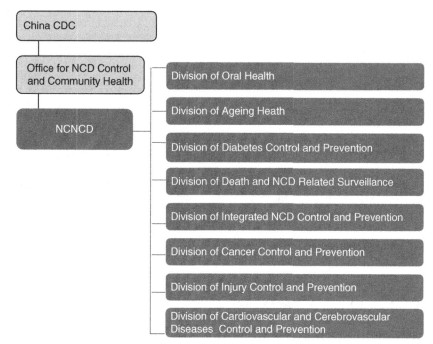

Figure 3.18 National Center for Non-communicable Diseases Control organizational structure

Figure 3.19 China CDC core functions

CDC History

China CDC was established in 2002. Its immediate predecessor was the Chinese Academy of Preventive Medicine (CAPM), which, in turn, had developed from the National Center for Preventive Medicine (NCPM). The precursor to the country's CDC was the Shanghai CDC. The latter was established in 1998 by the Shanghai Municipal Health Bureau to consolidate seven existing institutions into a new agency and then emulated in other provincial regions. These CDC structures were established in recognition of changing disease patterns in China, along with changing perceptions of disease and governmental roles.

Following the privatization and decentralization efforts begun in the late 1970s, monies to fund public health and healthcare delivery largely devolved to provincial and local government. Regional variations in funding resulted in regional variations in attention to public health issues and variations in the population's access to public health services. Combined with few national administrative mandates, the limited financial flows and limited bureaucratic control exerted by the CDC over local CDC offices meant a diminished role of the MOH and CDC in developing public health.

The CDC's funding history is presented in Figure 3.20. Global funding has been shrinking

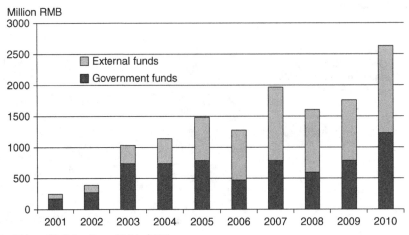

Figure 3.20 China CDC funding, 2001–2010

due to the boom in China's economy, leaving a greater share to domestic sources. Nevertheless, the government has been engaged in rebuilding CDC facilities in 31 provinces at a cost of $1.3 billion; the central government is only investing 28 percent of the needed funds, with the remainder to come from governments at lower levels. Overall, public health remains an underfunded activity, particularly with regard to health education and rural public health.[101] Such funding issues have motivated public health officials, who are typically underpaid compared to medical personnel, to engage in revenue-generating activities and extra-agency income from international agencies. Some of these revenue activities include charging fees for services that are supposed to be free.

Manpower Issues

There is an undersupply of public health personnel, although their numbers have grown in recent years. Personnel increased from less than 4.50 per 10,000 population (2009) to 4.60 (2010), to 4.70 (2011) and then to 4.96 (2012 data). The CDC itself currently has about 2,267 staff. The vast majority of CDC personnel are health professionals; the remainder are managerial and logistics staff.

In addition to supply, there is the issue of training. On average, only 0.6 percent of CDC personnel have graduate degrees, and only 12.6 percent have undergraduate degrees. The training level diminishes as one descends the geographic divisions of the CDC hierarchy. At the provincial level, only 7.3 percent of personnel have graduate degrees and only 35.6 percent have undergraduate degrees; at the prefecture level, the percentages are lower (2.1 percent and 24.5 percent, respectively); and they are lower still at the county level (0.3 percent and 12.6 percent, respectively). Unlike graduate health training in the United States, most medical and public health education in China occurs at the undergraduate level, with degrees in preventive medicine. Most of these bachelor's programs focus on clinical medicine rather than population medicine and health policy.

Information Infrastructure

Prior to the new millennium, China's disease surveillance system was based on monthly, paper-based reports (1950–1985) and then on monthly digital reports (1985–2003). Following the SARS outbreak in late 2002 and early 2003, the information infrastructure for public health in China was substantially improved. The major achievement here was the development of the web-based Notifiable Disease Reporting System, implemented on January 1, 2004 (see Figure 3.21). The reporting system serves several functions, including unified information collection, outbreak surveillance, information analysis and

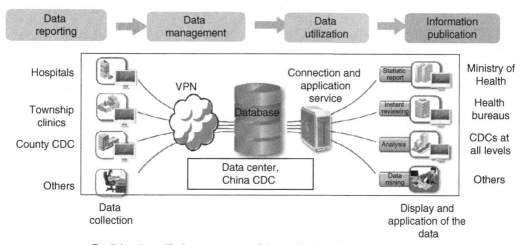

Realizing the unified management of data collection, data management, data utilization, and data publication

Figure 3.21 Working principle of the web-based reporting system
Source: Xiaofeng Liang: China's Public Health System and Infrastructure.

feedback, modularized analysis and reporting, and dynamic quality evaluation.

By the end of 2006, 94.9 percent of medical institutions at the national level, 80 percent of institutions at the provincial level, and 70.3 percent of township hospitals and clinics served as direct reporting entities. By the end of 2010, 100 percent of CDCs filed reports through the web-based reporting system, as did 98 percent of hospitals at county or higher levels and 87 percent of clinics at the township level. All of these institutions feed information into an expanding CDC network. The total number of users of the reporting system reached 68,000. About 25,000 infectious disease cases are reported daily through the web-based system.

This surveillance system was jointly financed by central government (250 million RMB) and local government (480 million RMB). Such investments covered system hardware and software, web access, personnel training, and programmer salaries.[102] Despite the investment (nearly $100 million), some remote areas of the country lack the infrastructure (e.g., computers and web access) needed to fully utilize the system, and instead must telephone their reports.

The surveillance system for reporting infectious diseases has some reported operating issues,

however. A small survey of CDC personnel at provincial city and county levels found that accurate reporting is hampered by the fact that case definitions for some diseases are unclear and too broad, making it difficult for clinicians to report. Accuracy is also thwarted by political influence and social pressure, which lead to underreporting.[103] There are also varying reporting standards across regions, and difficulties faced by local county CDC staff in conducting laboratory tests (since most reference labs are in hospitals at the prefecture level and higher). Moreover, focus on a large number of mild cases of disease may increase the workload and divert CDC staff attention away from more severe and fatal cases.[104]

China also has enhanced disease-specific surveillance systems, covering 26 diseases and four vectors (rat, mosquito, fly, and cockroach). Using over 1,000 surveillance sites across the country, these systems undertake active surveillance via case investigation, in-depth epidemiology field investigation, and data collection (on the host, immunity, pathogen variance, drug resistance, and vector density). As one illustration, the Beijing authorities discovered that problems with toilets improperly flushing led to an accumulation of flies. The new regulations specified a maximum of two flies per toilet.

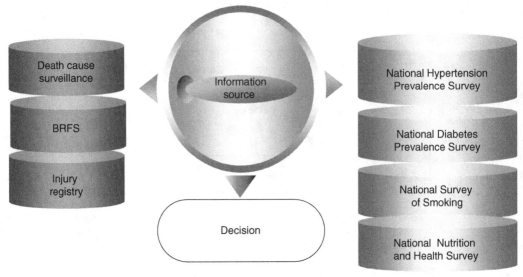

Figure 3.22 The information system for NCDs in China
Source: Xiaofeng Liang: China's Public Health System and Infrastructure.

Infectious diseases pose a great danger to public health internationally. The outbreak of SARS exposed China's fragile public health system and its limited ability to detect and respond to emergencies in a timely and effective manner. In order to strengthen its capability of responding to future public health emergencies, China is developing a public health emergency response information system (PHERIS) to facilitate disease surveillance, detection, reporting, and response. PHERIS provides nationwide, internet-based, and real-time reporting, and serves as the country's basic emergency reporting mechanism. It collects the information on emergency occurrence, impact, and response covering 11 categories of public health crises. In 2011, roughly 77 percent of these public health emergencies were due to infectious diseases; another 15 percent were due to food poisoning.

Finally, China's public health system includes additional information systems and mechanisms. Figure 3.22 depicts the information system for NCDs including the Death Cause Surveillance, Injury Registry, and Behavioral Risk Factor Surveillance (BRFS). Beyond this, there is a case management information system for HIV/AIDS, TB,

and sexually transmitted diseases; a laboratory information network (Food-Net, Pulse-Net); food-borne disease surveillance; media surveillance; and population surveys and cross-sectional investigations at different levels.

China's Key Public Health Strategies and Measurements

Strategies and Measurements for Combating Infectious Diseases

The basic legal basis for infectious disease control is the *Infectious Diseases Prevention and Treatment Act of People's Republic of China,* which was enacted by the National People's Congress in 1989 and revised in 2004. The general principle places emphasis on prevention, combined with disease-specific strategies pursued under a national strategic framework. This framework for infectious disease prevention and control includes the following:

• Top-priority diseases: This category includes HIV/AIDS, TB, malaria, and schistosomiasis. Each has a national disease-specific program including clear targets, strong government commitment and budget support, multi-sector cooperation, and active measures.

- Intensified monitoring diseases: This category covers plague, cholera, SARS, HPAI, and pulmonary anthrax. The common goal is timely detection of each occurrence, application of powerful public health measures, and prevention of transmission.
- EPI-targeted diseases/vaccine-preventable diseases: This category consists of 15 vaccine-preventable diseases. Strategies are intended to improve the quality of immunization service, and achieve and maintain adequate coverage of vaccination for each EPI-target disease. One obstacle here has been the lack of reimbursement for vaccines by the two large insurance schemes (URBMI and UEBMI). Poor families cannot afford the rabies vaccine. One dose of the pneumonia vaccine available from Pfizer costs roughly 800 RMB; four doses are required for a full schedule.
- Emerging infectious diseases: This category involves SARS (2003), HPAI (2005), EV71 (2008), and novel H1N1 (2009). The strategy is to enhance scientific research; improve capacity for detection, identification, and early warning; improve capacity for investigation and control preparedness; and establish new methodology to improve the performance of surveillance.

China's strategy is also legally based in the three categories of notifiable diseases that entail mandatory reporting and management. The law allows the MOH and provincial governments to adjust the list of Class B and Class C diseases based on actual situations.

Chronic Diseases/Non-communicable Diseases

To combat the rise of chronic illness NCDs, the central government has developed a national plan for NCD prevention and treatment (2012–2015). The plan was issued by 15 ministries and commissions.[105] The plan aims to fulfill the goals of the 2009 healthcare reform[106] to actively conduct NCD prevention and control, to curb the rapidly growing prevalence of NCDs in China, protect and promote the health of the people, and facilitate sustainable economic and social development.

The NCD control and prevention strategy focuses on three populations, three stages and three measures of intervention, and three enablers (see Figure 3.23). The main contents of the plan include 8 targets, 24 indicators, 7 measures, and 5 safeguards. The goal is to promote healthy behavior among all Chinese people, enhance early detection and treatment, and reduce NCD prevalence, disability rates, and mortality rates.

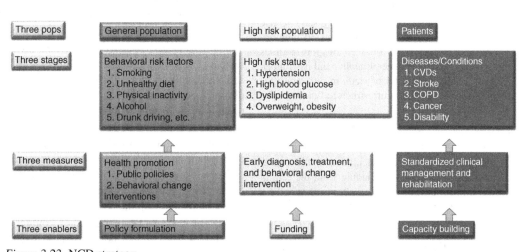

Figure 3.23 NCD strategy

The central government will take the lead in plan implementation, with multi-sector cooperation and societal-wide participation. Led by the government, implementation consists of a series of actions and major projects for combating NCDs in China, using the platform of Healthy City Initiative. Main measures include public access to exercise facilities, free hypertension screening at pharmacies, healthy education, healthy services, healthy food, physical and cultural activities/entertainment, and healthy environment.

- *Demonstration sites for comprehensive NCD prevention and control*

  This project is designed to promote NCD control by developing comprehensive measures and using demonstration sites with government support. The key challenge here is how to exercise the government's responsibility, prioritize prevention and control of risk factors, and promote a good experience. As of June 2014, 265 sites had been certified by the National Commission of Health and Family Planning.

- *Healthy lifestyles for all initiative*

  All the provinces in China launched the healthy lifestyles initiative, covering 80% of counties/districts across the nation. The initiative implemented many model communities/workplaces and supportive physical environments.

- *Health campaign for all*

  The National Fitness Campaign Plan was issued by the State Council (2011–2015). Nearly one-third (32%) of residents participate in physical exercise three times per week for more than 30 minutes. The government has encouraged all sport facilities to be opened to the general public, and has funded over 1.5 square meters of stadium per capita for outdoor exercise, with infrastructure funded by the government.

- *Early diagnosis and treatment of cancers*

  Since 2005, about 2.5 million people have been identified as a high-risk population in 115 cancer epidemic regions. Using funding from the central government budget, they have been examined for early detection and treatment.

- *Promotion of family health and NCD self-management*

  Over time, more people in the Chinese population are becoming aware of the importance of health management. Self-care and self-help are useful when clinical resources are limited. Activities to foster this growing awareness include forming self-care management teams of hypertension patients, appointing family health managers and health coordinators, and establishing cancer rehabilitation associations, cancer control corners, and diabetes patient clubs.

- *Project of Salt Consumption Reduction*

  In March 2011, Shandong's provincial government and the MOH jointly initiated a five-year project to reduce salt consumption and improve hypertension control. Shandong is the biggest province and the largest consumer of salt (12 grams per day vs. 10-gram average nationwide). Targeted activities include the reduction of salt in cooking and improved food labeling. Measures include supportive government policy making and environment; public education programs regarding salt consumption reduction and hypertension control; promotion of hypertension control techniques; and the development of surveillance and evaluation systems.

- *National Plan on Tobacco Control (2012–2015)*

  A national plan on tobacco control was issued by eight ministries. A corollary project promotes a smoke-free environment.

Future of China's Public Health System

Going forward, China's public health system faces several challenges. First, the public health issues are complex: globalization, an aging society, a huge migrant population, emerging and re-emerging infectious diseases, the growing threat of NCDs, and frequently occurring natural and industrial disasters. Second, the public health issues must be tackled in the face of China's huge territory and population, as well as the geographic and economic diversity of its population. Third, China's healthcare system suffers from major disparities in service delivery. Fourth, capacity building (surveillance, lab network, research, training, etc.) needs to be enhanced to deal with the above issues.

The key tasks to be performed are outlined in Figure 3.24. They include new legislation regarding mental illness and smoking control, sustainable financial support for public health as international agencies withdraw from China, multi-sector cooperation across government ministries, and multi-level cooperation across national, provincial, and local governments. The rapid rise of NCDs suggests the country's need for training new health workers in such diverse specialties as psychiatry, rheumatology, rehabilitation medicine, and ophthalmology. They also suggest the need for a primary care workforce that can help to implement behavior modification programs that a hospital-based system is ill-equipped to handle. These will need to be supplemented by new regulation, taxation, and information campaigns to encourage more healthy lifestyles.[107]

- *Strengthen legislation and establish effective legal regulation mechanism*
- *Sustainable financial support*
- *Multi-sector cooperation and linkage*
- *Strengthen institutional construction*
- *Play more important roles in healthcare system reform*
- *Enhance capacity and strengthen experts' advantage*
- *Enhance research and evidence-based policy making*
- *Community mobilization and empowerment*
- *International cooperation and interaction*

Figure 3.24 Key tasks for improving public health systems

According to the 2009 reform, China needs to establish a basic healthcare system covering urban and rural residents by 2020. Across all provinces, the goal is to set up a fairly complete public health service system and healthcare delivery system, a comparatively sound medical security system, a secure and relatively well regulated pharmaceutical supply system, and a comparatively sound healthcare institution management and operational system – depicted in Figure 3.25 (8 pillars, 4 points, 1 goal). The end result should be the formation of a multi-sponsored medical configuration to (at least preliminarily) meet the multilayer demands of the population for healthcare services, such that everyone has access to basic healthcare services that help to enhance the health status of the population.

An important element of this system reform is the continued development of the public health service system. Efforts should be made to establish and improve professional public health service networks, which include disease prevention and control, health education, maternity and child care, mental health, emergency response, blood collection and supply, hygiene supervision, and family planning. Efforts are also needed to improve (a) the public health system's functioning, including a clear-cut division of work, information-exchange, resource-sharing, coordination and interaction; (b) capacity to deal

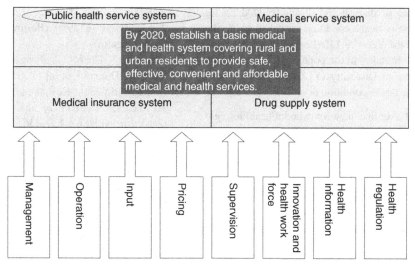

Figure 3.25 Framework for healthcare system reform

with public health emergencies; and (c) equalized access to basic public health services for urban and rural residents (gradually over time). A third set of efforts should be made to identify the scope of public health services, clarify the basic public health service items to be provided nationally, increase step by step the content of these services, and encourage local governments to likewise increase the content of their public health services on the basis of the service items defined by the central government and in accordance with the local economic development and prominent public health problems.

Notes

1. Chinese Center for Disease Control and Prevention. Data available online at: www.chinacdc.cn/tjsj/fdcrbbg/201303/t20130327_79057.htm. Accessed on March 27, 2013.
2. State Council. 2012. *Medical and Health Services in China* (Beijing: Information Office of the State Council).
3. According to the World Health Organization,

   one DALY can be thought of as one lost year of 'healthy' life. The sum of these DALYs across the population, or the burden of disease, can be thought of as a measurement of the gap between current health status and an ideal health situation where the entire population lives to an advanced age, free of disease and disability. DALYs for a disease or health condition are calculated as the sum of the Years of Life Lost (YLL) due to premature mortality in the population and the Years Lost due to Disability (YLD) for people living with the health condition or its consequences.

   Available online at: www.who.int/healthinfo/global_burden_disease/metrics_daly/en/. Accessed on October 9, 2015.
4. Gonghuan Yang, Yu Wang, Yixin Zeng et al. 2013. "Rapid Health Transition in China, 1990–2010: Findings from the Global Burden of Disease Study 2010," *The Lancet* 381: 1987–2015.
5. Jiang He, Dongfeng Gu, Xigui Wu et al. 2005. "Major Causes of Death Among Men and Women in China," *New England Journal of Medicine* 353: 1124–1134.
6. Lei Zhang and David Wilson. 2012. "Trends in Notifiable Infectious Diseases in China: Implications for Surveillance and Population Health Policy," *PLoS ONE* 7(2): e31076. doi: 10.1371/journal.pone.0031076. Epub 2012. Feb 16.
7. Zhang and Wilson. 2012. "Trends in Notifiable Infectious Diseases in China."
8. Yang et al. 2013. "Rapid Health Transition in China, 1990–2010."
9. Zhang and Wilson. 2012. "Trends in Notifiable Infectious Diseases in China."
10. Joan Kaufman. 2009. "Infectious Disease Challenges in China," in Charles Freeman and Xiaoqing Lu (Eds.), *China's Capacity to Manage Infectious Diseases* (Washington, DC: Center for Strategic & International Studies).
11. Kaufman. 2009. "Infectious Disease Challenges in China."
12. Yang et al. 2013. "Rapid Health Transition in China, 1990–2010."
13. Kaufman. 2009. "Infectious Disease Challenges in China."
14. Ibid.
15. World Health Organization. 2006. *Global Tuberculosis Control*. WHO Report (Geneva, Switzerland: WHO).
16. Ministry of Public Health of the People's Republic of China. 1992. *Nationwide Random Survey for the Epidemiology of Tuberculosis in 1990* (Beijing: Ministry of Public Health).
17. Xianyi Chen, Fengzeng Zhao, Honglin Duanmu et al. 2002. "The DOTS Strategy in China: Results and Lessons After 10 Years," *Bulletin of the World Health Organization* 80(6): 430–436.
18. Ministry of Public Health of the People's Republic of China. 2002. *Report on Nationwide Random Survey for the Epidemiology of Tuberculosis in 2000* (Beijing: Ministry of Public Health).
19. Kaufman. 2009. "Infectious Disease Challenges in China."
20. Daiyu Hu, X. Liu, J. Chen et al. 2008. "Direct Observation and Adherence to Tuberculosis Treatment in Chongqing, China:

A Descriptive Study," *Health Policy and Planning* 23(1): 43–55.

21. Liya Wan, Shiming Cheng, and Daniel Chin. 2007. "A New Disease Reporting System Increases TB Case Detection in China," *Bulletin of the World Health Organization* 85 (5). Available online at: www.who.int/bulletin/volumes/85/5/06-036376/en/. Accessed on May 12, 2014.

22. Ministry of Public Health of the People's Republic of China. 2002. Report on Nationwide Random Survey for the Epidemiology of Tuberculosis in 2000.

23. Xiaoqing Lu. 2009. "The Challenge of Tuberculosis Control in China," in Charles Freeman and Xiaoqing Lu (Eds.), *China's Capacity to Manage Infectious Diseases* (Washington, DC: Center for Strategic & International Studies).

24. Yang et al. 2013. "Rapid Health Transition in China, 1990–2010."

25. Lu. 2009. "The Challenge of Tuberculosis Control in China."

26. Yuanli Liu. 2009. "The Anatomy of China's Public Health System," in Charles Freeman and Xiaoqing Lu (Eds.), *China's Capacity to Manage Infectious Diseases* (Washington, DC: Center for Strategic & International Studies).

27. Lu. 2009. "The Challenge of Tuberculosis Control in China."

28. Janet Vail. 2009. "Managing Infectious Diseases Among China's Migrant Populations," in Charles Freeman and Xiaoqing Lu (Eds.), *China's Capacity to Manage Infectious Diseases* (Washington, DC: Center for Strategic & International Studies).

29. Lu. 2009. "The Challenge of Tuberculosis Control in China."

30. Vail. 2009. "Managing Infectious Diseases Among China's Migrant Populations."

31. Paul Goss, Kathrin Strasser-Weippl, Brittany Lee-Bychkovsky et al. 2014. "Challenges to Effective Cancer Control in China, India, and Russia," *The Lancet* 15: 489–538.

32. Vail. 2009. "Managing Infectious Diseases Among China's Migrant Populations."

33. Ibid.

34. Lu. 2009. "The Challenge of Tuberculosis Control in China."

35. Ibid.

36. 45 percent of the country's population was infected with the TB bacilli by 2008. Among these, a sizeable percentage can be expected to contract the disease during their lifetime. Lu. 2009. "The Challenge of Tuberculosis Control in China."

37. Lu. 2009. "The Challenge of Tuberculosis Control in China."

38. A 2008 MOH survey found that 61 percent of the population who reported being ill during the prior two weeks also suffered from chronic disease; in 1998, only 39 percent reported chronic illness.

39. Ping Zhao, Min Dai, Wanqing Chen et al. 2010. "Cancer Trends in China," *Japanese Journal of Clinical Oncology* 40(4): 281–285.

40. Goss et al. 2014. "Challenges to Effective Cancer Control in China, India, and Russia."

41. Yuanli Liu, Gonghuan Yang, Yixin Zeng et al. 2013. "Policy Dialogue on China's Changing Burden of Disease," *The Lancet* 381: 1961–1962.

42. Yang et al. 2013. "Rapid Health Transition in China, 1990–2010."

43. The World Bank. 2011. *Toward a Healthy and Harmonious Life in China: Stemming the Rising Tide of Non-Communicable Diseases* (Washington, DC: World Bank).

44. International Agency for Research on Cancer. 2012. *GLOBOCAN 2012: Estimated Cancer Incidence, Mortality and Prevalence Worldwide in 2012*. Available online at: http://globocan.iarc.fr/Pages/fact_sheets_population.aspx.

45. Goss et al. 2014. "Challenges to Effective Cancer Control in China, India, and Russia."

46. The World Bank. 2011. *Toward a Healthy and Harmonious Life in China.*

47. Yang et al. 2013. "Rapid Health Transition in China, 1990–2010."

48. Ibid.

49. Zhao et al. 2010. "Cancer Trends in China."
50. X.J. Ma, C. Lin, and W. Zhen. 2008. "Cancer Care in China: A General Review," *Biomedical Imaging and Intervention Journal* 4(3): e39.
51. Goss et al. 2014. "Challenges to Effective Cancer Control in China, India, and Russia."
52. Xiao Zou, Xia Wan, Zhen Dai et al. 2012. "Epidemiological Characteristics of Cancer in Elderly Chinese," *ISRN Oncology*. Available online at: www.hindawi.com/jour nals/isrn/2012/381849/. Accessed on October 8, 2015.
53. Zhao et al. 2010. "Cancer Trends in China."
54. Goss 2014. "Challenges to Effective Cancer Control in China, India, and Russia."
55. The World Bank. 2011. *Toward a Healthy and Harmonious Life in China.*
56. Ibid.
57. Dongfeng Gu, Xigui Wu, Kristi Reynolds et al. 2004. "Cigarette Smoking and Exposure to Environmental Tobacco Smoke in China: The International Collaborative Study of Cardiovascular Disease in Asia," *American Journal of Public Health* 94(11): 1972–1976.
58. Zhao et al. 2010. "Cancer Trends in China."
59. Ted Alcorn. 2013. "Winds Shift for Tobacco Control in China," *The Lancet* (November): 679–680.
60. Goss et al. 2014. "Challenges to Effective Cancer Control in China, India, and Russia."
61. Theo Vos, Rob Carter, Jan Barendregt et al. 2010. *Assessing Cost-Effectiveness in Prevention: ACE Prevention* (Brisbane, Australia: University of Queensland).
62. Staff. 2014. "Government Coughers," *The Economist* (March 1): 39.
63. Alcorn. 2013. "Winds Shift for Tobacco Control in China."
64. Michael Phillips. 2013. "Can China's New Mental Health Law Substantially Reduce the Burden of Illness Attributable to Mental Disorders?" *The Lancet* 381: 1964–1966.
65. Michael Phillips, Jingxuan Zhang, Qichang Shi, Q et al. Prevalence, treatment, and associated disability of mental disorders in four provinces in China during 2001–05: an epidemiological survey. *Lancet.* 2009; 373: 2041–2053.
66. Ibid.
67. Alzheimer's Disease International. 2010. *The World Alzheimer Report 2010* (London: ADI).
68. Kit Yee Chan, Wei Wang, Jing J. Wu et al. 2013. "Epidemiology of Alzheimer's Disease and Other Forms of Dementia in China, 1990–2010: A Systematic Review and Analysis," *The Lancet* 381: 2016–2023.
69. Yang et al. 2013. "Rapid Health Transition in China, 1990–2010."
70. Hon-Ming Lam, Justin Remais, Ming-Chiu Fung et al. 2013. "Food Supply and Food Safety Issues in China," *The Lancet* 381: 2044–2053.
71. Lam et al. 2013. "Food Supply and Food Safety Issues in China." The stability of the food supply chain has been an issue in China's past, going back to the widespread famine during the 1950s. This issue was voiced again in the 1990s by the publication of *Who Will Feed China?*
72. Lam et al. 2013. "Food Supply and Food Safety Issues in China." See Table 2.
73. Goss et al. 2014. "Challenges to Effective Cancer Control in China, India, and Russia."
74. Jiaying Zhao, Edward Jow-Ching Tu, Christine McMurray et al. 2012. "Rising Mortality from Injury in Urban China: Demographic Burden, Underlying Causes, and Policy Implications," *Bulletin of the World Health Organization* 90: 461–467.
75. Zhao et al. 2012. "Rising Mortality from Injury in Urban China."
76. According to the MOH, the country has 16 million companies and factories with poisonous or hazardous operations, exposing some 200 million workers to occupational health problems.
77. Shanghai. 2008. *Report on the Epidemiology of Injury in Shanghai* (Shanghai: Shanghai Municipal Center for Disease Control and Prevention).
78. Goss et al. 2014. "Challenges to Effective Cancer Control in China, India, and Russia."

79. Perhaps the most notable expression of the environmental problem is the recent acknowledgment of the existence of "cancer villages." These include 459 villages in 29 of China's 32 provinces.

80. Goss et al. 2014. "Challenges to Effective Cancer Control in China, India, and Russia."

81. Gwynn Guilford. 2013. "China Now Has Up to 400 Cancer Villages, and the Government Only Just Admitted It" (February 22). Available online at: http://qz.com/55928/china-now-has-up-to-400-cancer-villages-and-the-government-only-just-admitted-it/.

82. Goss et al. 2014. "Challenges to Effective Cancer Control in China, India, and Russia."

83. Ted Alcorn. 2013. "China's Skies: A Complex Recipe for Pollution with No Quick Fix," *The Lancet* 381: 1973–1974.

84. Sung Cho, Jonathan Li, and Leea Tiusanen. 2013. "The Effects of Outdoor Air Pollution on National Healthcare in China," Research paper prepared for Wharton Course on China's Healthcare System and Reform. Guanghua School of Management, Peking University.

85. Goss et al. 2014. "Challenges to Effective Cancer Control in China, India, and Russia."

86. Jing Zhang. 2012. "The Impact of Water Quality on Health: Evidence from the Drinking Water Infrastructure in Rural China," *Journal of Health Economics* 31: 122–134.

87. Goss et al. 2014. "Challenges to Effective Cancer Control in China, India, and Russia."

88. Ibid.

89. Ibid.

90. Ibid.

91. Ibid.

92. Liu. 2009. "The Anatomy of China's Public Health System."

93. Kaufman. 2009. "Infectious Disease Challenges in China."

94. Jesse Huang. n.d. *The Health Care System and Public Health in China*. Available online at: www.pitt.edu/~super4/37011-38001/37901.ppt. Accessed on October 6, 2015.

95. Huang. *The Health Care System and Public Health in China.*

96. Kaufman. 2009. "Infectious Disease Challenges in China."

97. Institute of Medicine. 2003. *Microbial Threats to Health* (Washington, DC: IOM).

98. Charles Freeman. 2009. "Introduction," in Charles Freeman and Xiaoqing Lu, *China's Capacity to Manage Infectious Diseases* (Washington, DC: Center for Strategic & International Studies).

99. Yan Ding, Helen Smith, Yang Fei et al. 2013. "Factors Influencing the Provision of Public Health Services by Village Doctors in Hubei and Jiangxi Provinces, China," *Bulletin of the World Health Organization* 91: 64–69.

100. Liu. 2009. "The Anatomy of China's Public Health System."

101. Ibid.

102. Long-De Wang, Yu Wang, Gong-Huan Yang et al. n.d. *China Information System for Disease Control and Prevention (CISDCP).* National Bureau of Asian Research: Center for Health and Aging.

103. Zhang and Wilson. 2012. "Trends in Notifiable Infectious Diseases in China."

104. Futang Pan, Biyun Chen, Wiedong Zhang et al. 2013. "Challenge of Notifiable Infectious Diseases Reporting System in China," *African Journal of Pharmacy and Pharmacology* 7: 2617–2621.

105. They include the National Commission of Health and Family Planning, National Development and Reform Commission, Ministry of Education, Ministry of Science and Technology, Ministry of Industry and Information Technology, Ministry of Civil Affairs, Ministry of Finance, Ministry of Human Resources and Social Security, Ministry of Environmental Protection, Ministry of Agriculture, Ministry of Commerce, State Administration of Radio Film and Television, General Administration of Press and Publication, General Administration of Sport, and the State Food and Drug Administration.

106. "Recommendations of the Communist Party of China (CPC) Central Committee and the State Council on Deepening the Medical and Healthcare System Reform."

107. Yang et al. 2013. "Rapid Health Transition in China, 1990–2010."

PART II

Healthcare Reform

Epidemiological Transition and Health System Reforms in China

GORDON G. LIU AND SAM KRUMHOLZ

Introduction

Over the past 30 years, China's economy has grown at an unprecedented rate.[1] This growth, combined with underlying demographic and societal trends, has speeded China's epidemiological transition. Today, the large majority of population mortality and morbidity in China are caused by non-communicable diseases (NCDs). The growth of NCDs has placed serious strains on the existing Chinese healthcare financing and delivery systems.

The Chinese government has recently embarked upon a wide-ranging healthcare reform to strengthen the capacity of its healthcare system and better prepare it to face future challenges. Foremost among these challenges are the aging of China's population and rise of NCDs in the Chinese population. The reforms focused on five areas: insurance reform, pharmaceutical reform, public health reform, primary care reform, and public hospital reform. However, although these reforms have achieved remarkable successes in some areas, much remains to be done.

For many Chinese, access to care is limited and remains prohibitively expensive. Additionally, the pressures placed on the healthcare system by a large population with chronic illness will continue to increase as China becomes older, wealthier, and more urbanized. Thus, ensuring that the Chinese healthcare system has the capacity to provide effective affordable care to patients with NCDs must be the primary goal of Chinese health policy over the coming decades.

This chapter provides a comprehensive examination of the issues addressed above. We first describe China's epidemiological transition and the underlying societal, economic, and demographic trends that have caused it. We next outline and evaluate the government's responses to improve the population's access to healthcare and address this epidemiological transition over the past two decades, highlighting both successes and areas still in need of improvement. We particularly emphasize government reforms in healthcare financing. Finally, we conclude by recommending several future health and social policies intended to slow the growth of NCDs in the Chinese population while also better preparing the healthcare system to efficiently and effectively care for the NCD population.

Although previous research has addressed China's epidemiological transition,[2] the dramatic economic and social shifts within the country, and the success and failures of China's recent healthcare reforms,[3] no report has yet provided a full comprehensive synthesis of these three topics. This chapter attempts to fill this gap.

China's Epidemiological Transition

Over the past 60 years, China has passed through a multistage epidemiological transition. In pre-revolutionary China, the vast majority of deaths were caused by communicable diseases, tropical diseases, diseases related to poor sanitation, perinatal illness, and natural and man-made disasters.[4] Life expectancy was low and infant mortality was extremely high. After the founding of the People's Republic of China in 1949, the central government placed a strong emphasis on improving population health. Greater centralization, political campaigns against unhealthy and unsanitary habits, an increase in "village doctors," and near-universal health insurance coverage led to large decreases in many infectious and sanitation-related diseases, as well as neo-natal and maternal deaths.[5]

In 1978, China implemented open-market reforms, beginning a period of rapid economic growth that has continued to the present day. Since the reforms, falling death rates from communicable and perinatal diseases have been accompanied by another more alarming trend: a sharp increase in the numbers of Chinese suffering and dying from NCDs.[6] This section outlines the extent of the shifts in China's population health, disease burden, and NCD risk factors in the years since 1978, and describes projections for future prevalence of NCDs.

examination of more recent trends finds a similar pattern; between 2003 and 2008, the prevalence of physician-diagnosed chronic diseases (e.g., heart disease, stroke, cancer, and COPD) all increased, while the prevalence of infectious diseases remained unchanged.[9] Chapter 6 (see Table 6.2) shows the distribution of the leading causes of death in the Chinese population in 2012.

Shift in Overall Death and Disease Burden

Deaths caused by NCDs have increased dramatically over the past three decades. Between 1973 and 2006, the share of deaths caused by noncommunicable diseases increased from 41.7 percent to 74.1 percent, while those caused by communicable and perinatal diseases fell from 28 percent to 5.2 percent.[7] Over the past 20 years, the absolute number of deaths caused by NCDs has increased due to China's aging and growing population, even as age-standardized mortality rates have fallen.[8] An

Shift in Individual NCDs

The leading causes of death in China today are stroke, ischemic heart disease, cancer, chronic obstructive pulmonary disease (COPD), and diabetes. However, among these five NCDs there exists significant heterogeneity in trends in mortality and prevalence (see Figure 4.1). While the absolute number of deaths caused by cancer and stroke increased between 1990 and 2010, the age-standardized mortality rates for these diseases fell (see Figure 4.2).[10] Epidemiological studies measuring shorter-run trends in stroke mortality found that age-standardized rates increased until 1998 and then fell in subsequent years, although

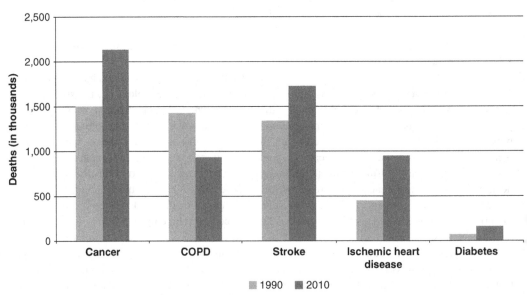

Figure 4.1 Change in number of deaths of five major chronic diseases, 1990 and 2010
Source: Yang et al. 2013.

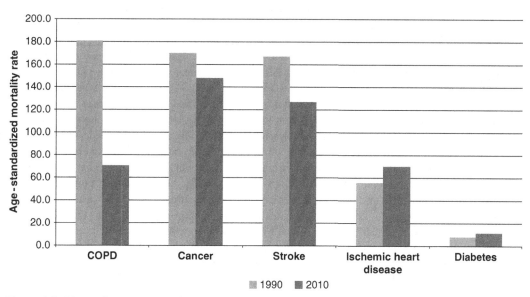

Figure 4.2 Change in age-standardized mortality rates of five major chronic diseases, 1990 and 2010

there is evidence that rates may again be beginning to rise.[11] Age-standardized cancer mortality rates increased dramatically between the 1970s and 1990s, but showed a slight decline between 1990 and 2005 with significant heterogeneity in trends by cancer type.[12] If these trends continue, absolute mortality rates for cancer and stroke will remain high as China's population continues to age, but the overall proportion of deaths caused by these two diseases may begin to decrease. By contrast, both age-standardized mortality rates and absolute mortality rates for COPD fell between 1990 and 2010. If this trend continues, COPD will afflict lower numbers of Chinese in the future.

Finally, age-standardized and crude mortality rates for ischemic heart disease and diabetes rose between 1990 and 2010. Age-standardized mortality from heart disease has been increasing at a steady rate since the mid-1980s, with larger increases among men.[13] Projections based off current mortality and population data suggest that absolute number of deaths attributable to cardiovascular disease in China will increase by 50 percent between 2010 and 2030 if population risk factors remain at 2000 levels, and by 64 percent if risk factors continue to increase at the present rate.[14] A

recent study estimated that China's diabetes prevalence more than tripled between 2002 and 2008, from 2.6 percent to 9.7 percent.[15] Even more alarming, 61 percent of men and 60 percent of women with diabetes are unaware of their condition.[16] These trends are extremely worrisome. Given China's aging population, they suggest that diabetes and heart disease prevalence and mortality will grow rapidly in China over the next several decades.

Shift in Risk Factors

Concurrent with the increase of non-communicable diseases over the past 30 years, there has been an even more dramatic increase in NCD risk factors. Hypertension is a major risk factor for stroke and cardiovascular disease. In 2005, hypertension was estimated to be responsible for 60 percent of Chinese deaths from cardiovascular disease and 20 percent of all deaths.[17] Between 1991 and 2001, the prevalence of hypertension among 35–74-year-olds rose from 19.7 percent to 26.6 percent.[18] By 2008, Yang et al. (2012) estimated that 30 percent of Chinese adults had hypertension.[19] Additionally, large numbers of Chinese with hypertension are unaware of their condition, putting them at even greater risk for stroke and cardiovascular disease.[20]

Obesity and sedentary behavior are both associated with increased probability for stroke, cardiovascular disease, cancer, and many other NCDs. The prevalence of obesity and overweight among Chinese adults has increased from 11.7 percent in 1991 to 29.2 percent in 2009.[21] Similarly, between 1991 and 2006 overweight and obesity rates among Chinese youth more than doubled, increasing from 5.2 percent to 13.2 percent.[22] Physical activity among Chinese adults has also decreased over the past two decades; between 1997 and 2006, total metabolic equivalent time (MET) per week fell by nearly a third for both men and women.[23] Chinese occupation-related physical activity has also decreased, falling by a third for men and by nearly a half for women between 1991 and 2006.

Smoking is a major risk factor for cancer, stroke, and cardiovascular disease. China currently consumes 30 percent of the world's cigarettes and has long been one of the world's largest producers of tobacco products.[24] Smoking rates have been falling slowly in China since the early 1990s; 32 percent of the adult population reported smoking in 1993 compared to 26 percent in 2003.[25] However, recent estimates suggest that this decline has stabilized, while smoking intensity has increased.[26]

Age is a significant predictor for NCD risk. China's population has aged significantly over the past 30 years (see Figure 1.6). Between 1982 and 2010, the proportion of the Chinese population between the ages of 0 and 14 years fell from 33.9 percent to 16.6 percent, while the proportion of the population aged 65 and over almost doubled.[27] By 2050, the 65 and over population is projected to make up more than a quarter of the total Chinese population.[28]

Diets high in fats and animal products have been linked to hypertension and obesity. Although the average amount of calories consumed by the Chinese population decreased throughout the 1990s,[29] the percent of the population consuming high-fat diets (>30 percent of calories from fat) increased dramatically between 1989 and 2006, from 14.7 percent to 44.1 percent.[30] This change was accompanied by a drop in the amount of tubers

and cereals consumed and a corresponding increase in the consumption of animal products.[31]

In sum, China has undergone a dramatic epidemiologic transition over the past thirty years. The greatest threats to the Chinese population's well-being are now diseases of old age and affluence; infectious and tropical diseases have ceased to become major drivers of disability and death. Research indicates that ischemic heart attacks and diabetes may be especially large drivers of mortality and morbidity over the next few decades. Additionally, the increasing prevalence of high blood pressure, obesity, and insufficient physical activity in conjunction with the aging of the Chinese population has put more and more Chinese at risk for NCDs. Thus, the Chinese government must prepare for increasing NCD mortality and morbidity for the foreseeable future.

China's Healthcare Reforms: What Are They and Have They Worked?

High levels of patients with NCDs create unique challenges for healthcare systems. To provide high-quality care to such patients, a health system must provide well-run primary and preventive care centers offering disease prevention, diagnosis, and management, as well as secondary and tertiary hospitals capable of performing complex interventions and procedures. Additionally, in order to make this treatment affordable, a health system must also offer a health insurance system with sufficient depth and breadth, while still maintaining systemic checks on the growth of total medical expenditures. In the 1980s and 1990s, China's health system lacked many of these features; its primary care system shrank, hospital and physician supply failed to keep pace with demand, physicians faced distorted prescribing and diagnosing incentives, and patients largely bypassed primary care clinics for secondary and tertiary hospitals.[32]

Over the past decade, China has begun a wide-ranging series of healthcare reforms. These reforms were aimed at addressing the many inefficiencies and distorted incentives embedded in the old Chinese health system, many of which also contributed to inadequate care for China's NCD patient population. This healthcare reform has five major components: insurance reform, pharmaceutical drug reform, public health reform, primary care reform, and public hospital reform.[33] We describe these reforms and evaluate their effectiveness in improving the Chinese healthcare delivery and financing systems' capacity to handle patients with NCDs and decrease NCD prevalence. We conclude with a series of recommendations for the direction of future reforms with an emphasis on policies focused on China's NCD population.

Insurance Reform

Access to health insurance should increase healthcare utilization and decrease risk of catastrophic health expenditures. Widespread health insurance coverage is an important step in decreasing the financial and health burdens related to acute as well as NCD diseases. However, prior to the recent reforms Chinese health insurance rates were extremely low; in 2000, less than 10 percent of the rural population and less than half of the urban population had access to health insurance.[34] This lack of coverage led to high levels of out-of-pocket spending, lack of access to quality care, and widespread dissatisfaction with the Chinese healthcare system.[35] Over the past decade, the Chinese government has implemented a series of health insurance reforms intended to achieve universal coverage by 2020.

In an effort to increase health insurance coverage in rural areas, the Chinese government created the New (Rural) Cooperative Medical Scheme (NCMS) in 2003. By 2010, NCMS reached 2,716 counties and more than 800 million people.[36] NCMS is a voluntary, household-based health insurance system. Risk-pooling is performed at a county level and each county has significant leeway in designing benefit packages and reimbursement rates. NCMS is heavily subsidized; individual premiums are kept extremely low to maintain high participation rates and minimize adverse selection. Government investment in NCMS has increased dramatically since implementation; per beneficiary contributions from the central and local government increased from 40 RMB in 2008 to 200 RMB in 2011, with greater subsidies going to poorer and western counties.[37] Most NCMS plans currently cover both

inpatient and outpatient care, but real reimbursement rates remain low and exhibit wide variation by county. NCMS packages also provide progressively lower reimbursement rates as patients enter higher level hospitals, incentivizing patients to seek care at primary health centers and township hospitals.[38]

Prior to the Chinese healthcare reforms, many urban residents not working in the formal sector had no access to government health insurance. This population included children, the retired, the unemployed, and workers in the informal sector. To reach this population, the Chinese government created Urban Resident Basic Medical Insurance (URBMI). URBMI was begun as a pilot project in 2007 and implemented nationwide in 2009.[39] URBMI is structured similarly to NCMS; funds are pooled at the municipal level, and reimbursement rates and covered procedures vary by city.[40] Initially, most municipalities did not cover outpatient procedures. Similar to NCMS, government investment in URBMI has increased since the program began. In 2011, URBMI was financed at an average of 170 RMB per enrollee, with estimates of average reimbursement rates ranging from 47 percent–60 percent.[41]

Chinese health insurance reforms have achieved enormous success in expanding insurance coverage, reaching more than 95 percent of the Chinese population by 2011 (see Figure 2.2). However, it is less clear if these programs have exerted a commensurate impact on patient health spending and utilization. Early appraisals of NCMS have generally found that the reforms have increased healthcare utilization, but have had a limited effect on healthcare spending.[42] Preliminary analyses have also reported mixed impacts on the prevalence of NCDs and health outcomes. Researchers reported that NCMS lead to a significant decrease in several chronic diseases, and that NCMS status positively influenced NCD risk factors (e.g., lower likelihood of abnormal glucose and cholesterol levels).[43] However, an earlier study found no effect of NCMS on self-reported health status or sickness/injury over the prior four months.[44]

Analyses of the effects of URBMI on health utilization, out-of-pocket spending, and health status are more limited. Lin et al. (2009) found that

URBMI had a positive effect on relieving enrollees' financial burdens,[45] while Liu and Zhao (2012) found that URBMI had an uncertain effect on patients' out-of-pocket spending while increasing healthcare access.[46] Although these preliminary studies appear to indicate that URBMI has had an overall positive effect on patients' ability to access and pay for care, more comprehensive studies are necessary. Further, no studies have yet specifically focused on URBMI's effects on health outcomes or financial effects on chronic disease patients.

Extending insurance coverage to the vast majority of the Chinese population may serve to improve the health system's capacity to handle patients with NCDs in the following manner. Access to insurance should incentivize patients to seek outpatient care to help keep their diseases under control, thereby improving their health, reducing their risk of catastrophic health events, and decreasing the risk of catastrophic health spending for patients with chronic disease.

The empirical evidence shows that Chinese insurance reforms may not be meeting these goals. Although healthcare utilization is increasing, the reform's effect on out-of-pocket spending is less clear, especially among NCMS enrollees. Most researchers speculate that the reason for the insurance expansion's small effect on out-of-pocket spending is NCMS' and URBMI's low reimbursement rates and limited coverage areas. However, much of the recent literature has focused on the effects of NCMS and URBMI in 2007 and 2008. Since that time, government subsidies have increased, reimbursement rates have gone up, and coverage has broadened. Thus, the true effects of the current iterations of NCMS and URBMI may be significantly different than those of 2007/2008. Therefore, although the insurance expansion appears to have only a limited effect on the finances of NCD patients and their families, more evidence on the current versions of NCMS and URBMI is necessary before any strong conclusions can be drawn.

Pharmaceutical Drug Reform

Access to cheap and effective pharmaceuticals can lower both the risk factors for NCDs and the risk of catastrophic health events among NCD patients. An effective pharmaceutical distribution system should encourage rational prescribing of pharmaceuticals while making these pharmaceuticals affordable to all patients. China's pre-reform pharmaceutical system accomplished neither of these goals. In the years after the open-market reforms, the government withdrew the majority of its support from public hospitals and clinics while continuing to mandate below-market prices for many basic medical services. To make up for the loss in revenue, providers were allowed to charge up to 15 percent markups on pharmaceuticals and high-tech procedures. Salaried physicians' income was also tightly tied to their financial performance; bonuses linked to physician revenues made up more than 50 percent of physicians' salaries in some settings (see Chapters 2 and 7).[47] This system created a direct financial incentive for providers to oversupply expensive drugs and procedures and undersupply essential medical services. For much of the 1990s, pharmaceutical spending made up more than half of total medical expenditures. Even by 2008, pharmaceuticals made up 54 percent of total inpatient spending and 44 percent of total outpatient spending.[48] Not only were pharmaceutical costs high, but the prescriptions themselves were often irrational; numerous studies documented extremely high prescription rates of antibiotics, injectables, and steroids.[49] However, even as antibiotics and other drugs were over-prescribed, the low diagnosis and control rates of Chinese patients with NCDs indicate that antihypertensives and anti-diabetic drugs were under-prescribed. One study found that only 28.2 percent of patients with hypertension took antihypertensive medications; another reported that only 20.3 percent of patients with diabetes were taking any kind of treatment, pharmaceutical or non-pharmaceutical.[50]

In order to rationalize this system and control overall health costs, the Chinese government began a pharmaceutical drug reform in 2009 (see Chapter 2). Beginning in 2009, the government created an Essential Drugs List (EDL). The EDL originally included 307 drugs: 205 western pharmaceuticals and 102 traditional Chinese medicines (TCMs).[51] This list has now been expanded to 520 drugs. All drugs on the list are generic;

inclusion is based on expected frequency of use, evidence base, safety, and affordability.[52] EDL drugs are procured at the provincial level using a bidding process intended to be open and transparent. Provincial governments have the right to supplement the national EDL with additional drugs for their provincial EDLs.

Concurrent with the creation of the EDL, the government also began implementing the "zero mark-up policy." This policy mandated that: (1) all community health centers (CHCs), township health centers (THCs), and village clinics stock all drugs on the EDL; (2) drugs on the EDL be prescribed before non-EDL drugs; and (3) these drugs be sold with no markups. The government has also strongly recommended that all health insurers reimburse EDL drugs. Beginning in 2012, this policy was expanded to cover county hospitals. Additionally, to increase rational prescribing a healthcare reform committee has promulgated clinical guidelines for 18 common conditions.

The Chinese government has had reasonable success in rolling out the EDL and zero mark-up policies. By early 2012, 99.8 percent of THCs and 58.1 percent of village clinics had adopted the zero mark-up policy and nearly all counties and municipalities had made EDL drugs reimbursable.[53] Preliminary studies have also suggested the policy has been successful in increasing EDL drug use and decreasing prescription cost per visit at THCs.[54] However, early analyses also found some negative unintended consequences of pharmaceutical reform. For instance, Tian et al. (2012) found that most drugs included on the national EDL had a rational basis for inclusion, but provincial supplements to the EDL averaged 207 drugs, many of which were not evidence-based.[55] Provincial drug procurement systems have been criticized for lack of transparency.[56] Qualitative studies have also found numerous patient and physician complaints over drug access. In one survey, 30.4 percent of patients reported difficulty accessing drugs for hypertension and diabetes at their THC.[57] The same survey found that prices for 70 percent of the drugs on the EDL increased after the reform, though they remained below the government-set bid ceilings. Many physicians also reported their income decreased while their workload increased after the zero mark-up

policy came into effect. Early reports have also shown an ambiguous effect on rational prescribing, with an observed slight fall in antibiotic prescriptions but an increased use of injectables.[58]

The existing preliminary evidence indicates that pharmaceutical reform has been marginally successful in decreasing patients' prescription spending at THCs and CHCs, but may also have decreased patients' access to some necessary pharmaceuticals and decreased physician income. Additionally, since many of these results are based on non-random surveys and "pre-post" (before and after) comparisons, they must be approached with caution. More rigorous studies are needed to ascertain the true effect of the EDL, especially in patients suffering from chronic disease.

Public Health Reform

Creating a sustainable public health system is a crucial component in China's fight against both infectious disease and NCDs. Public health workers can reduce the frequency of NCDs and improve the health of chronically ill patients through identifying those at risk, developing programs of chronic disease management, and educating the population on healthy lifestyle habits. Prior to the open-market reforms in 1978, China's grassroots public health system was one of the most successful in the world.[59] However, the open-market reforms of 1978 reduced available government tax revenues, leading to a dramatic fall in financial support for village doctors, and the number of public health workers fell dramatically. The number of health workers in rural areas fell from 3.5 million in the late 1970s to around 500,000 by the late 1990s.[60] The number of village doctors alone fell from 1.8 million in 1977 to 1.2 million in 1984.[61] Many remaining village doctors chose to open private clinics, relinquishing any public health responsibilities.

The Chinese government has recently instituted a new policy to rebuild its public health system, with a special focus on NCD and chronic disease patients (see Chapter 3). In 2009, the government began paying primary care providers a small subsidy to provide public health services to all residents in their catchment area. The subsidy was originally set at 15 yuan/person, increased to 25 in 2011, 30 in 2013, and is targeted for continued increases in the future.[62] In exchange for the subsidy, providers are expected to deliver extensive packages of public health services ranging from establishing health archives and chronic disease management to infectious disease control and immunization.[63] This public health reform has the potential to greatly help patients with NCDs and residents at risk for NCD conditions.

However, like the other components of health-care reform, the implementation of the public health reform has yielded mixed results. Early critics suggested that the government subsidy was insufficient to compensate village doctors and physicians for their greater workload.[64] Doctors and clinic managers interviewed in Hubei and Jiangxi provinces echoed such concerns. Village doctors felt that while subsidies incentivized them to focus more on public health, a larger subsidy would encourage an even greater focus.[65] Managers in local THCs and CDCs felt that supervision of village doctors was difficult; they had no way of holding village doctors accountable if they did not perform their public health responsibilities. A more quantitative review of the public health reform using government statistics found that the program was largely successful in increasing immunizations and child and maternal health, but had only limited effectiveness in increasing chronic disease management and care for the mentally ill.[66]

These findings suggest that although the public health reform has succeeded in reorienting village doctor and primary care physicians' focus toward public health issues, it has not yet created a cadre of health workers with the capacity to improve chronic disease prevention and management. Chronic disease prevention and management are complex activities; village doctors likely fear that taking on the responsibility for these would take too much time away from other, more remunerative activities. It is also possible that best practices in chronic disease prevention and management are unfamiliar to many village doctors and rural physicians, especially given their low levels of medical training. Thus, the government may benefit from creating additional, targeted public health subsidies for chronic-disease-related public health activities, as well as from increasing training of health workers on best practices within these areas.

Primary Care Reform

A well-functioning primary care system is essential to managing the health and financial risks of patients with NCDs. Primary care physicians are frontline health workers; they are responsible for diagnosing and managing chronic disease, judging whether patients should seek more advanced care at higher-level hospitals, and working with at-risk patients on disease prevention. A strong primary care system should increase the health of patients with NCDs, decrease the prevalence of chronic disease, and prevent unnecessary and wasteful health spending.

Prior to the current healthcare reform, primary care in China faced three related challenges. First, in the years following the open-market reforms, many government-operated primary care centers closed, decreasing residents' access to primary care. Second, many primary care physicians were much less educated than their colleagues in secondary and tertiary hospitals. Only 31.8 percent of doctors in community health centers have a bachelor's degree or above; the rate is even lower in township health centers.[67] One estimate found only .7 percent of doctors in village clinics have a bachelor's degree or above, while 78.3 percent have less than a technical school education.[68] Less educated doctors and health workers may not have the skills necessary to perform the complex tasks required for chronic disease management and treatment. Third, perhaps due to the problems posed by the first two challenges, many Chinese patients choose to seek primary care at secondary or tertiary hospitals.[69]

To address these problems, the Chinese government implemented a three-part reform in 2009. First, the government made large investments in primary care infrastructure and human resources. Specifically, the government pledged to build or renovate 13,000 community healthcare facilities to train more than 500,000 healthcare professionals at rural health centers and institute programs incentivizing primary care physicians to practice in rural areas.[70] Second, the reform aimed to change the financing model of primary care centers away from reliance on prescription and medical procedure revenues. The most popular way of enacting this reform is the "separating revenue from expenditures" (SRE) policy.[71] Under SRE, the primary care center passes on all revenues, including pharmaceutical prescribing and medical services revenues, to the healthcare financing bureau. In return, the center receives a global budget and the opportunity for performance-based bonuses, encouraging more patient-centric care. Third, the reform aims to provide primary care centers with an unofficial gatekeeping role; primary care centers will be patients' first contact with the medical system, after which the primary care physician should direct the patient to the most appropriate place to seek care.[72]

These three reforms have had mixed success. The government's greatest accomplishments have been in increasing the number of care sites that patients can access. Between 2008 and 2011, the number of CHCs increased from 24,260 to 32,860 and the number of village clinics grew from 613,143 to 662,894, although the number of township health centers fell slightly (see Figure 4.3).[73] Whether or not patients utilized these sites rather than hospitals is a critical issue. One study found that the rate of outpatient visits per year and access to a health facility increased significantly between 2003 and 2011; however, the rate of increase was fairly small.

Increased utilization of rural primary care sites is constrained by the availability of manpower to staff them. The government has enjoyed much less success enticing physicians to come to the countryside to practice than in building practice sites. Attracting qualified participants into any government program may be difficult, particularly since physicians in the countryside work longer hours for less pay than their urban counterparts.[74] The separation of primary care revenue from pharmaceutical revenue is still in its early stages. However, just as in the EDL drug reform, properly implementing SRE will require local governments to find a funding source sufficient to replace revenues from pharmaceuticals. In the absence of a sufficient funding source, physicians may engage in other revenue-enhancing behavior such as soliciting bribes or refusing to see time-intensive patients such as those with NCDs. There is little information available about the quality of the investments into medical education. Finally, the success of optimizing patient flow between different levels of care will largely depend on the success of the first two parts of the primary care reform. Patients will only be willing to visit primary care centers if the centers are accessible and they are staffed with physicians that patients can trust.

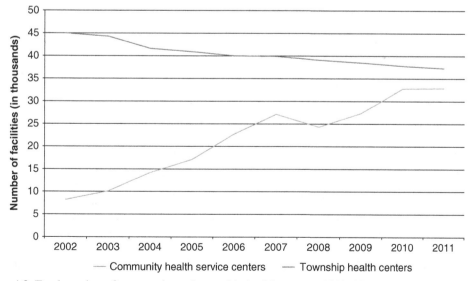

Figure 4.3 Total number of community and township health centers, 2002–2011

Primary care reform is essential to bolster China's health system's capacity to handle its increasing NCD population. Early analysis shows that the government has had success in building physical infrastructure, but has struggled to improve physician quality and financially incentivize physicians to focus on quality of care. The government must be willing to continue to make long-term investments to train new primary care physicians and find alternate sources of revenue for primary care centers for the reforms to truly be a success.

Public Hospital Reforms

As a country's NCD population grows, the capacity of secondary and tertiary hospitals also becomes increasingly important. Treating NCDs requires complex medical interventions and pharmaceutical treatments with high levels of physical infrastructure and human resources. These procedures and treatments are also expensive; if proper incentives are not in place for providers, they are liable to be overused, with serious financial and health consequences for payers and patients.

Until recently, China's public hospital system had most of the shortcomings and few of the benefits of a centrally planned system. Hospitals in China operated in the midst of a great bureaucracy. Researchers have estimated that Chinese hospitals are accountable to more than eight different government agencies, each of which has conflicting interests and preferences.[75] In many localities, the same department regulates the local health market and operates the local hospital, providing incentives to constrict healthcare supply and competition. Promotion of physicians is typically non-performance related and almost entirely based on seniority. Public hospitals receive less than 10 percent of hospital revenues from government subsidies, but are required to adhere to government prices. These prices are set at below-market rates for many basic services, leading hospitals to induce demand in areas where they can earn a profit, mainly pharmaceuticals and high-tech medical procedures.[76]

The Chinese government has attempted to address many of these problems in a wide-ranging public hospital reform. This reform has four major components. First, the government has begun pilot projects separating hospital regulation and hospital management. The specifics of this separation vary by place, with some local governments moving control of hospital operations out of the health department entirely and others creating independent hospital management agencies within the health department.[77] Second, the government has attempted to give hospitals more autonomy in hiring, promotion, and capital acquisition decisions, including the institution of performance-based promotions and the loosening of physician practice restrictions. Third, in order to better align patient and provider incentives, the government has encouraged hospitals to move away from a fee-for-service (FFS) model and toward a case-based or capitation system. A number of studies have documented extensive waste in the Chinese system. One estimated that 30 percent–50 percent of hospital admissions are unnecessary;[78] another study found that unnecessary care constitutes 20 percent–30 percent of Chinese health spending.[79] Through realigning provider incentives, the government hopes to eliminate much of this waste while improving the overall quality of care for patients. Finally, the government hopes to stimulate increased private sector investment in the healthcare sector.[80] More private sector investment should create more health supply, leading to greater competition. Although the literature on the effects of greater hospital competition is mixed, it is the hope that forcing public sector hospitals to compete for patients will lead to increased quality of care and/or decrease costs. Increasing supply is also likely to lead to induced demand by providers, resulting in increased utilization, increased costs, and perhaps more unnecessary care.

There are few systematic evaluations of the overall effects of public hospital separation reforms. One study found that enacting separation reform had a positive impact on healthcare supply in two of three pilot cities, but did not investigate changes in managerial practice or quality of care.[81] Recent Ministry of Health reports have also provided some indications that the reform may be having success. Currently more than 3,467 medical facilities utilize clinical pathway management guidelines to standardize care and more than 94 percent of hospitals have instituted pre-registration procedures, which should decrease waiting times.[82]

Other studies have examined the effects of the changes in physician and provider payment schemes. By 2011, more than 1/3 of tertiary hospitals had adopted case-based payments, and many local governments had begun experimenting with different types of physician payment schemes, including a province-wide pilot project in Guangxi.[83] A recent review of the Chinese-language literature on physician payment reforms found that switching from fee-for-service to a diagnostic related group (DRG) or case-based reimbursement method was associated with decreased costs without decreasing quality of care.[84] However, the authors caution that many of these evaluations are not empirically rigorous. A recent World Bank report cites several case studies where adoption of physician payment reform has led to a drop in expenditures and irrational prescriptions, but these results have again not been rigorously tested.[85]

If true, these results indicate that moving toward case-based payments might be an important tool in increasing the affordability of healthcare for the growing NCD population. These results also accord with the experiences in many developed countries, although rigorous empirical research in these

countries is also limited.[86] However, researchers have expressed concern that many of China's case-based payment schemes only include a small selection of diseases, incentivizing providers to classify inexpensive patients as having case-based diseases and more expensive patients as having diseases requiring fee-for-service treatment. Further, if a provider has wholly adopted a case-based or DRG payment system, the hospital may turn away the more complex cases, whose treatment is associated with financial losses. Early positive reports are tempered by the lack of rigorous evaluation techniques and the lack of focus on patient satisfaction and quality of care. More research is necessary to test the validity of these concerns. Finally, there has been little research on whether reform policies have led to increased competition and whether increased competition affects the accessibility and affordability of healthcare.

With regard to hospital capacity, between 2009 and 2011 the total number of hospitals increased from 20,291, to 21,979, while the number of beds in medical institutions per 1,000 population also increased from 3.31 to 3.51 (see Figure 4.4).[87] Such increases cannot necessarily be attributed to reform policies, however. Like many Chinese reforms, the public hospital reforms were

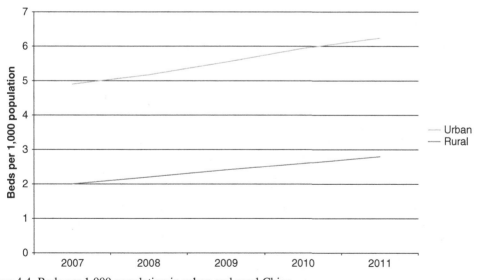

Figure 4.4 Beds per 1,000 population in urban and rural China

implemented at a local level in a manner adapted to local conditions and often implemented simultaneously with other reforms. While this may increase the reforms' theoretical effectiveness, it also makes it extremely difficult to measure their effects. Thus, although early reports suggest that public hospital reforms have been largely positive, especially in the shift away from fee-for-service payment, more systematic research is necessary to understand the reforms' true effects.

Moreover, the success of these reforms is at present limited to increases in physical capacity, utilization of guidelines and pre-registration procedures, and changes in provider payment and reimbursement methods. It is not known whether such reforms have impacted the cost, quality, and accessibility of care by patients with NCDs.

Recommendations and Conclusions

China's health system reforms have touched on every aspect of the Chinese healthcare system. Some reforms have seen remarkable success; China has achieved near-universal insurance coverage and has witnessed a dramatic increase in construction of community health centers and village clinics. However, the reforms also remain incomplete. Although the number of Chinese with insurance has increased dramatically, some studies suggest that the effect of this insurance in decreasing out-of-pocket costs may be limited. Public health subsidies have had some effect in reorienting the focus of village doctors and community health centers toward primary care, but their effect on chronic disease management and treatment has been negligible. And although pharmaceutical reform has successfully increased EDL prescribing, it has done too little to address supply shortages and under-treatment of chronic disease patients. In many other areas, the effects of the reform are unclear, making evidence-based recommendations difficult. This concluding section offers a series of recommendations for the next stage of China's healthcare reforms with a holistic focus on improving the health system's capacity to treat Chinese patients with NCDs and decrease the country's NCD burden.

For any reform to truly address the problems associated with China's growing NCD burden, it must improve chronic disease management and chronic disease prevention. China's healthcare reform takes several important steps in this direction. The increased subsidies to primary care doctors and public health workers in exchange for public health work, the renewed focus on building primary care centers, and the creation of an Essential Drugs List all should improve the health of chronically ill and at-risk patients – if implemented correctly. However, these reforms must be strengthened. Specifically, the subsidy for public health providers must increase; 25 yuan per person per year is insufficient to truly incentivize providers to focus on public health rather than on other, more profitable areas of medicine. The government might also consider giving public health providers targeted bonuses for conducting health education sessions on behavioral changes intended to reduce the risk of chronic disease or for performing chronic disease management. However, the evidence base for health education or disease management programs to actually change patient behaviors, let alone impact their health status, is really limited. Second, grassroots primary care providers and other health workers should receive extra training on chronic disease management and treatment. Early evidence indicates that although some public health goals have been met, those related to chronic disease treatment are lagging behind. Combined with evidence of high rates of under-diagnosing and undertreating chronic diseases and chronic disease risk factors, these findings suggest that more education on chronic diseases for primary care health workers is necessary. Third, China would be well served by increasing investment in pharmacist training. As NCD rates continue to rise, both demand for drugs and the number of individuals engaging in "poly-pharmacy" (i.e., taking numerous medications) will increase. Well-trained and knowledgeable pharmacists can play an important role in directing patients to appropriate pharmaceuticals and ensuring that these patients take these pharmaceuticals safely. Thus, investing in pharmacists may be a cost-effective way to increase safe and rational pharmaceutical treatment of chronically ill patients. However, despite the recent growth in retail pharmacies in China, the system for training pharmacists is undeveloped, and the rate of licensed pharmacists per capita is extremely low.[88] Moreover, retail pharmacies dispense only a small percentage of all drugs prescribed in China.

Another major problem is the financial burden attached to NCD treatment. These costs affect patients and their family members, but also threaten the financial solvency of newly created social insurance programs. The rapid rise of insurance coverage in China has been an important step in minimizing patients' financial risks. However, some evidence suggests that despite wide coverage, reimbursement rates for many beneficiaries remain low and out-of-pocket payments remain high, especially for rural individuals enrolled in NCMS. This is likely because of a relatively low per capita funding rate; on average NCMS receives only around 250 RMB/beneficiary/year, limiting the program's ability to provide full coverage. Continuing to strengthen NCMS, either through increased government subsidies or increased individual premiums, would be an important step toward lowering patient financial risk. In recent years, NCMS and URBMI have expanded insurance packages to include reimbursements for many outpatient expenditures.[89] However, as funding becomes available, insurance programs may also consider creating targeted programs to specifically incentivize patients with NCDs and at-risk individuals to seek outpatient care.

Although insurance coverage addresses individual financial risk, it does nothing to slow rising national healthcare costs. Indeed, by introducing moral hazard and physician-induced demand, insurance may lead healthcare costs to increase at an even faster rate. For instance, between 2000 and 2009, per capita healthcare spending more than tripled in China (see Table 2.4). To prevent this, insurance plans have included high co-pays and deductibles. The Chinese government has also encouraged hospitals and local governments to move from fee-for-service toward capitation or case-based payment. These reforms should reduce physicians' incentives to oversupply unnecessary care. However, current reforms may be limited by case-based payments being applied to only certain diseases, insufficient payment, and insufficient

clinical information to create fairly valued payments. Accordingly, we recommend the government spearhead an effort to create national guidelines for case-based payments, similar to the role Medicare plays for DRGs in the United States. Although this would be an enormous undertaking, we believe an effort of this magnitude is necessary in order to create a well-functioning physician payment system.

Although steps to divorce provider income from pharmaceutical prescribing revenues are well intentioned, local governments too often lack sufficient resources to appropriately compensate providers for lost revenue. Ultimately, this revenue may come from capitation agreements with local insurance providers; however, currently funding is too limited for this source of income to fill the gap created by the loss of prescribing revenue. The government may speed this process – either through providing bonuses to insurers and local providers who enter into capitation agreements, through increasing subsidies to insurers, or through increasing direct case-based or capitation-based subsidies to providers themselves.

Finally, we believe a crucial aspect of any reform process is a strong infrastructure for program evaluation. To ensure that resources are being allocated most efficiently and to improve the effectiveness of current and future programs, rigorous empirical evaluations are necessary. Although the Chinese government has performed evaluations of many aspects of the healthcare reforms, these evaluations typically lack good comparison groups to understand what would have happened in the absence of the intervention and do not use rigorous econometric methods to correct for potential sources of bias. We believe that there are several specific actions the government could take to improve this state of affairs. First, the government frequently nominates cities as pilot groups to implement reforms. However, if the government doubled the size of this "pilot group" and then randomly assigned some cities to implement pilot projects and some cities to act as controls, researchers would be able to more rigorously determine the effects of reform. Second, the Chinese government's reports often focus on process rather than outcomes. For instance, while trends in insurance coverage are important, trends in average out-of-pocket payment per patient are more important. Although many academic researchers have investigated these topics, a greater government emphasis on outcomes instead of process may lead local governments to focus more on accomplishing the end goals of the reform: providing accessible, affordable, and quality care to China's citizens.

Over the past 30 years, China has undergone the final stage of an epidemiological transition. Underlying demographic, economic, and environmental trends have combined to create a growing burden of NCDs among the Chinese population. Without improving the capacity of the Chinese healthcare system to affordably care for NCD patients and to slow the rate of NCD growth, the human and financial costs of NCDs threaten to challenge China's three decades of constant economic growth. Over the past five years, the Chinese government has begun a wide-ranging comprehensive health system reform intended to dramatically improve its healthcare delivery and financing systems. Although this reform has been on the whole successful, especially in expanding insurance coverage and slowing out-of-pocket medical expenditures, much remains to be accomplished. Specifically, over the next decade, the Chinese government must educate its primary care providers and its citizens about chronic disease management and prevention. At the same time, the government must increase investments in public health and physician payment reform in order for the early gains in these areas to grow larger. Finally, the government must employ rigorous evaluations of current and future reforms in order to give policymakers and researchers the tools necessary to create the next iteration of reforms. China's NCD population will grow dramatically over the next 30 years; the actions of the current government will dictate the size of this effect on China's growth, sustainability, and overall economic prosperity.

Notes

1. World Bank Global Development Indicators. "China, GDP Per Capita (Current US$)." Available online at: www.google.com/public data/explore?ds=d5bncppjof8f9_#!ctype=l&strail=false&bcs=d&nselm=h&met_y=ny_gdp_pcap_cd&scale_y=lin&ind_y=false&rdim=region&ifdim=region&tdim=true&hl=en_US&dl=en_US&ind=false. Accessed on July 1, 2013.

2. Gonghuan Yang, Lingzhi Kong, Wenhua Zhao et al. 2008. "Emergence of Chronic Noncommunicable Diseases in China," *The Lancet* 372(9650): 1697–1705. Gonghuan Yang, Yu Wang, Yixin Zeng et al. 2013. "Rapid Health Transition in China, 1990–2010: Findings from the Global Burden of Disease Study 2010," *The Lancet* 81(9882): 1987–2015.

3. Winnie Yip, William Hsiao, Wen Chen et al. 2012. "Early Appraisal of China's Huge and Complex Health-care Reforms," *The Lancet* 379(9818): 833–842.

4. Ian G. Cook and Trevor J. B. Dummer. 2004. "Changing Health in China: Re-evaluating the Epidemiological Transition Model," *Health Policy* 67(3): 329–344.

5. David Hipgrave. 2011. "Communicable Disease Control in China: From Mao to Now," *Journal of Global Health* 1(2): 224.

6. Hipgrave. 2011. "Communicable Disease Control in China."

7. Ibid.

8. Yang et al. 2013. "Rapid Health Transition in China, 1990–2010."

9. Hongpeng Sun, Qiuju Zhang, Xiao Luo et al. 2011. "Changes of Adult Population Health Status in China from 2003 to 2008," *PloS One* 6(12): e28411.

10. Sun et al. 2011.

11. Dong Zhao, Jing Liu, Wei Wang et al. 2008. "Epidemiological Transition of Stroke in China: Twenty-One–Year Observational Study from the Sino-MONICA-Beijing Project," *Stroke* 39(6): 1668–1674. Ming Liu, Bo Wu, Wen-Zhi Wang et al. 2007. "Stroke in China: Epidemiology, Prevention, and Management Strategies," *The Lancet Neurology* 6(5): 456–464. Haixin Sun, Xinying Zou, and Liping Liu. 2013. "Epidemiological Factors of Stroke: A Survey of the Current Status in China," *Journal of Stroke* 15(2): 109–114.

12. Ping Zhao, Min Dai, Wanqing Chen et al. 2010. "Cancer Trends in China," *Japanese Journal of Clinical Oncology* 40(4): 281–285. Yang et al. 2008. "Emergence of Chronic Non-communicable Diseases in China."

13. Julia Critchley, Jing Liu, Dong Zhao et al. 2004. "Explaining the Increase in Coronary Heart Disease Mortality in Beijing Between 1984 and 1999," *Circulation* 110(10): 1236–1244.

14. Andrew Moran, Dongfeng Gu, Dong Zhao et al. 2010. "Future Cardiovascular Disease in China: Markov Model and Risk Factor Scenario Projections from the Coronary Heart Disease Policy Model–China," *Circulation: Cardiovascular Quality and Outcomes* 3(3): 243–252.

15. Hang Li, B. Oldenburg, C. Chamberlain et al. 2012. "Diabetes Prevalence and Determinants in Adults in China Mainland from 2000 to 2010: A Systematic Review," *Diabetes Research and Clinical Practice* 98(2): 226–235.

16. Wenying Yang, Juming Lu, Jianping Weng et al. 2010. "Prevalence of Diabetes Among Men and Women in China," *New England Journal of Medicine* 362(12): 1090–1101.

17. Jiang He, Dongfeng Gu, Jing Chen et al. 2009. "Premature Deaths Attributable to Blood Pressure in China: A Prospective Cohort Study," *The Lancet* 374 (9703): 1765–1772.

18. Y. Wang, J. Mi, X. Shan et al. 2006. "Is China Facing an Obesity Epidemic and the Consequences? The Trends in Obesity and Chronic Disease in China," *International Journal of Obesity* 31(1): 177–188.

19. Zhao-Jun Yang, Jie Liu, Jia-Pu Ge et al. 2012. "Prevalence of Cardiovascular Disease Risk Factor in the Chinese Population: The 2007–2008 China National Diabetes and Metabolic Disorders Study," *European Heart Journal* 33 (2): 213–220.

20. Yangfeng Wu, Rachel Huxley, Liming Li et al. 2008. "Prevalence, Awareness, Treatment, and Control of Hypertension in China: Data from the China National Nutrition and Health Survey 2002," *Circulation* 118(25): 2679–2686.

21. Lindsay Jaacks, Penny Gordon-Larsen, Elizabeth Mayer-Davis et al. 2013. "Age, Period and Cohort Effects on Adult Body Mass Index and Overweight from 1991 to 2009 in China: The China Health and Nutrition Survey," *International Journal of Epidemiology* (June 14): 1–10.

22. Zhaohui Cui, Rachel Huxley, Yangfeng Wu et al. 2010. "Temporal Trends in Overweight and Obesity of Children and Adolescents from Nine Provinces in China from 1991–2006," *International Journal of Pediatric Obesity* 5 (5): 365–374.

23. Shu Wen Ng, Edward C. Norton, and Barry M. Popkin. 2009. "Why Have Physical Activity Levels Declined Among Chinese Adults? Findings from the 1991–2006 China Health and Nutrition Surveys," *Social Science & Medicine* 68(7): 1305–1314.

24. Jing Zhang, Jia-Xian Ou, and Chun-Xue Bai. 2011. "Tobacco Smoking in China: Prevalence, Disease Burden, Challenges and Future Strategies," *Respirology* 16(8): 1165–1172.

25. Juncheng Qian, Min Cai, Jun Gao et al. 2010. "Trends in Smoking and Quitting in China from 1993 to 2003: National Health Service Survey Data," *Bulletin of the World Health Organization* 88(10): 769–776.

26. Qiang Li, Jason Hsia, and Gonghuan Yang. 2011. "Prevalence of Smoking in China in 2010," *New England Journal of Medicine* 364 (25): 2469–2470.

27. Xizhe Peng. 2011. "China's Demographic History and Future Challenges," *Science* 333 (6042): 581–587.

28. Qiang Li, Mieke Reuser, Cornelia Kraus et al. 2009. "Ageing of a Giant: A Stochastic Population Forecast for China, 2006–2060," *Journal of Population Research* 26(1): 21–50. Feng Wang. 2011. "The Future of a Demographic Overachiever: Long-term Implications of the Demographic Transition in China," *Population and Development Review* 37(s1): 173–190.

29. Shufa Du, Thomas Mroz, Fengying Zhai et al. 2004. "Rapid Income Growth Adversely Affects Diet Quality in China – Particularly

for the Poor!" *Social Science & Medicine* 59 (7): 1505–1515.

30. Barry M. Popkin. 2008. "Will China's Nutrition Transition Overwhelm Its Health Care System and Slow Economic Growth?" *Health Affairs* 27(4): 1064–1076.

31. Fengying Zhai, Huijun Wang, Shufa Du et al. 2007. "Lifespan Nutrition and Changing Socio-economic Conditions in China," *Asia Pacific Journal of Clinical Nutrition* 16(Suppl 1): 374–382.

32. Karen Eggleston, Li Ling, Meng Qingyue et al. 2008. "Health Service Delivery in China: A Literature Review," *Health Economics* 17(2): 149–165.

33. Zhu Chen. 2009. "Launch of the Health-Care Reform Plan in China," *The Lancet* 373(9672): 1322–1324.

34. Sarah L. Barber and Lan Yao. 2011. "Development and Status of Health Insurance Systems in China," *The International Journal of Health Planning and Management* 26(4): 339–356.

35. Jens Leth Hougaard, Lars Peter Østerdal, and Yi Yu. 2011. "The Chinese Healthcare System," *Applied Health Economics and Health Policy* 9(1): 1–13.

36. China Health Statistical Yearbook. Available online at: http://tongji.cnki.net/overseas/EngNavi/HomePage.aspx?id=N2010042070&name=YSIFE&floor=1. Accessed on May 23, 2015.

37. Lincoln Chen and Dong Xu. 2012. "Trends in China's Reforms: The Rashomon Effect," *The Lancet* 379: 782–783.

38. Lin Chen, Arjan de Haan, Xiulan Zhang et al. 2011. "Addressing Vulnerability in an Emerging Economy: China's New Cooperative Medical Scheme (NCMS)," *Canadian Journal of Development Studies/Revue canadienne d'études du développement* 32: 399–413.

39. China Health Statistical Yearbook.

40. Barber and Yao. 2011. "Development and Status of Health Insurance Systems in China."

41. Shenglan Tang, Jingjing Tao, and Henk Bekedam. 2012. "Controlling Cost Escalation of Healthcare: Making Universal Health Coverage Sustainable in China," *BMC Public Health* 12 (Suppl 1): S8. Yip et al. 2012. "Early Appraisal of China's Huge and Complex Health-care Reforms."

42. Adam Wagstaff, Winnie Yip, Magnus Lindelow et al. 2009. "China's Health System and Its Reform: A Review of Recent Studies," *Health Economics* 18(S2): S7–S23. Baozhen Dai, Jianzai Zhou, Y. John Mei et al. 2011. "Can the New Cooperative Medical Scheme Promote Rural Elders' Access to Health Care Services?" *Geriatrics & Gerontology International* 11(3): 239–245.

43. Slawa Rokicki and Katherine Donato. 2013. "Measuring the Impact of China's Rural Insurance Scheme on Health: Propensity Score Matching Valuation Using Biomarkers," *The Lancet* 381: S127. Xueling Chu, Qihui Chen, and Xiangming Fang. 2013. "Can National Health Insurance Programs Improve Health Outcomes? Re-examining the Case of the New Cooperative Medical Scheme in Rural China." *Joint Annual Meeting Agricultural and Applied Economics Association (AAEA) & Canadian Agricultural Economics Society (CAES), Washington (DC).*

44. Xiaoyan Lei and Wanchuan Lin. 2009. "The New Cooperative Medical Scheme in Rural China: Does More Coverage Mean More Service and Better Health?" *Health Economics* 18(S2): S25–S46.

45. Wanchuan Lin, Gordon G. Liu, and Gang Chen. 2009. "The Urban Resident Basic Medical Insurance: A Landmark Reform Towards Universal Coverage in China," *Health Economics* 18(S2): S83–S96.

46. Hong Liu and Zhong Zhao. 2012. "Impact of China's Urban Resident Basic Medical Insurance on Health Care Utilization and Expenditure." *IZA Discussion Paper* (6768).

47. Weiyan Jian and Yan Guo. 2009. "Does Per Diem Reimbursement Necessarily Increase Length of Stay? The Case of a Public Psychiatric Hospital," *Health Economics* 18 (S2): S97–S106.

48. Xuan Yu, Cheng Li, Yuhua Shi et al. 2010. "Pharmaceutical Supply Chain in China: Current Issues and Implications for Health System Reform," *Health Policy* 97(1): 8–15.

49. Eggleston et al. 2008. "Health Service Delivery in China." Janet Currie, Wanchuan Lin, and Wei Zhang. 2011. "Patient Knowledge and Antibiotic Abuse: Evidence from an Audit Study in China," *Journal of Health Economics* 30(5): 933–949.

50. Dongfeng Gu, Kristi Reynolds, Xigui Wu et al. 2002. "Prevalence, Awareness, Treatment, and Control of Hypertension in China," *Hypertension* 40(6): 920–927. Dongsheng Hu, Pengyu Fu, Jing Xie et al. 2008. "Increasing Prevalence and Low Awareness, Treatment and Control of Diabetes Mellitus Among Chinese Adults: The InterASIA Study," *Diabetes Research and Clinical Practice* 81(2): 250–257.

51. Yip et al. 2012. "Early Appraisal of China's Huge and Complex Health-care Reforms."

52. Xiaodong Guan, Huigang Liang, Yajiong Xue et al. 2011. "An Analysis of China's National Essential Medicines Policy," *Journal of Public Health Policy* 32(3): 305–319.

53. Yang Li, Cui Ying, Guo Sufang et al. 2013. "Evaluation, in Three Provinces, of the Introduction and Impact of China's National Essential Medicines Scheme," *Bulletin of the World Health Organization* 91(3): 184–194.

54. Lianping Yang, Chaojie Liu, Adamm Ferrier et al. 2012. "The Impact of the National Essential Medicines Policy on Prescribing Behaviours in Primary Care Facilities in Hubei Province of China," *Health Policy and Planning* (November): czs116. Li et al. 2013. "Evaluation, in Three Provinces, of the Introduction and Impact of China's National Essential Medicines Scheme."

55. Xin Tian, Yaran Song, and Xinping Zhang. 2012. "National Essential Medicines List and Policy Practice: A Case Study of China's Health Care Reform," *BMC Health Services Research* 12(1): 1–8.

56. Yip et al. 2012. "Early Appraisal of China's Huge and Complex Health-care Reforms."

57. Li et al. 2013. "Evaluation, in Three Provinces, of the Introduction and Impact of China's National Essential Medicines Scheme."

58. Yang et al. 2012. "The Impact of the National Essential Medicines Policy on Prescribing Behaviours in Primary Care Facilities in Hubei Province of China." Li et al. 2013. "Evaluation, in Three Provinces, of the Introduction and Impact of China's National Essential Medicines Scheme."

59. Hipgrave. 2011. "Communicable Disease Control in China."

60. Houli Wang, Tengda Xu, and Jin Xu. 2007. "Factors Contributing to High Costs and Inequality in China's Health Care System," *JAMA: The Journal of the American Medical Association* 298(16): 1928–1930.

61. Hipgrave. 2011. "Communicable Disease Control in China."

62. Karen Eggleston. 2012. "Health Care for 1.3 Billion: An Overview of China's Health System," *Asia Health Policy Program.* Available online at: http://iis-db.stanford.edu/pubs/23668/ahppwp_28.pdf. Accessed on October 8, 2015.

63. Yip et al. 2012. "Early Appraisal of China's Huge and Complex Health-care Reforms."

64. David Hipgrave. 2011. "Perspectives on the Progress of China's 2009–2012 Health System Reform," *Journal of Global Health* 1(2): 142.

65. Yan Ding, Helen Smith, Yang Fei et al. 2013. "Factors Influencing the Provision of Public Health Services by Village Doctors in Hubei and Jiangxi Provinces, China," *Bulletin of the World Health Organization* 91(1): 64–69.

66. Yip et al. 2012. "Early Appraisal of China's Huge and Complex Health-care Reforms."

67. Onil Bhattacharyya, Yin Delu, Sabrina Wong et al. 2011. "Evolution of Primary Care in China 1997–2009," *Health Policy* 100(2): 174–180.

68. Leiyu Shi, Li-Mei Hung, Kuimeng Song et al. 2013. "Chinese Primary Care Physicians and Work Attitudes," *International Journal of Health Services* 43(1): 167–181.

69. Sarah L. Barber, Michael Borowitz, Henk Bekedam et al. 2014. "The Hospital of the Future in China: China's Reform of Public Hospitals and Trends from Industrialized Countries," *Health Policy and Planning* (May) 29(3): 367–378.

70. Eggleston. 2012. "Health Care for 1.3 Billion."

71. World Bank. 2010. "Experiences with Health Provider Payment Reform in China," *China Health Policy Notes*. Available online at: http://siteresources.worldbank.org/HEALTHN UTRITIONANDPOPULATION/Resources/ 281627-1285186535266/HealthProviderPaym ent.pdf. Accessed on October 8, 2015.

72. Qian Liu, Bin Wang, Yuyan Kong et al. 2011. "China's Primary Health-care Reform," *The Lancet* 377(9783): 2064–2066. Winnie Yip, William Hsiao, Qingyue Meng et al. 2010. "Realignment of Incentives for Health-care Providers in China," *The Lancet* 375(9720): 1120–1130.

73. China Ministry of Health. 2012 Statistical Health Yearbook.

74. Shi et al. 2013. "Chinese Primary Care Physicians and Work Attitudes."

75. Yip et al. 2012. "Early Appraisal of China's Huge and Complex Health-care Reforms."

76. Qun Meng, Ling Xu, Yaoguang Zhang et al. 2012. "Trends in Access to Health Services and Financial Protection in China Between 2003 and 2011: A Cross-sectional Study," *The Lancet* 379(9818): 805–814. Hougaard et al. 2011. "The Chinese Healthcare System."

77. Pauline Allen, Qi Cao, and Hufeng Wang. 2013. "Public Hospital Autonomy in China in an International Context," *The International Journal of Health Planning and Management* 29(2): 141–159.

78. World Bank. 2010. Health Provider Payment Reforms in China: What International Experience Tells Us (Vol. 2 of 2): Main Report. Available online at: www.worldbank .org/research/2010/07/13246497/health-provi der-payment-reforms-china-international-experi ence-tells-vol-2-2-main-report. Accessed on September 29, 2015.

79. Yu et al. 2010. "Pharmaceutical Supply Chain in China."

80. Yip et al. 2010. "Realignment of Incentives for Health-care Providers in China."

81. Jay Pan, Gordon G. Liu, and Chen Gao. 2013. "How Does Separating Government Regulatory and Operational Control of Public Hospitals Matter to Healthcare Supply?" *China Economic Review* (December) (27): 1–14.

82. Yip et al. 2010. "Realignment of Incentives for Health-care Providers in China."

83. Allen et al. 2013. "Public Hospital Autonomy in China in an International Context."

84. Jin Pingyue, Nikola Biller-Andorno, and Verina Wild. 2013. "Case-Based Payment System in the Chinese Healthcare Sector and Its Ethical Tensions," *Asian Bioethics Review* 5 (2): 131–146.

85. World Bank. 2010. Health Provider Payment Reforms in China.

86. T. Gosden, F. Forland, I.S. Kristiansen et al. 2000. "Capitation, Salary, Fee-for-service and Mixed Systems of Payment: Effects on the Behaviour of Primary Care Physicians," *Cochrane Database Systematic Reviews* 3(3): 1–29. DOI 10.1002/14651858.CD002215.

87. China Ministry of Health. Health Statistical Yearbook 2012.

88. Yu Fang, Shimin Yang, Siting Zhou et al. 2013. "Community Pharmacy Practice in China: Past, Present and Future," *International Journal of Clinical Pharmacy* 35(4):520–528.

89. Barber and Yao. 2011. "Development and Status of Health Insurance Systems in China."

China's Healthcare Reform
Status and Outlook

CLAUDIA SÜSSMUTH-DYCKERHOFF AND FLORIAN
THEN

Introduction

China's healthcare system is undergoing a major reform, one of the most complex and far-reaching efforts ever undertaken by any public health system in the world. It is designed to tackle a number of issues, including substantial inconsistencies in healthcare provision, the burden of chronic diseases, and rising costs.

This chapter provides an overview of China's healthcare context, the reforms that the government has put in place at national, provincial, and city levels, and the outlook for the next stages of reform. It is intended to inform discussion on future choices and actions taken by government, healthcare leaders and professionals, and private sector players.

The reforms are rooted in the specific context for healthcare in the country. First, China's healthcare services vary considerably between rural and urban areas, between one city and another, and even within one city. Second, the country faces a major challenge from chronic diseases: for instance, diabetes affects 11.6 percent of the population compared with the US rate of 9.3 percent. One in four Chinese has high blood pressure. China also accounts for a third of the world's smokers.[1] Third, healthcare costs are rising, out-of-pocket expenditures still account for 34 percent of all healthcare spending, and inequalities in income mean that advanced medical treatment and drugs are still out of reach for many people.

Healthcare reform deliberations conducted between 2005 and 2009 drew on internal input from the Ministry of Health (which has since evolved into today's National Health and Family Planning Commission, or NHFPC) along with external input from Peking University and Fudan University, the State Council's Development Research Center, the World Bank, and the World Health Organization. In 2009, the government announced a new system. The overall objective of the reform was defined as providing every Chinese citizen with access to healthcare at an affordable cost by establishing a basic universal system of safe, effective, convenient, and low-cost services – with full rollout by 2020. To achieve this objective, the government set five priorities:

1. *Medical insurance*: Expand basic medical insurance programs
2. *Drug supply security*: Establish a national system for essential drugs
3. *Medical service provision*: Develop a primary healthcare service
4. *Public health service*: Provide equal access to urban and rural dwellers
5. *Operating environment*: Accelerate reform of public hospitals

Figure 5.1 shows the key milestones of the reform and the progress achieved to date.

While formulated at a high level by the central government, the implementation of healthcare has been, and still is, carried out at provincial or city levels. This approach allows provinces the flexibility to tailor healthcare to their socio-demographic and fiscal needs. It also creates an ecosystem of pilot projects that might eventually uncover best practices relevant for the broader system. Not surprisingly, the healthcare reform landscape has evolved into a heterogeneous patchwork. A few examples illustrate this variety:

- Elimination of drug markups in all public hospitals is a key policy designed to curb physicians' over-prescription of drugs and to limit use of expensive

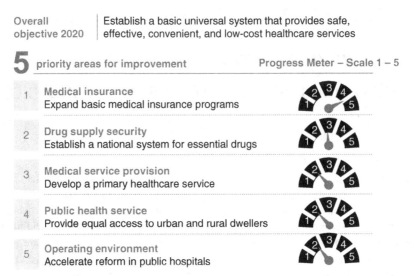

| Overall objective 2020 | Establish a basic universal system that provides safe, effective, convenient, and low-cost healthcare services |

5 priority areas for improvement   Progress Meter – Scale 1 – 5

1 Medical insurance
   Expand basic medical insurance programs

2 Drug supply security
   Establish a national system for essential drugs

3 Medical service provision
   Develop a primary healthcare service

4 Public health service
   Provide equal access to urban and rural dwellers

5 Operating environment
   Accelerate reform in public hospitals

Figure 5.1 Progress on the five key priorities
Source: Healthcare reform 12th Five-Year Plan; McKinsey analysis.

drugs. While 100 pilot cities can claim that they have carried out this policy, others have yet to do so.

- Changing patients' self-referral to Class III hospitals is another important policy. Guangzhou initiated a guideline in April 2015 to promote the establishment of referrals from primary care clinics to Class II/III hospitals. Reimbursement at Class II/III is only available for patients if they have been referred through primary care facilities. Only a few cities follow this model.
- Fee-for-service hospital reimbursement is also a big issue. While most hospitals in the country are reimbursed on a fee-for-service basis, Beijing has been experimenting with diagnosis-related groups (DRGs) for several years. Tianjin is piloting capitation models (fixed annual budget for each patient treated) to encourage prevention and cost-effective care.
- Implementation of the Provincial Reimbursable Drug List (PRDL) varies. The list may feature 2,342 molecules, as in Jiangxi, or include 2,051 traditional Chinese medicine (TCM) products, as in Shanghai.
- There is also considerable variation in drug reimbursement. Drugs may be fully reimbursable according to one city's ruling, but may be an out-of-pocket expense for patients in a nearby city.

Heterogeneity has thus become a key characteristic of China's healthcare system – an important fact to keep in mind as we reflect on the progress of reform and consider what developments to expect in this dynamic stage of the process.

The Chinese government has taken numerous steps to accelerate the healthcare reform since the first announcement in 2009. These adjustments have been consistent with the initial objectives and overall direction of the program. Table 5.1 describes the key announcements around the main schemes.

Medical Insurance: Objective 1

The backbone of China's public health insurance system consists of three insurance schemes: Urban Employee Basic Medical Insurance (UEBMI) covering city dwellers who are employed, Urban Resident Basic Medical Insurance (URBMI) covering retirees and students in cities, and the New Cooperative Medical Scheme (NCMS) covering rural residents. The three programs cover more than 95 percent of the Chinese population, but how they work varies widely between different cities and rural areas. For instance,

Table 5.1 Key announcements on major themes

Major Themes	Key Announcements
Medical insurance	• "Opinions on Further Implementing Critical Disease Insurance (CDI) for Urban and Rural Residents" released by the central government in 2015 to push for the full rollout of CDI • Supportive policies for Private Health Insurance (PHI) development released by central government, including encouragement for PHI to offer CDI service and run PHI pre-tax deduction pilots • Convergence of three BMI schemes is under way, while the combination of URBMI and NCMS has been successfully piloted in many regions
Drug supply security	• First national Essential Drugs List (EDL) published in 2009 with updates and expansion in 2013 • Low-cost drug list released by NDRC in 2014 to ensure the supply of low-margin drugs • NDRC lifts price controls on most medicines in 2015 to promote medicine price reform and encourage reasonable prices
Public health service	• "Opinions on Establishing General Practitioners System" released in 2011 to address talent shortage in primary care facilities • "Opinions on Further Improving Drug Supply and Management in Primary Care Facilities" released in 2014 to permit Non-EDL drug usage in primary care facilities, thus improving access to medication • Mandatory referral system announced in pilot regions (e.g., Guangzhou: reimbursement ratio at Class II/III is lowered if patient is not referred through primary care institutions)
Hospital reform	• "Guidance on the Comprehensive Reform of City Public Hospitals" released in 2015 to increase the number of public hospital reform pilot cities from 33 to 100 nationally • Pilot reform to separate management and operation in hospitals has already been implemented in some regions (e.g., Shanghai Shenkang Hospital Development Center) • "National Planning Guidelines for the Healthcare Service System (2015–2020)" released in 2015 with emphasis on the opening up of the hospital space to private investments
Compliance environment	• NHFPC issued two sets of regulations in 2013 to prohibit misconduct and to push for ethical behavior – "Blacklist Regulations" targeting pharmaceutical manufacturers and distributors – "9 Prohibitions" targeting healthcare providers and institutions

Source: Government policies.

a worker in Shanghai will have a different public health insurance scheme from a worker in Guangzhou. Chapters 4 and 11 describe the three main national medical insurance schemes in detail (see Table 11.1).

The National Reimbursement Drug List (NRDL) plays an important role in the insurance system. The NRDL is issued by the Ministry of Human Resources and Social Security (MoHRSS). The NRDL determines which drug is reimbursed and to what extent. The current list, which dates to 2009, covers 2,127 molecules in two sublists. Its "A list" is centrally determined; a "B list" is also centrally determined but allows up to 15 percent substitution by the provincial government. For patients with basic medical insurance, drugs on RDLA are fully reimbursable, whereas drugs on RDLB are 50–80 percent reimbursable.

The government's stated goal is to cover 100 percent of the population by 2020. Recent statistics indicate that coverage has already reached more than 95 percent.[2] The government has advanced a goal to reduce out-of-pocket spending from the current levels – in 2013, out-of-pocket spending stood at 34 percent of healthcare expenses – to below 30 percent. The effective reimbursement coverage through the basic insurance schemes still varies significantly by city and province, and

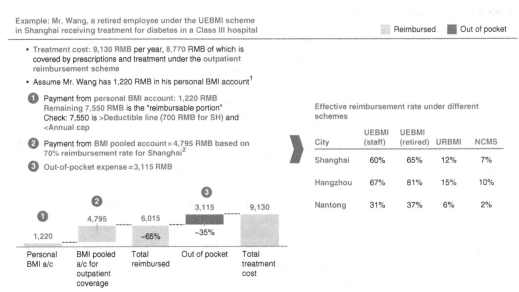

Example: Mr. Wang, a retired employee under the UEBMI scheme in Shanghai receiving treatment for diabetes in a Class III hospital

■ Reimbursed   ■ Out of pocket

- Treatment cost: 9,130 RMB per year, 8,770 RMB of which is covered by prescriptions and treatment under the outpatient reimbursement scheme
- Assume Mr. Wang has 1,220 RMB in his personal BMI account[1]

1 Payment from personal BMI account: 1,220 RMB
Remaining 7,550 RMB is the "reimbursable portion"
Check: 7,550 is >Deductible line (700 RMB for SH) and <Annual cap

2 Payment from BMI pooled account = 4,795 RMB based on 70% reimbursement rate for Shanghai[2]

3 Out-of-pocket expense = 3,115 RMB

Effective reimbursement rate under different schemes

City	UEBMI (staff)	UEBMI (retired)	URBMI	NCMS
Shanghai	60%	65%	12%	7%
Hangzhou	67%	81%	15%	10%
Nantong	31%	37%	6%	2%

1,220 — Personal BMI a/c
4,795 — BMI pooled a/c for outpatient coverage
6,015 ~65% — Total reimbursed
3,115 ~35% — Out of pocket
9,130 — Total treatment cost

[1] Average fund in a Shanghai resident's personal BMI account is estimated at 1,217 RMB
[2] (7,550 RMB–700 RMB deductible line) x 70% = 4,795 RMB

Figure 5.2 Reimbursement rates vary even at the same location
Source: Government policies.

co-payments (the fixed amount that the health insurer requires a patient to pay for a medical service) can be hefty. Figure 5.2 illustrates the burden using an example of a retiree with diabetes. The differences are more marked for patients needing high-priced oncology drugs, where the effective reimbursement rates vary between 15 percent and 30 percent depending on provincial policies and the cost of the drug treatment.

Gradual Improvement of Basic Insurance Schemes

Overall, reimbursement levels have risen and annual caps raised in many areas over the past few years. For example, the URBMI schemes in Kunming and Shaoxing have reduced co-payments for outpatient services. Kunming has reduced the co-pay from 80 percent to 50 percent and increased the annual cap by 50 percent to 400 RMB; Shaoxing has reduced the co-pay from 65 percent to 50 percent and increased the annual cap to 500 RMB.[3] In addition, Kunming has increased the annual

inpatient cap to 60,000 RMB, while Shaoxing has lowered the deductible for inpatient service from 400 to 200 RMB. Reimbursement now covers at least 50 percent of self-paid bills for procedural costs, drugs, and medical devices.

Critical Disease Insurance

Another high-impact initiative has been the implementation of Critical Disease Insurance (CDI). The intent is to provide the groups most vulnerable to large healthcare expenses – such as individuals insured under NCMS and URBMI – with additional protection against catastrophic illnesses. The government set up a funding and operational model for this "top-up insurance" that provides secondary reimbursement for all or part of patients' out-of-pocket spending over the standard basic medical insurance reimbursement ceiling. It asked private insurance companies to bid for providing the desired coverage, essentially using public funds to buy private group insurance at scale for certain populations. Several large, local private health insurance companies followed suit and have since become important parts of the CDI system including China Pacific Insurance Group (CPIC) and China Life.

The CDI system was issued in 2012 for the NCMS-covered population and started with a list of 20 critical diseases to be reimbursed at higher rates.[4] It has evolved toward an add-on insurance broadly covering healthcare costs for life-threatening diseases that exceed certain limits, irrespective of the diagnosis. The government has requested that CDI reimburse at least 50 percent of the total medical bill for critical diseases for rural and non-working urban residents. Participants do not need to pay extra fees for the new insurance coverage. By April 2015, CDI had been piloted in all 31 provinces, covering roughly 700 million people. At the recent State Council summit (July 22, 2015) hosted by Premier Li Keqiang, the government announced that CDI programs should be rolled out to all provinces by the end of 2015 to cover all rural and non-working residents. By 2017, a robust CDI system should be established to form a solid network with other existing medical assistance programs.

Risk-Sharing Arrangements with Pharmaceutical Companies

Some cities have explored innovative ways to work with pharmaceutical companies to improve access to expensive therapies that are not yet covered by the NRDL or the PRDL. For instance, Qingdao has negotiated access programs in which the pharmaceutical company donates a proportion of the medication used in the city to patients who meet certain physician evaluation and financial criteria. The remainder of the treatment cost is covered by the Qingdao government. Diseases and drug treatments covered by these schemes include multiple sclerosis (recombinant interferon beta-1b), leukemia (Dasatinib), breast cancer (Trastuzumab), and rheumatoid arthritis (Adalimumab). Established in 2012, the Qingdao scheme was extended to additional drugs in 2015, suggesting that the model is sustainable for both the public payer and partnering companies alike.

Convergence of NCMS and URBMI

The government is now contemplating a merger of the NCMS and URBMI schemes that would elevate NCMS coverage to URBMI standards. Just as important, the administration of NCMS would move under the umbrella of MoHRSS, creating a large "super-payer" in charge of all public insurance in China (at present, NCMS is administered by the NHFPC). Pilots are under way in several regions, including Sichuan, Tianjin, and Zhejiang.

Promotion of Private Health Insurance

While China has executed its public health insurance agenda, the government also sees an important role for private health insurance (PHI). For example, it has initiated measures such as tax breaks for PHI plans and relaxation of long-standing rules limiting foreign health insurers to minority ownership or 50–50 joint ventures with local players. Foreign insurers can now operate majority-owned businesses in Shanghai's Free-Trade Zone.

There is a clear need for approaches that promote faster access to appropriate care, guaranteed quality of care, and (for select consumer segments) improved hardware and infrastructure (such as advanced diagnosis and treatment devices and high-end hospital wards). Nevertheless, the PHI market in China is still nascent (see Chapter 11). This stems from several systematic challenges, such as differing standards of treatment in public hospitals, lack of data transparency required for needs-based product design and proper claims management, and high-cost distribution models.

Outlook for Reform Objective 1

The government's stated goal is to expand the coverage of basic medical insurance and steadily improve the level of security it provides. However, each province or city has to work within basic medical insurance budgets that could limit the depth of coverage that can be achieved. This has led to a fragmentation of reimbursement schemes. Whether innovative patented drugs, which are expensive yet potentially lifesaving, will ever be reimbursed at the national level, local level, or not at all is unclear. Innovative approaches like Qingdao's patient access programs for specific therapies will therefore be of interest to manufacturers of high-cost drugs and medical devices. We expect further activity and innovation as industry and public payers explore win–win partnerships to provide access to patients. Basic medical insurance seems to have found its way as a pillar of health insurance, making full coverage by the end of 2015 a credible scenario.

As for PHI, several local and multinational companies are excited about its future, and substantial investments are being made in the quest for pole position in this largely untapped market. The emergence of digital channels and a growing private healthcare sector offer support for the optimism of PHI players.

Drug Supply Security: Objective 2

In 2004, the Chinese government set up a national Essential Drugs List (EDL) to define the minimum number of molecules needed to cure the broadest spectrum of diseases at the lowest possible cost. At that time, China had no systems to manage the cost, availability, and quality of these drugs, nor did it have any policies in place to cover tendering, supply, or distribution.

The initial EDL was revised in 2009 following the announcement of the healthcare reform. The revised list covered 307 molecules with more than 2,600 formulations, outlined new policies for tendering, and described a purchasing and delivery system that would be linked to the reimbursement system. All 307 molecules were fully reimbursed, and all community health centers (CHCs) were expected to use the EDL for all medication needs. Pharmaceutical companies with molecules on the EDL had to decide if they wanted to bid. If they chose to participate and won, they had to accept price cuts. While they would almost certainly see an increase in sales volume, they had no guarantee that the gain would compensate for the price cuts.

In 2010, the market was dominated by the Anhui model, which was initially supported by the central government, and which specified "double envelope" bidding and "the lowest price wins." Double envelope refers to the bidding method: "first envelope" covers the technical evaluation focusing on product quality, while the "second envelope" covers the price evaluation. Under this model, price was the initial criterion for screening, and the offer with the lowest price made it to the next round. Only then were criteria such as quality and guaranteed supply amount considered. However, downward pressures on price prompted some manufacturers to stop supplying at low cost, creating shortages of some drugs. Moreover, some CHC physicians wanted more drug options or were concerned about the quality of EDL drugs. Concerns about access and quality stirred a public debate. Some pharmaceutical companies argued that quality be given a higher priority than cost.

In response, the government adjusted its initial policy. In March 2012, the government issued a new document (State Council No. 11) that altered the winning criterion from "lowest price" to "quality first, appropriate price." In March 2013, the State Council General Office issued a revised EDL policy (State Council No. 16) that contained further adjustments. First, quality was reaffirmed as the primary criterion and reasonable price as the second, with evaluation taking place through the "double envelope" process. Second, the EDL was to be adjusted every three years to reflect actual usage and needs. Finally, there was to be a centralized purchasing mechanism for certain types of drugs, notably EDL drugs that (a) have been on the market for a long time and (b) have relatively stable prices, enabling uniform prices to be determined by the government. National pricing advocates are also supporting experiments with price and volume agreements as a way to reduce prices further. These policies would help to increase transparency over EDL procedures.

In May 2013, a new version of the EDL was released with 520 molecules. Disease coverage was broadened to include cancer and involved more drugs for certain areas such as blood disease and psychiatric disorders. The government further extended access to EDL drugs and pricing beyond grassroots institutions to Class II/III hospitals. More than 20 provinces launched EDL usage requirements for their hospitals. Provinces followed the requirements set by the central government on EDL revenue share (by value): 100 percent in grassroots institutions, at least 40 percent in Class II hospitals, and 25–30 percent in Class III hospitals. In September 2014, the NHFPC released a guideline allowing the use of non-essential drugs in grassroots medical facilities, although essential drugs were still given priority.

An important trend causing concern among pharma companies is the proposed linkage between EDL and non-EDL tendering, which has been implemented on a pilot basis in regions such as Qinghai and Shandong. As a result of this linkage, a pharmaceutical company that loses an EDL tender (or decides not to participate in the EDL) will automatically lose the RDL tender altogether if the molecule is EDL listed. Another concern triggered by the current tendering dynamic is that prices could be driven down to levels that are simply not sustainable for pharmaceutical companies, eventually putting supply of medication at risk.

Outlook for Reform Objective 2

Although we cannot predict what future versions of EDL will look like, we can safely assume that the molecule list will expand further and that the government will continue to push for its adoption as a mainstay of hospital prescribing beyond grassroots facilities and Class III maximum-care providers. Hospitals' tendency to prescribe drugs outside the EDL is likely to be challenged by a mandate for a specific percentage of prescribed value to come from EDL drugs. Given the much lower prices of these drugs, the great majority of prescribed daily doses and volumes would be EDL drugs under such a mandate. The impact of these trends will depend on the number of molecules included on EDL, the relative weighting of quality and price, and the extent of EDL adoption across hospital levels (classes).

Medical Service Provision: Objective 3

Public institutions underlie China's healthcare system. According to the recent available data, 90 percent of inpatient cases were treated in the public system in the first five months of 2015. The public system is organized by levels, with Class III hospitals representing large maximum-care providers and academic medical centers, often with over 1,000 beds, and boasting China's best medical talent. The lack of any steering mechanism for referrals has led to over-use and crowding of these hospitals – at the expense of Class I and II hospitals which are under-utilized (see Figure 5.3). This likely impedes the achievement of good patient outcomes, as Class III hospitals are neither designed nor able to provide the continuous care and patient education needed to treat the millions of people suffering from chronic diseases (for example, diabetes, hypertension, and cardiovascular disease).

The mismatch of care settings partly explains why some diseases are under-diagnosed, or diagnosed at a relatively late stage, in China. The unbalanced medical allocation leads to the low efficiency of disease treatment and management. For example, 70 percent of cancers are mid- or end-stage at the time of first diagnosis.[5] Fewer than 20 percent of patients suffering from depression are diagnosed.[6] The control rate of hypertension is less than 10 percent across the nation, compared with 48 percent in the United States.[7] Beyond poor clinical outcomes, the lack of a patient referral network leads to several economic inefficiencies: minor diseases are treated in maximum-care settings, tests and examinations are duplicated across multiple healthcare facilities, and patients fail to comply with the treatments that have been prescribed and paid for. Moreover, the combination of long wait times and time-short physicians has stressed patient–doctor relationships (see Chapter 7).

From a reform perspective, one government policy to redress this misallocation of demand and supply is the establishment of a primary care infrastructure. The government envisions a broad network of CHCs that act as primary care units. They are designed as the first point of contact for healthcare where some minor diseases are treated

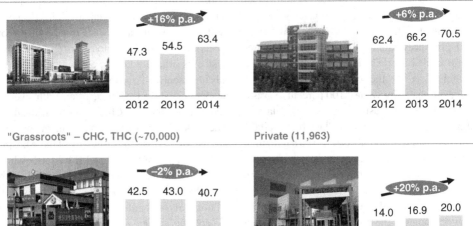

(No. of facilities, 2014)

Class III hospitals (1,875)

+16% p.a.

47.3   54.5   63.4

2012   2013   2014

Class II hospitals (6,764)

+6% p.a.

62.4   66.2   70.5

2012   2013   2014

"Grassroots" – CHC, THC (~70,000)

−2% p.a.

42.5   43.0   40.7

2012   2013   2014

Private (11,963)

+20% p.a.

14.0   16.9   20.0

2012   2013   2014

Note: 2014 volume is extrapolated based on January–November data.

Figure 5.3 Medical facilities' inpatient flow, in million patients
Source: NHFPC, Team analysis.

directly, while patients with other and more serious conditions are referred to appropriate specialists in Class II and III hospitals. More importantly, they are the principal provider for continuous management of chronic diseases.

To date, more than 33,000 CHCs and CHSs (community healthcare stations) across China have not yet diverted patient flow from larger hospitals. In fact, CHCs may actually be waning in relevance as hospital patient flows outgrow those of CHCs in both absolute and relative terms. For example, in the first five months of 2015, Class III hospitals had to accommodate 52 million more patients compared with the same period in the previous year, a 10 percent increase year over year. In that same period, patient loads at CHCs and CHSs grew by 5 percent, or 12 million visits.

Outlook for Reform Objective 3

China needs a robust primary care system to sustain its healthcare in the long run. The government might pursue several avenues to bolster this system. First, it could close ailing CHCs, consolidate

the remaining centers, and continuously upgrade those with stable patient flow. Second, the government could grant more authority to hospitals to operate the CHCs. This essentially would create referral networks for large public hospitals, and in turn commit them to steer patients to those centers and relieve the congestion in their outpatient areas. Third, the government could open the CHC market to private investment to draw needed entrepreneurship, talent, and capital.

For its part, the government would perform a steering role, managing cost (for example, through capitation models) and monitoring clinical quality and outcomes. Indeed, about 15 percent of patients are already being treated in CHCs that operate outside the public system and are outgrowing their government-run counterparts (7 percent year over year for the first 5 months of 2015 compared with 4.7 percent growth last year). In sum, evidence from China and elsewhere suggests that a more diverse CHC landscape and continued efforts by the government to strengthen the role of county hospitals on the one side and increasing operational and financial pressure at Class III hospitals on the other side will eventually lead to a sustainable primary care system.

Public Health Service: Objective 4

While patients in urban areas face significant challenges to obtain access to the right level of healthcare, they pale in comparison with the daunting task China confronts in providing access to its vast and dispersed rural population. Rural patients must deal with both a lack of hospitals (3.4 beds per 1,000 inhabitants in rural areas compared with 7.4 in cities) and a low ratio of healthcare workers to local people (3.6 healthcare workers per 1,000 inhabitants in rural areas compared with 9.2 in cities).[8] Logistics are especially challenging in more remote areas.

In its desire to provide more equal access to healthcare, the government has invested massively in rural provider infrastructure. An initiative from 1965 to 1970 undertook the construction of about 56,500 township healthcare centers (THCs); these were intended to be the cornerstone of frontline healthcare delivery in rural areas. The extensive bricks-and-mortar infrastructure suffered from a lack of clinical talent, modern equipment, and patient acceptance. As part of the current Five-Year Plan 2011–2015 (FYP), the government has invested another 30 billion RMB (roughly $5 billion) in improving infrastructure, upgrading medical talent, and implementing population health programs; the latter programs include increasing the examination rate of common diseases among rural women to deepen the impact of rural healthcare reform. The number of THCs fell from roughly 38,500 to 37,000 between 2009 and 2013, since the government focuses more on the quality of THC instead of pursuing blind expansion; 94 percent of those remaining were upgraded to comply with the latest standards and requirements of healthcare reform.[9]

To develop talent, the government has invested in rural training programs, including 2–3 billion RMB of spending by the end of 2012.[10] The programs encompass (a) clinical training for 4.95 million physicians, nurses, and other healthcare workers, (b) training in common diseases for some 4 million healthcare workers, and (c) general practitioner training for 36,000 physicians in grassroots medical institutions. The government has also introduced a subsidy of 6,000 RMB per person to encourage medical students to work in grassroots medical institutions. The proportion of those physicians with undergraduate degrees working in CHCs increased from 30.8 percent to 35.3 percent in 2013. A notice on national basic public health services issued on June 5, 2013, specifies several targets to be met by the end of 2013; many have been revised in the new 2015 plan. The goals were (are):

- Increase health information record system coverage to 80 percent of the population, and electronic medical record (EMR) coverage to 65 percent (75 percent in the 2015 plan)
- Cover 30 percent of the population with TCM-based health management offerings such as providing regular TCM-based consultation and offering healthcare instruction to the elderly (40 percent in the 2015 plan)
- Extend the national immunization program to vaccinate more than 90 percent of children, including the migrant population
- Extend health management to more than 80 percent of children such as regular family visits of families with newborn babies and health check programs for those in early childhood (85 percent in the 2015 plan)
- Extend health management to more than 80 percent of pregnant women (85 percent in the 2015 plan), ensuring that each receives five prenatal examinations and two postnatal checks; also improve provision for pregnant women in grassroots medical institutions
- Extend health management to 65 percent of people over the age of 65
- Secure the health management of 70 million hypertensive patients and 20 million diabetes patients (80 million and 30 million, respectively, in the 2015 plan)
- Enhance health education, mental illness management, communicable diseases and public health emergency management, health supervision, funding management, and evaluation programs
- Improve the role of grassroots medical institutions in all the above areas.

Outlook for Reform Objective 4

The difficulty of assessing progress toward these targets makes it even harder to predict future developments. As in other areas of the reform, the interpretation of the guidelines and the determination to implement them vary widely across the country. Nevertheless, there are indications that progress has been made. For example, the WHO estimates that vaccination rates for Class I vaccines (BCG, DTP3, HepB3, and HCV) have risen by about 5 percent since 2009 to reach almost 100 percent. The incidence of measles has plummeted from more than 50,000 cases in 2009 to roughly 6,000 in 2012, representing about five cases per million people, an incidence lower than, e.g., Germany's.

In other areas, the picture is more mixed. EMRs have been on the agenda since the tenth FYP 2001–2005, but the development of a multitude of approaches in isolation has produced a fragmented landscape that lacks interoperability. That puts the initial goal of EMR implementation – smooth and efficient documentation, storage, and exchange of patient data across hospitals – out of reach except in a few pilot areas in large cities.

Overall, progress seems most marked in areas with one-dimensional goals and key performance indicators (KPIs) such as vaccination rates and infrastructure delivery. These respond well to appropriate funding and do not require a highly skilled workforce or complex coordination across regions and stakeholders. It remains to be seen whether similar success rates can be achieved in areas requiring longer-term coordination and balanced incentives across different stakeholders – such as disease management for chronic diseases, implementation of a truly integrated EMR system, and educational efforts capable of changing people's behavior at scale.

Operating Environment: Objective 5

A main objective of the reform is to build a sustainable, cost-effective, and high-quality public hospital system. This involves four core elements:

- Funding mechanism: moving to a zero markup (ending the current margins on drugs and medical devices used in hospitals), increasing government subsidies and medical service charges as the main sources of funding, and reducing dependence on drug sales
- Cost control: capping budgets and establishing payer–provider relationships with effective cost-control mechanisms, such as DRGs and a cap on total costs
- Management transformation: setting clear KPIs for service quality and operational efficiency
- Improvement in resource balance: reallocating resources from large hospitals in big cities to grassroots institutions such as CHCs.

To date, none of these measures has been broadly implemented. However, major elements of the reform are being tested in pilots at the level of hospital classes (such as Class III), counties, and individual cities. An examination of a few examples yields some insight into the depth and breadth of the reform.

Counties

The National Development and Reform Commission – China's economic planning and management agency – and the Ministry of Health plan to invest RMB 40 billion in upgrading more than 2,000 county hospitals. The first-wave pilot, including 311 county hospitals, was planned in three phases:

- *By the end of 2011*, at least one hospital per county should have reached the Class IIA level; county hospitals should have been capable of treating common diseases, severe or emergency diseases, and some complex diseases; and physicians should have been trained in THCs and village clinics.
- *By the end of 2015*, all county hospitals should reach the Class IIA level and be able to provide sufficient care to their local population.
- *By the end of 2020*, the quality gap between county and Class III hospitals should be closed; patient care conditions, treatment skills, and hospital management should have been upgraded; and there should be continuous improvement in medical care to county level populations.

Another 700 county hospitals joined the pilot in April 2014. In early 2015, NHFPC minister Li

Rationale	Pilot situation	Initial results

• **Control cost**
• **Improve service quality** by giving each disease a clinical pathway
• **Enhance hospital management** by changing the business model and mind-set
• **Speed up IT** by standardizing the first page of medical records
	• 2004: launch of the management model for the DRG prospective payment system
	• 2007: standardization of the DRG medical record template
	• 2008: setting up of Beijing DRGs
	• 2011: official start of the DRG pilot in 6 hospitals,[1] including 108 diseases in 26 major diagnostic categories
	• Initial pricing based on historical data
		Average hospital stay
		  – Pilot hospital: 7 days
		  – Class III average: 10 days
		• **2 week rehospitalization rate**
		  – Pilot hospital: 6.5%
		  – Class III average: 7.4%

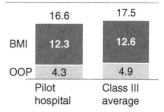

Average inpatient cost
Thousand RMB

	Pilot hospital	Class III average
	16.6	17.5
BMI	12.3	12.6
OOP	4.3	4.9

• **Hospitals had 18% surplus**

1 Peking University 3rd (the first to pilot, starting in November 2011), Peking University People's, Youyi, Chaoyang, Xuanwu, and Tiantan

Figure 5.4 Early success with DRGs in Beijing Class III hospital pilots
Source: 2012 Xiamen H-CEO Conference.

Bin commented on the 2015 healthcare reform plan, stating that the county hospital upgrade program would be a priority for the coming year. The focus would be implementing the zero mark-up policy and improving quality of county hospitals.

Cities

Building on the DRG model it set up in 2008, Beijing introduced a pilot in six Class III hospitals in 2011 (there were still six pilot hospitals based on the latest announcement). The results have been encouraging (see Figure 5.4).

Shenzhen's public hospital reform focuses on changing the funding mechanism and introducing measures to control costs. The plan is to introduce a zero markup in two stages, the first limited to local patients and the second extended to all patients, including migrants. The funding mechanism will be improved by gradually increasing government contributions and increasing the service fee according to the hospital's level (class). The payment mechanism will be improved by moving to disease- or category-based payments for inpatients and to mostly capitation payments for outpatients.

Competition will be introduced by allowing patients to use their prescriptions to purchase drugs at pharmacies: patients now can buy drugs in medical insurance-designated pharmacies, thus further lowering the healthcare cost. Drug purchasing will be reformed by centralizing purchasing and distribution and allowing manufacturers to sell directly to hospitals; this has been piloted in selected hospitals such as the University of Hong Kong-Shenzhen Hospital.

Outlook for Reform Objective 5

Progress to date in hospital reform has been the slowest of the five pillars. Many pilots have been launched, but they have not yet been fully evaluated.

In addition, the government should consider focusing on implementing treatment standards that are unified and linked to an appropriate funding mechanism that ensures hospital solvency. At this stage, hospitals other than those in Class III seem to have difficulty offering care at reimbursed fees; their real costs are higher than the sums they receive from the various public programs.

Experience from other, more mature health systems suggests that it will be helpful for the government to consider whether and how a division between medical and managerial leadership roles, supported by clear KPIs in service quality and operational efficiency, could support delivery of its objectives for transforming hospital management.

When discussing the status of hospital reform in China, we also must reflect on the progress made in the private sector. The objective of treating 20 percent of the patient population in private hospitals by the end of 2015 may not be achieved. But several regulatory changes may accelerate the provision of private offerings: (1) the official guideline that allows physicians to work at multiple sites helps to relieve the talent challenges of the private hospital sector; (2) the option to set up private hospitals as wholly foreign-owned entities; and (3) the possibility that public insurance programs might also be used to pay for treatment at private hospitals.[11] Regulatory changes are pointing in the right direction. Yet all the administrative requirements facing private hospitals and clinics in China create challenges and roadblocks.

Summary

There is an enormous effort under way at central, provincial, county, and city levels to implement the main content areas of a universal healthcare system that ensures affordable access to quality care and offers choices in the private sector for those who can afford it. The healthcare system's major stakeholders share an understanding of what has to happen next to further implement the reform and to live up to its vision. While funding reform is a continuing issue among decision-makers, one can argue that China, as an economy, has the means to pay for a reasonable system offering universal access to care. China is at present spending 5.6 percent of its gross domestic product on healthcare and has room to continue on its trajectory of offering access to quality healthcare for its population.

The biggest challenges will involve management of chronic diseases and rigorous prevention programs, development of the medical workforce at the speed required, and system levers (see Figure 1.7) such as steering mechanisms to the appropriate level of care. The government's reform program has identified many of the healthcare system levers that have proven effective in other countries. These levers include an increase in public-private partnerships, which is leading to an acceleration of the private sector's ability to offer increased healthcare choices and improved outcomes.

We remain optimistic that China will select the system levers that have proven effective in other countries. The open question is how long this journey will take and how radical some of the changes will be. The unique situation of population size, geographic scale, and urban–rural dynamics creates a level of complexity that no other country faces. We anticipate a significant increase in public-private partnerships and acceleration of the private sector's ability to offer healthcare choices to individuals. The sector will remain dynamic, providing private enterprise unique opportunities to participate in improving the healthcare of the Chinese people.

Notes

1. Xu Yu et al. 2013. "Prevalence and Control of Diabetes in Chinese Adults," *Journal of the American Medical Association* 310 (9):948–958. Centers for Disease Control and Prevention. 2014. *National Diabetes Fact Sheet*.
2. NHFPC of the People's Republic of China. 2014. *China Health Statistics Yearbook 2014*.
3. Local BoHRSS website.
4. Including severe pediatric conditions, certain cancers, infectious diseases such as tuberculosis and AIDS, and severe mental disorders.
5. China Anti-Cancer Association. Available online at: www.chinacdc.cn/jlm/mxfcrxjbxx/200612/t20061211_38640.htm.
6. Wei Hao, Chairman of Neurologist Society of Chinese Medical Doctor Association. Available online at: www.yiqib.net/car/2015/07/03/108.html. Accessed on November 21, 2015.

7. Lisheng Liu, Honorary chairman of China Hypertension League. Available online at: www.heartonline.cn/HeartOnLine_web/servlet/ MeetingController;jsessionid=A7265D164ED86 A1F227E29A5385DCCEA?method=detail&id= b3865686-278b-46be-9a15-6ce0531451f6& type=10. Cathleen D. Gillespie and Kimberly A. Hurvitz. 2013. "Prevalence of Hypertension and Controlled Hypertension – United States, 2007–2010," *MMWR Surveill Summ* 62 (03):144–148.

8. NHFPC of the People's Republic of China. 2014. *China Health Statistics Yearbook 2014.*

9. NHFPC of the People's Republic of China. 2015. Healthcare Reform Progress Report, 83, May 25, 2015. Available online at: www.nhfpc .gov.cn/tigs/ygjb/201505/2f9a3505457d4179b8 822c7444da2f6a.

10. Bingli Zhang. 2013. *Rural Medical System Development and Reform Report.* Available online at: www.ccms.org.cn/UpLoads/News/ 2013-07-03-10-34-22.ppt.

11. Ministry of Human Resources and Social Security of the People's Republic of China. 2014. Notice on Implementing Market-regulated Price for Service of Non-public Medical Facilities, 503, NDRC, March 25, 2014. Available online at: www .mohrss.gov.cn/gkml/xxgk/201404/t20140422_ 128933.htm.

The Challenge of Non-communicable Diseases (NCDs) in China

Government Responses and Opportunities for Reform

TSUNG-MEI CHENG

Introduction

China had a population of 1.38 billion and a per capita income of $13,217 in 2014 (in purchasing power parity, or PPP, international dollars).[1] The United Nations lists China as an "upper middle-income country."[2] The country has had solid economic growth for over three decades, beginning with the market reforms of the late 1970s. The country has also made impressive gains in several dimensions of population health, including health status and life expectancy. Life expectancy increased from 36.3 years in 1950 to today's 75.2, close to the figure in many advanced economies.[3]

However, China now confronts a grave challenge in the form of the growing prevalence of non-communicable disease (NCD). Unless reversed and controlled, that trend threatens to derail the continued growth of China's economy and improvements in the health of its population. As early as 2011, vice chairman of China's National People's Congress and former minister of health Chen Zhu called NCDs "the single biggest health challenge to the Chinese."[4]

Overview of NCDs

Prevalence of NCDs

NCDs accounted for 70 percent of China's total disease burden in 2012.[5] The leading NCDs in China today are cancer, cardiovascular disease, cerebrovascular disease (stroke), chronic obstructive pulmonary disease (COPD), and diabetes. Osteoporosis is also commonly seen. According to the 2015 Report on Nutrition and Chronic Disease in Chinese Residents, NCD prevalence rates are estimated to be 25.2 percent for hypertension (over 300 million people), 9.7 percent for diabetes, and 9.9 percent for COPD among those 40 years of age and older.[6] An earlier study found that 50.1 percent (493.4 million) of the adult Chinese population are prediabetic.[7] The 2015 report also showed that the incidence of cancer, the leading cause of deaths in China since 2012, was 235 per 100,000 population.

NCDs are now striking Chinese at younger ages as in low- and middle-income countries, and are a major cause of not only poverty and household impoverishment but also morbidity and premature deaths. This poses serious implications for China's economy going forward.[8]

Table 6.1 shows the changes in prevalence of chronic disease (both infectious and non-infectious) in China by gender, age, and urban–rural residence for 1993, 1998, 2003, and 2008 (years the Chinese government had collected such data).[9] The prevalence of NCDs has been consistently higher among urban than rural residents and higher among women than men. Significantly, large numbers of relatively younger adults (those aged 35–64) of both genders are afflicted with NCDs.

Table 6.1 Changes in the prevalence of chronic diseases in China, by gender, age, and place of residence, 1993–2008

	1993			1998			2003			2008		
	Total	Urban	Rural	Total	Urban	Rural	Total	Urban	Rural	Total	Urban	Rural
Overall												
Prevalence	169.8	285.8	130.7									
Men	152.3	254.4	119.0	141.6	251.1	106.3	133.5	215.4	106.4	177.3	266.2	147.0
Women	187.6	316.2	142.9	173.9	294.9	131.1	169.0	262.7	135.3	222.5	298.6	194.4
Age (Years)												
0–4	19.2	23.5	18.3	13.4	8.0	14.4	6.3	5.3	6.5	6.4	7.9	6.1
5–14	19.2	26.3	17.6	18.6	22.1	17.9	9.6	8.7	9.7	8.7	7.0	9.0
15–24	26.0	35.0	23.9	25.8	25.6	25.9	18.0	14.5	18.9	20.2	15.1	21.7
25–34	66.4	64.0	67.1	72.5	69.0	73.5	58.3	48.9	61.6	51.3	35.6	57.5
35–44	162.0	167.2	159.7	142.2	174.9	128.2	117.1	118.6	116.5	121.7	105.0	127.3
45–54	263.4	358.1	227.2	232.0	327.3	195.2	219.5	261.7	203.1	259.5	272.7	254.0
55–64	430.5	618.7	335.0	386.5	573.4	296.4	362.1	497.1	302.6	419.9	522.5	379.7
65 and over	540.3	789.3	398.2	517.9	793.1	355.1	538.0	777.1	391.7	645.4	851.8	523.9

Sources:

1. Author's analysis based on data from the 2013 China Health Statistics Yearbook.
2. National Health and Family Planning Commission Center for Statistics and Information.
3. National Health and Family Planning Commission, China. Beijing, 2014. Tables 9-6-1, 9-6-2, 9-6-3, 9-6-4.

Health and NCD Prevalence among China's Migrant Workers

China's rapid industrialization and urbanization in the past three decades saw large-scale migration of rural residents to urban areas in search of better jobs and escape from the hard agricultural life. China's National Bureau of Statistics estimated there were 278 million migrant workers in China as of 2014. Premier Li Keqiang has acknowledged they are the driving force behind China's "economic miracle."[10]

Migrant workers appear to be at greater risk for developing NCDs despite their relative youth and presumed good health when they left home. Possible explanations range from mental and psychological stress from being homesick to difficulties in adjusting to industrial jobs and urban life. More importantly, perhaps, urban migrant workers have far less generous health insurance coverage – despite the overall health insurance coverage rate of approximately 95 percent – compared to formal sector employment, which comes with the best health insurance coverage in China (Urban Employee Basic Medical Insurance, or UEBMI; see Chapters 2 and 11). They are instead enrolled in either the Urban Resident Basic Medical Insurance Scheme (URBMI) or the New Cooperative Medical Scheme (NCMS). Because the latter schemes have less financing and therefore offer fewer covered benefits, many Chinese covered by these schemes lack the means to access needed care.[11]

During July–December 2012, two Chinese agencies (the former Ministry of Health and the China Centers for Disease Control, or CDC) conducted a survey of chronic disease prevalence among China's migrant workers.[12] The surveys focused on risk factors (smoking, harmful drinking, poor diet, and physical activities), physical measurements (height, weight, waistline, blood pressure), and laboratory measurements (blood glucose, cholesterol, HbA1C, and insulin level).[13]

Survey findings released in December 2014 highlighted several important differences in the prevalence of risk factors and health status between migrant workers and local residents (those with household registration in the cities and towns where they live):

• More migrant workers consume alcohol (although their level of alcohol overuse is lower)
• Fewer migrant workers (44.1 percent) do not consume enough fruits and vegetables, a rate lower than local residents
• More migrant workers (nearly 40 percent) consume too much red meat
• More migrant workers are either overweight (30.4 percent) or obese (10.9 percent), but only among males
• More migrant workers have abnormal (high) levels of total blood cholesterol and triglyceride, but comparable levels of low-density cholesterol and lower levels of high-density cholesterol
• Fewer migrant workers suffer from hypertension (15.6 percent) and diabetes (4.8 percent), and their control rate for these conditions is higher; but their awareness of having these two chronic conditions is lower and they are less likely to be treated

Another key set of findings highlights the importance of gender: more than half of male migrant workers smoked (55.3 percent) compared to women (1.9 percent; 32.5 percent overall) – a situation not much changed from 2010. Male migrants aged 18–59 also had higher rates of being overweight compared to women (35.1 percent vs. 24.1 percent; 30.4 percent overall) and being obese compared to women (13.5 percent vs. 7.3 percent; 10.9 percent overall), a higher incidence of hypertension (20.6 percent vs. 8.9 percent; 15.6 percent overall), and a higher prevalence of diabetes (6 percent vs. 3 percent; 4.8 percent overall). Male construction workers exhibited the worst risk factors and health status levels: they had the highest rates of smoking and drinking, and the highest prevalence of obesity.

Under-treatment and lack of control of these chronic conditions were also more common among male migrant workers. Among those with a definite diagnosis of hypertension, males were less likely than females to receive treatment (44.7 percent vs. 56.4 percent; 47.8 percent overall) and were less likely to have their condition under control (2.5 percent vs. 4.2 percent; 2.9 percent overall). Only 24.3 percent of migrants (26.4 percent men, 23.7 percent women) were aware they were hypertensive, and just 12 percent (11 percent men, 15.4 percent women) were being treated for it. Among those with a definite diagnosis of hypertension the treatment rate was 47.8 percent (44.7 men, 56.4 percent women).

The picture is slightly more favorable for diabetes. The overall treatment rate was 23.8 percent; among those with a definite diagnosis, 83.4 percent were being treated. The rate of control of HbA1C (glycated haemoglobin) was 28.6 percent (27.2 percent for men, 32.4 percent for women); the overall diabetes control rate was 34.8 percent.[14] Gender differences were not as apparent here (34.7 percent for men vs. 35.2 percent for women).

The survey found that in 2012, the majority of those migrant workers 18–59 years of age diagnosed with hypertension (82.8 percent) and diabetes (83.4 percent) were not enrolled in active health management schemes. Low staffing and inadequate staff training are two main explanations. Moreover, the conduct of health management plans was seldom carried out according to guidelines: 16.2 percent for hypertension, 23 percent for diabetes. These rates were lower than those for local residents. Clearly, additional staffing, staff training, and use of evidence-based clinical guidelines are needed to carry out effective health management of migrant workers.

Mortality from NCDs

According to World Health Organization (WHO) data published in 2013, the absolute number of deaths due to NCDs fell 27.8 percent between 1990 and 2010 from 7.09 million to 5.94 million in China.[15] However, *as a percentage of the total*, deaths from NCDs have increased from 85 percent in 2012 to 86.6 percent in 2014, according to a 2015 China report on Nutrition and Chronic Disease – a rate far higher than the global average of 67.9 percent.[16]

Table 6.2 ranks the ten leading causes of death by volume, gender, percentage of total deaths, and absolute number of deaths in China in 2012. The 2015 report reveals that three major NCDs – cardio- and cerebrovascular diseases, cancer, and COPD – accounted for 79.4 percent of all deaths. This accords with WHO estimates that deaths from

cancer, cardio- and cerebrovascular diseases, diseases of the respiratory, endocrine-nutrition-metabolic, digestive, nervous, and urinary and reproductive tract systems accounted for 87.6 percent of total deaths in China in 2012.[17]

An additional 2015 report released by the WHO suggests that 3 million Chinese die prematurely each year from preventable diseases.[18] Premature deaths from NCDs in China accounted for 35.8 percent of total NCD mortality (39.7 percent for men and 31.9 percent for women) in 2012. By contrast, premature NCD deaths are much lower in developed countries (discussed next).

Drivers of NCDs

NCD risk factors in China fall into four categories: behavioral, environmental, institutional, and other (e.g., urbanization, aging). Table 6.3 compares the prevalence of the major NCD risk factors and the rate of premature mortality from NCDs in China with select countries belonging to the Organisation for Economic Co-operation and Development (OECD) and other emerging market countries (Brazil, India, Thailand, and Vietnam).

Lifestyle-related Behavioral Risks

The 2015 Report on Nutrition and Chronic Disease shows both positive and negative changes in the health and nutrition status of the Chinese population. Positive changes since 2002 include (a) significantly declining rates of stunting, underweight, anemia, and malnutrition, (b) significantly improving nutritional status and stature of children aged 6–17 and young men and women 18+ years old, and (c) significantly declining rates of anemia among pregnant women (17.2 percent, down 11.7 percentage points). Today 18.7 percent of adults engage in regular physical exercise, compared to only 11.9 percent in 2011.[19] The biggest negative change is an increased number of people suffered from NCDs during the period 2002–2012.[20]

Several drivers underlie these trends. Rapid economic growth over three decades led to a 6.3-fold growth in urban household disposable income and a 4.7-fold growth in rural household income in the

Table 6.2 Leading causes of deaths in China, by rank, percent of total deaths, and number of deaths per 100,000 population, 2012

	Total			Men			Women		
	Rank	Percent of Total Deaths	No. of Deaths per 100,000	Rank	Percent of Total Deaths	No. of Deaths per 100,000	Rank	Percent of Total Deaths	No. of Deaths per 100,000
Cancer	1	26.81	164.51	1	29.64	208.11	2	22.95	120.12
Cardiovascular disease	2	21.45	131.64	2	19.42	136.38	1	24.22	126.80
Cerebrovascular disease	3	19.61	120.33	3	18.61	130.68	3	20.97	109.80
Respiratory system disease	4	12.32	75.59	4	12.47	87.55	4	12.11	63.41
Injuries, poisoning, and other external causes	5	5.67	34.79	5	6.5	45.66	6	4.53	23.72
Other diseases	6	3.88	23.82	6	3.4	23.85	5	4.54	23.78
Endocrine, nutrition, and metabolic diseases	7	2.82	17.32	8	2.27	15.96	7	3.57	18.69
Digestive system diseases	8	2.48	15.25	7	2.67	18.78	8	2.23	11.65
Nervous system diseases	9	1.12	6.86	9	1.04	7.28	9	1.23	6.43
Urinary and reproductive system diseases	10	1.03	6.3	10	1.00	7.01	10	1.07	5.58

Source: Data based on the 2013 *China Health Statistics Yearbook*. National Health and Family Planning Commission, China. Beijing. 2014. Table 11-1-6.

Table 6.3 Major risk factors in China and select OECD countries – Brazil, India, Thailand, and Vietnam – as percent of total population (male and female), 2010, 2012, and 2014

	Obesity BMI ≥ 30 (aged 18+ years) (2014)	Overweight (BMI ≥ 25) (aged 18+ years) (2014)	Raised Blood Pressure (aged 18+ years) (SBP ≥ 140 and DBP ≥ 90) (2014)	Raised Blood Glucose (fasting glucose ≥7.0 or on glucose drug or diabetic) (2014)	Smoking (aged 15+ years) (2012)	Insufficient Physical Activity (adults 18+ years) (2010)	Per Capita Use of Pure Alcohol (liters) (2012)	Premature NCD Mortality as Percent of Total Mortality (2012)
China	7.3	35.4	18.8	10.1	26.8*	23.8	8.8	39.7	31.9
Australia	29.9	66.4	15.4	8.1	15.9	25.8	11.9	28.4	18.9
Brazil	20.1	54.2	23.3	7.6	16.6	27.2	10.1	50.7	41.4
Canada	30.1	67.7	13.3	9.1	16.5	25.9	8.9	31.9	22.1
France	25.7	64.1	21.0	8.6	27.4	26.4	12.3	32.5	16.2
Germany	22.7	59.7	19.5	9.0	28.8	23.4	11.5	28.8	14.7
India	4.7	21.4	25.4	8.5	12.9	12.1	5.2	62.0	52.2
Japan	3.5	26.5	16.9	11.2	…	38.7	6.6	27.2	14.7
Mexico	27.6	63.4	21.0	9.9	15.7	25.4	7.2	51.7	42.7
South Korea	6.3	35.5	10.8	9.4	…	34.7	10.5	40.2	19.9
Thailand	9.2	31.6	21.3	10.9	…	14.6	6.5	45.5	38.7
United Kingdom	29.8	66.7	15.2	10.1	19.9	40.0	11.4	29.1	19.2
United States	35.0	69.6	13.4	10.5	18.0	35.0	9.1	37.2	25.1
Vietnam	3.5	20.4	22.2	6.0	24.3	23.6	7.2	54.3	30.0

* denotes an increase in smoking prevalence from 2010. All other countries in this group showed reductions in smoking prevalence.
In 2010, smoking prevalence in China was 25.9 percent.

Source: Author's analysis based on data in Global Status Report on Non-communicable Diseases 2014. World Health Organization, Geneva. 2014.

period 1995–2012 alone.[21] Such growth resulted in an increased ability to pay for healthcare and better nutrition. However, rapid urbanization occurred in tandem with rising income and prosperity. Together, these forces fostered sedentary lifestyles, poor diets, higher smoking rates, and alcohol use – all known major risk factors for NCDs like cancer, heart disease, stroke, COPD, and diabetes. These risk factors are reflected in increased body mass and serum cholesterol levels.

According to the 2015 report, smoking, excessive drinking, lack of exercise, and other health risks still prevail among the Chinese population. Such problems are not limited to the migrant worker population. Between 2002 and 2012, the percentage of Chinese adults (18+ years) who were overweight increased 7.3 percent to reach 30.1 percent; the percentage who were obese rose 4.8 percent to reach 11.9 percent.[22] In 2014, there were 300 million smokers in China, including 52.9 percent of Chinese men. Equally significant, 740 million Chinese (72.40 percent of non-smokers) were exposed to secondhand smoke.

Environmental Risk Factors

Environmental pollution plays an important role in major NCDs such as cancer, cardiovascular disease, and COPD. China's economic transformation in the past three decades has led to one of the most severe cases of environmental degradation the world has ever seen. Data on the environmental impact on health in China are not readily available.[23] Glimpses may be had, however, from published reports. For example, the *Lancet* reported that air pollution is estimated to cause 500,000 premature deaths in urban China,[24] and China-CDC has estimated that total deaths (urban and rural combined) attributable to air pollution range between 960,000 and 970,000.[25] Another *Lancet* study, based on 2010 data, reported that China had significantly higher levels of ambient and household air pollution, compared to G20 nations.[26]

Polluted water poses an additional serious threat to the health of the population. According to China CDC director-general Wang Yu, 50 percent of the water supply in rural China today does not meet WHO standards for clean water.[27]

Institutional Risk Factors

Lack of health insurance coverage can delay or prevent access to needed healthcare and thus serves as an institutional risk for NCDs. In 2000, only 15 percent of China's population had health insurance coverage.[28] The 2009 health reform dramatically elevated the level of health insurance coverage to over 95 percent of the population by 2012[29] see Figure 2.2. Nevertheless, benefits vary by type of insurance. The UEBMI offers the most generous coverage, followed by the NCMS and URBMI schemes (see Chapter 11). The benefit levels offered by URBMI have been catching up with those in NCMS in recent years. The higher out-of-pocket costs borne by beneficiaries in these two schemes create financial barriers to needed healthcare for those who cannot afford the expense.

Other NCD Risk Factors: Aging, Nutrition, and Socioeconomic Status

In 1999, China officially became an "aging society." The proportion of its population 60+ years old reached 10.1 percent; the percentage of those 65+ years reached 7 percent.[30] By 2013, Chinese aged 65+ years constituted 9.7 percent of the population, compared to an average of 15.7 percent among OECD countries.[31] China is thus a relatively younger country. However, the rate of aging in China has been rapid. It took 46 years for the percentage of the population 65+ to double in the United Kingdom (from 7 percent to 14 percent), 68 years in the United States, and 116 years in France; it took only 26 years in China.[32] Driven by both a low birth rate and an increase in life expectancy, that trend is likely to continue in China.[33]

Why is this important? The risk of NCDs increases with age. As a result, aging is a major driver of the increased prevalence of NCDs and their associated healthcare costs.[34] In 2005, healthcare costs for the elderly accounted for 21.8 percent of China's total health spending; by 2010, that share had risen to 36.4 percent.[35]

In developing countries, a host of other risk factors drive NCDs, often occurring later in life. For example, shortages of natural resources (arable land, water) impact the food supply, nutrition, and thus disease. Malnutrition, stunting, anemia, and parasitic infections all affect the health of mothers, infants, and children – exposing them to greater risks for certain NCDs later in life. Research has shown that fetal and early childhood malnutrition predisposes those affected to becoming overweight and obese, or to develop heart disease, stroke, and diabetes.[36] Parental socioeconomic status and educational attainment – especially the education of the mother – similarly affect child health, with implications for health status later in life.[37]

Economic Burden of NCDs

NCDs impose several types of cost on different stakeholders. Patients and their households incur the physical costs of pain and suffering, medical costs in the form of out-of-pocket spending, disability costs and potential losses in productivity, and premature death. The country incurs macroeconomic costs in terms of aggregate healthcare spending, crowding out of other social spending, lost productivity, and lower gross domestic product (GDP) (see Chapter 1). Many studies have demonstrated the strong causal relationship between economic growth and health, and vice versa.[38] A 2009 survey of world business leaders on global risks conducted by the World Economic Forum identified chronic disease as "one of the leading threats to global economic growth."[39]

Household Costs

In 2012, household out-of-pocket spending comprised 34.3 percent of China's total national health expenditures. This represented a 24.6 percent reduction from the high of 58.8 percent in 2000.[40] Out-of-pocket payment for NCD prevention and treatment, on the other hand, accounted for 47.3 percent of China's total NCD-related healthcare expenditure in 2010. In some provinces, such spending exceeded 50 percent.[41]

Out-of-pocket spending for NCD-related prevention and treatment constitutes a heavy financial burden on some households, especially low-income families and the poor. This burden is especially high for NCD inpatient care. In 2010, the average cost of an inpatient episode was 6,978 RMB, or

36 percent of the average annual disposable income for urban residents.[42] Treatment costs for complicated diseases such as stroke and post-acute follow-up care impose continuing heavy financial burdens, especially on households in rural areas. This burden is a major source of poverty and impoverishment, despite the significantly improved health insurance coverage and access to medical services following the 2009 health reform.[43]

Nevertheless, discussions with senior health officials in Beijing suggest that out-of-pocket spending for NCD care is not an economic burden for the average Chinese.[44] Essential medicines for NCDs are inexpensive and nearly universally affordable. For example, one month's supply of antihypertensive drugs costs only several RMB (approximately $1–$1.50).[45]

Societal Costs

In 2010, total spending on NCDs accounted for 70 percent of China's total national health spending. This represented 3.2 percent of China's total GDP that year.[46] According to the 2011 Report on Cardiovascular Diseases in China released by the National Center for Cardiovascular Diseases, treatment costs for heart attacks, stroke, diabetes, and COPD will rise by 50 percent from 2010 to 2030.[47]

In addition to the added public and private spending on healthcare, NCDs also impose certain other costs on society. One is lost labor productivity and thus a decline in GDP. The other is the economic value of the disability-adjusted life years (DALYs) lost.[48] For 2010, dietary risk factors alone generated an estimated 16.3 percent of the total DALYs from all risk factors in China and 30.6 percent of all deaths.[49] Hypertension generated the second highest number of DALYs (12 percent) and 24.6 percent of all deaths. Tobacco use generated 9.5 percent of DALYs and 16.4 percent of all deaths.[50]

The WHO estimates that for the period 2011–2015, cumulative economic losses due to NCDs in low- and middle-income countries (LMICs) amounted to $7 trillion, a sum far larger than the estimated annual $11.2 billion cost of implementing effective interventions to reduce the NCD burden.[51] Certain diseases account for major shares of total lost output during this period in

LMICs: cardiovascular disease (51 percent), respiratory disease (22 percent), cancer (21 percent), and diabetes (6 percent).[52]

Analysts have developed estimates of the economic cost of the five major NCDs in China (diabetes, cardiovascular disease, respiratory disease, cancer, and mental illness) using the WHO's EPIC model of economic growth. The EPIC model, developed by Abegunde and Stancioli and applied by Bloom et al., builds on Nobel Laureate Robert Solow's seminal 1956 neoclassical theory of economic growth as a function of two main factors of production: capital formation and labor supply.[53] The EPIC model adds a third factor, the health of the population, which along with education comprises a major component of what economists call "human capital." NCDs cause a diversion of savings from capital investment into nonproductive healthcare; and NCD mortality leads to reduced stocks of available labor. In other words, NCDs impose a negative cost on economic growth because they affect both capital formation (through reduced savings) and labor supply (through lower labor productivity due to illness and premature mortality), the two most important factors of production in any national economy. This enhanced model shows that for the period 2012–2030 the cost of foregone societal output resulting from four major NCDs in China (cardiovascular disease, cancer, COPD, diabetes) will total $18.5 trillion. If mental health is included as a fifth NCD, the total is estimated at $23.0 trillion (in 2010 US$).[54] This cumulative GDP loss due to NCDs is staggering, considering that in 2014 China's total GDP was $10.4 trillion.[55]

Additional analyses suggest the relative contribution of these five NCDs to overall lost output for China for the period 2012–2030: cardiovascular disease (33.1 percent), cancer (24.4 percent), respiratory disease/COPD (20.8 percent), mental health (19.6 percent), and diabetes (2.1 percent).[56] To be sure, the estimates from the EPIC model have serious limitations. A major drawback is that the estimates are derived from mortality data alone. Failure to include the morbidity component of NCDs significantly understates the true magnitude of the overall costs of NCDs in China. Additional limitations of the EPIC model are described elsewhere.[57]

Can China's Health System Cope Adequately with the Growth of NCDs?

In the face of rapidly rising healthcare spending, rapid aging, a rising dependency ratio, a slowing macro economy, a shrinking labor force, and large numbers of premature deaths from NCDs, one may ask whether China's healthcare system has the financial capacity and physical infrastructure to adequately cope with NCDs? The proper answer to this question is, "it depends." China certainly will not be able to cope adequately with its growing NCD burden unless several actions are simultaneously undertaken. It must allocate more financial resources to its healthcare system. It must also dedicate more physical resources (e.g., land) and infrastructure (labor, capital equipment). Third, it must reform its delivery system to become more cost-effective. Fortunately, the Chinese government has embarked upon a multipronged, proactive policy to achieve these goals. The following section and the appendix provide an overview of these policy and program initiatives.

Government Response: Policies and Program Initiatives

As early as the mid-1990s, China's central and provincial governments began implementing a variety of measures and guidelines to prevent and control NCDs. These initiatives targeted tobacco control, along with diabetes and stroke prevention, and laid the foundation for NCD mitigation efforts in the coming years.[58]

In January 2002, China CDC was established to help the country follow international best practices then advocated by the WHO. The CDC also sought to increase prevention and control of three groups of diseases in developing countries: communicable diseases, non-communicable diseases, and injuries.[59]

The neglect of NCDs in favor of acute care has been a worldwide phenomenon in the twentieth century, even in advanced nations. The worldwide NCD control and prevention campaign is thus a nascent effort in learning mode. The effort involves a potpourri of programs overseen by different organizations. Continued experimentation with different approaches may yield a more streamlined administration, as appears to be happening now in China.

China has pursued numerous initiatives to fight NCDs, distinguished by their institutional origin, objectives, financing, and administration. The lengthy list of initiatives suggests the Chinese government and its agencies are fully aware of the NCD threat and aim to develop China's health policy accordingly. Reported findings further suggest that many of the demonstration projects have yielded positive results.

The Chinese government's current (2015) focus on NCD prevention and control has several targets: social mobilization in such areas as health education and healthy lifestyle promotion; a ban on smoking in public places; NCD surveillance through monitoring of causes of deaths, nutrition, and cancer registries; early detection and treatment; active community-based NCD management such as hypertension and diabetes disease management in both urban and rural areas; and NCD prevention and control through equal emphasis of both western and traditional Chinese medicine.[60]

Two of the more recent top-level policy initiatives covering the period of 2012–2020 and two nationwide initiatives, which serve as the main platforms for the government's NCD prevention and control efforts, are discussed below. Lest readers lose sight of the forest for the trees, other important initiatives are described in the appendix. Many of these initiatives have targeted individuals and families to enhance their health literacy and make them better managers of their own health and healthcare. Others have targeted providers to improve the quality of the medical and preventive care they render to patients. Still others emphasize data collection as an inherent part of healthcare that is "crucial for evaluating disease trends, planning health services, and monitoring progress," as recognized in the 2006 Report on Chronic Disease in China.[61]

The China National Plan for NCD Prevention and Treatment (2012–2015)

The China National Plan for NCD Prevention and Treatment ("the plan") represents the first-ever national effort to target NCD prevention and control formally articulated by the Chinese government. The importance attached to the NCD issue by the government lies in the fact that it was *jointly* issued by 15 ministries and state administrations, including the powerful National Development and Reform Commission (NDRC) in the State Council. Since its issuance, provincial and local governments throughout China have followed suit with their own efforts based on the national plan.

The plan is a clearly articulated national roadmap to comprehensive NCD prevention and control in China. Its goal is to "protect and promote the health of the people, and facilitate sustainable economic and social development."[62] The plan adheres to the basic principles of government leadership, intersector cooperation and coordination, and social participation. To achieve its goal, the plan emphasizes primary prevention along with the integration of prevention and treatment through a strengthening of primary care. The plan targets key NCDs for intervention (cardiovascular diseases, cancer, diabetes, COPD), their key behavioral risk factors (tobacco use, imbalanced diet, insufficient physical activities, excessive drinking), and their key biological risk factors (elevated blood pressure, elevated blood sugar [HbA1C], dyslipidemia, overweight-obesity).

The plan also aims to increase the number of NCD prevention and control professionals to more than 5 percent of the professionals in disease control institutions at all levels nationally. As an ultimate aim, the plan sets a target to increase the average life expectancy of the Chinese by one year at the end of the plan period (2015). To carry out this ambitious effort, the government has allocated a budget nearly twice the size of its fiscal commitment for 2011.

The State Council Framework for Food and Nutrition Development in China 2014–2020

Earlier initiatives in NCD control and prevention originated primarily at the cabinet ministerial level. In January 2014, China's State Council issued its "Framework for Food and Nutrition Development in China 2014–2020 (Office of the Premier Document [2014] No. 3)".[63] This framework clearly articulated the State Council's vision and ambition for population health improvement for all Chinese. With the backing of the full power and prestige of the highest administrative office of the land, the framework document will serve as the highest guideline for all levels of governments in all 31 provinces (including the autonomous regions and municipalities and the Xinjiang Production and Construction Military Corps), all ministries and national commissions, and all state agencies under the State Council on matters relating to food and nutrition development in China.

The document outlines priority areas such as food production and supply, residents' nutrition status, and awareness regarding health and nutrition. The objectives are to safeguard the effective supply of foods and improve food composition to improve the nutrition and health status of the Chinese.[64]

Earlier dramatic successes in improving population health through national government nutrition policies provide a strong evidence base for the State Council's bold move in the same direction. The effort is reminiscent of the highly successful Finnish national nutrition policy implemented in the 1980s to address the unacceptably high rates of morbidity and mortality from cardiovascular diseases.[65]

National Campaign on Healthy Lifestyle for All

The National Campaign on Healthy Lifestyle for All is an ongoing initiative that started in 2007. Its goal was to promote health knowledge, awareness, and healthy behaviors among all Chinese. Unlike the State Council framework, the initiative was not a formal top-down government plan, but rather was organized by the Ministry of Health, the China CDC, and the National Commission for Patriotic Health Movement – all of whom share responsibility for healthcare.

The initiative focused at first on (a) promoting healthy lifestyles through reasonable diet and physical exercise, and (b) building a supportive and health-enhancing physical environment. The latter included healthy restaurants, healthy school cafeterias, public parks, designated pedestrian walkways, and even innovations such as gas stations equipped with blood pressure gauges and scales. Smoking cessation, oral and mental health, and accident and injury prevention activities were added in 2011. The initiative also trained volunteer "advisors" – often retired healthcare workers – to organize activities, public lectures, and speech contests for the public. As of April 2015, Beijing had trained close to 10,000 "healthy lifestyle advisors."[66] A 2012 evaluation showed that compared to those areas that had not participated in the initiative, participating sites had much higher levels of health literacy, use of health-promoting equipment, and adoption of healthy behaviors.[67]

In 2011, the initiative was included in the national basic public health service package and became a major platform of the government's stepped up efforts to promote healthy lifestyles – a key strategy in the National Plan for NCD Prevention and Control 2012–2015. The government also began more formal evaluations of the program's effectiveness. In 2012, the Ministry of Health (National Health and Family Planning Commission since 2013) included the initiative's performance as a measure of overall performance evaluation on NCD prevention and control.[68] By the end of 2013, 71.4 percent of China's counties were participating in the initiative.[69]

National Demonstration Sites for Integrated NCD Prevention and Control

In 2011, before the 2012–2015 National Plan was announced, the Chinese government began testing a new working model for NCD prevention and control. The model was based on the WHO Health-in-All-Policies (HiAP) approach, which was a key WHO strategy in NCD prevention and control. HiAP seeks to engage all sectors of society beyond just healthcare and urges policy makers to include consideration of health impact in all public policies. HiAP was introduced in the European Union in 2006. In China, policy makers created a series of demonstration sites nationwide to implement the HiAP approach.

This new working model takes a formal top-down approach, with government leadership at the top, followed by "inter-sector cooperation and societal participation."[70] Local governments have been supportive of the project, which helped the model to quickly gain momentum. As of March 2015, there were 265 demonstration sites in both urban and rural areas in all 31 provinces (including the autonomous regions and municipalities), with over 500 provincial-level NCD prevention and control demonstration districts in operation.[71]

Batteries of metrics have been developed to monitor and evaluate the various dimensions of the demonstration sites' programs. The metrics include risk factors, health education, high-risk population screening, disease management, and the environment. Overall results of this "Chinese HiAP in action" are reportedly encouraging. The project is considered a model for NCD prevention and control "with Chinese characteristics."[72]

Challenges and Policy Recommendations

As health reformers around the world know only too well, there is a disjunction between designing health policies and actually implementing them and making them work in practice. When the Chinese government introduced its first NCD initiative, the China National Plan for NCD Prevention and Treatment (2012–2015), it faced serious challenges. These included low public awareness about NCDs and the threats they pose, low public participation in control efforts, lack of coordination among multiple government sectors, inadequate NCD prevention and treatment infrastructure (including personnel at every level), counterproductive payment mechanisms for providers, and misallocation of healthcare resources across sectors. Recognizing the need for more forceful change, China's 12th Five-Year Plan (2011–2015) designated NCD prevention and control as priorities for government intervention. Some of the major challenges to NCD intervention are discussed below.

Constraints on the HiAP Approach

Despite the recognized importance of the HiAP approach in pursuing NCD prevention and control, implementing HiAP in public policies and programs in China is still a challenge. According to Wang Yu, China needs time to deal with several constraints.

These include constrained natural resources (insufficient arable land, water, and energy supply), the country's rapidly aging population, the population's growing appetite for more of everything including unhealthy foods, and rising consumer expectations.[73] There are also institutional constraints such as the absence of or insufficient levels of coordination and cooperation within and between governmental bodies.[74] Perhaps most important, HiAP in China still lacks a coordinating mechanism at the top, as well as a national health law to serve as a legal framework to guide the next steps in China's health reforms.[75]

Other constraints include the lack of regulation over products and services closely linked with health risk factors. Such products and services encompass salt, sugar, food labeling, restaurant hygiene, tobacco, and tobacco warning labels. HiAP in China thus remains a work in progress.

Inadequate Budgets for NCD Prevention

China needs to increase its budget for NCD preventive services. Of the total spending on NCD prevention and control in China, *preventive* services account for a paltry 1.26 percent.[76] The bulk of this funding comes from the central government's public health services equalization program.[77] The Chinese government has been steadily increasing the per capita budget allocation for public health services; however, greater allocations are needed. By contrast, treatment costs (inpatient and outpatient services) account for the bulk (83.85 percent) of the total healthcare spending on NCDs.[78] Figure 6.1 decomposes total spending on NCD treatment by type of service: inpatient- and outpatient services, healthcare products, administrative expense, preventive services, and auxiliary services.

Inadequate Primary Care Workforce

While the 2009 health reform has greatly increased the supply of China's health workforce, manpower levels remain woefully inadequate to handle the vastly increased demand for healthcare services.[79] Table 6.4 compares the number of general practitioners per 1,000 population and the number of

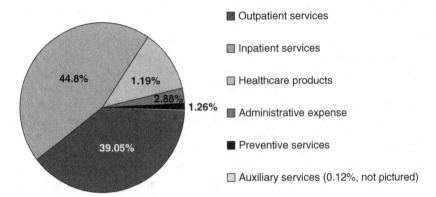

Figure 6.1 Health spending on NCDs in China, by type of service, 2013
Source: China National Health Development Research Center. Strategies for Healthcare Expenditure and Financing for Chronic Disease. China National Health Development Research Center, Ministry of Health. Beijing, China. 2012.

nurses per 1,000 population in OECD countries versus China. Among China's 2.5 million doctors (2015), only 130,000, or 5 percent, are primary care physicians. This translates into one primary care doctor for every 10,000 Chinese.[80] China's nursing supply also remains quite low, despite a 46.7 percent increase in nurses per 1,000 population between 2009 and 2013 – largely due to the 2009 healthcare reform.

Why is this important? Good primary care is a cost-effective way to improve patient outcomes and population health. One barrier is that primary care doctors are the lowest paid and have the lowest standing of all specialties in China. Higher salaries and prestige are needed to incentivize more medical students and doctors to go into primary care.

The Role of Evidence-based Clinical Guidelines and Clinical Pathways

As part of the 2009 healthcare reform, the Chinese government has invested heavily in its healthcare system. As an illustration, the central government investment in healthcare facilities during 2009–2010 exceeded the sum of all government investments in the prior 30 years (i.e., since China's economic reform). During 2009–2011, the Chinese government invested more than US$ 204 billion (PPP$) in the health sector.[81] Financial

investments are necessary but insufficient, however. Policy makers must make sure the new money is efficiently spent, and not just poured into a dysfunctional system.

Two major instruments are crucial in this endeavor. First, there must be a parallel effort in healthcare technology assessment (HTA) to discover which treatments and practice arrangements work better than others (see Chapter 13). Second, there must be evidence-based clinical pathways derived from clinical guidelines to help physicians navigate and follow best practices in patient treatment. These clinical pathways can help reduce unnecessary and inappropriate care, but generally leave sufficient room to allow physicians' clinical judgment and discretion. Such pathways now exist in computer-based algorithms.

With its health reform beginning in 2009, the government has adopted health technology assessment to bring about quality and efficiency improvements, albeit on a limited basis. China's Ministry of Health established an HTA unit within its China National Health Development Research Center (CNHDRC, a policy think tank that serves multiple government ministries and agencies involved with healthcare in China). China might consider developing its nascent HTA capacity and applying HTA techniques to health insurance benefits design, coverage (including public health services), and payment models.

Table 6.4 Number of general practitioners and nurses per 1,000 population in select OECD countries, 2014 or nearest year, and China, 2015 (GP) and 2013 (nurse)

	General Practitioner	Nurse
China	0.0001	2.01
Australia	1.53	11.52
Austria	1.64	7.87
Canada	1.21	9.48
Czech Republic	0.70	7.99
Denmark	0.69	16.3
France	1.56	–
Germany	1.69	12.96
Italy	0.89	–
Japan	–	10.54
Korea	0.60	5.61
Mexico	0.77	2.62
Netherlands	1.45	8.4
New Zealand	0.94	10.39
Norway	0.87	16.67
Spain	0.75	5.14
Sweden	0.64	11.15
Switzerland	1.11	17.36
United Kingdom	0.80	8.26
United States	0.31	–

Source: Data for OECD countries from OECD Health Statistics 2015. Data for the number of general practitioners per 1,000 population for China from Chen Zhu, vice chairman of China's National People's Congress and former minister of health; and that for nurses per 1,000 population from OECD Health Statistics 2015.

Soon thereafter, the Ministry of Health collaborated with the UK's National Institute for Care Excellence (NICE) to develop evidence-based clinical pathways for single diseases treated in rural public hospitals. These evidence-based clinical pathways were paired with changes in provider reimbursement from fee-for-service to case payment and achieved several important results: lower costs, reduced lengths of stay, reduced use of drugs (including overly prescribed antibiotics), improved patient outcomes, and increased satisfaction among patients, providers, and payers.[82] These encouraging results

prompted the government to roll out this reform model nationally. The Chinese government (again in collaboration with NICE) is currently developing and implementing evidence-based clinical pathways for key chronic diseases, beginning with stroke and COPD.

Financial Access to NCD Care

Another constraint to NCD prevention and control is the continuing high level of out-of-pocket spending in China. Such spending accounts for 41.6 percent of the cost of outpatient visits, 51.5 percent of the cost of inpatient care, and 72 percent of the cost of drugs at retail pharmacies.[83] High out-of-pocket spending constitutes a financial barrier to needed care. In his report to the 12th China's National People's Congress held in March 2015, Premier Li Keqiang stated that the government will increase (a) subsidies to health insurance for both urban and rural residents by 19 percent, from 320 RMB to 380 RMB per person; and (b) public health budgets by 14 percent, from 35 RMB to 40 RMB per person.[84] Such continuing investments in the government's 13th Five-Year Plan (2016–2020) in public health and NCDs are expected, barring unforeseen circumstances.

Need for Measurement, Monitoring, and Evaluation

One final constraint is the nascent stage of development of NCD program measurement and evaluation. As of 2012, systematic evaluation of program efficacy and outcomes has not kept pace with new program implementation.[85]

To be sure, China CDC has engaged in a number of important monitoring and measurement programs (see Chapter 3). For example, it fielded the national causes of death surveys, the national NCD and nutrition surveys, and cancer registries. As of 2011, systematic measuring and monitoring appear concentrated in the 265 NCD demonstration sites spread throughout China's 31 provinces including the autonomous regions and municipalities and the Xinjiang Production and Construction Military Corps.

As of 2015, the National Health and Family Planning Commission has been actively conducting evaluations of the effectiveness of the various NCD prevention and control programs implemented in preparation for the 2016 national work plan as well as for either the 13th Five-Year Plan (2016–2020) or a ten-year plan 2015–2025. The length of the next-phase NCD plan had not yet been determined as of March 2015.[86] Overall, however, more evaluations of program efficacy are needed to determine the value of the government's increased resource allocations for NCD prevention and control.

Potential of Public-Private Partnerships[87]

As recently as 2013, the Chinese government has regarded NCD prevention and control as part of the public health system. It has therefore chosen to play the leading role in this effort, supported by collaborations with multiple government agencies and social (private sector) participation. Since the 2009 health reform, governments at all levels have expanded work in NCD prevention and control – including "purchasing services" from private providers to deliver certain services such as management of hypertension and diabetes – and borne all of the associated costs. At the same time, the Chinese government has also explored additional sources to finance its expanded efforts at NCD prevention and control. Unable to marshal the huge financial resources required to meet the NCD challenge in a timely manner, the government has recently solicited greater participation from the private sector. That policy goes hand in hand with the belief that the private sector can solve many social problems more efficiently.

There are a number of opportunities for engaging in public-private partnerships (PPPs) in healthcare. These include:

- Engage private information technology (IT) companies to establish bridges between patients and healthcare providers. These companies can also serve as vehicles to teach population health and develop behavioral economics strategies to incentivize healthy behaviors.
- Enlist private employers to help employees guard and enhance their own health. This approach, now

widely used in the United States, includes education, websites, and on-site checkups to catch NCDs early in their etiology.
- Engage the manufacturers of health products (e.g., drugs and medical devices) to meet the growing demand from rising NCDs.
- Partner with the private sector (including for-profit firms) in the *production and delivery* of healthcare. Such partnerships have long existed in the United States and Germany.

In October 2015, at the Fifth Plenum of the 18th CPC Central Committee, the Chinese Communist Party adopted China's 13th Five-Year Plan (2016–2020), which includes promoting the building of a "Healthy China" and deepening health system reform. In this regard, commercial health insurance is to play an important, albeit supplementary, role to the government-run basic health insurance schemes and will include such services as long-term care, healthcare delivery, health management, and elder nursing care.

Private versus Social Goals

Fostering PPPs in healthcare, however, is more challenging than might be imagined. The goals of private enterprises tend to conflict with the social goals of government. Government policy is focused mainly on (1) maintaining and improving the health of the population, (2) protecting individuals and households from the financial risk of ill health, and (3) achieving both in an equitable manner to promote a "harmonious society." Private enterprise – especially investor-owned for-profit enterprise – is not structured to pursue social goals but rather to maximize shareholder wealth. Practically, this means maximizing the difference between *revenues* and *costs* over time, without violating the laws of the land.

This mandate implies that on the production side, management should seek to minimize the cost of production – e.g., by using productive inputs as sparingly as possible and paying for them the lowest prices and wages sufficient to attract an adequate supply of the resources. It is this feature of private enterprise that leads many economists, management consultants, and bureaucrats to believe that private enterprise is more efficient than public enterprise.

On the revenue side, however, the mandate to maximize profits implies that the managers of private enterprises should seek to extract from buyers the maximum revenue possible for the products being sold. In healthcare, this can be done by recommending and delivering more healthcare than is clinically necessary (a phenomenon widely known as supplier-induced demand). It can also be achieved by charging buyers the highest prices possible. That certainly occurs in the United States, where prices in the private healthcare sector tend to be much higher than comparable prices in Europe and Canada.[88]

This latter point is often overlooked by advocates of private enterprise and private markets in healthcare. Buyers – be they patients, government, or private health insurers – care primarily about the prices they are charged for healthcare. It does not help them to know that production costs are minimized or, as economists put it, when production is economically efficient. It is the main reason why in most developed nations the prices for healthcare are not left to the market but instead are regulated by government.

Governments do so because spending on healthcare entails significant opportunity costs. For government spending, these opportunity costs include education of the nation's young at all levels, infrastructure building, including social programs and institutions, and external and internal national security. For households facing health insurance premiums and out-of-pocket outlays on healthcare, the opportunity costs consist of all the other desirable goods and services.

What are the policy implications for China? If the government (a) seeks to enlist private enterprise in healthcare – particularly investor-owned, for-profit enterprises – and (b) wants the healthcare system to achieve the *social goals* for healthcare – that "everyone enjoys" access to needed basic healthcare as a means to achieving a "harmonious society"[89] – it cannot avoid regulating the behavior of private enterprise, especially prices. Switzerland's widely admired private health insurance system is a model in this regard; for example, in Switzerland the Ministry of Health sets drug prices.[90]

Moreover, the government and private information technology companies must combine their efforts to monitor the *quality* of healthcare delivered by all sectors of the health system, including not only the private sector, but the government sector as well. Efforts to do so are now under way in many parts of the developed world. One approach is the development and implementation of evidence-based clinical pathways mentioned above; other means to monitor are now being developed worldwide.[91]

Conclusion

China's top leadership appears to be committed to improving the health of the Chinese population. The country's population health policy is promoted both for humanitarian reasons and because it is recognized that healthy people are an important factor in production that helps drive economic growth.

In the view of many Chinese and international experts, the next few years will be crucial for China to prevent and control NCDs.[92] China has taken many important steps toward meeting its NCD challenge, but much more needs to be done to tackle the enormous obstacles ahead.

First, because of the unequal distribution in China's growing average per capita income, China will have to undertake a sizeable income transfer from the well-to-do population to low-income residents to manage NCDs successfully. This will be politically difficult, even in countries with strong central governments.

Second, although China is far more prosperous now than when it began its economic reforms in 1978, the government is still not in a position to finance a major assault on NCDs without a partnership with the private sector. While there are many opportunities for developing such partnerships, the divergence in goals may make both sides wary of each other. Certainly, the government will need to carefully watch and control the activities of the private sector.

A strong government, such as China's, can be helpful in the war on NCDs. If the rapid eradication of infectious diseases in China's earlier years is any indication, one has good reason to be optimistic about the prospects of China meeting the challenge of NCDs. In the process, China can provide valuable lessons for other low- and middle-income countries.

Appendix: Program Initiatives for NCD Prevention and Control

Health Education and Health Awareness

Health education is a key government tactic in China's NCD prevention and control efforts. Increased health literacy will hopefully foster healthier lifestyle choices and the ability to better manage one's own health. "Health literacy" is defined as accurate knowledge of disease and treatment efficacy, ability to identify appropriate treatment facilities, compliance with provider's post-visit-treatment instructions, and utilization of basic public health services.[93]

There are many community-based health education programs throughout the country today. Results from a pilot program involving 300 diabetic and 300 hypertensive patients carried out at a community health center in Zhengjiang (Jiangsu province) showed that health education and disease management significantly increased patients' knowledge about NCDs and was further associated with marked improvement in these patients' disease biomarkers.[94]

Overall, however, health literacy in China remains low. According to a 2013 report, the overall basic healthcare literacy rate among Beijing residents was only 22.1 percent in 2012.[95] Literacy is higher among urban than rural Beijing residents (23 percent vs. 16.7 percent), among women than men (23.8 percent vs. 20.5 percent), and among younger (20- and 30-year-olds) than older residents (25.6 percent vs. 25 percent).[96]

National Health Awareness Promotion Action Plan 2014–2020

Recognizing that low health literacy may contribute to NCDs, the National Health and Family Planning Commission issued an action plan for the 2014–2020 period to provide the public "evidence-based knowledge."[97] Major NCDs chosen for this plan include cerebral- and cardiovascular disease, diabetes, COPD, and cancer; tobacco control is included as well.

The "Four Reductions" Program

The Four Reductions program is a population-wide NCD risk factor reduction effort. In full swing by 2015, the program targets reductions in four important dietary and lifestyle risk factors: salt, sugar, oil, and alcohol intake. Results have been encouraging: daily salt intake declined 32 percent among urban residents between 1992 and 2010 and by 17 percent among rural residents.

Early Diagnosis and Treatment

Nationwide screening for breast and cervical cancers, diabetes, and hypertension is now part of the public health program. Systematic screenings are detecting millions of new cases, often early on, thus providing opportunities for early intervention. As national systematic screening continues, more cases will be found and treated.

Expansion of Public Health Services and Health Management for High-risk Populations

Diabetes and hypertension management have been part of China's basic public health service package since 2009. Recent initiatives to further strengthen the package include efforts to detect and manage NCDs in high-risk populations: those with hypertension, high blood sugar, high blood lipids, smokers, heavy drinkers, and the overweight and obese. Specific targets have been set for intervention: increase the *management rate* of hypertensive and diabetic patients to 40 percent, increase the *control rate* of these same patients to 60 percent, limit the increase in stroke incidence to 5 percent, and reduce stroke mortality by 5 percent.

Currently 25 million diabetic and 85 million hypertensive patients are under disease management using clinical guidelines and protocols.[98] These represent major increases over 2009, when just 14.8 million hypertensive and 4.6 million diabetic patients were in disease management programs.[99]

Tobacco Control

China is currently the world's largest producer and user of tobacco products. In 2003, China signed the WHO Framework Convention on Tobacco Control, an international treaty signed by 180 parties in response to the global tobacco epidemic. China ratified the treaty in 2005, but has been slow to take strong anti-tobacco actions such as imposing higher cigarette taxes. Cigarette taxes are approximately 32 percent–40 percent of the cost of retail prices in China, far lower than the average of 65 percent–75 percent in developed countries and far lower than the taxes imposed in fellow developing countries such as India (72 percent), Thailand (63 percent), and Vietnam (45 percent).[100] China's reluctance to tackle the rampant use of tobacco is largely financial: the tobacco industry is one of the largest sources of tax revenue for the Chinese government, generating 7 percent–10 percent of the central government's annual revenues.[101] Higher tobacco taxes may actually reduce total government tax revenues.

It was not until March 2011 that a ban on smoking in all interior public places was included in the 12th Five-Year Plan (2011–2015). However, by November of that same year, the ban remained a goal "to be implemented," according to the then health minister Chen Zhu.[102] Nearly a year later in September 2012, China still had no national tobacco control legislation and has not been able to ban tobacco advertisement.

Nevertheless, the times may be changing. On December 29, 2013, the China State Council and the Chinese Communist Party Central Office jointly issued a decree entitled, "Regarding the Notice to Ban Smoking in Public Places Led by the Leadership." The document demonstrated the emphasis on population health by the highest government leadership, lending a significant push toward tobacco control to improve population health.[103]

Patriotic Health Campaign Committee Office

The Patriotic Health Campaign Committee Office (PHCCO) is a nationwide network of "patriotic health campaign committees" led by a central government committee in Beijing under the direct leadership of China's Communist Party and the State Council. The PHCCO's origin dates back to the 1940s and 1950s as the government platform for (a) eradicating disease-causing agents such as flies and rats, (b) preventing infectious diseases (e.g., plague and cholera) through coordinated mass mobilization of the public and the military, and (c) safeguarding and promoting the population's health. The national committee and its network of local committees are vested with the power to mobilize and help the public engage in health promotion activities including health education, environmental and food hygiene, rural drinking water quality improvement, sewage treatment, and infrastructure construction to improve urban hygiene.

The PHCCO national commission is one of three government agencies sponsoring the "national healthy lifestyle for all" initiative. As part of the PHCCO effort, Shanghai's municipal government in 2008 distributed millions of free "salt spoons" – a small spoon of 6-grams capacity, the Chinese recommended daily allowance for salt – to teach families what 6 grams of salt looks like. The initiative won top public praise for the government that year.[104]

Healthy Cities and Healthy Communities

In response to the impact of rapid urbanization on people's health, the WHO inaugurated a global initiative in the early 1980s called Healthy Cities and Healthy Communities. Thousands of cities around the world now participate in this initiative. China's initiative began with the construction of healthy environments for residents of participating cities. For example, Healthy Beijing incorporated health promotion in public policy by addressing the social determinants of health such as smoking, noise, pollution, sewage, waste, traffic and occupational safety.[105] The patriotic health committees now serve as a major vehicle to promote healthy cities throughout China. All regions and cities applying to participate in the initiative are required to establish one or more national NCD prevention and control demonstration areas within their jurisdiction.

Role of Traditional Chinese Medicine

Traditional Chinese Medicine (TCM) has been practiced in China for over 2,000 years and remains highly popular today. The Chinese government considers TCM an important part of its overall NCD prevention and control strategy and program. Every public hospital in China has a TCM department that offers both TCM outpatient visits and inpatient care. There are also general hospitals that offer what is called "integrated medicine" – a combination of both western medicine and TCM in the treatment of chronic diseases such as cardiovascular disease, hypertension, and diabetes. In addition, every township must have at least one TCM clinic or a TCM hospital that offers community-based NCD prevention and control.

As of 2013, China had 505,917 TCM workers, constituting 7.03 percent of its total technical health workforce and 41,906 TCM provider organizations which constituted 4.3 percent of total provider organizations.[106] TCM visits and treatments are covered under the various health insurance schemes.

The WHO and numerous TCM societies in China have been cooperating on various fronts in efforts at NCD prevention and control. This demonstrates the increasing regard in the international community for TCM's role in fighting NCDs. For example, acupuncture, massage, and exercise to counter osteoporosis among the elderly are efficacious complements to western medical treatments. A research project conducted during 2007–2011 at the 2nd Affiliated Hospital of Guangzhou University of Chinese Medicine yielded several studies documenting the value of TCM. The studies showed that for 11 diseases, use of clinical pathways for treatment using both western medicine and TCM (integrated medicine) resulted in greater reduced length of stay, lower costs, and higher satisfaction compared to clinical pathway treatment using western medicine alone.[107]

Since 2013, treating asymptomatic illness through TCM – a central tenet of TCM – has been a part of the basic public health services equalization package. The National Health and Family Planning Commission (NHFPC), in close collaboration with the China State Administration of Traditional Chinese Medicine, has designated pilot sites to study the efficacy of TCM in NCD prevention and control.[108]

International Cooperation

International cooperation has played an important role in China's overall healthcare development and reform. One example is China's decade-long partnership with the Global Fund to Fight AIDS, Tuberculosis, and Malaria. According to Ren Minghui, a high NHFPC official, the partnership has "measurably improved China's management of these three diseases, but it also created benefits that extend far beyond the metrics usually used to assess public health programs."[109] These benefits included "deeper engagement with civil society organizations, stronger public health systems, and the implementation of innovative approaches for disease management."[110] Other examples of fruitful international cooperation include the close collaboration between the US Centers for Disease Control and Prevention (US CDC) and the China CDC. In 2009, the Chinese government specifically requested the US CDC's help to address China's NCD challenge. The two countries have cooperated on a range of NCD projects in China (chronic disease survey, behavioral risk factor surveillance, salt reduction, hypertension control, reduction of tobacco use, injury prevention and control).[111]

Chronic Disease and Nutrition Surveillance in Chinese Residents National Pilot Working Plan (2014)

Diet, hypertension, and tobacco exposure are risk factors that contribute heavily to DALYs in China.[112] Recognition of this close link has prompted China's policy makers to address primary prevention as a means to combat NCDs. One instrument used is field surveys of national nutrition status conducted four times since the founding of the People's Republic in 1949. Another related instrument, begun recently in 2010–2012, is nutrition and health status monitoring. Data from both efforts provide the important basis for subsequent government policies to improve the nutrition of the Chinese population. Finally, the Chinese government conducted four waves of national adult chronic disease and behavioral risk factor monitoring (in 2004, 2007, 2010, and 2013). These field surveys and monitoring are among the most important instruments in China's national adult chronic disease surveillance system.[113] Through them, the Chinese government has gained a basic understanding of NCD prevalence and mortality, NCD risk factors, and the level of nutrition and health among its population. As of 2013, there are 302 monitoring sites throughout China.

However, there are several challenges. The continuing expansion of the scope of work of these national surveys with an ever-growing number of indicators used, as well as a growing number of government agencies involved in conducting the surveys and monitoring, has made coordinated effort more difficult. The different government agencies have used the same set of indicators but different methodologies, which has led to inconsistencies in the survey and monitoring results. That, in turn, has made it difficult for the government agencies involved to interpret the data obtained and make policy decisions based on these data.

A national pilot working plan, The Chronic Disease and Nutrition Surveillance in Chinese Residents National Pilot Working Plan, issued on October 11, 2014, by the NHFPC aims to rectify this problem. The plan will establish coordination mechanisms and standard operating procedures to streamline and unify surveillance processes and methodologies among the multiple government agencies involved in the surveys and monitoring. It will also build a national common information platform for electronic data collection, entry, sharing, and in-depth statistical analyses to form the evidence base for policy making regarding nutrition improvement and NCD prevention and control. Survey staff has received scientific and technical training in preparation of the nationwide field survey to take place in 2015 at the 302 sites. A test run of the 2015 field survey was conducted on April 22–26, 2015, in Jinan, Shangdong, with satisfactory results.

In June 2015, the National Health and Family Planning Commission made public the Chronic Disease and Nutrition Surveillance in Chinese residents 2015 report. The report was based on the latest data from China's Center for Disease Control and Prevention, National Center for Cardiovascular Diseases, National Cancer Center, and the National Bureau of Statistics, and produced using sophisticated statistical methodology such as weighted averages and meta analyses, followed by multiple rigorous reviews by both domestic and international expert agencies to insure the report's scientific validity.

Notes

1. World Bank. 2015. *World Development Indicators Database*. Data updated on April 14, 2015. Available online at: http://data.worldbank .org/indicator/NY.GDP.PCAP.PP.CD?order=w bapi_data_value_2014+wbapi_data_value+wba pi_data_value-last&sort=desc. Accessed on November 9, 2015.

2. United Nations Department of Economic and Social Affairs Population Division. 2015. *World Population Prospects the 2015 Revision: Key Findings and Advance Tables*. Available online at: http://esa.un.org/unpd/wpp/Publications/Files/ Key_Findings_WPP_2015.pdf. Accessed on July 3, 2015.

3. OECD. 2015. OECD Economic Surveys: China. Available online at: www.oecd.org/eco/surveys/ China-2015-overview.pdf. Accessed on July 8, 2015.

4. Feng Pan. 2011. "Health Minister Chen Zhu: Chronic Disease Becoming the Biggest Health Challenge," ScienceNet.cn. June 6, 2011. Available online at: http://news.sciencenet.cn /htmlnews/2011/6/248179.shtm. Accessed on July 20, 2015.

5. Chinese Center for Disease Control and Prevention (China CDC). 2012. *China National Plan for NCD Prevention and Treatment (2012–2015)*. Available online at: www.chinacdc.cn/en/ne/ 201207/t20120725_64430.html. Accessed on November 30, 2015.

6. Xinhua. 2015. *Chronic Disease on Rise in China: Health Survey*, June 30, 2015. Available online at: www.china.org.cn/china/

Off_the_Wire/2015-06/30/content_35946728
.htm. Accessed on July 26, 2015. Source of the
300 million statistic: Author's meeting with Yu
Wang, director-general, China CDC,
March 19, 2015. Beijing, China.

7. Yu Xu, Limin Wang, Jiang He et al. (China
Noncommunicable Disease Surveillance
Group 2010). 2013. "Prevalence and Control
of Diabetes in Chinese Adults," *JAMA*
September 4 310(9):948–959. Available online
at: www.ncbi.nlm.nih.gov/pubmed/24002281.
Accessed on July 26, 2015.

8. David E. Bloom, Elizabeth T. Cafiero, Mark
E. McGovern et al. 2013. "The Economic
Impact of Non-Communicable Disease in
China and India: Estimates, Projections, and
Comparisons," National Bureau of Economic
Research Working Paper 19335. Available
online at: www.nber.org/papers/w19335.
Accessed on July 22, 2015.

9. NHFPC of the People's Republic of China.
2013. China Health Statistics Yearbook 2013.

10. Lucy Hornby. 2015. "China Migration: Dying
for Land. Financial Times Series on China
Society." Available online at: https://next.ft
.com/33ae0866-3098-11e5-91ac-a5e17d9b4cff.
Accessed on July 27, 2015.

11. See, for example, Peng Gong, Song Liang,
Elizabeth J. Carlton et al. 2012. "Urbanisation
and Health in China," *The Lancet* 379(9818):
843–852. Available online at: www.thelancet
.com/journals/lancet/article/PIIS0140-6736%
2811%2961878-3/abstract. Accessed on July
27, 2015.

12. The survey sample size was 48,704 persons,
including 55.2 percent male and 44.8 percent
female respondents. The sample covered workers in manufacturing, retail, hotel and food
services, construction, and other sectors.
The population sampled was 18–59 years of
age in 170 counties and districts in the 31
provinces and Xinjiang Production and
Construction Military Corps.

13. Chinese Center for Disease Control and
Prevention (China CDC). 2014. *Main
Findings of the 2012 Survey on Chronic
Disease and Risk Factors among Migrant
Workers in China*. Briefing, December 29,
2014.

14. The "control rate" is defined as when the disease
progression is halted or slowed; ideally there is
no evidence of end-organ damage such as reti-
nopathy or kidney failure. Control is achieved
through control of blood cholesterol, lipids, and
overweight-obesity, which are common in
patients with type 2 diabetes and which play
important roles in disease progression. For
more on overall control of type 2 diabetes, see
Mark W. Stolar. 2010. "Defining and Achieving
Treatment Success in Patients with Type 2
Diabetes Mellitux," *Mayo Clin Proc* 85(12
Suppl): S50–S59. Available online at: www
.ncbi.nlm.nih.gov/pmc/articles/PMC2996162/.
Accessed on November 3, 2015.

15. Gonghuan Yang, Yu Wang, Yixin Zeng et al.
2013. "Rapid Health Transition in China,
1990–2010: Findings from the Global Burden
of Disease Study 2010," *The Lancet* 381(9882):
1987–2015. Available online at: www
.thelancet.com/journals/lancet/issue/vol381no
9882/PIIS0140-6736(13)X6028-3. Accessed
on July 20, 2015.

16. Chinese Center for Disease Control and
Prevention. 2012. *China National Plan for
NCD Prevention and Treatment (2012–2015)*.
Xinhua. 2015. "Chronic Disease on Rise in
China."

17. World Health Organization. 2014.
*Noncommunicable Diseases (NCD) Country
Profiles*. Available online at: www.who.int
/nmh/countries/en/. Accessed on August 2,
2015.

18. China Daily. 2015. "Chronic Disease Takes
High Toll on China," January 20. Based on
findings in WHO Global Status Report on
Noncommunicable Diseases 2014. Available
online at: www.china.org.cn/china/2015-01/
20/content_34602999.htm. Accessed on
August 3, 2015.

19. Zhu Chen. 2011. "China's Response to NCDs."
Keynote presentation to the 7th Sino-US
Conference on Medicine in the Twenty-first
Century. La Jolla, California. September 23,
2011.

20. Xinhua. 2015. "Chronic Disease on Rise in China."

21. NHFPC of the People's Republic of China. 2013. *China Health Statistics Yearbook 2012*. Figures based on author's calculations using data on household incomes in Appendix 1-6-1 Urban and Rural Household Incomes.

22. National Health and Family Planning Commission. 2015. *2014 Report on Nutrition and Chronic Disease in Chinese Residents.*

23. China National Health Development Research Center. 2012. *Strategies for Chronic Non-communicable Disease Control and Prevention in China.*

24. Zhu Chen, Jin-Nan Wang, Guo-Xia Ma et al. 2013. "China Tackles the Health Effects of Air Pollution," *The Lancet* 383(9909): 1559–1960. Available online at: www.thelancet.com/journals/lancet/article/PIIS0140-6736(13)62064-4/fulltext. Accessed on August 5, 2015. It is significant that the lead author of the *Lancet* report was the former minister of health and currently vice chairman of the National People's Congress, China's highest legislative body.

25. Author's meeting with Maigeng Zhou, deputy director of the NCD Center, China CDC. March 20, 2015. Beijing, China.

26. Yang et al. 2013. "Rapid Health Transition in China, 1990–2010."

27. Author's meeting with Yu Wang, director-general, China CDC. March 19, 2015. Beijing, China.

28. Chen. 2011. "China's Response to NCDs."

29. Tsung-Mei Cheng. 2012. "Early Results of China's Historic Health Reforms: The View from Minister Chen Zhu," *Health Affairs* 31 (11): 2536–2544. Available online at: http://content.healthaffairs.org/content/31/11/2536.full.pdf+html. Accessed on July 20, 2015.

30. Liming Lee. 2004. "The Current State of Public Health in China," *Annual Review of Public Health 2004* 25:327–339. Available online at: www.annualreviews.org/doi/pdf/10.1146/annurev.publhealth.25.101802.123116. Accessed on July 22, 2015.

31. OECD. 2015. *OECD Economic Surveys: China 2015*. Available online at: www.oecd.org/eco/surveys/China-2015-overview.pdf. Accessed on July 3, 2015.

32. Martin J. Prince, Fan Wu, Yanfei Guo et al. 2015. "The Burden of Disease in Older People and Implications for Health Policy and Practice," *The Lancet* 385(9967): 549–562. Available online at: www.thelancet.com/pdfs/journals/lancet/PIIS0140-6736(14)61347-7.pdf. Accessed on July 8, 2015.

33. National Institute on Aging, U.S. Department of Health and Human Services. 2011. *Global Health and Aging, October 2011*. Figure 2. Available online at: https://d2cauhfh6h4x0p.cloudfront.net/s3fs-public/global_health_and_aging.pdf. Accessed on November 30, 2015.

34. Prince et al. 2015. "The Burden of Disease in Older People and Implications for Health Policy and Practice."

35. China National Health Development Research Center. 2012. *Report on Cost Accounting for Chronic Disease Health Care Expenditure and Financing Strategies.*

36. Janet Currie and Tom Vogl. 2012. "Early-life Health and Adult Circumstances in Developing Countries," National Bureau of Economic Research Working Paper 18371. Available online at: www.nber.org/papers/w18371. Accessed on July 28, 2015. Subgroup on Maternal and Child Nutrition (SMCN). 2011. *The Influence of Maternal, Fetal and Child Nutrition on the Development of Chronic Diseases in Later Life*. London: TSO (The Stationary Office). Available online at: www.gov.uk/government/uploads/system/uploads/attachment_data/file/339325/SACN_Early_Life_Nutrition_Report.pdf. Accessed on August 26, 2016.

37. Janet Curry and Joshua Goodman. 2010. "Parental Socioeconomic Status, Child Health, and Human Capital," *International Encyclopedia of Education* (Third Edition): 253–259. Available online at: www.sciencedirect.com/science/article/pii/B9780080448947012689. Accessed on July 26, 2015.

38. Bloom et al. 2013. "The Economic Impact of Non-Communicable Disease in China and India."

39. World Health Organization and World Economic Forum. 2011. "From Burden to 'Best Buys': Reducing the Economic Impact of Non-Communicable Diseases in Low- and Middle-Income Countries." World Economic Forum. Cologny/Geneva, Switzerland. Available online at: http://apps.who.int/medicinedocs/documents/s18804en/s18804en.pdf. Accessed on August 1, 2015.

40. OECD and World Health Organization. 2014. *Health at a Glance: Asia/Pacific 2014; Measuring Progress towards Universal Health Coverage.* November 27, 2014. Available online at: www.oecd.org/health/health-at-a-glance-asia-pacific-23054964.htm. Accessed on July 30, 2015.

41. China National Health Development Research Center. 2012. *Report on Cost Accounting for Chronic Disease Health Care Expenditure and Financing Strategies.*

42. Ibid.

43. Ibid.

44. Author's meetings with Yang Hongwei, vice director-general of the China National Health Development Research Center; officials at the National Health and Family Planning Commission; and Chen Zhu. March 19 and 20, 2015. Beijing, China.

45. Author's meeting with Chen Zhu, vice chairman, China National People's Congress and former minister of health, China. March 19, 2015. Beijing, China.

46. China National Health Development Research Center. 2012. *Report on Cost Accounting for Chronic Disease Health Care Expenditure and Financing Strategies.*

47. Xinhua. 2012. "Report Predicts Rapid Chronic Disease Growth in China," August 11, 2012. Available online at: www.china.org.cn/china/2012-08/11/content_26205246.htm. Accessed on March 12, 2015.

48. According to the WHO,

    one DALY can be thought of as one lost year of "healthy" life. The sum of these DALYs across the population, or the burden of disease, can be thought of as a measurement of the gap between current health status and an ideal health situation where the entire population lives to an advanced age, free of disease and disability. DALYs for a disease or health condition are calculated as the sum of the Years of Life Lost (YLL) due to premature mortality in the population and the Years Lost due to Disability (YLD) for people living with the health condition or its consequences.

    Available online at: www.who.int/healthinfo/global_burden_disease/metrics_daly/en/. Accessed on October 10, 2015.

49. China National Health Development Research Center. 2012. *Report on Cost Accounting for Chronic Disease Health Care Expenditure and Financing Strategies.*

50. Ibid.

51. World Health Organization. 2014. *Global Status Report on Noncommunicable Diseases 2014.* Available online at: http://apps.who.int/iris/bitstream/10665/148114/1/9789241564854_eng.pdf?ua=1. Accessed on July 20, 2015.

52. World Health Organization and World Economic Forum. 2011. *From Burden to "Best Buys": Reducing the Economic Impact of Non-Communicable Diseases in Low- and Middle-Income Countries.* Available online at: http://apps.who.int/medicinedocs/documents/s18804en/s18804en.pdf. Accessed on July 22, 2015.

53. Bloom et al. 2013. "The Economic Impact of Non-Communicable Disease in China and India." Dele Abegunde and Anderson Stanciole. 2006. *An Estimation of the Economic Impact of Chronic Noncommunicable Diseases in Selected Countries.* World Health Organization, Department of Chronic Diseases and Health Promotion (CHP). Available online at: www.who.int/chp.

54. David E. Bloom, Elizabeth T. Cafiero-Fonseca, Mark E. McGovern et al. 2014. "The Macroeconomic Impact of Non-Communicable Disease in China and India: Estimates, Projections, and Comparisons," *The Journal of the Economics of Aging* 4(December): 100–111. Available online at: www.sciencedirect.com/science/article/pii/S2212828X14000206. Accessed on July 26, 2015.

55. Data based on The World Bank. GDP (current US$) for China 2014. Available online at: http://data.worldbank.org/indicator/NY.GDP .MKTP.CD. Accessed on August 1, 2015.

56. Bloom et al. 2014. "The Macroeconomic Impact of Non-Communicable Disease in China and India."

57. For more on the limitations of the EPIC model, see Bloom et al. 2014. "The Macroeconomic Impact of Non-Communicable Disease in China and India."

58. China CDC, Ministry of Health. 2006. *Report on Chronic Disease in China.* Available online at: www.chinacdc.cn/jdydc/200605/P02006051232 17538575667461530.pdf. Accessed on July 27, 2015.

59. Lee. 2004. "The Current State of Public Health in China."

60. Author's meeting with Guanglin Li, deputy director, Division of Noncommunicable Disease Prevention and Control, Bureau of Disease Prevention and Control, National Health and Family Planning Commission. March 20, 2015. Beijing, China.

61. See China CDC, Ministry of Health. 2006. *Report on Chronic Disease in China.*

62. Chinese Center for Disease Control and Prevention. 2012. *China National Plan for NCD Prevention and Treatment (2012–2015).*

63. The State Council. 2014. *Framework for Food and Nutrition Development for Chinese Residents (2014–2020).*

64. Ibid.

65. See, for example, Tiina Laatikainen, Julia Critchley, Erkki Vartiainen et al. 2005. "Explaining the Decline in Coronary Heart Disease in Finland between 1982 and 1997," *Am. J. Epidemiol* 162(8): 764–773. Available online at: http://aje.oxfordjournals.org/content/ 162/8/764.full. Accessed on July 5, 2015.

66. "Beijing Trained 10,000 Healthy Lifestyle Advisors." *Beijing Daily.* Available online at: www.gov.cn 2015-03-13. Accessed on November 30, 2015.

67. Yuan Li, Juan Zhang, Jing-Lei Wang et al. 2014. "Effects of the National Healthy Lifestyle for All Campaign on China's NCD

Prevention and Control," *China J Prev Med* 48 (8): 741–743.

68. Li et al. 2014. "Effects of the National Healthy Lifestyle for All Campaign on China's NCD Prevention and Control."

69. Ibid.

70. Author's meeting with Yuan Li, associate professor at the Division of NCD Control and Community Health, China CDC. March 20, 2015. Beijing, China.

71. Author's meeting with Guanglin Li, Deputy Director, Division of Noncommunicable Disease Prevention and Control, Bureau of Disease Prevention and Control, National Health and Family Planning Commission. March 20, 2015. Beijing, China.

72. Ibid.

73. Author's meeting with Yu Wang, director-general, China CDC. March 19, 2015. Beijing, China.

74. China National Health Development Research Center. 2012. *Strategies for Chronic Non-communicable Disease Control and Prevention in China.*

75. Author's meeting with Zhu Chen, vice chairman, China National People's Congress, and former minister of health, March 19, 2015. Beijing, China.

76. China National Health Development Research Center. 2012. *Strategies for Healthcare Expenditure and Financing for Chronic Disease.*

77. Ibid.

78. Ibid.

79. For more on China's progress on health workforce supplies through 2012, see Cheng. 2012. "Early Results of China's Historic Health Reforms." Available online at: http://content .healthaffairs.org/content/31/11/2536.full.pdf +html. Accessed on August 6, 2015.

80. Author's meeting with Zhu Chen, vice chairman, China National People's Congress, and former minister of health, March 19, 2015. Beijing, China.

81. Cheng. 2012. "Early Results of China's Historic Health Reforms."

82. For more on the role of HTA on healthcare costs, quality, and outcomes in China's rural

public hospitals, see Tsung-Mei Cheng. 2013. "A Pilot Project Using Evidence-Based Clinical Pathways and Payment Reform in China's Rural Public Hospitals Shows Early Success," *Health Affairs* 32(5): 1–11. Available online at: http://content.healthaffairs.org/content/early/2013/04/01/hlthaff.2012.0640.full.html. Accessed on August 5, 2015.

83. China National Health Development Research Center. 2012. *Strategies for Healthcare Expenditure and Financing for Chronic Disease.*

84. Keqiang Li, Premier, The State Council, People's Republic of China. 2015. *Premier's Government Work Report to the 12th National People's Congress 3rd Plenary. March 5, 2015.*

85. China National Health Development Research Center. 2012. *Strategies for Chronic Non-communicable Disease Control and Prevention in China.*

86. Author's meeting with Guanglin Li, deputy director, Division of Noncommunicable Disease Prevention and Control, Bureau of Disease Prevention and Control, National Health and Family Planning Commission. March 20, 2015. Beijing, China.

87. This section draws on earlier work, mainly by Tsung-Mei Cheng and Uwe Reinhardt. 2012. "Perspective on the Appropriate Role of the Private Sector in Meeting Health Care Needs," in Benedict Clements, David Coady, and Sanjeev Gupta (Eds.), *The Economics of Public Health Care Reform in Advanced and Emerging Economies* (Washington, DC: International Monetary Fund, 2012): chapter 5. Available online at: www.imf.org/external/pubs/ft/books/2012/health/healthcare.pdf. Accessed on August 9, 2015.

88. Gerard F. Anderson, Uwe E. Reinhardt, Peter S. Hussey et al . 2003. "It's the Prices, Stupid: Why the United States Is So Different from Other Countries," *Health Affairs* 22(3): 89–105. Available online at: http://content.healthaffairs.org/content/22/3/89.full.pdf. Accessed on August 16, 2015. See also Miriam J. Laugesen and Sherry A. Glied.

2011. "Higher Fees Paid to US Physicians Drive Higher Spending for Physician Services Compared to Other Countries," *Health Affairs* 30(9): 1647–1656. Available online at: http://content.healthaffairs.org/content/30/9/1647.abstract. Accessed on August 16, 2015.

89. Tsung-Mei Cheng. 2008. "China's Latest Health Reforms: A Conversation with Chinese Health Minister Chen Zhu," *Health Affairs* 27(4): 1103–1110. Available online at: http://content.healthaffairs.org/content/27/4/1103.abstract. Accessed on August 20, 2015.

90. Tsung-Mei Cheng. 2010. "Understanding the 'Swiss Watch' Function of Switzerland's Health System," *Health Affair* 29(8): 1442–1451. Available online at: http://content.healthaffairs.org/content/29/8/1442.full.pdf+html. Accessed on August 6, 2015.

91. See, for example, a list of the health watchdogs and regulators in the UK National Health Service and their functions in the NHS Health Watchdogs and Authorities. Available online at: www.nhs.uk/NHSEngland/thenhs/healthregulators/Pages/health-watchdogs-explained.aspx. Accessed on August 15, 2015. Another example is Outcome-Based Quality Monitoring (OBQM) Centers for Medicare and Medicaid, U.S. Department of Health and Human Services. 2010. *Outcome-Based Quality Monitoring (OBQM) Manual.* Available online at: www.cms.gov/Medicare/Quality-Initiatives-Patient-Assessment-Instruments/HomeHealthQualityInits/Downloads/HHQIOBQMManual.pdf. Accessed on August 15, 2015.

92. China National Health Development Research Center. 2012. *Strategies for Chronic Non-communicable Disease Control and Prevention in China.*

93. Beijing Municipal Government. 2014. *Health Care and Population Health in Beijing 2013.*

94. Zhi-Xia Jia. Jiangsu Zhengjiang. China NCD Management Net (NCD.ORG.CN). 2015. *Standardized NCD Management, Happy NCD Patients.*

95. Beijing Municipal Government. 2014. *Health Care and Population Health in Beijing 2013.*
96. Ibid.
97. Mao Qunan: 2014. "Fully Realizing the Strategic Role of Health Education and Health Promotion in NCD Prevention and Control," Address by Mao Qunan, director-general, Department of Communications, National Health and Family Planning Commission to the 2014 China National Conference on NCD Management. Beijing, China. July 4, 2014.
98. Author's meeting with Guanglin Li, deputy director, Division of Noncommunicable Disease Prevention and Control, Bureau of Disease Prevention and Control, National Health and Family Planning Commission. March 20, 2015. Beijing, China.
99. Chen. 2011. "China's Response to NCDs."
100. China National Health Development Research Center. 2012. *Strategies for Healthcare Expenditure and Financing for Chronic Disease.*
101. Cheng Li. 2012. *The Political Mapping of China's Tobacco Industry and Anti-Smoking Campaign* (Washington, DC: John L. Thornton Center at Brookings. The Brookings Institutions). Available online at: www.brookings.edu/research/papers/2012/10/25-china-tobacco-li.
102. Chen. 2011. "China's Response to NCDs."
103. National Health and Family Planning Commission. 2014. *Progress on China's Tobacco Control in Accordance with Treaty Agreement.*
104. Author's meeting with Chen Zhu, vice chairman, China National People's Congress and former minister of health. March 19, 2015. Beijing, China.
105. Chen. 2011. "China's Response to NCDs."
106. State Administration of Traditional Chinese Medicine. 2013. *2013 China Statistical Yearbook of Chinese Medicine.*
107. Author's personal email communication with Darong Wu, professor, Department of Clinical Epidemiology; director, Program for Outcome Assessment in TCM, Department of Clinical Epidemiology; and physician, Internal Medicine of Traditional Chinese Medicine, 2nd Affiliated Hospital of Guangzhou University of Chinese Medicine, and Guangdong Provincial Hospital of Chinese Medicine, Guangzhou, China. November 5, 2015. The 11 diseases include chronic heart failure, peripheral neuropathy (a complication of diabetes), chronic renal failure, ulcerative colitis, acute ischemic stroke, acute myocardial infarction, sudden hearing loss, vertebral artery type of cervical spondylosis, leiomyoma of uterus, herpes zoster, and hyperplasia of mammary glands.
108. Author's meeting with Guanglin Li, deputy director, Division of Noncommunicable Disease Prevention and Control, Bureau of Disease Prevention and Control, National Health and Family Planning Commission. March 20, 2015. Beijing, China.
109. Minghui Ren, Fabio Scano, Catherine Sozi et al. 2015. "The Global Fund in China: Success beyond the Numbers," *Lancet Global Health* 3 (2):e75–e77. Available online at: www.thelancet.com/pdfs/journals/langlo/PIIS2214-109X%2814%2970366-3.pdf. Accessed on July 20, 2015.
110. Ren et al. 2015. "The Global Fund in China."
111. U.S. Centers for Disease Control and Prevention Center for Global Health. 2011. *U.S. CDC in China: Healthy People in a Healthy China. 2010–2011 Annual Report.*
112. Yang et al. 2013. "Rapid Health Transition in China, 1990–2010."
113. China CDC. 2015. *Chinese Adult Chronic Disease and Health Survey 2015 First Phase Successfully Completed.*

PART III

Healthcare Providers

CHAPTER 7

China's Physician and Nurse Workforce

LAWTON ROBERT BURNS

Introduction

Does China have a medical "profession"? Western dictionaries define a profession as a calling requiring specialized knowledge obtained through long and intensive academic training. Medical sociologists in the West define a profession as a group of practitioners who control the content of their work and resist outside efforts to do so. Others describe professionals in terms of traits such as honesty, competence, integrity, ethics, altruism, duty, and accountability.

It is not clear that China's physicians can be accurately described using any of these definitions. The training of Chinese physicians is variable in length and has been (until recently) more apprentice-based than academic; the practice environment has been more hierarchical than collegial and autonomous; and Chinese physicians have induced demand to increase their incomes. During much of the twentieth century, the Chinese language reportedly contained no synonym for "profession," "professional," or "professionalism." In recent years, the medical community has initiated efforts to "professionalize," and the government has begun to encourage greater occupational mobility and adoption of ethical practices. At the same time, the Chinese public has expressed growing distrust of physicians through verbal disputes and physical attacks.

China has a large community of physicians, trained according to both allopathic and traditional medicine standards. Chinese physicians differ from their western counterparts on several dimensions: (a) many Chinese physicians practice both styles of medicine; (b) the medical population slightly outnumbers the nursing population, resulting in greater reliance on the former with fewer opportunities for substitution using the latter; (c) most Chinese physicians are already vertically integrated with and employed by specific hospitals; (d) because the practice models and business models of China's physicians are closely intertwined with China's hospital industry, there is greater potential to align the interests and activities of the two major providers of healthcare in the country. This chapter examines these developments.

Milestones in the History of Allopathic Medicine

Pre-revolutionary China

Traditional Chinese medicine (TCM) has existed for thousands of years. Initially based on apprenticeship, formal training commenced in the seventh century A.D. during the Tang Dynasty under the auspices of the Imperial Medical Bureau, which trained physicians for the imperial court.[1] Medical education, like Chinese education in general, was rooted in Confucianism and the associated ethics of morality, self-control, and respect for human life.[2]

TCM was widely used due to several factors: it was the only type of medicine available, it was inexpensive, and it was widely perceived by the population to be efficacious. TCM was seriously challenged in the nineteenth and twentieth centuries by western medicine by virtue of having a competitor that had relatively higher perceived efficacy in the eyes of coastal city inhabitants exposed to it. This competitive threat was limited in two ways, however: (1) there were few practitioners of western medicine compared to the mass of TCM providers; and (2) in contrast to western medicine, the population believed that TCM treated the causes of disease rather than the symptoms. The competitive threat was also blunted by a third factor: efforts by western-leaning Chinese physicians to integrate modern medicine into TCM practice.

Western missionary societies employed apprenticeship models to train medical aides to staff mission hospitals and introduce allopathic medicine into China in the first half of the nineteenth century. The first missionary hospital was established in 1834 at Guangzhou, followed by the establishment of the first western medical school in 1866 at the Canton Medical School and the first university-based medical school at St. John's University in Shanghai in 1880. The Chinese government began to establish its own western and TCM medical schools thereafter.[3] By 1914, the central government had two medical schools: Peking Medical Special College and Peiyang Military Medical College (Tientsin); several provinces operated their own schools as well.[4]

Western incursions exposed the primitive state of domestic training in TCM, and by contrast, the modern revolution in germ theory and the curative effects of the allopathic approach. Those seeking to upgrade Chinese education advocated the western training model. During the late nineteenth century, the government sent many Chinese abroad to study medicine who returned zealous to upgrade the state of medical training in China. Formal medical school programs began to supplant apprenticeship as the primary route for physician training. China's first president under the republic, Sun Yat-Sen, was born in China but grew up in Hawaii. Upon returning to China, he trained in western medicine at the Hong Kong College of Medicine for Chinese, established by the London Missionary Society in 1887. Following the establishment of the republic in 1912, a spate of government (e.g., military), missionary, and private medical colleges opened. Several of these floundered as the republic descended into conflicts between the national government and regional warlords (1912–1927).

In 1914, the Rockefeller Foundation surveyed the state of health and medical education in China. Many colleges followed a Japanese model of vocational training in short-term programs (accepting middle-school graduates), largely due to Japanese incursions in northern China in prior years. In 1917, the Rockefeller Foundation established the nation's

first modern allopathic medical school at Peking Union Medical College (PUMC), purchased from the London Missionary Society in 1915. The foundation sought to upgrade medical education and improve the practice of medicine, much in the manner of the Carnegie Foundation's effort to improve US medical education via the Flexner reforms. PUMC adopted the western model of laboratory-based clinical training, encompassing both research and teaching.[5] The PUMC model replaced the missionary model of biomedical education and served as a training ground for staff in other medical colleges.

Western incursions not only introduced allopathic training. Along with the industrialization of the eastern coastal cities, these incursions exposed the population to contagions and laid bare the inability of TCM practice to deal with these problems. With the help of western-trained physicians, the Nationalist government began initiatives to improve public health, including "mass health campaigns" (e.g., anti-cholera campaign in Fuzhou in 1920) and midwifery training in basic hygiene, that were to serve as the basis for Maoist reforms decades later in the 1950s.[6]

The formation of the Nationalist government in 1927–1928 led to more central coordination of medical education reform. The government organized ministries of education and health, both staffed by those seeking to reform China's system. The two ministries appointed a Committee on Medical Education (CME) to set up a string of national university medical colleges and upgrade training standards, all based on the western biomedical model. In part, this effort served to counteract the closure of approximately one-third of the country's medical colleges during the latter years of government conflict with the warlords.

The challenge was monumental. A committee-sponsored report found only 4,000–5,000 physicians trained in biomedical medicine, compared with 1.2 million TCM practitioners.[7] The demand for biomedical training was low. In 1930, there were only 3,500 students in 24 colleges listed by the committee. The low attendance reflected the high cost of training, the high entrance requirements, and the meager training resources (e.g., staff, equipment). Demand for the services of western physicians was concentrated primarily in the eastern coastal cities; after nearly a century of western medical training, few Chinese knew of or valued the biomedical approach.

To deal with this situation, the committee report recommended the continued use of the vocational schools and expanded enrollment in them to supplement the western institutions. It further advised that western-trained practitioners not be sent to compete with traditional practitioners in rural China, noting that biomedical practices were creeping into the training and practice of TCM.[8]

The Ministry of Health, dominated by those with western training, did not view the vocational schools or the traditional practitioners favorably. Both of the latter lacked a foundation in laboratory science. Indeed, the period saw efforts to undermine TCM (including a 1929 legislative proposal, "A Case for the Abolishment of Old Medicine to Thoroughly Eliminate Public Health Obstacles"), based on the belief that TCM was rife with "charlatan, shamanic, and geomancing ways."[9] The legislation sought to restrict the practice of TCM, the establishment of TCM schools, and advertisement of TCM products. The legislative thrust proved unfruitful due to protests by TCM practitioners who enjoyed considerable public support (due to their low cost, easy access, and ease of use) in the form of street protests, as well as to the shortage of allopathic physicians. Instead, the Ministry of Health reached an accommodation by continuing with China's two-tier system of medical education: allopathic western training and vocational (i.e., short term) training. In 1930, the government established a Central College of Chinese Medicine.

During China's civil war (1927–1949), Mao maintained an ambivalent attitude toward TCM. On the one hand, he believed the TCM practitioners were shamans (as portrayed in the 1929 legislative proposal) that should be replaced by village public health stations. On the other hand, Mao's rural base included TCM practitioners who served as a foil against the urban-based, bourgeois, and western allopathic practitioners. Mao used this latter approach for political purposes after the founding of the People's Republic to distinguish the Chinese model of socialism from the USSR model, as well as to build self-reliance and patriotic fervor among the population to support his mass campaigns.[10]

The war with Japan and the Japanese occupation (1931–1945) disrupted the operations of most of the country's medical, pharmacy, and dental schools; some closed, others were destroyed, and still others were forced to relocate to western China. The wartime hardships included infectious disease outbreaks, famine and starvation, and rapid inflation. The western biomedical approach offered two avenues to deal with these hardships: the curative practices offered in hospitals, and the prevention and health promotion advocated in public health. The former was reactive, expensive, slow, and resisted by the population; the latter was proactive, affordable, and more aligned with Chinese culture. The latter also offered one avenue to counteract contagion and improve the health status of the population, particularly in its emphasis on hygiene and prevention. The biomedical approach was also better suited than TCM to deal with the soldiers and civilians wounded in the conflict.[11] Ironically, graduates of China's more elite medical schools championed the prevention and public health approach.

In this manner, the western model of public health diffused to China's central and western regions. This diffusion was abetted in several ways. Starting in 1927, China's Red Army introduced training programs to deal with injury and disease among their soldiers and local populations. As part of these programs, they developed preventive health services and promoted public hygiene. A number of the medical personnel came from the lower-tier vocational medical colleges set up by the Japanese in northern China. Other medical volunteers joined the Red Army effort from foreign countries. Dr. Norman Bethune, a Canadian surgeon and member of the Canadian Communist Party, served in the Spanish Civil War and then traveled to China during 1938–1939. He treated Red Army soldiers, died from blood poisoning, and was later lionized by Mao as an example of medical professionalism and public service.

The public health approach was financially supported by the Rockefeller Foundation, endorsed by the Nationalist government in 1935 as "State Medicine," and served as a cost-effective substitute for the more expensive hospital-based practice in the eastern coastal cities. State Medicine was an approach developed earlier in Europe to deal with the ravages of World War I and imported to China by PUMC leaders. During the 1930s, the new national medical colleges trained thousands of students in public health and prevention. An experimental school to demonstrate the training in State Medicine was established in 1937 in Jiangxi Province. All of these developments were consistent with China's cultural heritage of educational training in support of public service.

In the period leading up to the founding of the People's Republic of China (PRC) in 1949, medicine was based on a private practice, fee-for-service model in which physicians were autonomous solo practitioners. The high level of inflation during this turbulent period induced many medical college faculty to moonlight as private practitioners, serve paying patients, apply curative practices ("medical relief," as opposed to public health), or leave the medical education arena altogether.

Medical school training and resources were further disrupted. Schools that had been geographically displaced earlier sought to relocate back to their original sites, only to find destroyed buildings and no equipment. Now there were no longer missionary societies and foundations to support the rebuilding of infrastructure. In this vacuum, public health and prevention (State Medicine) easily supplanted biomedical training based on curative hospital-based care. While this was the only avenue that was affordable, it was perhaps the better avenue to deal with the aftermath of poverty and disease in the war-ravaged country.

The total number of medical schools remained low: 35 colleges with 5,300 students. In the two years immediately after the Japanese surrender, the Ministry of Education increased the number to 42 schools with 9,000 students. Of these students, roughly half attended 21 national medical colleges, another cohort attended 8 vocational and provincial schools, while the remainder attended 13 private and missionary schools. Already, the shift away from foreign-dominated schools was apparent. Modern biomedical education was now largely in the hands of various levels of Chinese government. The total number of western-trained practitioners remained small, however, numbering anywhere from 40,000 to 85,000 doctors.[12]

Post-revolutionary China: 1949–1975

The public health model established in the prior two decades became institutionalized under Mao and the Communist Party. It now also became infused with the political ideology of public service by physicians and the goal of improving public satisfaction in rural areas (as opposed to physical healing through restorative services offered in urban areas).[13] Mao nevertheless retained TCM as a counterweight to western medicine for two reasons: to distinctly brand China's socialist system with third-world approaches to medicine and to reduce Chinese dependence on Soviet medical goods such as drugs and equipment. TCM herbal products and treatments (e.g., acupuncture) were inexpensive and easily available from domestic suppliers. Along with TCM, public health and prevention became mainstays of medical education and delivery in rural China.

Following the revolution, Mao adopted a Soviet model for the Chinese economy. By 1953, state enterprises had become the major employers of the urban population; by 1956, the private sector had been eliminated.[14] This general economic transformation extended to healthcare training and delivery as well. The early five-year plans included developing healthcare infrastructure to increase the supply of practitioners. Medical schools were established as separate universities; the handful of private medical schools (e.g., PUMC) were nationalized. In contrast to the traditional university-based curriculum of five to six years training, medical education was now shortened in some schools to three-year vocational (polytechnic school) programs.

The Ministry of Health (MOH) promoted the development of medical universities, public hospitals, and public health services – all of which were entirely lacking. He Cheng, the director of the General Medical Department in the Red Army, was appointed the first director of the MOH in 1949. Cheng was a western-trained physician who favored the western education model and sought to professionalize China's medical community.[15] This included establishment of educational institutions, the imposition of licensing requirements, and the issuance of regulations on the infrastructure required in private medical clinics (e.g., separate waiting and examination rooms, patient record keeping, labeling of drugs).

He Cheng also established "improvement schools" that traditional practitioners were required to attend to gain knowledge of basic anatomy and physiology, pass an examination, and thereby receive a license to continue practice. Many of these practitioners naturally failed the examination. He Cheng utilized many TCM practitioners in MOH public health campaigns to improve sanitation and hygiene, as well as in frontline efforts to prevent infectious diseases using vaccinations and education. The TCM practitioners were thus relegated to a less prestigious role of public health doctor.

The MOH efforts ran counter to Mao's historical alliance with rural-based practitioners during the pre-revolutionary period, the central role they played in his mass campaigns, and their role in caring for the largely rural population in order to maintain worker health and social harmony. During the early 1950s, Mao began to shift away from the Soviet model and began to suspect leanings toward western science and institutions inside the governmental bureaucracy. This suspicion led to conflict with He Cheng. Mao accused him of acting contrary to the Communist revolution and replaced him in 1956.

Mao also subscribed to the view that physicians should serve the population and were, in fact, part of the working-class proletariat (as the allopathic and TCM physicians serving the Red Army were during the civil war). The PRC's first constitution in 1954 emphasized public and collective ownership by the people. The doctor–patient relationship was thus cast as one of service and patients first. To emphasize this model, Mao's writings cited the example of Dr. Bethune's service to the Chinese masses. This model received expression in state ownership of all medical facilities and personnel (including training), the demotion of the medical profession, and the institution of the Rural Cooperative Medical System of health insurance (see Chapters 2 and 11).[16]

China's transition to a publicly owned and operated system did not commence immediately after the founding of the PRC. Private practice was still allowed and was still necessary to render medical care to the population. But private physicians were encouraged by local health departments to join "united clinics," or group practices, that were gradually pushed into public ownership by 1957.[17] Starting in 1950, the government instituted a system of "unified job assignment" whereby students of the medical colleges were assigned positions upon graduation to balance the government's need to fill managerial and technical posts in the growing public sector. Graduates accepted these positions not only because the government sent the assignments down to their schools, but also because the newly dominant public sector had totally replaced the private sector as the source of employment, because few possessed information on job opportunities elsewhere, because personal connections now counted for little, and because many of the young graduates had patriotic fervor.[18] Physicians became salaried employees in work units (hospital wards and clinics), not independent fee-for-service practitioners. This placed the Chinese physician in a descending hierarchical order of "state, work-unit, professional, and patient" which further contributed to the demise of private practice and private sector medicine.[19]

Mao re-emphasized the TCM model, described traditional medicine as a national treasure, and advocated an educational model that rested on basic medical training. In 1952, a Department of Chinese Medicine was established within the MOH. By 1956, Mao established four TCM colleges in Shanghai, Beijing, Guangzhou, and Chengdu; by 1960, there were at least 19 institutions teaching TCM. In 1958, Mao also declared that western and traditional medicine should be united – much in the way that nineteenth-century reformers sought to integrate western practices into traditional medicine. Mao announced a national search for allopathic physicians to help assist the evolution of TCM.[20]

These steps elevated TCM in the short term but may have undermined TCM in the long term.[21] By 1962, TCM training consisted of 2.5 years of allopathic training followed by 2.5 years of TCM education, followed by an additional year of internship training in both fields.[22] But rather than have just TCM physicians train in western medicine, now allopathic physicians had to train in traditional medicine as well. Some historians surmise that Mao's goal was more social control over physicians rather than the integration of traditional and allopathic medicine. TCM departments were now established in many urban hospitals. However, the champions of TCM now suspected that the allopathic training was diluting TCM principles. They urged the curriculum be abolished and replaced by a new curriculum that began with three years of TCM training. This reform was implemented but soon thwarted by the Cultural Revolution, which terminated all medical education.[23]

The tumult of the Cultural Revolution (1966–1975) undermined China's allopathic and TCM medical communities. All medicine was now suspect, due to the anti-intellectual bias of the time. Mao asserted that formal medical education was elitist and exclusionary. All medical training and research was suspended for nearly ten years; universities were shut down; and all medical association activities were banned. Eminent university-based practitioners were relocated to the rural areas, or subjected to "weekly struggle sessions" with subordinates.[24] The net effect was the stagnation of allopathic training and a growing undersupply of western-trained physicians. The champions and prominent practitioners of TCM were likewise viewed as part of the establishment and publicly ridiculed. TCM practitioners abandoned their academic pursuits to avoid persecution, thus allowing western medicine to reassert its primacy.

Mao countered the elitism of university training and the urban bias of the MOH bureaucracy with the barefoot doctors program of 1968. The program trained paramedics to serve as rural healthcare providers, using short three–six months training at local county hospitals. The doctors provided services to members of China's agricultural communes whose care was financed by the new cooperative medical system. To support this, Colleges for Workers, Peasants, and Soldiers were established in 1972 to offer three-year rudimentary vocational training in both TCM and western medicine. The increased supply promoted timely treatment and access to immunizations, rudimentary obstetrical services, some western medicines and simple procedures, and sanitation – and at half the salary cost of a regularly trained physician.[25]

The barefoot doctors program fit with Mao's effort to "proletarianize" China's doctors and reduce any status differentials within the population. Mao believed that health workers ought to be detailed to the local work units to support their labor effort. This placed the work of physicians more under state control and as part of the nation's state-building effort. Physician employment became publicly based, commune- or hospital-based, and salary-based rather than privately based, community office-based, and independent.

As a result, during these three decades healthcare became more government-financed through a large rural insurance scheme and two smaller urban schemes (GIS, LIS – see Chapter 1). Healthcare resources became largely nationalized through the establishment of public training institutions and public hospitals. Healthcare professionals increasingly became government workers and bureaucratic employees. Underlying all of these changes was the new Maoist belief that healthcare (and thus health workers) must serve the population and public needs.

Medicine in the Reform Era

In the post-Maoist era, the government's policy of economic liberalization precipitated the collapse of the rural communes and the rural cooperative insurance scheme. This undermined the institutional and financial foundation for the barefoot doctors. In response, the doctors left medical work for agricultural work, transitioned from the public to the private sector, shifted their attention from public health and prevention to the treatment of acute conditions, and charged fees for these acute care services. The result was a dramatic decline in rural healthcare institutions and personnel (see Figure 7.1).[26]

The Chinese government also relaxed its constraints on allopathic medical training and practice. Medical schools reopened, curricula lengthened from three to five years, and undergraduate and graduate training programs resumed. Private practice was encouraged by the State Council in 1985 to deal with the shortage in manpower supply; in 1989, the Ministry of Health allowed public doctors to engage in part-time private practice in public facilities.

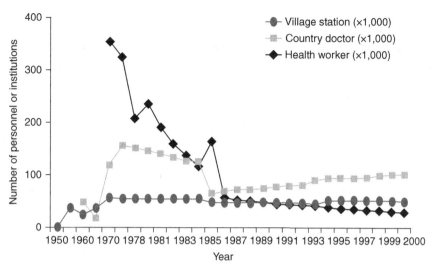

Figure 7.1 Rural healthcare infrastructure, 1950–2000
Source: Zhang and Unschuld (2008).

An increasing number of medical exchanges with the West brought the Chinese medical community into contact with more allopathic practitioners, their academic research orientation, and standards of western medical professionalism. In 1992, the government allowed foreign physicians to engage in short-term medical practice. Starting in 2000, collaborations between western pharmaceutical firms (e.g., Novo Nordisk) and the Chinese Academy of Medical Sciences and Beijing Union Medical School further increased this exposure. In 2004, Chinese medical schools introduced English-language courses in undergraduate courses and opened up instruction to foreign students; this provided an attractive opportunity to aspiring medical students in other countries where the tuition costs were much higher.[27]

During this period, the government also undertook some efforts to upgrade and professionalize the practice of medicine. The Chinese Medical Association (CMA) was allowed to resume in 1984 and supplemented in 2002 by the formation of the Chinese Medical Doctors Association (CMDA). In 1998, the government enacted the Law on Licensed Doctors of the PRC.[28] The following year, it issued regulations concerning qualifying examinations and provisional medical licensing as part of an effort to develop

a census of physician supply and standards of competence.

The major transition during this period was the growing economic interdependence between China's physicians and public hospitals. Economic liberalization meant a withdrawal of government funding of public hospital operating costs and healthcare in general. In 1989, the government allocated block grants to fund healthcare with fixed budgets to fund hospital operations. Government funding as a percentage of hospital revenues dropped from 30 percent in the 1970s and 1980s to only 7–8 percent by 2000.[29] Hospital prices were also fixed for many services to make them affordable: regulated prices allowed hospitals to recover only 50 percent of their costs and price above cost for less than 10 percent of their services.[30] Hospitals and their salaried physicians now had to rely on private financing via patient out-of-pocket payments for their services (e.g., markups), as well as commissions from suppliers for using their products. The same economic dictates applied to TCM practitioners and their hospitals: they too had to become profitable through the provision of services and expensive herbal treatments for which patients could be billed, rather than through the prescription of cheap herbal medicines and the use of TCM diagnostics.[31]

To further hospital commercial efforts, the government (a) encouraged hospitals to set up special clinics offering higher quality and higher cost care to those who could afford it; (b) allowed hospitals to charge fees above cost for using modern technologies and equipment; and (c) encouraged public hospitals to adopt a "responsibility system" and offer "performance wages" to their medical staffs that linked physician remuneration with hospital economic performance (e.g., through drug prescribing, performing procedures, and utilizing equipment).[32] In this way, physician salaries now contained a guaranteed component and a contingent component that could be a 30–70 percent mix.

Such commercial activities turned China's public hospitals into de facto profit-making institutions. The activities ran counter to the public service ethos promulgated by Mao, spawned corruption among hospitals and their physicians, and began to create tensions between physicians and their patients.[33] Declarations by the Central Committee and State Council in 1997, as well as by the 2004 Chinese Constitution, emphasized the original goals of serving the people and ensuring the public's health. However, these goals were now to be somehow pursued through a socialist market economy rather than government ownership.[34]

Physicians thus transitioned from an employed public servant in rural communes to salaried employees of public hospitals whose financial interests they now served. But in both settings, they were hierarchically controlled by the state, organizationally restricted to a single site of practice, and expected to serve the commonweal and protect its health. Beginning in the late 1980s, the government began to slowly relax the restriction of physician practice to a single site (covered below).

This historical review suggests that the medical staff of a typical public hospital in China contains three cohorts of physicians who trained in quite different epochs.[35] Older medical staff members (aged 60 and over) lived through the Cultural Revolution, likely had no research track available to them (due to the closure of universities and medical training), and likely attended the polytechnic schools. Middle-aged physicians (aged 40–60) trained after the Cultural Revolution, perhaps in five-year programs, and were likely promoted to

mid-level positions of "attending doctor" and categorized as experts and specialists. By contrast, only the younger cohort of physicians (under the age of 40) trained during the recent period of licensing and registration (covered below), as well as the emphasis on academic research.

Medical Practice: China versus the West

The foregoing chronicle reveals a sharp contrast between medical practice in China and the United States. In China,

- physicians are primarily public sector employees, not practitioners residing in the private sector.
- physicians are primarily hospital-based, not community-based practitioners.
- physicians work in hierarchies, not in solo practice or collegial small groups.
- physicians are primarily specialists attached to one hospital, not a mix of generalists and specialists that are primarily office-based and affiliated with multiple hospitals.

Only in the past few years has a new governmental policy encouraged physicians with five or more years of practice after receipt of a national license to open their own clinics. Chinese physicians are thus tightly integrated with Chinese hospitals, unlike in the United States where hospitals have sought to vertically integrate and align with physicians for the past three decades. Chinese physicians practice a mix of allopathic medicine and TCM, whereas US physicians are primarily allopathic. Finally, most Chinese physicians have a college education or less (e.g., three- or five-year medical degrees), compared to US physicians who have a college degree, four years of medical school, and one to seven years of additional specialty training in residencies, often supplemented by fellowship programs.

There are nevertheless some interesting similarities between the two. Both Chinese and US physicians earn higher incomes through the use of advanced technology, which helps to fuel the healthcare quadrilemma (see Figure 1.10). Both sets of physicians prefer to practice in hospitals with high technology that attract patients and

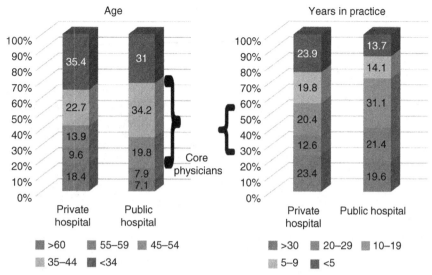

Figure 7.2 Physician demography in public and private hospitals
Source: Adapted from Citi Research.

research opportunities. Both sets of physicians view the awarding of academic titles as a measure of prestige and technical competence; and both sets of physicians earn higher incomes through fee-for-service practice than through hospital salaries.

Physician Supply

Medical Colleges and Students

In 2006, China had approximately 180 medical schools.[36] The largest number (77) was free-standing medical colleges; the next largest number (64) was university-based programs with five to eight years training; the remainder (39), offering three-year programs, were known as "secondary medical schools." These schools are publicly owned and government funded;[37] some are independent and operated by the provinces.[38] More than 150 of these schools teach allopathic medicine; the Ministry of Education has categorized the majority of these as "first class" level schools and targeted them (through receipt of grants) to become internationally recognized as top tier research institutions.

China expanded its medical education system starting in 1998. The number of medical college graduates increased from 75,000 in 1998 to 450,000

annually by 2008, and then to roughly 600,000 by 2013. As a result of this growth, a large block of graduates working in public hospitals are less than 35 years old; two-thirds of hospital physicians are less than 45 years old (see Figure 7.2).

Physician Manpower

In 2011, China had 2.47 million physicians: 2.02 million medical practitioners (including 267,000 practitioners of TCM) and 446,000 assistant medical practitioners. This represents an increase over the 1.95 million practitioners in 2005 (1.3 million in urban areas, 650,000 in rural areas) and the 2.08 million in 2008. An additional 917,000 village health workers previously known as barefoot doctors supplemented this workforce.[39]

Similar to its supply of general practitioners (see Table 6.4), China's ratio of 1.9 physicians per 1,000 population is near the bottom of the distribution in the OECD statistics (data for 2011).[40] China's medical supply ranks lower than such neighboring countries as Korea, Japan, and Singapore, but higher than other populous countries in the region such as India and Indonesia.

During the period 1990–2009, China's physician-population ratio remained nearly constant,

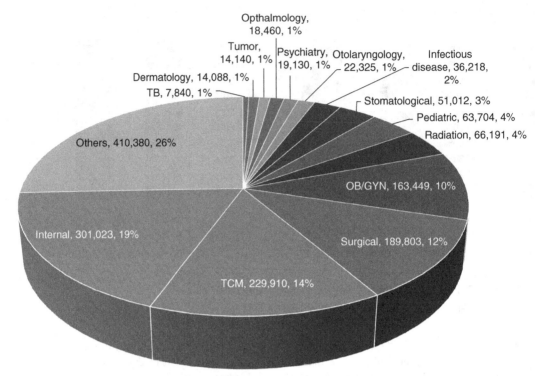

Figure 7.3 Number and percentage of doctors by specialties in 2005
Source: Adapted from MedTech Insight. *China Hospital Report 2011.*

despite the surge in the economy, increased demand for healthcare services, and thus rising healthcare expenditures. Research suggests that China's low level of medical manpower and low increase in medical supply is partly due to the low wage levels earned by physicians.[41] Such low wage levels reflected their employment as salaried medical staff in public hospitals, governmental restrictions on how much hospital profit (30 percent maximum) could be allocated to wage payments, and the historical lack of occupational mobility across different sites of practice.

The distribution of Chinese physicians by specialty is depicted in Figure 7.3 (data for 2005). The largest departments within Chinese hospitals are internal medicine (19 percent), TCM (14 percent), surgery (12 percent), and obstetrics/gynecology (10 percent). Most departments have declined in their share of physicians, suggesting the addition of other departments and specialties in Chinese hospitals.

What is missing in China is a cadre of primary care physicians (PCPs). Such physicians used to be the foundation of rural healthcare delivery during the Maoist era. They were trained initially in the vocational schools and then later in the barefoot doctor program. Economic reform resulted in a more urban-centered, hospital-based, and specialty-oriented medical workforce.

Since 1997, and leading up to the 2009 reform, the government has sought to refocus attention on community-based services as the foundation for healthcare delivery.[42] Such services rested on already existing infrastructure – e.g., community health centers (CHCs) and community health stations (CHSs) – as well as on newly developed residency programs in general practice and family medicine. Between 2001 and 2008, the number of CHCs and CHSs sharply increased from 11,700 to 29,127; the vast majority of these (20,224) were the smaller stations. The average number of physicians per CHS was 3.5; CHCs had an average of 18.1

physicians on staff. Three-quarters of the physicians in both sites were trained at the vocational school level or below.

Despite the increase in infrastructure, insurance barriers to primary care still persist. Social health insurance schemes reimbursed care in 86.6 percent of CHCs, but only 48.2 percent of CHSs;[43] reimbursement for outpatient care is higher in some insurance schemes (e.g., UEBMI) than in others (URBMI). Utilization of community health sites is low compared to inpatient care, accounting for only 14 percent of all visits in 2008. This low level reflects the lack of capacity, the low level of medical training, the lower level of insurance coverage, and the low degree of public knowledge about these fairly new services.[44]

The government has also sought to improve healthcare service delivery at the grassroots level. Objectives include construction of 2,000 county hospitals (including TCM facilities) so that each county has at least one hospital and construction of village clinics in remote areas such that each village has at least one clinic. Finally, the 2009 reform supports manpower training to staff township hospitals (360,000 workers), urban CHSs (160,000 workers), and village clinics (1.37 million workers). What the reform did not specify, however, was funding to improve medical education and physician training. The government has also not determined the best way to develop appropriate referral patterns between primary and secondary healthcare providers at the different geographic levels. Currently, of the 15,000 daily visits to Class III hospitals, an estimated 13,000 are for services that could be rendered at lower-level facilities.

Supply and Training of Nurses

Number of Nursing Personnel

The available statistics suggest the number of nurses in China has grown rapidly over time. This reflects the government's effort to expand education of healthcare professionals since 1998. In 2005, there were 1.35 million nurses; in 2008, the country had 1.65 million nurses; and in 2011, China had 1.85 million nurses.[45] More recent presentations suggest the number has grown to 2.49 million as of 2013.[46]

Nevertheless, like its supply of physicians, China's supply of 1.9 practicing nurses per 1,000 population is low compared to the rest of the world.[47] A 2007 study reported that China's top hospitals had a low ratio of nurses-to-beds (0.38), again far lower than other countries. According to the WHO, the statistic ranged from 1.1 in Africa to 1.25 in Europe. The nurse-to-bed ratio is an important structural indicator of quality of care. The vacancy rate was 27 percent at the end of 2008: 1.4 million positions for registered nurses were unfilled.[48] In recognition of this problem, the Ministry of Health published a Nursing Development Plan in China (2005–2010) to reduce the nursing vacancy rates in Chinese hospitals. The "Nursing Act" signed by Premier Wen Jiabao in 2008 mandated nurse-to-bed ratios for all hospitals in the country of at least 0.40; the act also stipulated that nurses should comprise no less than 50 percent of the total health workforce in a hospital. The gap may have closed in recent years, based on other indicators. The World Health Organization recommends two nurses per 1,000 people, or a total supply of 2.6 million nurses for a population size of 1.3 billion people. This is close to the size of the nursing workforce reported in 2013. Other reports indicate the country has 1.85 nurses per 1,000 population as of 2013.[49]

China has slightly fewer nurses per 1,000 population as physicians – estimated by some at 0.99:1.00.[50] This low ratio contrasts sharply with the 3.6 ratio observed in the United States. China's low ratio offers little opportunity to (a) substitute the former for the latter in underserved areas or (b) boost physician productivity.[51] This low ratio also contributes to the country's already existing shortage of primary care physicians. Moreover, the vast majority of China's nurses (97 percent) work in hospitals rather than in community settings.

Finally, as with physicians, there is a geographic maldistribution of the nursing workforce in China. Data from 2007 show a higher density of nurses in urban areas than in rural areas (18.8 vs. 5.5 nurses per 100,000 population).[52] Most nurses work in the more economically prosperous eastern region, while very few nurses work in the poorer western region.

Causes of the Shortage

There are several drivers of the nursing shortage. One is the moratorium on nursing education during the Cultural Revolution (see below). A second is that hospitals are more likely to hire physicians than nurses, since physicians are the key to revenue generation (see below); by contrast, nurses are an expense item. Third, the vast majority of Chinese patients (as high as 95 percent) receive informal care from family members during their long inpatient stays; this reflects the primacy of the family unit in Chinese culture and familial responsibility to care for sick family members. This confers on nurses the paradoxical role of "stranger" along with caregiver and may obviate the need for more nurses.[53] Fourth, Chinese patients rely more on the advice of physicians, particularly physicians at Class III facilities; nursing care is not regarded as highly. Fifth, nurses perform tasks of lower complexity and skill in Chinese hospitals and thus are not as highly trained as their counterparts in other parts of the world (see below). These tasks may include non-nursing tasks, including getting patients to pay for their hospital services. Thus, it is not as attractive as a profession.

The working conditions in Chinese hospitals further contribute to the low attraction: heavy patient workloads, patient attacks on providers (see below), the low status of ward nurses in the hospital hierarchy, low respect from physicians (reflected in a common saying, "the doctor's mouth directs the nurse's legs"), low respect from hospital administrators, and low prospects for promotion.[54] There is also considerable hierarchy within the nursing staff: nurse, master nurse, supervisor/charge nurse, vice chief nurse, and chief nurse. One study reported that ward nurses in Chinese hospitals tended to at least 10–14 patients, with some caring for more than 30 patients at a time; another study reported high patient loads particularly on the evening and night shifts.[55] Not surprisingly, several research studies suggest high levels of anxiety (43.4 percent of nurses) and burnout among Chinese nurses.[56]

An additional change in the employment relationships that nurses have with hospitals may exacerbate the supply problem. Traditionally, dating back to the start of the People's Republic, the government's planned economy included lifetime employment, steady salaries, and benefits for a designated number of personnel in a given employer (in a system known as *bianzhi*). Between 1949 and 1978, nearly all professional nursing jobs were categorized as *bianzhi* positions. Since the economic reforms of 1978, and particularly in recent years due to the nursing vacancy rates reported in hospitals, Chinese hospitals have used "contract-based" jobs to supplement their nursing workforce. Such contracts are struck with the employer (rather than the government) and do not include the same job tenure and compensation package.

Chinese hospitals have utilized such positions not only to supplement *bianzhi* positions, but also to reduce their outlays on nursing salaries. Nursing positions have reportedly been reclassified as temporary, contractual positions that receive lower pay. Beyond the lower pay, contractual nurses are not allowed to participate in continuing education or receive paid holidays.

Training Levels

Recent data suggest that the number of Chinese hospital nurses employed in these new contractual positions now accounts for anywhere from 20 percent to 54 percent of all nursing personnel. In a survey of 181 hospitals in six provinces, the utilization of contract nurses ranged from 0 percent to 91 percent, with an average of 51 percent. The remaining *bianzhi* positions are reserved for nurses with Bachelor of Science in Nursing (BSN) training rather than the vocationally trained nurses. Occupation of a contract-based position was associated with greater dissatisfaction with salary and benefits, and greater intention to leave the position.[57] Researchers report that the average salary of an entry-level nurse in some urban hospitals is comparable to that for a janitor.[58]

China has slowly moved to upgrade the technical qualifications of its nursing workforce. In the early 1950s, the government established nursing programs of only two and then three years length of training following junior high school. Most of these vocational programs were attached to hospitals, not colleges or universities. Like medical education, nursing education was curtailed during the Cultural Revolution, but took much longer to resume. Vocational (*zhuanke*) programs were first to resume. Associate (college and university) and baccalaureate programs did not restart until 1983; masters and doctoral programs did not emerge until much later (1992 and 2004, respectively). The government required graduates from non-university health schools (three years training after junior high school) and university programs (three years training after senior high school) to take the National Nurse Qualification Examination as of 1993. Since 2008, graduates from all levels of nursing schools (including baccalaureate and higher) must pass the examination in order to practice.

Nursing education programs in the health schools are being gradually phased out, although they still comprise a major supplier of nurses for Class I hospitals. Class II and III hospitals rely more heavily on higher-trained nurses, which comprise at least half of their nursing personnel; nationally, the country wants at least 30 percent of nurses trained at the university level (according to the 2005–2010 Nursing Development Plan). Those graduating from the vocational programs are typically only 18 years old – suggesting a relatively inexperienced workforce that is lacking in senior mentors.[59]

China's nursing workforce continues to suffer from problems of its skill mix, though the situation may be improving. Nursing education spans the following levels (from lowest to highest): diploma, associate, baccalaureate, masters, and doctoral training. The majority of China's nurses have traditionally had only vocational training.[60] A 2005 study found that 58 percent of nurses had vocational level training; 37 percent had associate degrees; 3 percent had baccalaureate degrees; and only 0.1 percent had masters degrees.[61] As of 2009, 52 percent were vocationally trained, compared to 39 percent with a university diploma and 9 percent with baccalaureate or higher training.[62] As of 2010, according to the Ministry of Health, 48.7 percent of nurses had only secondary training; 42.5 percent had associate degrees; 8.7 percent had

baccalaureate degrees; and only 0.1 percent had graduate degrees. As a result, they occupy subordinate roles of assisting patients, not diagnosis or treatment; unlike the physicians, who often come from outside the province, the nurses may speak to one another in their local dialect.

China has been busy expanding the number of professional training programs for nurses. The number of BSN programs, for example, grew from 1 in 1983 to 179 by 2005 and numbered 213 by 2009. One issue for the country will be matching the supply of nurses with the expansion of the country's hospital and community health center infrastructure. More specialized training programs have arisen since 2000 to develop "advanced practice nurses," including nurse practitioners, certified nurse midwives, certified registered nurse anesthetists, and clinical nurse specialists.[63]

Overall Manpower Levels

In 2012, China's physicians and nurses comprised roughly half of the country's healthcare workforce (see Figure 7.4).[64] The heavy representation of professional clinicians among the total workforce suggests that China may lack a sufficient number of ancillary and clerical workers to support physicians. This may leave physicians with the responsibility for more administrative work in addition to patient care. The growth in the supply of professional workers between 1950 and 2008 is depicted in Table 7.1. While the workforce has grown tremendously over time, most of the growth occurred between 1970 and 2000.

The vast majority of healthcare workers reside in government and state-owned enterprise (SOE) facilities; less than ten percent work in privately owned sites. Among physicians, the vast majority (estimated anywhere from 70 percent to 90 percent) work in the public sector in public hospitals.[65] Healthcare personnel are disproportionately located in the eastern region of China rather than the middle or western regions (see Figure 7.5). They are even more disproportionately urban based (7.62 per 1,000 population) rather than rural based (3.04 per 1,000). This is especially true of the distribution of physicians (2.5 urban vs. 0.4 rural). To address this imbalance, China's Development and Reform

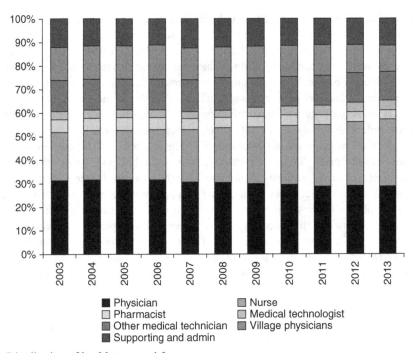

Figure 7.4 Distribution of healthcare workforce
Source: Adapted from Citi Research. China Healthcare Sector (December 2013).

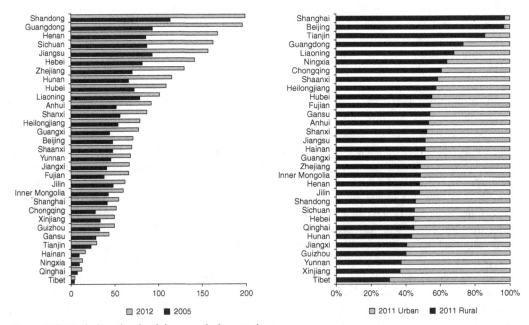

Figure 7.5 Variations in physician supply by province
Source: Adapted from Citi Research. China Healthcare Sector (December 2013).

Table 7.1 Number of doctors and other health professionals in China

Year	Doctors	Nurses	Pharmacists	Lab Technicians	Others	Total Health Professions
1950	380,800	37,800	8,080	NA	NA	555,040
1960	596,109	170,143	119,293	NA	NA	1,504,894
1970	702,304	295,147	NA	NA	NA	1,453,247
1980	1,153,234	465,798	308,438	114,290	756,481	2,798,241
1990	1,763,086	974,541	405,978	170,371	583,945	3,897,921
2000	2,075,843	1,266,838	414,408	200,900	532,814	4,490,803
2005	1,938,272	1,349,589	349,533	211,495	611,298	4,460,187
2008	2,082,258	1,654,297	330,525	212,618	751,340	5,030,038

Source: Ministry of Health (2009).

Commission instituted a free five-year training program for students agreeing to practice in underserved geographic areas for six years.

Medical Training, Licensing, and Continuing Education

China's cadre of physicians has been cultivated and selected since their high school days and channeled through medical college training of three to five years and hospital posting. Until recently, students enjoyed little career mobility both within and outside of this system. Moreover, Chinese medical education has been criticized for inculcating an examination mind-set, which bred rote learning and passive acceptance of what is taught. The result was a body of medical college graduates short on advanced training, short on problem-based learning and creativity, and long on caution and risk-aversion.[66] China has sought to correct these problems by increasing the number of doctoral-level training programs, merging medical education with more general education, and inculcating skills and learning among the students.

Medical College Preparation and Training

China's educational system includes six years of primary school, three years of junior middle school, and three years of senior middle school. Graduates of senior middle school, the equivalent of high school graduates in the United States, are candidates for medical school. Graduates prioritize the schools they wish to attend and their majors/specialties of choice, and take the National College Entrance Examination to qualify for admission. The Ministry of Education and the schools select the entering students, primarily based on the examination scores. Applicants for the higher-level degrees must have higher exam scores than applicants for the lower-level degree programs.

Many graduates historically entered three-year programs at vocational schools to earn associate degrees. These graduates became assistant doctors, resembling the physician assistants in the United States; as such, they must work under the supervision of a licensed physician. They can become independent practitioners following five years of practice and completion of a series of qualifying exams.[67]

Other graduates applied to five-year training programs in university medical schools. Those who spend four years in training plus a one-year clerkship obtain bachelors degrees (MBMS, Bachelor of Medicine and Bachelor of Surgery); those who spend seven years in training earn masters degrees; and those with eight years of training earn doctoral degrees. Most graduate training as interns and residents consists of apprenticeship under the tutelage of senior mentors.

Across all graduates, those with few years of training are heavily represented in the distribution, while those with many years of training are only lightly represented (see Figure 7.6). A 2001 survey of physicians in three provinces found that

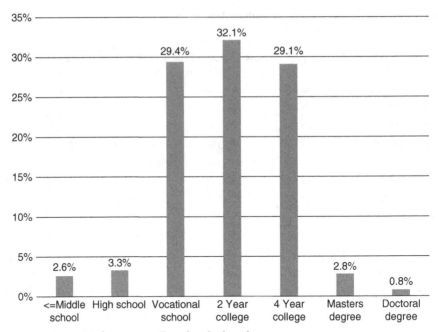

Figure 7.6 Physicians with four-year college level education
Source: China Ministry of Health, China Health Statistics, 2008 (2005 data).

37 percent had high school training or less, while 36 percent were college trained and 27 percent had university training; in terms of length, nearly 70 percent had five years or fewer medical training.[68] In 2003, for example, among the 300,000 graduates who took the qualifying exams, 80 percent or more had attended junior colleges and vocational schools; fewer than 15 percent had undergraduate training; and only a fraction (3.2 percent according to MOH data) had graduate level training.[69] The government has sought to increase the length of training and emphasize MBMS programs to meet growing demand for high-quality physicians. At present, the majority of schools offer five-year programs, which increased their share of medical graduates from 10 percent in the early 1970s to 65 percent by 2005.[70]

Post-college Training

Chinese medical school graduates have typically not attended residency programs in a certain specialty offered at a particular hospital. Western-style residency programs first began in 2003 at Sichuan University. In 2005, Sir Run Run Shaw Hospital in Zhejiang Province opened a three-year specialization in family medicine.

Generally, graduates of the three-year programs work in township and community health centers, while graduates of the five-year, seven-year, and eight-year programs work in hospitals as specialist physicians (see Figure 7.7).[71] Graduates are hired into a hospital and then slotted into a certain specialty. All specialists pass the same licensing examination following college without any formal training programs or certifications to demarcate their specialty competence. The only training programs that come close to resembling residencies are the seven-year degrees; the five-year programs train generalists, while the eight-year programs largely train PhD level researchers.

Following two to three years of practice at the initial hospital, graduates may move to more sophisticated facilities with higher reputations. However, lateral mobility across organizations has not been at the discretion of the individual but rather at the discretion of his/her superiors and the government. Rigid personnel systems (personnel quota system,

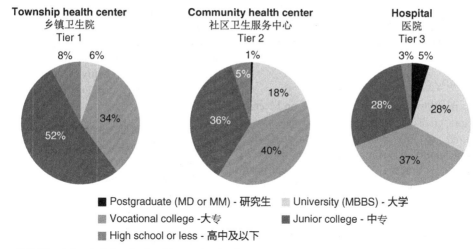

Figure 7.7 Physician training by healthcare institution
Source: Data from the People's Republic of China Ministry of Health (2010).

mandatory relocation of redundant workers) limit the physician's free movement across hospitals, but also limit the hospital's ability to dismiss physicians. Hospital directors are also loath to allow the physicians they have invested in and trained over time to leave their institution. Such exit behavior is negatively viewed and discouraged as disloyalty. Upward mobility and income may be restricted to the handful of physicians with eight-year degrees engaged in high-profile, government funded research.

Historically, "exit" behavior such as voluntary resignation of one's position was not permitted, given the possible imposition of penalties by superiors, the competitive market for positions in large tertiary hospitals, the difficulty of establishing a private practice, and the difficulty of finding a job elsewhere outside of healthcare. Thus, graduates might spend their entire career in one organization, encased within a steep hierarchy with few other prospects. Hospital physicians were thus stuck in environments where they were besieged by patient demands, heavy workloads, pressures to generate revenues, and stymied career advancement. Recently, several resignations from high-profile hospitals have sparked public controversy.[72]

Indeed, in recent years, China's medical colleges have reported more graduates leaving medicine. During the period 2006–2008, 40 percent of the

1 million students who passed the national licensing examination did not register in hospitals.[73] Additional evidence suggests that only one-sixth of the 600,000 doctors with medical licenses have been registered to a healthcare institution during the prior five years, suggesting that many graduates have sought employment elsewhere or sought out postgraduate medical training to improve their prospects.[74] Many have switched to more lucrative careers in the pharmaceutical and biotechnology industries, suggesting a waste of training resources.[75]

Part of the problem is that most medical graduates want to work in the top-tier hospitals in large cities, where the salaries, prestige, technological capabilities, and learning opportunities are higher. However, among graduating medical students, fewer than half locate positions in the large hospitals. They do not want to work in smaller hospitals and clinics at the county level or below; in their eyes (citing a Chinese proverb), to do so would be "to make little use of large talents."[76] Their reluctance to practice at the periphery of China's healthcare systems is one reason why the rural population bypasses their local (and now under-utilized or vacant) facilities to seek care at the large tertiary facilities in the cities. Rural medical care is thus left to lesser-trained physicians from the vocational colleges and the former barefoot doctors. To rectify this problem, the government may need to develop more western-model residency programs and improve the salaries of hospital-based physicians.

Licensing and Registration

After the 1999 enactment of the Law on Licensed Doctors, graduates of China's medical schools were required to (a) pass the Medical Doctors Qualification (Licensing) Examination to receive a license to practice, (b) register at local health departments, and (c) then begin work at a medical institution. Physicians are registered in terms of the 24 categories of qualifying examinations taken. Doctors can typically only practice in one category and one specialty within that category. Separate examinations were given for licensed doctors and licensed assistant doctors. Those choosing to work in rural areas were governed by the "Regulations on Medical Practice of Countryside Doctors," implemented in 2004; they too must be licensed doctors or assistant doctors.[77]

Licensed doctors may only practice in one of three registered locations: institutions for medical treatment, disease prevention, or health protection. Historically, government policy required physicians to practice only at the registered employer stated in the physician's practice certificate. Paralleling differences among the registered locations, licensed doctors are further distinguished according to whether they are registered to work at that site or come from the outside (e.g., trainees, foreigners, and "mobile" doctors who practice at multiple sites). Physician license categories encompass clinical (allopathic) medicine, TCM (including hybrid allopathic-TCM), dentistry, and public healthcare.

Thus, all doctors in China are specialists. There are virtually no primary care physicians and no recognizable distinction between generalists and specialists. Only in recent years has the MOH established in-service training for general practice in select cities.

Continuing Medical Education

Continuing medical education (CME) is recent in origin.[78] Regulations and an organizing structure developed in the 1990s under the supervision of the MOH. The National CME Commission and parallel commissions at the provincial level are responsible for guidance, coordination, and quality control of CME activities. According to the National Health and Family Planning Commission (formerly the MOH), the goals of the CME system are:

- keep the high professional morals of physicians
- improve their practice skills
- upgrade the quality of healthcare service
- help the development of public health and disease management

Like the physician population, the bulk of CME courses are concentrated in China's eastern provinces. The courses are often described as monotonous, outdated in both presentation and knowledge content, insufficiently resourced, and unsupervised. CME programs are not evaluated by outcome measures such as physician performance, patient care, or population health.

In 2000, the MOH published its "Regulation on Continuing Medical Education." CME is targeted at middle- and upper-level physicians. Completion of CME requirements serves as evidence for annual performance reviews and is a prerequisite for credentialing and promotions. National providers are evaluated and reaccredited every three years, though the process of evaluation is often conducted on an irregular basis. Each provincial department of health and CME commission can determine its own policy in terms of provider performance review.

While there are no official data, some estimate that the majority of funding comes from industry sponsors (e.g., pharmaceutical and device companies). CME is supposed to be free of commercial bias, but there are no detailed regulations on commercial support. A large proportion of CME registration fees comes indirectly from industry, since many physicians receive manufacturer kickbacks for prescribing their products. This practice may change as the government targets corruption.

Career Ladders, Science, and Research

Figure 7.8 provides one depiction of the career ladder for a clinical physician in China.[79]

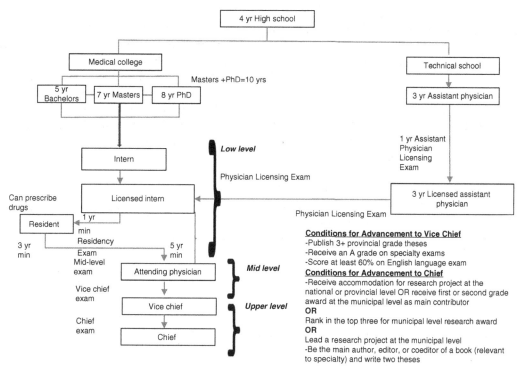

Figure 7.8 Physician career ladder
Source: Adapted from Ryan Leonard, *Working Lives of Chinese Physicians.*

Graduates with a bachelor's degree (five-year program) are known as "doctors," after passing the licensing examination, they are allowed to prescribe drugs. Those wishing to obtain masters or doctoral degrees must pass an entrance examination to enter postgraduate study (typically one year clinical work, two years of independent research).

Medical college graduates work their way up a hierarchy of lower, middle, and upper-level doctors. Lower-level doctors include (a) MBMS graduates who enter one-year hospital-based internship programs prior to licensure; (b) MBMS graduates who have taken the licensing exam and been licensed; and (c) licensed doctors in three-year hospital-based specialty training programs. Lower-level doctors who gain at least five years of clinical experience (which can include the three years of specialty training) and pass the Mid-level Physician Licensing Examination become "attending physicians" (middle-level physicians). The majority of Chinese physicians who practice

in inpatient settings remain at this level for most of their careers and serve as the bulk of the hospital medical staff. The pyramid inside the medical staff is reportedly quite steep, with very little upward mobility and very little clinical autonomy, particularly for the younger physicians.

Upper-level physicians are typically those who have obtained masters and doctoral degrees that entail clinical research (e.g., funded by the local Bureau of Science and Technology) that the graduates have published. Another set of exams and three years of additional clinical experience qualify these graduates to become vice chief and chief physician in their specialty.[80] The chief physician serves not only as the department head of his/her specialty but also as the chief administrator wielding decision-making power. Those with international research experience and collaboration occupy the apex of the hierarchy.

Physicians in this hierarchy are no longer just public employees of the government and servants of the country's health (as under Mao), but now also servants of the interests of the hospitals in which they work. One Chinese physician described their professional status in one word: "ox."[81]

Upon China's entrance into the World Trade Organization (WTO) in 2001, the country emphasized scientific development and provided financial incentives for academic research. China opened up its hospitals to foreign visitors and its medical schools to foreign students, which required raising the quality of the medical education system to meet international standards. China invested heavily in academic medicine and research, as well as access to modern technologies to facilitate that research.

"State Laboratory" is an honorific title bestowed on established research labs that conduct government-sponsored scientific research, provide key data to the government, and interface with western researchers.[82] These laboratories are affiliated with the country's top universities (e.g., Peking University, Qinghua University) and are funded with generous grants by the Ministry of Science and Technology to establish a foundation of competitive research. The labs also provide higher salaries and promotion opportunities to physicians pegged to academic output, but siphon away time spent in patient care.[83]

Not surprisingly, several issues have been raised about the integrity of the research conducted.[84] One academic physician has suggested that as much as 90 percent of published articles lack quality assessment.[85] There are also reports that physicians need to have influential supervisors as well as pay administrative fees as high as 3,000–9,000 RMB to have their research published in medical journals (instance of *guanxi*, or network relationships, in academia). Questions of plagiarism have motivated many State Laboratory researchers to work with colleagues in the West rather than researchers at home.

Another career consideration for Chinese physicians is whether or not to work in the private sector. With China's entrance into the WTO, there has been marked growth in the number of private facilities. However, private hospitals are much smaller in size than their public counterparts and are dwarfed in terms of their total numbers and bed capacity. There is also lingering patient suspicion that such

hospitals are lower in quality and more likely to engage in unethical practices. Finally, there is less clarity about the career ladder for physicians who work in private hospitals, and less likelihood they will be engaged in publicly funded academic research. As a result, the job security and compensation models are perceived as potentially risky and hence disruptive. Not surprisingly, 90 percent or more of China's hospital-based physicians work in public facilities.

Practice Models and Business Models

Private Practice

During the period of rapid economic growth after Mao, China had a shortage of both urban and rural hospital facilities to care for a growing population that increasingly could afford it. There was also a shortage of physicians, exacerbated by at least three factors: the moratorium placed on medical education during the Cultural Revolution, the demise of the Cooperative Medical Scheme (CMS), and the resulting decision by barefoot doctors to leave village practice for more profitable employment.

As one effort to deal with this shortage, the State Council encouraged private medical practice in 1982 and allowed physicians to have both public and private (dual practice) patients in 1987, while in 1989 the MOH allowed physicians to engage in part-time private practice in public facilities. Starting in 2009, the MOH issued several notices allowing multi-site practice (usually at multiple hospitals) on a trial basis for a small fraction of physicians in six cities; the trials began in 2010 and 2011. In November 2014, the National Health and Family Planning Commission issued the "Opinions on Encouragement and Regulation of Multi-Sited Practices of Physicians,"[86] which allowed physicians to practice at more than three sites within a given province. However, they specified two criteria to qualify: practice in specialty for five or more years and no disqualification record during the two most recent assessment periods. In addition, physicians still required the consent of their employer to pursue practice at other sites.

Since the 1980s, many Chinese physicians converted ownership (at least in part). Such conversions were more common in rural areas at the village level due to the collapse of the communes and CMS and the greater market opportunity and population to serve. Between 1980 and 1990, nearly half of village doctors became for-profit, compared to only a handful at the township health centers.[87] Between 1982 and 2002, the number of private practitioners mushroomed from 80,000 to 200,000.[88] Private for-profit clinics became quite prevalent by the end of the twentieth century (estimated at more than 70 percent, mostly in rural areas); privatization has been less prevalent among urban clinics (10 percent), outpatient departments (48 percent), and hospitals (15 percent).[89] In 2000, the government recognized for-profit hospitals by formally distinguishing them from nonprofit facilities.

Research suggests there were no substantive differences between the public village doctors and the converted private practice village doctors in terms of their equipment quality, prescribing behavior, or preventive measures.[90] Contrary to expectations, the public doctors were more likely to over-prescribe drugs, since drug sales accounted for 90 percent of their service revenues; by contrast, private doctors charged fees for all of their services. Other research suggests that private practices were more conveniently located, more responsive to patient schedules (e.g., flexible hours), more affordable and satisfying to patients, and higher in quality for minor illnesses. However, they were less able to treat major illnesses, less likely to be viewed by patients as highly skilled (due to perceptions of having fake credentials and using fake drugs), and less likely to be sought out by patients with higher education, income, and insurance coverage.[91]

Technological Sophistication and Hospital-based Care

Like their US counterparts, Chinese hospitals compete with one another based on the recruitment of well-known physicians and the availability of high-tech equipment and services. Patients are attracted to higher-cost, higher-tech facilities in order to receive the comprehensive array of therapies offered by their specialists. This has spawned a medical arms race among the elite hospitals in large urban areas. Without publicly available information on quality of care, patients associate hospital quality with availability of technology (as indicated by the hospital accreditation scheme: Class I, II, and III).

The medical arms race is reflected in several statistics. Class III hospitals comprise only 10 percent of facilities, but employ 35 percent of physicians and treat 37 percent of inpatients; by contrast, Class II hospitals have roughly equal percentages of facilities (45 percent), physicians (46 percent), and inpatients (49 percent) (see Figure 7.9). Between 2002 and 2005, there was a reported 90 percent increase in MRI machines and 55 percent increase in CT machines. Equipment costs came to represent as much as 60 percent or more of a hospital's fixed assets and could often lie unused (up to 40 percent of the time). This contributed to higher hospital costs and inefficiencies in resource allocation.

The large tertiary hospitals also feature large outpatient departments with multiple specialty clinics. Primary care physicians (PCPs) do not refer patients to these sites because PCPs do not exist in China; instead, patients travel to Class III facilities on a walk-in (self-referral) basis. They thus avoid the community health centers located closer to their homes, due to the lower degree of technical sophistication and patient trust in the skills of lesser-trained physicians. This explains why Class III hospitals have experienced the highest occupancy levels (see Figure 7.10) and the highest rates of outpatient growth (see Figure 7.11) and why provincial level hospitals have the highest number of patient visits per physician (see Figure 7.12).

On any given day, enormous waiting lines form in the cavernous outpatient area (and then spill outside) where patients register to see any available specialist. The environment is crowded, noisy, uncomfortable, public, and impersonal; researchers have likened the experience to visiting the division of motor vehicles in any US city.[92] Some patients hire "appointment touts" and "medical introducers" to help them jump the queue and avoid delays in seeing the physician.[93]

The impact on physician practice has been profound. Given the growth of the population, the undersupply of practitioners, and the lack of PCPs

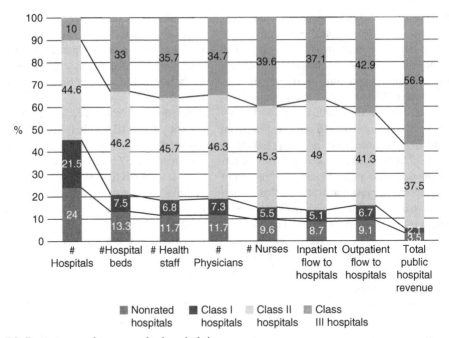

Figure 7.9 Resources and revenues by hospital tier
Source: Adapted from Citi Research. China Deep Dive (2013).

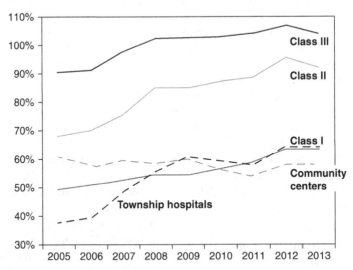

Figure 7.10 Occupancy levels by hospital tier
Source: Adapted from Citi Research. China Deep Dive (2013).

treating lower-severity cases in the community, physicians in the large urban hospitals developed enormous patient caseloads. Both inpatient and outpatient visits have outpaced physician supply (see Figure 7.13). According to one study conducted at Peking University, physicians worked ten or more hours per day and saw 100 or more patients daily.[94] According to another study, physicians treated

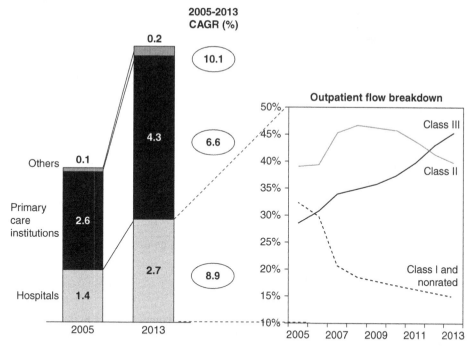

Figure 7.11 Distribution of outpatient visits
Source: Adapted from Citi Research. China Healthcare Sector (2013).

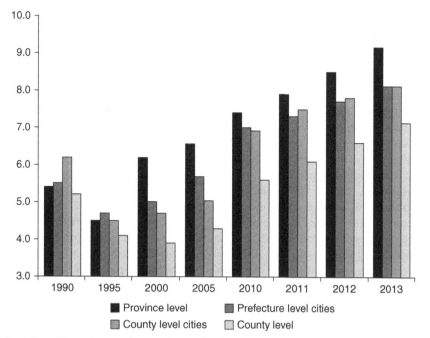

Figure 7.12 Daily patient visits per physician per level
Source: Adapted from Citi Research. China Healthcare Sector (2013).

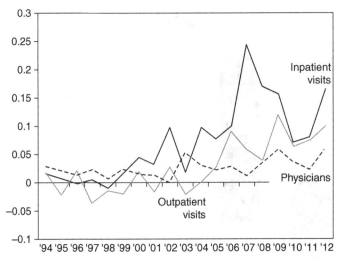

Figure 7.13 Growth of patient visits versus physician supply
Source: Adapted from Citi Research. China Deep Dive (2013).

anywhere from 40 to 60 patients a day in the outpatient clinics.[95] On average, physicians spent one minute or less with each patient; some patient encounters were group visits. Physicians have defended this brevity by stating that most patients did not have problems requiring specialist care and extensive workups.[96]

This assembly-line approach did not foster favorable patient impressions of the care they received and led to verbal disputes and even physical attacks on physicians. Precursors to such episodes included miscommunication (93 percent), inadequate quality (57 percent), unsatisfactory outcome (60 percent), heavy patient workload (43 percent), and high medical expenses (40 percent).[97] Two-thirds of physicians and 40 percent of nurses reported that they had "no cordial relationship with patients."[98]

Not surprisingly, Chinese physicians do not express a great deal of satisfaction with their career. In a 2001 survey of physicians in three provinces, very low percentages of respondents indicated they were satisfied or very satisfied with their job (27 percent), income (8 percent), skill level (30 percent), professional interaction (29 percent), ancillary backup (18 percent), and opportunity for continuing medical education (18 percent). Surprisingly, the highest-rated item was patient relationships, but even that was fairly low (60 percent).[99] Physicians

were also quite negative in their views of China's healthcare system (32 percent).

Base Wage Levels

Chinese physicians are poorly paid by western standards as well as by comparison with other occupations (see Figures 7.14 and 7.15). Between 1978 and 1997, physicians' wages in some provinces increased 28-fold but still remained low.[100] Low wages are partly a historical legacy of Mao's egalitarianism and status leveling effort.[101] They were exacerbated by economic liberalization and the withdrawal of government financing of hospitals. In 2002, public financing covered only 6–7 percent of hospital spending, while staff wages comprised one-quarter of hospital budgets.[102] Low wages also reflected the concentration of most physicians in salaried positions inside government hospitals. The low salaries paid to physicians have helped to keep hospital operating costs down; labor in Chinese hospitals accounts for only 25–40 percent of operating costs, compared to roughly 50 percent of US hospital operating costs (which do not even include doctor salaries).

Data from the 2009 National Bureau of Statistics placed the average monthly (annual) salary at 2,820 RMB (33,830 RMB).[103] In 2010, the average annual salary had risen to 2,956 RMB (35,468

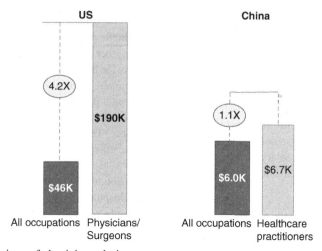

Figure 7.14 Comparison of physician salaries
Source: Adapted from Citi Research. China Deep Dive (2013).

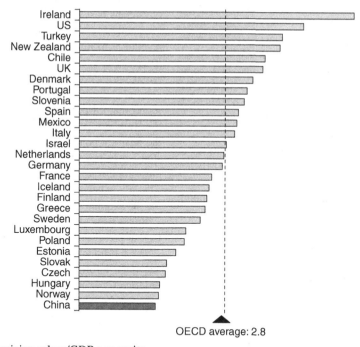

Figure 7.15 Physician salary/GDP per capita
Source: Adapted from Citi Research. China Deep Dive (2013).

RMB) – representing a 4.8 percent increase; this salary was only slightly higher than that earned by the average Chinese employee (32,244 RMB).[104] State salary standards are regulated by the Ministry of Health, Ministry of Finance, and General Bureau of Labor, and periodically adjusted as national standards of base pay in the Post Performance Payment System (PPPS). The base salaries, which represent a minority of physician compensation (see below), are comprised of a position wage based on promotion (13 grades), a seniority wage based on qualifications and performance (65 levels), incentive pay reflecting the physician's performance and contribution (largely replaced by the bonus system, discussed below), and a subsidy for work in "arduous remote areas." The position wage and seniority wage account for the majority of the base salary: they comprised 630 RMB monthly pay for a first-year junior resident (Grade 13, Level 1).[105]

There is reportedly not a lot of differentiation in base pay across hospitals and regions in China. Nevertheless, some public hospitals pay their physicians higher salaries than others. The MOH system of accreditation (begun in 1989) classifies Chinese hospitals by class (I, II, III) based on government administrative level and bed size, and by gradations within Class (A, B, C) based on local health bureau evaluations of service, technology, and equipment.[106] The government allocates more financial resources to higher-level hospitals, which are associated with higher quality and more advanced technologies. Such hospitals compete for more prestigious, senior physicians by paying them higher salaries. Different hospital classes may charge different levels of service fees.

According to one recent study, consultants in larger urban hospitals earn about 4,000 RMB per month (~$645), while their rural counterparts in smaller hospitals earn 3,000 RMB per month (~$485).[107] A second source distinguished the monthly salaries for younger physicians by hospital level (4,000 RMB at Class III; 3,000 RMB at Class II; 2,000 RMB at Class I hospitals), as well as the salaries of physicians at hospitals at different geographic levels (4,000–5,000 RMB at provincial hospitals; 2,000–4,000 RMB at municipal hospitals; 1,000–2,000 RMB at local hospitals).[108]

These salary levels serve as the fixed component of doctors' wages and account for roughly 30–50 percent of total compensation. The other two components of physician compensation include bonus payments and benefits; these represent the majority of hospital compensation and vary by geographic region, hospital size, and the profitability of the hospital and the physician's department.

Variable Income

Chinese physicians augment their low salaries in a number of ways. The first is the receipt of bonuses from the hospital for prescribing expensive pharmaceuticals, medical devices, and diagnostic tests to hospital patients.[109] The bonus system was inaugurated after 1979 by various government ministries with "The Opinion on the Pilot Work of Strengthening Economic Management of Hospitals."[110] Over time, the bonus system and the method of payment distribution has been refined.

Hospitals collect commissions (kickbacks) from manufacturers for using their products and then distribute them to physicians as bonuses. Hospital directors set revenue targets for the various clinical departments, which in turn set revenue targets for their physicians.[111] These distributions can take various forms. According to an earlier study, the distributions consisted of a flat bonus given to all physicians based on the hospital's financial status, a quantity bonus based on exceeding some target level of utilization (admissions, inpatient days, visits, procedures, etc.), or a revenue-related bonus based on exceeding some target achieved by the doctor.[112] Survey data from one province in 1997 found that 78 percent of county hospitals utilized the revenue-related bonus, while the remainder used the quantity bonus.[113] According to a more recent study, two major types of distribution methods are now employed: a "surplus pro-rata" model and a "workload count" model. The two models resemble the revenue and quantity bonus models.[114]

Bonus payments can also be based on the percentage of prescriptions written by the individual physician and filled at the hospital pharmacy. There is anecdotal information on the physician bonus for ordering CT scans ($2.50), laser surgery ($63), and pacemakers ($2,500), as well as the commissions paid to departments for the volume of prescriptions (3–5 percent).

More generally, physician incomes rise with increasing hospital revenues. Both sets of providers generate higher revenues through price and volume mechanisms. On the price side, Mao's government allowed physicians and hospitals to sell drugs to patients with 15 percent markups. In the post-Maoist era, hospitals increased revenues by

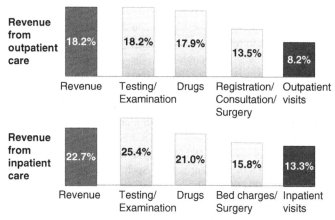

Figure 7.16 CAGR of hospital revenue sources, 2008–2011
Source: Adapted from Citi Research. China Deep Dive (2013).

marking up prices on drugs not on the Essential Drugs List (EDL), as well as on devices and other technologies (see Figure 7.16); Class III hospitals may depend more heavily than other hospitals on such markups. All of these incentives encouraged the importation of foreign drugs and devices, whose prices were higher and thus enjoyed greater markups. In 1980, imported drugs accounted for less than 1 percent of drug sales in China; by 1993, they had captured anywhere from 30 percent to 55 percent market share in China's major cities.[115]

Scholars note that herbal medicine in general and drug dispensing in particular have historically been more central to the physician–patient relationship in eastern cultures than in western cultures.[116] Doctors thus earned much of their income through the prescribing and dispensing of medications. As physician practice became more closely integrated with practice in public hospitals, the dispensing of medications shifted from community to hospital settings. Roughly 80 percent of all drugs are now sold through hospitals. Moreover, because of the freedom to charge markups and earn commissions, and because of the withdrawal of governmental financing, Chinese hospitals had incentives to diversify into inpatient and outpatient pharmacies to cover their operating costs and earn profit margins. Between 2000 and 2008, prescription drugs and biologics (not TCM products, which are low cost and low revenue) accounted for 50–60 percent

of hospital outpatient spending, 43–48 percent of inpatient spending, 40 percent of public hospital revenues, and anywhere from 40 percent to 50 percent of national healthcare spending.[117]

Much of this dispensing is unwarranted. According to one study, Chinese physicians prescribe antibiotics to nearly two-thirds of their patients (and three-quarters in village clinics).[118] Other research shows that intramuscular and intravenous injections are quite common in urban areas (13 percent and 32 percent of prescriptions, respectively) and especially in rural areas (30 percent and 35 percent, respectively).[119] According to the MOH, the average Chinese citizen is prescribed ten times more antibiotics than the average US citizen.[120] Some researchers estimate that 30–40 percent of drug expenditures for various conditions are unnecessary.[121]

Another avenue to augment physician income includes the pursuit of advanced medical training and academic research. Prestigious physician researchers can earn high salaries tied to government grants. Alternatively, physicians can climb the hospital hierarchy to occupy leadership positions (e.g., department chair) that control distribution of some of the hospital's surplus revenue. Finally, physicians can travel on weekends and moonlight in clinics in other parts of China, or work in the growing number of private hospitals. At present, the private hospitals have attracted older (and likely retired public hospital) physicians; younger physicians may perceive higher switching costs to moving from public to private hospitals, perhaps due to the fear of not being able to return.

Overall, these additional payments can double or triple a physician's total practice income. For example, on top of a base salary of 46,000 RMB, doctors could earn up to 10,000 RMB from the hospital as a monthly bonus and an annual bonus of several thousand yuan. As a result, the total income of a hospital specialist could be as much as 180,000 RMB, while the total income of a department head could be as much as 250,000–300,000 RMB.

China's physicians thus work under pay-for-performance incentives that are all tied to productivity, utilization, and revenue generation (the equivalent of the US fee-for-service model of "eat what you kill"). Hospitals reward their physicians for using their services and equipment. In this manner, the economic incentives of the manufacturer, hospital, and physician are entirely aligned: more is better. These incentives work against the traditional ethos of medical practice, cause divisions and income disparities among physicians, and now serve as a source of rising dissatisfaction among doctors. The dissatisfaction may be most acute among those specialists (e.g., pediatricians, pathologists, TCM practitioners) who are unable to perform procedures, conduct tests, or prescribe medications that entail kickbacks and markups.[122]

The financial incentives serve not only as a spur to technological development but also as a major driver of rising cost and over-utilization of healthcare. According to China's Development Research Center, as much as one-fifth of all healthcare spending in China may be due to supplier-induced demand.[123]

China's healthcare reform has sought to change these practices (see Chapter 2). In 2004, the MOH announced it would cancel the principle of tying bonus distributions to departmental revenues; over time, however, that principle has remained in place.[124] In 2012, the MOH ordered hospitals and patients to sign an agreement that bribes would not be accepted or offered for inpatient care. In 2013, the National Health and Family Planning Commission issued prohibitions on nine unethical practices dealing with augmentation of physician incomes (see Chapter 2). In 2013, the State Council issued guidelines stating that hospitals could no longer link patients' utilization of drugs or medical exams to physicians' incomes. The guidelines also called on hospitals to teach their physicians how to properly use basic medicines. Public sector physicians practicing at local levels were required to sell drugs on the EDL without any markup in price. Moreover, pilot programs encouraged separation of physician services from pharmaceutical sales in public hospitals in Beijing. Such initiatives may be intended to stem the effects of technological change on expanded insurance coverage which, in turn, spurs demand for that technology (the healthcare quadrilemma discussed in Chapter 1).[125] Separation policies have not yet been imposed on the mass of public hospitals, however.

Researchers suggest there are several barriers to installing quality-based and other performance appraisal models to motivate Chinese physicians. One barrier is the legacy of egalitarianism instituted by Mao. Wage differences and increases are reportedly too narrow to motivate and reward higher-performing physicians. A second barrier is the difficulty reported by hospitals in developing the proper evaluation metrics beyond just patient volume. Third, the low and declining government subsidy of public hospital operating costs (8.7 percent in 2007 vs. 8.2 percent in 2010) hampers any effort to decouple physician payment from hospital and departmental performance.[126]

Informal Payments

Another avenue taken by physicians to augment their low salary is the receipt of informal payments from patients ("red envelopes," "red packages"). According to one study, the average red envelope payment is 1,039 RMB, which represents roughly 14 percent of the physician's total fee. The specialties most likely to receive (and expect) such payments are surgeons, anesthesiologists, and obstetricians. Hospitals can also receive informal payments that amount to 140–320 RMB; payments can reach as high as 400 RMB in tertiary facilities.[127] Such payments are variously viewed as a vehicle to ensure being seen and treated by the physician in the overcrowded outpatient department, to receive better service, and/or to assure good treatment outcomes.

There are no firm data on the prevalence of such payments. An earlier research study reported that 21 percent of Chinese physicians accept such payments to compensate for their low salaries; 59 percent stated they refused on ethical grounds.[128] Another survey reported that nearly a third of recent medical school graduates consider these payments "normal."[129] These findings are likely subject to serious underreporting due to social desirability bias. A substantial number of inpatients report making such payments; the World Bank estimates they comprise 8.6 percent of all inpatients.[130] Patients most likely to pay these fees are those in bad health, younger in age, and higher utilizers of services.

Regulating Physician Behavior

Prior to the economic reforms, there was a general convergence in the personal and professional values of physicians. Following John Eisenberg's classification, Chinese physicians saw little conflict between their roles as "patient's agent," "society's agent," and their own "economic agent." According to one researcher, "medicine's primary goal [was] to serve and care for the health of the people. Medical professionals took pride in their work and were respected by the people."

Starting in the 1980s, the physician's compact with Chinese society and Chinese patients changed.[131] Physician salaries lagged behind those of other occupations; the government withdrew funding from public hospitals, requiring them to engage in for-profit behaviors and over-treatment of patients; and hospitals incentivized their medical staffs to facilitate this for-profit conversion. Doctors compensated for relatively low pay by accepting informal payments from patients and kickbacks from hospitals and their suppliers to over-utilize products and services. Chinese physicians began to emphasize their role as self-interested economic agents, as well as the agents of their hospital employers; this came at the expense of their role as the patient's agent or society's agent. What was once a normatively based exchange quickly transformed into a utilitarian-based exchange. The once dominant model of "State Medicine" via public health and prevention was not remunerative for either doctors or hospitals, and rapidly gave way to the (more expensive) biomedical model of cure and treatment.

Levers to Influence Physician Practice

Paradoxically, while Chinese physicians practice in pyramidal hierarchies as state employees, their behavior is not tightly supervised. Many of the system levers to influence and control practice behavior are lacking in China (see Figure 7.17).[132] First, education is quite variable, with most physicians trained below (or well below) the doctoral level. Second, there are enormous financial incentives to over-utilize drugs and other technologies in order to increase practice incomes. Third, there are few reported practice norms, in large part due to the absence of a well-functioning association to "professionalize" doctor behavior, exercise self-regulation, and instill medical ethics. Fourth, there are little data on physicians' practice patterns and thus little opportunity to conduct medical audits and monitor adherence to practice guidelines. Fifth, there is little group medical practice in China, and thus little opportunity to practice "shoulder to shoulder," monitor one another's behavior, and exert peer pressure over one's colleagues.

Many Chinese physicians (e.g., those in private practice) are paid on a fee-for-service basis, as in the United States. Fee for service incentivizes physicians to provide more care which, as noted in Chapter 1, is not necessarily better care. Other Chinese physicians are paid on a salaried basis; however, the salaries are so low that hospitals and physicians have responded in different ways to augment their incomes, often based on service volume incentives, which again have fostered over-utilization. As in the United States, China is now experimenting with other modes of physician payment to incentivize appropriate care and reduce overutilization. These modes include capitation, case-based payments, prospective case-based payments, and global budgets (among others). There is limited diffusion of these different payment methods and limited research evidence on their impact; the available evidence suggests they help to reduce expenditures per hospital admission.[133]

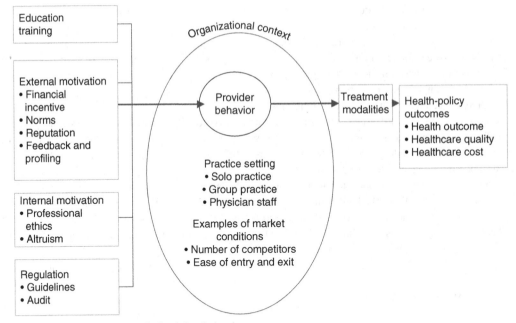

Figure 7.17 Levers to control physician behavior
Source: Adapted from Yip et al., *The Lancet* (March 27, 2010).

Government Regulation

The nascent and narrowly diffused professionalism in Chinese medicine prior to the civil war was undermined by Mao's anti-professionalism bias. Similarly, in Chinese society, the traditional emphasis on Confucianism as one source of ethics was replaced by a Communist ideology during the Maoist era. The government went beyond ideology to ban non-state organizations and professionalizing activities as potential sources of competition and loyalty with civic society. Urban physicians had become salaried employees in rigid hierarchies within public institutions who needed to be obedient to their superiors (who were often appointed by the government and/or Communist Party). There were no opportunities to form horizontal associations with one's colleagues in other institutions or cities.[134]

During the subsequent period of economic liberalization, the Communist ideology was dampened by the focus on economic growth and money. There was no concerted effort in existing medical associations or medical training to instill an ethos of patient-centered care, quality, or judicious use of societal resources.

The Ministry of Health and its administrative departments at various geographic levels (county level and above) oversee physician affairs. These departments are required to conduct physician assessments at regular intervals. They are also supposed to develop training programs for continuing medical education, with the support of the institutions where physicians practice. Doctors at the village level are subject to local government regulations. Enforcement here is also suspect; according to an earlier study of poor counties in China's western provinces, 65–70 percent of village doctors had only a high school education and only 20 months of medical training.[135]

Over time, the Chinese government has issued a series of codes to govern professional medical practice:

- In 1988, the MOH issued "Norms and Implementation of Medical Ethics for Healthcare Workers" to upgrade their ethics. That same year, the Chinese Medical Association issued a "Medical Ethics Manifesto" that emphasized the priority of the patient.[136]

- In 1989, the MOH promulgated seven principles for the medical profession in a "Code of Conduct." These codes included (1) rescue the dying and healing the wounded, humanitarianism, and keeping the patient's interest; (2) respect the patient's personality and rights, treat patients as equals; (3) serve the patient with dignity; (4) be honest and don't pursue selfish interests; (5) respect the patient's confidentiality; (6) learn from colleagues; and (7) be rigorous and dependable.[137]

- The 1998 Law on Licensed Doctors offered some general regulations governing physician behavior. The regulations are only ten pages long, and thus cannot encompass much in the way of specifics. The various chapters in the law cover examinations, registration, doctors' rights and obligations (e.g., including medical ethics, duties to patients), and prohibitions on taking monies illegally from patients.

- In 1999, the MOH issued requirements for good clinical practice (including ethical review) that were revised four years later.

- In 2007, the MOH issued a medical ethics code and ethics evaluation system.

However, the succession of codes suggests the desired behaviors have not been achieved or tightly monitored. Chinese scholars assert that the demotion of medical professionals under Mao, combined with hospital-based employment and the reliance on revenue generation, bonus systems, and profit making under economic reform, served to erode physicians' professional ethics and practice norms and trumped patient interests and patient-centric care.[138] Local health bureaus have not paid much attention to the cost and quality of care provided in healthcare facilities for several reasons, including the low priority on health relative to economic growth, the lack of regulatory capacity and staffing in local government, and the lack of funding from higher levels of government. The government has yet to systematically collect and post information on its medical workforce, education and training, and work experience. Such information could serve to help Chinese consumers in their selection of providers to visit for treatment.

Professionalism and Professional Associations

The Chinese Medical Association (CMA) was founded in 1915 as the oldest non-governmental medical organization in the country. However, it was open to all healthcare occupations, not just physicians, and thus was unlikely to promote physician-specific ethics. Moreover, the CMA historically acted as the academic/educational counterpart to the MOH due to being administered by governmental appointees, populated by Communist Party members, and plagued by party bureaucracy.[139]

To remedy this situation, a second body – the Chinese Medical Doctor Association (CMDA) – was established in 2002 to provide professional guidance, self-discipline, coordination, supervision, and evaluation of doctor qualifications. On a lesser basis, it functions to protect and represent the interests of the country's 2.1 million doctors.[140] CMDA, open only to physicians, has 39 local associations and 51 specialty subassociations.

CMDA is a voluntary association focused heavily on offering its members educational programs and exchange opportunities. These programs are funded by the hospitals in which physicians work and/or the local health bureaus that fund the hospitals. Educational events are organized for senior doctors only; like continuing medical education, the CMDA is more active in urban areas than in rural regions.

CMDA and China's medical workforce thus do not pose a countervailing force to hospitals, as they do in the United States. CMDA members view the association as an academic society, not a trade union to protect or advance their interests in the organizations they work for. They also have no influence over hospital management and no sway over the government bureaus that control them. Similar to the administrators of China's public hospitals, the senior leaders of CMDA are former officials of central and local government who are loyal to the Communist Party. Although they are "elected" by the membership, the government must approve any leadership appointments.

It is debatable whether CMDA plays any role in protecting the rights of its members in medical malpractice disputes, or as a lobbyist for medical reform and medical ethics. Clearly, these associations have not been effective in lobbying for higher wage levels for their members or for higher governmental support of the institutions in which they work. According to one physician, the "Medical Association is an organization that has no political power, no administrative power, no professional authority, and no financial management power. It is just a 'shadow organization' working for the State. It is insignificant in the healthcare system."[141]

In 2005, the CMDA did adopt an international code, the "Medical Professionalism in the New Millennium: A Physician Charter," published a few years earlier in the West. The charter contained three fundamental principles (primacy of patient welfare, patient autonomy, and social justice) and outlined ten professional commitments with which doctors should comply. Survey research showed that most Chinese physicians have attitudes consistent with the charter but not necessarily behaviors consistent with the attitudes.[142] For example, while nearly 100 percent of doctors stress the importance of maintaining professional competence, only 75 percent stated they were able to apply new medical knowledge and skills critically. As another illustration, while over 90 percent believe they should actively evaluate the quality of their peers, less than 50 percent report they have participated in such activity.

Finally, in 2000, the MOH and other ministries issued "Guidelines on the Reforms to Municipal and Township Pharmaceutical and Health Systems" to overhaul the urban healthcare system. These guidelines promised to gradually establish a system to manage medicine as a profession – phasing out the work-unit allocation of physician labor, the lock-in between physicians and specific hospitals, and the move to contractual-based employment. Years later, the guidelines had yet to be implemented.[143] Due to the fact that Chinese physicians cannot unionize and require (at least in the past) the permission of their hospitals to practice elsewhere, they have little bargaining power with their hospital employers.

Patients and Consumerism

At present, China has a weak malpractice system and even weaker consumerism movement. As noted above, the government has yet to publish national data on the quality of care rendered by the country's physicians that would help to foster some patient shopping. Most information on provider quality deals with "structural" indicators such as hospital size, physician credentials, and available technology and equipment ("technical qualifications") – denoted by the hospital accreditation and classification scheme. Along with the hospital's location, these structural factors are what patients consider in shopping, and what hospitals focus on in competing with one another.[144]

Consumerism may be presently limited to the patient's ability to pay. According to one physician, "Money is the biggest issue that patients face. Chinese people are very simple. They look for the cheapest alternative that works."[145] Patients may therefore forego recommended therapy in favor of other affordable treatments or no treatment at all. This is particularly true for lower-income patients, but also for those whose insurance provides little coverage for expensive tests, drugs, and services.

Moreover, some researchers claim there is an inherent conflict between (a) traditional Confucian values of mutual trust and benevolence and (b) modern consumerism that denotes an economic exchange between two parties on an equal footing. The former is cast as patient-centric; the latter is cast as profit-centric. Their juxtaposition and conflict has been occasioned by economic liberalization.[146] Chinese physicians claim that they have experienced greater pressure by patients and increased exhaustion as a result.

To the extent there is consumer behavior, it is largely negative, rooted in unpleasant physician encounters (e.g., long waiting lines, crowded outpatient departments, lack of privacy, lack of time with the provider), distrust of physician motives, and both verbal and physical clashes with physicians and nurses.[147] Patients' inability to pay may be one reason for clashes with physicians. For example, patients suspect that recommended tests are unnecessary, that physician decision making is distorted, and that their doctors are trying to cheat them.[148]

As another example, family members stabbed ten physicians in Shanghai allegedly after the hospital denied treatment based on inability to pay.[149] The situation may be aggravated by delays in care seeking on the part of patients with less ability to pay, which contributes to higher illness severity and greater likelihood of an adverse outcome.

There are other reasons for such clashes. Conflicts likely result from information asymmetry between doctor and patient, the provider's inability to fully explain the patient's condition (which increases expectations), and thus the latter's inability to understand the gravity of their condition.[150] Following this logic, clashes may be more likely in outpatient clinics rather than on inpatient wards for two reasons. First, patients and their families may more fully understand the severity of illness after admission; second, the inpatient admission may be better covered by insurance. Other explanations for clashes include uneven quality of care across Chinese hospitals, the public ownership of hospitals (whereby patients believe the government may step in to provide compensation), and media reports that highlight the conflicts.[151]

The number of medical disputes reportedly doubled between 2006 and 2008, reaching more than 1 million annually; on average, roughly 40 disputes occurred at each medical institution.[152] In 2010, the *China Daily* reported there were 10,000 violent incidents in the country's hospitals. Other testimony suggests that the number of violent incidents rose 70 percent between 2006 (10,248 incidents) and 2010 (17,243 incidents).[153] Some journalists put the number of physicians experiencing violent disputes with their patients as high as 70 percent.[154] The growing frequency of these attacks has led to hospitals being referred to as "high-risk workplaces."[155]

There are also high consumer expectations placed on physicians for quality care due to a host of factors: fee-for-service medicine, informal payments, high out-of-pocket costs, the one-child policy, and increased government funding of hospitals' technology upgrades. Patients have adopted a "client mentality" and view their physicians as instruments to cure them via timely medication and efficacious treatment, not as trusted agents who have patients' welfare at the center of their ethos.[156] They and their families may also bully the physicians. Errors are thus unacceptable.

Physicians have responded by taking a series of precautionary measures to avoid medical disputes with patients, including defensive medicine (e.g., order more diagnostic tests).[157] One of the more famous images was a group of Chinese physicians wearing combat helmets while dealing with a patient at the bedside (see Figure 7.18).

China does have two tracks for litigating medical malpractice. The first is governed by State Council regulations issued in 2002 whereby plaintiffs can file claims if the physician commits a "medical accident." This track does not favor patients: awards here are typically low and dependent on the determination of a medical review board (comprised of members of local medical associations) that an error was made. Resolution of disputes outside of this track does not favor hospitals: medical malpractice insurance typically only covers cases where the review board has found an error was committed, not when awards were made outside of court. The second track is to bring a tort claim that relies on civil law and judicial inspection agencies retained by both sides. The civil courts reportedly serve more as a state tool than a counterweight to state power. In 2010, China enacted a new tort liability law that placed the burden of proof on the plaintiffs.

Chinese patients have historically put less emphasis on pursuing claims in court and more emphasis on solving disputes through interpersonal means. According to a 2009 story in the *China Daily*, patients and their families file more than 10,000 malpractice cases annually; according to the Supreme People's Court, courts nationwide heard 17,000 malpractice claims in 2010, representing a 7–8 percent over the prior year. Regardless of the true magnitude, these are small numbers compared to the large population size and the number of medical disputes.[158] Instead of the courts, Chinese patients may hire protesters ("medical chaos professionals") to help them obtain better hospital settlements.

The Chinese government has sought to shield physicians from irate patients and malpractice lawsuits. One avenue has been to designate the hospital as the primary bearer of liability. Hospitals (and not

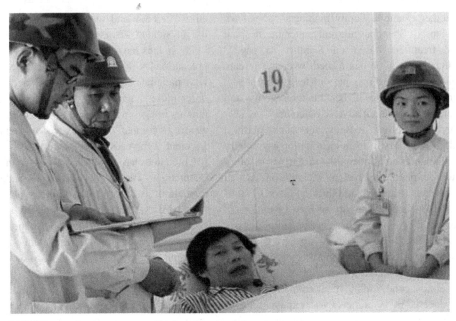

Figure 7.18 "Precautionary measures" taken by physicians

the professional associations) assist physicians in settling malpractice cases, and reportedly settle for higher amounts than would be awarded in court to avoid family protests.[159] A second avenue has been to regard malpractice as "moral negligence" rather than "personal injury negligence"; the former carries lower financial penalties in the form of compensation.

Nevertheless, there exists an uneasy relationship between the government, the physicians it employs, and the patients/citizens who rely on their services. On the one hand, doctors feel under-resourced by the public hospitals they work in and under-served by the government that pays them salaries below other occupational groups; this situation has not been addressed in China's healthcare reforms. On the other hand, doctors feel pressured by demanding patients who expect perfection and unfavorable media reports of physician negligence. This has led to China's own version of "the iron triangle of conflicting expectations."[160]

It may seem paradoxical that growing patient consumerism may not be what patients want or what patients are prepared for. Researchers claim that Chinese patients want their physicians to take responsibility for their treatment and make the important treatment decisions. They also prefer to follow their doctors' recommendations even when they do not agree with them.[161] This may result from the information asymmetry between doctor and patient, and the lack of public information on their providers. Thus, patients may want to trust their doctors as under the old Confucian model but are reluctant to do so based on the new economic model and incentives in medical practice. For their part, Chinese doctors want their patients' trust, as part of their need for professional satisfaction and fulfillment. Chinese doctors also want to support their patients' autonomy and have patients participate in decision making; however, much of this desire may be prompted by fears for their own physical safety.

Consumerism may nevertheless come to China's healthcare system. Both the wage levels and educational levels of the urban Chinese population have grown over time, both of which fuel shopping behavior. In the near term, such shopping may be restricted more to over-the-counter (OTC) products than to inpatient and outpatient hospital consumption, however.

Notes

1. Charlie Xue, Qing Wu, Wen Yu Zhou et al. 2006. "Comparisons of Chinese Medicine Education and Training in China and Australia," *Annals Academy of Medicine* 35 (11): 775–779.
2. Tai-Pong Lam, Xue-Hong Wan, and Mary Sau-Man Ip. 2006. "Current Perspectives on Medical Education in China," *Medical Education* 40: 940–949.
3. Lam et al. 2006. "Current Perspectives on Medical Education in China."
4. China Medical Commission. 2014. *Medicine in China* (New York: Rockefeller Foundation).
5. John Watt. 2012. *Public Medicine in Wartime China* (Boston, MA: Suffolk University).
6. Francis Hong. 2004. "History of Medicine in China: When Medicine Took an Alternative Path," *McGill Journal of Medicine* 8: 79–84.
7. The report also reviewed most of the 24 medical colleges listed by the National Medical Association of China in 1930. They were sponsored by a variety of organizations (13 private, 4 government, 3 military, and 2 provincial). The number of colleges grew gradually. A subsequent report by the CME identified 27 medical colleges, including 19 that offered six-year degree training and 6 offering vocational training of four years with no degree. In 1937, there were 14 missionary/private, 8 government, 7 provincial/vocational, and 3 military. Watt. 2012. *Public Medicine in Wartime China.*
8. Watt. 2012. *Public Medicine in Wartime China.*
9. Heiner Fruehauf. 2009. "Chinese Medicine in Crisis: Science, Politics, and the Making of 'TCM,'" Available online at: www.classical chinesemedicine.org/2009/04/chinese-medi cine-in-crisis-tcm/. Accessed on June 22, 2015.
10. Fruehauf. 2009. "Chinese Medicine in Crisis."
11. Watt. 2012. *Public Medicine in Wartime China.*
12. Some place the number much higher at 200,000. Yuanli Liu, Peter Berman, Winnie Yip et al. 2006. "Health Care in China: The Role of Non-Government Providers," *Health Policy* 77: 212–220.
13. Watt. 2012. *Public Medicine in Wartime China.*
14. Deborah Davis. 2000. "Social Class Transformation in Urban China: Training, Hiring, and Promoting Urban Professionals and Managers after 1949," *Modern China* 26 (3): 251–275.
15. Kim Taylor. 2005. *Chinese Medicine in Early Communist China 1945–1963: A Medicine of Revolution* (New York: Routledge).
16. Jianqing Yang. 2010. "Serve the People: Communist Ideology and Professional Ethics of Medicine in China," *Health Care Analysis* 18: 294–309.
17. Yang. 2010. "Serve the People."
18. Davis. 2000. "Social Class Transformation in Urban China."
19. Ibid. Yang. 2010. "Serve the People."
20. Ironically, the handful of allopathic doctors recruited served as the administrators of the new TCM institutions; this effectively left the promotion of TCM in the hands of allopathic physicians who typically suspected the traditional practices.
21. Fruehauf. 2009. "Chinese Medicine in Crisis."
22. Xue et al. 2006. "Comparisons of Chinese Medicine Education and Training in China and Australia."
23. Fruehauf. 2009. "Chinese Medicine in Crisis."
24. Ryan Leonard. 2010. *Working Lives of Chinese Physicians.* 2009–2010 Penn Humanities Forum on Connections (April).
25. Daqing Zhang and Paul Unschuld. 2008. "China's Barefoot Doctor: Past, Present, and Future," *The Lancet* 372: 1865–1866.
26. Zhang and Unschuld. 2008. "China's Barefoot Doctor." In parts of the country, however, the barefoot doctor delivery system remained intact for some time with practitioners salaried by local level brigades. Jeffrey Koplan, Alan Hinman, Robert Parker et al. 1985. "The Barefoot Doctor: Shanghai County Revisited," *American Journal of Public Health* 75(7): 768–770.
27. Krishna Kumar Vr. 2013. "Just What the Doctor Ordered," *China Daily Asia* (December 20).

28. *Law on Licensed Doctors of the People's Republic of China.* Available online at: www.asianlii.org/cn/legis/cen/laws/loldot proc467/. Accessed on June 18, 2015.

29. Yang. 2010. "Serve the People."

30. Ibid.

31. Fruehauf. 2009. "Chinese Medicine in Crisis."

32. Yang. 2010. "Serve the People."

33. Such tensions had already surfaced soon after the period of liberalization began, when the Chinese media began publishing stories of the impact of bureaucratic medicine on patient care. These stories mentioned the low quality, poor access and long waits, "rent seeking" (e.g., extracting fees from patients), and the poor physician attitudes toward patients ("callous," "crude," "confrontational") – which Chinese scholars attribute to the typical public servant stance. Yang. 2010. "Serve the People."

34. Yang. 2010. "Serve the People."

35. Belinda Tin Yan Chow. 2009. *Medical Doctors of the People's Republic of China: The Profession, Professionalization, Professionalism and Professional Commitment.* Master's Thesis, Hong Kong Polytechnic University (August). Available online at: http://repository.lib.polyu.edu.hk/jspui/bitstream/10397/5356/2/b2507241 9_ir.pdf. Accessed on June 20, 2015.

36. These schools train roughly equal numbers of "doctors" and "assistant doctors." Dong Xu, Baozhi Sun, Xuehong Wan et al. 2010. "Reformation of Medical Education in China," *The Lancet* 375(9725): 1502–1503.

37. For one listing of 150 schools, see the following: www.iime.org/database/asia/china.htm.

38. Xu et al. 2010. "Reformation of Medical Education in China."

39. Sudhir Anand, Victoria Fan, Junhua Zhang et al. 2008. "China's Human Resources for Health: Quantity, Quality, and Distribution," *The Lancet* 372: 1774–1781.

40. Note that the *2010 China Yearbook of Health Statistics* provides a higher estimate of nearly 1.8 physicians per 1,000 population for 2009.

41. Xuezheng Qin, Lixing Li, and Chee-Ruey Hsieh. 2013. "Too Few Doctors or Too Low Wages? Labor Supply of Health Care Professionals in China," *China Economic Review* 24: 150–164.

42. Onil Bhattacharyya, Yin Delu, Sabrina Wong et al. 2011. "Evolution of Primary Care in China, 1997–2009," *Health Policy* 100: 174–180.

43. Bhattacharyya et al. 2011. "Evolution of Primary Care in China, 1997–2009."

44. Ibid.

45. Sudhir Anand, Victoria Fan, Junhua Zhang et al. 2008. "China's Human Resources for Health: Quantity, Quality, and Distribution," *The Lancet*. Available online at: www.thelancet.com/journals/lancet/article/PIIS0140-6736(08)61363-X/references. Accessed on October 12, 2015. Hu Yun, Shen Jie, and Jiang Anil. 2010. "Nursing Shortage in China: State, Causes, and Strategy," *Nursing Outlook* 58(3): 122–128.

46. Shaunagh Browning. 2015. "A New Role for Chinese Nurses: The Clinical Research Nurse in Clinical Trials." Presentation to the International Association of Clinical Research Nurses. Available online at: www.nursinglibrary.org/vhl/bitstream/10755/338380/1/1_Browning_S_p67929_1.pdf. Accessed on October 12, 2015.

47. Here again there is a discrepancy in statistics. According to the OECD, China has 1.7 nurses per 1,000 population; according to the *2010 China Yearbook*, it is 1.4.

48. Yun et al. 2010. "Nursing Shortage in China." See also: H. Liu, Y. Gong, L. Yao et al. 2005. "Current Status of Nursing Manpower and Nursing Staff Post Capacity Standards Research," *Chinese Nursing Management* 5 (4): 22–25.

49. Author unknown. 2014. "Severe Nurse Shortage Continues in China," *Want China Times* (May 14). Available online at: www.wantchinatimes.com/news-subclass-cnt.aspx?id=20140514000011&cid=1103. Accessed on October 12, 2015.

50. Beatrice Kalisch and Yilan Liu. 2009. "Comparison of Nursing: China and the United States," *Nursing Economics* 27(5): 322–331.

51. Nigel Crisp and Lincoln Chen. 2014. "Global Supply of Health Professionals," *New England Journal of Medicine* 370: 950–957.

52. Yun et al. 2010. "Nursing Shortage in China."

53. Emily Eddins, Jie Hu, and Huaping Liu. 2011. "Baccalaureate Nursing Education in China: Issues and Challenges," *Nursing Education Perspectives* 32(1): 30–33. Derek Smith and Sa Tang. 2004. "Nursing in China: Historical Development, Current Issues and Future Challenges," *Oita University of Nursing and Health Sciences* 5(2): 16–20. Available online at: www.oita-nhs.ac.jp/journal/PDF/5_2/5_2_1 .pdf. Accessed on October 12, 2015.

54. Eddins et al. 2011. "Baccalaureate Nursing Education in China."

55. Yun et al. 2010. "Nursing Shortage in China." Kalisch and Liu. 2009. "Comparison of Nursing."

56. Yu-Qin Gao, Bo-Chen Pan, Wei Sun et al. 2012. "Anxiety Symptoms Among Chinese Nurses and the Associated Factors: A Cross Sectional Study," *BMC Psychiatry* 12: 141–149. Frances Lin, Winsome St. John, and Carol McVeigh. 2009. "Burnout Among Hospital Nurses in China," *Journal of Nursing Management* 17(3): 294–301.

57. Jingjing Shang, Liming You, Chenjuan Ma et al. 2014. "Nurse Employment Contracts in Chinese Hospitals: Impact of Inequitable Benefit Structures on Nurse and Patient Satisfaction," *Human Resources for Health* 12 (1): 1–10.

58. Yun et al. 2010. "Nursing Shortage in China."

59. Kalisch and Liu. 2009. "Comparison of Nursing: China and the United States."

60. Anand et al. 2008. "China's Human Resources for Health." Leonard. 2010. *Working Lives of Chinese Physicians.*

61. Liu et al. 2005. "Current Status of Nursing Manpower and Nursing Staff Post Capacity Standards Research."

62. Frances Wong and Yue Zhao. 2012. "Nursing Education in China: Past, Present, and Future," *Journal of Nursing Management* 20: 38–44.

63. Xu Tian, Jun-xiao Lian, Li-juan Yi et al. 2014. "Current Status of Clinical Nurse Specialists and the Demands of Osteoporosis Specialized Nurses in Mainland China," *International Journal of Nursing Sciences* 1: 306–313.

64. The workforce size has vastly increased since 1950 (less than 1 million); however, most of the personnel gains occurred between 1950 and 1980.

65. Meng-Kin Lim, Hui Yang, Tuohong Zhang et al. 2004. "China's Evolving Health Care Market: How Doctors Feel and What They Think," *Health Policy* 69: 329–337.

66. Tai Pong Lam and Yu Ying Bess Lam. 2009. "Medical Education Reform: The Asian Experience," *International Medical Education* 84(9): 1313–1317.

67. The Chinese government pursued a policy to phase out such programs, then reversed course in 2009 to encourage them as a feeder of rural healthcare manpower, but may seek to wind them down again.

68. Meng-Kin Lim, Hui Yang, Tuohong Zhang, et al. 2004. "Public Perceptions of Private Health Care in Socialist China," *Health Affairs* 23(6): 222–234.

69. Ge Jiangyi. 2008. "The System of Licensing Doctors in China," *Medicine and Law* 27: 325–338.

70. Lijuan Wu, Youxin Wang, Xiaoxia Peng et al. 2014. "Development of a Medical Academic Degree System in China," *Medical Education Online*, 19. Available online at http://med-ed-online.net/index.php/meo/article/view/23141.

71. Honglei Dai, Lizheng Fang, Rebecca Malouin et al. 2013. "Family Medicine Training in China," *Family Medicine* 45(5): 341–344. See also Hua Xu, Alex He Jingwei, Kai Zheng et al. 2012. "China," in James Johnson and Carleen Stoskopf (Eds.), *Comparative Health Systems Update: France, China, and Peru* (Sudbury, MA: Jones & Bartlett): chapter B.

72. Liu Xu, Yang Hongyang, and Zhang Lulu. 2013. "Chinese Doctors Leaving Public Hospitals – Brain Drain or Emancipation?" *The BMJ* (September 11). Available online at: http://blogs.bmj.com/bmj/2013/09/11/liu-xu-et-al-chinese-doctors-leaving-public-hospitals-brain-drain-or-emancipation/. Accessed on October 9, 2015.

73. Li-Mei Ran, Kai-Jian Luo, Yun-Cheng Wu et al. 2013. "An Analysis of China's Physician Salary Payment System," *Journal of Huazhong University of Science and Technology* 33(2): 309–314.

74. Jie Zeng, Xing Zeng, and Qi Tu. 2013. "A Gloomy Future for Medical Students in China," *The Lancet* 382: 1878. Jeffrey Hays. 2012. "Health Care in China – Doctors, Insurance, and Costs," *China – Facts and Details* (November). Available online at: http://factsanddetails.com/china/cat13/sub83/item335.html. Accessed on September 23, 2015.

75. Anand et al. 2008. "China's Human Resources for Health."

76. Hays. 2011. "Health Care in China."

77. Jiangyi. 2008. "The System of Licensing Doctors in China."

78. Information here is drawn from a presentation by Zeng Zhechun, "CME in China." Available online at: www.slideserve.com/nova/cme-in-china. Additional information is taken from Lewis Miller et al. 2015. "CME Credit Systems in Three Developing Countries: China, India and Indonesia," *Journal of European CME* 4. Available online at: www.jecme.eu/index.php/jecme/article/view/27411. Accessed on July 19, 2015.

79. Leonard. 2010. *Working Lives of Chinese Physicians*. Leonard's description is based on a field study and interviews at Guangzhou Medical College. This section of the chapter draws on his ethnographic research.

80. Leonard. 2010. *Working Lives of Chinese Physicians*.

81. Chow. 2009. *Medical Doctors of the People's Republic of China*.

82. Leonard. 2010. *Working Lives of Chinese Physicians*.

83. Bo Ye and Ae-Huey Jennifer Liu. 2013. "Inadequate Evaluation of Medical Doctors in China," *The Lancet* 381: 1984.

84. Author unknown. 2010. "Scientific Fraud: Action Needed in China," *The Lancet* 375: 94. Author unknown. 2015. "China's Medical Research Integrity Questioned," *The Lancet* 385: 1365.

85. Leonard. 2010. *Working Lives of Chinese Physicians*.

86. McDermott Will & Emery. 2015. "Chinese Government Further Encourages, Regulates Multi-Site Practice by Physicians" (Shanghai: MWE China law Offices).

87. Qingyue Meng, Xingzhu Liu, and Junshi Shi. 2000. "Comparing the Services and Quality of Private and Public Clinics in Rural China," *Health Policy and Planning* 15(4): 349–356.

88. Liu et al. 2006. "Health Care in China."

89. Karen Eggleston, Li Ling, Meng Qingyue et al. 2008. "Health Service Delivery in China: A Literature Review," *Health Economics* 17: 149–165. Xu et al. 2012. "China."

90. Meng et al. 2000. "Comparing the Services and Quality of Private and Public Clinics in Rural China."

91. Lim et al. 2004. "Public Perceptions of Private Health Care in Socialist China." Liu et al. 2006. "Health Care in China."

92. Leonard. 2010. *Working Lives of Chinese Physicians*.

93. Benjamin Liebman. 2013. "Malpractice Mobs: Medical Dispute Resolution in China," *Columbia Law Review* 113(1): 181–264.

94. Ping Xie. 2013. "Outpatient Workload in China," *The Lancet* 381: 1983.

95. Leonard. 2010. *Working Lives of Chinese Physicians*.

96. Ibid.

97. Wenzhi Cai, Ling Deng, Meng Liu et al. 2011. "Antecedents of Medical Workplace Violence in South China," *Journal of Interpersonal Violence* 26(2): 312–327.

98. Abdul Mbwah, Peng Xiaoming, and Chen Shaoxian. 2010. "Professional Analysis of Medical Staff in Public Hospitals in China," *Journal of Public Health and Epidemiology* 2(4): 60–70.

99. Lim et al. 2004. "Public Perceptions of Private Health Care in Socialist China."

100. Ibid.

101. Gerald Bloom, Leiya Han, and Xiang Li. 2001. "How Health Workers Earn a Living

in China," *Human Resources for Health Development Journal* 5(1–3): 25–38.

102. Xuebing Cao. 2014. "Submerged Discontent and Patterns of Accommodation: A Case Study of Doctors' Pay in Two Public Hospitals in China," *International Journal of Health Planning and Management* 29: 124–140.

103. Xuebing Cao. 2011. "The Chinese Medical Doctor Association: A New Industrial Relations Actor in China's Health Services?" *Industrial Relations* 66(1): 74–97.

104. Ran et al. 2013. "An Analysis of China's Physician Salary Payment System."

105. Ibid.

106. Eggleston et al. 2008. "Health Service Delivery in China."

107. Cao. 2014. "Submerged Discontent and Patterns of Accommodation."

108. Chow. 2009. *Medical Doctors of the People's Republic of China.*

109. Peter Wonacott. 2005. "Medical Companies See Troubling Side of Chinese Market," *Wall Street Journal* (October 21): A1, 8.

110. Ran et al. 2013. "An Analysis of China's Physician Salary Payment System."

111. William Hsiao. 2008. "When Incentives and Professionalism Collide," *Health Affairs* 27 (4): 949–951.

112. Xingzhu Liu and Anne Mills. 2005. "The Effect of Performance-related Pay of Hospital Doctors on Hospital Behaviour: A Case Study from Shandong, China," *Human Resources for Health* 3(11): 1–12.

113. Liu and Mills. 2005. "The Effect of Performance-related Pay of Hospital Doctors on Hospital Behaviour."

114. Ran et al. 2013. "An Analysis of China's Physician Salary Payment System."

115. Similarly, MRI and CT scanners diffused from 0 percent share to heavily penetrate county hospitals. Liu and Mills. 2005. "The Effect of Performance-related Pay of Hospital Doctors on Hospital Behaviour."

116. Karen Eggleston. 2011. "Prescribing Institutions: Explaining the Evolution of Physician Dispensing," Asia Health Policy Program Working Paper #24 (October).

117. Qin et al. 2013. "Too Few Doctors or Too Low Wages?." Karen Eggleston, Mingshan Lu, Congdong Li et al. 2010. "Comparing Public and Private Hospitals in China: Evidence from Guangdong," *BMC Health Services Research* 10: 1–11. Richard Yeh and Ziyi Chen. 2013. *China Healthcare Sector: Handbook 2014* (Citi Research, December 18).

118. Eggleston. 2011. "Prescribing Institutions." Janet Currie, Wanchuan Lin, and Wei Zheng. 2010. "Patient Knowledge and Antibiotic Abuse: Evidence from an Audit Study in China," Working Paper #16602, National Bureau of Economic Research (December). Hsiao. 2008. "When Incentives and Professionalism Collide."

119. K. Rao, Xu Ling, S.L. Barber et al. 2010. "Changes in Health Service Use and Expenditure in China During 2003-2008," Results from the National Health Services Survey (May).

120. Author unknown. 2014. "Physician, Heal Thyself," *The Economist* (February 1): 37.

121. Liu and Mills. 2005. "The Effect of Performance-related Pay of Hospital Doctors on Hospital Behaviour."

122. Lim et al. 2004. "China's Evolving Health Care Market."

123. Christina Ho. 2010. "Health Reform and *De Facto* Federalism in China," *China: An International Journal* 8(1): 33–62.

124. Lim et al. 2004. "China's Evolving Health Care Market."

125. Eggleston. 2011. "Prescribing Institutions."

126. Ran et al. 2013. "An Analysis of China's Physician Salary Payment System."

127. Eggleston et al. 2008. "Health Service Delivery in China."

128. Bloom et al. 2001. "How Health Workers Earn a Living in China."

129. Liu Jianrong et al. 1995. "An Analysis on 'Red Package' Phenomenon and Resolution Searching," *Chinese Journal of Hospital Management* 15: 25–26.

130. Wei Zhang. 2007. "Informal Payments in Health Care and Their Impact on Provider Performance: Evidence from China," Presentation on December 25.

131. Po-Keung Ip. 2005. "Developing Medical Ethics in China's Reform Era," *Developing World Bioethics* 5(2): 176–187.

132. This model was developed by Winnie Yip, William Hsiao, Qingyue Meng et al. 2010. "Realignment of Incentives for Health-Care Providers in China," *The Lancet* 375: 1120–1130.

133. Yip et al. 2010. "Realignment of Incentives for Health-Care Providers in China." Eggleston et al. 2008. "Health Service Delivery in China."

134. Davis. 2000. "Social Class Transformation in Urban China."

135. G. Wang and H. Xu. 2003. "Evaluation on Comprehensive Quality of 456 Doctors in Township Hospitals," *Journal of Health Resources* 6(3): 72–74.

136. E. C. Hui. 2005. "The Physician as a Professional and the Moral Implications of Medical Professionalism," *Hong Kong Medical Journal* 11(1): 67–69.

137. Ip. 2005. "Developing Medical Ethics in China's Reform Era."

138. Yip et al. 2010. "Realignment of Incentives for Health-Care Providers in China."

139. Leonard. 2010. *Working Lives of Chinese Physicians.*

140. Cao. 2011. "The Chinese Medical Doctor Association."

141. Chow. 2009. *Medical Doctors of the People's Republic of China.* Quote from page 138.

142. Jing Chen, Juan Xu, Chunmei Zhang et al. 2013. "Medical Professionalism Among Clinical Physicians in Two Tertiary Hospitals, China," *Social Science and Medicine* 96: 290–296.

143. Jingqing Yang. 2008. "Medical Practice in the Non-public Sector in China," *Journal of Asian Public Policy* 1(3): 346–351.

144. Mark Gilbraith, David Wood, Cipher Jia et al. 2010. *Emerging Trends in Chinese Healthcare: The Impact of a Rising Middle Class* (Beijing, China: PricewaterhouseCoopers).

145. Leonard. 2010. *Working Lives of Chinese Physicians.*

146. Yaming Li and Xiaoyan Wang. 2012. "Dilemma of Consumerism in China," *Journal of Cambridge Studies* 7(3): 11–24.

147. Sharon LaFraniere. 2010. "Chinese Hospitals are Battlegrounds of Discontent," *New York Times* (August 11).

148. Leonard. 2010. *Working Lives of Chinese Physicians.*

149. Li Mao. 2011. "Shanghai Moves to Fix Medical Disputes," *Global Times* (August 24).

150. Liebman. 2013. "Malpractice Mobs."

151. Ibid.

152. Ibid.

153. United States – China Economic and Security Review Commission. 2014. *China's Healthcare Industry, Drug Safety, and Market Access for U.S. Medical Goods and Services.* Hearing on April 3. Available online at: origin. www.uscc.gov/sites/default/files/transcripts/ USCC%20Hearing%20Transcript_April% 203%2C%202014_0.pdf. Accessed on July 15, 2015.

154. Michael Woodhead. 2014. "How Much Does the Average Chinese Doctor Earn?" *China Medical News* (March 31).

155. Xu et al. 2013. "Chinese Doctors Leaving Public Hospitals."

156. Chow. 2009. *Medical Doctors of the People's Republic of China.*

157. Mbawah et al. 2010. "Professional Analysis of Medical Staff in Public Hospitals in China."

158. Leonard. 2010. *Working Lives of Chinese Physicians.* Liebman. 2013. "Malpractice Mobs."

159. Liebman. 2013. "Malpractice Mobs."

160. Hamilton Moses, David Matheson, E. Ray Dorsey et al. 2013. "The Anatomy of Health Care in the United States," *Journal of American Medical Association* 310(18): 1947–1963.

161. Li and Wang. 2012. "Dilemma of Consumerism in China."

China's Hospital Sector

GERARD M. LA FORGIA AND WINNIE YIP

CHAPTER 8

Introduction

China's hospital sector absorbed the lion's share (62.6 percent) of the country's total health expenditure ($511.4 billion) in 2013.[1] As discussed in Chapter 2, the sector is plagued by distorted financial incentives and managerial inefficiencies that increase costs and retard quality improvement. The government recognized these problems in the 2009 healthcare reform by targeting public hospital operations as one of the five pillars of change (see Chapter 5). Specific areas targeted for reform include hospital governance, hospital financing, provider payment methods, and, more recently, encouraging the growth of the private hospital sector.

This chapter analyzes the structure, conduct, and performance of the hospital sector in China. The chapter opens with a brief discussion of the demographic profile of Chinese hospitals. It then analyzes the sources of hospital financing, methods of provider payment, structure of public hospital governance, hospital managerial practices, and public hospital performance. The chapter then discusses the growth of the private sector and profiles two institutions, as well as analyzes recent efforts to promote integrated delivery of healthcare services and care coordination. The chapter concludes with a brief discussion of current challenges and future policy directions.

Overview of Sector

Between 2005 and 2013, the total number of hospitals in China increased 32.5 percent from 18,644 to 24,709. This growth was driven exclusively by a growth in non-public hospitals from 3,220 to 11,313, as public hospitals actually decreased in number from 15,483 to 13,396 (see Figure 8.1).[2] Public hospitals comprise the near majority (54.2 percent) of hospitals compared to private hospitals (45.8 percent), but contain the vast majority of beds (84.4 percent vs. 15.6 percent in private facilities) (see Figure 8.2). For-profit private hospitals accounted for 8.6 percent, while not-for-profit hospitals accounted for 7 percent of all beds. Public hospitals also accounted for the majority of all hospital health professionals (4,606,153 or 85.8 percent), delivered close to 90 percent of the country's inpatient and outpatient services, and accounted for roughly 70 percent of all hospital expenditures.[3]

The majority of public hospitals (72.2 percent) are large, government-run institutions. By contrast, private hospitals are generally small. Almost all (96 percent) have fewer than 100 beds; only 60 percent of public hospitals fall into this category. This is probably because smaller facilities have lower capital investment and management requirements, enabling private sector expansion in this size range.[4]

In terms of service type (general medical-surgical vs. specialty), China's 24,709 hospitals included 15,887 general hospitals (64.3 percent), 5,127 specialty hospitals (20.7 percent), and 3,015 traditional Chinese medicine hospitals (12.2 percent). The majority of public (67 percent) and private (62 percent) hospitals are classified as general hospitals (see Figures 8.3 and 8.4). The private sector (29 percent) owns a greater share of specialty hospitals compared to the public sector (13 percent).

China's hospitals can also be distinguished according to their service capability (also known as hospital class or level). Class III hospitals are typically large hospitals (more than 500 beds) located in large cities and providing comprehensive (tertiary) services and advanced technologies; Class II hospitals are medium-sized hospitals (100–500 beds) in smaller cities at the county or district that provide secondary services; Class I hospitals are smaller facilities (less than 100 beds) located in

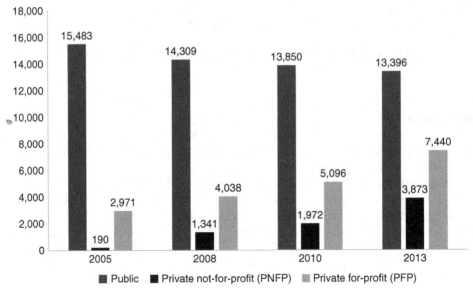

Figure 8.1 Growth in hospitals by ownership, 2005–2013

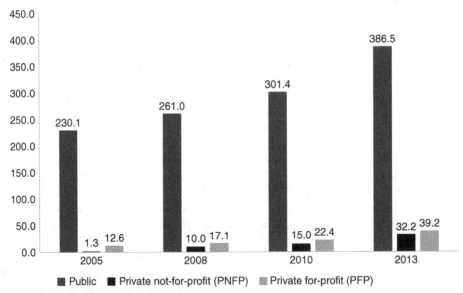

Figure 8.2 Growth in beds by ownership (Unit: 10,000), 2005–2013

the townships. Table 8.1 shows the changing distribution of hospitals across these three classes, as well as the changes in primary care institutions.

China's hospital capacity is geographically maldistributed. A relatively high proportion of both public hospitals (36.9 percent) and private hospitals (40.3 percent) are concentrated in eastern China (see Table 8.2). This is particularly true for specialty hospitals. Almost twice as many specialty hospitals are located in the higher-income eastern provinces compared to the lower-income western regions.

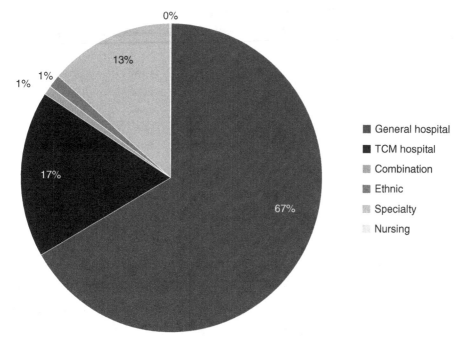

Figure 8.3 Type of hospitals operated by public sector, 2013

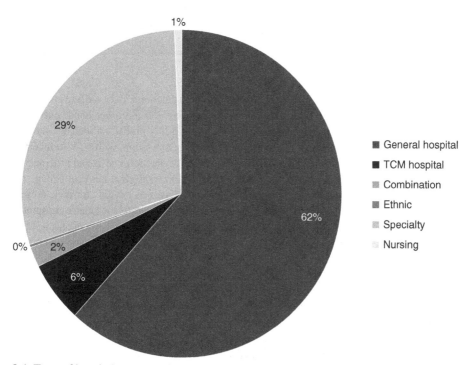

Figure 8.4 Type of hospitals operated by private sector, 2013

Table 8.1 Hierarchy of China's healthcare infrastructure

	2009	2010	2011	2012	2013
Medical institution					
Hospitals	20,291	20,918	21,979	23,170	24,709
Class III	1,233	1,284	1,399	1,624	1,787
Class II	6,523	6,472	6,468	6,566	6,709
Class I	5,110	5,271	5,636	5,962	6,473
Unclassified	7,425	7,891	8,476	9,018	9,740
Primary care facilities					
CHC	5,216	6,903	7,861	8,182	8,488
CHS	22,092	25,836	24,999	25,380	25,477
THC	38,475	37,295	37,097	37,015	

Source: NHFPC 2014 statistic yearbook. McKinsey & company.

Table 8.2 Regional distribution of hospitals in China, 2013

	Public Hospitals				Private Hospitals			
	Total Number	Region (%)			Total Number	Region (%)		
		Eastern	Central	Western		Eastern	Central	Western
General Hospital	8919	36.02	33.46	30.52	6968	38.12	22.22	39.67
TCM Hospital	2337	33.55	34.96	31.49	678	47.05	31.56	21.39
Specialty Hospital	1804	47.62	31.21	21.18	3323	42.76	32.11	25.13
Others	336	25.60	12.50	61.90	344	47.09	21.51	31.40
Total	13396	36.89	32.89	30.22	11313	40.29	25.66	34.05

Source: China Health Statistical Yearbook (2014), 1-2-2, 1-2-3.

Between 2005 and 2013, the number of hospital admissions grew 2.7-fold; public sector volume grew 2.5-fold while private sector volume (for-profit and not-for-profit combined) grew nearly 6-fold. However, the vast majority (88 percent) of inpatient visits were still concentrated in the public sector in 2013 (see Figure 8.5). Similarly, while outpatient visits almost doubled between 2005 and 2013, the vast majority (89.5 percent) of visits occurred in public facilities (see Figure 8.6).

Public Hospitals

Chinese public hospitals are an embodiment of both government and market failures. On the one hand, they are governed by bureaucratic rules and subject to conflicting policies from the many ministries that govern them. As a result, hospital directors have limited autonomy over staffing and other investment decisions. On the other hand, public hospitals are motivated by profits and behave like any other for-profit organization, with built-in incentives to over-prescribe diagnostic tests and pharmaceuticals. Such over-utilization generates profits that are distributed to physicians as rewards for their prescribing behavior and retained to finance hospital expansion. The subsections below discuss how public hospitals' financing, payment incentives, and governance help to explain their behavior and performance. The section that follows describes the government's latest effort to reform public hospitals, including some pilot tests of innovative models.

Financing

Public hospitals in China are financed through government subsidies, service charges, and

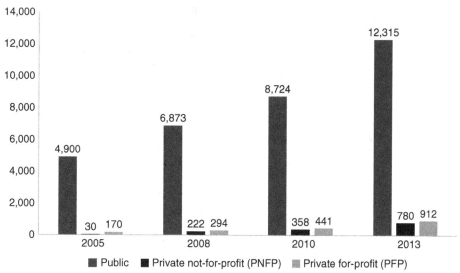

Figure 8.5 Growth of hospital admissions by ownership (Unit: 10,000), 2005–2013

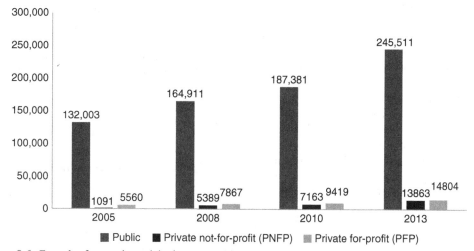

Figure 8.6 Growth of outpatient visits by ownership (Unit: 10,000), 2005–2013

markups on drug prices. In 2013, the government subsidy comprised 14.6 percent of total public hospital revenue, while business (non-subsidy) revenue contributed the rest.[5] Business revenue consisted of medical service charges (50.9 percent), income from drug markups (38.9 percent), and other sources (10.3 percent).[6] Among medical service charges, 69.6 percent came from inpatient services and 30.4 percent from outpatient services; with regard to sales of drugs, 59.8 percent came

from inpatient stays and 40.2 percent from outpatient visits.[7]

This pattern of financing does not distinguish Chinese public hospitals from private hospitals in China or elsewhere. What explains this? In 1978, when China liberalized its economy, it experienced a fiscal crisis. The government's revenue dropped sharply; government revenue as a percentage of GDP fell from 30 percent to 10 percent between 1978 and 1993.[8] As a result, government subsidies for public health facilities fell during that period from 50 percent to 60 percent to a mere 10 percent of the facilities' total revenues.[9]

The revenue model of public hospitals switched from government subsidies to patient charges. Revenues from the prescribing of medicines, imaging and laboratory tests, and other service charges accounted for 90 percent of hospital income. The government set fee schedules that priced office visits and hospital bed-days below cost and the latest diagnostic and medical technologies above cost. Hospitals were allowed to charge a 15 percent markup on drugs. The government's pricing policy created a leveraging effect whereby a provider had to sell seven dollars' worth of drugs to earn one dollar of profit. Physicians received bonuses tied to generating these revenues, which incentivized them to prescribe drugs and tests that were not clinically necessary. For the same reasons, hospital managers raced to introduce high-tech services and expensive imported drugs to boost revenues. According to a study of 21 Class III hospitals,[10] monthly bonuses paid to nurses and physicians on average comprised nearly 45 percent of their reported incomes; bonuses accounted for at least half of hospital managers' incomes.

Public facilities adopted a private sector business model and became de facto for-profit entities. Physician staff members became the residual claimants of profits generated by the public hospitals and thus public hospital shareholders. Their profit-making behaviors were formally legitimized in September 1992 when the State Council issued a document titled "Instructions on Health Reform."[11] Besides allowing charges to patients, the policy encouraged public hospitals to operate income-earning services and businesses alongside their regular medical services. Hospitals began to charge high user fees for special wards attended by more senior and more well-known physicians. To compound the problem, pharmaceutical and medical equipment companies provided financial incentives to hospitals and physicians to prescribe their products. As a consequence, public hospitals developed neither the motivation nor the incentive to make treatment decisions based on cost-effectiveness or population health.

Provider Payment Incentives

Public hospitals in China are typically paid on a fee-for-service (FFS) basis under the distorted, government-set fee schedule. The National Development and Reform Commission (NDRC) established the fee schedule, which contains over 4,000 items at the national level, with variations in the number of items and fees across provinces. At the provincial level, fees for the same item can vary across hospital classes. The NDRC also controls the prices of drugs on the Essential Drugs List (EDL); prices on most other drugs are set by negotiation between the government and manufacturers.

The 2009 healthcare reform sought to increase hospital reimbursement from social insurance funds and thereby reduce direct out-of-pocket payments by individuals. By 2013, 96 percent of the Chinese population was covered by one of the three public insurance schemes: the Urban Employee Basic Medical Insurance Scheme (UEBMI) covering employees in the formal sectors; the Urban Resident Basic Medical Insurance Scheme (URBMI) covering urban residents not already covered by UEBMI; and the New Cooperative Medical Scheme (NCMS) which covered the rural population. The depth of coverage varies across the three schemes and geographic locations, with UEBMI being most generous. In the coming years, the government aims to have reimbursement rates of URBMI and NCMS reaching 75 percent and 50 percent of expenditures for hospital admissions and outpatient visits, respectively.

In theory, the social insurance schemes can act as a purchaser to leverage behavioral change of hospitals through the use of more efficient provider payment incentives. However, as of today, FFS remains the dominant form of provider payment utilized by these schemes.

Governance

China's public hospitals are governed by an archaic and complex structure. The National Health and Family Planning Commission (NHFPC) has responsibility for the population's health. However, powers to (a) allocate public and

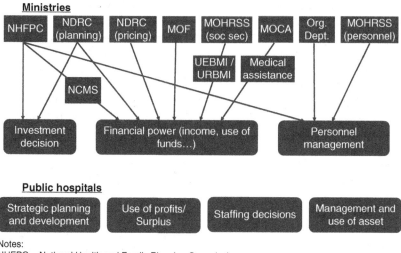

Ministries

Figure 8.7 Dispersion of power among ministries and public hospitals

Notes:
NHFPC = National Health and Family Planning Commission;
NDRC = National Development and Reform Commission (detailed function in parentheses);
MOF = Ministry of Finance; MOHRSS = Ministry of Human Resource and Social Security;
MOCA = Ministry of Civil Affairs; Org. Dept. = Organization Department of Chinese Communist Party;
NCMS = New Cooperative Medical Scheme; UEBMI = Urban Employee Basic Medical Insurance;
URBMI = Urban Resident Basic Medical Insurance.

insurance funds for healthcare, (b) set prices and payment methods, and (c) allocate human resources and capital investments are divided among various ministries (Figure 8.7). Competing ministries often pursue their own bureaucratic interests and issue policies and regulations contradicting the social purposes of public hospitals.

Public hospitals in China have enjoyed considerable financial autonomy since the market liberalization of the early 1980s in terms of residual claimant status (i.e., internal distribution of profits). However, they have had restricted decision-making authority regarding human resource management, service pricing, and asset management.[12] They are unclear about their social responsibilities and accountabilities while also faced with conflicting policies and rules from the many ministries that govern them. As an illustration, the NHFPC wants hospitals to prioritize healing patients and providing services at minimum cost (i.e., deliver value). However, distorted prices set by the NDRC's Price Bureau incentivize physicians to over-prescribe tests and drugs; civil-service rules set by the Ministry of Personnel give job guarantees to physicians and other personnel, regardless of

productivity; and the Organization Department of the Communist Party appoints hospital directors.

Hospital Managerial Practices

There is little empirical evidence or comprehensive understanding about management practices in Chinese hospitals. Most studies are qualitative and small in scale. Most studies focus on a single managerial function, such as staff performance assessment, patient flow management, and application of managerial tools originating in manufacturing and technology: e.g., the "Balanced Score Card" (BSC), the Toyota Production System (TPS) or "lean" management, and total quality management (TQM). This section reviews the literature on hospital management practices in public hospitals drawing on extant survey data and case studies.[13]

A recent pilot study measured management practices in a small sample of 35 Class II (secondary) and 75 Class III (tertiary) hospitals across 27 provinces.[14] The study utilized the World Management Survey (WMS), originally developed to measure managerial and organizational practices in manufacturing, but subsequently applied to and

1. *Standardizing care and operations*
    - Hospital layout and patient flow
    - Patient pathway management
    - Standardization and clinical protocols
    - Good use of human resources
2. *Performance monitoring*
    - Continuous improvement
    - Performance tracking
    - Performance review
    - Performance dialogue
    - Consequence management
3. *Target management*
    - Target balance
    - Target interaction
    - Clarity and comparability of targets
    - Time horizon of targets
    - Target stretch
4. *Talent management*
    - Rewarding high performers
    - Removing poor performers
    - Promoting high performers
    - Managing talent
    - Retaining talent
    - Attracting talent

Figure 8.8 Management practice domains

Source: Liu (2015); Bloom and Van Reenen (2007).

validated in hospitals in several countries.[15] The survey measured 20 management practices across four major management domains: standardizing care and operations, target setting, performance monitoring, and talent management (see Figure 8.8). The research team also interviewed 291 department directors and head nurses. Following the WMS methodology, practices were scored on a scale of 1–5 for each of the 20 practices; higher scores indicated better performance.

The weighted average management score was 2.69 (out of 5.00) with a highly dispersed distribution ranging from 1.85 to 3.35. Compared to OECD countries where the WMS has been applied, China is an average performer: China scores lower than the United States (3.0) and the United Kingdom (2.86) but higher than France (2.4) and Italy (2.48).[16] Figure 8.9 displays the average scores for each management practice across the four domains. Secondary hospitals scored significantly lower (2.66) than tertiary facilities (2.90), with considerable variation observed across provinces. Hospitals scored the highest in terms of human resources, promoting high performers, performance review, and attracting talented staff; they scored the lowest in standardization and protocols, continuous improvement, consequence management, rewarding high performers, and removing poor performers. Combined with findings from the interviews, the above-mentioned low scores highlight several managerial shortcomings:

- *Reactive management practices*: hospitals do not have systems to find and prevent potential problems or to continuously improve processes and services.
- *Poor performance management*: managers have little authority to reward high performers and dismiss low performers due to lack of autonomy in staffing and compensation. Talent management is not a high priority and there are few consequences for poor performance.
- *Poor performance feedback*: hospitals do not systematically analyze performance data or use data to provide feedback for improvement.
- *Poor performance improvement*: performance management is mainly used to allocate staff bonuses, not to improve individual or hospital performance. Bonuses are linked mainly to revenues and volume, not to improving quality of care or patient satisfaction.
- *Poor clinical integration*: lack of care standardization may indicate deficient clinical management that can negatively impact quality and outcomes.

The study also analyzed the determinants of variations in hospital management practices. It found that hospital bed size, competition from nearby hospitals, and autonomy in administrative decision making (human resources, asset management, financial management) were associated with higher management scores.

Research on specific management practices supports a subset of the WMS findings. For example, surveys show that the "Balanced Score Card" (BSC) is widely applied in China, but usually by tertiary public hospitals affiliated with medical schools.[17] Typical of BSC implementation internationally, Chinese hospitals reported using the BSC to develop

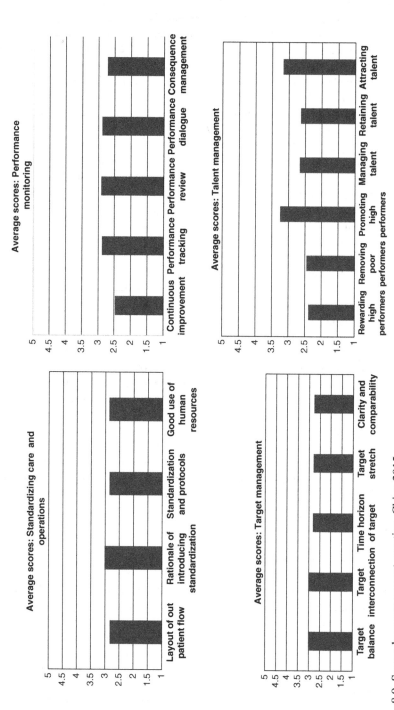

Figure 8.9 Scores by management practice, China 2015

performance measures along four dimensions: financial, patient satisfaction, service quality, and research and training. BCS implementation contributed to improved organizational performance and worker satisfaction. However, another (albeit small scale) survey found that BSC use in China focused on financial performance rather than quality and patient satisfaction.[18] The tool was mainly used for assessing performance of physicians in order to determine their bonuses.

Single-site case studies suggest that internationally recognized management tools are used to improve hospital operations and quality. For example, lean management techniques were used in provincial hospitals in Guangdong to improve efficiency and throughput of operating rooms.[19] Dongyang Hospital applied management tools such as TQM, "quality control" (QC) circles, and the "plan-do-study-act" (PDSA) cycle to improve clinical and non-clinical processes throughout the hospital.[20] The extent to which these tools are used elsewhere in China is unknown.

As mentioned earlier in this chapter, public hospital executives are appointed by higher-level party and government authorities in a process that is not merit based. Even within hospitals, promotions are usually based on tenure rather than competitive performance. Most hospital managers have received little formal training. For example, a 2004 study of managers in 96 hospitals across 21 provinces found that less than one-third had received short-term professional training; over one-half learned management on-the-job through their work experience. Nearly all presidents of public hospitals are responsible for all managerial, clinical, and academic activities. Largely clinicians by training, they tend to manage during their "spare time" or delegate managerial functions to junior staff. There are no standards or qualifications for hospital managers; most see managerial know-how as something that requires investment by government authorities rather than by the hospitals themselves.[21]

Performance of Public Hospitals

The consequences of the combined policies of financing, provider payment incentives, and governance, together with the managerial practices of public hospitals, have created a public hospital system that is plagued by rapid health expenditure inflation, low efficiency, and questionable quality. Between 1995 and 2014, the annual growth rate of total health expenditures was 16.5 percent, surpassing the growth rate of GDP by 2.7 percentage points (see Figure 1.21).[22] Such rapid growth of health expenditure reflects the poor efficiency of healthcare production. A huge portion of this expenditure was for high-tech tests and unnecessary drugs; about half of Chinese healthcare spending is devoted to drugs, as compared to only 10 percent in the United States and an OECD average of 16 percent.[23]

Systematic evidence on *process measures* of quality (care is provided according to best evidence or guidelines) and *outcome measures of quality* (patient health improvement as a result of treatment) is limited. However, over-prescription of drugs (especially antibiotics) is widespread in all facilities.[24] These medical practices contributed not only to the rapid growth in health expenditures; they also harmed patients with adverse reactions from the over-use of drugs, microbial resistance from the use of multiple drugs, and false-positives from poorly executed tests.[25]

There is also evidence of both underuse and overuse of other drugs.[26] For example, in a sample of 14,241 patients with acute myocardial infarction (AMI) from 162 hospitals, researchers found that β-blocker use in ideal patients was 54.3–67.8 percent between 2001 and 2011.[27] Use of β-blocker in patients with risk factors for cardiogenic shock was 42.6–59.5 percent during the same period. This shows both underuse in patients who could benefit and substantial use (and potential overuse) among those who might be harmed.[28] The researchers also found that hospital admissions for ST-segment elevation myocardial infarction increased fivefold between 2001 and 2011 from 3.5 to 15.4 per 100,000 individuals, with no reductions in in-hospital mortality rates.[29] By contrast, both the United States and the United Kingdom experienced marked declines in mortality rates during this period. This could be due to no change in the underuse of reperfusion therapy, β-blocker, angiotensin-converting enzyme inhibitors and delays in treatment.[30] Finally, patient experience with healthcare is suboptimal. Patients commonly complain about poor provider attitudes and lack of effort, short consultation time with doctors and nurses, and over-prescription of unnecessary medications.[31]

Recent Reform Policies and Pilots

In 2012, the government announced the Twelfth Five-Year Plan for Health (12th FYP), which set forth a program for reforming public hospitals. The 12th FYP stated clearly that the objective of public hospitals is to pursue "public interest" but did not define what public interest means. A package of policies was introduced with the intention to realign public hospitals' incentives with serving the public interest and to enable them to increase their efficiency. These policies included delinking hospital income and staff remuneration from drug revenues, changing provider payment methods, promoting rational drug use, testing alternative governance structures, improving human resource management, and adopting more efficient internal management.[32] Most of these have been implemented in various national or local reform pilots. The subsections below briefly summarize these policies and describe some of the more innovative pilot models in provider payment incentives and governance.

Financing

The government introduced the zero mark-up drug policy that delinked public hospitals' income from drug sales by eliminating the 15 percent markup on drug prices. First piloted among rural county hospitals, the policy has since then rolled out nationwide. However, the policy only applies to drugs on the Essential Drugs List (EDL); hospitals can continue to charge a markup on drugs not on the EDL. To compensate hospitals for the loss in drug revenue, local governments are encouraged to increase their direct subsidies to public hospitals. In addition, the schedule of hospital prices is to be revised, including a reduction in the prices for hi-tech diagnostic tests and an increase in the prices of services

that are more labor-intensive and previously underpriced.

Provider Payment Incentives

To accompany the set of financing policy changes, the three social health insurance (SHI) schemes are encouraged to change their reimbursement of public hospitals from retrospective FFS to prospective methods such as global budgets, capitation, and case-based payment methods. Such changes shift the financial risk of over-treatment to public hospitals and therefore incentivize them to increase their efficiency.

Recent government reviews show that progress in provider payment reform has been slow. Although more than 80 percent of counties/cities have piloted new payment methods, most only cover a small percentage (10 percent on average) of total hospital revenue and have not fundamentally changed providers' financial incentives.[33] In addition, because standard cost accounting is absent in most public hospitals, payment rates are typically estimated based on past expenditures rather than cost data. This effectively embeds inefficient incentives in the distorted price schedule.

Overall, most of the pilots are not scientifically designed, reflecting the lack of local technical capacity. For example, a few cities/counties claimed that they have introduced global budget payment methods; in reality, they have implemented a FFS system with expenditure caps. Others use capitation to pay for selected services rather than all services needed by an individual during a defined period of time. This further fragments the delivery system, as providers are incentivized to shift cost from services included in the capitation payment to those that are still paid by FFS. A number of pilots also introduce some form of performance-based incentives, in which the SHI scheme withholds a certain percentage of the total budget for each provider and ties the "withhold" to an assessment of the provider's performance. However, except for selected cases, most of the performance measurements are not related to quality. They are primarily based on service volume, inpatient days, visits per person, average expense of outpatient visit and inpatient days, etc. Three of the more innovative models are briefly described below.

Comprehensive Case-based Payment Based on Clinical Guidelines in Xi County, Henan Province

The NCMS in Xi County introduced case-based payment linked to clinical pathways. For each diagnosis, a fixed rate was set to include services as prescribed by clinical guidelines for standard (non-complicated) cases, known as Group A. The standard case payment rate was based on actual average FFS expenses over the past three years, and negotiated with providers. For more complicated cases (as measured by existence of secondary diagnoses, known as Group B), additional payment was included; and for rare cases that were deemed outliers (Group C), FFS would be used. To prevent hospitals from upcoding and classifying their patients as severe when in fact they are not, NCMS stipulated that on average for each hospital, the number of cases classified as Group A should exceed 70 percent while the number of cases classified as Group C should not exceed 10 percent annually.

NCMS prepaid 40 percent of total payments to providers, with the remaining 60 percent based on performance assessment. The main performance indicators include (among others) inappropriate prescription rate not exceeding 5 percent, positive rate of diagnostic tests greater than 70 percent, accurate rate of diagnosis greater than 90 percent, and percent of patients surveyed who are dissatisfied less than 5 percent. NCMS invited experts to assess provider performance. The contingent portion of payment is tied to performance according to the following schedule:

Performance Assessment Score	Percent Claim Payout
≧85	100%
80–85	95%
75–80	90%
70–75	85%
65–70	80%
60–65	75%

NCMS will cease contracting with providers whose scores fall below 60 for three consecutive years; such substandard performance will also trigger an investigation by NCMS.

Global Budget with Pay-for-Quality in Yanchi County, Ningxia Autonomous Region

A common phenomenon in rural China is that a significant share of hospital admissions (and therefore expenditures) occurs at costlier tertiary facilities than at county hospitals, even for health conditions that county hospitals are capable of treating. In 2012, the SHI in Ningxia Province piloted a new form of payment in Yanchi County. The primary objectives of this pilot are to incentivize county hospitals to play the role of gatekeeper for the local population's hospital care and to improve the efficiency and quality of their own service delivery.

The pilot changed provider payment for county hospitals from FFS to a global budget with a pay-for-quality component. The design of the global budget is innovative. Rather than being facility-based (the usual case), it is population-based and calculated to cover all hospital admissions from the county's residents, but limited to conditions that it is deemed capable of treating. The county hospital thus becomes the gatekeeper for all services and populations included in its budget. It is incentivized to keep patients it is able to treat, since it has the fiscal responsibility to pay the cost of patients treated at higher-level hospitals from its own global budget. At the beginning of each year, SHI prepays 70 percent of the budget to the county hospital, with the remainder as a withhold that is disbursed based on biannual quality assessments. This supply-side intervention is accompanied with demand-side incentives for patients designed to discourage self-referral to higher-level hospitals. Reimbursement rates for out-of-county secondary and tertiary hospitals are more generous for patients with a referral from county hospitals than for those without referrals.

The performance indicators for county level hospitals cover both quality and efficiency. There are 5 overall indicators and 18 disease-specific evaluation indicators (6 indicators for 3 diseases each), including mortality, CMI (case mix index), time consumption index, expense consumption index, and compliance with treatment protocol for 3 priority diseases (measured by 18 indicators). Performance assessment is conducted by a group of clinical experts appointed by the provincial department of health.

A pre-post trend analysis shows that before the reform, out-of-county share of total admissions and total inpatient expenditures were increasing from 18.7 percent to 21 percent and 53.7 percent to 58.3 percent, respectively, from 2010 to 2011. After the implementation of the global budget with pay-for-quality, out-of-county share of admissions and inpatient expenditures fell to 14.0 percent and 38.7 percent, respectively.[34] Baseline quality measures were low and quality improvement has been slow. County hospital directors initially only paid attention to how much money they lost without examining the reasons for performance penalties. Nearly one year elapsed before hospital directors began to review the quality assessment results with their department chairs to find ways to improve their quality.

Diagnosis-related Group Case-based Payment in Beijing

Beijing's UEBMI scheme pioneered the first DRG system in China in six hospitals in 2011, covering 108 diagnoses. An evaluation study compared hospital discharge data from the six pilot hospitals with eight comparison hospitals which continued to be paid by FFS. The evaluation found that the DRG payment led to a 6.2 percent reduction in health spending and a 10.5 percent reduction in patient out-of-pocket payments. However, hospitals continued to receive FFS payments for patients who were older and had more complications, thus limiting the effect of DRG payment.[35]

Governance of Public Hospitals

One of the core public hospital reform objectives is the "separation of government administration from hospital management." Policy directives have aimed to grant hospitals greater managerial autonomy from direct hierarchical control by the government's administrative apparatus but maintain their accountability to government priorities, particularly in terms of serving the public interest.[36] This section examines hospital governance models that have emerged from the reform pilots and the degree to

which they have made hospital operations more independent of government administration, while simultaneously instituting the accountability mechanisms and incentives to align hospital behaviors with government policies and reform objectives.

Building on pilot experiences initiated in 2010, recent State Council directives envision public hospitals as independent entities with legal personality and full decision-making authority over management and operations, thereby separating hospital management from the government's administrative apparatus.[37] Importantly, the central government also envisions putting in place an accountability framework through performance evaluation of several domains of hospital performance (e.g., administrative functions, quality, spending, patient satisfaction, access, and efficiency). However, as in the case of previous reform directives, it is not clear how such a framework will be designed or applied, or who will have the authority to assess performance and enforce compliance.

The proposed changes involving autonomy are complex. The international experience suggests that they would require setting up new organizational arrangements (such as boards), establishing an arms-length relationship between government and hospitals, making use of indirect tools of accountability (e.g., performance reviews, compliance monitoring, external audits, use of contracts, contract management), and establishing provisions for their enforcement.[38] However, China's experience along these lines is nascent at best.[39]

Four Governance Models in Comparative Perspective

Figure 8.10 presents major components and characteristics of pilot governance models in four mostly urban areas: Shanghai, Zhenjiang/Kangfu, Dongyang, and Sanming.[40] Following a framework developed to analyze public hospital governance reforms,[41] the remainder of this section examines these cases by addressing the following questions: (i) what is the organizational makeup of the governance models? (ii) to what extent have these models promoted greater decision-making autonomy, separating hospital management from government

Component	Shanghai (Shenkang)	Zhenjiang (Kangfu)	Dongyang	Sanming
New governance arrangement				
Organizational unit/name	Multi hospital management center	Multi facility "network" council	Hospital board	Prefecture health reform leadership group
Jurisdiction	Municipal	Municipal	Municipal	Prefecture
No. of hospitals	24	5[a]	1	22
Decision rights of new governance unit				
Hiring/firing hospital director	Partial[b]	No	Yes	Yes
Hiring/firing quota staff	No	No	No	No
Flexibility in setting HR remuneration for quota staff	No	No	Yes	Yes
Pricing	No	No	No	Yes
Residual claimant	No[b]	No[b]	Yes	Partial
Asset management	Partial[c]	Partial[c]	Yes	Yes
Accountability mechanisms				
Performance assessment of hospital directors[d]	Yes	No	Yes	Yes
Performance assessment of hospital(s)	No	No	Yes	No
Review/enforcement of safety and quality standards	No	No	Yes	No
Compliance supervision	Similar to other public facilities	Similar to other public facilities	Yes	Partial
Incentives				
Realigning staff incentives	Partial	No	Yes	Yes
Governance unit: members' position at risk	No	No	No	No
Hospital directors' position at risk	No	No	Yes	Yes
Sanctions for noncompliance with rules or for low performance	Similar to other public facilities	Similar to other public facilities	Yes	Yes

[a] Network includes nine ambulatory centers.
[b] Can recommend to government.
[b] Retained at hospital level.
[c] In consultation with government agencies.
[d] Usually involves signing a "responsibility agreement" between governance unit and hospital director.

Figure 8.10 Organizational, autonomy, and accountability characteristics of selected public hospital governance reform models, 2015
Source: Unpublished case studies commissioned by World Bank (2015); Ying (2014); Jin (2014).

administration? and (iii) how is the organization and its hospital members incentivized and made accountable to achieve government objectives and performance?

Organizationally, two of the models, *Shanghai* and *Zhenjiang*, are typical of governance reforms observed in the pilot reform hospitals in China and build upon earlier initiatives launched in Wuxi, Weifang, and other cities in the early and mid-2000s.[42] These cities legislated the creation of a new agency, usually referred to as a hospital management center or council (HMC), which is led by high-level municipal officials, consists of representatives of public agencies involved in health sector oversight, and staffed by civil servants. The HMCs oversee a group of affiliated facilities: 24 hospitals in Shanghai; 5 hospitals and 9 ambulatory units in Zhenjiang. The HMCs were granted legal personality but the hospital members also maintained their original legal personalities, which compromised the decision-making authority of the HMC vis-à-vis the hospitals. The HMCs in these cities differ in two respects. Shanghai aims to improve the operations and performance of a subset of tertiary hospitals. In addition to sharing Shanghai's objectives, Zhenjiang aims to promote greater vertical integration among a broader mix of facilities including tertiary, secondary, and primary facilities.

The *Dongyang* experience involves a single hospital that formed an independent board with government and non-government participation. The board consists of representatives of government agencies, private corporations, and local and foreign medical schools. The hospital has special legal status, and its statutes are similar to corporate governance models observed in private hospitals.[43] The model aims to create a corporate governance arrangement to improve the efficiency, capacity, and quality of services while maintaining the hospital's public nature through "social responsibility."

Finally, *Sanming* did not create a new agency, but decreed a fully empowered "leadership group" (LG) to enact health system reforms with an initial focus on the prefecture's 22 secondary and tertiary hospitals.[44] The aim was to contain runaway cost inflation in hospitals which contributed to a large deficit in the main social insurance scheme (UEBMI).

Decision rights display a bifurcated distribution across the four cases. Key decisions on human resource management, compensation, and service pricing remain with government agencies and are not transferred to HMCs (or member hospitals) in Shanghai and Zhenjiang. Also, residual claimant status and asset management are retained mostly by the hospitals themselves. In Zhenjiang, part of the problem relates to the fact that HMC spans independent municipal and district public administrative units. District administration controls asset management of primary care units and some secondary hospitals, while municipal administration together with hospital management does the same for larger tertiary hospitals. These entities were unwilling to relinquish control to the HMC.

By contrast, Dongyang's Board and Sanming's LG exhibit considerably more decision rights. Dongyang still abides by government pricing policies and rules governing hiring and firing of quota staff, but does determine the full compensation package for all staff. Sanming's LG has assumed the full range of decision-making authority except for recruitment and dismissal of quota staff. The LG has altered compensation policies for hospital directors and all medical professionals. For example, the government pays the salaries of hospital directors, and physician incomes are no longer linked to revenue-based bonuses. The LG makes all decisions regarding major asset investments, prices, and social insurance reimbursement rates. In terms of residual claims status, the LG has set caps on reimbursements for inpatient stays and outpatient visits

if hospitals spend below the caps; savings are shared with the social insurance schemes.

Turning to accountability mechanisms, three of the governance models aim to impact hospital behaviors by linking hospital director income to performance. However, it is uncertain how the performance assessment system differs from routine systems to evaluate leaders' performance. In the latter, hospital directors appear more accountable to the higher-level leaders who appointed them than to the government agencies responsible for reform implementation and on-the-ground performance.[45] Only Dongyang's Board has established a comprehensive hospital-based performance assessment system that embraces financial, efficiency, quality, patient satisfaction, and safety domains. In fact, the Dongyang Board is the only governance arrangement among the group to mandate a continuous quality improvement program, establishing a quality management department, medical record control committee, and a clinical assessment system for physicians and nurses.

Unlike Dongyang, Shanghai and Zhenjiang HMCs do not independently assess hospital performance or compliance with rules and standards, and appear to piggyback on supervisory practices performed by government agencies. Sanming's LG carefully supervises the implementation of the human resource, compensation, and pricing reforms it has crafted but relies on government agencies for other domains.

In terms of realigning incentives, Dongyang and Sanming have delinked physician "bonus" income from revenues derived from sales of drugs, medical supplies, and diagnostic tests, and instead placed doctors on salaries. Their salaries contain a fixed and variable component in which the latter is no longer linked to revenue but rather to a combination of measures of productivity, cost control, quality, and patient satisfaction.[46] As suggested above, altering physician compensation has been a major accomplishment and has addressed a cost escalating distortion widely observed in public hospitals. While Shanghai has placed a hard budget constraint on total personnel spending, it is uncertain whether they have eliminated the bonus system. Surplus revenues are still distributed to physicians at the discretion of hospital and departmental directors.

In part because most of the governance units consist of government officials, members' positions are not at risk in the two HMCs if hospitals perform poorly or do not comply with government policies. However, hospital directors can be dismissed for poor performance by Dongyang's Board and Sanming's LG. While Shanghai and Zhanjiang rely on government agencies to apply sanctions for non-compliance with standards and rules, Dongyang and Sanming governance arrangements are fully empowered to apply sanctions themselves. However, Sanming sanctions center on non-compliance with reforms which it has instituted.

Impact

Unfortunately, none of these cases (or any of the official pilots) has been rigorously or independently evaluated. Also, teasing the results of public hospital reforms from other health reforms is a difficult task. Public hospitals are often the platform for launching the latter as in the case of the zero mark-up reform policy. Based on available but limited administrative data, salient results of each case can be summarized as follows:

Shanghai: In comparison to similar hospitals in Shanghai, the HMC member facilities showed no difference in terms of trends in service volume (inpatient discharges), lengths of stay, or asset expansion from 2003 to 2013.

Zhenjiang: Compared to provincial and national averages, between 2009 and 2013, Zhenjiang was able to contain charges and spending on outpatient visits and inpatient admissions. The reduced growth in spending may relate to consolidation of sterilization, pathology, and logistics services for all network members by the HMC.

Dongyang: Compared to similar hospitals, Dongyang's income from drug sales was 10–15 percent lower than comparator hospitals before and after the introduction of the zero mark-up policy in 2012. Average per outpatient and inpatient costs were significantly lower than a sample of comparator hospitals over the same period. Restrictive use of antibiotics has exceeded national standards. The hospital reports surgical and overall hospital infection rates of 1 percent and 7 percent, respectively. These rates are closely monitored by the board.

Sanming: Sanming government has issued reports showing a significant reduction in hospital spending growth between 2009 and 2013 when compared to Fujian Province and national averages for outpatient visits and inpatient admissions. Drug revenues as a proportion of total hospital revenues decreased from 47 percent to 28 percent between 2011 and 2013. Over this same period, the prefecture reported a 3.9 percent reduction in average inpatient stay costs compared to cost increases of 11.6 percent and 14.7 percent in Fujian and nationally, respectively.

The Limits of Emerging Governance Models

The four cases suggest that the ability of governance reform in China to separate public hospital management from government administration is uncertain. An array of organizational arrangements has emerged, but all remain at a small scale or pilot stage. Each has aimed to consolidate decision-making within a single entity through coordinating the actions and policies of diverse government departments responsible for the health sector. The failure to rigorously evaluate these models, and public hospital reform interventions in general, limits the ability to draw lessons from the pilot experiences.

Variants of the HMC model observed in Shanghai and Zhenjiang are common among other pilots.[47] However, HMCs consist entirely of current or former government officials and appear to behave more as extensions of government than as independent agents of the same. Additional decision rights have not been transferred to the HMCs from government administration. Meanwhile, hospitals under HMC governance maintain their financial autonomy and do not appear answerable to the new government unit on financial matters. This may relate to the fact that affiliated hospitals have maintained their legal personality. Arms-length tools and mechanisms to foster accountability have not been developed. HMCs mostly rely on direct supervisory and oversight mechanisms traditionally operated by the relevant government agencies. The HMCs also do not have a robust track record in realigning incentives.

By contrast, Dongyang Hospital manifests many of the features of corporate governance observed internationally. It is operated by an independent board with government and non-government representation and enjoys considerably more decision-making authority than the HMCs. The board has created strong accountability mechanisms and incentives to control costs, increase quality, and improve the patient's experience. However, the origins of the Dongyang governance model, which involved external financing and technical support, may be difficult to reproduce elsewhere in China. After 20 years of existence, the model has yet to be replicated.

Facing a financial crisis, high-level leaders in Sanming created the LG with a broad reform mandate but with an initial focus on addressing cost escalation in prefecture hospitals. The LG was granted full autonomy and authority to alter accountabilities and incentives to successfully foster more efficient use of hospital resources. The hospitals themselves were not granted greater decision-making authority. However, as a governance model, the LG lacks institutionalization. The make-up of the group can be altered at any time due to rotation of government officials – a common occurrence in Chinese public administration. The effectiveness of LGs in other locations and sectors has suffered from the instability of personnel and therefore its sustainability is questionable.[48] Despite intense promotion by central government, the Sanming model has yet to be replicated in China.

Private Hospitals

The most striking announcement of the 12th FYP is the government's decision to promote private investment in the hospital sector, with the target of private hospitals reaching 20 percent market share by 2015.[49] Although not made explicit, the motivation behind privatization can be interpreted partly as (a) a strategic move to use private sector competition to stimulate changes in the otherwise stymied public hospital reform, (b) a swing back in government ideology toward a more pro-market approach for improving productivity in the health sector, and (c) a naïve view of healthcare as just another sector to boost the economy. The rationale for the 20 percent target and any future government

encouragement of the private market beyond 2015 remains unknown. Companion policies putting private hospitals on an equal footing with public hospitals are being introduced: for example, the three social insurance schemes would contract with private hospitals, and physicians working in the private hospitals would qualify for promotion within the medical professional ranking system.[50] At the same time, no new building projects or expansion of public hospital beds will be approved. How the government plans to regulate the private hospitals and, more importantly, whether regulations can be effectively enforced in the Chinese context are both open questions at this moment.

Although private hospitals are not new in China, their role has been limited. As discussed above, private hospitals accounted for just 12 percent of total hospital admissions and 10.5 percent of outpatient visits in 2013. Most are either high-end specialty hospitals that cater to the expatriate community and affluent Chinese or smaller scale hospitals providing elective services, such as cosmetic surgery for the general population. To reach 20 percent market share by 2015 requires rapid expansion.

The policy announcement has since attracted a flurry of interest from private investors. Recent trends suggest that most new entrants are current private hospital chains, pharmaceutical and medical device conglomerates, and real estate developers – all motivated by profit. While strategies vary from targeting provincial megacities to subprovincial urban centers, the emphasis has been on wealthier locations with strong household purchasing power and public insurance schemes that are more likely to cover a wider range of services. Investors describe a two-pronged strategy: (1) targeting high-end specialist hospitals that command high prices and (2) buying general public hospitals, typically contracting with SHI programs, to maximize sale volume. While some investors are building their own facilities, increasingly they enter the market by buying up existing hospitals to take over existing land and staff. Various joint ventures also seek prestige by association with brand-name medical universities.[51]

The existing literature on the impact of market competition on hospital efficiency and quality has yielded mixed results depending on the institutional context.[52] With few exceptions, most studies do not examine competition among different ownership types. Among those that do, some studies found that the presence of for-profit private hospitals led to a positive spillover effect on public hospital efficiency,[53] while others found that for-profit private hospitals cream-skim lucrative patients, leaving public hospitals to bear a larger share of the severely ill.[54]

Reviews comparing quality and cost of care of hospitals with different ownership status have in general found that for-profit status is associated with higher costs and lower (or similar) quality than private nonprofits, although the reported differences vary according to a study's data source, time period, and geographic region.[55] Some recent evidence in the management literature suggests that for-profit private hospitals are more efficient in management, and that competition can lead to management efficiency gains.[56] However, in the case of China, if public hospitals continue to be subject to bureaucratic governance, competition will be less likely to promote management improvements.

Public-private hospital competition in China is more akin to competition among for-profit hospitals. We speculate that private for-profit hospitals entering the market will compete with established public hospitals by (a) offering higher compensation to attract the best public sector physicians, and (b) acquiring the latest expensive high-tech equipment to signal a higher quality of healthcare to both physicians and patients. The higher costs will be passed onto patients or the social insurance programs. In response, public hospitals will have to raise the salaries of their own medical staffs and enter the medical arms race.

This scenario predicts that the entrance of private hospitals will likely exacerbate the excessive use of high-tech diagnostic tests and expensive pharmaceutical products. This is particularly true if such utilization generates profits for the hospital and patients are unable to judge the quality of care provided. If the parent company of a private hospital is a pharmaceutical or medical device firm, the incentives to over-prescribe may be even stronger.[57]

Although the government introduced a Certificate of Need (CON) policy in 2005 to regulate the purchase of expensive medical equipment, it has not been effectively enforced.[58] A study of four Chinese cities showed that the number of computerized tomography (CT) and magnetic resonance imaging (MRI) machines increased by 50 percent on average between 2006 and 2009.[59]

Management Practices in Private Hospitals

Similar to public hospitals, studies of the managerial practices of private hospitals are limited. Several high-end private hospitals have adopted management practices and service models that distinguish them from other private (and public) hospitals in China and resemble practices of hospitals in OECD countries. Two examples are Wuhan Asia Heart Hospital and Aier Eye Hospital Group. To maintain and expand their market position, these facilities have created an enabling organizational and managerial environment of continuous improvement in order to provide high quality care in an efficient manner. While not representative of private sector hospitals in China, these facilities can serve as learning platforms for improving clinical and non-clinical management in public hospitals.

Wuhan Asia Heart Hospital

Founded in 1999, Wuhan Asia Heart Hospital[60] (WAHH) is owned and operated by Wuhan Asian Industrial Co., a wholly owned foreign enterprise engaged in hospital and hotel investment and management. While WAHH is the company's flagship facility, it owns a second facility and manages a third under a contract with a state-owned enterprise.

WAHH specializes in the treatment of cardiovascular disease. In 2013, the facility had 750 beds, 1,735 total staff, 450 full-time physicians, and 850 nurses. Significantly, and unlike many private sector facilities in China, WAHH has been certified by all the social insurance schemes from whom it derives about 70 percent of its revenues. Private insurance (15 percent) and self-payment (15 percent) comprise the remaining revenue sources. Between 2010 and 2013, WAHH averaged about 4,140 surgeries annually; in 2014, WAHH provided 375,000 outpatient consultations, placing the facility among the top three cardiovascular facilities in terms of volume.

1. Medical departments: hospital bed turnover rate, degree of patient condition, quality of work, quality of the medical record, compliance with quality standards, and patients' satisfaction
2. Diagnostics: workload, the complexity of the work, the work quality, patient satisfaction results, etc.
3. Nursing: operation, hospitalization days, level of patient severity, number of shifts (night and day), quality, patient satisfaction results
4. Administration: hospital's overall workload, staffing level coefficient, regular assessment results for employee by each department

Figure 8.11 Categories and indicators used for performance appraisal and bonuses

Facility managers report a 10 percent profit margin. The hospital is governed by a corporate governance board.

WAHH exhibits a "differentiated management model" in which clinical and academic responsibilities rest with the facility president, while non-clinical matters are handled by a general manager. In public hospitals, the hospital president performs both responsibilities. This model is repeated at the departmental level where each departmental clinical director has an administrative manager to support non-clinical activities and facilitate coordination with other departments. Each department also possesses a medical assistant (usually a nurse) who is responsible for patient communication, post-discharge follow-up care and promoting patient self-care management.

WAHH has established a "patient service center" to make appointments, provide medical advice, triage patients, and assist patients with navigation among the hospital's service departments. For long-term post-discharge care, the facility operates a "lifelong" follow-up program in which about 60 percent of discharged patients participate. The facility has also developed standard operating procedures to facilitate patient flows and demarcate staff responsibilities in outpatient clinics, operating theatres, diagnostic areas, and patient wards.

WAHH has implemented a number of measures to improve and maintain quality standards. It received ISO9000 certification and is in the process of seeking international accreditation. It established a Clinical Quality Management Center to accompany its hospital infection control and pharmacy management committees. Consisting of a physician and four quality control specialists, the center tracks 40 indicators (such as rates of misdiagnoses, complications, and mortality) across departments, conducts root cause analysis on adverse events, and works with staff to take corrective measures.

Performance management for the hospital president and medical staff is delinked from hospital revenues and volume, and instead centers on quality performance measures such as time taken for surgical procedures, postsurgical complication rates, and bleeding. Figure 8.11 displays the areas of assessment used to determine bonuses and promotions offered to different personnel categories. Importantly, seniority is not a criterion used in promotions. Medical professionals must pass an examination for promotion to a higher position and pay grade.

WAHH does not work in isolation from the broader delivery system. It has also established a technical cooperation program with more than 100 public primary care centers and county hospitals providing on-site technical support, short-term resident training in WAHH, and academic seminars for physicians staffing these facilities. A two-way referral system has also been established with these facilities.

Finally, WAHH has established cost control measures in part because it must keep within the reimbursement rates of social insurance schemes. Measures include (i) uniform bar codes to track all drugs and consumables and affix them to the patient's medical record; (ii) standardized cost accounting which determines costs per procedure; (iii) a tracking system which identifies 20 percent cost deviations, which in turn trigger an audit (management aims to keep such deviations to less than 5 percent of patients); (iv) package pricing for ambulatory and short-stay surgical procedures; (v) application of clinical pathways; and (vi) strict pharmaceutical procurement and management, which lowers total drug spending to less than 14 percent of treatment costs for inpatients and 25 percent of outpatient treatment costs.

Aier Eye Hospital Group

Aier Eye Hospital Group[61] (AEHG) is China's largest ophthalmology hospital chain, with 70 hospitals in 23 provinces. Founded in 1997 and headquartered in Changsha (capital of Hunan Province), AEHG has become a major player among *private* hospitals in ophthalmology with 3.2 percent of China's market share and 2.5 billion RMB in annual business revenue.[62] In 2014, AEHG treated 2.5 million outpatients and performed over 250,000 surgeries. It employs nearly 8,000 people, including 5,200 medical professionals such as physicians, technicians, and nurses. Table 8.3 displays AEHG's main service lines. About half of AEHG's patients are covered by social insurance. The hospital has been recognized nationally and internationally for quality of medical treatment, human resource development, and research.

AEHG adopted a corporate governance arrangement and management structure found in private hospital systems in the OECD whereby major decisions and a number of key functions (e.g., procurement,[63] human resource management, asset management) are centralized at the headquarter level. AEHG's board of directors oversees all operations of the conglomerate and has four specialized committees: strategic, audit, compensation, and managerial supervision. Management is structured along seven main domains: strategic investments, medical devices, marketing, medical management, operations, human resources, and finance. Individual hospital management teams are appointed by the board and are responsible for the development and implementation of business plans that are aligned with corporate objectives and

policies. AEHG also applies a "unified management framework" in which standardized reports – including financial statements, customer analysis, production, and quality – are submitted at set intervals by individual facilities. Monthly audits are conducted on five randomly selected hospitals.

AEHG further employs a "chain model" to link care, including referrals, across three facility levels: (i) a flagship Class III hospital in Shanghai that focuses on providing complex care, clinical research, and providing technical support to lower-level facilities; (ii) secondary Class II hospitals located in provincial capital cities serve as the core business operating platform, offering full-scale ophthalmology services to patients while supporting both Class I and Class III facilities; and (iii) primary Class I hospitals and ambulatory units located in smaller, peripheral cities, focusing on optometric services and diagnosis and treatment for general eye diseases. Physicians are deployed across the facility network to support provincial and local facilities. Such support is both physical and virtual. To streamline management, AEHG created seven regional business offices headed by a CEO and responsible for managerial support and oversight of Class I and Class II hospitals. According to AEHG executives, the regional offices and "chain model" have enabled the conglomerate to reduce the time period for new facilities to achieve a profit. Finally, AEHG is moving to expand the network of ambulatory clinics at the county level with the aim that 60 percent of first contacts occur at these facilities.

Similar to Wuhan Asia Heart Hospital, AEHG's hospitals separate clinical from non-clinical management. Experienced managers are recruited for

Table 8.3 AEHG's main service lines

Category	Service Lines
Optometry	• Vision testing • Eyeglass sales • Identification of ophthalmic (and other) conditions
LASIK	• Correction of shortsightedness
Cataract surgery	• Extraction and replacement of opaque lens
Specialist eye treatments	• Treatment of complex ophthalmic condition (e.g., corneal transplants)

CEO positions and are responsible for hospital administration, business operations, patient service, government relations, and external corporate affairs. Hospital presidents and vice presidents are responsible for clinical management, training, and research, but report to the CEO. Staff compensation consists of a base salary combined with performance-based incentives. The criteria for the latter include quality of care, financial revenue, managerial efficiency, patient satisfaction, patient safety, and research publications. AEHG has recently introduced a shareholding program in which top physicians and executives share up to 30 percent ownership in new facilities. Promotions are not based on seniority but rather on a formal performance assessment system.

AEHG places considerable importance on ensuring high quality care and patient satisfaction. For example, AEHG requires all hospitals to operate six quality-related committees: medical quality control, quality of nursing management, ethics, pharmaceutical management, hospital infection control, and medical record management. These committees are responsible to monitor and assess relevant practices, conduct monthly reviews, and conduct biannual inspections. Every month each hospital submits a medical quality report to the leading quality group at headquarters. Each department operates a quality control team composed of the director, deputy director, and head nurse who are responsible for reviewing and reporting adverse events (among other things). AEHG has crafted standard clinical pathways and operating procedures, including checklists for diagnostic services, surgical procedures (including pre- and postsurgical care), infection control, prescriptions, and medical records. Finally, AEHG has implemented several measures to enhance patient satisfaction and communication including internet appointment scheduling, flexible walk-in appointments for the frail and elderly, WeChat[64] registration, daily limits on the maximum number of outpatients ($n=40$) seen by a doctor, limits on patient waiting time (20 minutes), a 24-hour hotline, free shuttle service for people with disabilities, and a patient service team to inform patients of risks and involve them in their treatment and recovery.

Emerging Models of Hospital Integration

Across the globe, many countries are implementing service delivery reforms to coordinate care among providers to address a similar set of challenges currently faced by China: rising costs, fragmentation of services, an aging population, and growing prevalence of chronic diseases. While these reforms use different nomenclatures such as "patient centered medical home," "enhanced general practice," and "integrated care" (to name a few), a more or less common set of features has emerged. These include strengthening primary healthcare to include gatekeeping and care coordination roles, establishing multidisciplinary teams across specialties and professions, developing individual care plans especially for chronic disease management, and promoting patient self-management.[65] Reforms also envision a new role for hospitals, focusing on providing high complexity care, shifting low complexity care to lower-level providers, providing training and technical support to primary care providers, sharing personnel as part of multidisciplinary teams, and establishing stronger links with the broader delivery system through shared medical records, community and home outreach through mobile devices, post-discharge coordination, and strengthened referral systems.[66] Reforms may be accompanied by experimentation with new payment systems such as shared savings and bundled payments.[67]

While not a major component of the 2009 reforms, recent central government policy reform plans and policy directives increasingly emphasize strengthening primary care along the dimensions cited above.[68] Similar to other reforms, the government aims to draw on the lessons from pilots. A number of mostly hospital-led and small-scale initiatives have emerged which seek to coordinate care, or at least link hospitals with other providers. Most of the initiatives include other reforms; care integration is usually one of multiple service delivery improvement objectives. This section reviews a subset of these experiences that provide insights into opportunities and constraints to greater hospital integration with the delivery system.

Characteristics of Integrated Care Initiatives in China

Drawing on case studies commissioned by the World Bank, Table 8.4 compares salient features of five recent initiatives in China that sought to strengthen care integration between hospitals and primary care providers. Except for Xi County in Henan Province, the initiatives took place in large cities and involved tertiary (Class III) hospitals, usually as the lead facility. Four were managed by hospital management groups or councils (HMCs) as described above, one by a county health bureau, and another by the lead hospital.

Objectives were broad and varied. All sought to improve the capacity of affiliated primary care providers – community health centers (CHCs) in urban areas and township health centers (THCs) in rural areas – mainly through rotating specialists, providing training and technical support, improving referral systems, and establishing rapid, "no wait" access to hospital-based specialty care (known as "green channel") to facilitate upward referrals from affiliates. However, the flow of upward referrals continues to dwarf downward referrals, while green channel admissions represented a fraction of total admissions.[69] Two initiatives, Shanghai-Rujin-Luwan and Zhenjiang-Kangfu, horizontally integrated a subset of diagnostic services in a single location. All involved some degree of electronic ("ehealth") innovation such as e-consultations among providers for diagnostics and teleconferencing for training and clinical guidance. However, two programs (Xi County and Hangzhou) established e-consultations between hospital specialists and patients attending primary care facilities, while Zhenjiang and Henan implemented an electronic medical record (EMR) system which affiliated providers can access.

With some exceptions (detailed below), care integration was limited. Gatekeeping, use of multidisciplinary teams, individualized care plans coordinated by primary care facilities, patient tracking, and post-discharge care were largely absent or restricted to a subset of conditions. Care-shifting from higher-level hospitals to lower levels was minimal. Chaoyang arranged for follow-up in CHCs for rehabilitating a subset of patients but was not active in the follow-up care. Most of the initiatives did not design payment systems to incentivize care coordination.

Nevertheless, three cases presented more vigorous examples of care integration, though the scope was limited.

- Zhenjiang-Kangfu established multidisciplinary "family health" teams consisting of hospital, CHC, and public health personnel to support integrated management of non-communicable diseases (NCDs) and maternal/child care. The program established a rehabilitation ward in four CHCs for patients discharged from geriatric and neurology departments and implemented a payment system to incentivize chronic care management at CHCs.
- Hangzhou created 46 collaborative care centers ("joint centers") in CHCs staffed by hospital specialists (from four municipal hospitals) and primary care physicians to manage patients with diabetes and hypertension. Features included tracking and coordinating care across the delivery chain, using integrated care pathways, crafting individual care plans, and fostering active involvement of hospital specialists in post-discharge care delivered in CHCs. The "joint centers" also established a peer-to-peer mentorship program pairing hospital endocrinologists and cardiologists with CHC-based physicians to improve NCD management.
- In Xi County, integrating care between the county hospital, THCs, and village clinics (VCs) was one component of an externally financed project that broadly aimed to improve accessibility, affordability, and quality of rural healthcare. Planners introduced integrated care pathways that specified the course of treatment and criteria for referrals and post-discharge care for over 100 conditions at each provider level. "Liaison officers" were hired by the THCs to manage care coordination and referrals and oversee the use of customized care plans for follow-up at the community level (VCs). The project developed metrics to assess the application of integrated pathways. EMRs were introduced that are accessible county-wide. Service agreements among county hospitals, THCs, and VCs reflect the above features. While there are no

Table 8.4 Characteristics of care integration initiatives involving hospitals

	Beijing Chaoyang Hospital Alliance	Beijing Renmin Hospital Integrated Care Delivery System	Shanghai Ruijin-Luwan Hospital Group	Zhenjiang Kangfu Network	Hangzhou NCD Joint Centers	Henan Xi County Integrated Care
Basic Features						
Administrative level	Municipal and district	Municipal but with significant national reach	Municipal and district	Mainly district	Municipal and district	County, township, and village
Initiation date	2012	2007	2011	2009	2013	2012
Participating facilities	Tertiary, secondary hospitals and CHCs	Mainly tertiary and secondary hospitals and CHCs	Tertiary, secondary hospitals and CHCs	Tertiary, secondary hospitals and CHCs	Tertiary hospitals and CHCs	County hospitals, THCs, and VCs
Lead facility	Tertiary hospital	Tertiary hospital	Tertiary hospital	Tertiary hospital	Tertiary hospital	County hospital
Lead organization to oversee and manage coordination	Hospital alliance "council"	Lead hospital	Hospital group council	Hospital management council	Informal municipal "leading team"	Informal (county health bureau)
Payment system to support care integration	Subsidy to hospital physicians to consult in CHCs	No	No	Payment to CHCs for NCD management	No	Yes
Main innovation	Formation of a "hospital alliance" to improve care at CHCs	Academic seminars, clinical research exchanges, and technical training (teleconferencing)	Horizontal integration of lab, imaging and radiotherapy services	Rehabilitation/recovery wards in CHCs; horizontal integration of lab, imaging and pathology services	Joint outpatient centers in CHCs for hypertension and diabetes	Integrated care pathways, "service agreements," and liaison officers to coordinate care
Elements of Integrated Care						
Tracking patient contacts with delivery system	Referrals only	No	Referrals and subset of diagnostic tests	Referrals and tests	Yes	Yes
Gatekeeping	No	No	No	For NCMS and URBMI	No	No
PHC-based care coordination across providers	No	No	No	No	For diabetes and hypertension management at CHCs	Partial: THC physician monitors care provided by VC

Table 8.4 (cont.)

	Beijing Chaoyang Hospital Alliance	Beijing Renmin Hospital Integrated Care Delivery System	Shanghai Ruijin–Luwan Hospital Group	Zhenjiang Kangfu Network	Hangzhou NCD Joint Centers	Henan Xi County Integrated Care
Use of integrated care pathways and/or individual care plans	No	No	No	No	Care plans for hypertension and diabetes	Yes
Use of metrics to measure care coordination	No	No	Limited to referrals and diagnostic tests	Limited to referrals and diagnostic tests	Limited to referrals and diagnostic tests	Compliance with integrated pathways; referral tracking
Hospital-related Activities and Roles						
Use of multidisciplinary care teams with participation of hospital professionals	No	No	No	Yes	Hospital specialists only	No
Hospital involvement in post-discharge follow-up care	No	No	No	Information provided to lower levels	Inpatients with diabetes and hypertension	Yes
Two-way referral system	Limited	Limited	Yes	Yes	Yes	Yes
Hospital "green" channel	Yes	Very limited	Yes, but limited	Yes, but limited	Yes	Yes
Care shifted out of hospitals to appropriate levels	Limited: subset of patients requiring rehabilitation	No	Some shifting of tests from tertiary to secondary hospitals	Limited to one hospital department	No	No
Technical support, training, or supervision provided by hospitals to lower levels	Yes	Yes	Yes	Yes	Yes	Yes
e-health	E-consultations for imaging services	Remote laboratory testing and imaging; teleconferencing for training/technical support	Teleconferencing for training/technical support	EHRs accessed by providers at different levels	E-consultations with hospital specialists	EHRs accessed county-wide; e-consultations with hospital specialists

penalties for non-compliance with the service agreements, Xi County introduced a payment mechanism in which insurance payments for inpatient care are shared between the county hospital and THCs, incentivizing a shift of care out of the hospital, post-discharge care, and hospital-THC coordination.

None of the initiatives has been evaluated. Based on administrative data, Zhenjiang reports improvements in the number of patients under NCD management; Xi County reports a significant increase in follow-up care by hypertensive patients and flows of two-way referrals. In other cases, referral systems appear to have strengthened upward patient flows rather than downward flows.

Constraints to Care Integration

Interviews with planners and personnel in hospitals and primary care centers (CHCs and THCs) identified several constraints to improving care coordination in China.[70] First, hospitals have strong financial incentives to capture inpatients and outpatients because of their heavy financial dependency on FFS revenues. Under these conditions, shifts in care will usually involve low-margin patients such as geriatric patients with long lengths of stay where revenues do not cover costs. Hospitals have few incentives to restrict the flow of *new* inpatients and outpatients. Each facility is paid separately for the care it provides, and except for the Xi County experiment there have been few attempts to share earnings or savings from improved coordination.

Second, integrated care is not compensated or fully compensated. For example, Beijing Chaoyang provides a small yearly stipend to physicians that rotate to CHCs on a part-time basis; however, the amount is insufficient to cover what some specialists claim to be "loss income" resulting from the reduced time available to them to provide hospital-based care. Primary care physicians usually receive no additional income for activities related to care coordination, and primary care facilities cannot retain savings earned from efficiency gains through improved care or disease management.

Third, patients have few incentives to use primary care as a first point of entry. Government policy allows patients direct access to all hospitals and primary care facilities for all care. Compared to hospitals, primary care facilities have limited drug formularies and lower qualified professionals, which limits demand from patients with complex conditions. Also, there are only minimal differences among the copayments charged at hospital outpatient departments and primary care facilities that might deter "hospital first" care-seeking behaviors by patients.

Finally, integration requires administrative coordination. However, networks of facilities that span different political-administrative jurisdictions (municipality, district, county) have a difficult time coordinating decision making, patient flows, overlapping services, financing arrangements, human resources, and logistics. The formation of HMCs has not overcome these constraints. The two sites with arguably the best examples of care coordination, Xi County, and Zhenjiang-Kangfu, operate within a single administrative jurisdiction.

Remaining Challenges and Future Directions

In 2015, the State Council affirmed that reforming the public hospitals is a top priority in order to achieve its healthcare reform objective of providing affordable, equitable access to quality basic healthcare for all its citizens by 2020.[71] It maintains that the public hospitals' objective is to pursue the public interest rather than profits. It further clarifies that public hospitals play a role in providing "basic" services for the people. However, what is basic is not defined, except for the principle that it should not be so broad as to exclude any role for private hospitals. In addition to the policies initiated in the 12th FYP, it further highlighted the direction of building an integrated delivery system and creating performance assessment for hospital directors and managers that are consistent with the pursuit of the public's interest.

Global experience shows that reforming public hospitals is a difficult and long-term process. China's situation is further complicated by several decades' exposure to a number of irrational policies. As a result, public hospitals are embodiments of both government and market failures. The main challenge to reforming Chinese public hospitals is not technical; it is vested interests. The ability of current reform policies to restore public hospitals' objectives and roles in serving the public interest remains unknown. Also unclear is the government's definition of "public interest" and its rules of behavior for private hospitals. Finally, as with all kinds of reform, the government must establish objectives along with scientifically conducted monitoring and evaluation to support evidence-based mid-course adjustments, including how the current entry of private hospitals affects the healthcare system.

Notes

1. This statistic includes all services rendered in hospitals, including use of drugs.
2. National Health and Family Planning Commission (formerly Ministry of Health). 2014. *China Health Statistics Year Book* (Beijing).
3. National Health and Family Planning Commission. 2014. *China Health Statistics Year Book.*
4. Xiaohui Hou and Joseph Coyne. 2008. "The Emergence of Proprietary Medical Facilities in China," *Health Policy* 88(1): 141–151.
5. National Health and Family Planning Commission. 2014. *China Health Statistics Year Book.*
6. Ibid.
7. Ibid.
8. Barry Naughton. 2014. "China's Economy: Complacency, Crisis & the Challenge of Reform," *Daedalus* 143(2): 14–25.
9. Winnie Yip and William Hsiao. 2008. "The Chinese Health System at a Crossroads," *Health Affairs* 27(2): 460–468.
10. Gordon Liu and Jiefu Huang. 2014. *Global Hospital Management Survey – China, Management in Healthcare Report* (Beijing: China Centre for Health Economic Research, Peking University).
11. State Council. People's Republic of China. 1992. *Instructions on Health Reform.*
12. Winnie Chi-Man Yip, William C. Hsiao, Wen Chen et al. 2012. "Early Appraisal of China's Huge and Complex Health-Care Reforms," *Lancet* 379(9818): 833–842.
13. Single-site studies do not provide sufficient information or analysis of the overall quality of management practices and therefore caution is advised in making inferences to the hospital system.
14. Gordon Liu. 2015. *Quality of Hospital Management Practices in China – China Hospital Management Survey (Chms).* Unpublished Manuscript. The survey was commissioned by the World Bank and the preliminary findings are reported here.
15. Nicholas Bloom, Christos Genakos, Raffaella Sadun et al. 2012. "Management Practices across Firms and Countries," *Academy of Management Perspectives* 26(1): 12–33. Nicholas Bloom, Carol Propper, Stephan Seiler et al. 2015. "The Impact of Competition on Management Quality: Evidence from Public Hospitals," *The Review of Economic Studies* 82(2): 457–489. Nicholas Bloom and John Van Reenen. 2007. "Measuring and Explaining Management Practices across Firms and Countries," *The Quarterly Journal of Economics* 122(4): 1351–1408.
16. Country comparisons should be taken with caution. 79 percent of the hospitals originally contacted in China refused to participate. This may have contributed to a sampling bias in which the surveyed hospitals were those with best management practices. The researchers did not examine the association between management scores and hospital performance indicators because validation of the latter was impossible.
17. Zhijun Lin, Zengbiao Yu, and Liqun Zhang. 2014. "Performance Outcomes of Balanced Scorecard Application in Hospital Administration in China," *China Economic Review* 30: 1–15.
18. Tian Gao and Bruce Gurd. 2015. "Meeting the Challenge in Performance Management: The Diffusion and Implementation of the

Balanced Scorecard in Chinese Hospitals," *Health Policy and Planning* 30(2): 234–241.

19. Jinshuai Guo, Shijun Ma, and Xun Zhang. 2014. *A Healthcare Experiment in China.* Available online at: http://planet-lean.com/lean-management-to-transform-a-chinese-hospital. Accessed on December 11, 2015.

20. Weiping Li and Jianxiu Wang. 2015. *China's Public Hospital Governance Reform: Dongyang Case Study* (Beijing: National Health Development Research Center). Unpublished report commissioned by the World Bank.

21. Dai Tao, Loraine Hawkins, Huihui Wang et al. 2010. *Fixing the Public Hospital System in China* (Washington DC: The World Bank).

22. National Bureau of Statistics of China. 1995–2014. *China Statistical Yearbook* (Beijing: China Statistics Press).

23. Organization for Economic Cooperation and Development. 2013. *OECD Health Statistics, 2013.* Available online at: http://stats.oecd.org/index.aspx?DataSetCode=HEALTH_STAT. Accessed on December 11, 2015. As noted earlier, much of the dispensing and spending on drugs occurs in China's hospitals.

24. Yongbin Li, Jing Xu, Fang Wang et al. 2012. "Overprescribing in China, Driven by Financial Incentives, Results in Very High Use of Antibiotics, Injections, and Corticosteroids," *Health Affairs* 31(5): 1075–1082. Xiaoyun Sun, Sukhan Jackson, Gordon A. Carmichael et al. Sleigh. 2009. "Prescribing Behaviour of Village Doctors under China's New Cooperative Medical Scheme," *Social Science & Medicine* 68: 1775–1779. Wenqiang Yin, Zhongming Chen, Hui Guan et al. 2015. "Using Entropy Weight RSR to Evaluate Village Doctors' Prescription in Shandong Province under the Essential Medicine System," *Modern Preventive Medicine* 42(3): 465–467. Xiao Yin, Fujian Song, Yanhong Gong et al. 2013. "A Systematic Review of Antibiotic Utilization in China," *Journal of Antimicrobial Chemotherapy* 68(11): 2445–2452. doi: 10.1093/jac/dkt223.

25. Li et al. 2012. "Overprescribing in China." Yip et al. 2012. "Early Appraisal of China's Huge and Complex Health-Care Reforms."

26. Lixin Jiang, Harlan M. Krumholz, Xi Li et al. 2015. "Achieving Best Outcomes for Patients with Cardiovascular Disease in China by Enhancing the Quality of Medical Care and Establishing a Learning Health-Care System," *The Lancet* 386: 1493–1505.

27. "Ideal" candidates are a group without any risk factors for cardiogenic shock, those for whom maximal benefit may be derived if β-blocker is given within the early stages of AMI.

28. Haibo Zhang, Frederick A. Masoudi, Jing Li, et al. 2015. "National Assessment of Early B-Blocker Therapy in Patients with Acute Myocardial Infarction in China, 2001–2011: The China Patient-Centered Evaluative Assessment of Cardiac Events (PEACE)–Retrospective AMI Study," *American Heart Journal* 170(3): 506–515.e501.

29. ST-segment elevation myocardial infarction is the most serious type of heart attack, where there is a long interruption to the blood supply. This is caused by a total blockage of the coronary artery, which can cause extensive damage to a large area of the heart. It is what most people think of when they hear the term "heart attack" (www.nhs.uk/Conditions/Heart-attack/Pages/Diagnosis.aspx).

30. Jing Li, Xi Li, Qing Wang et al. 2015. "St-Segment Elevation Myocardial Infarction in China from 2001 to 2011 (the China PEACE-Retrospective Acute Myocardial Infarction Study): A Retrospective Analysis of Hospital Data," *The Lancet* 385: 441–451.

31. Center for Health Statistics and Information. Ministry of Health. People's Republic of China. 2009. *An Analysis Report of National Health Services Survey in China, 2008.* Available online at: www.nhfpc.gov.cn/cmsresources/mohwsbwstjxxzx/cmsrsdocument/doc9911.pdf. Accessed on December 11, 2015.

32. State Council. People's Republic of China. 2012. *The Twelfth Five-Year Plan for Health Sector Development.* Available online at: www.gov.cn/zwgk/2012-10/19/content_2246908.htm. Accessed on December 11, 2015. State Council. People's Republic of China. 2012. *On Deepening Medical and Health System: Notice of the Work Arrangements.* Available

online at: www.gov.cn/zwgk/2012-04/18/con tent_2115928.htm. Accessed on December 11, 2015.

33. National Health and Family Planning Commission. People's Republic of China. 2015. *Report on the Assessment of County-Level Public Hospital Reform*. Available online at: www.nhfpc.gov.cn/tigs/ygjb/201507/ 7a73fe3715d94959a99cab2ce864b893.shtml. Accessed on December 11, 2015. National Health and Family Planning Commission. People's Republic of China. 2015. *Report on the Assessment of Urban Public Hospital Reform*. Available online at: www.nhfpc.gov .cn/tigs/ygjb/201507/bd39f973732849dea9e0a 1ede3a10577.shtml. Accessed on December 11, 2015.

34. Weiyan Jian, Winnie Yip, William Hsiao et al. 2014. "A Win-Win-Win Provider Payment Policy Innovation: The Case of Yanchi County Hospital," *China Health Economics* 11: 8–10.

35. Weiyan Jian, Ming Lu, Kit Yee Chan et al. 2015. "Payment Reform Pilot in Beijing Hospitals Reduced Expenditures and Out-of-Pocket Payments per Admission," *Health Affairs* 34(10): 1745–1752.

36. Public hospitals operate with considerable autonomy in most countries. Like China, a number of countries that historically directly administered public hospitals have taken steps to grant them greater independence, including UK, Brazil, Netherlands, Spain, Norway, and others.

37. State Council. People's Republic of China. 2015. *Guiding Opinions on Pilot Comprehensive Reform of County-Level Public Hospitals*. Available online at: www .gov.cn/zhengce/content/2015-05/08/con tent_9710.htm. Accessed on December 11, 2015. State Council. People's Republic of China. 2015. *Guiding Opinions on Pilot Comprehensive Reform of Urban Public Hospitals*. Available online at: www.gov.cn/ zhengce/content/2015-05/17/content_9776.htm. Accessed on December 11, 2015.

38. Gerard Martin La Forgia and Bernard Couttolenc. 2008. *Hospital Performance in Brazil: The Search for Excellence* (Washington DC: The World Bank). Alexander S. Preker and April Harding. 2003. *Innovations in Health Service Delivery: The Corporatization of Public Hospitals* (Washington DC: The World Bank). Richard Saltman, Antonio Durán, and Hans F. W. Dubois. 2011. *Governing Public Hospitals. Reform Strategies and the Movement Towards Institutional Autonomy* (Copenhagen Denmark: European Observatory on Health Systems and Policies). Sanming Prefecture Government. 2015. *Compensation System of Public Hospitals*. Available online at: www.sm.gov.cn/ztzl/shyywstzgg/zcwj/ 201508/t20150814_310859.htm. Accessed on December 11, 2015.

39. Pauline Allen, Qi Cao, and Hufeng Wang. 2014. "Public Hospital Autonomy in China in an International Context," *The International Journal of Health Planning and Management* 29(2): 141–159. Tao et al. 2010. *Fixing the Public Health System in China*.

40. As already suggested, a number of local governments have launched pilots involving alternative governance arrangements for public hospitals. Some are official pilots sanctioned by the central government; others are not. Shanghai and Zhenjiang were official pilots. Dongyang and Sanming were local initiatives.

41. Adapted from Gerard Martin La Forgia, Loraine Hawkins, April Harding, and Eric De Roodnebeke. 2013. *Framework for Developing and Analzying Public Hospital Reforms Involving Autonomy* (Washington, DC: World Bank HD Learning Week).

42. Tao et al. 2010. *Fixing the Public Health System in China*.

43. This arrangement was part of a special agreement made between city leaders and a Taiwanese businessman who made a substantial donation to rebuild the hospital in 1993.

44. A prefecture is an administrative unit common to all China's provinces and usually consisting of both urban and rural areas. Located in Fujian Province, the Sanming Prefecture has a population of about 2.7 million and consists of 2 districts and 10 counties. The prefecture had 166 healthcare facilities in 2013, of which

22 were secondary and tertiary hospitals, with a total of about 8,000 beds.

45. Jiwei Qian. 2015. "Reallocating Authority in the Chinese Health System: An Institutional Perspective," *Journal of Asian Public Policy* 8 (1): 19–35.

46. Sanming Prefecture Government. 2015. *Compensation System of Public Hospitals.*

47. Tao et al. 2010. *Fixing the Public Health System in China.*

48. Qian. 2015. "Reallocating Authority in the Chinese Health System."

49. National Development and Reform Commission, Ministry of Health, Ministry of Finance, Ministry of Commerce, and Ministry of Human Resources and Social Security. People's Republic of China. 2010. *Further Encouraging and Guiding the Establishment of Medical Institutions by Social Capital.* Available online at: www.gov.cn/zwgk/2010-12/03/content_1759091.htm. Accessed on December 11, 2015. National Health and Family Planning Commission and State Administration of Traditional Chinese Medicine. People's Republic of China. 2015. *Accelerate the Development of Establishing Hospitals with Social Capital.* Available online at: www.moh.gov.cn/tigs/s7846/201401/239ae12d249c4e38a5e2de457ee20253.shtml. Accessed on December 11, 2015. State Council. People's Republic of China. 2012. *The Twelfth Five-Year Plan for Health Sector Development.* State Council. People's Republic of China. 2012. *On Deepening Medical and Health System.*

50. General Office of the State Council. People's Republic of China. 2015. *Several Policies and Measures for Promoting the Accelerated Development of Private Health Facilities.* Available online at: www.gov.cn/zhengce/content/2015-06/15/content_9845.htm. Accessed on December 11, 2015.

51. Winnie Yip and William Hsiao. 2014. "Harnessing the Privatisation of China's Fragmented Health-Care Delivery," *Lancet* 384(9945): 805–818.

52. Gwyn Bevan and Matthew Skellern. 2011. "Does Competition between Hospitals Improve Clinical Quality? A Review of Evidence from Two Eras of Competition in the English NHS," *British Medical Journal* 343:d6470. Carol Propper and George Leckie. 2011. "Increasing Competition between Providers in Health Care Markets: The Economic Evidence," in S. Glied and P. C. Smith (Eds.), *Oxford Handbook of Health Economics* (Oxford: Oxford University Press) Chapter 28, 671–688.

53. Jason R. Barro, Robert S. Huckman, and Daniel P. Kessler. 2006. "The Effects of Cardiac Specialty Hospitals on the Cost and Quality of Medical Care," *Journal of Health Economics* 25(4): 702–721. Daniel P. Kessler and Mark B. McClellan. 2002. "The Effects of Hospital Ownership on Medical Productivity," *RAND Journal of Economics* 33(3): 488–506.

54. Zack Cooper, Stephen Gibbons, Simon Jones et al. 2012. "Does Competition Improve Public Hospitals' Efficiency?: Evidence from a Quasi-Experiment in the English National Health Service," *LSE Centre for Economic Performance Discussion Paper 1125.*

55. P. J. Devereaux, Holger J. Schünemann, Nikila Ravindran et al. 2002. "Comparison of Mortality between Private for-Profit and Private Not-for-Profit Hemodialysis Centers: A Systematic Review and Meta-Analysis," *Journal of American Medical Association* 288 (19): 2449–2457. P. J. Devereaux, Peter T. L. Choi, Christina Lacchetti et al. 2002. "A Systematic Review and Meta-Analysis of Studies Comparing Mortality Rates of Private for-Profit and Private Not-for-Profit Hospitals," *Canadian Medical Association Journal* 166(11): 1399–1406. P. J. Devereaux, Diane Heels-Ansdell, Christina Lacchetti,. 2004. "Payments for Care at Private for-Profit and Private Not-for-Profit Hospitals: A Systematic Review and Meta-Analysis," *Canadian Medical Association Journal* 170 (12): 1817–1824. Karen Eggleston, Yu-Chu Shen, Joseph Lau et al. 2008. "Hospital Ownership and Quality of Care: What Explains the Different Results in the Literature?" *Health Economics* 17(12): 1345–1362. Yu-Chu Shen, Karen Eggleston,

Joseph Lau et al. 2007. "Hospital Ownership and Financial Performance: What Explains the Different Findings in the Empirical Literature?" *Inquiry* 44(1): 41–68. Elaine M. Silverman, Jonathan S. Skinner, and Elliott S. Fisher. 1999. "The Association between for-Profit Hospital Ownership and Increased Medicare Spending," *New England Journal of Medicine* 341(6): 420–426.

56. Bloom et al. 2012. "Management Practices Across Firms and Countries." McKinsey & Company. 2013. *In Search of New Growth Models for Big Pharma in China.* Available online at: www.mckinseychina.com/in-search-of-new-growth-models-for-big-pharma-in-china/. Accessed on December 11, 2015.

57. Allen et al. 2014. "Public Hospital Autonomy in China in an International Context."

58. Ministry of Health, National Development and Reform Commission, and Ministry of Finance. 2004. *Regulation on Large Medical Equipment Allocation and Utilization.* Available online at: www.moh.gov.cn/mohghcws/s3585/200905/40572.shtml. Accessed on December 11, 2015.

59. Laurence C. Baker. 2010. "Acquisition of MRI Equipment by Doctors Drives Up Imaging Use and Spending," *Health Affairs* 29(12): 2252–2259. Da He, Hao Yu, and Yingyao Chen. 2013. "Equity in the Distribution of CT and MRI in China: A Panel Analysis," *International Journal for Equity in Health* 12(1): 39. Bruce J. Hillman and Jeff C. Goldsmith. 2010. "The Uncritical Use of High-Tech Medical Imaging," *New England Journal of Medicine* 363(1): 4–6. John K. Iglehart. 2009. "Health Insurers and Medical-Imaging Policy – a Work in Progress," *New England Journal of Medicine* 360(10): 1030–1037. Eun-Hwan Oh, Yuichi Imanaka, and Edward Evans. 2005. "Determinants of the Diffusion of Computed Tomography and Magnetic Resonance Imaging," *International Journal of Technology Assessment in Health Care* 21: 73–80.

60. Vivian Chen and YueXia Gao. 2015. "Wuhan Asia Heart Hospital Case Study." Unpublished report commissioned by the International Finance Corporation, World Bank, Beijing. April.

61. Chen and Gao 2015. "Wuhan Asia Heart Hospital Case Study."

62. However, ophthalmological care is still dominated by public hospitals. Of an estimated *total* market of 60 billion RMB, public hospitals account for about 94 percent. Headquarter approval is needed for equipment purchases and service contracts over certain amounts.

63. 80 percent of procurement of goods and services is managed centrally and the remainder by the hospitals.

64. WeChat is a very popular mobile text and voice messaging communication service in China.

65. The main features are similar to the "coordinated/integrated health services delivery" model proposed by WHO/Europe, "medical home," "coordinated care," and "chronic care" models that have emerged in OECD countries. Most are small scale. See World Health Organization. 2013. *Global Action Plan for the Prevention and Control of NCDs 2013–2020.* Available online at: www.who.int/nmh/events/ncd_action_plan/en/. Accessed on December 11, 2015. Natasha Curry and Chris Ham. 2010. *Clinical and Service Integration: The Route to Improved Outcomes* (London, UK: The King's Fund). Edward H Wagner. 1998. "Chronic Disease Management: What Will It Take to Improve Care for Chronic Illness?," *Effective Clinical Practice* 1(1): 2–4. John W. Williams, George L. Jackson, Benjamin J. Powers et al. 2012. *The Patient-Centered Medical Home: Closing the Quality Gap: Revisiting the State of the Science* (Rockville: Agency for Healthcare Research and Quality, U.S. Department of Health and Human Services).

66. Sarah Purdy. 2010. *Avoiding Hospital Admissions: What Does the Research Evidence Say?* (London: The King's Fund). Bonnie Sibbald, Ruth McSonald, and Martin Roland. 2007. "Shifting Care from Hospitals to the Community: A Review of the Evidence on Quality and Efficiency," *Journal of Health Services Research & Policy* 12(2): 110–117.

67. In part due to their recent implementation, small scale, and the scarcity of robust evaluations, impact remains an open question. Emerging evidence from programs adapting care integration models in OECD countries suggests gains in efficiency (e.g., decreased admissions, readmissions, and lengths of stay), improved access to appropriate care, greater use of preventive services, improved patient experience and satisfaction, and higher patient compliance with therapies and healthier lifestyles. However, evidence of impact on cost containment is thin. See Ellen Nolte and Emma Pitchforth. 2014. *What Is the Evidence on the Economic Impacts of Integrated Care?* (Copenhagen, Denmark: European Observatory on Health Systems and Policies). John Øvretveit. 2011. *Does Clinical Coordination Improve Quality and Save Money?* (London: The Health Foundation). Deborah Peikes, Arnold Chen, Jennifer Schore et al. 2009. "Effects of Care Coordination on Hospitalization, Quality of Care, and Health Care Expenditures among Medicare Beneficiaries: 15 Randomized Trials," *Journal of American Medical Association* 301(6): 603–618.

68. State Council. People's Republic of China. 2012. The Twelfth Five-Year Plan for Health Sector Development. State Council. People's Republic of China. 2012. On Deepening Medical and Health System. State Council. People's Republic of China. 2015. Guiding Opinions on Pilot Comprehensive Reform of County-Level Public Hospitals. State Council. People's Republic of China. 2015. *Guiding Opinions on Pilot Comprehensive Reform of Urban Public Hospitals.*

69. For example, green channel admissions accounted for less than 1 percent of total admissions in Beijing-Renmin.

70. Interviews were conducted as part of case study research.

71. State Council. People's Republic of China. 2015. *Guiding Opinions on Pilot Comprehensive Reform of County-Level Public Hospitals.* State Council. People's Republic of China. 2015. *Guiding Opinions on Pilot Comprehensive Reform of Urban Public Hospitals.*

CHAPTER 9

United Family Healthcare (Chindex International)

A Case Study

VANESSA FOLKERTS AND ROBERTA LIPSON

Introduction

United Family Healthcare (UFH) is a private health-care system with hospitals and clinics in five cities in China and one city in Mongolia. Founded in Beijing in 1997 as the healthcare services arm of Chindex International, UFH was the first foreign-invested, for-profit healthcare provider in China. In the ensuing decades, it developed from a modest primary care facility in Beijing into a chain of acute-care general hospitals and community-based clinics, scattered across the metropolitan areas of China's east coast. Chindex was listed on NASDAQ from 1994 until 2014, when it was acquired by a consortium including US private equity firm TPG Capital, the Chinese conglomerate Fosun Pharma, and Chindex management for $463 million.

UFH remains the largest system of high-end private hospitals in China and the only one to be accredited by Joint Commission International. The brand is known for premium service, a multinational clinical staff, and an elite clientele. At the outset, UFH drew its patients primarily from the expatriate community but, with the growth of the Chinese economy and rising levels of domestic wealth, it now serves more local patients than foreign. In 2015, UFH launched an insurance product to pave the way toward becoming China's first health maintenance organization.

Company History

From Equipment Supplier to Healthcare Provider

UFH's CEO, president, and co-founder Roberta Lipson began her career in China in 1979 at the cusp of the country's economic liberalization, working for an American trading company. In 1981, she founded an equipment import and distribution business, U.S.-China Industrial Exchange, with Elyse Silverberg, a fellow New Yorker in her twenties. Lipson and Silverberg ran their fledgling company out of a room at the Beijing Hotel – private residences were not permitted for foreigners at the time – helping Chinese trade agencies to source and import capital equipment from US manufacturers. They acquired two typewriters and a motorcycle, taking turns to communicate with the outside world via the mechanical telex machines at the post office. Pragmatically, the name of their company was shortened to Chindex. By the end of the decade, they were granted some of the first residence permits to be issued to foreign citizens. More than 30 years later, they are still working in Beijing.

Though it served many industries initially, Chindex came to specialize in capital medical equipment, bringing the first ultrasound and MRI machines to China. Lipson recalls demonstrating ultrasonic imaging to physicians who were moved to tears at the sight of a fetus they had previously only been able to assess by hand. The professional network Lipson and Silverberg created within the Chinese medical establishment, initially travelling through China by train with a portable ultrasound in hand, became a valuable asset to their transition into healthcare services. Chindex also distinguished itself with the quality of its after-sales service, foreshadowing the company's move into the service sector.

In 1994, Lipson and Silverberg listed Chindex on NASDAQ (CHDX) in order to raise money for their first hospital. The 50-bed facility, housed in a repurposed office building, opened under the name Beijing United Family Hospital (北京和睦家医院) in 1997. As Chindex's pace of growth accelerated, and the vision of a United Family hospital group began to look viable, they divided the leadership of the healthcare and equipment divisions between them. Lipson became the CEO of the healthcare services brand, United Family Healthcare, and the listed parent company, Chindex, while Silverberg served as head of medical products distribution. UFH opened a second hospital in Shanghai in 2005 and a clinic in Guangzhou in 2008. The advent of Chinese healthcare reform in 2009, including the government's encouragement of private investment in the sector, accelerated this expansion. Targeting the top 5 percent of income earners among China's population of 1.3 billion, as well as UFH's traditional expatriate market, the system began to open a new facility every other year. Financial support was obtained through the management-backed buyout of Chindex in 2014, in which the principal investors, TPG Capital and Shanghai Fosun Pharmaceutical Group (Fosun Pharma), committed $130 million in additional equity financing for the development of new UFH hospitals. Chindex began to divest itself from the medical equipment business in 2011, eventually completing the company's shift into healthcare services by selling the equipment division to Fosun Pharma.

Improving Public Health

In the 1980s, when Lipson and Silverberg began selling medical equipment to Chinese hospitals, local healthcare lagged significantly behind international standards in quality and accessibility. The "barefoot doctor" system of primary healthcare established under Mao Zedong had been disbanded, and instead, patients were flocking to large city hospitals staffed by specialists. These hospitals were overcrowded, underfunded, and unable to meet demand, especially in the absence of the screening and gatekeeping traditionally performed by primary care. Upgrading the medical equipment at Chinese hospitals was an important step toward raising the standard of care, but equipment alone

could not close the quality gap. The promotion of best practices in healthcare delivery – models of evidence-based medicine and patient-centered care – became Lipson's next priority in improving public health.

Chinese medical leadership, whom Lipson and Silverberg accompanied on delegations to major hospitals in the United States, admired these practices but considered them impossible to implement in China's uniquely challenging environment. Having experienced healthcare firsthand in China, Lipson recognized both the business opportunity and the public service imperative to prove better care was possible. With the credibility of a decade's industry experience at the helm of Chindex, Lipson began lobbying in 1992 for Chinese government support to establish the country's first foreign-invested, for-profit hospital. Leveraging relationships with the Academy of Medical Sciences and Ministry of Health, she found an influential audience willing to consider the radical proposition. More than 180 government stamps were required – from the healthcare bureaucracy on the one hand and the commercial government oversight agencies on the other (including the Ministry of Commerce, National Development and Reform Commission, State Administration of Industry and Commerce, and their municipal branches) – in order to receive the license for operating a healthcare facility. Having persuaded the Beijing Health Bureau, the final hurdle in the development process, Lipson and her team opened Beijing United Family Hospital (BJU) in the presence of the US secretary of commerce, William Daley, Chinese vice-minister of health, Cao Ronggui, and Chinese vice-minister of commerce, Ma Xiuhong.

The case that Chindex made was that the availability of international-style healthcare would help to make China a more attractive destination for foreign talent, thereby contributing to the country's economic development. Serving mostly non-Chinese patients, the hospital would not threaten the politically sensitive healthcare sector: it was posited as a "contained" experiment from which the public system might learn international best practices without overt disruption. Moreover, operating on a modest scale and starting with primary care services, UFH would amass a patient base with limited risk of poor outcomes threatening its reputation. The key was to excel in relatively low-complexity care with high potential for added value through better service. Thus Chindex's healthcare operations made their start by delivering mainly obstetric and pediatric care to the diplomatic and expatriate business communities of Beijing.

UFH was established with the approval of the highest government authorities and has continued its development under the scrutiny of Chinese policy makers. The SARS epidemic in 2003 thrust the weaknesses of the Chinese healthcare system into the international spotlight and initiated the process of domestic healthcare reform, in which Lipson has played an advisory role. UFH hospitals frequently host public hospital leaders seeking new ideas, from facility design to management practices. The ability of UFH to influence public health beyond the direct treatment of its patients has helped to attract important leadership talent to its ranks, including former deputy surgeon general of the United States, Dr. David Rutstein, who now serves as Executive Vice President of Medical Affairs (UFH's chief physician).

Bringing Back Primary Care

A key feature of the UFH mission is to re-introduce primary care to China, starting with UFH's own patients. To this day, the paucity of trained primary care practitioners in the public system forces those seeking care into a labyrinth of trial and error that can be both wasteful and dangerous (see Chapter 7). Without a generalist to meet most clinical needs and point the patient in the direction of an appropriate specialist, the patient is left to guess the organ system behind any symptoms and self-select a specialist accordingly. If this turns out to be the wrong kind of specialist, the patient must try another, losing time and money – particularly in the Chinese public system, where patients may wait hours for consultations and in which bribes to "jump the queue" are rife. A patient with stomach pain, for instance, may spend significant personal resources fighting to see a gastroenterologist at a large city hospital, only to be sent to a cardiologist after a brief consultation. No one oversees the patient's medical journey, follows up with the specialist and checks that a coherent plan of treatment is conveyed to the patient. Instead, the patient is thrown deeper into a morass of uncoordinated, discontinuous care.

The dearth of primary care and extreme reductionism of the public system have not improved significantly since Chinese healthcare made its first impression on Lipson in the 1980s. The 12th Five-Year Plan set an ambitious target of adding 150,000 general practitioners to the workforce between 2010 and 2015.[1] In 2015, the National Health and Family Planning Commission estimated that 180,000 new general practitioners would be needed by 2020 in order to provide every 10,000 citizens with two to three of these doctors.[2] The challenge is great – not least given the low pay and humble standing of general practitioners compared to specialists in China, at a time when the medical profession has fallen into disfavor overall.[3]

By focusing initially on pediatrics, obstetrics, and family medicine, UFH was from its inception able to provide patients with primary care doctors to coordinate their care, including referrals for services outside the system. Now that UFH offers secondary and tertiary care, with many patients arriving to avail themselves of specialists at their first appointment, the system has a policy of automatically assigning a primary care physician to each patient, regardless of the cause for their visit. Besides the direct benefit to patients – many of whom (particularly Chinese patients accustomed to the public system) are unfamiliar with primary care and would not otherwise seek out the service – the automatic assignment increases accountability and cohesion within the UFH system, as specialists round with primary care providers to provide team-based, multidisciplinary care.

UFH's freestanding clinics also bring primary care closer to patients, obviating the need to go to the hospital to be seen by a doctor in non-acute cases. The proximity fosters close physician–patient relationships, which are known to improve health maintenance by increasing patient compliance with medical recommendations.[4]

Having foreign family medicine physicians in these clinics lends some prestige to the discredited field of community care in China, disproving the local conviction that good doctors are only found in hospitals.

In 2012, responding to the national need for primary care physicians and UFH's interest in securing a talent pipeline, the UFH Center for Primary Care Practice and Education (CPCPE) was carved out of the company's operating budget to design and run fellowships to the standards of the Accreditation Council for Graduate Medical Education (ACGME) in the United States. Due to regulatory constraints, UFH's fellowships are intended for fully licensed Chinese physicians – specialists who wish to retrain as western-style primary care providers, and upon successful completion of their training, take up employment in the UFH system. The center's inaugural class matriculated in 2013 and is now in its third and final year. Fellowships in emergency medicine, pharmacy, and radiology are also under way.

Alongside UFH's commitment to training is its support for translational research with practical benefits for patients in China. The UFH Center for Clinical Research awards seed money and the system-wide Institutional Review Board evaluates protocols according to National Institutes of Health (NIH) standards. In 2016, UFH expects to receive government certification as a site for clinical trials recognized by the China Food and Drug Administration (CFDA), which will enable it to collaborate with pharmaceutical companies seeking to bring US FDA-approved drugs to the Chinese market.

UFH is the first private healthcare provider in China to undertake training and research, on the principle that these will help to underpin its quality while moving into increasingly complex disciplines and support its development into a fully comprehensive care provider. To that end, management is currently exploring the establishment of China's first international health professions university, in partnership with a US medical school and a Chinese university. The mission will be to standardize clinical training for the country's next generation of clinicians, with an emphasis on UFH's greatest strength: primary care.

Capacity and Performance

Geographical Footprint

Over the course of 18 years, Beijing United Family Hospital has grown into a general hospital of 120 beds and the flagship of a system that operates 6 hospitals and 14 clinics in Beijing, Shanghai, Tianjin, Guangzhou, Qingdao (China), and Ulaanbaatar (Mongolia) (Figure 9.1). The UFH system in China – the focus of this case study – comprises 500 licensed beds, of which 400 are active and 100 in reserve, all in private rooms. Currently under construction, or otherwise in the pipeline, are an additional 200-bed hospital in Guangzhou, two 100-bed hospitals in Shanghai, a 100-bed hospital in west Beijing, and several community-based clinics. UFH is prioritizing expansion in China's first- and second-tier cities, where the country's wealth is concentrated. Shanghai (population of 24.3 million),[5] Beijing (21.5 million),[6] and Tianjin (13 million),[7] along with Chongqing, are the country's four largest cities. Guangzhou (13 million)[8] and Qingdao (9 million)[9] are close behind, and the latter, with its yacht clubs and German colonial architecture, is disproportionately upscale. There is no lack of demand or funding for new hospitals; the rate of expansion is limited primarily by the supply of top clinical and management talent.

Satellite clinics are strategically dispersed in a "hub-and-spoke" pattern to extend the reach of the hospitals in their catchment areas, and in some cases, the clinics cultivate patient bases before the hospitals arrive. Distance and traffic deter patients in west Beijing from traveling to Beijing United Family Hospital in the east; however, a clinic in the western Haidian district is attracting patients into the system ahead of the new hospital planned to open there in 2018. In Guangzhou, a large clinic has been the only UFH facility for eight years, but in 2016, it will be joined by the largest new hospital in the system. Recruitment and marketing for the upcoming Guangzhou United Family Hospital have been boosted by the clinic's roots in the city.

Facilities in the UFH system are majority-owned by Chindex and operated by UFH as a group organized into geographic service areas. Each area is led by a local management team and overseen by UFH

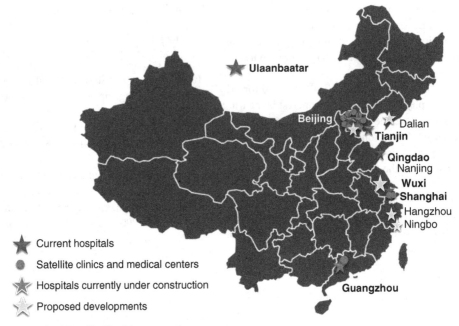

Current hospitals

Satellite clinics and medical centers

Hospitals currently under construction

Proposed developments

Figure 9.1 United Family Healthcare roadmap

corporate management, which provides centralized functions such as human resources, procurement, information technology (IT), and finance. This ensures tight-knit synchrony among the facilities as the company's geographical footprint expands. Demonstrating the scalability of the UFH management model beyond China, Chindex entered into a management contract and minority shareholding of the first high-end private hospital in Mongolia in 2014.

Ownership Structure

Though the UFH system is centrally managed, Chinese law requires each facility to be incorporated as a discrete legal entity. The entities are established as either joint ventures (JVs) between Chindex and a passive local partner, or, where possible, wholly foreign-owned enterprises (WFOEs). Chindex ownership of the JV hospitals ranges from 70 percent in Shanghai to 90 percent in Beijing. The percentages vary with government policy on foreign ownership limits, which has vacillated over time. During the founding of

Beijing United Family Hospital in the early 1990s, the government required at least 50 percent, but no more than 90 percent, foreign investment. When UFH's next hospital opened in Shanghai in 2005, a 70 percent cap on foreign ownership was imposed. Following healthcare reform in 2009, the cap was removed altogether in the free trade zones (FTZs). This was intended to stimulate investment in private hospitals and help reduce the government's burden of providing better healthcare for the nation. Chindex responded by establishing Qingdao United Family Hospital in April 2015 as the first wholly foreign-owned hospital in China.

Yet, later in 2015, foreign-invested private healthcare providers like UFH were returned to the FTZ "Negative List," disqualifying them from establishing WFOEs in the FTZs or elsewhere in China. This may have been done in tandem with the ongoing Sino-US negotiations over the Bilateral Investment Treaty, whose time horizon will span at least another year: re-admitting private healthcare companies to the FTZs would be an easy concession for the Chinese side to make. Given the limited competition between the private and public health-care sectors, the concession would not raise strong local industry objections. In the meantime, the uncertainty imposes costs on Chindex, which had been contemplating new facilities in Pudong and other zones, and is forced to navigate an unpredictable regulatory environment.

Centralized Management

It is challenging to deliver standardized services in a geographical area as diverse as that covered by UFH, from Ulaanbaatar in the subarctic north to Guangzhou in the tropical south. Yet standardization is crucial to maintaining the integrity of the UFH brand, which in recent years has encountered growing competition in its core services and chronic intellectual property infringement. Centralized management is needed to oversee standardization across disparate facilities.

Corporate UFH management, based at Beijing United Family Hospital, is divided into three strands of equal standing: medical, nursing, and operational (see Figure 9.2). Endowing nursing with its own management hierarchy reaching to the executive level was considered a key step toward increasing the autonomy of nurses, and thus the capacity of the nursing profession in China as a whole. Each hospital has its own chief medical officer, chief nursing officer, and general manager, who report to the UFH

VP of Medical Affairs, VP of Nursing, and CEO, respectively. The triumvirate of Rutstein, Shen Xiaoyan (who was in the first cohort of UFH nursing staff), and Lipson set the tone for the system, along with Chindex veterans who lead the hospital development and finance departments, and Sylvia Pan, general manager of the Beijing service area.

Representatives from each facility and corporate management sit on the UFH Board of Business, chaired by Lipson, and Board of Quality and Safety, chaired by Rutstein, which meet monthly to share updates across the system and approve policies. The UFH Office of Quality and Safety selects and analyzes clinical performance indicators ranging from the level of the individual physician to the level of departments, facilities, and the system as a whole. Upon announcing in 2014 to the Board of Business the terms of Chindex's buyout, Lipson stressed that Fosun and TPG had committed to maintaining UFH's signature quality and that cost-cutting measures, if any, would not impede the continued implementation of best practices in the system.

Integrated Information Technology

The cohesion of the UFH group is enhanced by a centrally managed, comprehensive and integrated digital system, InterSystems' TrakCare, which links the facilities across China. Though Chinese law still

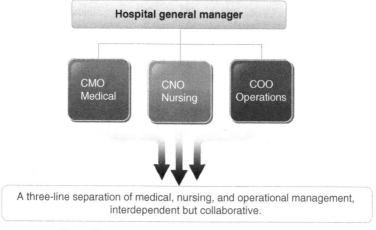

Figure 9.2 Three separate lines of management

requires hospitals to maintain paper records, UFH transitioned to the electronic medical record (EMR) starting in 2007. The relatively small scale of the facilities and low complexity of care being managed at that early stage of UFH's development made digitization less difficult than in more mature medical centers. The TrakCare platform, which includes patient registration, appointment scheduling, clinician notes, orders, picture archiving and communication system (PACS), and billing, is integrated with a system for inventory management, financial analysis, and customer relationship management (CRM). The UFH call center handles appointments for all service areas except Shanghai, and enters the information directly into TrakCare. Inter-facility videoconferencing enables management meetings, training, and telemedicine with participants from all six service areas joining simultaneously. The "Morning Rounds" and "Noontime CME" gatherings initiated in the early days of Beijing United Family Hospital have evolved into regular "virtual" gatherings of UFH medical staff scattered across China, enhancing their sense of belonging to the system.

The EMR is at the heart of UFH's structure as a system, rather than a network of independent hospitals. Each patient has one UFH medical record which can be read at any UFH facility. This makes it easy for physicians to refer patients elsewhere in the system, typically to centers of excellence – for example, IVF at Tianjin United Family Hospital or sports medicine at Shanghai United Family Hospital – while continuing to track their care. The universal platform also brings operational efficiency by creating economies of scale: nighttime radiology readings at smaller UFH hospitals, such as in Tianjin and Qingdao, are covered by the mature departments in Beijing and Shanghai. The smaller facilities also benefit from the larger hospitals' partnerships, such as Beijing United Family Hospital's telepathology arrangement with University of California, Los Angeles.

Investment in IT is needed to save costs, maintain an interactive relationship with patients, and stay ahead of the competition. Much as with radiology, the use of tele-ICU is being considered as a means of extending critical care services to facilities without having to staff them to the same level of intensity. A portal for patients to access their medical records, receive results, and make appointments online is also under construction – a priority given that these functions are already available to public hospital-goers through companies such as Guahao .com (a Fosun subsidiary). The TrakCare system is not yet fully bilingual, a need that grows as the proportion of UFH's Chinese staff and patients increases. International telemedicine is impeded by the "Great Firewall," the government filter on the internet which causes slow speeds and loss of quality. And as the acuity of care at UFH rises, the digital platform will need to be expanded to keep up with the growing complexity of the records.

Facility Design

The project management of opening new facilities – including site selection, design, construction, fit-out, and licensing – is the responsibility of a dedicated, multidisciplinary unit at UFH comprised of government relations experts, engineers, finance specialists, and project managers. Depending on the availability of land, buildings are repurposed or constructed de novo. In Beijing and Shanghai, the first UFH hospitals were built from converted office buildings and public hospital facilities, respectively; in Guangzhou and the Pudong district of Shanghai, the hospitals currently under development are greenfield projects. All facilities are designed to conform to a signature UFH aesthetic and high standard of safety, functionality, and comfort.

Pleasant clinical environments are UFH hallmarks and have proved commercially viable investments. Visitors have commented that the facilities more closely resemble hotels than hospitals. They combine elegant interior design with layouts tailored to best-practice clinical workflows. Local demand for UFH's family-centered birthing experience, for example, has made obstetrics one of the company's most profitable service lines. Chinese patients have revealed their preferences by paying out of pocket at UFH for added comfort rather than utilizing their government medical insurance at public hospitals. In principle, attractive healthcare settings not only draw in patients, but improve clinical outcomes as well.[10]

All UFH inpatient rooms are private occupancy including en-suite bathrooms and sofa beds for visitors, who are welcome to stay at the discretion of the patient without restriction on visiting hours. Suites and duplexes with kitchen facilities are also available. Public spaces are enhanced with discrete waiting areas, high-end coffee shops, soft furniture, free reading material, and colorful children's play areas. Lipson personally approves the design of every facility. Qingdao United Family Hospital, with its etched glass, natural lighting, and curved reception areas created by Robarts Spaces – the design firm behind over 100 global blue-chip companies' offices and several embassies in China – won an international award for interior design in healthcare in 2015. This stands in marked contrast with the typical Chinese public hospital environment.

Some practices introduced by UFH into China have been adopted by public hospitals, demonstrating an increased sensitivity on the part of public providers to patients' needs. In obstetric wards, UFH pioneered the country's first convertible delivery beds, which allow expectant mothers to receive care in labor, delivery, recovery, and post-partum (LDRP) in one room, thereby eliminating the separation of mother and newborn in most cases. The LDRP model has been adopted in some public hospitals as well. UFH also introduced four-handed dentistry – adding an assistant to work alongside the dentist for procedures and maneuvers such as suctioning – which boosts the speed and comfort of dental work. The pneumatic tube system at Beijing United Family Hospital, which delivers medications and consumables throughout the facility, was the first in China. Unfortunately, the central air purification in regular wards and hand-sanitizer dispensers at every door – standard defenses against hospital-acquired infections that UFH has championed – still appear lacking in the public system.

New models of care are not always readily accepted, even when presented in world-class settings. Opening dedicated facilities for rehabilitation and outpatient cancer treatment, services rarely found in China, were among the company's boldest moves. UFH's New Hope Center in Beijing – "oncology" was removed from the name to protect patient privacy – was established in 2011 as the first LEED-certified "green" healthcare facility in China. It has partnered with Peking University Cancer Hospital to access the talent bench of one of the country's leading academic centers. But public medical insurance covers only inpatient cancer care, deterring local patients from seeking outpatient cancer services. These payers are also primed by the public system to expect hospitalization during cancer treatment, even though outpatient care can provide a better quality of life.

Likewise, Beijing United Family Rehabilitation Hospital, opened in 2013, is housed in the edifice originally intended as Google's China headquarters, with picture windows and terraces overlooking a private park. The president of the International Society of Physical and Rehabilitation Medicine, Dr. Li Jianan, was hired as its chief medical officer. Yet rehabilitation remains undervalued in China, and while UFH strives to build its reputation in acute care, the Rehabilitation Hospital must depend on outside referrals for business. In both cases, UFH faces the challenge of convincing local payers and providers to buy into new types of care.

Clinical Personnel

The system is served in China by a medical staff of over 450 full-time physicians, 55 percent of whom are Chinese citizens and 45 percent are from overseas. In addition, UFH employs 550 part-time Chinese physicians, most of whom also work at public hospitals. A further 350 Chinese physicians are on the UFH roster for rare cases. All physicians must be licensed in China, credentialed by UFH, and privileged by the Medical Advisory Board of the UFH facility in which they plan to practice. The requirements for foreign physicians to receive Chinese licenses vary by city. In Beijing, written and oral exams (available in Chinese and English) are compulsory. In Shanghai, only a paper application is needed. These physicians maintain their home country licenses while working in China by fulfilling continuing medical education (CME) requirements, for which UFH provides each physician with an allowance.

The nursing staff across the system numbers 800 (see Table 9.1). The nurse licensing exam, unlike the physician equivalent, is administered only in Mandarin Chinese. Consequently, most UFH nurses are hired locally. Many have prior experience working overseas, such as in Saudi Arabia and Singapore, and all receive up to three years of in-house training at UFH, tailored to their experience level. This includes simulation lab practice, communication techniques such as SBAR (Situation, Background, Assessment, and Recommendation) and AIDET (Acknowledge, Introduce, Duration, Explanation, and Thanks),[11] and a mentorship system pairing new entrants with experienced nursing staff. UFH invests in nurse training on the principle that quality nursing care has been shown to correlate positively with clinical outcomes and patient satisfaction.[12] Competitors have also realized the effectiveness of UFH's training programs and made the retention of junior nurses challenging for the company, particularly in Beijing, where nurses have received offers of up to double their UFH salaries.

Table 9.1 Staff composition

Full-time doctors	450
Part-time doctors	550
Visiting doctors	350
Nurses	800
Administrative staff	1,050
Total headcount	2,780

Patient Profile

UFH received 380,000 outpatient visits and 7,000 admissions at its facilities in China in 2014. While UFH is widely regarded as catering to the expatriate community – reflecting its initial business model – revenue generated from local patients has exceeded that from foreign patients since 2013. The past 30 years of China's rapid economic ascent have given rise to a new cohort of Chinese consumers with the means to purchase a better quality of life in areas traditionally controlled by the government, including education, housing, and healthcare. Meanwhile, the expatriate population in China has been growing at a diminishing rate due to hazardous pollution and rising living costs. UFH has thus turned its sights on capturing the growth in the local healthcare market.

In Guangzhou and Shanghai, where many multinational companies have their China offices, UFH's foreign patients still outnumber Chinese patients (see Figure 9.3). However, the source of revenue growth, as in all UFH service areas, is among local payers. Most of these pay out of pocket, as public insurance does not cover UFH's services and the commercial insurance market in China is still in its infancy (see Figure 9.4). Chinese demand is strongest in obstetrics and pediatrics, where UFH's Chinese patients significantly outnumber foreign patients. Although the UFH system is equipped to serve all ages, in 2014 one-third of its patients were under the age of 12. This is expected to increase

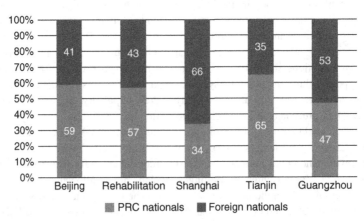

Figure 9.3 Patient nationality mix, by net revenue

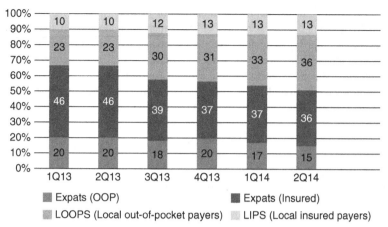

Figure 9.4 Revenue composition, by payer type, 2014

further with the end of the one-child policy in late 2015, leading affluent couples to have a second child. Recognizing the demand and low barrier to entry, many of UFH's competitors in high-end private healthcare are also focusing on obstetrics and pediatrics, and driving down prices. Amcare, a foreign-invested women and children's hospital established in 2004 one city block away from Beijing United Family Hospital, has grown into a group that includes hospitals in Tianjin, Shenzhen, and Hangzhou.

The elderly healthcare market, by contrast, has proven difficult to tap despite the rapidly aging population: only 4 percent of UFH's patients are over 60. UFH's Home Health services, rolled out in 2013 to address this segment, was forced to re-orient its products toward postpartum care in light of the booming demand for obstetric services and the low uptake of geriatric care. Whereas local payers are willing to pay out-of-pocket premiums on obstetric and pediatric care, public insurance coverage (for which UFH is ineligible) seems to be a "must" for elder care. Perhaps the dual factors of the one-child policy, which made children a focal point for spending, and the difficult political and economic circumstances in which the pre-1960 generation grew up, which made today's retirees frugal, have created this trend in discretionary spending.[13]

UFH's largely insurance-carrying expatriate clientele remains an important source of revenue and the historical reason for UFH's fee-for-service pricing system using CPT codes, the medical code set maintained by the American Medical Association. Although the percentage of revenue from insurance dropped steadily from 56 percent in 2013 to 49 percent in 2014, due to the declining proportion of insured expats, it remains a sizable part of UFH's business. To serve this segment, UFH maintains direct billing arrangements with more than 30 of the international insurance companies which foreign patients typically carry, including Aetna (United States), Cigna (United States), BUPA (United Kingdom), AXA (France), and Allianz (Germany). It provides standby medical services to foreign dignitaries visiting China and treats international sports and media celebrities. The Patient Services team at Beijing United Family Hospital translates into 15 languages. This also fosters UFH's international brand image, which resonates with local patients skeptical of the public system, drawing them to UFH.

Financial Performance

In the 18 years since the opening of its first facility, UFH revenues have grown at a compound annual rate greater than 20 percent, reaching RMB 1.4 billion in 2014. In 2014, year-on-year net revenue growth stood at 20 percent and year-on-year earnings before income, taxes, depreciation and amortization (EBITDA) at over 35 percent.

UFH's revenue comprises outpatient services (59 percent) and inpatient services (41 percent). The price of an outpatient consultation with a primary care physician is around RMB 1,000 and with a specialist from RMB 1,700 to 2,600. The estimated prices are posted online for transparency.[14] Per hospital admission, the average charge is RMB 83,000 and average length of inpatient stay is 3.7 days. Increasing the conversion rate of outpatient consultations into inpatient surgeries is a strategic priority. UFH has built community-based outpatient clinics to feed referrals to UFH hospitals, and in 2015 introduced an HMO-style insurance product in partnership with Yong An insurance, a Fosun subsidiary, in order to stimulate utilization of its inpatient services. It is thought that the HMO structure would help to create a sustainable business model in which UFH is contributing to the long-term health of patients, not just providing episodic care.

Medical service fees contribute 60 percent to total revenue, more than all ancillary services combined (see Figure 9.5). By contrast, Chinese public hospitals rely heavily on pharmaceutical sales and laboratory services to fund their operations, reportedly leading to over-prescription of medications, over-utilization of laboratory studies, and endemic corruption. This has soured the patient–doctor relationship in China and engendered significant

mistrust of physicians, as evidenced by violent attacks on doctors in the public system and the presence of armed guards at large city hospitals (see Chapter 7).[15] UFH removes the perverse incentives to over-prescribe by excluding drug and other ancillary revenue from the performance evaluations of its physicians.

Company Culture

The patient- and family-oriented service culture that Lipson championed was formalized in 2015 as the "UFH Way," a daylong training administered to all employees and incorporated into the three-day orientation of newcomers, centered around the mnemonic I-CARE ("innovative, caring, accountable, respectful, and excellent"). Company rhetoric speaks of the staff as a "united family," warmly invoking the lifelong *danwei* work units of the past (see Chapter 2). UFH staff recount their own experiences as patients in an internal video designed to heighten empathy and dedication to patient advocacy as part of the UFH Way training. Healthy competition is encouraged through internal "Quality Star" competitions held each month, and management uses the regular gathering of the system's medical staff as a platform to laud exemplary patient care. An "Art of Medicine" course, held in monthly rotation at UFH hospitals and conducted by UFH physician volunteers, teaches bedside manners via role-play; with enrollment geared toward external physicians, it has also proven to be a successful recruitment tool. The Quality and Safety team reports daily on safety events discussed at the staff morning huddle and propagates a "No Blame" culture to encourage openness about errors, which facilitates their timely rectification.

While corporate social responsibility appears to hold relatively little sway over the commercial choices of Chinese consumers, it can contribute to the development of patient-centeredness among UFH's medical staff. Physicians and nurses receive compensation for serving Chindex's charitable arm, the United Foundation for China's Health (UFCH), and participating in medical missions to underprivileged areas in China. The UFH Center for Disaster and Emergency Medicine Education was founded in

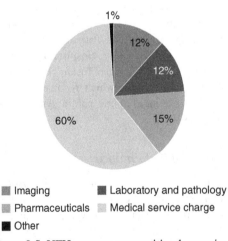

1%
12%
12%
15%
60%

- Imaging
- Laboratory and pathology
- Pharmaceuticals
- Medical service charge
- Other

Figure 9.5 UFH revenue composition by service type

part to develop UFH's ability to provide disaster relief, such as following the 2008 Sichuan earthquake, when it dispatched infection control and mental health personnel to the affected zone. Since 2001, UFH has donated 1 percent of its gross revenues as in-kind medical care to UFCH, mainly in support of Chinese orphans and the families of migrant workers. In 2014, the foundation sponsored 2,199 patient visits and 37 surgeries. In 2015, UFCH also acquired a mobile clinic bus, which carries out health screenings in underserved communities. A six-month telemedicine program developed by UFH and Stanford Children's Health in 2015 focused on the care of orphans enrolled by UFCH, many abandoned at birth with complex medical conditions.

Patient Education

Patient education is arguably UFH's most effective marketing tool, used to recruit patients as well as improve their understanding of, and compliance with, doctors' recommendations. The company encourages UFH physicians to acquire social media followings which allow UFH-branded health information to be shared with large audiences on a personal platform. The 4.77 million Weibo social media followers of Beijing United Family Hospital's chief of pediatrics, Dr. Cui Yutao, has made him one of the most influential primary care physicians in China. It is speculated that he boosted the country's vaccination rate simply by advocating for vaccination on his popular blog. In-person lecture tours by Dr. Cui, the popular obstetrician Dr. Chang Ling, and other well-known UFH physicians also increase brand recognition across the country. A quarterly UFH magazine on health topics is distributed in the facilities and automatic reminders are emailed to patients due for mammograms and other screenings. A UFH-branded online database of health topics (in the style of WebMD and Mayo Clinic) in Chinese is planned for the future.

Patient education is also emphasized to help local patients, accustomed to the idiosyncratic practices of the public system, adapt their expectations to the evidence-based style of medicine delivered at UFH. The 20- to 30-minute appointment slots at UFH

afford the luxury of time to the doctor–patient encounter. For instance, a patient who expects intravenous antibiotics for a head cold, a common practice in Chinese public hospitals, must be persuaded of the benefits of conservative care (such as rest and drinking fluids) by a UFH doctor. Public hospitals have so little time for patients and are so reliant on drug sales for revenue that rarely a patient leaves without a prescription in hand, necessary or not. Prescriptions and laboratory studies have come to substitute for thorough examination, and patients in turn have come to expect them as the main deliverable of physician encounters. At UFH, these patients learn to leave appointments ostensibly empty-handed. The positive outcome, however, is good antibiotic stewardship.

Growth Strategy

Centers of Excellence

Wherever a specialty of medicine is unavailable at a UFH facility, physicians are encouraged to refer patients to colleagues elsewhere within the system. While most UFH hospitals (aside from the rehabilitation facility) are general medical-surgical hospitals, they have developed centers of excellence around locally available talent and operational licenses. Licenses are elusive, as they are granted individually according to specialty – and the licenses for high-acuity disciplines are typically reserved for hospitals of 500 beds or more, which rank highest in the Ministry of Health's hospital classification system. With sizes ranging from 30 beds in Tianjin to 100 beds in Beijing, UFH hospitals must appeal on a case-by-case basis for licenses that exceed their classification. They would otherwise be confined to primary and secondary care.

Tianjin United Family Hospital is home to the system's in-vitro fertilization (IVF) facilities, as the Tianjin municipal government was the first to grant an IVF license to UFH. Beijing United Family Hospital conducts robotic surgery because the Beijing Health Bureau made an unprecedented exception for the use of surgical robots at a hospital of its size. Shanghai United Family Hospital became the sports orthopedics center of

UFH, thanks to the popularity of an American orthopedic surgeon, formerly of Massachusetts General Hospital, who moved to Shanghai.

The pursuit of licenses and recruitment of talent are mutually reinforcing: cutting-edge medical technology draws senior physicians to UFH, while the presence of high-level recruits practicing at the hospital gives license-issuers confidence in the company's ability to handle complex procedures. For instance, UFH's acquisition of the Da Vinci surgical robot – of which Chindex is the exclusive distributor in China – attracted Beijing University Cancer Hospital into a resource-sharing partnership, to which UFH contributed facilities and Beijing University Cancer Hospital contributed specialist talent. Moreover, nationally acclaimed names on UFH's physician roster, particularly Dr. Hu Dayi in cardiology and Dr. Lin Feng in neurosurgery, have helped Beijing United Family secure groundbreaking licenses for interventional cardiology and neurosurgery. These have permitted the company to move into higher-acuity care and pioneer the concept of small but excellent general hospitals in China.

Physician Recruitment

As local demand fuels UFH's growth, the need to recruit Chinese physicians becomes more urgent. While the presence of foreign doctors legitimizes UFH's international brand status, which is a key selling point in a competitive field, and helps to spread best practices from overseas, ultimately, local physicians are able to communicate best with local patients. The tendency of Chinese patients to trust individual physicians, rather than hospitals – symptomatic of the lack of faith in the public system – has given rise to the phenomenon of celebrity doctors. With patient followings that seek them out personally, these doctors can significantly boost volume wherever they practice. Recently, some have parlayed this power into private physician groups, such as the Dr. Smile Medical Group, founded in 2014 by vascular surgeon Dr. Zhang Qiang, which collaborates with UFH and other hospitals on a consultant basis.

At the same time, the high cost of recruiting foreign physicians is rising in parallel with China's mounting living costs. Shanghai and Beijing were ranked as the world's 6th and 7th most expensive cities for expatriates in 2015, compounded by some of the world's worst pollution in Beijing.[16] Thus the proportion of foreign physicians on UFH's medical staff is shrinking as UFH updates its cost model and accommodates the rising proportion of Chinese patients. Nonetheless, UFH continues to hire almost exclusively foreign physicians in family medicine and emergency medicine, as the training for these specialties in China differs substantially from international practices. However, this policy too may change with the accumulation of graduates of UFH's fellowships.

Top Chinese medical talent is concentrated in the large public hospitals, which, despite shortcomings, retain a firm grip on senior doctors. Domestic recruitment is typically the greatest obstacle for new high-end private hospitals in China. Mainstream medical career progression is defined as rising through the academic ranks of a single institution (see Figure 7.8); lateral moves – particularly out of the public system and into the private – risk the loss of both job security and prestige. Private hospitals may offer attractive compensation packages but cannot be the "iron rice bowls" (lifetime employment and family benefits of the Maoist era) that still characterize state institutions, including public hospitals.

Moreover, unlike in India and other developing countries, public opinion in China is prejudiced against private hospitals, which are suspected of being profit-oriented at the patient's expense and lacking the talent of big-city public hospitals. Though Beijing United Family Hospital was the first foreign-invested private hospital in China, locally-invested private healthcare predated UFH and was negatively regarded. Its front-runner was a Fujian Province-based chain of clinics specializing in venereal diseases known for the unscrupulous over-treatment of patients. Since then, such family-owned companies have branched into private specialty hospitals (under new brand names) and made efforts to professionalize, but some of the old reputation and practices prevail.

Through its emphasis on quality and service, UFH has taken pains to increase the respectability of the private healthcare sector and its desirability as a workplace. It has attracted doctors from Chinese public hospitals by offering respite from those hospitals' entrenched flaws: too many patients, too little time, and too little above-board pay (see Chapter 7). UFH's attractions are its modern and friendly practice environment, exposure to a multinational medical staff and international best practices, training opportunities, as well as comparatively high base salaries that obviate the need for illegal kickbacks and bribes. The chance to practice medicine in more than two-minute slots, and engage in teaching and research, can persuade specialists to leave tenure-track positions at public hospitals to join the private sector.[17] In terms of national repute, two successive directors of the State Council's Healthcare Reform Office have publicly cited UFH as a model to be emulated since the launch of healthcare reform. The positive spotlight enhances UFH's attractiveness to potential patients and staff.

Partnerships

UFH's partnerships serve many purposes, among them broader access within the four areas of medical talent (HR), consumers (marketing), clinical services not available within UFH's system (referrals), and training and research opportunities. Domestic partnerships often involve the privileging of public hospital doctors for practice at UFH. The majority of Beijing United Family Hospital's neurosurgery cases, for instance, come from Xuanwu Hospital, the major neurosurgery hospital in Beijing: Xuanwu neurosurgeons bring patients seeking a high-end care environment to UFH and perform the surgery there for a fee. Hospital associations such as that between Beijing United Family Hospital, Anzhen Hospital, the major cardiac hospital, and Sino-Japanese Friendship Hospital, allow physicians to practice at any "sister" facility in the association without requiring additional registration of their licenses.[18] Removing the cumbersome registration requirement enhances the mobility of talent between sites, which is useful for UFH while it ramps up volume in tertiary care.

Online-to-offline partnerships are crucial to UFH's outreach in marketing and recruiting; though reputations in healthcare are made by word of mouth, China's online platforms are too large to be ignored. On Tmall.com, the Alibaba subsidiary, UFH has created an online shop selling treatment packages, such as deliveries, home healthcare, and bundled-payment surgeries (see below). It has established a presence on Hao Daifu ("Good Doctor"), the interactive directory of hospitals and physicians, and is planning collaboration with Dxy.com, the patient education database. A new mobile application linked to Baidu's search engine is under design. In a marketing stunt for United Family Home Health, UFH partnered with Didi Dache, the taxi-hailing application, to send its home health clinicians to customers' homes for free. It is hoped that an innovative mobile appointment and payment system, paired with an efficient means of navigating traffic on the roads, could increase the demand for home health in the longer term.

International partnerships facilitate integrated patient access to clinical trials, quaternary treatments, and particular oncology drugs which are approved overseas but not in mainland China. UFH has established green channels with leading academic medical centers in the United States, including Cedars-Sinai Medical Center, City of Hope, Massachusetts General Hospital Cancer Center, New York Presbyterian, Seattle Children's, Stanford Children's, and University of California Los Angeles. They are keen to receive affluent Chinese patients and have invested in developing Chinese patient services. Though focused on treating patients in China, UFH can contribute to the growing outbound medical tourism field by providing screening and follow-up care to patients traveling overseas. It is uniquely able to facilitate international collaboration through its English-language staff and EMR.

Partnerships diversify the training options UFH can offer its staff, such as public hospital rotation sites for fellows, international observerships for junior doctors and functional area managers, nurse training partners, CME conferences, and life support certification. UFH's training center, established adjacent to its hospital in Qingdao in 2015, hosted the first international conference in China to be accredited for both American and Chinese CME. It has also offered a training course co-sponsored by the Chinese Congress of Neurosurgeons and the American Association of Neurosurgeons, with hands-on surgical skills training in UFH's cadaveric dissection lab. UFH is the only official international training center in China affiliated with the American Heart Association, allowing it to certify its staff in China and Mongolia, as well as generate revenue from unaffiliated participants.

Value-based Pricing

Since 2014, UFH has experimented with bundled payments in place of traditional fee-for-service pricing in an effort to boost surgery volume. The objective was to boost UFH's surgery volumes by attracting local cash-pay patients with competitive deals. The bundles would be an alternative to the traditional fee-for-service pricing designed for insurance reimbursement. This was inspired by Geisinger Health Systems' success in pioneering the bundled payment model, which increased revenue, reduced costs, and improved clinical outcomes at the same time.[19]

With fee-for-service pricing, which is the mainstream form of reimbursement in the United States, hospitals generate revenue by giving more care, not necessarily better care. Providers are inherently incentivized to err on the side of excessive and expensive treatments. By contrast, with bundled payments, the provider receives a lump sum for a clinically defined episode of care – for example, removal of the gallbladder. The bundle covers everything associated with the specified procedure, including preoperative tests, surgical and nursing fees, inpatient stay, and postoperative care up to 90 days after treatment. Given that the revenue per bundle is fixed, providers are incentivized to minimize costs by opting for cheaper and faster treatments – essentially, making the patient well as quickly as possible – without compromising quality, which would lead to complications paid out of the bundle and reduce the provider's profit. UFH shares the margin on bundles with the participating doctors and nurses in order to give them a direct financial stake in the outcome.

UFH had three aims in piloting bundled payments. First, to dispel the common misperception – sometimes propagated by competitors – that UFH prices are 50–100 percent higher than they really are. This is seen as significantly impeding UFH's

inroads into the cash-pay surgery market, and publicizing fixed, transparent prices is a promising antidote. Second, it aimed to increase profits by incentivizing physicians to be cost-aware. Third, it expected to improve clinical outcomes, such as readmission rates, by incentivizing efficiency – reducing errors, standardizing clinical workflows, and maximizing patient engagement. The volume of bundled payment surgeries at UFH has not yet been sufficient to evaluate the extent to which the model lives up to expectations in China.

Macroeconomic Factors

The convergence of macroeconomic factors in China has propelled UFH's growth, particularly through the rise of the domestic consumer. The first factor is increased economic prosperity brought by annual economic growth over 7 percent. The top 5 percent of income earners in China are able to opt out of the public system and purchase private services. Second, the government is focused on stimulating domestic consumption in order to rebalance the economy. Third, the rapidly aging population is facing greater medical needs. Fourth, the one-child policy (in place until late 2015) gave rise to parents with a doting willingness to spend on children's well-being, including on pediatric care. In short, demand for UFH's premium medical care has increased as the needs and the purchasing power of the Chinese population have grown.

Healthcare Reform

The 2009 Chinese healthcare reform heralded a liberalization of government policy toward foreign investment in private healthcare. The government sought to increase the accessibility of public healthcare in part by redirecting the attention of public hospitals toward serving the general populace, shifting luxury services from their VIP wards to the private sector. The target was set at doubling the market share of private hospitals from 10 percent to 20 percent by 2015 and satisfying the needs of higher-income consumers in particular. Accordingly, restrictions on investment, licenses, leases, and the recruitment of talent from the public system were relaxed. This enabled UFH to grow its services in line with local demand, particularly in obstetrics and pediatrics, where Chinese consumers were most willing to pay out of pocket for upgraded service. As the first mover in an area with high unmet needs, UFH was able to build a strong brand image, establish a patient-centered company culture, standardize practices, and garner a reputation that attracted top talent. These were the enablers that put UFH at the head of the pack in premium private healthcare, and which it leveraged to grow into a system of acute-care general hospitals.[20] Nonetheless, UFH still suffers from the vagaries of Chinese healthcare policy.

Challenges

Intellectual Property Rights (IPR)

In 2015, a UFH physician traveling in the southwestern province of Guizhou was surprised to come upon a UFH hospital in the remote city of Weining. He snapped a photo of "Weining United Family Hospital," with a large UFH logo by the entrance, and posted it to the company's internal message board, where it quickly came to the attention of the legal team. The website of "Weining United Family Hospital" also featured a falsified letter of congratulations from President Obama, and it turned out that there was a video loop in the lobby showing Lipson and the UFH executive team. With support from the US Commercial Service, UFH undertook legal action; this induced the logo to be removed, but the hospital was allowed to keep "United Family" in its name. It appeared that the local government favored the economic boost a UFH look-alike could bring to the region, in the country's poorest province. With strong political support for the offender, little could be done.

Intellectual property protection in China is particularly weak outside of the manufacturing industries, both legislatively and in enforcement. Despite a nearly 20-year history in China, UFH has been unable to obtain "national brand" designation, without which it does not have IPR protection outside of the cities where it conducts business. Legal action against infringers is mostly futile and has little deterrence value. Simply substituting a single character in UFH's Chinese name can make them

immune from accusation. The danger is that in healthcare, unlike manufacturing, a single mistake at the hands of an impostor can threaten a human life and an institutional reputation which took decades to build. The UFH call center received one complaint from a patient dissatisfied with care at "Weining United Family Hospital" before UFH launched a local campaign to disassociate itself from the counterfeit hospital.

Public Insurance

UFH has sought for years to be eligible for reimbursement by China's social health insurance schemes (*yibao*), to no avail. The obstacle is a stipulation by the State Council that requires healthcare facilities to conform to government-set prices in order to be covered. In effect, this means UFH would need to command prices as low as public hospitals to qualify. As a point of comparison, regular consultation at a public hospital in a secondary care specialty can be as low as RMB 14, roughly 1 percent of the cost at UFH. A typical lab test, such as the complete blood count, costs RMB 20 at a public hospital, compared to RMB 350 at UFH. The company would become financially unviable if it tried to satisfy the current requirements for social insurance reimbursement.

The low official price point of the public hospitals belies the true price to patients. This can include non-indicated testing and medication, which is the largest source of revenue for public hospitals; unofficial payments to doctors (known as "red envelopes"), which is one of the largest sources of revenue for doctors; as well as longer than necessary in-patient hospital stays, scalper fees for scarce appointments, and missed time at work throughout the process.

UFH incurs higher operational costs than public hospitals in order to maintain international-standard quality. Back-office services such as internal auditing, physician credentialing, and training contribute to the system's integrity and the advancement of its medical staff. But the biggest cost is salaries, wages, and benefits: in order to attract top talent, UFH is pressed to match the take-home income of physicians in the public system. Public hospitals knowingly push the cost of doctors' pay onto corrupt payers, turning a blind eye to kickbacks from the pharmaceutical and medical device industries, and doing little to prevent bribes from patients. A number of public hospital presidents have been jailed for embezzlement of public funds, and a former head of the China FDA, Zheng Xiaoyu, was executed in 2007 for taking RMB 6.5 million in bribes from pharmaceutical companies.[21] Public hospitals also benefit from the government's commitment to invest in capacity-building through subsidies in construction and rent.

Exclusion from public insurance limits UFH's accessibility to local patients, particularly older individuals who have paid into the public scheme for decades and are unwilling to forgo their savings. If they choose to be treated at UFH, or any premium-price private hospital, they must bear the full out-of-pocket cost of services or buy commercial insurance, of which there are a limited number of products on offer. In discussion with the government, UFH has proposed that private hospitals be allowed to set prices at their discretion and public insurance reimburse them only up to the level commensurate with government prices. The difference between the government price and the hospital price is one that individuals could elect to pay out of pocket, or with a supplementary private insurance. UFH believes that many consumers of healthcare would be willing to go this route in exchange for the additional level of service provided by UFH. It would also encourage the growth of the private health insurance market and reduce pressure on the public system by making private healthcare more accessible.

Corporate Tax

Despite the invitation to private investment in Chinese healthcare, publicized by the government in the context of healthcare reform, business taxation gives an inhospitable welcome. Rather than receiving the 15 percent corporate tax rate bestowed on "encouraged industries" such as information technology and new energy, healthcare faces a rate of 25 percent – the highest tax rate applied to businesses in China. Moreover, since foreign JV medical institutions are not allowed to have branches, current tax law does not allow the consolidation of

accounts at all the UFH facilities, with the consequence that the financial losses at one facility cannot be offset against the profits at another. New hospitals and clinics can face an effective tax rate over 100 percent given the typical three- to five-year start-up period.

Opening Hospitals

Even with the government's target of increasing the number of private hospital beds from 5 percent of all hospital beds to 20 percent by 2020, the process of opening a new hospital remains onerous. Land lease approval is the first hurdle and one that is never firm: even Beijing United Family Hospital, UFH's flagship of 18 years, has repeatedly faced the threat of eviction from some of its buildings as ownership of the land changed hands among government entities. Likewise in Shanghai, a public hospital with backing from the municipal government reclaimed UFH's lease before it expired. New properties must pass environmental and safety inspections, neighborhood consent, and numerous politically sensitive government approval processes – besides fulfilling UFH's criteria of price and location in a commercially attractive area – before being secured for construction.

Recruitment of doctors and nurses is the next hurdle. Until 2011, physicians were only allowed to register their licenses at one healthcare facility, which restricted them to practicing at that facility. This meant that private hospitals had to accept moonlighting doctors or persuade them to give up their prestigious and secure faculty posts. Subsequently, the restriction was lifted and doctors are now permitted to register in more than one facility. Nonetheless, in some cities, the local regulations still require Chinese physicians to receive written approval from their hospital president to register at another hospital. This is a deterrent for physicians who worry that the hint of disloyalty could reduce their chances of career advancement. Once a candidate is identified, UFH's recruitment team often faces resistance from hospitals while performing checks on their credentials, as ongoing professional practice evaluation (OPPE) is not yet standard in China. Hiring nurses is also made difficult by a limited local supply and the fact that it is more difficult for private hospitals to provide local residence permits (*hukou*) to employees from other cities.

Conclusion

Today's interest in investing in Chinese healthcare comes as the world takes note of the growing purchasing power of Chinese consumers and the scale of demand for better healthcare services. Lipson and her team embarked on the establishment of the first high-end private healthcare facility in China 15 years before healthcare reform acknowledged the appropriateness of such an endeavor. This foresight provided an enormous lead time over other market entrants, which was spent developing IT systems, quality practices, company culture, and most importantly, a brand, which have laid the foundation for UFH's cohesive growth as a system.

The initially quiet, "contained" experiment of international-standard healthcare pioneered by UFH has become an influential model permeating the national system. Comfortable environments, attention to service, accreditation of quality, and an international brand culture are now the hallmarks of top-of-the-line healthcare in China, inducing patients to demand higher standards of the public system as well. UFH's trajectory is proof that, despite the unique challenges of the Chinese healthcare system, international best practices *can* be implemented and those with the patience and dedication to handle the regulatory environment are likely to see a return on investment in the long run.

Notes

1. "China's 12th Five-Year Plan: Healthcare Sector," *KPMG* (May 2011). Available online at: www .kpmg.com/CN/en/IssuesAndInsights/ArticlesPub lications/Documents/China-12th-Five-Year-Plan-Healthcare-201105-3.pdf. Accessed on December 20, 2015.

2. "Can the Number of General Practitioners in China Be Doubled?" *MedSci.* (September 8, 2015). Available online at: www.medsci.cn/arti cle/show_article.do?id=1b3f5594116.

3. "China's Doctors Not Part of Society's Elite," *Financial Times* (October 6, 2013). Available online at: www.ft.com/intl/cms/s/0/35a081ae-2653-11e3-8ef6-00144feab7de.html#axzz3tuH qPQl3.

4. Ngaire Kerse et al. 2004. "Physician-Patient Relationship and Medication Compliance: A Primary Care Investigation," *Ann Fam Med.* September 2(5): 455–461. Available online at: www.ncbi.nlm.nih.gov/pmc/articles/ PMC1466710/.

5. "Population of Shanghai Expands to 24.3m," *Shanghai Daily* (March 1, 2015). Available online at: www.shanghaidaily.com/metro/ society/Population-of-Shanghai-expands-to-243m/shdaily.shtm.

6. "Beijing to Limit Population Growth This Year," *China Daily* (January 24, 2015). Available online at: www.chinadaily.com.cn /china/2015-01/24/content_19394117.htm.

7. "Exploring Tianjin – General Facts," *China Daily.* Available online at: www.chinadaily .com.cn/m/tianjin2011/2011-10/14/content_14 131615.htm.

8. "Guangzhou's Permanent Population Hits 12.7 Million," *Guangzhou International News* (May 12, 2011). Available online at: http://eng lish.gz.gov.cn/gzgoven/s4171/201105/817256 .shtml.

9. "Qingdao's Population Soars to 9 Million," *China Daily* (February 13, 2015). Available online at: www.chinadaily.com.cn/m/shan dong/e/2015-02/13/content_19582180.htm.

10. "The 21st Century Hospital: Role of the Physical Environment," *Center for Health Design* (September 2004). Available online at: www.healthdesign.org/sites/default/files/Role %20Physical%20Environ%20in%20the% 2021st%20Century%20Hospital_0.pdf. See also E. R. C. M. Huisman, E. Morales, J. van Hoof et al. 2012. "Healing Environment: A Review of the Impact of Physical Environmental Factors on Users," *Building and Environment* 58: 70–80.

11. SBAR (Situation, Background, Assessment, and Recommendation) and AIDET (Acknowledge, Introduce, Duration, Explanation, and Thanks) are standard

handover scripts used for communicating essential elements of a patient's care during handoff from one clinician to another.

12. Evridiki Papastavrou, Panayiota Andreou, Haritini Tsangari et al. 2014. "Linking Patient Satisfaction with Nursing Care: The Case of Care Rationing – A Correlational Study," *BMC Nursing* 13: 26. Available online at: www .biomedcentral.com/1472-6955/13/26#B14.

13. "Understanding Chinese Consumers," *China Business Review* (July 1, 2011). Available online at: www.chinabusinessreview.com /understanding-chinese-consumers/.

14. For prices at Beijing United Family Hospital, visit http://pbj.ufh.com.cn/.

15. "China's Doctors Are Under Attack," *The Atlantic* (December 3, 2013). Available online at: www.theatlantic.com/china/archive/ 2013/12/chinas-doctors-are-under-attack /282002/.

16. "Shanghai Becomes Most Expensive City in Asia for Expats," *CNBC* (June 12, 2015). Available online at: www.cnbc.com/2015/06/ 12/shanghai-becomes-most-expensive-city-in- asia-for-expats.html.

17. "Doctors See Patients for an Average of 2.4 Minutes," *The China Healthcare Research Network* (June 30, 2014). Available online at: http://yy.chinairn.com/news/20140630/ 175348670.htmlhttp://yy.chinairn.com/news/ 20140630/175348670.html.

18. January 12, 2015, *National Health and Family Planning Commission.* Notification for the issuance of "the opinions on promoting and standardizing physicians' multi-site practice." Available online at: www.nhfpc.gov.cn/yzygj/ index.shtml.

19. "Where Surgery Comes With a 90 Day Guarantee," *The Atlantic* (September 26, 2012). Available online at: www.theatlantic .com/health/archive/2012/09/where-surgery- comes-with-a-90-day-guarantee/262841/.

20. "Investing in China Hospital Market," *The Boston Consulting Group* (June 2013). Available online at: http://58.30.31.200:9999/ www.bcg.com.cn/export/sites/default/en/files/ publications/reports_pdf/BCG_Investing_in_ China_Hospital_Market_June_2013_ENG .pdf.

21. "China Executes Ex-food Safety Chief," *The Financial Times* (July 10, 2007). Available online at: www.ft.com/intl/cms/s/0/ 86ea503c-2eb4-11dc-b9b7-0000779fd2ac.html# axzz3uUwWViLm.

Providing and Financing Elder Care in China

JOHN WHITMAN AND LAWTON ROBERT BURNS

Introduction

China currently has two broad systems available to provide care for its elderly population: a medical care system (the subject of Chapters 7, 8, 9) and a social welfare system. The medical system broadly encompasses physicians, hospitals, and primary care clinics; the social welfare system encompasses community-based elder services, community residential facilities, and nursing homes.[1] This chapter is concerned with the latter. These two systems are overseen by different government ministries with different financing mechanisms, policies, and workforces. There is some minor overlap in that hospitals provide care to the elderly for their acute and chronic conditions; they have also recently begun to develop rehabilitation units and geriatric programs.

The Chinese government and its official statistics have historically included all social welfare services under one global category. This chapter distinguishes them as follows. We define "senior care services" (SCS) as the array of social, medical, and community-based services excluding institutional care. Long-term care (LTC) encompasses institutional care in non-acute settings with significant levels of medical and support services required. LTC is not senior housing but rather a higher level of care for seniors with significant care needs, usually provided in a nursing home.

It is important to recognize the difference between SCS and LTC. SCS are provided at the community level with the goal of allowing seniors to stay home, at lower cost, and to avoid nursing home placement. LTC placement is necessitated when community-based services are no longer safe for the senior, or when family members and other caregivers are physically unable to render the care.

While a high percentage of China's senior population will need and benefit from community-based SCS, a smaller but significant percentage will eventually requires LTC. Both care models are absolutely needed in China.

This chapter examines the current level of SCS and LTC in China, the forces that have shaped them, and their evolution. The chapter then analyzes the various barriers to this sector's evolution, including the significant financing hurdles on both the supply and demand side. Given the rise in life expectancy, the growing number of seniors, the eroding ability of families to care for seniors at home, the lack of effective primary care, and threats to the Chinese pension system, the Chinese government is now confronting a serious challenge of enormous proportions.

China's Aging Population

China's population is one of the most rapidly aging worldwide. Figure 10.1 charts the dramatic shift in both the number of seniors and the distribution of age cohorts in China from 1950 through 2050. The number of elderly in China is rapidly rising due to population aging, decreasing mortality rates, improvements in public health, and longer life expectancy. Between 1960 and 2010, male life expectancy rose from 41.9 years to 72.3 years. Life expectancy is expected to increase going forward to roughly 80 years old. The rising proportion of the elderly in the population is also growing due to declining fertility rates.

There are two different ways to define China's elderly population. The conservative approach is to define the elderly as those 65+ years old, as is done in the United States. In 2010, China's elderly

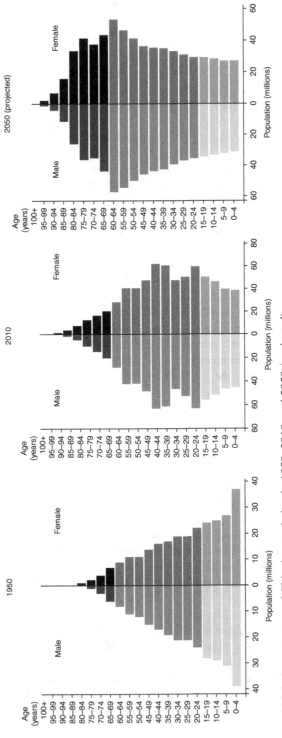

Figure 10.1 Age structure of China's population in 1950, 2010, and 2050 (projected).
Source: United Nations Population Division, World Population Prospects.

population totaled 117 million people, or 8.8 percent of the population. By 2030, this cohort will grow to 260 million (18.2 percent of the population); by 2050, it will grow to 396 million people, or 28.9 percent of the nation's projected population.[2] To put this into perspective, the entire US population was approximately 319 million in 2014.

A more liberal definition of the elderly is the population 60+ years old, a standard established in 1996 Chinese law.[3] Using this definition, the elderly population in 2010 totaled 173 million people, or 13 percent of the population; this segment will grow to 372 million (26 percent) by 2030 and then to 510 million (37.2 percent) by 2050.[4]

China is characterized as an "aging nation" not only because of the significant increase in seniors, but also because of the dramatic growth of the oldest group (80 years and older), typically the greatest users of SCS and LTC. In 1990, China's senior cohort aged 80+ years included some 11 million seniors; by 2007, that number had grown to 19.5 million; and is estimated to grow to over 40 million by 2030.[5] Figure 10.2 displays the growth of the elderly using the different definitions above.[6]

The aging of the Chinese population is troubling due to its impact on health status and utilization of healthcare services. Cross-sectional data from the China Health and Retirement Longitudinal Survey (CHARLS) show that older Chinese suffer from declines in episodic memory and intact mental status. Aging is also associated with lower health status, depression, and physical limitations.[7] Finally, as noted in earlier chapters, age is associated with the presence of multiple chronic diseases that require frequent provider visits – in China, usually to hospitals.

The Disabled

Moreover, there is a growing number of disabled.[8] Researchers define old-age disability in terms of difficulties in performing one or more of the "activities of daily living" (ADL, such as bathing, dressing, toileting, or moving around) or "instrumental activities of daily living" (IADL, such as shopping, cooking, or housekeeping). In China, old-age disability has usually been assessed using ADLs and other measures of physical function (e.g., lifting a certain weight, walking a specific distance); IADL measures have been introduced in recent years.[9] An estimated 33 million Chinese elderly (60+ years old) suffered limitations in ADLs in 2009, and roughly one-third depend on others for assistance.[10] By 2014, the number of disabled reached 40 million.[11] SCS and LTC typically

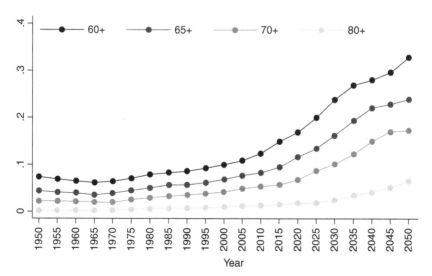

Figure 10.2 Aging of China's population, 1950–2050
Source: United Nations, 2012. Smith, Strauss, and Zhao (2014).

provide patients with assistance with both ADL and IADL.

Disability in China is associated with age and chronic illness. Both are increasing rapidly in the country. Previous chapters in this volume have chronicled the spread of diabetes, hypertension, stroke, and cardiovascular disease. Disability is also associated with certain unhealthy behaviors – such as smoking and lack of exercise – which are also quite prevalent. Finally, some disability measures like ADL have been found to be associated with fewer years of schooling, lower levels of savings and pensions, and lower socioeconomic status in childhood.[12]

Recent research projects the number of disabled (1+ ADL/IADL) and severely disabled (3+ ADLs) in China will increase fivefold between 2008 and 2050 under the status quo.[13] In urban areas, the number of disabled will rise from 11 million to 50 million; the number of rural disabled will increase from 14 million to nearly 63 million. Moreover, the ratio of disabled elders to possible caregivers will also rise due to declining family sizes. In urban areas, the number of disabled per 1,000 caregivers will rise from 26 to 81; in rural areas, the ratio will increase from 29 to 215. Urban migration is expected to exacerbate the situation in rural areas.

Some Questions

These statistics on aging and disability, along with the evidence presented in Chapter 3 on public health, have led analysts to pose three questions. First, will China grow old before it grows rich?[14] Second, will China get sick and die before it gets wealthy?[15] Third, will the increasing elderly population serve as a dragging anchor on China's economic growth ("slower, lower, and weaker")?[16] These are non-trivial questions. To answer them, this chapter will consider China's ability to finance the economic cost of caring for this surging population.

Current Delivery of Elder Care

As described in prior chapters, China's hospital system has three tiers (Class I, II, and III; see Chapter 8), as does its systems of urban and rural healthcare delivery (see Chapter 2). The same is true for the country's delivery of elderly care. Analysts commonly define three levels of elderly care: home-based care, community-level care services, and institutional care. The first two levels map onto what we have labeled here as SCS; the third level reflects what we call LTC. Each level has its own history and dynamics. The oldest model of elderly care is home care; institutional care developed in the early years of the People's Republic; community-based models have emerged only recently. The government has enunciated a goal of "90-7-3": 90 percent of elderly care in home-based settings, 7 percent in community service settings, and 3 percent in nursing home institutions. These three models are briefly summarized below in the order of their historical emergence.

Home-based Care

As in other countries, family members have traditionally rendered most healthcare in China, with only minimal support from the government. This approach is rooted in the traditional Chinese values of "filial piety" and respect for elders taught by Confucius over 2,000 years ago, deeply embedded in Chinese culture and even articulated in the Chinese Constitution, the Criminal Code, and the 1996 Elders' Protection Law.[17] Filial piety has served as China's version of the Medicare, Social Security, and long-term care systems in the United States.[18]

There has traditionally been some mutual social embarrassment for not adhering to the practice of filial piety. It was embarrassing for the elderly to not be cared for by one's family; it was also embarrassing for the family to not assume this responsibility. However, urbanization, mobility, and dwindling family size have made it more difficult for Chinese families to continue with three generations under the same household: from 2000 to 2011, the number of such households declined from 201 million to 61 million.[19]

In 2006, an estimated 59 percent of elderly lived with their children or relatives; the remainder may not have shared the same dwelling but nevertheless relied on family members for financial support.[20]

Moreover, survey data suggest that most Chinese elderly (85–90 percent) want to and, in fact, receive care in their own homes from family members.[21] This pattern of family-based care provision is more evident in rural China, where families are larger (due to the earlier relaxation of the one-child policy) and both retirement pensions and healthcare facilities are less prevalent. According to one study, rural seniors were heavier users of informal care (91.8 percent) than urban seniors (87.7 percent). Rural seniors received 378 hours of "informal care" from family caregivers and 533 hours of "formal care" from paid caregivers per month; by contrast, urban seniors received 613 hours of informal care and 612 hours of formal care.[22] Rural men spent more per month on formal care (4,020 RMB) compared to urban men (2,370 RMB) and spent less per month on informal care (1,319 vs. 2,991 RMB).[23] In terms of income that can be used to pay for such services, urban residents rely heavily on pensions, while rural residents rely on family support.

Several trends have undermined this "home health" approach. One is the decline in the sheer number of family members available to care for the elderly – partly a legacy of the one-child policy. Between 1990 and 2008, the average household size in China decreased from 3.5 to 2.9 persons, suggesting a shift from an "extended family" to a "nuclear family" model.[24]

A second trend is the growing mobility of the (younger working) population, due to both the migration of rural workers to seek employment in cities and the growing job opportunities in a market economy. The emerging role of women in the workforce is one factor contributing to the breakdown of the Chinese tradition of caring for one's parents and adding to the need for increased community and social support services. Married women, who traditionally assumed the primary caregiver role, have joined the ranks of the employed. Today, 71.1 percent of women aged 18–64 are employed. In urban areas, 60.8 percent are employed as compared to 82 percent in rural areas. Chinese women are no different from women around the world fighting for equality in education, jobs, and salaries. As women become equal players in the workplace, they have less time and desire to remain in the home.[25]

A third trend, partly resulting from the second, is the growing number of "empty nest families" where the elderly live alone or with spouses, but not with their children. Survey data from 2006 suggest that 8.3 percent of elderly lived alone while 41.4 percent lived only with their spouse. More recent data present similar statistics: 9 percent of elderly live alone and 37 percent live with a spouse (38 percent live with children, and 16 percent live with others).[26] There are urban versus rural differences here. One study estimates the percentage of empty-nest households as high as 70 percent in urban cities, but 50 percent of elderly households across both urban and rural China.[27]

This pattern is reinforced by a growing preference, among both the elderly and their children, to live autonomously (particularly in urban areas): the children may not wish to care for their elderly parents, and the latter may not wish to care for the children of their children. The percentage of elderly preferring not to live with their children may be as high as 40 percent.[28]

Institutional Care

Nursing Homes

Residential-based care in China emerged in the late 1950s primarily as a resource for the destitute. The government assumed responsibility for citizens falling into three categories (the *three no's*; also known as *wubao* elders): no family or relatives to support them, no physical ability to work, and no source of income. These individuals received daily custodial and medical care in residential "welfare institutions" operated by local governments free of charge.[29] This became the start of China's nursing home sector.

As part of the post-1978 market reforms, China embarked on the "socialization of social welfare." In the acute healthcare sector, hospitals and physicians assumed primary responsibility for generating their own revenues from patient fees rather than government subsidies. Likewise, in the LTC sector, the government opened up the residential welfare institutions to the broader population beyond the *three no's* to include patients (and their families) who could afford the fees for their care. However, non-*wubao* elders could face exclusion from admission for certain pre-existing conditions (infectious disease, mental illness, and bedridden status).

By the 2000s, private facilities also emerged with government encouragement. In 2001 and 2006, the Ministry of Civil Affairs inaugurated successive five-year projects (*Xing Guang* and *Xia Guang*) to encourage local level authorities to construct residential facilities for the *rural wubao* elderly, financed by 20 percent of social welfare lottery funds.[30] In 2005, the government introduced the "Beloved Care Engineering" program to broaden sponsorship by the private sector by offering subsidies on a per-bed, per-month basis.

By 2008, welfare institutions had 1.93 million beds to serve 1.61 million elderly.[31] By 2010, the country had 5,413 institutions to provide elder care in *urban* areas, with 567,000 beds and a service population of 363,000 patients.[32] Nationally, 1 percent of the rural elderly population lived in one of these institutions. By 2009, anywhere from 60 pecent to 78 percent of residents of residential homes were the three no's population, while those paying fees constituted only 17 percent.

Nursing facilities have three types of sponsors: the government, nongovernmental organizations (NGOs, typically charities), and private investors. Government-owned facilities are sponsored at the provincial and local township level. To date, most nursing homes in China have been government supported, with financial support (and bed capacity) that varies widely across the country. Data from 2004 indicate that government subsidies ranged from 800 RMB to 2,400 RMB per patient per year.[33] These institutions mainly served older adults with poor financial situations. Private institutions relied on fees paid by the patient's family and were not required to admit the *wubao* elders.

In terms of capacity, nursing homes range from as few as ten beds to large facilities with 100 or more beds. Facilities serving the *wubao* elders tend to be smaller in size. In terms of utilization, only 1–2 percent of the Chinese elderly use institution-based care (up from 0.8 percent in 2006); the government has set targets of 3 percent and 4 percent utilization in its last two five-year plans (FYPs), respectively.[34] Municipal surveys suggest the interest level among the elderly may range as high as

8–10 percent in eastern China.[35] In terms of actual numbers, national surveys suggest that 8.1 million elderly needed LTC in 2010; by 2050, that number is projected to increase to 27–43 million.[36]

The institutionalized *wubao* patient population is often bedridden with dementia and other serious chronic conditions; a significant percentage is also incontinent. While this level of care is the least desirable from a social and cost perspective, it is often necessitated by elder care needs that exceed the capabilities of families and community care facilities. Compared to community-based senior care services, nursing home services are institutionally based, focused on patients with serious medical conditions, and entail much higher costs.

Acute-Care Hospitals

China's healthcare system is hospital-centric; there is little formal provision of primary care or organized community-based care. The centricity of the hospital, particularly on the inpatient side, is embedded in existing insurance schemes that reimburse expensive episodes of hospitalization. Few reimbursement schemes use diagnosis-related groups (DRGs) or capitation, which incentivizes hospitals to increase use of inpatient days and other expensive inputs (see Chapter 8).

This institutional focus encourages expensive hospital utilization for any medical need. The average length of stay for seniors treated by the geriatric department at Peking University First Hospital in Beijing in 2005 was as follows (by age cohort): 27.5 days (age 60–69), 36.4 days (age 70–79), 44.3 days (age 80–89), and 52.5 days (age 90+).[37] Lengths of stay increased as the patient's diagnosis changed from cardiac disease (two weeks) to medical conditions (four weeks) to psychiatric (months). By contrast, the average stay for US seniors (65+ years) was 5.2 days.[38] Long stays are a function of the lack of post-acute care facilities, lack of DRG and capitation incentives to discharge patients earlier, and expectations on the part of both patients and providers. Similarly, utilization levels for both outpatient services and inpatient hospital days are far greater among the elderly (60+ years) population than any other age cohort.[39]

Community-based Care

Prior to the 1978 economic reform, communities made available formal assistance for elder care in the home. The work units (*danwei*) in urban areas organized committees to help their retired workers in the form of relief funds and hands-on care for daily needs. Economic reforms after 1978 undermined these work units and their assistance efforts. Another form of assistance was in-home care in urban areas overseen by municipal committees. Such assistance was rendered by a caregiver (*bao hu zhu*) to elders without children, in the form of meal preparation, errands, and help with visits to healthcare providers.[40]

Starting in the late 1980s, and then picking up in the 1990s, local communities built upon the "socialization of social welfare" ideology and established multiple SCS providers including home help services, community service centers, and community healthcare services. These services were administered by the local department of health and encompassed public health services (see Chapter 3) as well as outpatient care, rehabilitation, and chronic disease treatment. The services were administered by community residents' committees, similar to neighborhood associations acting as an auxiliary of local government, and offered home health and day care assistance.[41] Currently, community-based services in China are of a social nature only and do not include any significant level of medical care.

As one illustration, Shanghai's Municipal Civil Affairs Bureau developed two types of community-based elder care services starting in the late 1990s.[42] One type was "community service centers" established by street station committees. These centers provided counseling, shopping, meals on wheels, home maintenance, ADL assistance, and referral services – typically by migrant workers, retired workers, or laid-off factory workers. A second type was "coordination/service centers" organized by nonprofit and for-profit organizations that served to link the elderly with homemakers (*bao mu, jai zheng*).

Shanghai also sponsored government residential care centers for the elderly, both citywide and at the city district level. These centers – the descendants of the welfare institutions serving the "three no's" –

had broadened their client populations and services rendered to include community-based functions (meals on wheels, homemakers, adult day care).

In 2001, the Ministry of Civil Affairs promoted an urban-based initiative called the Starlight Program to assist local governments to build community activity centers and stations. These sites served as a platform to offer community care services and support home-based services. The program was financed by a portion of the proceeds of the welfare lottery. In the first three years of its operation, the Starlight Program supported the construction of 32,490 facilities in provincial capitals, major cities, and ultimately lower-level cities and townships. Total government funding amounted to $2.1 billion. After 2005, the program lost steam due to dwindling government financial support. It has been supplanted by a new "Virtual Elder Care Home" (or "Elder Care without Walls") model where home health agencies render services in patients' homes.[43] The first virtual home opened in 2007. These arrangements have quickly spread due to their lower cost and wider access.

The legacy of these developments has been a complex sprawl of service centers with pluralistic sponsorship, organization, and financing. The sponsors include local government, government auxiliaries, and the private sector (including real estate developers and insurance companies); organizational models include independent living, assisted living, and skilled nursing facilities; and funding sources include government subsidies, private fees, and donations.

Aggregate Capacity and Utilization

There are no definitive statistics on the volume or sponsorship of China's residential facilities and nursing homes, but the numbers are large and growing. In 2009, there were an estimated 38,000 homes of all types with 2.66 million beds; by 2010, there were 40,000 homes with 3.15 million beds; by 2013, there were 44,304 institutions with 4.16 million beds.[44] The vast majority of these beds (87 percent) are found in public institutions. There is clearly an imbalance in the supply of beds and the distribution of the population. Depending on the data source, roughly one-quarter of the facilities and roughly one-third of the total beds are in urban areas; by contrast, urban areas contained roughly half of the population.[45]

According to the Ministry of Civil Affairs, there were 21.5 beds per 1,000 elderly; according to a survey conducted by the China Research Center on Aging, the number of beds per 1,000 elderly was 26. Total admissions at the end of 2012 were 2.936 million patients; occupancy rates have hovered around 75 percent for over a decade.

Supply and Demand Issues

Infrastructure Capacity

It is difficult to accurately assess the balance of supply and demand for SCS and LTC in China. One problem is the difficulty in distinguishing the supply of community-based residential facilities from nursing homes in terms of their numbers and bed capacity. The population of Chinese elderly 65+ years old (117 million in 2010) was served by 40,000 homes with 3.15 million beds; China thus had a ratio of one senior facility for every 2,925 seniors and 26.92 beds per 1,000 elderly. By contrast, in 2012, the United States had 37,900 residential care facilities and nursing homes with 2.52 million beds, serving an elderly population of 43 million. Thus, the United States had one facility for every 1,135 elderly and a ratio of 58 beds per 1,000 elderly. This suggests that expanded nursing home capacity as well as senior housing options are needed to meet the growing needs of China's exploding senior population. In 2013, the director of the Department of Social Welfare and Charity Promotion in the Ministry of Civil Affairs, Wang Hui, estimated the country needed 10 million more nursing home beds.[46]

Manpower Capacity

There is a massive undersupply of SCS and LTC workers in China. The government estimates that 10 million LTC workers are needed to provide proper support for the elderly; this contrasts with the current supply of only 300,000 now employed.[47] This suggests a 33-fold gap in supply. Moreover, among the 300,000 workers, as few as one-third

(and perhaps as many as two-thirds) are nurses; of these, only 10 percent hold nursing licenses.[48]

Inadequate manpower levels are exacerbated by the high turnover in personnel. There are manifold reasons for high turnover, but they commonly center on low pay, low social status and occupational prestige, and the social stigma associated with such employment. In Shanghai, the monthly salary for a *bao mu* homemaker in the early 2000s was only 500–600 RMB (including board). Such conditions further contribute to the general public's perception that nursing facilities provide poor care; the high turnover rate also exacerbates the poor quality of care rendered (covered below).

Quality and Staff Training

Another factor affecting demand for nursing home services is the general public's perception of the poor level of quality available in the nation's nursing facilities. In 2002, the Ministry of Labor and Social Security issued "Professional Standards of Carers of Older Persons." This document prescribed detailed knowledge and skill requirements for the daily, medical, rehabilitation, and psychological care for older people. These new guidelines accorded a higher priority to recruiting and training of workers within nursing facilities.

Nevertheless, the current level of training and skills among workers in home healthcare, senior housing, and nursing homes in China appears deficient. Home care is largely a "homemaker" service focused on supporting seniors with ADL functions: bathing, toileting, feeding, etc. Home care workers receive no training in performing such functions; in Shanghai, training for *jia zheng* lasted only two days.[49] In nursing homes, the basic hands-on worker is often a displaced factory worker with little or no training in senior care.[50] Other nursing home workers are migrant farmers with also little or no training – even in the basics of caring for an elderly patient. According to a recent survey by the China Research Center on Aging, many nursing home personnel are between 40 years and 50 years of age and have little education. They are more oriented to providing physical care rather than emotional or medical care. Anecdotal evidence from 34 elder facilities in Shanghai's Changning district revealed that 241 of 554 workers had only primary school education, while 97 were illiterate. Only one-quarter of the staff had three or more years of experience.[51]

Some companies (e.g., International Senior Services) have attempted to develop skilled care services modeled after proven western home care companies (e.g., Bayada Home Health Care). Their efforts to upgrade skill levels have confronted regulations that restrict them from expanding beyond homemaker services; however, they believe these restrictions will be removed, thereby allowing a medical homecare model similar to that offered in the United States. Providing medical services in the home will have a major impact by enabling medical conditions to be identified and treated early, rather than allowing such conditions to go untreated and escalate to the point of hospitalization.

Geriatrics as a Medical Subspecialty

Geriatrics as a subspecialty has been very slow to develop in China. The first geriatric department was established in the Capital University of Medical Sciences only in 2007. The country has few training programs that lag well behind the geriatric training programs offered by western countries.[52] Due to the complexity of the aging patient, geriatrics by its very nature requires a multidisciplinary approach covering gerontology, medicine, sociology, ethics, environmental sciences, and other fields. Given the unprecedented increase in the number of seniors in China, developing a well-trained and specialized physician workforce is needed. One reason for the slow development is the belief that every hospital in China is able to admit and care for geriatric patients.

Attracting Private-Pay Patients

The number of nursing homes has dramatically increased in China over the past decade to partially address the undersupply. The majority of these facilities have sought to attract private-pay residents rather than patients with government support.[53] However, many of these new projects have not been financially successful. A review of several nursing facilities in Beijing in 2015 confirmed the difficulty private nursing facilities

were having in attracting residents. One for-profit facility in particular was built as a 400-bed private-pay nursing home. After almost five years of operations, the facility achieved only 51 percent occupancy. Explanations for low occupancy include the lack of cultural acceptance of placing the responsibility of caring for one's parents with a facility and not the family, the cost of a private nursing facility, and the lack of government financial support.

Another reason for not attracting patients is the fact that many elderly Chinese with economic means would rather leave their money to their children and (one) grandchild rather than spend it on themselves. Leaving a legacy for their children and grandchild is a very strong factor that restricts the number of Chinese seniors willing to spend their income on themselves.

Regulatory Complexity

While China has made efforts to increase senior centers and social services (i.e., the Starlight Program), the creation of medically focused community-based and home-based SCS has been largely ignored. There are several existing regulations that complicate or impede the development of medically oriented community-based services for seniors.

One set of barriers relates to the complexity of the regulatory landscape (see Chapter 2). This landscape includes both national and local agencies. At the national level,

- the Ministry of Civil Affairs governs the licensing and administration of senior care facilities at the national level;
- the National Health and Family Planning Commission (NHFPC, formerly Ministry of Health) governs health facility approvals at the national level along with administration of medical related issues;
- the Ministry of Commerce governs approval for foreign investment;
- the Administration for Industry and Commerce governs business registry for for-profit business;
- the China Insurance Regulatory Commission regulates insurance company activities relating to senior housing;

- the Ministry of Housing and Urban-Rural Development governs construction standards for senior housing;
- the Ministry of Land Resource governs land-use right policies for senior housing;
- the State Administration of Foreign Exchange governs foreign exchange (paid-in capital, foreign debt, etc.);
- the National Development and Reform Commission controls approval of project construction; and
- the Ministry of Human Resources and Social Security oversees caregiver qualifications.

The above list indicates that different ministries oversee elder care (Civil Affairs) and medical care (NHFPC) – roughly paralleling the social versus medical aspects of care. This poses some barrier to the integration of these two aspects of care. Current regulations further complicate bringing medical staff into elder facilities, since the former need to practice in facilities with medical licenses.

At the local level, approvals are made by the Municipal Bureau of Civil Affairs and cover the following: accreditation, licensing requirements, construction standards, requirements for medical treatment, safety and hygiene, caregiver qualifications and level of service, and assessment of seniors' need for care. National policies are reportedly vague; local policies vary widely and are often severely underdeveloped.

Another set of regulatory hurdles concern real estate and construction laws. Land is scarce and expensive. Given the long-standing imperative for economic growth, local governments tend to favor for-profit enterprise when approving land deals. On the other hand, to lower their operating costs and make their services more affordable, many elder care facilities tend to register as nonprofit entities and thereby achieve tax-exemption. This situation has stymied private sector development and investment.

Many senior housing projects are so big they encounter construction obstacles in the form of land quotas imposed by local government. There are also different types of land-use rights that influence the appropriate development and financing models for senior housing projects, which in turn affect their product and fee structures. Moreover,

there is no specific category of land-use right for senior care facilities, although some municipalities have recently established special land provision plans for senior care projects (see below).

Another regulatory barrier is directly tied to licensing criteria for healthcare services in China. The two major licensure levels in China include hospitals and home care services. Unfortunately, the services that home care agencies are allowed to provide are governed by what is referred to as "Rule 88," which prevents home care service workers from "piercing the skin" or from using "medical devices that are used within the hospital setting." Because of these restrictions, home care agencies in China are really no more than support services offering absolutely no medical monitoring or services that simply help in the activities of daily living. As long as the restrictive requirements of Rule 88 exist, the supply of medically oriented home care services will stagnate and seniors will continue to use the nation's hospitals for primary care services.

Impact on Hospital Utilization and Chronic Disease

China's healthcare system relies heavily on a hospital-based delivery model (see Chapter 8). Such an acute-care, institutionally based focus necessarily limits the current level of medical services available to seniors in the community. By offering the right mix of medical, social, and support services to seniors in community settings, China could reduce costly hospital utilization, relieve patient congestion, and simultaneously increase access to those truly in need of both long-term care and acute-care services. In addition, improving basic social and medical services available in the home and community could improve early detection and treatment of noncommunicable diseases (NCDs, or chronic illnesses) which, under the current system, too often go unrecognized (see Chapter 5 and Case Study 1 below). Left untreated, NCDs can escalate to an acute level requiring hospitalization. At the same time, there is an absolute need for quality nursing home services for those seniors in need of support services beyond what can be safely and cost-effectively given in the community.

The availability of both home-based and community-based SCS and LTC is thus critical to the successful care of China's aging population, the effective treatment of chronic illness, and the efficient use of healthcare resources. The case study provides a realistic view of one problem with Chinese SCS and the potential benefits available by offering primary medical services in the home.

Case Study 1: Linda Len's mother – 62 years old, post-stroke

Linda is a 36-year-old single woman working as an executive for an international company in Beijing. Linda's mother, who had been a practicing physician, suffered a massive stroke almost three years ago that left her in need of regular support to perform activities of daily living. Linda and her aging father have been the primary caregivers, although the level of help her father can offer is limited. When her mother experienced her stroke, she was admitted to a Class III hospital and from there was transferred to a hospital with stronger rehabilitation services. After almost two months, she came home permanently in need of significant support. Upon her mother's discharge, Linda took a leave of absence from work to care for her. After 60 days, Linda needed to return to her job. To enable her to do so, she hired a "hugong" (a young, unskilled girl typically from the country) to help care for her mother. Without any formal training, the hugong's primary responsibilities were providing basic services like cleaning, dressing, bathing, and feeding her mother. To do so on an ongoing basis, the hugong moved into Linda's home, a small, two-bedroom apartment on the fourth floor of an apartment building without an elevator. Her parents lived in one bedroom, while Linda and the hugong now shared the other.

Linda has been caring for her mother for three years now, and several patterns have emerged. Approximately every six to eight weeks, her mother is re-admitted to the hospital for congestive heart failure or other chronic disease issues that flare up. Each time, Linda is forced to call an ambulance to bring her mother to the hospital. Because they live on the fourth floor with no elevator, Linda is forced to call friends to literally help carry her mother down a narrow stairwell on a stretcher. Linda confided that her biggest fear in sending her mother back to the hospital is that she will be dropped in the stairwell while being carried up and down the staircase. Linda is extremely frustrated with the current healthcare system because she recognizes that her mother's repeat admissions to the hospital are a direct result of the lack of medical supervision or monitoring of her mother at home.

Note: This case study was developed through personal interviews conducted by John Whitman in Beijing, China, in July 2015.

Home-based SCS can be rendered either at the senior's home or at a unit within a large senior housing project. SCS includes a wide array of both medical and social services: physician home visits, both skilled and unskilled nursing services, rehabilitation services (physical, occupational, respiratory, speech), social services, companionship, meals, and other services that enable seniors to remain at home. The needs of seniors vary in terms of their medical and social needs, location (rural vs. urban), gender, marital status, level of available family support, and other factors. A well-designed system will be able to evaluate and respond to the senior's situation and modify the services offered as care and support needs change over time. The goal of a good senior care service is to allow clients to remain safely in their own homes as long as possible and prevent/delay nursing home placement. This approach respects the wishes of most seniors to remain in their homes and represents a lower-cost approach for both the government and caretaking families.

With a growing senior population, China also needs to provide nursing home (institutional) services. Despite the fact that the vast majority of seniors would prefer home-based care, some percentage of seniors will require a level of care that can no longer be safely, physically, or economically provided in the home. There is also a growing number of elderly in China that either have no family or have no family living nearby who can help in their care and allow them to live at home.[54] In the absence of adequate nursing home capacity, these seniors may be forced to utilize acute-care hospitals.

The second case study highlights several problems with China's healthcare system that arise from the continual reliance on hospitals for medical services. Allowing community-based medical services would have a major impact on improving care for seniors and reducing costs for the government and patient families.

Case Study 2: Mr. Zhang – 72-year-old man with permanent catheter

Mr. Zhang is a 72-year-old, retired government official living in a high-rise building in Beijing. Mr. Zhang has several chronic medical conditions and requires a full-time catheter that must be changed every three days. Because there is no skilled home care in China and primary care is only provided at the hospital, Mr. Zhang must return to the hospital every three days to have his catheter replaced.

On those days, Mr. Zhang spends almost seven hours in care-seeking. The seven hours encompass time spent on travel to and from the hospital, hospital registration, waiting to be seen, and the actual 30 minutes required to replace his catheter. By the end of the day, Mr. Zhang is understandably exhausted and mentally stressed, knowing he must repeat this same routine three days later.

Affordability of Elder Care

A major subset of the supply and demand issues concern financing and investment. On the *demand side*, there is the issue of whether China's growing number of elderly can afford SCS and LTC. Given that pensions are a major source of the urban elderly's income, pension funding is critical to affordability. This issue is discussed in this section. On the *supply side*, there is the twofold issue of encouraging the private sector to invest in developing the needed capacity in this sector and their ability to do so profitably. This issue is discussed in the section that follows.

Cost of SCS and LTC

Available statistics indicate that the 2012 monthly expenditures on paid caregivers are non-trivial for both urban residents (2,370 RMB) and rural residents (4,020 RMB). Such costs are heavily financed by the pensions of the urban elderly and by family funds of the rural elderly. More recent survey data released in 2015 by the China Research Center on Aging indicate the average monthly cost for nursing home care is 2,134 RMB. By contrast, the average monthly pension for urban retirees is only 2,061 RMB; rural retirees only recently benefited from pension reform and have low monthly stipends that average 75 RMB per month.[55] On an annual basis, this translates into 21,000 RMB for urban retirees and 900 RMB for rural retirees. The high cost limits the affordability of high-end senior housing. Consultants estimate that less than 10 million elderly can currently afford such housing, growing to perhaps 22 million by 2020.[56]

There is little research on the public's "willingness to pay" for LTC. One official survey conducted in Shanghai suggested the acceptable monthly payment for service in a senior care facility was <1,000 RMB (31.9 percent of those sampled), 1,000–2,000 RMB (51.6 percent), 2,000–3,000 RMB (13.4 percent), and >3,000 RMB (3.1 percent).[57]

To be sure, the elderly Chinese population has other assets. Younger family members transfer money to their parents to help finance their daily expenditures; the total transferred annually is estimated at nearly 5,000 RMB for urban elderly and over 3,300 RMB for rural elderly.[58] According to the National Bureau of Statistics, the country has a home ownership rate of 80 percent, one of the highest in the world. However, given the cost of housing and real estate, and the preference to pass wealth on to future generations, the elderly may prefer to transfer these assets to their children rather than consume them (e.g., using reverse mortgages) to pay for SCS and LTC. In 2014, four large municipalities (Beijing, Shanghai, Guangzhou, Wuhan) initiated a two-year pilot program called the "home for pensions plan" to allow elderly to take out bank loans against their homes to pay for their living expenses.[59] Obvious barriers to such a plan include the strategy of passing on assets to children to avoid poverty, the desire not to foment family disputes, any public concerns over bank insolvency, and Chinese law that caps all private home ownership at 70 years.

The Chinese are notoriously thrifty with a high savings rate. In 2013, the urban elderly had 14,700 RMB in assets, while the rural elderly had 3,466 RMB. Such assets were conservatively invested in bank deposits and held as cash for purposes of accessibility. Both the urban and rural elderly spend two-thirds of their income on food and household items, with much of the remainder going to medical expenses and utilities. There is little income left for more discretionary items such as education or travel.

Origins of China's Pension System

The roots of China's old-age pension system lie in the country's planned Soviet-style economy and its first healthcare insurance schemes (see Chapter 2) enacted in the 1950s.[60] Workers in urban-based state-owned enterprises (SOEs) and collective enterprises were covered by the Labor Insurance Scheme (LIS) for healthcare needs. An important part of this scheme was a "Pay As You Go" (PAYG) retirement system funded by the state. Enterprises had unlimited liability for employee health, old age, sickness, disability, and death. Workers did not have to pay into the pension fund, which covered roughly 80 percent of the worker's last wage. However, to contain the liabilities, the pensions were limited to workers who worked for at least 30 years and retired at age 50 to 55 (for females) or 60 (for males). Given that life expectancy was quite low at the time, the retirement age requirement was quite high. Government workers received healthcare coverage under the more generous Government Insurance Scheme (GIS) which covered inpatient and outpatient care. They also received retirement insurance under a civil service pension system that did not require any employee contribution.

After the initiation of economic reform in 1978, China retreated from this pension system.

It abolished lifetime employment at SOEs and introduced an "enterprise responsibility system" whereby firms rather than the state had to accumulate and pay out pensions. However, most SOEs suffered operating losses and could not afford to make such pension contributions; this financing problem was compounded by the relatively small risk pool and exclusion of workers in private firms. In 1991, the government issued its "Decision on the Reform of Enterprise Pension System" that called for a three-tiered pension system that split financing between the state, firms, and citizens.

The proposal culminated in the 1997 establishment of the Urban Employee's Basic Old-Age Insurance (BOAI). This mandatory scheme had two components: (a) social pooling via an employer-financed pension and (b) an individual account based on a defined contribution. The employer contributed 20 percent of the employee's wage, while employees contributed 8 percent of their wages to the individual account. The employer portion was paid into a social pooling fund at the local level, and was to be used to finance current benefits as part of the PAYG system. The individual contribution was designed to be deposited into the worker's account and then distributed monthly upon retirement (using an annuity factor of 139 months). By the end of 2012, the scheme had 304 million members, including 74 million pensioners (who received an average monthly payment of 1,731 RMB). This amount constituted roughly 54 percent of per capita gross domestic product (GDP), well below China's 2011 poverty line of 2,300 RMB. The replacement rate of the original retirement system was too high and was subsequently lowered to 59 percent: 35 percent was paid by the pooling mechanism, 24 percent was paid by the individual account.

The 1997 reform extended coverage to those in the private sector, foreign-funded enterprises, and joint ventures, with further coverage extended in 2005 to the self-employed and those with "flexible" employment. Their contribution rate of 20 percent of wages consisted of 12 percent payments into the social pooling fund and 8 percent into the individual account. The scheme became known as "old age insurance for all labors."

BOAI was a mandatory social insurance that represented the first pillar in a three-tiered system. It was supplemented by a second pillar introduced in 2004, an enterprise-sponsored individual account (Voluntary Employer Enterprise Annuity and Group Pension Scheme), with contributions by sponsoring employers and voluntary contributions by workers. This pillar is roughly comparable to the 401(k) account found in the United States. This vehicle has experienced very slow adoption and covers very few (18 million workers in 2012, or roughly 6 percent of what BOAI covers), partly due to the lack of tax incentives for employers and workers. A third pillar is individual retirement savings using voluntary personal pensions and commercial pension insurance.

In 2009, the government introduced a pension system for rural retirees called "The New Rural Social Pension Scheme" (NRSPS). By 2012, the scheme had 450 million members (contributors), including 124 million pensioners. The scheme had two components – a social funding mechanism and an individual contributory account. The former included a basic monthly pension payment of 55 RMB to the elderly 60+ years old, funded entirely by the central government for the central and western regions and half-funded for the eastern region; local governments were also expected to make annual "co-contributions" of at least 30 RMB. The individual account is a voluntary annual contribution of anywhere from 100 RMB to 500 RMB.

Compared to BOAI, the NRSPS is clearly inadequate. The estimated benefit for an individual making an annual contribution of 100 RMB (the most popular choice by members) will be only about 95 RMB per month after 15 years of participation. This represents only 16 percent of average income.[61]

Issues with the Pension System

The BOAI has suffered from several problems. First is the aging population, the decline in the size of the workforce, and the country's growing "old-age dependency ratio," i.e., the number of elderly 65+ years old per 100 working people aged 15–64. Figure 10.1 displays the aging of the population. As a percent of the population, the Chinese workforce will fall from 72 percent

in 2010 to 61 percent by 2050. As the dependency ratio grows, existing workers will need to support a growing number of pensioners. When measured in 1990, the old-age dependency ratio was only eight; since then, the ratio grew to 11 by 2010 (compared to 20 in the United States); the ratio is projected to reach 39 by 2050 (surpassing the US rate of 36). Stated differently, in 1997 there were 3.42 workers to support each retiree; by 2011, that number fell to 3.16. If one defines the elderly as those aged 60+ years (as does the Chinese government), there were 4.9 people of working age for each elderly person in 2013; by 2050, that number is expected to fall to 1.6.

In the presence of underfunded pensions, there will be fewer workers to support pension payments. In the presence of smaller families and greater numbers of elderly living without their children, there will be greater pressure on family members to subsidize the LTC needs of their parents. There will also be greater pressure on the government to either reinforce or replace home-based care as the dominant form of elder care.

Second, the 28 percent contribution rate was excessive and one of the highest in the world. The high level hampered the scheme's capacity to increase the contribution rate to match the aging of the population. It also burdened the workforce as a high tax on wages (which precipitated problems with worker participation) as well as a barrier to enterprise formation.

Third, there is the growing problem of pension underfunding, which increases pressure on central and local governments to make up the shortfalls. Existing retirees as of 1997 continued to receive their legacy benefits; those working in 1997 received a blend of previous and new benefits. Most local governments found that the social pooling funds were insufficient to pay the legacy benefits due to the low number of workers paying into the funds. These payouts also competed with other public financial commitments. The local governments dipped into the individual worker accounts to pay the current benefits, as well as relied on transfers from central government. More generally, public pension spending accounts for only 3 percent of China's GDP, compared to 7 percent in the United States.

Chinese media labeled the practice of using current contributions to pay legacy benefits as the "empty accounts" phenomenon. One estimate of the shortfall in the individual accounts is 90 percent. In response, both employers and workers sought to minimize their participation (by not contributing, by underreporting wages, etc.).

An estimated one-half of China's provinces cannot pay their retiree costs and rely on central government transfers. Deutsche Bank estimated the shortfall in future pension payouts at $3 trillion in 2013; the government countered by stating that despite shortfalls in many provinces, there was a $500 billion pension surplus. A report published in December 2013 by the Chinese Academy of Social Sciences (CASS) estimated the accumulated shortfall would amount to 90 percent of the country's gross domestic product. This has fueled considerable worker distrust of the pension system as well as public discontent, as reflected in worker protests over a decade of unpaid pension contributions by their employer.[62] Workers doubt they will receive any pension payouts (plus interest) from their individual accounts.

Between 2005 and 2010, the pension deficit grew at 25 percent CAGR. The deficits are partly due to underfunding and partly due to the low contribution participation rate on the part of employees paying into the individual accounts. In 2009, only 57 percent of the 280–311 million urban workers contributed; only 15 percent of the 460–470 million rural workers participated. According to the Human Resources and Labor Protection Survey, 23 percent of insured employees suspended contributions in 2011.

Fourth, the replacement rate has gradually declined to 44 percent in 2011 as wage growth has outstripped growth in pension benefits. Between 1997 and 2008, the compound annual growth rate (CAGR) in wages was 15 percent compared to the 10 percent growth in pensions. This will make it increasingly hard for retirees to maintain their living standards, particularly as the cost of living increases. The declining replacement rate means less basic financial protection for retirees, particularly as they have few other income sources and typically spend a relatively high percentage of their pension income on food.

Fifth, there are great inequities in pensions between urban and rural workers, as well as between workers in different sectors. CASS reported that annual pension benefits for retired urban employees dwarfed those for retired agricultural workers (20,900 RMB vs. 859 RMB). This partly reflects the different levels of contribution noted above. It also reflects the fact that pensions historically were awarded to urban workers. In 2010, over 90 percent of urban workers received a government pension, compared to only 25 percent of retirees in rural areas. To correct these inequities and achieve social harmony, the government has vowed to "unify" the urban and rural retirement schemes. Within the urban pension schemes, there are also inequities favoring retired civil servants (who did not have to contribute to their pension benefits) and those in wealthier cities (who receive larger pension benefits due to differences in the average cost of living).

Sixth, the pension funds have earned very low returns. Liquidity and credit rating requirements have led firms at provincial and municipal levels to invest pension funds in banks and government bonds earning a nominal 2 percent return. Interest rates on such "safe investments" have been held low for years by the government for policy reasons. By doing so, however, the government has contributed to the projected replacement rate issue discussed above. Simultaneously, inflation in China is running at 3 percent.

Seventh, China's pension system is quite fragmented. In addition to the separate schemes for urban employees at large companies and those in the civil service, the government has instituted two additional schemes – a voluntary pension system for rural workers (2009) and another for non-employed rural residents. This patchwork system mirrors the patchwork system that has evolved for health insurance: UEBMI, URBMI, and NCMS (see Chapters 2, 4, and 11). Some estimate that there are as many as 3,000 different pension pools across China, which make monitoring them difficult for the central government.[63] Such fragmentation inhibits the mobility of labor, due to administrative barriers to transferring the accrued benefits. Labor mobility is further hampered by long vesting rules and the *hukou* system. There is also fragmentation within the BOAI scheme due to differences in financing and administration across provincial and municipal governments.

Solutions to the Pension Problem

One solution to the pension mess is the government's recent decision in late 2015 to relax the one-child policy. As discussed in Chapter 2, however, it is unclear how Chinese couples will respond. Another solution is the government's decision in early 2015 to gradually hike the retirement age to 65, starting in 2017. This solution will have a greater effect on the urban elderly than the rural elderly, among whom retirement is an alien concept.[64] Another response is for the government to fund the unfunded pension contributions, perhaps through higher income taxes or issuance of debt.

Investment in Elder Care

There has been growing interest among government agencies in supporting investment in SCS and LTC to increase their supply. The government's Five-Year Plan (2011–2015) established a target of providing institution-based care to 3 percent of the total senior population by the end of 2015. In 2013, the National Development and Reform Commission and the Ministry of Commerce jointly announced the *Catalogue of Priority Industries for Foreign Investment in Central and Western China.* The *Catalogue* accorded SCS and medical institutions preferential status for foreign investment (including exemption from taxes on imported equipment and refunds of value-added taxes in domestic equipment). In November 2014, the Ministry of Commerce and Ministry of Civil Affairs jointly issued the *Announcement Encouraging Foreign Investors to Establish For-Profit Senior Care Institutions to Engage in Senior Care Services in China.*

In 2015, ten ministries in the Chinese government jointly issued the *Implementing Opinions on Encouraging Private Capital to Participate in the Development of Senior Care Service Industry* in an effort to encourage private sector investment in both SCS and LTC. The National Development and

Reform Commission issued guidance for regulating pricing of such services by reliance on the market. The Ministry of Civil Affairs and China Development Bank jointly issued *Implementation Opinions on the Financing Support for Establishment of Senior Care Service System.* And the Ministry of Land Resources issued its *Guiding Opinion on the Utilization of Land Use Right for Senior Care Facility.* As noted above, land is a particularly scarce and expensive resource input needed to develop the SCS and LTC sector. Beginning in 2015, major cities in China (Nanjing, Shenzen, Beijing) began to grant land-use rights specifically for the purpose of operating senior facilities.[65]

The Ministry of Civil Affairs has also worked with the Ministry of Finance in allocating government funds annually along with funds from a special central lottery to support the construction of senior care facilities in rural areas. Provincial Ministries of Finance also allocate funds to construct a range of SCS and LTC facilities.

Despite the government's encouragement and supporting financial policies, the private sector has not deeply penetrated the sector. Roughly 90 percent of senior services are still rendered by public sector providers. China's nursing homes have suffered from low profit margins and long-term returns on investment; nearly half of the homes surveyed by the China Research Center on Aging broke even, one-fifth earned a profit, and roughly one-third operated at a loss. Part of the problem may be the market segmentation strategy pursued by nursing homes. Some homes appear to target the lower end of the market by providing only basic food and living necessities, without any medical equipment or entertainment facilities – for example, in rural elderly homes and welfare houses. By contrast, other homes target the higher end of the market with better facilities, equipment, and service standards – and at a much higher cost. Some recent construction appears to be pursuing the latter market in an effort to more quickly recoup their investment; however, these homes may be beyond the financial reach of most seniors. The higher-end homes reportedly have the lowest occupancy rates, reflecting not only their high price (up to 5,000 RMB per month) but also their location in distant suburbs that are not easily accessible to family members. The majority of homes appear to be targeting the middle range of the market with recently constructed homes for the middle class.

Summary and Conclusion

China currently faces a multitude of issues in senior services and long-term care, including:

- More than 2,000 years of Confucian teaching and tradition that stresses filial piety
- A rapidly expanding senior population expected to reach 450 million by 2050
- The negative stigma that currently exists surrounding nursing facilities
- A healthcare system that is currently hospital-centric and does not recognize home-based skilled care services
- The growing imbalance of older to younger people in China
- A changing workforce that includes more woman
- A nation with tremendous numbers of seniors yet a healthcare system lacking solid geriatric training for medical students and others responsible for caring for these seniors
- A lack of good hands-on quality in nursing facilities due to poorly trained and poorly paid staff resulting in high turnover rates
- Historical regulations restricting the development of skilled care home-based services

China is in a serious race to ensure that the massive senior population receives the highest quality of care while preventing negative economic ramifications. Changing dynamics will shift elder care from families, who have historically taken on primary responsibility, to retirement communities, nursing facilities, and other forms of housing. For years, China's economic growth was driven by an enormous supply of young labor, cheap labor, and capital; this is now changing. The aging of the population has resulted in a growing old-age dependency ratio with fewer workers to support more elderly; cheap labor has been undermined by rising living standards and labor mobility; and, due to population aging, the population segment that were the highest savers (age 30–50) will decline from 50 percent in 2010 to 46 percent by 2020 and further to 40 percent by 2030. This will mean a decline in the national savings rate.[66]

At the same time, the aging of the population will serve as a stimulus to China's healthcare system. Chinese experts predict the senior market will explode in the coming years for several reasons.[67] They include the decline in traditional cultural barriers, the development of alternative models, and the entrance of foreign healthcare companies seeking to develop high-end western-style medically-oriented home healthcare services, retirement communities, as well as high-end nursing facilities specifically targeting the private-pay market.

Notes

1. Bei Wu, Zong-Fu Mao, and Renyao Zhong. 2009. "Long-Term Care Arrangements in Rural China: Review of Recent Developments," *Journal of American Medical Directors Association* 10: 472–477.
2. Bei Lu, Wenjiong He, and John Piggott. 2014. "Should China Introduce a Social Pension?" *Journal of the Economics of Ageing* 4: 76–87.
3. *Law of the People's Republic of China Regarding the Protection of the Rights and Interests of the Elderly.* Lin Wenyi. 2014. "Challenges of Long-Term Care Provisions for the Elderly in Urban China," *China: An International Journal* 12(2): 144–160.
4. Lu et al. 2014. "Should China Introduce a Social Pension?"
5. Wu et al. 2009. "Long-Term Care Arrangements in Rural China." James Smith, John Strauss, and Yaohui Zhao. 2014. "Healthy Aging in China," *Journal of the Economics of Ageing* 4: 37–43.
6. Smith et al. 2014. "Healthy Aging in China."
7. Ibid.
8. Jianhui Hu. 2012. *Old-Age Disability in China* (Santa Monica: RAND Corporation).
9. Ibid.
10. Yu Cheung Wong and Joe Leung. 2012. "Long-Term Care in China: Issues and Prospects," *Journal of Gerontology Social Work* 55(7): 570–586.

11. No author. 2015. "Research Highlights Challenges for China's Senior Care Market," *CRI English News* (July 17).

12. Hu. 2012. *Old-Age Disability in China*.

13. Ibid.

14. Richard Jackson and Neil Howe. 2004. *The Graying of the Middle Kingdom: The Demographics and Economics of Retirement Policy in China* (Washington, DC: Center for Strategic and International Studies).

15. James Huang. 2012. Presentation to Wharton-Guanghua Class.

16. Feng Wang. 2012. "Racing Towards the Precipice," *China Economic Quarterly* (June). Abstract available online at: www.brookings .edu/research/articles/2012/06/china-demo graphics-wang. Accessed on December 23, 2015.

17. Bei Wu, Mary Carter, R. Turner Goins et al. 2005. "Emerging Services for Community-Based Long-Term Care in Urban China: A Systematic Analysis of Shanghai's Community-Based Agencies," *Journal of Aging and Social Policy* 17(4): 37–60.

18. Zhanlian Feng, Chang Liu, Xinping Guan et al. 2012. "China's Rapidly Aging Population Creates Policy Challenges in Shaping a Viable Long-Term Care System," *Health Affairs* 31 (12): 2764–2773.

19. Paul Gordon. 2014. "American Senior Living Goes to China," Presentation to Session on "Long Term Care and the Law," American Health Lawyers Association Meeting (Las Vegas: February 19–21).

20. Chris Kaye, Richard Huang, Juan Triola et al. 2012. *From Silver to Gold: How Insurers Can Capitalize on Aging in China* (April). Boston Consulting Group and Swiss Re. Available online at: www.bcg.com.cn/en/files/publica tions/reports_pdf/From_Silver_to_Gold_Apr_ 2012_ENG_FINAL.pdf. Accessed on December 17, 2015.

21. Zhihong Zhen, Qiushi Feng, and Danan Gu. 2015. "The Impacts of Unmet Needs for Long-Term Care on Mortality Among Older Adults in China," *Journal of Disability Policy Studies* 25(4): 243–251.

22. Mei Li, Yang Zhang, Zhenyu Zhang et al. 2013. "Rural-Urban Differences in the Long-term Care of the Disabled Elderly in China," *PLOS ONE* 8(11): e79955.

23. Li et al. 2013. "Rural-Urban Differences in the Long-term Care of the Disabled Elderly in China."

24. Wenyi. 2014. "Challenges of Long-Term Care Provisions for the Elderly in Urban China."

25. Li et al. 2013. "Rural-Urban Differences in the Long-term Care of the Disabled Elderly in China."

26. Jacques Penhirin and James Yang. 2015. *More Than Fifty Shades of Grey* (Hong Kong: Oliver Wyman).

27. Heying Jenny Zhan. 2013. "Population Aging and Long-Term Care in China," *Generations – Journal of the American Society on Aging* 37 (1): 53–58.

28. Wenyi. 2014. "Challenges of Long-Term Care Provisions for the Elderly in Urban China."

29. Ministry of Labor and Social Security. 2002. Professional Standards of Carers for Older Persons.

30. Wu et al. 2009. "Long-Term Care Arrangements in Rural China."

31. Ibid.

32. Wenyi. 2014. "Challenges of Long-Term Care Provisions for the Elderly in Urban China."

33. Wu et al. 2009. "Long-Term Care Arrangements in Rural China."

34. By comparison, bed capacity in western countries serves 5–7 percent of the elderly population.

35. Helen Chen and Ken Chen. 2013. "The Coming Senior Housing Boom," *Business Now* (March): 10–13.

36. Bei Wu. 2012. "Development of China's Long-Term Care Finance and Delivery System," *China Health Policy Report* (September 6).

37. Joseph Flaherty, Mei Lin Liu, Lei Ding et al. 2007. "China: The Aging Giant," *Journal of American Geriatric Society* 55: 1295–1300.

38. Agency for Healthcare Research (AHRQ) Center for Delivery, Organization, and Markets, Healthcare Costs and Utilization Project (HCUP), National Inpatient Sample (NIS) 2012.

39. Yuting Song, Ruth A. Anderson, Kirsten N. Corazzini et al. 2014. "Staff Characteristics and Care in Chinese Nursing Homes: A Systematic Literature Review," *International Journal of Nursing Sciences* 1(4): 423–436.

40. Wu et al. 2005. "Emerging Services for Community-Based Long-Term Care in Urban China."

41. Wenyi. 2014. "Challenges of Long-Term Care Provisions for the Elderly in Urban China."

42. Ethnographic evidence from Shanghai is taken from Wu et al. 2005. "Emerging Services for Community-Based Long-Term Care in Urban China."

43. Feng et al. 2012. "China's Rapidly Aging Population Creates Policy Challenges in Shaping a Viable Long-Term Care System."

44. Ibid. Data from Ministry of Civil Affairs. 2013. *China Senior Housing and Care* (August): p. 4.

45. Wong and Leung. 2012. "Long-term Care in China." Gordon. 2014. "American Senior Living Goes to China."

46. Sarah O'Meara. 2014. "Aging Population in China: Having a Senior Moment," *CKGSB Knowledge* (July 22). Available online at: http://knowledge.ckgsb.edu.cn/2014/07/22/finance-and-investment/the-aging-population-in-china-having-a-senior-moment/. Accessed on December 22, 2015.

47. Penhirin and Yang. 2015. *More Than Fifty Shades of Grey.*

48. O'Meara. 2014. "Aging Population in China."

49. Wu et al. 2005. "Emerging Services for Community-Based Long-Term Care in Urban China."

50. Li et al. 2013. "Rural-Urban Differences in the Long term Care of the Disabled Elderly in China."

51. Zhang Qian. 2012. "China's Elder-Care Woes," *Shanghai Daily* (June 26). Available online at: https://nursing.duke.edu/sites/default/files/centers/ogachi/chinas_elder-care_woes_feature_shanghai_daily_06262012.pdf. Accessed on December 22, 2015.

52. Flaherty et al. 2007. "China."

53. Susan B. Brecht, Sandra Fein, and Linda Hollinger-Smith. 2009. "Preparing for the Future: Trends in Continuing Care Retirement Communities," *Senior Housing and Care Journal* 17(1): 75–90.

54. Some estimate that upwards of 25 percent of China's current senior population fall in these two categories, making them more likely to need nursing home support sooner than those seniors with strong family support.

55. No author. 2015. "Research Highlights Challenges for China's Senior Care Market." Penhirin and Yang. 2015. *More Than Fifty Shades of Grey.*

56. Helen Chen and Ken Chen. 2013. "Looking After China's Elderly," *China Business Review* (June 11).

57. Michael Qu and Joseph Christian. 2015. *Doing Business in China – Senior Housing Industry* (November 17).

58. Penhirin and Yang. 2015. *More Than Fifty Shades of Grey.*

59. Xiaoyi Shao and Koh Gui Qing. 2014. "China to Start Reverse Mortgage Pilot Programme for Senior Citizens," *Reuters* (June 23). Available online at: www.reuters.com/article/china-economy-mortgages-idUSL4N0P429D20140623. Accessed on December 22, 2015.

60. This section draws heavily on the following sources: Robert Pozen. 2013. *Tackling the Chinese Pension System* (Chicago, IL: Paulson Institute, July). Zhen Li. 2014. *The Basic Old-Age Insurance of China: Challenges and Countermeasures.* Available online at: www.worldpensionsummit.com/Portals/6/Zhen%20Li_Basic%20old%20age%20insurance%20in%20China.pdf. Accessed on December 18, 2015. Wang Dewen. 2006. "China's Urban and Rural Old Age Security System: Challenges and Options," *World Economy* 14(1): 102–116. Kaye et al. 2012. *From Silver to Gold.*

61. Lu et al. 2014. "Should China Introduce a Social Pension?"

62. Jennifer Baker. 2014. "China: Thousands of Yue Yuen (Nike Adidas) Factory Workers Strike Over Unpaid Pensions" (April 15). Available online at: http://revolution-news.com/china-thousand-yue-yuen-nike-adidas-factory-workers-strike-unpaid-pensions/. Accessed on December 18, 2015.

63. Dexter Roberts. 2013. "Chinese Rage at the Pension System," *Bloomberg Business* (October 31). Available online at: www .bloomberg.com/bw/articles/2013-10-31/chi nese-rage-at-the-pension-system. Accessed on December 19, 2015.

64. Smith et al. 2014. "Healthy Aging in China."

65. Michael Qu and Jane Zhang. 2015. China Senior Housing and Health Care Newsletter (June).

66. Wang. 2012. "Racing Towards the Precipice."

67. Findings are based on site visits by John Whitman to multiple nursing facilities in China in July 2015.

PART IV

Insurers and Reimbursement

Health Insurance in China

AMBAR LA FORGIA AND LAWTON ROBERT BURNS

Introduction

As of 2012, China had achieved nearly universal. health insurance with approximately 95 percent of the population covered through three government insurance programs: the Urban Employee Basic Medical Insurance (UEBMI), the New Cooperative Medical Scheme (NCMS), and the Urban Resident Basic Medical Insurance (URBMI).[1] Private health insurance revenue in China also experienced astonishing growth, increasing from $13.8 billion in 2012 to $18.2 billion in 2013, providing additional coverage for 7 percent of China's 1.36 billion citizens.[2] Despite this breadth of coverage, insurance options have been criticized for their lack of depth in both the public and private sector. Those insured still face large out-of-pocket costs, low quality of medical care, and inequitable access – what we have labeled the "iron triangle of healthcare" (see Chapter 1).

This chapter examines the history, evolution, and future opportunities for public and private health insurance in China. The chapter is organized as follows. The next section provides a primer on the basics of health insurance. The subsequent sections describe the development of public health insurance in China, the series of reforms and their ongoing challenges, and the more recent emergence of private health insurance and its market prospects. The last section outlines future directions for health insurance in China to assure effective and efficient provision of healthcare.

Health Insurance Primer

Most countries can be classified under three models of health insurance: the predominantly tax-funded

The authors wish to thank the Wharton Global Initiatives program for financial support to write this chapter. They also thank Rong Li for excellent research assistance.

insurance model, the predominantly social insurance model, and the predominantly voluntary insurance model. The tax-funded model (also called the Beveridge model or national insurance model) is a single-payer system where healthcare is provided and financed by the government through tax payments. Such a model is found in England, Hong Kong, and Canada. The social insurance model (sometimes referred to as the Bismarck model) is a multi-payer system with competing insurance funds (e.g., "sickness funds") jointly financed by employers and employees through payroll deductions. Variations of this model have been implemented in Germany, France, Japan, and the Netherlands. The voluntary insurance model is dominated by private insurance purchased voluntarily either through one's employer (group insurance) or individually. This model, used in the United States and Switzerland, now requires compulsory private insurance for those not covered by government insurance programs.

Private health insurance (PHI) is an insurance scheme financed through private health *premiums*, or payments that an insured individual agrees to make to receive coverage. The insurance policy generally consists of a contract that is issued by the insurer to the *beneficiary* (insured or covered person) and specifies the *covered benefits* (medical services covered under the contract). Take-up is often, but not always, voluntary. The pool of financing is not channeled or administered through the government, even when the insurer is government-owned.[3]

PHI has various forms, including duplicate, complementary, supplementary, and primary/comprehensive coverage. *Duplicate* PHI offers coverage for health services already included under government health insurance while also offering access to different providers (private hospitals) or levels of service (faster access to care). It does not exempt individuals from contributing to government health coverage. *Complementary* PHI, as expected, complements coverage of government-insured services by paying all or part of the residual costs not otherwise reimbursed, such as the co-payments. *Supplementary* PHI provides coverage for additional health services not covered by government insurance. Lastly, *primary or comprehensive* PHI completely replaces government insurance for those ineligible for it or those who have opted out of it, usually for higher quality coverage and care.

Most emerging countries do not follow any one of the three models, but instead employ a hybrid approach to health insurance. China has implemented a mix of the public insurance models: mandatory public insurance for urban employees (who share the costs with their employers), voluntary public insurance for non-working urban residents, and voluntary insurance for rural residents. Private health insurance is mostly supplemental in nature and purchased by less than 7 percent of the population.[4] The main benefit covered by health insurance is inpatient coverage. Special types of insurance are also available for particular illnesses (e.g., cancer) or special populations (e.g., children).

Typically, insurance companies have at least two different methods for determining the appropriate premium to charge for coverage. Under *community rating*, insurers rate all people in a community at the same rate and charge them the same premium; under *experience rating*, insurers evaluate different segments of the community as higher (lower) risk and charge them higher (lower) premium levels based on their past utilization.[5] The health status or risk level of individuals purchasing insurance is fundamental to the profitability of insurance companies. *Favorable selection* occurs when a population segment's use of health services is lower than expected; *adverse selection* occurs when a segment of higher-risk people enroll in the insurance plan, remain there longer than other types of risk groups, and utilize more health services.[6]

Insurance companies protect themselves against adverse selection by offering *group insurance*, which creates a large pool of insured enrollees. Group insurance is typically obtained through one's employer or union and is known as employer-based health insurance. With a large, diverse risk pool, the insurer can calculate the predictable rates of acute and chronic illness (e.g., diabetes) and can charge insurance premiums that reflect the costs of treating these conditions. *Individual insurance*, by contrast, is typically purchased out of pocket by the self-employed, individuals employed in the informal sector, and/or businesses that are too small to pool risk or afford group insurance. Since this insurance is voluntary, healthy individuals often forgo insurance and take their chances with illness; those who purchase insurance do so because they are less healthy and face higher risk. The cost of insuring these people will be higher, so insurance companies have to charge them higher rates, which drives away the healthier individuals. Adverse selection is the primary reason why individual coverage is so much more expensive than large group coverage (an issue in China discussed below).

A major policy concern is *out-of-pocket* costs, which are the additional costs borne by the insured beyond payment of the premium. In order to protect themselves from financial risk, plan sponsors (government, employers) require their insured enrollees to bear a portion of the cost of their care. Research shows that patient cost sharing reduces utilization of healthcare services and lowers the outlays by plan sponsors. Cost sharing can take multiple forms: (1) a *deductible*, which is the amount the insured must pay before any benefits are paid by the insurer; (2) *co-insurance*, which is the proportion of total medical costs that the insured has to pay each time care is received; and (3) *co-payment*, which is a fixed sum paid by the insured at the time of each provider visit.[7] In order to protect the insured enrollees from financial risk, insurance plans often set a ceiling on the out-of-pocket costs borne by the insured. In order to protect themselves from financial risk, insurance plans can also reinsure, establish stop-loss provisions, and set annual ceilings and lifetime limits on the benefits paid out.

Plans contract with *provider networks* of hospitals, doctors, and clinics from whom the insured enrollees are allowed to receive treatment. These contracts specify what services are covered, the method by which the provider is paid (see below), and at what rate. Until recently, China's public insurers only covered visits to public providers.

The occasion of a provider visit generates a *claim*, i.e., a medical bill generated by the provider for its services forwarded to the insurer for payment.

Insurance companies utilize different methods to reimburse providers for these claims. Traditional indemnity policies in the past required patients to pay the provider on a fee-for-service (FFS) basis and then seek reimbursement from the insurer. Over the past decade, this method has been supplemented by the addition of a third party administrator (TPA) who pays the provider and then submits the claim to the insurer for reimbursement.[8]

FFS reimbursement methods can create incentives for providers to induce demand that increases utilization and costs. Induced demand includes providing more services than necessary, choosing more costly alternatives (e.g., inpatient instead of outpatient care), performing more costly procedures, ordering more diagnostic tests, and prescribing more pharmaceuticals. For example, 40 percent of Chinese hospital revenue is tied to drug spending (e.g., via the over-prescription of antibiotics), compared to an average of 12 percent in other countries.[9] This situation underscores the need to set appropriate reimbursement rates for providers, to develop utilization and medical management programs, and to have effective bargaining between insurers, their TPAs, and providers. Establishing these processes and rates can be very difficult, given the lack of transparency of provider costs in China and the insurer's lack of visibility into the delivery system.

Evolution of Public Health Insurance in China

History from 1951 to 1998

China's health insurance coverage has oscillated between universal coverage and high levels of uninsurance as a result of various government initiatives (see Chapter 2). Between the 1950s and mid-1970s, health insurance was organized around urban sites of employment and rural communes, which achieved near-universal levels of insurance and low out-of-pocket spending.[10]

The first formal health insurance for the urban population, the Labor Insurance System (LIS), was established in 1951 for employees of state-owned enterprises (SOEs) and collectively owned enterprises and their dependents.[11] The Government Insurance System (GIS) was established in 1952

for government staff, government retirees, and university students. The Cooperative Medical System (CMS) was inaugurated during the 1950s to serve the rural population and quickly covered 90 percent of Chinese villages. CMS was funded by contributions from enrollees and subsidized by the collective welfare funds.[12] Together these programs achieved nearly universal insurance with low out-of-pocket payments.

The CMS became an internationally recognized innovation for tackling the healthcare needs of rural populations. The goal of the communal system was mainly to support the country's five-year plans for industrialization and agricultural development by providing nurseries, schools, entertainment, and healthcare.[13] The covered care was basic, relying heavily on traditional Chinese medicine and medical treatment rendered by barefoot doctors, but was remarkable for achieving broadly available, low-cost coverage.

After 1978, the government quickly transitioned from a closed, centralized, and planned economy to a market economy. The central government sought to decrease its role in provincial affairs through the introduction of the Household Responsibility System, resulting in local governments taking on the responsibility for healthcare. This led to the dissolution of the rural cooperatives, which in turn led to the loss of health insurance coverage among rural households. Coverage sharply declined from nearly universal levels in 1978 to 7 percent in 1999.[14] An initial effort to re-establish the CMS in 1997 failed due to a lack of financial commitment, political will, and sound management.[15]

Government statistics reported growing gaps in insurance coverage, under-utilization of providers, and growing inequities in healthcare access and outcomes between rural and urban areas. By 2003, the proportion of urban residents without health insurance rose to 50 percent; among rural residents, the percentage without coverage rose to 79 percent.[16] Moreover, between 1993 and 2003, the proportion of urban residents who did not visit a doctor when ill rose from 42 percent to 57 percent; among rural residents, the proportion rose from 34 percent to 46 percent.[17]

Low utilization of health services was due not only to the lack of insurance coverage, but also to the rising price and cost of healthcare. Between 1993 and 2003, the cost of a doctor visit increased from 14 RMB to 120 RMB, which accounted for 19 percent and 43 percent of per capita monthly income for urban and rural residents, respectively. The majority of the cost was paid out of pocket. Out-of-pocket health spending as a percent of private health expenditures exceeded 90 percent in the 1990s and 88 percent in 2003.[18] Not surprisingly, 30 percent of poor households reported healthcare costs as a main cause of their poverty.

The public became increasingly vocal about unaffordable healthcare, impoverishment from medical expenses, and inequalities across regions.[19] The SARS outbreak in 2002–2003 shed additional light on China's healthcare problems and brought unwelcome international attention. In part as a response to the SARS outbreak, and in part to address the rising discontent among the populace, the Chinese government began to institute large-scale health reforms in 2003 to once again achieve universal health insurance.

Health Insurance Reforms

UEBMI

As in many other policy areas in China, healthcare initiatives (both delivery and insurance) need to be distinguished by urban and rural settings. In 1994, the State Council carried out pilot changes to the basic medical social insurance scheme for urban employees established in the 1950s. The first health sector reform was the creation of the Urban Employee Basic Medical Insurance (UEBMI) in 1998.[20] The UEBMI covered those eligible under the older GIS and LIS schemes set up in the 1950s (see Chapter 2): employees in private and state-owned enterprises, government, social organizations, and nonprofits.

UEBMI employs three primary forms of insurance payment: (1) "integrated social pooling" and individual medical savings accounts for the formally employed; (2) "solitary social pooling" accounts for the informally employed; and (3) "lower-level social pooling" accounts for migrant workers (see below). The Social Insurance Law, enforced by the Ministry of Human Resources and

Social Security (MoHRSS), stipulates that all enterprises and employees must participate in UEBMI. However, enforcement is difficult for informal and migrant workers due to the lack of control on self-identification.[21]

For the formally employed, the integrated social pooling works like an employer-based insurance scheme consisting of both an individual account and social pooling with fixed contribution rates set by the central government. The premium is collected in the form of a payroll tax where employers contribute 6 percent and employees contribute 2 percent. UEBMI pools risk at the municipal rather than the firm level and thereby provides more stable financing. This evokes the principal of *community rating*, where the government rates all people in a community (municipality) at the same rate based on salary and thus the same premium. All contributions from employees are put into personal medical savings accounts while employer contributions are divided into two parts: 70 percent is placed in a pooled fund and 30 percent is placed in the individual employees' personal medical savings account. The individual account is used to cover employee outpatient expenses, emergency services, and outpatient drug costs; the pooled fund covers inpatient costs (with restrictions). Taxation levels vary with the local economic environment: Shanghai levies the highest tax at 10 percent for employers and 2 percent for employees.[22]

The solitary social pooling fund applies to the informally employed such as retirees, employees of ailing enterprises, and workers with partial or flexible employment. These individuals only pay premiums for the social pooling accounts and have no individual medical savings accounts. Due to difficulty in verifying eligible employees, contributions are based on the average salary in the region. A similar insurance scheme, the lower-level social pooling, was established for migrant workers because of their lower income. These require lower employer and employee contributions, which are based on average salary levels in that region and have no individual medical savings accounts.[23]

Despite heterogeneity in insurance payment, the UEBMI offers the most comprehensive coverage of the existing insurance schemes: deductibles average

3 percent of an employee's annual salary, while the coverage ceiling is roughly six times the employee's salary. The co-payment percentage is lower for primary care and secondary care received at lower-level hospitals in order to mitigate moral hazard. Retiree co-payments are about half that of regular full-time employees, lessening the financial burden on retirees.[24] In 2011, around 79 percent of the fund went to pay for inpatient treatment, while deductibles and outpatient medical costs were paid from personal accounts or out of pocket.[25] UEBMI has thus played a significant role in reducing individual out-of-pocket health expenditures.

By 2012, UEBMI covered approximately 95 percent of the eligible population.[26] As expected, the rapid expansion in UEBMI enrollment and coverage has been accompanied by an enormous increase in insurance funds: between 1998 and 2012, fund revenues rose from 1.95 billion RMB to 696.2 billion RMB.[27] The bulk of premium contributions came from employers (73 percent) and employees (21 percent), with smaller contributions from government financing (3 percent) and other income (3 percent). Despite these achievements, challenges in financing, management, and coverage persist and continue to impact the quality of care delivered (see below).

NCMS

After the initiation of UEBMI in the late 1990s, the Chinese government addressed the large inequalities in rural insurance through the creation of the New Cooperative Medical Scheme (NCMS) in 2003. This replaced the Cooperative Medical Scheme (CMS) of rural health financing system. The NCMS sought to provide low-cost, basic healthcare services, including inpatient, catastrophic, and some types of outpatient care.[28] By the end of 2008, NCMS covered 93 percent of the rural population in China.[29]

The NCMS is funded jointly by beneficiaries, county government, and the central government. Under broad guidelines issued by the central government, the NCMS is operated at the county level by the local bureau of health; as a result, program design and benefit packages vary geographically. A typical package involves a modest household medical

savings account (MSA) for outpatient expenditures and a social pooling account for inpatient expenses with high deductibles; overall, coverage is typically shallow.[30] In 2012, average premium contributions were around 300 RMB; in 2014, the per capita premium was around 410 RMB. Central and local governments contributed 320 RMB ($50), while individuals contributed 90 RMB ($15).[31] This varies greatly by region: poorer regions of western and central China rely more on the central government, while the affluent local governments of eastern China are able to contribute more.

The insurance fund is mainly used for hospitalizations and outpatient expenses incurred in the treatment of critical diseases. Reimbursement levels reached 70 percent in 2011, while the coverage ceiling increased to six times the net annual income of rural residents, providing greater financial protection.[32] However, given the shallow funding, many counties do not cover outpatient services at all. Moreover, the co-payment for inpatient services can be almost 60 percent and the deductible around 500 RMB – large amounts by rural Chinese standards.[33] Thus, the NCMS still leaves low-income enrollees exposed to large financial risks.[34] While the NCMS is designed as a modern substitute for the CMS, in reality most rural residents cannot afford the up-front payment for major illnesses and do not understand how to get reimbursed on the back end after treatment.

As an illustration, researchers studied NCMS financing of inpatient care in Longyou County from 2004 to 2012.[35] Similar to UEBMI, the deductible varies by hospital level (class): township hospital (300 RMB), special hospital (600 RMB), and county hospital (1,000 RMB). In Longyou County, the average government contribution was 260 RMB, compared to the average individual contribution of 120 RMB. For NCMS insured inpatients, the average expenditure per admission rose from 4,389 RMB in 2004 to 6,853 RMB by 2012. By comparison, the average expenditure per admission for UEBMI enrollees rose from 7,799 RMB in 2004 to 8,456 RMB in 2012. Spending by both groups has increased over time, yet a large gap still remains in reimbursement levels. The average reimbursement rate under NCMS rose from 12.9 percent in 2004 to 51.3 percent in 2012; the average reimbursement rate for UEBMI enrollees rose from 51.7 percent in 2003 to 76.1 percent in 2012. These differences are important: Longyou County is far below the mandatory reimbursement ceiling of 70 percent.

URBMI

UEBMI covered 64 percent of the urban employed, but only 31 percent of the total urban population. Following the implementation of UEBMI and NCMS, 420 million urban residents remained ineligible for health insurance by 2007, mostly due to employment in the informal sector of the economy. This led to the creation of Urban Resident Basic Medical Insurance (URBMI) in 2007 to cover informal labor and the urban unemployed (children, students, the elderly, and disabled) who had not been covered by the UEBMI. Unlike UEBMI, the URBMI program is voluntary, but has achieved a high level of coverage because of large government subsidies that have increased annually since 2007. Individual contributions have not increased significantly, meaning that government subsidies make up over 80 percent of the total fund.[36]

The URBMI is managed by the MoHRSS. It follows a policy framework similar to UEBMI with respect to administration and social pooling, provider payment, and management of insurance funds: URBMI pools risk at the municipal/prefectural level. The major difference is that the URBMI by design has no medical savings account and consists of only a social pooling account. Furthermore, the benefits package of URBMI is shallower than the UEBMI and includes only hospitalization and catastrophic illness. However, the goal of URBMI is to cover catastrophic events and thereby prevent medically induced poverty; it does not focus on preventative care, though some cities cover outpatient services for chronic diseases (i.e., diabetes). Based on 2008 data from pilot cities, inpatient deductibles ranged from 0 RMB to 2,700 RMB, while reimbursement caps ranged from 25,000 RMB to 100,000 RMB.[37]

Table 11.1 compares the various features of UEBMI, NCMS, and URBMI. Figure 11.1 depicts their respective coverage levels, reimbursement rates, and fund surpluses over the period from 2011 to 2014.

Medical Assistance Program

In addition to UEBMI, NCMS, and URBMI, the government launched the Medical Assistance (MA) program to cover catastrophic health expenses for the poor (as well as a $2 billion Rural Health Services Construction and Development Program to develop rural health infrastructure and equipment).[38] Separate rural and urban pilot MA programs were launched in 2003 and 2005, and then expanded nationwide in 2006 and 2008. The MA program initially provided a subsistence allowance to low-income elderly and disabled residents, but transitioned to fund comprehensive care for the poor. The MA program pays a portion of the medical bill that is not reimbursed by the NCMS and URBMI. The Ministry of Civil Affairs manages the MA program and pools risk through its county level bureau.[39]

Enrollment in MA is free and voluntary. In 2009, urban and rural MA programs covered 93.4 million poor residents. Approximately one-third of enrollees are urban poor (30.7 million, or 4.9 percent of urban residents); the remaining 62.7 million are rural poor (8.8 percent of rural residents).[40] Central, provincial, and county governments heavily finance the MA program's budget; the central government's share (15 billion RMB) increased to 80 percent in 2011.[41] There are also supplementary contributions from townships, lotteries, donations, and development assistance.

In 2011, MA paid the premiums for 5.8 percent of NCMS enrollees (48.3 million people) and the premiums for 7 percent of URBMI enrollees (15.5 million people). In so doing, the MA program increased the coverage rate of the NCMS and URBMI. However, once the poor were enrolled in the health insurance schemes, only one-third of them received financial assistance paying for medical bills (1.8 percent of NCMS, 3 percent of URBMI). Expanded coverage is needed to provide more financial protection to the poor.

Coverage Gaps

Expansions of these programs, along with investments in infrastructure, technology, and personnel, resulted in near-universal coverage by 2012.

Table 11.1 Comparison of UEBMI, NCMS, and URBMI

	UEBMI	NCMS	URBMI
Overseeing ministry	MoHRSS	MOH/NHFPC	MoHRSS
Year of pilot/formal launch	1994/1998	2003/2006	2007/2009
Target population	Urban	Rural	Urban unemployed, elderly, students, children
Level of pooling	Prefecture/municipality	County	Prefecture/municipality
No. of risk pools (approx.)	330	2,566	330
Enrollment rate (%)	95	98.3	92.4
Unit of enrollment	Individuals	Households	Individuals
Type of enrollment	Compulsory	Voluntary	Voluntary
Total revenue (100 million RMB)	6,061.9	2,484.7	876.8
Enrollees (millions, 2013)	274	802	296
Enrolled as percent of total population	19.6	59.5	20.1
Per capita premium (RMB)	2,287.51	308.5	322.35
Fund financing	8% of employees' monthly payroll (2% from employee, 6% from employer)	Central and local governments contribute 80–90% of premium, individuals contribute remainder	Minimum government subsidies 40 RMB per person per year (average subsidies increased to 280 RMB in 2013 but varies by city)
Expenditures (100 million RMB)	4,868.5	2,408	675.1
Benefits package	Inpatient and outpatient care	Inpatient and critical outpatient care	Inpatient and critical outpatient care
Mandated reimbursement :			
inpatient care	No	70%	75%
actual inpatient rates	<88.5%	<50%	<48%
outpatient care	No	No	No
mandated reimbursement ceiling	No less than six times the local worker's annual average wage, and national annual average less than 60,000 RMB	No less than eight times the income of a farmer, and no less than 60,000 RMB	No less than six times a local resident's annual disposable income, and no less than 60,000 RMB

Source: Adapted from China Statistical Yearbook 2013, McKinsey, and multiple sources.
Notes
- Revenue of the insurance program refers to payments made by employers and individuals participating in the medical care insurance program in accordance with the basis and proportion stipulated in state regulations, and income from other sources that become source of medical insurance fund, including income paid by units, individual paid income, financial assistance's income (including individual income from medicaid), financial subsidies' income, interest income, and other income.
- The total population of China was 1.354 billion in 2012.
- Expenditure of the insurance program refers to payment made to people covered in basic medical care insurance program within the scope and standards of expenditure according to related national policies and medical care payment and other expenses, including medical expenses of hospital inpatients, medical expenses for outpatients and emergency patients, payment from individual accounts, and other expenditure.

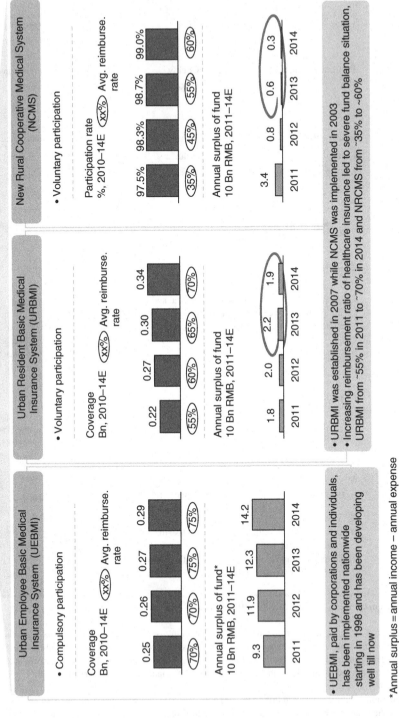

*Annual surplus = annual income – annual expense

Figure 11.1 Coverage, reimbursement, and fund surplus of UEBMI, URBMI, and NCMS

Source: Statistical Yearbook of NHFP (2009–2014); General Office of the State Council; National Bureau of Statistics.

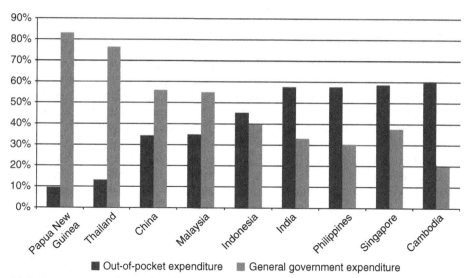

Figure 11.2 Government and out-of-pocket spending on health as a percent of total health expenditures in select countries, 2012
Source: World Health Organization Global Health Expenditure Database.

Moreover, following the expected pattern, higher government spending led to lower out-of-pocket spending (as a percentage of the total spending on healthcare). Compared to other Asian countries, China's out-of-pocket spending is at the lower end of the distribution (see Figure 11.2). Out-of-pocket spending still comprised 35 percent of total health expenditures by 2012, though this has decreased considerably from the 60 percent level of 2001.[42]

According to the World Health Organization (WHO), households are protected from catastrophic health payments only when the average out-of-pocket payment falls below 15–20 percent of total health expenditures.[43] China's out-of-pocket payment percentage is almost twice this amount. This high burden disproportionately affects the low-income and rural populations, whose out-of-pocket costs for intensive treatment can easily exceed annual disposable income.[44] This could be attributed to relatively low reimbursement caps and rates, high deductibles and co-payments, and provider incentives to over-prescribe drugs and over-utilize technology. The problem is exacerbated by large geographic variations in coverage, subsidies, and reimbursement rates.

Despite accomplishing near-universal health insurance, the Chinese people still protest "Kan bing gui, kan bing nan": the perception that

healthcare is expensive and hard to get. Many surveys find widespread dissatisfaction with medical care and affordability.[45] This is because the coverage is "wide but shallow," creating a state of underinsurance for most low- to middle-income families.[46] In other words, despite universal health insurance, the financial protection provided by the benefit plans is insufficient. As seen in Figure 1.2, per capita health expenditures have increased considerably, while out-of-pocket spending has remained high.

Inequities in Financial Risk Protection

These aggregate numbers obscure the large disparities in the out-of-pocket spending levels between urban and rural populations and across China's provinces. In a sample of 13 provinces, rural residents paid 50 percent of total health spending out of pocket, while the urban population paid 36 percent (2011 data).[47] In Longyou County, out-of-pocket spending among NCMS insured inpatients decreased from 88.8 percent in 2004 to 45.3 percent in 2012. Nevertheless, their out-of-pocket burden was still higher than the national average (35 percent) and that of UEBMI insured inpatients, whose out-of-pocket spending decreased from 48.3 percent to 23.9 percent during the same period.[48]

Furthermore, the ratio of out-of-pocket spending to disposable personal income remains high and is expected to increase.[49] In 2008, out-of-pocket spending for inpatient care amounted to 56 percent of the income of an NCMS enrollee and 38.2 percent of the income of a URBMI enrollee. In addition, illness-related poverty rose from 30 percent in 2003 to 34.5 percent in 2008; of this amount, 9.2 percent was due to catastrophic health expenses.[50] This reflects the fact that NCMS and URBMI only cover severe illnesses, leaving the insured the responsibility to pay for basic healthcare and outpatient care. Therefore, despite widespread access, the cost of care continues to burden the lower income population.

Government data suggest that out-of-pocket spending per outpatient visit and inpatient stay has not decreased and that the risk of catastrophic spending has increased.[51] The joint phenomena of augmented insurance coverage and higher risk of catastrophic spending are due to moral hazard. Insurance makes healthcare cheaper, and thereby encourages people to not only seek care when sick but also seek care from higher-level (and higher-cost) hospitals.[52] Since 2010, service coverage has increased, but URBMI and NCMS beneficiaries still bear responsibility for more than 50 percent of their inpatient expenditure and 60–70 percent of their outpatient expenditure (taking into account deductibles, co-payments, and reimbursement ceilings).

The government now aims to reduce the co-payment for inpatient services to 30 percent.[53] However, this intervention may not be sufficient, especially for the poorest enrollees. Recent studies show that patients with higher medical bills received lower reimbursement rates; moreover, the incidence of catastrophic medical payment is highest among the poorest areas and the lowest quintiles of wealth.[54] This suggests that social insurance fails to provide adequate risk protection to the people most at risk.

Benefit Plan

Insurance plan benefits can be very limited, often covering only hospitalizations and outpatient care for critical and chronic diseases. Exclusion of general outpatient care, which is fundamental to the prevention and treatment of non-communicable diseases, reduces the effectiveness of financial risk protection.[55] As a result, the government has prioritized benefit expansion. From 2008 to 2010, the percent of local benefit plans including general outpatient care increased from 12.5 percent to 57.5 percent for URBMI, and from 29.1 percent to 78.8 percent under NCMS.[56]

Additionally, the government is trying to expand benefit options to focus on cancer, common ailments, and preventative medicine. For example, in 2010, co-payments were reduced for the following priority diseases: hypertension, diabetes, cirrhosis, nephritis, arthritis, asthma, cancer, and cardiovascular disease. The government has also heavily subsidized hospital maternity services in an effort to reduce infant and maternal mortality.[57]

Financing and Management

There are 2,800 NCMS offices responsible for collecting premiums, managing funds, contracting providers, and reimbursing patients. Such complexity has bred bureaucratic inefficiency in fund management. The offices receive government per capita subsidies through the Ministry of Finance, which transfers budgets to the designated bank account held by the county Bureau of Finance. Unfortunately, the process of earmarked transfers from central to local government is usually prolonged and unmonitored.[58] This leads to funding delays from 3 to 12 months. As a result, service providers often wait long periods before receiving reimbursement for their services.

Similarly, county level variations in claims processing leaves patients vulnerable to large out-of-pocket costs. In many counties, enrollees have to pay the full bill upfront and then submit claims to get reimbursed by the NCMS office, the Bureau of Human Resources, or other government agencies at their city/county of enrollment.[59] This can be difficult for rural or migrant workers who live and work in different areas, especially when reimbursement offices have limited hours of operation. These factors have reduced the number of beneficiaries willing or able to submit claims.[60] By contrast, other counties require patients to pay their share of the bill at the time of discharge.

Provider Reimbursement Issues

The predominant reimbursement model in China is fee for service (FFS): the services rendered by providers to enrollees are unbundled and paid for separately. This model incentivizes physicians to focus on quantity over quality, and to see more patients (volume) and provide more treatments per visit (intensity), often unnecessarily. FFS also de-emphasizes the provision of preventative care, since such care generates little reimbursement from insurers and little demand from patients.[61] FFS is associated with increased access to care, since providers do not have an incentive to turn away patients. However, an inadequate supply of qualified providers combined with rising demand across all age and income groups has constricted access in the country.

The FFS system received an enormous boost in the 1980s and 1990s as the government began to reduce its funding of public hospital operating costs. To compensate for the lost subsidies, the government allowed providers to charge payers more than average cost for certain services, such as prescription drugs and high technology diagnostic and surgical procedures, while keeping necessary services at or below average cost.[62] This allowance, combined with the FFS payment model, led Chinese hospitals to increase investment in high technology medicine and incentivize their physicians to utilize it.

An alternative reimbursement system to substitute for FFS and its distorted incentives is "prospective payment": providers receive a fixed, predetermined payment regardless of the intensity of the actual services they render. This gives providers an incentive to lower utilization, since providers retain the difference between the fixed payment and their costs. Hainan Province implemented prospective payment on a trial basis in six high-cost hospitals. The new payment model led to a slower rate of growth of expenditures on services that were profitable under FFS, particularly expensive drugs and high-technology procedures.[63] Prospective payment can also include some distorted incentives: cream skimming (seeking out healthier patients), shirking (reducing services provided to sick patients), and dumping (explicitly avoiding sick patients) to keep costs low.[64]

Another alternative to FFS is to pay physicians a salary plus a bonus (see Chapter 7). Because physicians not only diagnose illness but also provide medical care, salaried payment might limit the FFS incentive to over-utilize care. At the same time, a bonus tied to quality and productivity metrics would counteract any tendency under strictly salaried payment to work less or do less.

A pilot study conducted in rural Guizhou Province in southwest China tested the impact of this payment model. The FFS system for village doctors in the NCMS program was replaced by salary plus bonus payment for doctors achieving quality and performance goals.[65] Moreover, village doctors could no longer supplement their income by dispensing drugs. The study found that the new payment model reduced spending, curbed unnecessary care for healthier patients, and decreased the prescribing of unnecessary drugs. However, doctors referred sicker patients to township and county facilities, where costs were higher. As a result, total healthcare spending was not significantly reduced.

The pilot studies described above are just two examples of the multiple payment reforms under way that seek to curb rising healthcare costs. Since the 1990s, many efforts have been undertaken to shift away from the traditional FFS system. As of 2011, more than 70 percent of counties/cities had experimented with new methods such as prospective payment and capitation.[66] Each method (FFS, salary, capitation, prospective payment) has its own strengths and weaknesses in terms of addressing the challenges of the iron triangle. Figure 11.3 depicts the relative merits of physician payment methods, while Figure 11.4 depicts the merits of hospital payment methods. Such experiments have not led to a fundamental, national change in provider reimbursement or incentives.

One exception is the implementation of an Essential Drugs List (EDL) and zero-markup drug policy (see Chapters 2 and 4). Historically, providers sold drugs directly to patients with a 15 percent markup over the acquisition price. This phenomenon was known as "yi yao yang yi": compensation for hospital medical costs through drug-selling profits.[67] To correct this practice – and its incentive to over-prescribe drugs (which accounts for more

	Fee for service (FFS)	Salary	Capitation
Quality	Same observed quality as found in capitation Incentive to provide lots of services and over-utilize Patients are more satisfied	Likely the same quality No incentive to: • over-utilize or under-use • skimp on quality • provide higher quality	Same observed quality as found in FFS Possible incentive to under-utilize Patients are less satisfied
Access	Easy to access provider Rewards volume Render more services Lower wait times	Possibly better access than capitation but less than FFS Volume same/lower than FFS Perhaps better access than under capitation No incentive to restrict access	Harder to access provider and longer wait times Disincentivizes volume: • Fewer hospital services • More provider services • Higher wait times • Use of gate-keeper provider May incent preventive care May disincent referrals
Cost	Highest cost and volume Provider has no incentive to cut cost	Lowest utilization of the three models... but Provider has no incentive to cut cost	Lower volume versus FFS: • Lower cost of hospital care • Higher cost of provider care • Lower costs overall Provider has incentive to cut cost

Figure 11.3 Iron triangle impacts of physician reimbursement

than 40 percent of hospital revenue)[68] – the government required physicians to prescribe only drugs on the EDL and sell them at wholesale prices with no markup in 2012. This initiative was accompanied by a purchaser (insurer) intervention, which increased the patient reimbursement rate for essential medicines by 10 percent. The Ministry of Health published an updated EDL in 2013 that includes a subset of drugs (317 chemical medicines and biological products, 203 Chinese patent medicines) from the National Drug Reimbursement List.[69] Initial studies of the reform report favorable results: a reduction in unnecessary drug dispensing, a 25 percent increase in outpatient visits, and a decrease in drug-related revenue.[70]

Evolution of Private Health Insurance in China

Role of Private Health Insurance

Given the gaps left by public insurance and general dissatisfaction with insurance coverage, a strong private health insurance (PHI) sector could emerge to relieve the burden of out-of-pocket payments. PHI can reinforce existing public insurance by offering complementary or supplementary insurance, as well as promote competition with public insurance by providing comprehensive primary insurance. Additionally, private insurance could provide primary health coverage for wealthier segments of the populations, freeing up limited government resources to provide public health insurance for low-income individuals.[71] However, such an insurance scheme has yet to gain traction in China.

Compared to Latin America, Africa, the Middle East, and Eastern Europe, Asia presents a particular challenge and opportunity for private coverage. According to the WHO, out-of-pocket expenditures account for the highest share of total health spending in the Asian region, while private insurance comprises the lowest amount of total health spending.[72] As seen in Figure 11.5, despite the country's status as an upper-middle-income country and the world's second largest economy, China's expenditures on PHI as a share of total expenditures are low. What is even more striking is that the PHI in China has been in a fledgling stage since the early

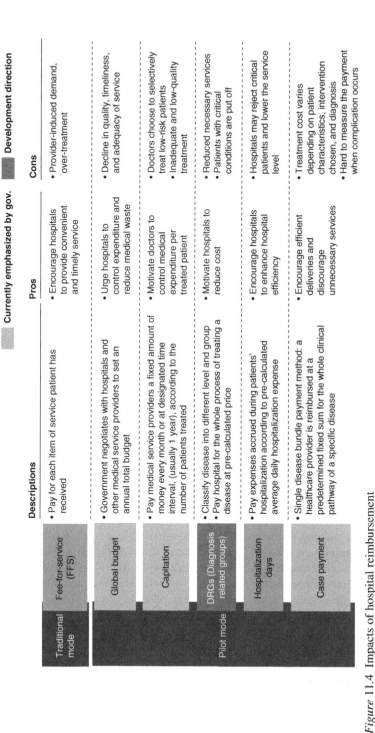

Legend: Currently emphasized by gov. | Development direction

Mode		Descriptions	Pros	Cons
Traditional mode	Fee-for-service (FFS)	• Pay for each item of service patient has received	• Encourage hospitals to provide convenient and timely service	• Provider-induced demand, over-treatment
	Global budget	• Government negotiates with hospitals and other medical service providers to set an annual total budget	• Urge hospitals to control expenditure and reduce medical waste	• Decline in quality, timeliness, and adequacy of service
	Capitation	• Pay medical service providers a fixed amount of money every month or at designated time interval, (usually 1 year), according to the number of patients treated	• Motivate doctors to control medical expenditure per treated patient	• Doctors choose to selectively treat low-risk patients • Inadequate and low-quality treatment
Pilot mode	DRGs (Diagnosis related groups)	• Classify disease into different level and group • Pay hospital for the whole process of treating a disease at pre-calculated price	• Motivate hospitals to reduce cost	• Reduced necessary services • Patients with critical conditions are put off
	Hospitalization days	• Pay expenses accrued during patients' hospitalization according to pre-calculated average daily hospitalization expense	• Encourage hospitals to enhance hospital efficiency	• Hospitals may reject critical patients and lower the service level
	Case payment	• Single disease bundle payment method: a healthcare provider is reimbursed at a predetermined fixed sum for the whole clinical pathway of a specific disease	• Encourage efficient deliveries and discourage unnecessary services	• Treatment cost varies depending on patient characteristics, intervention chosen, and diagnosis • Hard to measure the payment when complication occurs

Figure 11.4 Impacts of hospital reimbursement
Source: Literature review, expert interview.

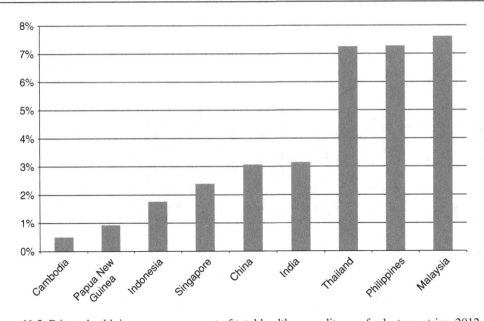

Figure 11.5 Private health insurance as percent of total health expenditures of select countries, 2012
Source: World Health Organization Global Health Expenditure Database.

1990s: the sector has enjoyed little growth, particularly when compared to other domestic insurance markets such as life and property insurance. In 2013, private health insurance revenue in China was $18 billion, less than one-fifth of the $101 billion in revenue from property insurance and less than one-eighth of the $153 billion in revenue from life insurance companies.[73]

The composition (e.g., forms and functions) of PHI hinges on the available public insurance schemes, the delivery system, and the culture and history of medical practice.[74] The main demand and supply barriers to PHI development include regulatory hurdles, heterogeneous actuarial standards, cultural barriers, insufficient medical data, and inability to contract with providers. Once these issues are resolved, PHI may grow alongside the rising demand for healthcare (and quality healthcare, per the "healthcare quadrilemma" presented in Chapter 1) in China.

Indeed, both public and private insurers face demand-side pressure as healthcare costs increase, as China's socioeconomic and health indicators improve, and as China's disease profile evolves. Between 2000 and 2012, disposable income per capita rose from 6,280 RMB to 24,565 RMB for urban households and from 2,253 RMB to 7,917

RMB for rural households, while health expenditures of urban households rose from 318 RMB to 1,064 RMB. Life expectancy at birth has also dramatically increased from approximately 40 to 70 years in the past half century, although progress has slowed.[75] Finally, the ailments of the Chinese people are evolving from communicable diseases to chronic conditions (e.g., respiratory and heart disease) which require more specialized, expensive, and managed care.[76]

Before the mid-1990s, there were no PHI companies in China.[77] They eventually formed as segments of life insurance companies, as in many developing nations.[78] As a result, much of the private healthcare coverage that individuals obtained was bundled with life or accident insurance products.[79] Bundled services constitute affordable add-ons to enrollees in normal life insurance policies and help insurers to reduce financial risk by increasing the size of the pool of consumers. Consequently, this type of health insurance mostly served as supplementary insurance for people covered by public health insurance.

However, these bundled services are very restrictive and do not offer much financial protection. The most common bundled offerings are accident

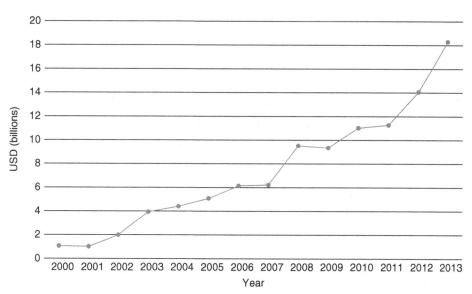

Figure 11.6 Annual private health insurance premium income
Source: China Insurance Yearbook 2013.

insurance and short-term health insurance, neither of which offers meaningful coverage if there is no accident or catastrophic illness. Additionally, many long-term care plans pay a lump sum payout to insurees who contract a severe disease, but no coverage of routine or preventative services.[80]

In 1999, there were 26 life insurance companies offering commercial health insurance, which covered only 5 million people.[81] Since then, annual private health insurance premium income rose rapidly but was still modest until after 2003 (see Figure 11.6). Yet even in 2003, PHI premiums accounted for only 3.6 percent of national healthcare expenditures and 6.3 percent of total insurance revenue.[82]

The China Insurance Regulation Commission (CIRC) regulates insurance companies. In terms of total insurance revenue, eight domestic companies controlled 96.3 percent of the market in 2004.[83] The largest insurance companies were China Life Insurance Company (55 percent share), Ping An Life Insurance (17 percent), and Pacific Life Insurance (11 percent).[84] All three are life insurance companies offering bundled health insurance packages; by contrast, the first companies to focus strictly on health insurance were not founded until after 2004 (see below).

In terms of numbers, the majority of insurance companies in 2004 were foreign-owned. Among the foreign firms, American International Assurance (AIA) was the largest life insurance company offering health insurance, with 1.5 percent market share in 2004.[85] The other foreign-owned companies commanded less than 1 percent of the market.[86] It is thus evident that foreign-owned companies have played a minor role in PHI development, primarily because government regulatory policy did not fully support the entry of private insurers.[87]

This situation has slowly changed. In 2001, China entered the World Trade Organization (WTO); in 2002, the Chinese government passed the Foreign Insurance Company Regulatory Law. This allowed joint ventures with increasing levels of foreign ownership: up to 50 percent foreign ownership before 2004 and up to 51 percent beginning in 2004. The law also stipulated a minimum total asset base for the insurer ($5 billion) and the local insurance broker ($500 million). In addition, the foreign insurer must have more than 30 years of established experience in a WTO member country.[88] As a result, only very large international corporations could qualify, thereby continuing to limit the entry of foreign insurers.

Insurer-Consumer Tension

While these supply-side barriers have limited the growth of China's PHI sector, demand factors have also stunted demand for insurance. One key factor is culture: "Chinese are not used to the concept of insurance and as a consequence, it is very difficult for the citizens to voluntarily pay the premiums up front and bear the risk of not using it at all."[89] According to the head of the China office for insurer British United Provident Association, trying to convince consumers of the benefit of paying premiums now for care later, rather than saving to pay for care as they do now, is a hard sell. Those who can't afford better care than that offered by the government won't be able to afford private insurance; those whose income is sufficient to buy supplemental coverage can typically afford to pay for care out-of-pocket anyway.[90] There is thus limited demand for PHI in both income groups.

Another barrier to demand for PHI is the high cost. A lack of reliable data on the health status of the population makes it difficult for insurers to offer customized benefit plans at an affordable price. Premiums must be adjusted to account for health risks; without sufficient data and historical claims experience, insurance schemes set high premiums to avoid losses on claims. Consequently, for the majority of the population, premiums exceed disposable income, leaving a small pool of potential enrollees to spread the risk. This potentially subjects private insurers to adverse selection whereby those who expect high medical costs select into high coverage plans.

Insurers impose many restrictions and limitations to mitigate adverse selection. For example, starting in 2004, most private insurers required enrollees to buy life insurance prior to health insurance. Insurers also limited coverage to those under the ages of 60–65, initiated waiting periods of three to six months before processing claims, and enforced a stop-loss ceiling on reimbursement.[91] In addition, insurance companies might discontinue insurance coverage in the year following reimbursement of a major claim, even for policies covering catastrophic diseases.[92] Such efforts to address adverse selection ultimately create dislike of insurers (as in the United States), engender distrust between consumers and insurers, and hinder prospective consumers from purchasing insurance. According to

economists at the World Bank, Chinese consumers have an unfavorable image of the private health insurance industry. They believe the industry does not really protect them against major financial loss when a major illness occurs or remove financial barriers for patients seeking healthcare services.

As noted above, only a small portion of the Chinese population has purchased PHI coverage. In 2004, the World Bank conducted a household survey in four cities in two provinces to study the determinants of PHI enrollment. Workers in government or state-run institutions were less likely to purchase PHI, while self-employed individuals or private sector individuals were more likely to purchase PHI. Moreover, the purchase of PHI by those with public insurance is infrequent; that is, private health insurance in China is not a supplement to public health insurance. PHI purchase was higher among individuals under 60 (which is expected given insurance age restrictions on PHI), the better educated, those in poor to fair health (evidence of adverse selection), and those in the top income quartile.

The World Bank also surveyed the population's willingness to pay for health insurance. Heads of households were asked about their hypothetical willingness to pay for three different insurance programs: major catastrophic disease insurance (covering 80 percent of expenditures on a catastrophic illness), inpatient expenses insurance (covering 100 percent of services), and outpatient expenses insurance (covering 60 percent of services). They found that respondents preferred coverage for inpatient services (48 percent of sample), followed by catastrophic insurance (43 percent), and then outpatient services (24 percent); for such coverage, they were willing to pay an associated mean monthly premium of 68.1 RMB, 42.9 RMB, and 37.8 RMB, respectively. For respondents in the top income quintile, the inpatient premium constituted 8 percent of income, while the catastrophic premium constituted 5 percent of income. By contrast, among the lowest income quintile, the monthly inpatient premium represented 50 percent of income, while the catastrophic premium represented 30 percent of income. Given this willingness to pay, only the top income quintile would be able to afford PHI.

It should be noted, however, that all insurance demand curves were inelastic: the estimated price elasticity of demand was –0.271 for catastrophic coverage, –0.342 for inpatient coverage, and –0.412 for outpatient coverage. This indicates that catastrophic and inpatient coverage would be the priority in PHI, but only the wealthiest in the country would afford it.[93]

In summary, from its inception in the 1990s to the introduction of health reforms in 2003, PHI in China did not experience significant development. Growth was stymied by regulatory hurdles imposed on insurance companies, the lack of viable private insurance options for consumers, and mistrust of insurers. A parallel problem has been the general lack of public insurance options, especially for the lower income population, despite the great need for protection against rising healthcare costs.

Private Health Insurers Today

Domestic Insurers

The government's difficulty in solving the iron triangle of healthcare – providing affordable, accessible, and high quality healthcare – has rekindled interest in privatization. Domestically, private businesses own an increasing number of the country's urban outpatient clinics and hospitals; in 2011,

investors built 1,372 new private hospitals. In September 2013, China launched an experimental "free trade zone" in Shanghai, allowing (a) foreign and private investment in financial institutions, medical services, and health insurers; (b) direct entry by private health insurers; and (c) full foreign ownership of hospitals.[94]

The shortcomings of public insurance, the increasing focus on privatization, and the growing demand for quality healthcare would suggest that the PHI market is poised to take off in China. Indeed, the number of health insurance plans in the market increased from around 300 to more than 1,000 between 2008 and 2012, as did their total premiums (see Table 11.2).[95] In 2013, the premium income from commercial/PHI totaled $18.23 billion, an increase of 30.2 percent over the prior year.[96] As depicted in Figure 11.7, this growth is encouraging. Nevertheless, PHI growth pales in comparison to the growth in premium revenue from property and life insurance companies ($100.8 billion and $152.9 billion in 2013, respectively).[97]

Profitability has also been a challenge. The four local insurers marketing only PHI have struggled to stay afloat. In 2012, all independent health insurers lost money (see Table 11.3). It is important to point

Table 11.2 Premium revenue for the top domestic health insurers ($ millions)

Health Insurance Company	2009	2010	2011	2012	2013
PICC Health Insurance	$292.9	$267.2	$436.7	$867.2	$845.5
Kunlun Health Insurance	$13.7	$15.2	$13.1	$53.0	$66.1
Ping An Health Insurance	$10.8	$10.1	$21.4	$34.4	$50.2
Hexie Health Insurance (Harmony)	$4.4	$0.5	$0.3	$3.5	$16.1

Source: Company annual reports.

Table 11.3 Top domestic private health insurers, 2012 ($ millions)

Health Insurance Company	Total Income in 2012	Total Benefits, Claims, and Expenses in 2012	Operating Profits in 2012
PICC Health Insurance	$1,033.44	$1,154.42	–$121.03
Kunlun Health Insurance	$63.06	$83.53	–$20.47
Hexie Health Insurance	$34.23	$88.17	–$53.94
Ping An Health Insurance	$29.39	$40.41	–$11.02

Note: Total income includes net earned premiums, reinsurance commission income, investment income, and other income. Total benefits, claims, and expenses include claims and policyholder benefits, handling charges and commissions, finance costs, and other operating and administrative expenses.
Sources: Company annual reports, China Insurance Yearbook 2013.

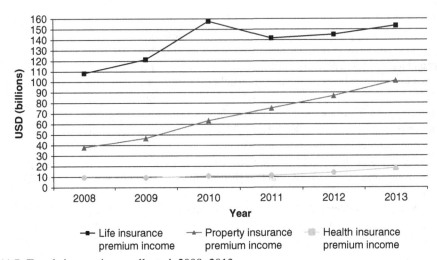

Figure 11.7 Trends in premiums collected, 2008–2013
Source: China Insurance Yearbook 2013 and 2013 Insurance Statistics Report. Conversion from Yuan to USD, exchange rate of .162823.

out these data are from the health insurance subsidiary only; the parent companies of these insurers also provide life insurance that offers short and long-term health insurance bundled into life insurance plans. PICC Health Insurance has the greatest market share but also the largest losses. PICC's parent company, the People's Insurance Company of China Limited, added 1 billion RMB (US$154.4 million) in 2011 to boost the health insurer's solvency ratio above 150 percent.[98]

It is also important to note that these companies are relatively young. PICC was founded in 2004, Ping An in 2005, Kunlun in 2006, and Hexie Health in 2006. Typical of health insurers in China, they also offer very specific insurance packages. PICC currently offers children's medical coverage, accidental individual injury, hospital expense reimbursement, supplemental specialist services, lifelong dread disease, and long-term care insurance plans. The recency of such specialized benefits suggests growing demand for more benefits.[99] Many health insurers are beginning to explicitly cater to foreigners, as well as the residents of Hong Kong, Macao, and Taiwan.[100] For example, Ping An offers bilingual customer services.

Ping An has pursued growth along a number of avenues. It entered into a joint venture in August 2010 with Discovery, the largest health insurer in South Africa. Discovery provides Ping An its financial support and expertise as a strategic investor.[101] With the help of Discovery, Ping An Health has taken steps to focus on the mid-to-high-end medical insurance business by introducing new products such as the "Vitality" program, which focuses on preventive health by rewarding members for making healthy choices. As a result, Ping An Health is the largest writer of new business in the high-end group market.[102] Such business development efforts have enabled Ping An to increase its premium income by 46 percent between 2012 and 2013 (from $34 million to $50 million).[103] Ping An's life insurance branch also bundles long-term care insurance into its life insurance offering for a fixed monthly fee and covers specific catastrophic illnesses such as cancer. Its 2013 premium revenue for long-term insurance was $2.37 billion – an amount 47 times greater than the income from its entire health insurance subsidiary.

Thus, despite the rapid growth of independent health insurance companies, companies that bundle their health insurance offerings with other insurance services produce much higher revenues. As of 2013, the largest life insurers offering health insurance are the China Life Insurance Company (CLIC)

(30.4 percent market share), Ping An Life (13.6 percent), New China Life Insurance Company (9.6 percent), China Pacific Life Insurance (8.9 percent), and PICC Life Insurance Company (7.0 percent). The largest property insurers offering health insurance include subsidiaries of these same companies: PICC (34.9 percent share), Ping An (17.9 percent), and China Pacific (12.6 percent). Life insurance companies tend to offer supplementary health insurance and long-term health insurance options, while property insurance subsidiaries tend to offer short-term health insurance coupled with accident insurance.[104]

Foreign Insurers

Foreign insurers have also increased their presence in China. China's life insurance market is currently home to 28 foreign companies. However, compared to other countries into which they have diversified, their role in China is still small. In 2010, the share of foreign companies in China's life insurance market was around 4 percent, compared to Hong Kong (86 percent), Malaysia (83 percent), Singapore (63 percent), Taiwan (24 percent), Korea (22 percent), and Japan (17 percent).[105] The space is still dominated by domestic players.[106]

The largest foreign insurers in China offering health services are American International Assurance (AIA), followed by CIGNA & CMB Life Insurance Company, and Chartis Insurance Company (also known as American International Group).[107] These companies traditionally have focused on high-end local elites and foreigners in China, but are trying to expand their clientele especially as domestic insurers become more competitive in the mid-to-high-end market.[108] Foreign insurers typically set up a third party administrator (TPA) office for a period of time before establishing a local office. This office must be set up as a Sino-foreign joint venture to receive a commercialization certificate. Wellpoint followed this model and entered the market as WPMI, LLC in April 2008 but closed down its subsidiary company, Kangzhong, after five years of exploration beyond the TPA model.[109]

A more successful model for foreign insurer entry has been partnerships with domestic companies. In these arrangements, foreign insurers bring in proven expertise and global experience, while domestic companies acclimate them to China's unique health sector. As noted above, Discovery is supporting Ping An Health with innovative programs such as Vitality. German insurance group Allianz has invested in China Pacific Insurance with plans to set up a joint health insurance company. Another model is the group collaboration started in 2011 between Roche, Swiss Re Insurance, and China Pacific Insurance to provide cancer insurance.[110] Other examples include Prudential Financial's life insurance joint venture with Fosun International in 2011 and Insurance Australia Group's investment in Bohai Property Insurance.[111]

The most unique and successful joint insurance venture in China is known as Cigna & CMB Life Insurance Co. Ltd. In 2003, Cigna, an American health insurer, entered the Chinese market by partnering with a leading retail lender, China Merchants Bank (CMB), known for its deft handling of consumers. This venture marked a sharp departure from the brokerage model used by many other foreign insurers that utilize local insurers as their distribution channel; such a model can lead to high commission costs as local firms compete on price in a market share grubbing contest. In 2012, the joint venture had revenues of $331 million, up 32 percent from the year before, but still a small fraction of the company's overall $29 billion in sales. Not all of this income is strictly from health insurance; roughly 70 percent is in the supplemental health, life, and accident market.[112]

Overall, China's health insurance industry has witnessed tremendous growth over the past few years in terms of premium revenue, foreign investment, and joint ventures. However, PHI revenue in China is just a fraction of that in other countries and is an insignificant part of total revenue for the large life and property insurers in China. More importantly, independent health insurers and health subsidiaries are struggling to remain profitable. This is unfortunate, since these flexible and comprehensive

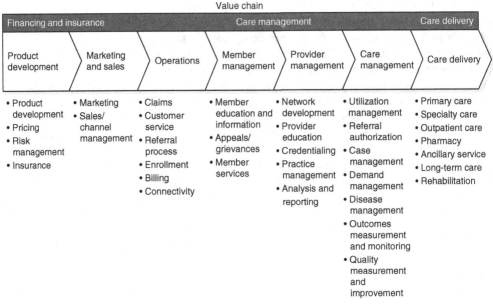

Figure 11.8 Insurer value chain

health plans are able to provide meaningful coverage, in contrast to the supplementary plans provided through life and property insurance.

Private Health Insurance Challenges

Domestic and foreign health insurers confront a variety of hurdles to selling PHI products in China. These include marketing challenges, lack of product differentiation, ineffective distribution channels, inadequate data to assess and price health risks, contracting problems, and regulatory barriers. This section reviews these hurdles and potential solutions to them. In order to understand these hurdles, it is first necessary to understand the "value chain" of activities that comprise a private health insurance company.

Insurer Value Chain of Activities

Insurance plans exist for two basic reasons: to provide healthcare coverage to enrollees and protect them against unaffordable losses. To do so, the insurers need to develop a value chain of activities –

skill sets and managerial infrastructure – that allows them to meet these enrollee needs. Figure 11.8 depicts the activities found in western insurers. These activities include the design of the product (benefit package, price), marketing and sales efforts, operations (enrollment, claims processing, patient billing), member management (questions, grievances) and provider management (network development, education, claims analysis), care management (utilization review), and in some instances the actual care of delivery. At present, a number of Chinese entrepreneurs are seeking to establish insurance plans with their own self-contained provider networks, modeled after the Kaiser system in the United States (see Chapter 9).

Marketing Hurdles: Uninformed Consumers

A 2012 McKinsey survey of 1,000 upper-class consumers (annual income over 80,000 RMB) found that 30 percent of China's urban population possess some kind of private health insurance and that an additional 20 percent would purchase PHI in the future. This finding is consistent with earlier results that the higher income population is more likely to purchase PHI. However, most persons with coverage are unclear about the scope of conditions covered, a symptom of the bundled packages usually offered to consumers. This lack of awareness is somewhat surprising, given that those covered are likely to be better educated. Consumers are thus uninformed about and underexposed to the western model of PHI.

Product Differentiation Hurdles

Most insurance coverage options are limited, sometimes only offering lump-sum payments when a critical illness is diagnosed. According to the McKinsey survey, financial protection from health costs is not the main concern; instead, consumers care about the quality of coverage and care offered at a given price – what is referred to as "value" (quality divided by cost).[113] Two-thirds of respondents expressed dissatisfaction with their access to quality care. In addition to addressing quality concerns, insurers must broaden their coverage and benefit options, and offer more flexible and comprehensive plans.

For example, the large local insurers all offer a homogenous portfolio with little product differentiation. As a result, competition is based on price and brokerage commissions.[114] Such competition drives down profit margins, which explains the lack of profitability among insurers. Ping An's partnership with Discovery and marketing of its Vitality program is one sign of product differentiation. This program tries to help members lead healthier lifestyles through a personalized rewards program. "Vitality points" are awarded for healthy activities such as health checkups and fitness assessments; these points can be used as price discounts on produce such as fresh fruit and vegetables. Such an innovative product has helped Ping An increase sales, making it the largest writer of new business in the domestic high-end group market.

Ineffective Distribution Channels

The majority of health insurance companies rely on large, in-house sales forces or brokers as key distribution channels. While large sales forces can be efficient and direct ways to reach consumers, their widely used method of cold calling tends to be ineffective in garnering new customers, especially those lacking exposure to PHI. Furthermore, with rapidly rising wages, it can be difficult for these smaller health insurance companies to recruit sufficient talent to hit sales quotas.

A successful model of an in-house sales force is found in the Cigna-CMB partnership, where CMB is a retail lender with a strong customer service reputation. The two companies have developed technology to revolutionize consumer targeting in China. Cigna uses proprietary software that sifts through 300 data points such as credit card use and demographics to help its marketers fine-tune their pitch.[115] They then employ advanced cold calling, where the consumers contacted are identified as strong prospects and offered insurance products tailored to their needs. For example, when the software detects considerable foreign travel charged to credit cards, it associates that cardholder with a health policy that is designed specifically for Chinese overseas travelers.[116] Cigna & CMB even have a call center in Shenzhen with predictive dialing, where the telemarketer's computer screen automatically cues up the customer's background, the customized products to sell, and a tailored pitch. Cigna & CMB are selling 80,000 policies a month at the Shenzhen site alone.[117] Given their success, other foreign companies may turn to innovative partnerships that marry their foreign expertise to the domestic insurance climate.

Such innovations should also take advantage of the digital boom. In 2014, China had approximately 620 million online users (not including Hong Kong, Macao, or Taiwan), comprising 46 percent of the population and 49 percent of all users in Asia.[118] Insurers could use less-expensive and more far-reaching digital distribution channels such as telemarketing and internet advertising instead of in-house sales forces and brokers. This represents a marked departure from current practice. However, it may be a suitable avenue to better inform a tech-savvy population about insurance alternatives.

Inadequate Medical Data

Consumer level health data are crucial to optimal insurance pricing. In particular, insurers require extensive data across segments of the Chinese population that include individual data on morbidity and health risks to properly conduct actuarial and underwriting calculations. Unfortunately, given the underdeveloped state of disease registries and electronic medical records, it is difficult to access comprehensive medical data. There is also little transparency in the healthcare system as a whole. The lack of standardized clinical data, disease statistics, and accounting information such as inpatient utilization and drug costs make it difficult for insurers to price and offer complex products.[119] As a result, health insurance is priced in a manner similar to life or accident insurance: a predetermined lump-sum payment is made when consumers suffer a disease.

Accurate pricing of policies requires better databases that incorporate both external data (population statistics) and internal data (claims history). Morbidity data are especially important for pricing calculations, as they suggest the total amount of financial loss due to injury and illness incurred by enrollees over a certain period. Coupled with historical claims data, actuaries in the United States also use a "continuance table" that depicts the probability that a claim will continue by time and amount, given morbidity and other observable factors. In China, health actuaries rely on external data to create their tables, and therefore have a large contingency margin in the premium calculation to avoid claims exceeding the expected amount. The calculated premiums are unaffordable to most, or simply overpriced for the given benefits.

A bigger issue in China is the lack of experienced health actuaries. Currently, most actuaries apply standards used in pricing life and property insurance policies to health insurance. In fact, Chinese actuaries say that pricing health insurance in China is impossible, because of insufficient data, unsound regulation, and a dramatically changing environment.[120] It would be beneficial for the China Insurance Regulatory Commission to update and deepen the Actuarial Regulation of Health Insurance to promote practices that price products fairly without driving insurers out of business.

Contract Problems with Healthcare Providers

Health insurers need to develop networks with a sufficient number of high-quality healthcare providers to offer coverage. Unfortunately, the healthcare reform has only recently targeted the delivery sector to expand the number of providers and promote higher quality care. One reform thrust is encouragement of the private sector to satisfy rising demand. However, many private hospitals struggle to recruit skilled physicians and remain profitable. This is partly due to a 70 percent cap on ownership (in effect until 2010), as well as the public's distrust of for-profit providers. This helps explain why the private sector handled less than 10 percent of total patient volume in 2011.[121] The lifting of the ownership cap is only a small step in the right direction.

Another problem is that insurers may need different sets of infrastructure to manage public and privately insured patients. Research shows there are no economies of scope in insuring both public sector and private sector patients: each set of patients requires their own value chain of activities (e.g., different infrastructure for claims processing). For those insurers wishing to expand into PHI, such diversification may require expensive investments. A related issue is that hospitals may likewise lack the infrastructure to "integrate" with PHI: accept patients with PHI, process their claims, and receive reimbursement. Many Class III hospitals are so overburdened with patients they are reluctant to incur the costs to integrate private insurance; moreover, there may be few benefits to incurring these costs, since revenues from PHI patients may not be high. Finally, patients have not embraced PHI for several reasons discussed above. Beyond these, PHI entails an additional reimbursement process for patient compensation, which can deter consumer purchase of PHI.

Insurers need to build high-quality provider networks where all three parties – insurer, provider/hospital, and patient – can benefit. At the same time, hospitals have to develop the appropriate administrative systems. Foreign companies and joint ventures have paved the way for such collaborations: MSH International has 180 providers in its network, while Cigna & CMC have built a network of 150 providers in two years.[122]

In addition to network contracting, private insurers face problems of medical management. Under the current FFS payment model, physicians are incentivized to prescribe expensive drugs and implant medical devices in order to compensate for lower wages (see Chapter 7). At present, because insurers have no control over such utilization, none cover chronic diseases and most cover only the shortfall for drugs that are partially reimbursed by public insurance.

Barriers to Foreign Entry

According to the most recent Foreign Investment Industrial Guidance, the Chinese government still categorizes the insurance industry as a "restricted foreign investment industry." Investment in medical institutions is now open, but limited to equity and contractual joint ventures. As a result, insurance companies face long waiting periods and serial approvals from the former Ministry of Health, the Ministry of Commerce (MOFCOM), and the National Development and Reform Commission (NDRC).[123] Foreign insurers need to first set up a third party administrator office that is a Sino-foreign joint venture, establish a local office, and then obtain a commercialization certificate. These regulatory barriers not only inhibit needed foreign expertise and investment, but also make it difficult for foreign companies to acclimate to the Chinese insurance culture and learn while doing.

Lack of Tax Incentives

The historical experience of the United States and other mature health markets suggests that tax incentives are crucial for encouraging employers to purchase PHI and offer it to their employees. Such tax incentives do not currently exist in China, thereby excluding PHI from the group insurance market and restricting it to the more risky individual insurance market. This represents a form of crowd-out: public health insurance dominates the group insurance market because of its affordability, while private insurers cannot compete with the subsidized prices in the public sector.

Traditionally, crowd-out occurs when the expansion of subsidized public programs encourages people at the margin to switch from private to public arrangements.[124] The World Bank reported that the expansion of URBMI did not crowd out private health insurance. Instead, private health insurance played a supplementary role in meeting those health demands not adequately covered under the general public scheme. Tax incentives may be necessary to encourage private insurers to offer primary instead of just supplementary health insurance, which would also promote competition between private and public offerings. This competition could promote both lower cost and higher quality care.

Insurers need to proactively engage regulators to shape the future of insurance in China. Options for improvement include establishing tax incentives, removing operational barriers, and allowing administrative simplification (e.g., allow beneficiaries to sign electronic agreements). In March 2012, the National Development and Reform Commission (NDRC) clearly stated its intention to increase the role of PHI. The State Council has also explicitly supported the implementation of preferential tax policies and simplification of claims settlements as next steps.[125] Joint planning by insurers and regulators can help to establish the proper regulatory environment for a successful private health insurance industry.

Future Directions

To address the shortcomings in the public and private health sector, the government aims to increase health spending from $357 billion in 2011 to $1 trillion in 2020, with the goal of decreasing out-of-pocket costs and improving quality over quantity of care.[126] China's largest reform initiatives, which began in 2009, are widespread and ongoing. They include broadening basic healthcare coverage, establishing a national essential drug system, expanding infrastructure for grassroots medical networks, providing equal access to basic public healthcare services, and implementing pilot reforms for public hospitals.

Though these reform proposals are clearly delineated, implementation has proved more difficult. Consequently, in February 2015 the World Bank and the World Health Organization launched a new collaboration with the Government of China to support the next phase of China's health system reforms.[127] According to Dr. Vivian Lin, director of Health Systems in the WHO Western Pacific Regional Office, "China is now entering the deep water phase of the health reform project, where crossing the river will require more than just feeling the stones." The most challenging aspects of reform are yet to come, leading to China's partnership with the World Bank and WHO for guidance.

As for private insurance, according to McKinsey, premiums are to grow from $18 billion to an estimated $90 billion between 2013 and 2020.[128] Despite these predictions, foreign insurers are still holding back on entering the Chinese market due to restrictions on foreigners, difficulties in establishing networks with Chinese hospitals, lack of access to patient health data, and hurdles to educating Chinese consumers about health insurance. These factors have prompted several companies to say the market is not yet ready for a comprehensive health insurance product.[129] United Healthcare (UIIC), one of the largest health insurers in the United States and globally, is watching China carefully but is not yet seeking a joint venture to sell insurance.[130] UHC set up an office in Beijing in 2007 but currently only sells insurance products to expatriates in China and Chinese nationals working in the United States.

On the domestic side, insurers and regulators also confront enormous opportunities and challenges. One opportunity lies in employer-sponsored group health insurance. As competition for qualified workers intensifies, employee benefits will become a tool for attracting scarce talent. A growing number of employers are searching for health benefit products for their employees, and requiring from their insurance vendors unique service capabilities and tools to assist them in managing costs and benefits.[131] Employers are increasingly relying on commercial insurers to provide TPA services such as enrollment, billing, claims processing, and customer relations (e.g., communications, grievances, and appeals). Additionally, commercial insurers are providing TPA services to local authorities for the administration of social insurance. This increased public-private collaboration is an explicit goal of the China Insurance Regulatory Commission to strengthen the private health insurance sector.[132]

Another opportunity has arisen from China's epidemiological transition from communicable diseases to chronic conditions. Chronic disease requires specialized and ongoing care, and is not amenable to a one-time, lump-sum payment upon diagnosis. The introduction of managed care plans could serve to integrate the needed care offered across providers. Managed care plans can create a provider network of physician and healthcare facilities, align provider payment incentives to substitute ambulatory for inpatient care as well as offer preventative care, and incentivize enrollees to use healthcare more efficiently and take better care of their own health status. The benefits are dependent on specific terms of the policy and can include value-added services such as claim reporting, healthcare consultation, and wellness education programs.

Despite these opportunities, the PHI market lacks the historical cost data and utilization experience needed for product development and pricing. Other insurer issues include volume-oriented business plans that drive up sales costs, high competition as a result of homogenous products, and low profitability. Insurers also face a host of technical barriers such as lack of insurance infrastructure, standardized underwriting and claims adjudication practices, uniform coding systems, and prepaid services in the current health system.

Beyond insurance specific issues, broader issues within the healthcare system will affect the development of the health insurance market. The current FFS payment model leads to over-utilization of certain medical services and drugs, over-burdened providers, inefficient allocation of medical resources, and the lack of evidence-based medical practices. This has limited insurers' ability to develop and manage products. Consequently, the government must continue health reforms with the goal of aligning incentives across the entire healthcare system, certainly not an easy task (for any country). However, China in particular would benefit from health reforms focusing on transparency and standardization.[133]

Price transparency, quality transparency, and insurance company scorecards (encompassing both regulatory and quality benchmarks) would help consumers better navigate the health sector and promote higher quality products. Standardization of data collection, care delivery protocols, and health insurance pricing practices (among many other reforms) would help increase quality, decrease variability, and ultimately reduce costs. Health insurers, who serve as the bridge between consumers and providers, need to play a crucial role in undertaking these initiatives. Only through collaboration with the public sector and other industry participants can the health insurance industry realize its potential in the Chinese market.

Notes

1. Robert Marten, Diane McIntyre, Claudia Travassos et al. 2014. "An Assessment of Progress Towards Universal Health Coverage in Brazil, Russia, India, China, and South Africa (BRICS)," *The Lancet* 384(9960): 2164–2171; *China Statistical Yearbook 2013*. National Bureau of Statistics of China. Available online at: www.stats.gov.cn/tjsj/ndsj/2013/indexeh .htm. Accessed on October 9, 2015.

2. *China Statistical Yearbook 2013*. Helen Chen and Yanyan Lin. 2012. "The Rise of Private Health Insurance," *China Economic Review*. Available online at: www.chinaeconomicre view.com/node/56670. Accessed on October 9, 2015.

3. OECD. 2014. "Definitions, Sources and Methods: Private Health Insurance," *OECD Health Statistics*. Organisation for Economic Co-operation and Development. Available online at: www.oecd.org/els/health-systems/ Table-of-Content-Metadata-OECD-Health-Statistics-2014.pdf. Accessed on October 9, 2015.

4. Chen and Lin. 2012. "The Rise of Private Health Insurance."

5. Lawton R. Burns, Aditi Sen, and Jessica Pickett. 2014. "The Health Insurance Sector in India: History and Opportunities," in Lawton R. Burns (Ed.), *India's Healthcare Industry: Innovation in Delivery, Financing, and Manufacturing* (New Delhi: Cambridge University Press): chapter 10.

6. Burns et al. 2014. "The Health Insurance Sector in India."

7. Ibid.

8. Ibid.

9. Arthur Daemmrich. 2013. "The Political Economy of Healthcare Reform in China: Negotiating Public and Private," *SpringerPlus* 2: 448.

10. Sarah Barber and Lan Yao. 2010. *Health Insurance Systems in China: A Briefing Note*. World Health Report Background Paper 37. World Health Organization. Available online at: www.who.int/healthsystems/topics/finan cing/healthreport/37ChinaB_YFINAL.pdf. Accessed on October 9, 2015.

11. Barber and Yao. 2010. *Health Insurance Systems in China.*

12. Hai Zhong. 2011. "Effect of Patient Reimbursement Method on Health-care Utilization: Evidence from China," *Health Economics* 20(11): 1312–1329.

13. Adam Wagstaff and Magnus Lindelow. 2005. "Can Insurance Increase Financial Risk? The Curious Case of Health Insurance in China." The World Bank Policy Research Working Paper. Available online at: http://eli brary.worldbank.org/doi/abs/10.1596/1813-9450-3741. Accessed on October 9, 2015.

14. X. Feng, S. Tang, G. Bloom et al. 1995. "Cooperative Medical Schemes in Contemporary Rural China," *Social Science and Medicine* 41: 1111–1118 Qun Meng, Ling Xu, Yaoguang Zhang et al. 2012. "Trends in Access to Health Services and Financial Protection in China between 2003 and 2011: A Cross-sectional Study," *The Lancet* 379(9818): 805–814.

15. Barber and Yao. 2010. *Health Insurance Systems in China.* Zhong. 2011. "Effect of Patient Reimbursement Method on Health-care Utilization."

16. Teh-Wei Hu and Xiao-Hua Ying. 2010. "Opportunities for the Future: China," in Alexander S. Preker, Peter Zweifel, and Onno Schellekens (Eds.), *Global Marketplace for Private Health Insurance: Strength in Numbers* (Washington, DC: World Bank): 263–292.

17. Xiaohui Hou and Jing Zhang. 2010. "Does Public Health Insurance Expansion Crowd-out Private Health Insurance in Urban China?" World Bank Publications.
18. "Out-of-Pocket Health Expenditures." World Bank: Data. Available online at: http://data .worldbank.org/indicator/SH.XPD.OOPC.ZS /countries. Accessed on October 9, 2015.
19. Xuedan You and Yasuki Kobayashi. 2009. "The New Cooperative Medical Scheme in China," *Health Policy* 91(1): 1–9. Hu and Ying. 2010. "Opportunities for the Future."
20. Barber and Yao. 2010. *Health Insurance Systems in China.*
21. The World Bank. 2010. *The Path to Integrated Insurance Systems in China.* China Health Policy Notes No. 3. (June). Available online at: http://siteresources.worldbank.org/ HEALTHNUTRITIONANDPOPULATION/ Resources/281627-1285186535266/ThePathto IntegratedIsurance.pdf. Accessed on October 9, 2015.
22. Swedish Agency for Growth Policy Analysis. 2013. *China's Healthcare System– Overview and Quality Improvements* (April). Available online at: http://docplayer.net/storage/17/ 150831/150831.pdf. Accessed on October 9, 2015.
23. The World Bank. 2010. *The Path to Integrated Insurance Systems in China.*
24. Ibid.
25. Ibid.
26. Lilin Liang and John C. Langenbrunner. 2013. "The Long March to Universal Coverage: Lessons from China." World Bank Universal Health Coverage Studies Series (UNICO) No. 9.
27. Labor and Social Security Development Statistics Bulletin, 1998 and 2010. Ministry of Human Resources and Social Security. *China Statistical Yearbook 2013.*
28. Hong Liu, Gao Song, and John A. Rizzo. 2011. "The Expansion of Public Health Insurance and the Demand for Private Health Insurance in Rural China," *China Economic Review* 22(1): 28–41.
29. Meng et al. 2012. "Trends in Access to Health Services and Financial Protection in China Between 2003 and 2011."
30. Zhong. 2011. "Effect of Patient Reimbursement Method on Health-care Utilization."
31. The World Bank. 2010. *The Path to Integrated Insurance Systems in China.* Ni Yuan. 2014. *Basic Social Medical Insurance in China.* Available online at: https://regulatory.usc .edu/files/2014/11/016NY_Basic-social-medi cal-insurance-in-China_Symposium_20143.pdf. Accessed on October 9, 2015.
32. Liang and Langenbrunner. 2013. "The Long March to Universal Coverage."
33. Adam Wagstaff, Magnus Lindelow, Gao Jun et al. 2007. "Extending Health Insurance to the Rural Population: An Impact Evaluation of China's New Cooperative Medical Scheme." World Bank Policy Research Working Paper 4150.
34. Karen Eggleston, Jian Wang, and Keqin Rao. 2008. "From Plan to Market in the Health Sector?: China's Experience," *Journal of Asian Economics* 19(5–6): 400–412.
35. Chiyu Ye, Shengnan Duan, Yuan Wu et al. 2013. "A Preliminary Analysis of the Effect of the New Rural Cooperative Medical Scheme on Inpatient Care at a County Hospital," *BMC Health Services Research* 13: 519.
36. Swedish Agency for Growth Policy Analysis. 2013. *China's Healthcare System.*
37. Barber and Yao. 2010. *Health Insurance Systems in China.*
38. Ibid.
39. Liang and Langenbrunner. 2013. "The Long March to Universal Coverage."
40. Barber and Yao. 2010. *Health Insurance Systems in China.*
41. Liang and Langenbrunner. 2013. "The Long March to Universal Coverage."
42. World Health Organization. *Indicators and Data: Global Health Expenditure Database.* Available online at: http://apps.who.int/nha/ database/Select/Indicators/en. Accessed on October 9, 2015.
43. Ke Xu, Priyanka Saksena, Matthew Jowett et al. 2010. *Exploring the Thresholds of Health Expenditure for Protection Against Financial Risk.* The World Health Report Background Paper 19.

44. Pinar Akpinar and Xiaofeng Li. 2014. "Private Health Insurance in China: Keeping Up With the Evolving Payor System," *In Vivo*. Available online at: https://invivo.pharmamedtechbi.com/IV004205/Private-Health-Insurance-In-China-Keeping-Up-With-The-Evolving-Payor-System. Accessed on October 26, 2016.

45. Dongmei Liu and Barbara Darimont. 2013. "The Health Care System of the People's Republic of China: Between Privatization and Public Health Care," *International Social Security Review* 66(1): 97–116.

46. Karen Eggleston. 2012. "Health Care for 1.3 Billion: An Overview of China's Health System." Walter H. Shorenstein Asia-Pacific Research Center, Stanford University. Available online at: http://iis-db.stanford.edu/pubs/23668/AHPPwp_28.pdf. Accessed on October 9, 2015.

47. Qian Long, Ling Xu, Henk Bekedam et al. 2013. "Changes in Health Expenditures in China in 2000s: Has the Health System Reform Improved Affordability," *International Journal for Equity in Health* 12(1): 40.

48. Ye et al. 2013. "A Preliminary Analysis of the Effect of the New Rural Cooperative Medical Scheme on Inpatient Care at a County Hospital."

49. Lufa Zhang and Nan Liu. 2014. "Health Reform and Out-of-pocket Payments: Lessons From China," *Health Policy and Planning* 29(2): 217–226.

50. Liang and Langenbrunner. 2013. "The Long March to Universal Coverage."

51. Qiang Sun, Xiaoyun Liu, Qingyue Meng et al. 2009. "Evaluating the Financial Protection of Patients with Chronic Disease by Health Insurance in Rural China," *International Journal for Equity in Health* 8: 42. Xiaoyan Lei and Wanchuan Lin. 2009. "The New Cooperative Medical Scheme in Rural China: Does More Coverage Mean More Service and Better Health?" *Health Economics* 18(2): S25–S46.

52. Adam Wagstaff and Magnus Lindelow. 2008. "Can Insurance Increase Financial Risk?: The Curious Case of Health Insurance in China," *Journal of Health Economics* 27(4): 990–1005.

53. Winnie Yip, William C. Hsiao, Wen Chen et al. 2012. "Early Appraisal of China's Huge and Complex Health-care Reforms," *The Lancet* 379(9818): 833–842.

54. Dan Liu and Daniel Tsegai. 2011. "The New Cooperative Medical Scheme and Its Implications for Access to Health Care and Medical Expenditure: Evidence from Rural China." Discussion Paper on Development Policy No. 155, Center for Development Research, Bonn. Available online at: http://papers.ssrn.com/sol3/papers.cfm?abstract_id=1945173. Accessed on October 9, 2015. Meng et al. 2012. "Trends in Access to Health Services and Financial Protection in China between 2003 and 2011."

55. Winnie Yip and William Hsiao. 2009. "Non-evidence-based Policy: How Effective is China's New Cooperative Medical Scheme in Reducing Medical Impoverishment?" *Social Science & Medicine* 68(2): 201–209.

56. Yip et al. 2012. "Early Appraisal of China's Huge and Complex Health-care Reforms."

57. Ibid.

58. Hana Brixi, Yan Mu, Beatrice Targa et al. 2010. "Equity and Public Governance in Health System Reform: Challenges and Opportunities for China." World Bank Policy Research Working Paper No. 5530, World Bank, Washington, DC. Available online at: https://openknowledge.worldbank.org/bitstream/handle/10986/3303/WPS5530.pdf?sequence=1. Accessed on October 9, 2015.

59. Liang and Langenbrunner. 2013. "The Long March to Universal Coverage."

60. Linxiu Zhang, Hongmei Yi, and Scott Rozelle. 2010. "Good and Bad News from China's New Cooperative Medical Scheme," *IDS Bulletin* 41(4): 95–106.

61. Barber and Yao. 2010. *Health Insurance Systems in China*.

62. Winnie Yip and Karen Eggleston. 2004. "Addressing Government and Market Failures with Payment Incentives: Hospital Reimbursement Reform in Hainan, China," *Social Science & Medicine* 58(2): 267–277.

63. Ibid.
64. Randall P. Ellis. 1998. "Creaming, Skimping, and Dumping: Provider Competition on the Intensive and Extensive Margins," *Journal of Health Economics* 17(5): 537–555.
65. Hong Wang, Licheng Zhang, Winnie Yip et al. 2011. "An Experiment in Payment Reform for Doctors in Rural China Reduced Some Unnecessary Care but Did Not Lower Total Costs," *Health Affairs* 30(12): 2427–2436.
66. Liang and Langenbrunner. 2013. "The Long March to Universal Coverage."
67. Zhongliang Zhou, Yanfang Sub, Benjamin Campbell et al. 2015. "The Impact of China's Zero-Markup Drug Policy on County Hospital Revenue and Government Subsidy Levels," *Journal of Asian Public Policy* 8(1): 102–116.
68. Philip Leung, Grace Shieh, and Ellon Xu. 2014. "Embracing China's Brave New Pharmaceutical World," Bain and Company (June 4). Available online at: www.bain.com /publications/articles/embracing-chinas-brave-new-pharmaceutical-world.aspx. Accessed on October 9, 2015.
69. China Food and Drug Administration. March 2013. "National Essential Medicine List (2012 edition) Released." Available online at: http://eng.sfda.gov.cn/WS03/CL0757/ 79154.html. Accessed on October 9, 2015.
70. Zhou et al. 2015. "The Impact of China's Zero-Markup Drug Policy on County Hospital Revenue and Government Subsidy Levels."
71. Hu and Ying. 2010. "Opportunities for the Future."
72. Neelam Sekhri and William D. Savedoff. 2005. "Private Health Insurance: Implications for Developing Countries," *Bulletin of the World Health Organization: The International Journal of Public Health* 83(2): 127–134.
73. Akpinar and Li. 2014. "Private Health Insurance in China."
74. Hou and Zhang. 2010. "Does Public Health Insurance Expansion Crowd-out Private Health Insurance in Urban China?"
75. *China Statistical Yearbook 2013.* Such an increase in life expectancy took 100 years in Western countries. Feng Wang. 2012. "Racing towards the Precipice," *China Economic Quarterly* (June): 17–21.
76. Eggleston. 2012. "Health Care for 1.3 Billion."
77. Hu and Ying. 2010. "Opportunities for the Future."
78. Akpinar and Li. 2014. "Private Health Insurance in China." Hu and Ying. 2010. "Opportunities for the Future."
79. Alexander Ng, Claudia Süssmuth Dyckerhoff, and Florian Then. 2012. "Private Health Insurance in China: Finding the Winning Formula." Health International, McKinsey Health Care Systems and Services Practice.
80. Chen and Lin. 2012. "The Rise of Private Health Insurance."
81. Hou and Zhang. 2010. "Does Public Health Insurance Expansion Crowd-out Private Health Insurance in Urban China?"
82. Liu et al. 2011. "The Expansion of Public Health Insurance and the Demand for Private Health Insurance in Rural China."
83. Hu and Ying (2010). "Opportunities for the Future."
84. Ibid.
85. Ibid.
86. Ibid.
87. Hou and Zhang. 2010. "Does Public Health Insurance Expansion Crowd-out Private Health Insurance in Urban China?"
88. Hu and Ying. 2010. "Opportunities for the Future."
89. Hou and Zhang. 2010. "Does Public Health Insurance Expansion Crowd-out Private Health Insurance in Urban China?"
90. Shirley S. Wang and Avery Johnson. 2011. "Health Insurers Face China Puzzle," *Wall Street Journal* (January 14). Available online at: www.wsj.com/articles/SB10001424052970 2035132045760475831390061 72. Accessed on October 9, 2015.
91. Hu and Ying. 2010. "Opportunities for the Future."
92. Ibid.
93. This is not necessarily an unjust scenario, as those who could afford private insurance would purchase it and free up limited government resources to provide public health insurance for low-income individuals.

94. Akpinar and Li. 2014. "Private Health Insurance in China."

95. Chen and Lin. 2012. "The Rise of Private Health Insurance."

96. China Insurance Regulatory Commission. 2013. *Insurance Statistics Report.*

97. Ibid.

98. Author unknown. 2011. "China's PICC to Inject US $154 MLN into PICC Health Insurance," *Asia Pulse Businesswire* (June).

99. China Insurance Report. 2008. *China Daily* No. 51 (September 1–30).

100. Company Overview of PICC Health Insurance Company Limited. *Bloomberg Businessweek.* Available online at: www .bloomberg.com/research/stocks/private/snap shot.asp?privcapId=12961883. Accessed on October 9, 2015.

101. Author unknown. 2009. "South Africa's Discovery Plans to Take a Stake in Ping An Health." *Ping An News* (December 1).

102. Discovery Group. *Integrated Annual Report 2013.* Available online at: www.discovery.co .za/discovery_coza/web/linked_content/pdfs/ investor_relations/discovery_integrated_an nual_report_2013.pdf. Accessed on October 9, 2015.

103. *Annual Report 2013.* Ping An Insurance Group Company of China, Ltd. Available online at: www.pingan.com/app_upload/ images/info/upload/5e41531f-63f0-4428-a00a-0625327ee293.pdf. Accessed on October 9, 2015.

104. Chen Tao. 2004. "Pricing Private Health Insurance Products in China." Southwestern University of Finance and Economics. Available online at: www.actuaries.org /IAAHS/Colloquia/Dresden/Tao%20presenta tion.pdf. Accessed on October 9, 2015.

105. Tom Ling, Peter Whalley, and Shu-Yen Liu. 2012. *Foreign Insurance Companies in China* (December). PriceWaterhouseCoopers (December). Available online at: www .pwccn.com/webmedia/doc/63490843800500 7110_foreign_insurance_cn_dec2012.pdf. Accessed on October 9, 2015.

106. Chen and Lin. 2012. "The Rise of Private Health Insurance."

107. Ibid.

108. Akpinar and Li. 2014. "Private Health Insurance in China."

109. Ibid.

110. Ibid.

111. Chen and Lin. 2012. "The Rise of Private Health Insurance."

112. Charles Wallace. 2013. "Cigna's Unlikely Partnership to Change Chinese Health Care," *Fortune* (May 28). Available online at: http://fortune.com/2013/05/28/cignas-unli kely-partnership-to-change-chinese-health-care/. Accessed on October 9, 2015.

113. Ng et al. 2012. "Private Health Insurance in China."

114. Ibid.

115. Wallace. 2013. "Cigna's Unlikely Partnership to Change Chinese Health Care."

116. Ibid.

117. Ibid.

118. Asia Internet Use, Population Data and Facebook Statistics. Internet World Stats: Usage and Population Statistics. Available online at: www.internetworldstats.com/stats3 .htm#asia. Accessed on October 10, 2015.

119. Tao. 2004. "Pricing Private Health Insurance Products in China."

120. Ibid.

121. Akpinar and Li. 2014. "Private Health Insurance in China."

122. Ng et al. 2012. "Private Health Insurance in China."

123. Lingling Jiang. 2013. "Foreign Investment in Restricted Industries," *China Business Review* (January 1). Available online at: www.china businessreview.com/foreign-investment-in-restricted-industries/. Accessed on October 9, 2015.

124. Linda Gorman. "Public Insurance Expansions Crowd Out Private Health Insurance," National Bureau of Economic Research. Available online at: www.nber.org/digest/aug07/w12858 .html. Accessed on October 10, 2015.

125. Ng et al. 2012. "Private Health Insurance in China."

126. Ibid.

127. World Bank. 2015. "China, World Bank and WHO Collaborate to Support 'Deep Water'

Phase of Health Reforms" (February 17). Available online at: www.worldbank.org/en/news/feature/2015/02/17/china-world-bank-and-who-collaborate-to-support-deep-water-phase-of-health-reforms. Accessed on October 10, 2015.

128. Claudia Süssmuth Dyckerhoff and Jin Wang. 2010. Identifying Private-Sector Opportunities in Chinese Health Care. *McKinsey & Company – Insights and Publications.* (November). Available online at: www.mckinsey.com/insights/health_systems_and_services/identifying_private-sector_opportunities_in_chinese_health_care. Accessed on October 9, 2015.

129. Wang and Johnson. 2011. "Health Insurers' China Puzzle."

130. Ibid.

131. John Domeika and Zha Yan. 2009. *Health Insurance Development in China* (AmCham China) (December 7). Available online at: www.amchamchina.org/article/5363. Accessed on October 9, 2015.

132. John Morrison and Karen Eggleston. n.d. "Developing Commercial Health Insurance in China: The CIRC-NAIC Joint Seminar on Health Insurance." CIRC-NAIC China-US Health Insurance Seminar. Available online at: http://aparc.fsi.stanford.edu/sites/default/files/CIRC-NAIC.pdf. Accessed on October 10, 2015.

133. Domeika and Yan. 2009. *Health Insurance Development in China.*

Health Insurance and Chronic Disease Control

Quasi-experimental Evidence from Hypertension in Rural China

KAREN EGGLESTON, M. KATE BUNDORF, MARGARET
TRIYANA, YAN WANG, AND SEN ZHOU

Introduction

Hypertension (i.e., high blood pressure) is the epitome of a prevalent risk factor for chronic disease in China (as noted in prior chapters). This condition could be better controlled by successful implementation of the country's reform effort to expand health insurance. This chapter makes the case for addressing hypertension through improved diagnosis and treatment funded by insurance.

We first summarize previous literature studying the impact of insurance coverage in rural China. We then present empirical evidence from two quasi-experimental settings: (1) the rollout of insurance

Karen Eggleston and Yan Wang thank the Shorenstein Asia-Pacific Research Center at Stanford University for supporting the data collection for the two-county anti-hypertensive control study (approved by the Stanford IRB as part of a broader study entitled "Health and Living Arrangements of the Elderly in Rural China"). Eggleston and Wang also gratefully acknowledge the excellent research assistance of Jinan Zhang in preparing the preliminary results presented at a meeting of the International Health Economics Association in 2014. This chapter also uses data from the China Health and Nutrition Survey (CHNS). We thank the National Institute of Nutrition and Food Safety, China Center for Disease Control and Prevention, Carolina Population Center (5 R24 HD050924), the University of North Carolina at Chapel Hill, the NIH (R01-HD30880, DK056350, R24 HD050924, and R01-HD 38700) and the Fogarty International Center, NIH for financial support for the CHNS data collection and analysis files from 1989 to 2011 and future surveys, and the China-Japan Friendship Hospital, Ministry of Health for support for CHNS 2009.

coverage across almost 40 counties in nine provinces and (2) two counties in Shandong Province, one of which adopted an initiative to offer free antihypertensive medications. Given the high and growing prevalence of hypertension in China, diagnosis, treatment, and control might serve as good metrics for assessing whether government-subsidized insurance such as the New Cooperative Medical Scheme (NCMS) can improve the control of chronic non-communicable diseases (NCDs) among China's rural residents.

Why Hypertension?

Hypertension is a major risk factor in China that is prevalent, underdiagnosed, and undertreated. The large and growing burden of NCDs in China is fueled by the prevalence of uncontrolled hypertension alongside other prominent risk factors such as (male) smoking, increasingly high-fat and calorie-rich diets, air and water pollution, and physical inactivity (cf. Chapters 3, 4, 6). In 2011–2012, 40 percent of men and 44 percent of women aged 45+ years in China were hypertensive, according to the China Health and Retirement Longitudinal Study (CHARLS).[1] About 40 percent of China's hypertensives are undiagnosed, and almost half of Chinese hypertensives aged 45+ years (both diagnosed and undiagnosed) are not receiving any treatment for their condition.[2] Among people aged 60+ years, 54 percent have hypertension; 30–40 percent of them remain undiagnosed.

Underdiagnosis is also common for diabetes, a serious and incurable chronic disease that is often comorbid with hypertension. The prevalence of diabetes among Chinese aged 45+ years is 16.0 percent for men and 16.1 percent for women; the high rates of undiagnosed patients are alarming (61 percent of men, 53 percent of women) according to the CHARLS data.[3] Nationally across all ages, the age-standardized prevalence of diabetes was 9.7 percent in 2007–2008 (20.4 percent among the elderly).[4]

Hypertension is more prevalent in urban China than among rural residents. According to CHARLS, 41 percent of those aged 45+ years with rural *hukou* (household registration) were hypertensive, compared to 49 percent of those with urban *hukou*.[5] Diabetes is also more prevalent among urban than rural residents (11.4 percent vs. 8.2 percent), although the prevalence of prediabetes was greater in rural areas in 2007–2008.[6]

There is mixed evidence about whether these disparities in prevalence between urban and rural China have arisen because hypertension is a "disease of affluence." Hypertension may be an equal opportunity risk factor plaguing the rich and poor alike. Researchers have documented the association of socioeconomic status with prevalence, awareness, treatment, and control of hypertension among people aged 45–80 using the 2004 and 2006 waves of the China Health and Nutrition Survey (CHNS).[7] They find no wealth or education gradients in the prevalence of hypertension; however, controlling for educational attainment, wealth seems to enable better treatment and control. An association exists between education and diagnosis/treatment/control in urban areas but not in rural areas. Using CHARLS 2011–2012 data, these researchers have documented socio-demographic gradients in hypertension prevalence, but only for men and for urban residents.[8]

Nevertheless, rural Chinese residents clearly are a vulnerable group for undiagnosed hypertension. According to the CHARLS baseline data, 44 percent of hypertensives with rural *hukou* were undiagnosed, compared to 36 percent of hypertensives with urban *hukou*.[9] Because the prevalence of hypertension is lower among rural residents, this lower diagnosis rate in rural areas implies almost identical rates of undiagnosed hypertension among rural and urban residents. According to the CHARLS data on middle-aged and elderly Chinese, 18.0 percent with rural *hukou* suffer undiagnosed hypertension (41 percent prevalence*44 percent undiagnosed = 18.0 percent), compared to 17.6 percent of Chinese with urban *hukou* (49 percent prevalence*36 percent undiagnosed = 17.6 percent).[10] Treatment rates for hypertension, conditional on diagnosis, are also lower in rural than in urban areas (77 percent vs. 86 percent).

Research further indicates that lower educational attainment is significantly associated with underdiagnosis (and undertreatment) among those with rural *hukou*, but greater income/wealth (as measured by higher household per capita expenditures) is not.[11] These mixed results highlight the need to control for education and income when examining the impact of insurance coverage on the diagnosis and treatment of hypertension.

This high prevalence of hypertension, combined with high rates of under-diagnosis and treatment, points to the importance of programs that increase awareness, screening, access to treatment, and treatment adherence. Prior chapters have noted the challenge of increasing public health awareness among the Chinese population. The recent expansion of health insurance in both urban and rural China holds out the promise of reducing the financial barriers to diagnosis and treatment. In particular, NCMS expansion may strengthen hypertension management among rural Chinese where, as noted above, prevalence of hypertension and related conditions (including pre-hypertension and prediabetes) is not only high, but rates of undiagnosed (and therefore untreated and uncontrolled) disease are higher than for their urban counterparts.[12] Moreover, the observed effects of NCMS coverage capture the impact of newly acquired health insurance coverage and not just the "crowding-out" of other forms of insurance. This is because pre-existing levels of health insurance coverage were either low or nonexistent prior to NCMS adoption in rural areas.

Prior Research on the Impact of NCMS Coverage

Populations Studied

Following the 2003 initiation of NCMS pilot programs, the rate of uninsurance in rural China decreased from about 80 percent to only 4 percent by 2010, eventually covering 836 million rural residents.[13] As befitting one of the largest expansions of health insurance in the world, the impact of China's NCMS program has attracted considerable research attention. Many prior studies examined the early implementation experience using various populations and sources of data: (1) household data from ten counties that adopted NCMS in 2003 and five counties that did not;[14] (2) survey analysis of the 2000, 2004, and 2006 waves of the CHNS;[15] (3) analysis of the 2006 China Agricultural Census covering 5.9 million people living in 8 low-income rural counties;[16] and (4) analysis of the 2005 and 2008 waves of the Chinese Longitudinal Healthy Longevity Survey.[17] This chapter analyzes the CHNS survey data through 2011, which covers the large group of counties that adopted NCMS from 2006 to 2011, thereby achieving universal coverage across China's rural counties.

Impact of NCMS

The growing literature provides mixed evidence about the impact of NCMS on the use of healthcare services by rural residents. Many studies (especially those conducted after the pilot program phase) found that NCMS was associated with greater utilization of some kinds of health services. For example, one study found that NCMS increased outpatient and inpatient utilization.[18] It also found that the program increased township health centers' (THC) ownership of expensive equipment but did not impact cost per case. Another study documented that NCMS increased the intensity of inpatient care at THCs and improved their financial status, but did not increase the overall number of patients served or the likelihood that a sick person would seek care at the THC site.[19]

NCMS also appears to have increased the use of medical services by sick and elderly enrollees.[20]

A literature review concluded that NCMS increased healthcare utilization by rural elders, but that affordability challenges remained, especially among the poorest.[21] Another study of NCMS' impact found an increased use of preventive care, but not of formal healthcare services.[22]

Studies to date have also reported conflicting evidence on the effects of NCMS on risk protection. One study found that NCMS coverage did not reduce out-of-pocket expenses per outpatient visit, per inpatient admission, or overall.[23] Others found no evidence that NCMS reduced catastrophic spending or out-of-pocket expenditure.[24] However, some of the most convincing evidence to date suggests that insurance did provide financial risk protection.[25] Using data from 2005 and 2008, the researchers measured exposure to financial risk by (a) whether out-of-pocket spending exceeded the 90th percentile of spending among the uninsured and (b) whether medical care was financed by borrowing or selling assets. They found that NCMS participation led to a 19 percent decline in out-of-pocket spending, and a 24–63 percent decrease in the two measures of exposure to financial risk. This increased level of risk protection did not come at the expense of foregone utilization. NCMS participation was associated with a 5 percent increase in village clinic use, but no change in overall medical care use.

Benefit Design and Utilization

China's NCMS includes national standards for basic parameters of coverage, such as the minimum total RMB yuan per person per year – the minimum premium amount that must be covered by a combination of premium contributions from households and the government – and the structure of premium subsidies from central and local government. However, NCMS is not a single uniform program. Many details of benefit design depend upon local level decision making; coverage varies across counties and also within counties over time. Several studies have catalogued local NCMS variations and their association with healthcare utilization. For example, one study of households in 2006 from 25 counties in Anhui and Jiangsu found that more generous coverage (i.e., higher NCMS reimbursement ceilings) led families with more elderly members to choose hospitals that were larger and more expensive (i.e., at higher administrative levels).[26] Higher deductibles reduced utilization at a given level of facility, although inpatient care was relatively inelastic to deductible level (which ranged from 0 RMB to 1,500 RMB in the counties they studied).

A second study of NCMS in 27 counties using data from 2004 to 2005 found that counties with lower per capita income chose to implement NCMS with less generous coverage.[27] Insured individuals in the least generous plans paid an average out-of-pocket amount of roughly $3.50 to cover an outpatient visit and $77.70 to cover an inpatient visit; patients with more generous (outpatient and inpatient) coverage paid only $0.40 and $8.10, respectively.

A third study of seven provinces in northern China in 2010 found that NCMS programs that provided more generous coverage (especially outpatient services) experienced higher utilization. Coverage generosity for outpatient services at the village and township levels had even larger impacts on utilization among the poorest.[28]

The above studies suggest that more generous NCMS coverage increases healthcare utilization, perhaps through a reduction in financial barriers to care. However, few studies have found an association between more generous coverage and improved health status and survival. One study in rural China found that the introduction of NCMS had no positive effect on child mortality, maternal mortality, and school enrollment for the overall population aged 6–16 years, although it did help improve the school enrollment of six-year-olds in the studied counties.[29] Another study found NCMS was not associated with any improvements in self-reported health status.[30]

Studies using more recent data report that NCMS might improve health outcomes, however. For example, one study found that NCMS was associated with significantly improved functional status and cognition of elderly enrollees, but not with lower mortality among the previously uninsured rural elderly.[31] Another study using mortality data from 2004 to 2012 from 85 rural counties found that

NCMS was associated with lower mortality from heart disease among rural men.[32]

Research Contribution of Chapter

The next section examines the effects of NCMS on healthcare utilization. We extend existing work examining the effects of NCMS on healthcare use and outcomes using more recent CHNS data from nine provinces.[33] The aim is to update (and hopefully resolve conflicting) estimates of NCMS effects from prior studies and address whether these effects hinge on the non-random implementation of the NCMS program across counties. Using the same dataset, we also examine the effects of NCMS on the diagnosis, treatment, and control of hypertension. The subsequent section reports on a natural experiment from two counties in Shandong Province to improve medication adherence for hypertension control. We provide evidence about whether a local program providing free antihypertensive medications to rural elderly is associated with lower out-of-pocket medical spending and improved hypertension control.

Survey Evidence from Nine Provinces

Survey Data and Measures

The China Health and Nutrition Survey (CHNS) sampled roughly 4,400 households with a total of 26,000 individuals in nine provinces that vary substantially in geography, economic development, public resources, and health indicators.[34] The survey does not merely rely on respondents' self-report of diagnosed hypertension, but also directly measures the blood pressure of respondents. We can thus study whether NCMS coverage is associated with measures of hypertension prevalence and control that include the substantial fraction of Chinese who are unaware that their blood pressure is high.

We categorized survey respondents as *hypertensive* in two groups: (1) those whose average measured blood pressure was above the threshold for diagnosis of hypertension – systolic blood pressure ≥140 and/or diastolic blood pressure ≥90 mm Hg; and (2) those who report taking any antihypertensive medication, whether or not those taking medications achieved blood pressure control. Hypertensives thus include those unaware and undiagnosed. *Treatment* of hypertension was defined as self-reported use of a prescription medi-. cation for management of hypertension. *Control* of hypertension was defined as average systolic blood pressure <=140 mm Hg and average diastolic blood pressure <=90 mm Hg among those with hyperten- sion. Therefore, by definition, control is conditional on hypertension diagnosis. Survey respondents are defined as not hypertensive if they have blood pres- sure less than 140/90 and do not report having been diagnosed with hypertension.

We classify counties sampled in the CHNS based on the year they officially initiated the NCMS program.[35] "Early adopters" are counties that adopted NCMS in the pilot phase before 2005 (including the few counties in which the old CMS was adapted into NCMS); "middle adopters" are counties that adopted NCMS in 2005 or 2006; "late adopters" are counties that started NCMS in 2007 or later.

Expansion of Insurance Coverage in Rural China

Consistent with government reports, CHNS data document a dramatic increase in insurance coverage among rural residents between 2000 and 2011 (see Table 12.1). The implementation of NCMS was associated with large, discrete increases in insurance coverage among rural residents, particularly in coun- ties characterized as middle or late adopters. For middle adopters, the proportion of residents with

coverage increased from 6.7 percent to 62.6 percent between 2004 and 2006. For late adopters, rates of coverage increased from 1.3 percent to 95.5 percent between 2006 and 2009. Among the early adopter counties, the rates of coverage also increased, but the baseline level of coverage was much higher. This suggests that the early adopters included counties with some pre-NCMS insurance coverage such as the old CMS (Table 12.1, wave 2000).

The top panel of Table 12.1 assesses insurance coverage based on an indicator of any coverage. The bottom panel considers only CMS or NCMS coverage. We find relatively little difference between the two indicators. This confirms that NCMS coverage accounted for the vast majority of the increase in insurance levels, particularly among the middle and later adopters.

Characteristics of Counties Implementing NCMS

NCMS implementation was temporally staggered across the CHNS counties. This allows us to describe how the early adopters differed from the middle and later adopters in terms of pre-existing levels of economic development, socio- demographic characteristics, healthcare infrastruc- ture, and health status. The top panel of Table 12.2 (Panel A) summarizes differences based on year 2000 county characteristics from the statistical year- book data and the 2000 census, drawing from a careful construction of life tables for all China's counties based on the 2000 census.[36] The bottom panel (Panel B) summarizes differences based on

Table 12.1 Insurance coverage expanded dramatically between 2000 and 2011, predominantly from NCMS

		Counties	Wave 2000	Wave 2004	Wave 2006	Wave 2009	Wave 2011
The percentage of individuals reporting having health insurance in different waves	Early adopters	7	32.15	51.46	84.44	95.70	98.42
	Middle adopters	20	2.67	6.71	62.58	96.77	98.84
	Late adopters	9	0.87	3.88	1.33	95.50	97.98
The percentage of individuals having CMS or NCMS insurance in different waves	Early adopters	7	30.07	48.68	82.17	91.06	89.98
	Middle adopters	20	0.84	5.30	60.28	95.27	96.75
	Late adopters	9	0.00	3.12	0.31	92.70	95.70

Sample: Rural residents with rural *hukou*, age 18 or older, China Health and Nutrition Survey.
Note: "Early adopters" are counties that adopted NCMS in the pilot phase before 2005; "middle adopters" are counties that adopted in 2005–2006; and "late adopters" are counties that started NCMS in 2007 or later.

Table 12.2 Counties that adopted NCMS early differed from counties that adopted NCMS later

	Early	Middle	Late	Testing Differences		
Number of CHNS counties	7	20	9	Middle vs. early	Late vs. early	Joint test
A. County characteristics in year 2000 (before NCMS), statistical yearbook data for the CHNS counties						
GDP per capita in 2000	8,239.65	5,879.24	5,887.20	0.192	0.186	0.293
Survival to age 70, from county-specific life table for year 2000	71.88%	67.94%	68.83%	0.010	0.027	0.016
Number of hospital beds in 2000 per 10,000	20.48	18.92	15.11	0.235	0.008	0.010
Total population	1,066,964	686,936	637,057	0.048	0.035	0.097
Percentage of population age 0–14	21.30%	22.68%	23.16%	0.434	0.418	0.653
Percentage of population age 15–64	69.41%	70.15%	68.94%	0.581	0.802	0.763
Percentage of population age 65 or above	9.30%	7.17%	7.90%	0.040	0.145	0.076
Percentage of population with no schooling	7.86%	6.17%	6.40%	0.071	0.283	0.177
Percentage of population with primary education	34.61%	41.15%	39.06%	0.006	0.011	0.010
Percentage of population with lower secondary education	36.83%	35.68%	36.26%	0.523	0.670	0.759
Percentage of population with upper secondary education	7.92%	6.02%	6.27%	0.060	0.064	0.134
B. Characteristics of the CHNS sampled population in year 2000 (before NCMS) in CHNS counties						
Percentage of individuals with poor health status	2.71%	5.11%	4.49%	0.022	0.264	0.071
Log income	8.47	8.31	7.88	0.267	0.002	0.001
Percentage of individuals reporting sick in the last 4 weeks	6.05%	6.93%	7.42%	0.745	0.666	0.908
Average years of schooling for individuals age 25 or older	5.69	6.48	5.76	0.029	0.853	0.039
Percentage of individuals at school	0.39%	1.78%	2.31%	0.002	0.101	0.004
Percentage with education not available	5.00%	10.52%	7.19%	0.046	0.183	0.106
Average age	42.40	41.60	42.04	0.406	0.723	0.666
Percentage female	51.39%	49.27%	49.76%	0.204	0.366	0.406
Percentage currently married	78.33%	72.68%	73.12%	0.224	0.269	0.460
Percentage single	12.17%	19.06%	15.12%	0.002	0.105	0.009
Percentage with marital status missing	3.33%	2.32%	5.63%	0.724	0.520	0.325
Percentage of Han ethnicity	99.79%	80.23%	80.56%	0.007	0.109	0.009
Percentage with ethnicity missing	0.10%	0.44%	0.41%	0.126	0.383	0.241
Average family size	2.58	2.64	2.70	0.610	0.274	0.471

Table 12.3 Descriptive statistics

	Mean	SD	N
Seeks medical care	0.158	0.364	14,740
Folk doctor visit	0.049	0.216	14,719
Preventive care	0.019	0.138	19,720
High blood pressure (HBP)	0.201	0.401	17,477
HBP drug	0.058	0.234	18,673
Diagnosed HBP	0.084	0.277	18,696
HBP under control	0.018	0.133	18,696
HBP under control among diagnosed HBP	0.216	0.411	1,571
Health status poor	0.071	0.257	11,954
Insurance	0.471	0.499	19,822
NCMS	0.451	0.498	19,801
NCMS available	0.508	0.500	19,980
Age	49.323	14.731	19,694
Gender	0.513	0.500	19,971
Married	0.832	0.374	19,980
Years of education (Yuan)	5.850	3.746	19,478
Household income	¥19,430.52	¥29,155.75	19,799
Household size	4.796	1.916	19,980
wave_2000	0.280	0.449	19,980
wave_2004	0.198	0.399	19,980
wave_2006	0.186	0.389	19,980
wave_2009	0.175	0.380	19,980
wave_2011	0.162	0.368	19,980

the household survey data from CHNS for those same counties.

Before NCMS was implemented anywhere in China, the counties that shortly became early adopters differed from subsequent adopters in several ways. According to Panel A, they had slightly higher gross domestic product (GDP) per capita, higher survival rates (as measured by survival from birth to age 70 from county-specific life tables), and more hospital capacity. They were also more populous with a larger percentage of population aged 65+ years. According to Panel B, the early adopters also exhibited higher pre-existing health status, higher household income, and a more homogeneous (Han ethnic) population. These differences in population, wealth, and health status confirm that

NCMS implementation was indeed not random: early adopters differed in several significant ways from subsequent adopters.[37]

Table 12.3 describes the levels of utilization, diagnosis, and control of hypertension among the pooled rural adult sample for CHNS waves 2000–2011. Some of the salient observations are as follows:

Utilization
- 16 percent reported seeking (formal) medical care in the past four weeks
- 5 percent reported visiting a folk doctor, and
- 2 percent reported receiving preventive care

Prevalence and diagnosis
- 20 percent had high blood pressure (defined to include those taking antihypertensive

medications as well as those with measured high blood pressure), but

- only 8 percent were diagnosed hypertensive

Treatment and control

- only 6 percent reported taking antihypertensive medication
- only 2 percent of hypertensives had their measured blood pressure under control (at the time of the CHNS survey)
- even if we focus only on those whose blood pressure is diagnosed, only 22 percent had their measured blood pressure under control

Health status and coverage

- 7 percent reported poor health status
- 47 percent reported having health insurance (45 percent with NCMS)

The CHNS data confirm prior findings that the formal diagnosis of hypertension is relatively low (42 percent of hypertensives are diagnosed). Among those diagnosed, a comparatively large fraction receives some treatment: the percentage of diagnosed hypertensive patients who are taking drugs was 69.5 percent in the pooled CHNS sample. By comparison, other research reports that 78 percent of men and 82 percent of women aged 45+ years who are diagnosed with hypertension (among 2011–2012 CHARLS respondents) were taking medications.[38]

As others have documented, those taking antihypertensive medications do not necessarily adhere sufficiently to their medication schedule to keep their blood pressure under control. The CHNS data above suggest that roughly one in four diagnosed hypertensives had their measured blood pressure under control. In order for NCMS to make an impact, it should focus on screening and diagnosis of latent hypertensives, along with improving medication adherence to keep blood pressure under control. The empirical analysis below considers these impacts and reveals some encouraging trends.[39]

Table 12.4 presents the estimates of the effect of NCMS coverage on the overall population using the pooled CHNS data (waves 2000–2011). The results are largely consistent with prior research on health-care utilization:[40] NCMS is not associated with

increased care-seeking (utilization) but is associated with increased use of preventive care and decreased use of folk doctors (i.e., providers without any formal training in biomedical sciences). These findings suggest slightly greater use of village clinics and THCs and lesser use of informal care providers, keeping overall utilization relatively constant. What is puzzling is that, contrary to prior research, NCMS respondents are more likely to report poor health status.[41] This may reflect the differences in sample and the influence of coverage on perceptions of need for care. These effects are even more pronounced among respondents in the middle- and late adopter counties.

We also examined the impact of NCMS on diagnosis, treatment, and control among CHNS respondents with hypertension, defined to include those taking any anti-hypertensive drug as well as those with measured high blood pressure ("the HBP sample" in Table 12.5). Consistent with the earlier results regarding greater preventive care, the analyses indicate that NCMS coverage is associated with greater diagnosis of hypertension and greater probability of having blood pressure under control. These results suggest that, over time, NCMS coverage may be helping to improve detection and management of hypertension in rural China.

Comparison of Two Counties

Does Lowering Medication Cost Improve Hypertension Control?

Whether patients faithfully take their antihypertensive medications can be critical for translating diagnosis into improved health and survival. However, the out-of-pocket spending burden can be a barrier to adherence, particularly for lower-income people. Moreover, since hypertension is largely an asymptomatic condition, individuals may question the necessity of continuing medication. Given the widespread financial incentive in China for physicians to over-prescribe (see Chapter 7), patients may be especially reluctant to adhere to long-term medication treatment for asymptomatic chronic conditions like hypertension.[42]

Table 12.4 Regression results for correlation of NCMS adoption with health and healthcare utilization, CHNS waves 2000–2011

Variables	Seeks medical care			Visits folk doctor			Uses preventive care			Poor health status		
	Basic reg	County FE	IV: NCMS	Basic reg	County FE	IV: NCMS	Basic reg	County FE	IV: NCMS	Basic reg	County FE	IV: NCMS
NCMS coefficient, all counties	0.00853	−0.00783	−0.0353	−0.0167***	−0.00206	−0.0130	0.0146***	0.0104***	0.0229**	0.0104*	0.00981*	0.0444***
	(0.00898)	(0.00981)	(0.0225)	(0.00546)	(0.00606)	(0.0140)	(0.00340)	(0.00361)	(0.00932)	(0.00552)	(0.00519)	(0.0135)
Observations	14,091	14,091	14,091	14,082	14,082	14,082	18,456	18,456	18,456	18,631	18,631	18,631
R-squared	0.099	0.092		0.011	0.008		0.013	0.012		0.056	0.057	
Number of counties		36	36		36	36		36	36		36	36
NCMS coefficient, without early adopters	0.00909	0.00713	−0.0189	−0.0180***	−0.00701	−0.0597***	0.0173***	0.0238***	0.0303***	0.0160**	0.0117*	0.0447***
	(0.0112)	(0.0116)	(0.0262)	(0.00690)	(0.00746)	(0.0168)	(0.00454)	(0.00413)	(0.00950)	(0.00714)	(0.00643)	(0.0148)
Observations	11,623	11,623	11,623	11,533	11,533	11,533	15,168	15,168	15,168	15,323	15,323	15,323
R-squared	0.096	0.092		0.011	0.009		0.015	0.016		0.057	0.057	
Number of counties		29	29		29	29		29	29		29	29

Note: Regression model employs fixed effects.

Table 12.5 Among CHNS 2000–2011 respondents with hypertension (treated or undiagnosed), NCMS associated with some improvements in hypertension management

Variables	Basic reg	County FE	IV: NCMS	Basic reg	County FE	IV: NCMS	Basic reg	County FE	IV: NCMS
	Diagnosed as hypertensive			Taking antihypertensive drug			Blood pressure under control		
NCMS coefficient, HBP sample	0.0516**	0.0239	0.118*	0.0456*	0.0208	0.0815	0.0165	0.0153	0.0784**
	−0.0258	−0.0282	−0.0702	−0.0245	−0.0269	−0.0671	−0.0139	−0.0152	−0.0378
Observations	3,315	3,315	3,315	3,289	3,289	3,289	3,315	3,315	3,315
R−squared	0.105		0.015	0.111		0.106	0.013		
Number of counties	36	36		36	36		36	36	

This section reports on one experiment in rural China in which local officials attempted to improve hypertension control by lowering the insurance co-payment requirements, thereby making antihypertensive drugs cheaper for patients. In July 2010, one county in Shandong Province began making specific antihypertensive medications on the Essential Drugs List (EDL) available free of charge to all residents over age 60 with diagnosed hypertension. We compared this county with another county in the same province that did not. Using this natural experiment, we study the impact of lowering patient co-payments for antihypertensives on total costs and out-of-pocket medical spending, self-reported health status, and medication adherence.

Data and Methods

We collected patient-level healthcare spending, self-reported blood pressure, and other intermediate outcomes for six months prior to the free drug policy and six months post implementation among patients in both counties who had visited clinics. Our analyses are based on a simple "difference-in-difference" study design: we compare individuals in the intervention county before and after the policy, relative to individuals in a matched control county in the same province over the same period of time. We collected household survey data from 2,315 patients aged 50+ years who received some portion of their care from clinics in 24 villages. We then linked the survey data to health insurance claims administrative data for the two counties and provider data.[43] Between the household survey and the healthcare claims and provider data, we were able to match data on blood pressure readings for 901 of the 2,315 patients.[44]

Results

Our analysis suggests that the program was associated with a decline in out-of-pocket expenditures for the poorest quartile of patients in the sample. We also observed a decrease in medication spending and overall spending for the poorest quartile of patients. However, access to low-cost medications did not lead to lower medical spending among the overall sample or among the non-poor chronically ill.[45]

This natural experiment does not show much impact on health outcomes: self-reported blood pressure, self-assessed health status, and general well-being do not differ significantly between the intervention and comparison groups. The data may be unable to detect health impacts that accrue only in the intermediate or long run. Moreover, self-reports are not necessarily reliable in terms of accuracy and sensitivity, especially for a longer recall period. If lower spending leads to better adherence, then we have reason to expect that objectively measured blood pressure may be better under control in the future for this vulnerable population of elderly poor in rural areas.

Our interpretation of the results is also informed by interviews conducted with local health officials and health service providers by one of the authors. The interviews revealed that the program's impact was limited by the fact that some patients were taking a different antihypertensive drug and did not want to switch since they believed that the free drugs were less effective (see the list of drugs in Table 12A.1).

Despite the advantages of studying a "natural experiment" in rural China, this analysis has several limitations. The sample is small (two counties in one province), and any observed program effects may be confounded by other policies unfolding in China at the same time. Nevertheless, we did control for the most prominent confounding policy in this case – implementation of the EDL in each county. Overall, the analysis used here represents a relatively strong study design, compared to the previous literature: a pre-post comparison with control group, along with household survey data linked to administrative data.

Discussion and Conclusion

Hypertension is prevalent and underdiagnosed in China. Control of hypertension in rural China is a particularly challenging health issue. Rural residents are catching up with their urban counterparts in terms of prevalence seemingly at a faster rate than the health system is catching up with appropriate diagnosis, treatment, and control. Indeed, as noted above, rates of undiagnosed hypertension are just as high in rural China as in urban areas, despite lower prevalence, because of the poorer track record of diagnosis. And since undiagnosed hypertension is asymptomatic, festering untreated and uncontrolled, this risk factor contributes to high and growing rates of cardiovascular disease and diabetes, often only detected after patients have developed sequelae and complications.

Hypertension thus offers a compelling lens and metric for assessing the impact of China's recent policy reforms, including the largest expansion of health insurance in the world. It is therefore important to study whether expansion of health coverage for China's vast rural population, either through the voluntary NCMS program or supplemental programs for specific patient groups, has contributed to better hypertension control. We have addressed this issue with two related studies applying quasi-experimental designs.

Our first study – on the impact of NCMS rollout among CHNS counties – showed the importance of controlling for underlying differences in the localities and populations studied. The counties that adopted NCMS early on (the pilot phase before

2005) systematically differed from the vast majority of counties that adopted after the pilot phase. The early adopter counties had populations that already enjoyed better health and survival; they also had larger, more elderly, and more ethnically homogeneous populations; and they had higher household incomes. Our findings indicate that NCMS benefits vary over time within a county as well as across counties, and that evidence from the early adoption years is not always generalizable.

The more recent CHNS data (through the 2011 wave) reveal effects of insurance on utilization similar to prior studies.[46] By contrast, the new results also show improvements in hypertension diagnosis and control that may be evident only with the longer study period utilized here. In rural China, NCMS is associated with a reduction in visits to folk doctors and higher use of preventive care. Overall use of medical care did not change, suggesting that patients may be substituting providers in the formal sector (village clinics and THCs) for informal providers. Did the shift in utilization and greater use of preventive services translate into better detection and management of hypertension? Our evidence suggests a tentative "yes." NCMS adoption in a county contributed to better hypertension control through greater diagnosis among adult residents of that county. In addition, given the relatively high rate of medication use conditional on diagnosis (which appears not to have changed much with NCMS), NCMS coverage is also associated with improvement in the likelihood that adults with hypertension have their measured blood pressure under control. In sum, although we confirm prior research findings regarding the relatively limited impact of NCMS on overall healthcare use, we find some encouraging trends regarding detection and management of hypertension among China's rural residents.

The second study utilizing the small natural experiment shows that targeted interventions can promote access to essential medications for the poor, as well as possibly reduce out-of-pocket spending among elderly hypertensive patients in the lowest quartile of reported household income. In the long run, such initiatives could improve health outcomes through better medication adherence, although there is no evidence that it has done so to date.

Such programs to lower cost-sharing could be important components of better institutional supports for healthy aging in contemporary China, which arguably should include expanded efforts at risk factor control. One example of health education and action to improve risk factors is the Shandong-Ministry of Health Action on Salt and Hypertension (SMASH) program. Policy makers may consider complementary targeted programs for lower-income groups to promote equity by reducing the co-payment burden for chronic disease management.

In sum, both quasi-experimental studies yield evidence that China's expansion of health insurance and other interventions targeted to improve diagnosis and access to treatment are indeed having some positive impact. Considerable room for improvement in hypertension control in rural China still remains. Careful policy evaluations, combined with openness of local policy makers to evidence-based policy making (as illustrated here for Shandong), offer considerable promise for identifying how policies can best contribute to better health in contemporary China.

Appendix

Table 12A.1 Shandong antihypertensive study: List of antihypertensive drugs provided under the reduced cost-sharing policy (on Essential Drugs List)

- Compound Reserpine (复方降压片)
- Nifedipine（硝苯地平）
- Metoprolol（倍他乐克）
- Captopril（卡托普利）
- National EML antihypertensives (2012 update):
- Captopril (卡托普利)
- Enalapril (依那普利)
- Valsartan (缬沙坦)
- Sodium Nitroprusside (硝普钠)
- Magnesium Sulfate (硫酸镁)
- Nitrendipine (尼群地平)
- Nifedipine (硝苯地平)
- Amlodipine (氨氯地平)
- Bisoprolol (比索洛尔)
- Indapamide (吲达帕胺)
- Phentolamine (酚妥拉明)
- Compound Reserpine (复方利血平)
- Compound Hypotensive (复方利血平氨苯蝶啶)
- Prazosin (哌唑嗪)

Notes

1. James Smith, John Strauss, and Yaohui Zhao. 2014. "Healthy Aging in China," *The Journal of the Economics of Ageing* 4: 37–43.
2. Ibid.
3. Ibid.
4. Wenying Yang, Juming Lu, and Jianping Weng. 2010. "Prevalence of Diabetes Among Men and Women in China," *New England Journal of Medicine* 362: 1090–1101.
5. Xiaoyan Lei, Xiaoting Sun, John Strauss et al. 2014. "Health Outcomes and Socio-economic Status Among the Mid-aged and Elderly in China: Evidence from the CHARLS National Baseline Data," *The Journal of Economics of Ageing* 3: 29–43.
6. Yang et al. 2010. "Prevalence of Diabetes Among Men and Women in China."
7. Xiaoyan Lei, Nina Yin, and Yaohui Zhao. 2012. "Socioeconomic Status and Chronic Diseases: The Case of Hypertension in China," *China Economic Review* 23:105–121.
8. Lei et al. 2014. "Health Outcomes and Socio-economic Status Among the Mid-aged and Elderly in China."
9. Ibid. Appendix, Table 1.
10. Ibid.
11. Lei et al. 2014. "Health Outcomes and Socio-economic Status Among the Mid-aged and Elderly in China."
12. Ibid. Yang et al. 2010. "Prevalence of Diabetes Among Men and Women in China."
13. Lingguo Cheng, Hong Liu, Ye Zhang et al. 2015. "The Impact of Health Insurance on Health Outcomes and Spending of the Elderly: Evidence from China's New Cooperative Medical Scheme," *Health Economics* 24(6): 672–691.
14. Adam Wagstaff, Winnie Yip, Magnus Lindelow et al. 2009. "China's Health System and Its Reform: A Review of Recent Studies," *Health Economics* 18: 7–23.
15. Xiaoyan Lei and Wanchuan Lin. 2009. "The New Cooperative Medical Scheme in Rural China: Does More Coverage Mean More Service and Better Health?" *Health Economics* 18: S25–S46.

16. Yuyu Chen and Ginger Zhe Jin. 2012. "Does Health Insurance Coverage Lead to Better Health and Educational Outcomes? Evidence from Rural China," *Journal of Health Economics* 31: 1–14.

17. Cheng et al. 2015. "The Impact of Health Insurance on Health Outcomes and Spending of the Elderly."

18. Adam Wagstaff, Magnus Lindelow, Jun Gao et al. 2009. "Extending Health Insurance to the Rural Population: An Impact Evaluation of China's New Cooperative Medical Scheme," *Journal of Health Economics* 28: 1–19.

19. Kimberly Babiarz, Grant Miller, Hongmei Yi et al. 2012. "China's New Cooperative Medical Scheme Improved Finances of Township Health Centers But Not the Number of Patients Served," *Health Affairs* 5: 1065–1074.

20. Cheng et al. 2015. "The Impact of Health Insurance on Health Outcomes and Spending of the Elderly."

21. Baozhen Dai, Jianzai Zhou, Y. John. Mei et al. 2011. "Can the New Cooperative Medical Scheme Promote Rural Elders' Access to Health-care Service?" *Japan Geriatrics Society* 11: 239–245.

22. Lei and Lin. 2009. "The New Cooperative Medical Scheme in Rural China." This study used the 2000, 2004, and 2006 waves of CHNS data, and employed a variety of empirical strategies: ordinary least squares, individual fixed effects, using county NCMS enrollment as an instrumental variable, and propensity score matching with difference-in-difference estimation.

23. Wagstaff et al. 2009. "Extending Health Insurance to the Rural Population."

24. Hongmei Yi, Linxiu Zhang, Kim Singer et al. 2009. "Health Insurance and Catastrophic Illness: A Report on the New Cooperative Medical System in Rural China," *Health Economics* 18: S119–S127. Lei and Lin. 2009. "The New Cooperative Medical Scheme in Rural China."

25. Kimberly Babiarz, Grant Miller, Hongmei Yi et al. 2010. "New Evidence on the Impact of China's New Rural Cooperative Medical Scheme and Its Implications for Rural Primary Healthcare: Multivariate Difference-in-difference Analysis," *BMJ* 341(c5617): 1–9.

26. Philip Brown and Caroline Theoharides. 2009. "Health-seeking Behavior and Hospital Choice in China's New Cooperative Medical System," *Health Economics* 18: 47–64.

27. Yunqin Ma, Lulu Zhang, and Qian Chen. 2012. "China's New Cooperative Medical Scheme for Rural Residents: Popularity of Broad Coverage Poses Challenges for Cost," *Health Affairs* 31: 1058–1064.

28. Hong Wang, Yu Liu, Yan Zhu et al. 2012. "Health Insurance Benefit Design and Healthcare Utilization in Northern Rural China," *PLOS One* 7(11) (e50395): 1–7.

29. Chen and Jin. 2012. "Does Health Insurance Coverage Lead to Better Health and Educational Outcomes?"

30. Lei and Lin. 2009. "The New Cooperative Medical Scheme in Rural China."

31. Cheng et al. 2015. "The Impact of Health Insurance on Health Outcomes and Spending of the Elderly."

32. Maigeng Zhou, Shiwei Liu, Kate Bundorf, et al. 2015."The Impact of Health Insurance on Survival: Evidence from NCMS in Rural China." Working paper, Stanford University.

33. Lei and Lin. 2009. "The New Cooperative Medical Scheme in Rural China."

34. The China Health and Nutrition Survey (CHNS) is managed by the Carolina Population Center at the University of North Carolina at Chapel Hill and the National Institute of Nutrition and Food Safety at the Chinese Center for Disease Control and Prevention. The survey used a multistage, random cluster process to draw a sample of about 4,400 households with a total of 26,000 individuals in nine provinces that vary substantially in geography, economic development, public resources, and health indicators: Guangxi, Guizhou, Heilongjiang, Henan, Hubei, Hunan, Jiangsu, Liaoning, and Shandong. The multidisciplinary research team first stratified counties by income (low, middle, and high) and a weighted sampling scheme was used to randomly select four counties in each province. In addition, the provincial

capital and a lower-income city were selected when feasible, except that other large cities rather than provincial capitals had to be selected in two provinces. The sampling scheme then randomly selected villages and townships within the counties and urban/suburban neighborhoods within the cities. Since 2000, the primary sampling units included 36 urban neighborhoods, 36 suburban neighborhoods, 36 towns, and 108 villages. For more information, see the CHNS website, available online at: www.cpc.unc.edu/projects/china.

35. We collected the NCMS start year from a combination of the community-level CHNS survey results, the earliest year respondents in a county report NCMS coverage, and a double-check with an independently collected NCMS coverage dataset that we assembled for a large sample of counties in China that overlaps with the CHNS counties and was anonymously matched to the CHNS survey data to assure accuracy of the NCMS start date.

36. Yong Cai. 2005. "National, Provincial, Prefectural and County Life Tables for China Based on the 2000 Census." Number 05–03. Seattle, WA. Yong Cai. 2009. "Regional Inequality in China: Mortality and Health," in Deborah. Davis and Feng Wang (Eds.), *Creating Wealth and Poverty in Post-Socialist China* (Palo Alto, CA: Stanford University Press): 143–155.

37. This reinforces the importance of including data on middle- and late-adopting counties and county fixed effects in analyses of the impact of NCMS on health and healthcare utilization, as well as of the instrumental variable (IV) technique we apply in the same way as Lei and Lin (2009): the date the county adopted NCMS is used as an IV for the CHNS individuals' health insurance status.

38. Lei et al. 2014. "Health Outcomes and Socioeconomic Status Among the Mid-aged and Elderly in China."

39. To facilitate comparison with analyses confined to the 2006 and earlier data, we largely apply the same empirical specifications as Lei

and Lin (2009). In each table reporting regression results, we first show basic regression results using OLS, and then empirical specifications that include county fixed effects, and the IV for NCMS enrollment (using adoption date as an IV for individual enrollment in NCMS).

40. Lei and Lin. 2009. "The New Cooperative Medical Scheme in Rural China."

41. Ibid.

42. Janet Currie, Wanchuan Lin, and Wei Zhang. 2011. "Patient Knowledge and Antibiotic Abuse: Evidence from an Audit Study in China," *Journal of Health Economics* 30(5): 933–949. Winnie Chi-Man Yip, William Hsiao, Wen Chen et al. 2012. "Early Appraisal of China's Huge and Complex Health-care Reforms," *The Lancet* 379: 833–842.

43. The patient-level data analyses include patient fixed effects to account for characteristics of the individuals that we do not directly observe in the data but that we can account for because they do not change over time.

44. Among the 901 for which we could match blood pressure readings for the study of outcomes, mean systolic blood pressure (SBP) was 142.4 (standard deviation 24.6) and mean diastolic blood pressure (DBP) was 94.0 (SD 21.1) (see Table 12A.1 in the appendix). In the household survey questionnaires, the patients reported their highest-ever SBP (which averaged 166.2) and their highest-ever DBP (mean 104.0). We know that these matched patients do not represent a random sample of the population, but they did not have any observable characteristics that deviated from the overall sample.

45. To be concise and to focus on the more robust results from the CHNS data, we do not report the full regression analysis tables for the two-county study; for the interested reader, those results are available upon request from the authors.

46. Lei and Lin. 2009. "The New Cooperative Medical Scheme in Rural China."

Drug Pricing and Health Technology Assessment in China and Other Asian Markets

CHAPTER 13

GORDON G. LIU, NAN LUO, AND ZHONGYUN ZHAO

Introduction

During the past few decades, drug expenditures constituted more than 50 percent of total health spending in both outpatient and inpatient settings in China. Drug reimbursement in China is largely paid through the public health insurance programs. This has led to increasing public concerns and a central focus on drug policies as a core component of the state health reforms. Government interventions such as price regulation, tendering, and negotiation have served as primary tools to solve the problem of rising cost.

At the same time, China and other countries have increasingly used economic analysis (e.g., health technology assessment, or HTA) to inform decision making on drug reimbursement. Healthcare financing now plays a major role in the formulation of the country's drug pricing and reimbursement policies. This chapter describes these linkages in China and compares the Chinese context with that in four other Southeast Asian countries: Japan, South Korea, Singapore, and Taiwan. The leading pharmaceutical markets in Southeast Asia actually share some similarities with China in terms of changes in pricing, reimbursement policies, and use of HTA.

China

Healthcare Financing

As a core component of the government's healthcare reform, China has launched a universal health insurance system to finance essential healthcare services for all through four major medical insurance schemes. These include Urban Employee Basic Medical Insurance (UEBMI), Urban Resident Basic Medical Insurance (URBMI), the New Cooperative Medical Scheme (NCMS), and commercial medical insurance programs (see Chapter 11). The UEBMI is a mandatory insurance scheme for a wide range of employees in urban areas. It was implemented nationwide in 1998 to replace the former Government Insurance Scheme (GIS) and Labor Insurance Scheme (LIS) developed in the 1950s. UEBMI schemes are managed locally and organized with social pooling and medical savings accounts (MSA). Funding for UEBMI comes from premium contributions by employers and employees (6–8 percent and 2 percent of the beneficiary's base salary, respectively). Rendered medical services, if covered, may be reimbursed through the personal MSA or a social risk pooling account, depending on the nature of services and policy settings.[1] The personal MSA is made up of the individual's premium plus 30 percent of the employer's contribution; the social risk pooling account is funded by the remaining 70 percent of the employers' contributions.

The UEBMI currently covers over 280 million of the urban employed population. In terms of its balance sheet, UEBMI has accumulated a fund surplus that outweighs its expenses at the national level and exceeds international reserve levels. The recurrent surplus indicates that the risk pooling capacity is large enough to support an increase in benefit payments without undermining the scheme's sustainability. The accumulated reserves have challenged the government to better manage program funds while reducing people's high out-of-pocket payment for medical expenses. The Ministry of

Human Resources and Social Security (MoHRSS) is expected to reduce the UEBMI surplus by either raising benefit payment rates or expanding the drugs on the program formulary.

The NCMS was re-established in 2003 for the rural population. NCMS policy specifications include (1) a government major premium contribution coupled with individual minor contribution; (2) insurance coverage mainly for inpatient care; (3) voluntary enrollment on a family basis, stressing freedom of choice, openness, and transparency; and (4) risk pooling and insurance administration at the county level under the direction of the local bureau of health. NCMS inpatient coverage includes varied deductibles and caps, depending on area-specific policy settings. Some area-specific NCMS policies cover outpatient services, with a family medical savings account set up to pay for common diseases and minor illnesses. Some pilot schemes also cover an annual physical examination and a fixed level of assistance for labor and delivery.

NCMS has grown very rapidly following the government's five-year reform initiative to increase investment in building infrastructure and train rural health professionals. By 2014, the NCMS had enrolled over 800 million rural beneficiaries, or 99 percent of the rural population; a government premium contribution of 320 RMB coupled with a 60 RMB contribution by individuals has financed the scheme.

NCMS has made significant progress in providing benefits to the rural population. National statistics show an increase between 2003 and 2005 of 15.9 percent in total health costs and 45.3 percent in insurance expenses per rural enrollee, respectively. This suggests that an increasing share of the cost burden is being borne by the insurance program.

The most recent public program, the Urban Resident Basic Medical Insurance (URBMI), started in 2007. Similar to NCMS, URBMI policy settings include a government contribution of RMB 320 premium per enrollee, voluntary participation, and insurance coverage primarily for inpatient care relatively lower level of reimbursement compared to the UEBMI. URBMI has been well received by the targeted urban population, with over 315 million urban residents enrolled by 2014. Based on an evaluation study, the poor and those

with previous use of inpatient services are more likely to enroll in URBMI.[2] These two disadvantaged groups have gained more relative to others in terms of access to care and a reduction of their financial burden. The disadvantaged groups also tend to be more satisfied with URBMI policies. URBMI's experience yields two strong policy implications. First, the State Council is committed to increasing public financing for population health, primarily by allocating public funds through social insurance as a major part of the state health reform. Second, taken together, the three public programs serve as milestone steps toward universal health coverage for all Chinese.

In addition to the three public insurance programs, some private health insurance (PHI) plans cover approximately 6 percent of urban dwellers and 8 percent of the individuals living in rural areas. The revenue of the PHI market in China reached about 30 billion RMB in 2006, an amount dwarfed by the UEBMI's annual revenues of 180 billion RMB. Although relatively small, the PHI market has gained a foothold and could expand rapidly with the increase in disposable income, urbanization, and demand for quality service – provided appropriate supportive policies are in place. With PHI as a strong supplement to UEBMI, the financial burden on government would be reduced, thereby freeing up public funds to be used in rural areas or for those with lower incomes. Despite growth, PHI still has a very low penetration rate and only accounts for 2 percent of total health expenditure compared to 20 percent globally. The future development and dynamics of a voluntary health insurance market in China will depend on the future shape of the public system. From a societal perspective, PHI can mobilize additional resources within a financially constrained healthcare system.

Pricing and Reimbursement

In China, there are four government ministries involved in drug approval, pricing, and reimbursement policy decisions. Similar to other countries, the first step begins with the regulatory approval process overseen by the China State Food and Drug Administration (CFDA). Following regulatory approval, every product must file price documentation with the National Development and Reform Commission (NDRC). The NDRC does not regulate the initial price set by the manufacturer of a new drug, provided it is not included in the national drug listing for public insurance coverage. This situation may last for years until the manufacturer seeks possible inclusion of its drug on the list. Once the MoHRSS included a new drug in the reimbursement list, the NDRC followed up with a price ceiling that typically involved a substantial discount off the manufacturer's set price. In 2015, however, the government ended the NDRC's direct price control and moved toward greater market pricing and competition, public bidding for procurement, and efforts to pay for outcomes.

Under the supervision of the MoHRSS, the Department of Medical Insurance coordinates and administers China's National Reimbursement Drug List (NRDL). Over time, the Department of Medical Insurance has assembled a full set of expert panels with thousands of members covering different therapeutic areas. Panel experts are randomly selected to minimize possible human bias or corruption in reviewing and updating the NRDL. The review panels also have many layers with some gatekeeper roles restricting each other. This is designed to assure a fair and efficient selection process as well as obtain fair outcomes. In recent years, the review panels and processes have become more transparent. Two NRDLs are developed from the review process: List A and List B. In principle, List A is for drugs characterized by clinical necessity, widespread use, usefulness, and price advantage in the same category. List B drugs have better clinical efficacy and safety profiles, but usually are relatively more expensive, branded products. Although coverage depth is gradually increasing, many patented or innovative drugs are still not found on the two NRDLs.

Lists A and B are subject to different policy controls. In terms of payment policy, all List A drugs are fully reimbursed by the public insurance schemes without patient co-payment. Furthermore, the content of List A drugs and their reimbursement rates are uniform across China. By contrast, List B allows variations among provincial governments in the drugs listed. Specifically,

the central government leaves 15 percent room for local governments to determine what other drugs are included and their own patient co-payment rates. These products require patients to pay a certain portion (around 20 percent) of the drug's cost out of pocket. According to the 2009 NRDL Edition, there are a total of 2,151 drugs, including 503 List A drugs and 1,724 List B drugs (with the remaining 24 drugs a residual third category).

In the past, when a new product was listed and covered in the NRDL, two primary layers of government intervened. The first was the NDRC and its establishment of price ceilings for all drugs and devices that would be reimbursed by any publicly funded insurance programs; manufacturers could set prices for products not covered in public insurance programs. Second, subject to the NDRC ceiling, local governments would follow with a public bidding process, usually conducted at the provincial level.

When determining prices, NDRC usually would take into account drug production cost, efficacy, and (recently) economic value. Pricing for generic and patented brand products followed two differential approaches: (a) uniform pricing ceilings applicable to generic drugs that meet good manufacturing practice (GMP) standards; and (b) an "independent pricing policy" for most patented products, off-patent originator drugs, domestic primary generic drugs, and generics of obviously superior quality. In 2001, NDRC issued regulations allowing manufacturers to apply for independent pricing under a special pricing system for products of better efficacy at lower cost compared to generics or similar drugs. This system allowed higher prices for drugs that demonstrated greater safety, efficacy, and quality benefits compared to similar drugs. The "independent pricing policy" has played a positive role in motivating manufacturers to improve drug quality and undertake incremental innovation. More recently, the government issued several policy directives calling for economic evaluation to play a greater role in setting drug prices. Representatives from both industry and academia responded quite positively by increasing efforts and resources to promote the development of health economic assessment and outcomes research.

Under the most recent government policy initiated in 2015, NDRC will no longer exercise direct price control. This will leave greater room for local public bidding and insurance payment reforms (e.g., capitation, pay for outcomes by disease) to increase pressures for cost containment at provincial or regional levels.

Public Bidding in Drug Purchasing

Public bidding for drug purchasing and procurement is required and conducted primarily by provincial governments. In most provinces, the public bidding is organized through the provincial department of health, a local agency of the former national Ministry of Health. Drug manufacturers must submit a comprehensive dossier (including the price for each drug to be sold in that province) to bid for pricing and procurement.

Role of Health Technology Assessment

Under current policy, several products are usually selected for the bidding process for each chemical name product included in the NRDL. Most of the products selected include both an original product and two or three generics. Considering the assumed higher quality of originator products, the bidding competition often takes place among the generics, giving the originators the privilege to negotiate directly with the bidding expert panel for both inclusion and higher pricing. At this point, health technology assessment (HTA) data play little role in the local bidding for drug purchasing. In the near future, HTA studies are expected and encouraged to compare originator drugs with the leading generics. The bidding policies can then be more effectively and equally applied to both the originators and generics in the same therapeutic area and thereby improve health outcomes and drug pricing in China.

Two important developments have occurred to HTA. First, in the 2009 healthcare reform, the government's official policy documentation called for the use of pharmacoeconomics (PE) in pricing and reimbursement. Second, the National Health and Family Planning Commission (formerly the Ministry of Health) issued the State Essential Drug Policy, also calling for a better use of health economic evaluations, whenever possible, in selecting the essential drug package. Academic communities responded by drafting China's PE guidelines. A multidisciplinary effort led by Peking University China Center for Health Economic Research (CCHER) released the first edition of China PE guidelines in April 2011, followed by a revised edition accompanied with manuals published in 2015.[3] Given these developments, HTA studies in general and PE data in particular are expected to play increasing roles in both pricing and reimbursement policies in China.

Japan

Healthcare Financing

Japan's universal health insurance system consists of a number of insurance programs designed for different subgroups of its population. By and large, all the insurance programs can be divided into two categories: employee health insurance (covering 60 percent of the population) and national health insurance (covering the remaining 40 percent of the population).[4] All residents in Japan are required to join one of the two types of insurance programs. In 2012, Japan spent about 10.3 percent of the nation's GDP or $3,649 per capita on health; 87 percent of the total health expenditure was borne by the government.[5]

In Japan, company workers and their families are required to join the employee's health insurance program. The premium for such a program – roughly 9 percent of an employee's monthly salary – is shared equally by employees and employers. Such insurance covers 70 percent of the medical costs of the insured, with the remainder paid by the patients. However, there is a cap on patient out-of-pocket payment. Employee health insurance programs are either managed by private insurers or the central government. The government-managed insurance is partly financed through public tax revenues.[6]

The national health insurance programs cover those who are not eligible for the employee health insurance, such as farmers and the self-employed. Those programs are financed through a mix of government subsidies, premiums paid by insured households, and co-payments made by service users. The insurance premium is based on household income and size. It can be discounted up to 60 percent for low-income households. Public health insurance pays 70 percent of medical and drug costs, while patients pay the remainder; patient payments are capped.

Healthcare Delivery

In Japan, health services are predominantly provided by private hospitals or clinics owned by physicians. Large hospitals are usually run by the government or nonprofit organizations. For all health institutions in Japan, profit-making is prohibited. In 2012, the number of hospital beds per 1,000 population was 13.3; the number of physicians per 1,000 population was 2.3.[7]

Most health institutions provide health services to policyholders in both the employee health insurance and the national health insurance programs. Fees for all services and products that can be reimbursed by insurance are identical for all providers. The fee rates are set by a government committee and reviewed every two years through negotiations between the government and service providers. Outpatient care is reimbursed on a fee-for-service basis, while inpatient care is reimbursed based on diagnosis-related groups (DRGs). Patients have free access to all healthcare facilities, including tertiary hospitals. Such unrestricted access has induced excessive use of health services. In 2012, the number of outpatient visits per capita in Japan was 12.9, one of the highest in the world.[8]

Pricing and Reimbursement

Japan's Ministry of Health, Labor, and Welfare (MHLW) determines pricing for drugs and medical devices, based on recommendations by the Central Social Insurance Medical Council (Chuikyo). The council consists of seven representatives from healthcare providers, seven from healthcare insurers, and six representing the public's perspective. After being priced, the product is automatically listed on the National Formulary for reimbursement at a uniform rate of 70 percent by the public insurance programs. Re-pricing is conducted regularly every two years to lower prices based on actual wholesale levels. In general, the price of each drug is set at the mean wholesale price plus a reasonable margin for medical providers to cover the prescription transaction cost. It is currently determined as 2 percent of the previous price.

There are two pricing methods for new drugs. One is the similar efficacy comparison method (SECM) for new drugs that have existing comparators in the same therapeutic category with the same indication, pharmacological action, chemical structure, dosing form, and formulary category. For similar products, the base price of the new drug is set to allow its daily expenditure to equal the daily expenditure of the similar drug. For a new drug that is more effective than the comparators, the price can be higher depending on the incremental additions to usefulness or innovativeness (efficacy or safety). A cost calculation method (CCM) is employed for new drugs that lack comparisons with pharmacologically similar drugs. This method places little emphasis on the value of health outcomes. Following the CCM, the base price is derived from the sum of manufacturing cost, administration cost, operating profit, distribution cost, and consumption tax charges.

Price premiums for new drugs fall into three categories: innovation, usefulness I, and usefulness II. The premium for innovation can range from 70 percent to 120 percent of the base price, if a new drug meets the following conditions: (a) it has a clinically useful new mechanism of action; (b) it has an efficacy and/or safety profile that is superior to existing drugs; and (c) it has been shown to improve the therapeutic method for treating the target disease. The premium for usefulness I ranges from 35 percent to 60 percent if a new drug meets two of the three conditions; the premium for usefulness II ranges from 5 percent to 30 percent if a new drug meets one of the three conditions. From 1997 to 2008, a total of 404 new drugs obtained premiums through these two pricing methods: 322 drugs listed were based on SECM and 72 were based on CCM.

Role of Health Technology Assessment

Regarding the role of HTA in pricing and reimbursement, there is no formal requirement for companies to conduct and submit relevant studies as the fourth hurdle for market access. However, as early as the 1990s, the Japanese MHLW recommended that pharmacoeconomic studies consider both the clinical benefit and cost outcomes of a new drug when compared to an existing product. This has contributed to the further inclusion of value-based considerations in pricing new drugs. A new drug with identified clinical advantages, based on clinical experience and expert opinions, would be given a price premium over the price of the existing products. For example, in April 2012, among 15,447 products under price revisions, 624 newly created drugs were given price premiums for promotion. It should be noted, however, that the price premium for more effective drugs in Japan is still determined largely via subjective and political considerations rather than scientific evidence. There is thus considerable room for HTA to further develop and play a greater role.

Some recent observations suggest progress is being made. In April 2011, the new chair of the central committee of Chuikyo indicated his support for the cost-effectiveness approach. In June 2011, the Prime Minister's Advisory Board endorsed the use of the HTA approach to assess innovation of new drugs for pricing. The role of HTA in drug price determination is anticipated to increase in coming years, although the formal HTA process mechanism is still under development.

Republic of Korea

Healthcare Financing

In 1989, South Korea established a universal healthcare system which was subsequently reorganized as a single-payer national health insurance program. The government-managed National Health Insurance (NHI) program and the Medical Aid Program (MAP) collectively cover the entire Korean population.[9] The country's healthcare system is financed by both public and private funds. Public funds are used to subsidize the NHI program and finance the MAP; private funds include contributions from employers and employees, along with out-of-pocket payments by patients. South Korea's total healthcare expenditures have steadily

increased over the past 20 years. In 2013, South Korea spent 7.2 percent of its gross domestic product (GDP) on health; 53.4 percent of total health expenditures were financed by public tax revenues.[10]

The NHI program is compulsory for all employed residents and covers 96.3 percent of the Korean population. The NHI premium is set at a fixed proportion of the employee's monthly salary and is equally shared by the insured and the employer.[11] Co-payments are required whenever the insured or their dependents use medical services. Co-payment rates vary from 20 percent of total treatment costs for inpatient care to 60 percent of medical costs for specialists' consultations. Caps are set for out-of-pocket payments to alleviate the financial burden of patients undergoing high-cost therapies. Out-of-pocket payments reached 38.7 percent of the total healthcare cost in the NHI program in 2006.[12] Currently, public funds account for 20 percent of the total contribution income of the NHI program.[13]

The Medical Aid Program covers all Koreans who cannot afford the NHI program. The MAP is financed through tax revenues from central and local governments. Beneficiary coverage of the MAP is the same as that provided by the NHI program. However, under the MAP, patients who lose the ability to work are exempt from making co-payments.

In 2008, the Korean government introduced the Long-term Care Insurance (LCI) program to care for older citizens.[14] The LCI program covers institutional care and home care needed by older persons with moderate-to-severe disabilities. Those eligible to apply for LCI include individuals aged 65+ years and those younger than 65 years who cannot care for themselves due to chronic diseases. The LCI program is financed by premium contributions, beneficiary co-payments, and government subsidies.

Healthcare Delivery

In South Korea, medical services are mainly provided by private healthcare institutions: approximately 90 percent of clinics and most secondary hospitals are private providers. By law, all healthcare institutions are NHI providers. In 2013, the number of physicians and hospital beds per 1,000 people were 2.17 and 10.96, respectively.[15]

Korean patients have free choice of clinic or hospital for needed medical services. For services and products covered by insurance, patients pay a certain proportion of the total costs; providers are reimbursed from the NHI on a fee-for-service basis and a DRG basis for certain hospital services. The choice of services included in the benefit package is determined by the Health Insurance Policy Deliberation Committee (HIPDC); the fees for those services are determined annually based on negotiation between the NHI and the providers.

In South Korea, physicians do not function as gatekeepers to secondary and tertiary care, and most private hospitals operate on a for-profit basis. As a result, over-utilization of outpatient care is a concern: in 2013, the country's rate of consultations per capita was 14.6, one of the highest in the world.[16]

Pricing and Reimbursement

Compared to other OECD (Organisation for Economic Co-operation and Development) countries, Korea has historically devoted a high share of its total health expenditures to drugs. In 2013, for example, drug spending as a percentage of total health expenditures was 20.6 percent, compared to an average of 16.9 percent in OECD countries.[17] In response, Korea has recently undertaken drastic reform of its drug policies. From 2004, there have been increasing calls to adopt "value" and volume-price agreements in pricing new drugs. Following the 2006 Drug Expenditure Rationalization Plan, the government made the first important policy change, shifting from the traditional "Negative Listing" based on relative pricing to "Positive Listing" for new drugs based on cost-effectiveness.

The current Positive Listing policy for new drugs, overseen by the Health Insurance Review Agency (HIRA) funded in 2000, entails several steps. The first step is to determine if a new drug has alternatives. For a new drug with alternatives, the second step is to assess its relative clinical benefit based on clinical evidence under the current guidelines. If the new drug proves to be superior, then incremental cost-effectiveness follows. Only when the new drug exhibits an incremental cost-effectiveness ratio (ICER) less than $20,000 does the HIRA decide to list the drug for reimbursement. However, if the new drug lacks superiority over the existing drugs, a cost minimization analysis is conducted using the weighted average price of the alternative products. HIRA will list it for reimbursement only if the new drug costs less than the weighted average price. An innovative drug without any comparators is considered as an essential drug and goes directly on the reimbursement list.

Following the HIRA's initial decision to list the drug, the manufacturer and the government's National Health Insurance Corporation (NHIC) enter a price negotiation. Through a volume-price agreement (VPA) policy intervention introduced in 2007, NHIC negotiates the price based on the expected sales of the new drug, its budget impact, and any substitution effect of generics for high-cost medicines. If actual sales exceed anticipated sales during a specified period, the drug's price is reduced to an agreed-upon amount based on the VPA. VPA may be revised in subsequent years to accommodate greater than expected spending increases.

The seeming transparency of Korea's drug pricing and reimbursement process is actually more complicated. HTA and/or economic evaluations are only some of the many factors considered in the positive listing of drugs. Other factors include therapeutic benefits, reimbursement status in other countries, necessity, and severity of disease conditions, and budget impact. Indeed, reimbursement decisions decreased while denial decisions increased following the mandatory requirement for submission of pharmacoeconomics (PE) data in 2007. Between 2007 and 2009, of the 209 drugs that applied for reimbursement, HIRA recommended 154 drugs (73 percent) for reimbursement; 126 drugs (60 percent) reached a pricing agreement with NHIC. Most of the drug denials reflected a lack of evidence or unacceptable cost-effectiveness values.

Role of Health Technology Assessment

As noted above, a formal HTA process has been in place since 2007 with PE submissions required for drug reimbursement. Going forward, drug manufacturers expect some refinement in PE submission guidelines. In terms of methodology, guidelines may strongly recommend that manufacturers conduct cost-utility analysis (CUA) when the use of quality-adjusted-life-years (QALY) is appropriate. Other forms of cost-effectiveness analysis (CEA) would be accepted only when QALY is neither important nor feasible due to disease conditions. When conducting CUA, generic utility is preferred to disease-specific utilities and should be based on the Korean population. Cost estimates should employ a social perspective, although estimating indirect or intangible costs is challenging. When relying on expert opinions for data estimation, studies must specify who is consulted and how and why they are chosen. Following the VPA approach, further use of risk-sharing schemes may be introduced into the negotiation process for new and expensive products such as oncology drugs. This may lead to some win–win outcomes for all parties including patients, manufacturers, and perhaps public payers.

Republic of Singapore

Healthcare Financing

Singapore has a modified universal healthcare system financed by public funds and two schemes: (a) the Medisave, a compulsory medical savings scheme and (b) the MediShield, a health insurance scheme. The country's total expenditure on health as a percentage of GDP has been around 4.5 percent, with the government financing 30–40 percent of the total. Per capita total expenditure on health was $3,578 in 2013.[18]

Launched in 1984, the Medisave is a savings scheme providing account holders and their families with funds for medical services. Medisave is mandatory for employed residents, who contribute up to 7–9 percent of their monthly salaries into a personal account. In 2010, more than 80 percent of inpatients in Singapore used Medisave funds to pay for their hospitalization bills.[19]

MediShield (MediShield Life replaced MediShield on November 1, 2015) is a government-managed national health insurance plan established in 1990. MediShield covers policyholders' basic hospital care at the rates charged by public hospitals. Policyholders pay a deductible as well as a co-pay for each admission. The premium rates of MediShield vary greatly depending on policyholders' age. Although MediShield is not compulsory, more than 92 percent of the resident population in Singapore was enrolled in 2011.[20] MediShield payouts may cover up to 80 percent of medical bills incurred in public hospitals.[21]

The Singapore government subsidizes the cost of basic medical services provided in public healthcare institutions. The subsidized rates to which patients are entitled depend on patients' immigration status and household income. For citizens, the subsidy rates for basic hospital care range from 65 percent to 80 percent.[22] The government runs an additional program, the Medifund, to help patients who cannot afford their medical bills even with subsidies. The fund is distributed on a case-by-case basis by application.

Healthcare Delivery

Private general practitioners deliver about 80 percent of outpatient care in Singapore. Outpatient clinics owned by public hospitals provide the remaining 20 percent of primary care services.[23] The public sector is the major provider of secondary and tertiary care. In 2014, hospital beds in public hospitals accounted for 77 percent of total bed capacity[24]; approximately 80 percent of the beds in public hospitals are subsidized by the government. In 2013, the number of physicians per 1,000 population was 2.0;[25] in 2011, the number of hospital beds per 1,000 population in Singapore was 2.27.[26] The density of hospital beds has been decreasing since 2000 as bed capacity remained stable while the size of the population increased. The system rests on a fee-for-service model in which patients have free choice of private and public healthcare providers.

Pricing and Reimbursement

Singapore employs a free-market approach to pricing healthcare products. Following registration with the Health Sciences Authority, any drug or medical device can be marketed in the country. There are currently no regulations for controlling health technology pricing.

The Ministry of Health maintains a Standard Drug List (SDL) and subsidizes drugs on the SDL that are dispensed in public clinics and hospitals. The SDL includes drugs that are deemed as clinically essential and cost-effective for managing common diseases.[27] The SDL is further divided into SDL1 and SDL2 drugs, which public healthcare institutions are required to supply. Drugs on SDL1 are first-line products, usually generics that can be acquired at relatively low cost. Patients attending a public institution pay a standard fee of $1.4 per week for each drug on SDL1. More than 80 percent of SDL drugs were on SDL1.[28] Drugs on SDL2 are relatively more expensive and essential. The ministry allocates a budget each year to subsidize those drugs so that patients attending the public healthcare institutions pay only 50 percent of the total cost. As of November 2011, the SDL included 653 drugs.[29] In order to help needy patients pay for expensive non-standard drugs, the Ministry of Health set up a Medication Assistance Fund in 2010. In this manner, the government subsidizes 50 percent of the cost of expensive drugs for treating cancers and heart diseases for low-income patients.[30]

The formulary decision-making process for the Standard Drug List is not transparent.[31] Only sketchy information is publicly available on the administrative process. Currently, the SDL is reviewed every year by the Drug Advisory Committee, a panel of medical experts appointed by the Ministry of Health. The review is designed to ensure that the drugs listed are in line with current clinical practice. The committee reviews proposals from doctors working in the public healthcare institutions regarding the addition and removal of drugs. The main factors in SDL decision-making are whether the drug is clinically essential, effective, and cost-effective.[32] However, there is little public information about how cost-effectiveness is defined or assessed by the committee, and currently no mechanism exists for manufacturers to submit proposals to the committee.

Role of Health Technology Assessment

The Pharmacoeconomics and Drug Utilization Unit (PEDU), formed in 2001 by the Ministry of Health, is responsible for reviewing drugs for inclusion in the Standard Drug List. Under the Health Sciences Authority, this unit assists the Drug Advisory Committee to assess the cost-effectiveness and budget impact of such drugs.[33] Another HTA division under the Ministry of Health is the HTA Branch, staffed by a team of specialists. The HTA Branch is responsible for developing and updating clinical practice guidelines. It also supports the ministry's development of policies for introducing new health services and variations in subsidy and Medisave usage.[34] Usually an economic evaluation is conducted by the HTA Branch through collaboration with an academic institution. For example, cost-effectiveness analysis recently served as one input in a recent Ministry of Health policy allowing Medisave to pay for the pneumococcal vaccine.[35]

There is a lack of transparency regarding how HTA is conducted by the PEDU or how such evidence is used in formulary decision making for SDL2 drugs. According to general principles enunciated by policy makers, cost-effectiveness may be considered in HTA decision making; however, the technical criteria or formulas are not public knowledge. For example, how cost-effective a drug should be for inclusion in the SDL2 and the recommended method of cost-effectiveness analysis are not known.

As a possible explanation, policy makers are likely concerned about the rapid expansion of the SDL, especially the more expensive SDL2 drugs. Cost containment has been an important goal in Singapore's healthcare policy.[36] As a result, pharmaceutical companies are not actively conducting PE studies in Singapore. Pharmacoeconomic data are mainly used by large pharmaceutical companies to market their expensive products – for example, to support efforts to include their products in SDL2 or the formularies of public hospitals. For both types of listing, the pharmaceutical companies need to identify key opinion leaders in the clinician community who are willing to submit the application dossiers to the relevant committees. Since there are no guidelines for how to prepare cost-effectiveness evidence in Singapore, pharmaceutical companies usually follow the general recommendations for pharmacoeconomic studies used in the United Kingdom and Australia. How the Drug Advisory Committee for SDL2 listing and pharmacy and therapeutic (P&T) committee of hospitals use the pharmacoeconomic evidence is not known; they may or may not give feedback about the submitted pharmacoeconomic evidence. Generally, large pharmaceutical companies deploy only one specialist in their Singapore offices to handle health economics–related development.

In the foreseeable future, the application of HTA in healthcare decision making is likely to increase. Recent years have seen great improvement in the infrastructure of health services research in Singapore. The establishment of the first school of public health at the National University of Singapore represents a recent development. With more experts and analysts available, the ministry should be more confident in taking further steps to improve its HTA practices.

Taiwan

Healthcare Financing

Taiwan's healthcare system is funded through a single-payer social insurance scheme, known as the National Health Insurance (NHI). NHI is a compulsory insurance plan providing all residents with equal access to essential health services. The NHI currently covers 99 percent of Taiwan's population. In 2013, the country spent 6.6 percent of its GDP on health ($1,129 per capita).[37] Drug expenditures have typically accounted for roughly 25 percent of total healthcare spending.

Introduced in 1995, the NHI is administered by the Department of Health through the Bureau of the National Health Insurance (BNHI). The NHI is financed through a mix of out-of-pocket payments and insurance premiums. Responsibility for paying the premiums is shared by the insured, their employers, and central and local government. The premium rates are scaled to monthly salaries of the insured and currently stand at 5.17 percent. The proportions paid by the three parties vary from individual to individual depending on the profession and salary

scale of the insured. In 2010, 95 percent of NHI revenue was from premiums contributed by the insured (38 percent), employers (36 percent), and government (26 percent). Co-payment by the insured is required to receive treatment or services. To encourage rational usage of health resources, the co-payment rates differ for different types of services and providers. Co-payments for all services in the benefit package are capped to reduce financial burden to patients.

Taiwan's NHI offers a universal benefit package to the insured. Contracted healthcare providers render the services and are reimbursed by BNHI. Providers were initially reimbursed on a fee-for-service model that led to a rapid increase in medical costs. To contain these increasing expenditures, Taiwan introduced a global budgeting system in 1998 and a DRG payment system in 2010.

Healthcare Delivery

Medical care in Taiwan is primarily delivered by private providers. In 2010, nearly all of the country's 508 hospitals and 20,183 clinics were in the private sector (84 percent and 98 percent, respectively).[38] Regardless of ownership, 92 percent of all health institutions were contracted by the BNHI to provide services. The number of hospital and clinic beds per 1,000 population was 6.82 in 2013;[39] the number of physicians per 1,000 population was 1.77.[40]

NHI enrollees have free choice among contracted providers, with or without referrals. This freedom shortens patients' waiting times to visit a doctor or undergo surgical procedures. Beneficiaries have taken good advantage of this access to care to frequently visit doctors. The number of consultations per capita in Taiwan was 12.3 in 2004, higher than most member countries of the Organisation for Economic Co-operation and Development.[41]

Role of Health Technology Assessment

After receiving market approval by the Bureau of Pharmaceutical Affairs in the Department of Health, a new drug subsequently can apply for pricing and reimbursement by national health insurance through two primary agencies. The drug pricing and reimbursement application first begins with the Health Technology Assessment Division at the Center for Drug Evaluation (CDE), a private not-for-profit entity responsible for conducting and compiling an HTA evidence report. This report is based on both the drug manufacturer's own dossier and globally searched health outcomes research. Upon completion, the HTA evidence report is then forwarded to the Drug Benefit Committee (DBC) of the BNHI for review and appraisal. The DBC makes recommendations on the listing, coverage, and pricing of the new drug which are submitted to the BNHI president for final decision. In general, the DBC makes three recommendations: (1) whether a new drug is listed or not, (2) any restrictions on coverage for indications, and (3) reimbursement price.[42]

The drug manufacturer's application dossier for pricing and reimbursement must include the following information:

- The basic biomedical and clinical information on the product;
- An appropriate comparator's information on efficacy and pricing;
- Pricing information on both the product and the comparator in the ten reference countries (Australia, Belgium, Canada, France, Germany, Japan, Sweden, Switzerland, United States, and United Kingdom);
- Reimbursement information on the product;
- Domestic information on both clinical trials and PE studies if conducted in Taiwan;
- HTA information on the product from United Kingdom, Canada, and Australia;
- A literature review that assesses the economic benefit of the product;
- A budget impact analysis of the product.

When preparing the evidence report, the CDE HTA division gathers information from both the manufacturer's dossier and an independent search of evidence from CADTH (Canada), NICE (United Kingdom), PBAC (Australia), SMC (Scotland), the Cochrane library, PubMed, and EMBASE.[43]

When it comes to new drug pricing, the CDE HTA takes several factors into consideration. First, it considers the drug category: (a) break-through drugs, (b) me-too drugs, or (c) line-extension drugs. For a break-through drug, the price is usually set to the median of the ten reference prices. For a me-too drug, the price follows the similar reference product. For a line-extension product, it can be priced in several ways, including the minimum price of referenced products, or the method of international drug pricing ratio (BNHI price of reference product multiplied by the median price ratio of the product to the reference product). Second, to encourage local ethnic-specific clinical studies, a 10 percent price premium can be awarded to a new drug that conducted a clinical trial in Taiwan. For similar reasons, an additional 10 percent price markup can be granted to new drugs if a PE study is conducted in Taiwan. Nevertheless, the final price of both me-too and line-extension products must be capped at the median of the ten referenced prices.

In preparing the HTA evidence report for listing in drug formulary, the CDE also considers data on comparative effectiveness, budget impact, cost-effectiveness and cost-benefit analysis (CEA, CBA), and the drug's ethical/legal/social impact. All the studies require a benchmark comparator which, in principle, should be the most popular and best alternative product otherwise available in the same therapeutic category. In selecting the right comparator product, first priority is given to head-to-head comparison studies, although indirect comparative studies can also be used. If a new drug clearly demonstrates superior efficacy relative to existing therapies, it will be included in the insurance drug formulary. If a new drug is equally effective compared to the existing drugs, it is also considered for inclusion, but its price must be more competitive. A budget impact analysis is also required for every new drug submission. This analysis must provide a three-to five-year estimate of the product-specific drug expenditures, all drug expenditures, and total healthcare spending if covered by the public insurance system. For a new drug to be listed, a three to five-year quantity-price agreement will be made based on the budget impact analysis. Subject to the agreement, the manufacturer may need to return some funds to BNHI or reduce price accordingly over time if the total drug expenditures significantly exceed the estimated amount.[44]

In terms of the decision-making process, the CDE HTA division is given 42 days to prepare the HTA assessment report before submission to the Drug Benefit Committee (DBC) for review and recommendations. The DBC consists of 24 members, including 5 public officers and 19 healthcare professionals (physicians from different specialties, pharmacists, and economists). The DBC usually conducts a monthly group meeting to discuss the HTA evidence reports, with two primary reviewers selected from the 19 medical professional members to review each report. Within a two-week review period, the reviewers write a recommendation summary based on the full evidence report for the DBC group appraisal meeting for pricing and reimbursement decisions. Manufacturers may not have access to the assessment and review report until hearing the final decision; however, manufacturers can pursue an appeal process for failed cases in the first DBC meeting and make a re-submission to BNHI when new data become available.

Summary

There is considerable diversity in healthcare financing, pricing and reimbursement, and HTA roles across the five markets (China, Japan, South Korea, Singapore, and Taiwan). Although a universal health insurance system has been implemented in all five markets, the coverage depth and scope are quite different. China and Singapore tend to cover essential medical needs with a supplemental mechanism to cover catastrophic events. A large portion of costs for innovative drugs are still paid by patients out of pocket; so the patient self-pay sector (cash market) represents an important component of the markets, especially for expensive medications or those not included on essential drug lists. On the other hand, Japan's insurance system covers all regulatory approved drugs at 70 percent of the costs with a cap at patient level. Meanwhile, a formal HTA process has been in place in South Korea and Taiwan. Overall, value-based pricing and HTA are expected to play an even more important role in future pricing and reimbursement decision making in these markets.

Notes

1. Gordon G. Liu, Zhongyun Zhao, Renhua Cai et al. 2002. "Equity in Health Care Access: Assessing the Urban Health Care Reform in China," *Social Science & Medicine* 55(10): 1779–1794.

2. Wanchuan Lin, Gordon G. Liu, and Gang Chen. 2009. "Urban Resident Basic Medical Insurance: A Landmark Reform toward Universal Coverage in China," *Health Economics* 18(Supplement 2): S83–S96.

3. Gordon Liu. 2015. *China Guidelines for Pharmacoeconomic Evaluations and Manual* (2015 Edition) (Beijing: China Science Press).

4. Yen-Huei Tarn, Shanlian Hu, Isao Kamae et al. 2008. "Health-care Systems and Pharmacoeconomic Research in Asia-Pacific Region," *Value in Health* 11(Supplement 1): S137–S155.

5. Elias Mossialos and Martin Wenzl (Eds.). *2014 International Profiles of Health Care Systems* (New York: The Commonwealth Fund). Available online at: www.commonwealth fund.org/~/media/files/publications/fund-report/2015/jan/1802_mossialos_intl_profiles_4 _201v7.pdf. Accessed on October 23, 2015.

6. Tetsuo Fukawa. 2002. "Public Health Insurance in Japan," The World Bank Institute Working Paper. Available online at: http:// unpan1.un.org/intradoc/groups/public/docu ments/APCITY/UNPAN020063.pdf. Accessed on October 23, 2015.

7. OECD Health Statistics. 2015. Available online at: http://stats.oecd.org/Index.aspx. Accessed on October 23, 2015.

8. Ibid.

9. Chang Bae Chun, Soon Yang Kim, Jun Young Lee et al. 2009. "Republic of Korea: Health System Review," *Health Systems in Transition* 11(7). Available online at: www .euro.who.int/__data/assets/pdf_file/0019/ 101476/E93762.pdf. Accessed on October 23, 2015.

10. World Health Organization Global Health Observatory Data Repository. 2011. www .who.int/gho/en/. Accessed on October 22, 2015.

11. Chun et al. 2009. "Republic of Korea."
12. Ibid.
13. Ministry of Health & Welfare, Republic of Korea. 2012. "Learn about the Policies of the Ministry of Health & Welfare." Available online at: http://english.mohw.go.kr/front_eng/index.jsp. Accessed on October 12, 2015.
14. Young Joo Song. 2009. "The South Korean Health Care System," *Japan Medical Association Journal* 52(3): 206–209. Available online at: www.med.or.jp/english/journal/pdf/2009_03/206_209.pdf. Accessed on October 22, 2015.
15. OECD Health Statistics. 2015. Available online at: http://stats.oecd.org/Index.aspx. Accessed on October 12, 2015.
16. Ibid.
17. OECD Health Statistics. 2015. Available online at: https://data.oecd.org/healthres/pharmaceutical-spending.htm. Accessed on October 23, 2015.
18. World Health Organization Global Health Observatory Data Repository. 2015. Available online at: www.who.int/gho/en/. Accessed on October 20, 2015.
19. MOH Flyer. 2011. "Healthcare, We Can All Afford." Available online at: www.healthxchange.com.sg/healthyliving/SpecialFocus/Pages/Understanding-Medisave-MediShield-Medifund.aspx. Accessed on October 20, 2015.
20. Ministry of Health, Singapore. 2012. Available online at: www.moh.gov.sg/content/moh_web/home/pressRoom/Parliamentary_QA/2012/medishield_coverageofpopulation.html. Accessed on October 20, 2015.
21. Ministry of Health, Singapore. 2011. "MediShield." Available online at: www.moh.gov.sg/content/moh_web/home/costs_and_financing/schemes_subsidies/Medishield.html. Accessed on October 20, 2015.
22. Ministry of Health, Singapore. 2012. *Revised Healthcare Subsidy Rates for Permanent Residents*. Available online at: www.moh.gov.sg/content/moh_web/home/pressRoom/pressRoomItemRelease/2012/revised_health caresubsidyratesforpermanentresidents0.html. Accessed on October 20, 2015.
23. Hwee Sing Khoo, Yee Wei Lim, and Hubertus J.M. Vrijhoef. 2014. "Primary Healthcare System and Practice Characteristics in Singapore," *Asia Pacific Family Medicine* 13 (1): 8. Available online at: www.ncbi.nlm.nih.gov/pmc/articles/PMC4129466/#B14. Accessed on October 20, 2015.
24. Department of Statistics, Singapore. 2011. *Yearbook of Statistics Singapore 2015*.
25. The World Bank. 2015. Available online at: http://data.worldbank.org/indicator/SH.MED.PHYS.ZS. Accessed on October 20, 2015.
26. Department of Statistics, Singapore. 2011. *Yearbook of Statistics Singapore 2011*.
27. Shu-Chuen Li. 2007. "Health Care System and Public Sector Drug Formulary in Singapore," *ISPOR Connections*. Available online at: www.ispor.org/news/articles/oct07/hcs.asp. Accessed on October 20, 2015.
28. Li. 2007. "Health Care System and Public Sector Drug Formulary in Singapore."
29. Ministry of Health, Singapore. 2011. "Drug Subsidies." Available online at: www.moh.gov.sg/content/moh_web/home/costs_and_financing/schemes_subsidies/drug_subsidies.html. Accessed on October 20, 2015.
30. ChannelNews Asia. 2013. "Review of Healthcare Financing Will Involve Fundamental Shifts: Health Minister." Available online at: www.channelnewsasia.com/news/singapore/review-of-healthcare-fina/602900.html. Accessed on October 20, 2015.
31. Saskia Van der Erf, Jeremy Fung Yen Lim, Wai Leng Chow et al. 2009. "Formulary Decision Making Process in Five Countries: Implications for Singapore." Available online at: www.davejunia.com/chsr/files/Conf_Formulary%20Decision%20Making%20Process%20in%20Five%20Countries%20Implications%20for%20Singapore.pdf. Accessed on October 20, 2015.
32. Salma Khalik. January 29, 2010. "Medifund to Help Middle Income with Costly Drugs,"

The Straits Times. Available online at: www .healthxchange.com.sg/News/Pages/Medifund-to-help-middle-income-with-costly-drugs.aspx. Accessed on October 20, 2015.

33. Li. 2007. "Health Care System and Public Sector Drug Formulary in Singapore."

34. Ken Ho Pwee. 2009. "Health Technology Assessment in Singapore," *International Journal of Technology Assessment in Health Care* 25(Supplement 1): 234–240.

35. Karen Richards Tyo, Melissa M. Rosen, Wu Zeng et al. 2011. "Cost-effectiveness of Conjugate Pneumococcal Vaccination in Singapore: Comparing Estimates for 7-valent, 10-valent, and 13-valent Vaccines," *Vaccine* 29 (38): 6686–6694.

36. Meng Kin Lim. 2005. "Transforming Singapore Health Care: Public-private Partnership," *Annals Academy Medicine Singapore* 34(7): 461–467.

37. Tsung-Mei Cheng. 2015. "Taiwan's Health Care System: The Next 20 years," *Brookings Series: Taiwan-U.S. Quarterly Analysis* 17. Available online at: www.brookings.edu /research/opinions/2015/05/14-taiwan-national -healthcare-cheng. Accessed on October 25, 2015.

38. Department of Health, Executive Yuan, R.O.C. (Taiwan). 2011. *2010 The Statistical Annual Report of Medical Care Institution's Status & Hospital's Utilization.*

39. Statista. 2015. Available online at: www .statista.com/statistics/324721/taiwan-hospital -bed-density/; National Bureau of Statistics of China; Taiwan National Statistics. Accessed on October 25, 2015.

40. National Statistics, Republic of China (Taiwan). 2013. *Yearly Statistics.* Available online at: http://eng.stat.gov.tw/mp.asp?mp=5; Knoema. 2013. Development Statistics of Taiwan. Available online at: http://knoema .com/TWDS2014/development-statistics-of-tai wan-2013?location=1000000-taiwan. Accessed on October 25, 2015.

41. National Health Insurance Administration. 2009. "The National Health Insurance Statistics 2009." Available online at: www.nhi.gov.tw/ English/webdata/webdata.aspx?menu=11&men u_id=296&WD_ID=296&webdata_id=3419. Accessed on December 12, 2015.

42. Yen-Huei Tarn. 2012. "Taiwan Health Insurance and HTA Development." Presentation at the China Health Insurance Reform Forum, Dalian, May 27, 2012.

43. ISPOR Global Health Care Systems Road Map. 2012. Available online at: www.ispor .org/htaroadmaps/taiwan.asp. Accessed on December 12, 2015.

44. Cheng-Hua Lee. 2012. "Taiwan Health Insurance: How to Determine Drug Formulary." Presentation at the 4th Huaxia PE and OR Forum, Beijing, May 5, 2012.

PART V

Product Manufacturers

China's Pharmaceutical Sector

RACHEL LEE AND LAWTON ROBERT BURNS

Introduction

This chapter describes the market opportunities and competitive dynamics in China's pharmaceutical sector. The rewards for pharmaceutical firms – both multinational companies (MNCs) and local players – are high. However, despite robust recent growth, companies are finding it increasingly difficult to compete in the new environment. Winners who wish to separate themselves from losers require a new strategy – one that is radically different from the strategy they have successfully employed before or in other markets. This chapter examines how the pharmaceutical sector evolved historically, its commercial model and current R&D efforts, and the latest policy and industry trends that are reshaping the landscape. The latter part of the chapter analyzes the biologics and vaccine segments, as well as over-the-counter (OTC) drugs, which are unique markets in different stages of development.

Measurement Issues

China's pharmaceutical manufacturers come in a variety of shapes and sizes. This makes it difficult to compare their business mix, market share, and performance on "an apples to apples" basis. For example,

- few companies are publically listed
- companies have a varying degree of active pharmaceutical ingredient (API) business mixed in with formulation business
- many have both a distribution and a manufacturing business
- companies often sell both traditional Chinese medicines (TCM) and western medicines
- some companies have both an OTC and prescription business blended together

Data reliability is another issue. Better data are available for hospital sales of prescription drugs in the top-tier cities and large hospitals. The more diversified the business and/or the greater the company's focus on smaller cities and hospitals, the less reliable the information becomes. With this heterogeneity in mind, the next section compiles a picture of the sector using estimates from different sources.

Overview of the Pharmaceutical Sector

Sector Fragmentation and Market Concentration

China's pharmaceutical sector is fragmented and subscale. Researchers and analysts estimate there are anywhere between 5,300 and 7,000 local manufacturers, each with a small share of the market. Most firms have a small revenue base (e.g., less than $16 million) and produce only a handful of products. The top 100 companies account for roughly 45 percent of the total revenue, with a minimum revenue among these top firms of 800 million RMB (approximately $130 million) in 2011. More recent data (2014) from IMS suggests the top 5 players account for only 9.2 percent of revenues, while the top 20 contribute 25 percent of revenues. According to the Commercial and Industry Bureau, company self-reported data suggest an average net profit margin of 10 percent among the 1,000 pharmaceutical manufacturers. The top 136 players generate most (80 percent) of the total profits in this group. Market leaders have higher profitability and can achieve 20–30 percent net margins.

China's pharmaceutical sector is much more fragmented than in the United States and elsewhere in the world.[1] Such fragmentation heightens competition. Moreover, most of the products are generics, and many firms make the same products; both of these factors further increase rivalry and generate price wars. In the face of such fragmentation, the government has set ambitious goals to consolidate the industry to foster larger and stronger players.

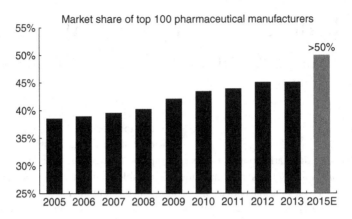

Figure 14.1 Growing concentration of pharma sector
Source: Jessica Li and Lillian Wan 2015. *China Healthcare Primer – The Immense Structural Upside.* Bank of America Merrill Lynch (July 9).

Specifically, the Chinese government hopes to achieve the following goals by the end of the 12th Five-Year Plan: (a) the top 100 companies should account for more than 50 percent of sector revenues by 2015, (b) 5+ companies should have revenues of 50 billion RMB, and (c) the top 100 companies should have revenues greater than 10 billion RMB. Admittedly, these goals have also been proposed in previous five-year plans. While they have not been fully met, the government's ambition to implement them has not abated. The sector has been slowly consolidating over time, due to the government's urging and a recent acceleration in company mergers from less than 5 in 2010 to roughly 60 by 2014 (see Figure 14.1).

Multinational Companies and Local Players

China's pharmaceutical sector includes both local domestic players and multinational corporations (MNCs). The MNCs include US, European, and Japanese firms such as Pfizer, AstraZeneca, and Sanofi-Aventis. They have typically been market leaders in terms of sales, with shares in the hospital market of 2–4 percent each (2013 data). As of 2014, there are 35 MNCs registered in China that belong to Research-Based Pharmaceutical Association (RDPAC). Leading local players include Qilu, Sino Biopharm, Hengrui, Fosun, and Shanghai Pharmaceuticals – which have

smaller shares of the hospital market (1–3 percent each). The top ten players have captured only 27 percent of the hospital market; the top 50 players have just slightly over half of the market (see Table 14.1).

Collectively, however, the local players control roughly three-quarters of pharmaceutical sales to large hospitals – a share that has been stable over the past five years (Figure 14.2). Since hospitals comprise roughly 70 percent of the Chinese pharmaceutical market, this suggests that local firms control more than half of all pharmaceutical sales in the country.

A Leading Pharmaceutical Market in the Making

The Chinese market grew from just $5 billion in 2000, when it was the 11th largest market in the world, to $55 billion in 2010, making it the number three market.[2] Between 2010 and 2014, the market grew at a compound annual growth rate (CAGR) of 16 percent and reached $108 billion in 2014. For the 2015–2019 period, analysts expect growth to continue but at a lower 9 percent CAGR, reaching an estimated $170 billion by 2019 (see Figure 14.3). Such growth will make China the number two market after the United States. China will also continue to contribute to roughly one-quarter of global growth in pharmaceutical sales.

Table 14.1 MNCs versus local players: hospital data

Rank ('13 sales)	Pharmaceutical Companies		Market Share		
			2013	2012	1H14
1	Pfizer	辉瑞	3.98%	3.03%	4.09%
2	Novartis	诺华	3.68%	2.39%	3.90%
3	AstraZeneca	阿斯利康	3.36%	2.91%	3.56%
4	Sanofi-Aventis	赛诺菲	2.90%	2.41%	2.66%
5	Roche	罗氏	2.63%	2.36%	2.58%
6	Merck/MSD	默沙东	2.40%	1.91%	2.35%
7	Qilu Pharma	齐鲁制药	2.31%	1.63%	2.25%
8	Sino Biopharm	中国生物制药	2.29%	1.96%	2.21%
9	Bayer	拜耳	1.95%	1.82%	1.95%
10	Hengrui	恒瑞	1.65%	1.14%	1.74%
11	Yangtze River Pharma	扬子江药业	1.51%	0.87%	1.63%
12	Fosun Pharma	复星医药	1.41%	1.03%	1.47%
13	GSK	葛兰素史克	1.41%	1.22%	1.20%
14	China Resources Pharma	华润医药	1.36%	1.13%	1.05%
15	Shanghai Pharma	上海医药	1.26%	0.77%	1.20%
16	Bristol-Myers Squibb	百时美施贵宝	1.08%	0.91%	1.12%
17	Eli Lilly	礼来	1.06%	0.79%	1.11%
18	Baxter	百特	1.01%	0.78%	0.87%
19	Beijing SL Pharma	北京双鹭药业	1.00%	0.96%	1.02%
20	Fresenius	费森尤斯	0.98%	0.85%	0.87%
21	Boehringer Ingelheim	勃林格殷格翰	0.93%	0.68%	0.91%
22	Aosaikang	奥赛康药业	0.91%	0.72%	0.95%
23	North China Pharma	中国北方医药集团	0.90%	0.70%	0.90%
24	Kelun Pharma	科伦药业	0.89%	0.51%	0.90%
25	Sihuan Pharma	四环医药	0.89%	0.81%	0.72%

		2013	2012	1H14
Market share of Top 10:		*27.2%*	*25.0%*	*27.3%*
Market share of Top 20:		*39.2%*	*37.5%*	*38.9%*
Market share of Top 50:		*58.8%*	*56.2%*	*57.7%*

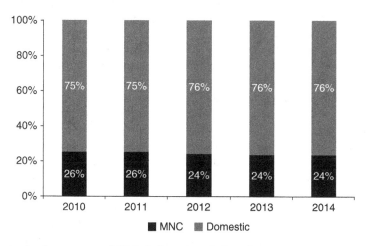

Figure 14.2 Domestic players versus MNCs in large hospital market
Source: Jessica Li & Lillian Wan 2015. *China Healthcare Primer – The Immense Structural Upside*. Bank of America Merrill Lynch (July 9).

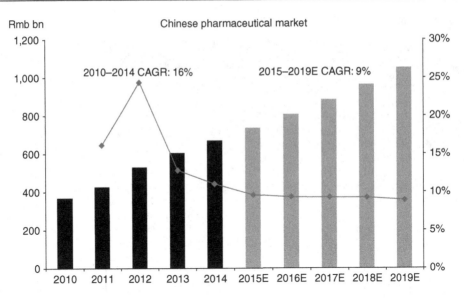

Figure 14.3 China's pharmaceutical market growth
Source: Jessica Li & Lillian Wan 2015. *China Healthcare Primer – The Immense Structural Upside.* Bank of America Merrill Lynch (July 9).

Growth Drivers

A number of factors drive expanding demand for pharmaceuticals in the country. As noted in Chapter 6, China is on an accelerated path as an aging society. Over the next 40 years, the population cohort 50+ years old will double from 22 percent to 44 percent of the total population. This process takes 100 years or more in many other countries. At the same time, changing lifestyles are contributing to a rise in chronic illness, which is also associated with older age. China already has the world's largest diabetic population of 92 million people. By 2020, one in three Chinese adults will have hypertension and one in ten will have type II diabetes. These changes in health status are accompanied by the rising wealth of the population: by 2020, the "middle and affluent population" will triple from 142 million to 401 million.[3] All of these trends create a strong underlying demand for pharmaceuticals. The 2009 healthcare reform extended access to public insurance coverage to the entire population, which in turn will result in realized demand. Previously uninsured or underinsured urban residents (retirees, students, children, etc.) and the rural population will increasingly present themselves to the healthcare system to seek care and treatment.

The Chinese government's 12th Five-Year Plan (2011–2015) set three overarching goals that suggest ambitious plans for the country's life sciences sectors. These include accelerating structural changes in the pharmaceutical sector, meeting the rising demand for healthcare services, and developing the biotechnology sector as one of the seven emerging strategic industries. Structural changes include targets for innovative products, technological capabilities, and manufacturing quality. With regard to product innovation, the goal is to have 30 innovative small molecule drugs for severe and highly prevalent diseases; 15 new biologic drugs to treat cardiovascular, central nervous system, gastrointestinal, AIDS, and immunological diseases; and 50+ new TCM drugs. With regard to technological capabilities, the goal for small molecule drugs is to improve active pharmaceutical ingredients (API), fermentation, and formulation. For biologics, the goal is to develop capabilities in antibodies, vaccines, cell culture technologies, and protein expression technologies. With regard to manufacturing, one goal is that all manufacturers meet the new good manufacturing practice (GMP) standards. To meet this goal, the pharmaceutical sector needs to consolidate into fewer but larger and stronger companies.

Market Segments: Diverse and Dispersed

Sales Channels

In contrast to the United States, China's pharmaceutical market relies heavily on the institutional channel (hospitals and clinics). The majority of total drug spending flows through hospital pharmacies; the remainder is sold in retail pharmacies across the country (see Figures 14.4 and 14.5). Figure 14.6 illustrates the market segments among the healthcare institution and retail channels. The six types of customer segments vary significantly in terms of drug purchase levels, patient profiles, and growth drivers. These segments are covered in detail below.

City Hospitals

City hospitals, particularly the large Class III institutions (cf. Chapter 8), are the most well-equipped facilities with highly trained doctors and more sophisticated treatment practices. On average, the 11,300 city hospitals spend about 30 million RMB on drugs annually. Moreover, most patients in these hospitals have either Urban Employee Basic Medical Insurance (UEBMI) coverage or higher levels of disposable income, which in turn make drugs and hospital services more affordable. Growth drivers in this population segment of hospital customers are primarily attributed to the rising prevalence of chronic illness stemming from economic development (noted above).

Community Health Centers and Stations

Urban-based community health centers (CHCs) and community health stations (CHSs) have on average only 3.8 million RMB in annual drug spending. Moreover, they are required to use only drugs on

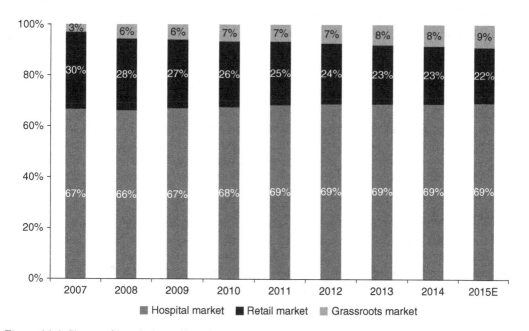

Figure 14.4 Shares of hospital, retail, and grassroots markets
Source: Jessica Li & Lillian Wan 2015. *China Healthcare Primer – The Immense Structural Upside*. Bank of America Merrill Lynch (July 9).

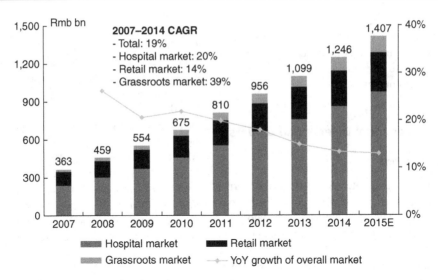

Figure 14.5 Sales and growth of end market
Source: Jessica Li & Lillian Wan 2015. *China Healthcare Primer – The Immense Structural Upside.* Bank of America Merrill Lynch (July 9).

the Essential Drugs List (EDL) (see Chapter 5 and below discussion). These care sites include 7,800 CHCs and their satellite CHSs that number about 25,000. The 2009 reform converted Class I hospitals and some Class II hospitals to CHCs/CHSs in order to serve as the country's new primary care system. The goal is to have this primary care system divert patient flow away from the crowded tertiary care settings (Class II and III hospitals) to less intensive and lower-cost sites with lower utilization. Patients who seek care in these community sites are typically elderly patients with chronic illnesses or patients with Urban Resident Basic Medical Insurance (URBMI) coverage.

Since the reform, however, these community sites have seen only a slow uptake in their patient volume. Despite free registration fees, low cost medications and services, and more convenient locations, patients are reluctant to seek care in the CHCs/CHSs. They are instead willing to wait in long lines to see doctors in the Class II and III hospitals. Nevertheless, there are some signs of change in the role these centers play. Instead of only refilling prescriptions initially written in the large hospitals, CHC doctors are now more confident to conduct the initial diagnosis, to write the scripts themselves, and to undertake disease management for chronic illnesses. The growth of this

market segment is driven by the government's mandate to use these facilities in order to obtain insurance reimbursement. Any fundamental changes to patient uptake will need to come from further upgrades in the quality of the centers' personnel and facilities.

County Hospitals

County hospitals serve as tertiary care centers for the rural population. Compared to the other rural care sites, county hospitals are larger, better equipped, and have more highly trained physicians. They are also the biggest beneficiaries of the 2009 healthcare reform. As part of the reform, the government spent $9 billion to upgrade their personnel (via training) and facilities in order to attract rural residents to seek quality tertiary care locally rather than travel to the city hospitals. Among the total of 10,300 county hospitals, 500 are slated to become Class III facilities by 2020.

County hospitals account for 17 percent of the pharmaceutical market today. Due to the reform, they are expected to grow at a faster rate than other segments and account for roughly 30 percent of the total market by 2020. These rural tertiary care hospitals have large spending power. The county

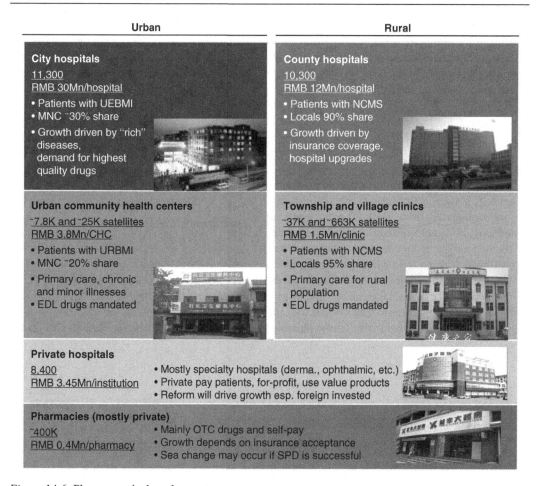

Urban	Rural
City hospitals 11,300 RMB 30Mn/hospital • Patients with UEBMI • MNC ~30% share • Growth driven by "rich" diseases, demand for highest quality drugs	**County hospitals** 10,300 RMB 12Mn/hospital • Patients with NCMS • Locals 90% share • Growth driven by insurance coverage, hospital upgrades
Urban community health centers ~7.8K and ~25K satellites RMB 3.8Mn/CHC • Patients with URBMI • MNC ~20% share • Primary care, chronic and minor illnesses • EDL drugs mandated	**Township and village clinics** ~37K and ~663K satellites RMB 1.5Mn/clinic • Patients with NCMS • Locals 95% share • Primary care for rural population • EDL drugs mandated

Private hospitals
8,400
RMB 3.45Mn/institution
• Mostly specialty hospitals (derma., ophthalmic, etc.)
• Private pay patients, for-profit, use value products
• Reform will drive growth esp. foreign invested

Pharmacies (mostly private)
~400K
RMB 0.4Mn/pharmacy
• Mainly OTC drugs and self-pay
• Growth depends on insurance acceptance
• Sea change may occur if SPD is successful

Figure 14.6 Pharmaceutical market customer segments

hospital segment is dominated by local Chinese companies, which command a 90 percent share of the generics market. As the gatekeeper for 600 million rural patients, these hospitals will be the next battleground for pharmaceutical manufacturers. However, affordability constraints, regional differences, and the large geographic dispersion of these facilities pose challenges to the traditional go-to-market approach. Cost-effective sales and marketing will be key competitive capabilities.

Rural Clinics and Township Centers

Village clinics and township health centers (THCs) represent the primary and secondary care sites for the rural population. There are an estimated 37,000 THCs with another 663,000 clinics that serve as village satellites. Collectively, these sites each account for an average of 1.5 million RMB spending on drugs. As in the county hospitals, prescribing drugs on the EDL is mandatory.

Private Hospitals

Private hospitals have historically played a minor role in China's healthcare system. While there are roughly 8,400 private hospitals today, they are typically small in size and command only 10 percent market share in patient utilization. Collectively, their drug spends account for an even smaller percentage (4 percent) of the total pharmaceutical market. Nevertheless, the government has encouraged the private sector to expand capacity, meet rising demand for healthcare services (in part driven by increased insurance coverage), and foster competition with the public hospital sector. This segment is expected to grow at more than 20 percent annually as a result – a rate faster than the public hospital segment.

Retail Pharmacies

The non-institutional (retail pharmacy) channel has long played a supplemental role in the dispensing of drugs in China. Only 20 percent of drug spending flows through non-hospital pharmacies. The major issue in this channel is that government insurance does not reimburse retail prescription drugs. Patients nevertheless seek drugs in this channel for purposes of convenience and/or privacy concerns (e.g., drugs to treat erectile dysfunction or hepatitis). In recent years, some pharmacy

chains have collaborated on coverage with the public insurance bureau to obtain reimbursement on selected drugs. Going forward, volume growth in this segment will depend on broader public insurance coverage. The real upside potential for this channel lies in current efforts to separate the dispensing and prescribing of drugs in public hospitals (see Chapter 8). This long-discussed initiative has been difficult to implement due to hospital reliance on drug sales to subsidize their operations.

Therapeutic Categories

Another way to segment China's pharmaceutical sector is by therapeutic category. Table 14.2 lists the top 20 therapeutic categories in China's pharmaceutical sector for 2013. Not surprisingly, based on analyses in prior chapters, antibiotics are the leading category. Figure 14.7 displays

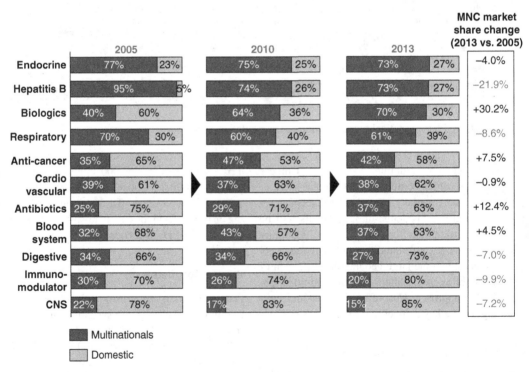

Figure 14.7 MNCs versus local players by therapeutic category
Source: Richard Yeh, Ziyi Chen, & Sean Lo. 2014. *Chinese Healthcare Sector Handbook 2015.* CitiResearch (December 9).

Table 14.2 Top 20 therapeutic categories

治疗小类	Therapeutic Class	2013 Market Share	'10-'13 CAGR	'13 yoy	1H14 yoy
抗感染药	Antibiotics	15.8%	0%	4%	11%
心血管系统用药	Cardiovascular	13.5%	16%	12%	10%
血液系统用药	Blood system	11.2%	15%	9%	11%
抗肿瘤药	Anti-cancer	9.7%	17%	11%	16%
消化系统用药	Digestive system	8.5%	17%	14%	15%
神经系统用药	Central nervous system	8.4%	25%	16%	16%
免疫调节剂	Immunomodulators	7.5%	17%	13%	12%
内分泌用药	Endocrine	5.8%	15%	13%	15%
生物技术药物	Biologics	3.0%	23%	18%	12%
呼吸系统药品	Respiratory system	2.9%	20%	13%	14%
骨骼与肌肉用药	Bone and muscular	2.5%	16%	8%	11%
精神障碍用药	Mental disorders	1.8%	20%	15%	14%
麻醉药	Anesthetics	1.7%	16%	12%	15%
生殖系统用药	Reproductive system	0.8%	17%	10%	18%
感觉器官用药	Sensory organ	0.7%	17%	9%	15%
皮肤科用药	Dermatology	0.6%	14%	11%	4%
泌尿系统用药	Urinary system	0.5%	11%	3%	3%

Source: Richard Yeh, Ziyi Chen, & Sean Lo. 2014. *Chinese Healthcare Sector Handbook 2015*. CitiResearch (December 9).

the market shares of MNCs versus local firms in selected categories.

A Land of Generics, but Slowly Changing

Until MNCs entered China with their branded innovative drugs, China's own pharmaceutical sector manufactured and sold generic products. Even today, 75 percent of the pharmaceutical market is still comprised of generics (15 percent unbranded, 60 percent branded); only 5 percent of the market value derives from sales of patented drugs, while another 20 percent derives from MNCs' sales of off-patent drugs. These percentages are expected to change to a slightly higher share for patented drugs as local firms increase their production of innovative products (see Figure 14.8). One interesting quirk is that only 15 percent of the generics market consists of unbranded products. This is due to legacy regulations whereby approved new drugs receive a brand unless the molecule is already in the pharmacopeia (see Figure 14.9 for the classification of new drugs).

The dominance of generics and the lack of patent protection heighten price competition, price wars, and susceptibility to government price-cutting to control rising healthcare costs. All of these factors suggest that the growth of China's pharmaceutical sector depends more on volume than on price. Over the period 2003–2013, volume growth doubled price growth (14 percent vs. 7 percent CAGR); in 2013, pharmaceutical prices actually declined for the first time (see Figures 14.10 and 14.11). While China enjoys a favorable global position in terms of its large population and volume potential, it is also distinguished by a low level of drug spending per capita (Figure 14.12).

Moving forward, the composition of the market will gradually shift (see Figure 14.13). Patented drugs will grow the fastest and are expected to double their presence. The driving forces behind this shift are twofold. First, MNCs are expediting global launches of new products in China, while local companies are endeavoring to generate domestic patented drugs. Second, improved insurance coverage and the general rise in drug affordability due to economic development will support the consumption of patented drugs.

The share of originator off-patent drugs will shrink, as the government actively reduces the premiums on these drugs marketed by MNCs. Rising volume may partially offset the price erosion due to growing affordability of drugs, trust in MNCs' brand quality, and perceived higher value. The market share currently enjoyed by off-patent brands can potentially shrink from 20 percent today to roughly 15 percent over the next decade.

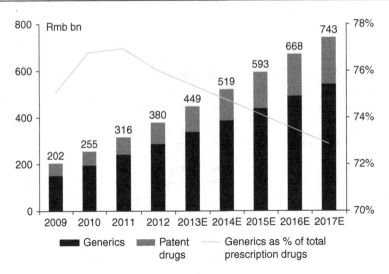

Figure 14.8 Sales of patent/off-patent originators versus generics
Source: Jessica Li & Lillian Wan 2015. *China Healthcare Primer – The Immense Structural Upside*. Bank of America Merrill Lynch (July 9).

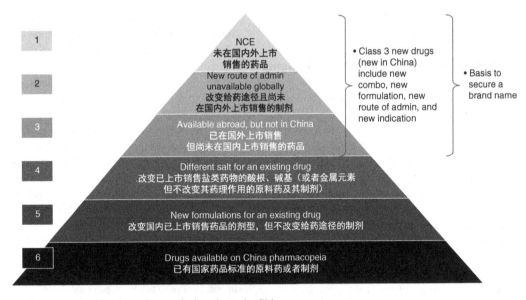

Figure 14.9 Classification of prescription drugs in China

What will happen to the 60 percent of the market controlled by branded generics? A portion of branded products will become unbranded: the China State Food and Drug Administration (CFDA) tightened the rules in 2006 to allow only Class I through III new drugs to be entitled to a brand. Another portion of branded generics will become differentiated generics as local companies strive for incremental innovation and quality for a price premium. This segment is likely to represent another 15 percent of the total market in ten years' time.

Another way to segment the market is by the product's reimbursement status. There will be products on the Essential Drugs List (EDL) and

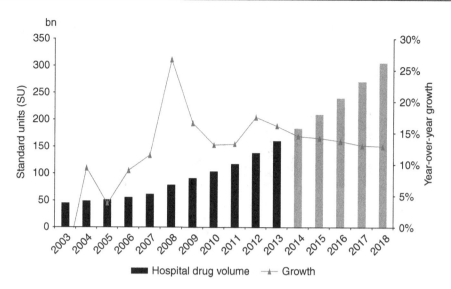

Figure 14.10 Sector growth: hospital volume
Source: Jessica Li & Lillian Wan 2015. *China Healthcare Primer – The Immense Structural Upside*. Bank
of America Merrill Lynch (July 9).

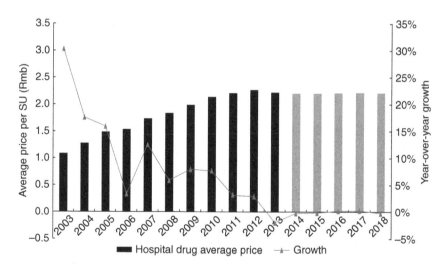

Figure 14.11 Trend in average drug price
Source: Jessica Li & Lillian Wan 2015. *China Healthcare Primer – The Immense Structural Upside*. Bank
of America Merrill Lynch (July 9).

products on the RDL (Reimbursement Drug List).
EDL drugs will experience strong growth as the
government continues to expand the list and mandate their usage – not only in basic healthcare institutions but also increasingly in tertiary care settings.
This segment may account for one-third of the total
market by 2020.

Complex Market Access Hurdles

Market access is a long and complicated process in
China (see Figure 14.14). Success demands long-
term investment in resources and careful navigation of the following steps: registration and
approval of new drugs, pricing and bidding,

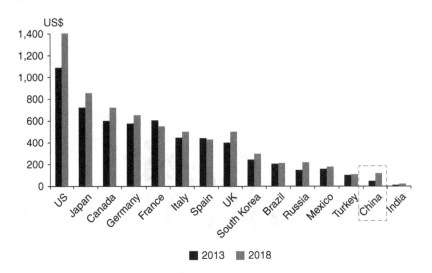

Figure 14.12 Per capita drug spend
Source: Jessica Li & Lillian Wan 2015. *China Healthcare Primer – The Immense Structural Upside*. Bank of America Merrill Lynch (July 9).

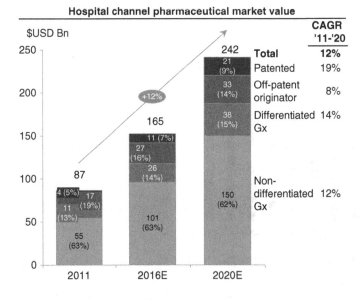

Notes: Sales are based on hospital purchase price and do not include retail pharmacies or TCM. Exchange rate 1USD = 6.2RMB

Figure 14.13 China's pharmaceutical market by product segment

reimbursement listing at the local and national level, and finally hospital listing. The process typically takes about four to six years for companies who are registering patented or differentiated generics. Provincial bidding takes place every two years or so; national reimbursement listing is every four to five years; the hospital listing process can take another two years' time. As a result, new

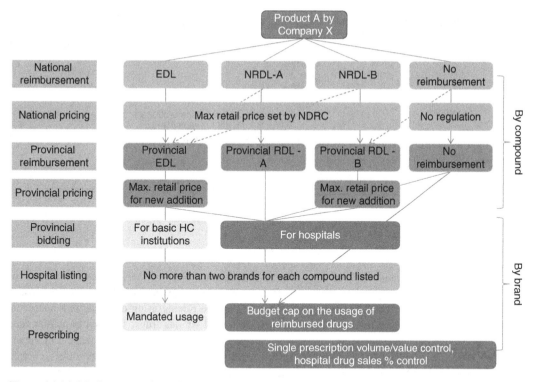

Figure 14.14 Market access in China

drug launches in China may wait an average of seven years for drug approval, launch, and listing in the target hospitals. Only upon completion of this process can companies commence sales activity in full force.

Depending on where the launch date falls during the five-year interval of national reimbursement listing, the company may wait another two to five years to see significant volume uptake from higher affordability. On the other hand, off-patent products have enjoyed higher premiums and do not see precipitous drop in revenue following the entry of generics. The volume and share largely depend on hospital economics – e.g., where higher-priced imported drugs are key to higher hospital profits. As a result, a product's life cycle in China looks dramatically different. Instead of a bell-shaped curve as in developed markets, it has a much slower ramp-up but maintains high growth for a long time. The total product life cycle can thus be as long as 20–30 years (see Figure 14.15).

Pricing

As with all other products in China, drug prices are regulated by the government's pricing bureau. The National Development and Reform Commission (NDRC) sets the maximum retail prices for drugs. GMP price is determined by surveying representative companies to obtain the average production price for a given molecule. Then a reasonable profit over the cost of production and business operations is added to reach the maximum retail price. For close to a decade, a second pricing mechanism existed whereby companies could apply for independent pricing for products they deemed as having original innovation or quality and technical differentiation. In this case, the price was determined through direct negotiation between the manufacturer and the NDRC. Historically MNCs were able to obtain independent pricing status for all of their drugs (globally patented or already off-patent); a few local companies managed to obtain

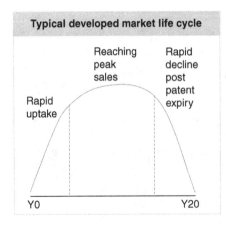
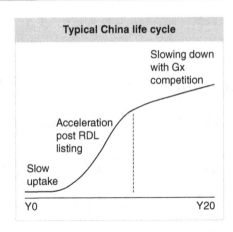

Figure 14.15 Product life cycle comparison

independent pricing status as well for selected drugs. The independently priced drugs often enjoyed a premium over the GMP price to 2–3x in the case of primary care treatments, 5–6x for drugs used in oncology and specialty care.

The rules have repeatedly changed in recent years, however. In 2007, the NDRC stopped granting independent prices to any drugs while they contemplated how to improve and enhance the overall drug pricing policy. The government revised its policy and put in place a five-step process for price-setting: regulators would visit the manufacturer to assess product cost and evaluate the proposed price, an expert group then evaluated the price, a public hearing gathered comments on the price, group discussions were convened, and a final price was determined. New drug imports generally obtained prices near the free-market price; imported generics obtained lower prices but higher than that enjoyed by local generic manufacturers. In 2010, the NDRC imposed price ceilings on the retail prices of selected drugs, rather than allow manufacturers to independently set prices. Most of the products that were targeted were made by MNCs and their joint ventures with local firms.

The new policy formulated conveyed a sense of balance between encouraging innovation (even if it is incremental innovation) and discouraging unnecessary generic duplication. More transparent and stringent criteria were applied when granting premiums over GMP prices. Under this new policy,

maximum retail prices for patented drugs were based on a combination of manufacturer costs and reference pricing using domestic and international prices of similar drugs. The first-to-market generic product would be priced at 90 percent of the originator's drug; prices for the first three generics to reach the market would be set at 90 percent of the predecessor's product. If a generic was not among the first three to market but presents evidence of differentiation, it could obtain up to 30 percent premium over the GMP price. The criteria needed to qualify for differentiation are still relatively vague but appear to be more stringent than before (e.g., those that have won a national technology award or those with higher quality).

In June 2015, the NDRC and six other government agencies issued a circular that removed many of its prior constraints on drug prices (e.g., price ceilings such as maximum retail prices or MRPs, or specific prices). The new policy extended to nearly 2,700 drugs included for reimbursement on public insurance schemes and included on the Reimbursement Drug List (see below); the number represents about 23 percent of all drugs sold in China. Now, with the exception of narcotics and certain psychotropic products (which would remain subject to MRPs), various market mechanisms would set drug prices; the government would also rely on a "pricing bureau" inside the NDRC to scrutinize illegal pricing behavior. These market mechanisms include (a)

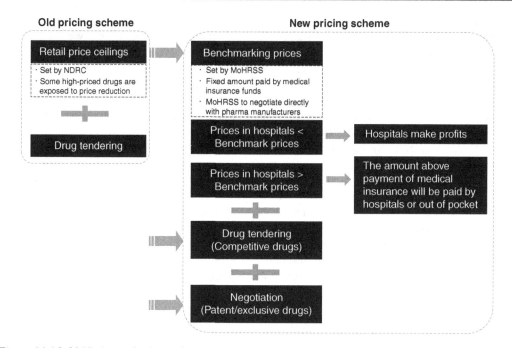

Figure 14.16 2015 change in drug pricing
Source: Jessica Li & Lillian Wan 2015. *China Healthcare Primer – The Immense Structural Upside*. Bank of America Merrill Lynch (July 9).

transparent negotiations involving hospitals, provincial governments, and insurance schemes for the purchase of patented drugs or TCM products made exclusively by one manufacturer; (b) negotiations between hospitals and public insurance schemes, which can set benchmark prices (rather than price ceilings) for products listed on the NRDL; (c) bidding processes or procurement negotiations for blood products outside of the NRDL; and (d) free pricing for other drugs, provided that prices accurately reflect cost and conditions of supply and demand (see Figure 14.16).[4]

Reimbursement

The Reimbursement Drug List (RDL) originated from the drug formulary for UEBMI enrollees. The national RDL (NRDL) is managed by the Ministry of Human Resources and Social Security (MoHRSS) and issued/updated every five years. The most recent NRDL was issued in 2009 and includes 987 TCM products and 1,164 western products. Criteria for listing on the NRDL include clinical need and utilization, safety and efficacy, reasonable pricing, average total cost, number of years on the market, and cost-effectiveness.

There have been four rounds to date, the latest in 2014. The formulary is divided into two lists (A and B) and goes by molecules rather than brands. The RDL-A list contains the most basic treatments and older generation drugs, supplied by multiple manufacturers, typically at fairly low prices. The RDL-B list contains more advanced treatments that carry higher prices and lower reimbursement. For example, for the oral treatment of diabetes, Metformin IR (regular release) is on the A list, while Metformin XR (extended release), Arcabose, and Pioglitizone are on the B list. The A list includes 349 western drugs; the B list includes 791 western drugs (the remaining drugs are for occupational injuries and contraception). An updated NRDL was anticipated in 2014 but was still delayed as of April of the following year.

The RDL-A list is national in nature; the RDL-B list can be modified locally by the Provincial Bureau of Human Resources and Social Security (BOHRSS). This results in a provincial reimbursement drug list, or PRDL. The government allows up to 15 percent variation in the number of molecules to accommodate variations across provinces in their economic development and fiscal strength.

RDL-A list drugs enjoy 100 percent reimbursement; reimbursement levels for RDL-B list drugs vary across provinces and typically range from 50 percent to 80 percent. Drugs on RDL-B list are categorized by active ingredient, not by brand name. This means there is one reimbursement for each active ingredient, regardless of brand name or price. This policy renders western medications more affordable to Chinese consumers, because the imported product and locally made generic receive the same level of reimbursement. Consumers also end up choosing the imported version due to preference for branded and western products.

The Essential Drugs List was created by the Ministry of Health (MOH) in 2009 as part of the healthcare reform initiative. The goal is to provide quality, low-cost medications to the entire population; the list reflects treatments for roughly two-thirds of the most common conditions in the country. The EDL list nearly overlaps the RDL-A list. However, the administration of EDL falls under the Pharmaceutical Policy Division (药政司) of the MOH, in collaboration with MOHRSS and several other related ministries. This is due to the fact that, historically, the MOH's Rural Administrative Division handled the provision as well as the financing for healthcare for the rural population. The national EDL expanded from 307 molecules in the 2009 version (including 5 western medicines) to 520 molecules in the 2012 version (with 317 western medicines). The latter version includes some of the most popular and best-selling MNC off-patent drugs (e.g., Pfizer's Norvasc and Diflucan, Novo Nordisk's Novolin, Bayer's Glucobay). If the MNC and its molecule participate on the EDL, the MNC originator premium will likely be eliminated and prices for the MNC brands will be 50–80 percent lower.

Provinces have latitude to modify the list to fit their fiscal conditions and local healthcare needs.

The 2009 National EDL contained an average of an additional 188 molecules than were on the provincial EDLs. When these molecules listed on the EDL, 45 percent of them had their maximum retail price reduced by 12 percent on average; 49 percent maintained their previous maximum retail price while on the RDL. EDL usage is mandated in the basic healthcare system (small public clinics and health centers); such clinics and centers are required to purchase only EDL products. There is also an effort to increase the EDL's usage in city hospitals (e.g., using a ratio of essential to non-essential pharmaceutical revenues: 45 percent of Class II hospital revenues, 25 percent of Class III hospital revenues); by 2020, all state-owned facilities are expected to be fully stocked by EDL products. Because EDL drugs are fully reimbursed, there is strong pressure to ensure that EDL drug prices are kept low.

Bidding

The practice of provincial level bidding began in 1995 and assumed its current format with the 2009 healthcare reform. The early impetus behind regional government bidding was the rising cost of drugs that resulted from distribution markups. China's drug distribution network gained notoriety for the multiplicity of small distributors and multiple points in the supply chain. In prior years, bidding rules varied significantly; some provinces even started municipal level bidding. Savings from bidding were passed onto hospitals, but not to patients. In 2009, the MOH and five other ministries issued guidance on public hospital purchasing practices. The provincial bidding is to benefit all Class II and III hospitals in the city. Once the results are finalized, prices to these hospitals in the province cannot exceed the provincial cap.

Drugs are separated into two groups: (a) non-differentiated or common generics and (b) differentiated generics (previously with independent pricing status). In the former (non-differentiated) group, typically two to four drugs of the same molecule with the lowest prices can win the bid. In the latter (differentiated) group, winners include the originator product and one to two differentiated generics.

Each province has its own sets of rules that balance between cost and quality. Some provinces set up quality tiers and give more weight to quality considerations. Companies are scored on various merits including the product itself, along with the company's standing and history. For example, companies can earn points and increase their score by being more highly ranked by the Ministry of Information and Industry, by having a manufacturing site located in a government planned high-tech zone, or by having a drug with a National Science and Technology award.

Provincial bidding typically opens every two years. However, there are no set dates; each province sets its own dates. There are no unified national timelines for bidding; provinces often change the timelines for various reasons. In the summer of 2013, due to the anti-corruption campaign, many provinces placed bidding on hold. Drugs launched during that summer and fall faced a much slower ramp-up due to a lack of market access. EDL drugs have a separate bidding process. Discussions were undertaken to unify the bidding, with some industry experts advocating for complete removal of provincial level bidding.

It is important to note that, unlike tendering in other markets, these bidding and tendering exercises require no volume purchasing commitment attached to a given bid. They thus serve effectively as ways to obtain lower prices from drug manufacturers. Discussions during the ongoing healthcare reform have considered whether EDL drugs should follow a true tendering process that exchanges volume commitment for price discounts.

Hospital Listing/Formulary

The hospital formulary listing is the last market access hurdle to overcome. Started in 2007, hospitals have implemented the policy whereby only two manufacturers (two brands) are allowed seats in the hospital formulary for any given drug with a specification (一品双规). The actual implementation of the policy varies, but typically a hospital gives one seat to the originator product and another seat to a local generic. It is uncommon to give both seats to two generics. Such a policy has helped to secure hospital access for MNC originator products

and made it more difficult for generics to win against each other or displace the incumbent.

Drug Cost Control Measures

Drug costs account for one-third of China's total healthcare expenditure and thus constitute a prime target for cost containment efforts. Cutting drug prices has been the strategy of choice to control drug costs for many years. Between 2000 and 2010, the government initiated 18 rounds of price cuts that yielded over $300 million in cost savings. The magnitude of the price cuts varied; they generally ranged between 10 percent and 15 percent for large spend therapeutic areas such as antibiotics, diabetes, and hypertension drugs. The expansion of health insurance coverage during the 2009 reform increased pressure on the government to further contain healthcare costs and reduce drug spend.

At the same time, however, the government recognized a need to balance cost containment with rewards for innovation. As a result, the NDRC formalized the price cutting policy in 2010 by specifying the frequency and magnitude. Drugs with patent protection or equivalent would face a 6 percent price cut every two to three years, while off-patent drugs would face a 15 percent price cut every two to three years. Under this new policy, the major issue facing the MNCs is the disappearance of the originator premium for their off-patent brands. Because these products often account for 70–80 percent of their total China business, the policy and the loss of premium pricing pose a very large risk. The government has previously indicated that they would like to reduce the originator premium to about 30 percent over the GMP price. Officials have also stated that while this is a goal, policy implementation will vary by drug. It is likely that the MNC originator premium will range between 30 percent and 100 percent by 2015.

Basic healthcare facilities (e.g., urban CHCs and CHSs, rural township hospitals, and village clinics) are required to use 100 percent EDL drugs; Class II and III hospitals have a minimum usage mandate which varies by province. Due to low medical service charges, hospitals have relied heavily on drugs

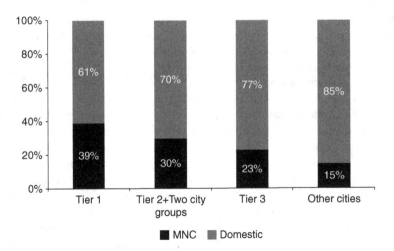

Figure 14.17 Domestic players versus MNCs by city tiers
Source: Jessica Li & Lillian Wan 2015. *China Healthcare Primer – The Immense Structural Upside*. Bank of America Merrill Lynch (July 9).

and diagnostic tests to generate revenues. Prescribing higher-priced drugs meant higher hospital profits. In the current reform era, local governments have deployed various cost containment measures to reduce hospital incentives to prescribe these higher-priced medicines. For example, the implementation of global budgeting by Shanghai reduced prescription volume and shifted the mix toward less expensive generic drugs.

Competitive Capabilities and Performance

As noted earlier, the government is seeking to consolidate the pharmaceutical sector and increase the average size of firms. The government has also pursued policies to support quality improvement and incentives to innovate in the sector. With regard to quality, the 2011 new GMP standard contains more stringent requirements than in previous versions; all manufacturers need to be qualified by 2015. While China has upgraded its GMP standards on a regular basis, the government issued its policy on bioequivalence in 2013 whereby all generic chemical drugs approved before October 1, 2007, need to conduct bioequivalence studies against their reference compounds. Failed drugs will no longer

be allowed on the market. The plan is to have all the EDL drugs go through bioequivalence testing by 2020. Both policies are geared toward the minimum quality standards for industry entry. With regard to innovation, the government has initiated a different set of policies using pricing and bidding levers to reward higher quality and more innovative players (discussed below).

Table 14.1 displays the performance of pharmaceutical companies in terms of their hospital market sales; Figure 14.17 shows that MNCs perform better relative to the local firms in the larger Tier 1 cities. The MNCs' average annual compounded growth rates ranged from 20 percent to 28 percent during the past few years. The other top performing group were the local private companies (e.g., Qilu, Sino Biopharm, Hengrui) which achieved a higher average CAGR around 25–35 percent during the same period. Large state-owned enterprises (SOEs) such as Shanghai Pharmaceuticals have come in a distant third with average growth rates hovering around 10 percent.

These three groups of companies have arrived at the top revenue positions by taking different approaches. For example, Shanghai Pharmaceuticals is an SOE with 600 molecules, the largest portfolio in the sector; however, only 12 of these molecules have some form of differentiation from other generics. Moreover, the average market size of its top ten western medicine drugs is 220 million RMB; by comparison, the market size of its top TCM drug is slightly better. The company achieved top market position by virtue of large scale and a large number of small products that are not the most competitive in their therapeutic class.

By contrast, the leading privately-owned companies have developed and promoted a handful of individual "blockbusters" that gained independent pricing status. Among the MNCs, success has been built on academic promotion of individual products that have originator premiums. They have also been more heavily engaged in continually educating the market and driving underlying demand.

The Chinese pharmaceutical market has undergone three major periods of development. In each period, different MNCs have out-competed the others using different success drivers. During the 1980s and early 1990s, China's pharmaceutical market was quite immature with loose regulation (e.g., blurry lines between OTC and prescription drugs). OTC drugs enjoyed coverage under the limited public insurance available, which enabled them to leverage both advertising (for patients but also doctors) and hospital reimbursement to drive adoption. Leading MNCs (e.g., Xi'an Janssen, Bristol Myers Squibb, and Tianjin SmithKline) gained first-mover advantage here, relied on *guanxi* (relationships) with government officials, and used heavy advertising to create a strong corporate brand.

During the mid-1990s to mid-2000s period, particularly after China entered the World Trade Organization (WTO) (see Chapter 2), the pharmaceutical sector was the target of increased government regulation and public policies that served to attract foreign investment and technology. The healthcare delivery sector (including demand for drugs) experienced rapidly growing demand in affluent urban areas. MNCs flourished in this period with a simple formula: develop a China-appropriate portfolio of products and heavily invest in a commercial arms race (sales force size and marketing budgets) to gain a share of voice and build the market. Companies that did particularly well in this era were AstraZeneca, Bayer, and Pfizer.

The third period (since 2009) was a turning point: significant issues with access to care triggered the 2009 healthcare reform. The new operating environment for pharmaceutical companies changed. Demand will continue to grow but will be more widely spread geographically. Due to rising utilization of drugs, MNCs will be subjected to pricing pressures. Local players aim to further close the gap with MNCs on additional competitive dimensions of quality and remote R&D. Going forward, the winning formula for MNCs will be more challenging, including portfolio management of all three categories of products, enhanced capability in market access, commercial model innovation, and talent management.

In contrast to the MNCs and their branded products, the global generics companies (e.g., Sandoz, Teva, Dr. Reddy) have had very limited presence in China. Their lack of success reflects time-to-market and cost disadvantages against locals: imported generics lag behind local versions by a couple of years, there are no cost advantages after importation, and it is harder for non-originator non-Chinese brands to obtain listing on hospital formularies. Sandoz started selling in China in 2005 and reached only $80 million in sales after six years; 80 percent of their sales derived from one drug (Sandostatin) that Novartis agreed to transition to them in 2007. Sandostatin is a well-established brand that was built up over many years by Novartis with independent pricing status and limited generic competition.

Commercial Models: Selling, Marketing, and Distribution

Sales Representatives

Commercial investments soared after China's entry into the WTO in 2001. Between 2002 and 2011, seven major MNCs added 16,000 representatives ("reps") in China to reach a combined total of 18,400 reps – nearly an eightfold increase. The increased size of sales forces has been the primary driver of the top MNCs' impressive growth in China (20 percent–35 percent CAGR). Such investments in the commercial arms race made good business sense. Due to the lack of patent cliffs, product life cycles are long in China (cf. Figure 14.15): the originators are rewarded with a price premium despite the fact that their products are off-patent. In addition, the market to serve is quite large: there are 700+ county level cities and 21,000 hospitals to cover. Most markets are still in an early stage of development where physicians need education about diseases and their treatment. Placing sales reps in front of doctors is the primary method of communicating such information to them. Furthermore, face time is important, as the Chinese doctors prefer person-to-person interactions. All of these factors require increases in sales reps. Lastly, the prevailing detailing model of single-line, specialized calls requires a large number of reps. AstraZeneca and Sanofi were among the first to adopt this sales force structure. The rationale is that both Chinese doctors and the reps themselves are less sophisticated and cannot handle too many products or complicated messages. The adage "one product, one rep" makes drug detailing more effective. MNCs employ this model for their important brands in major hospitals in the "core market" of large hospitals in large cities.

In the past, when the cost of sales reps was low, adding more sales people was a cheap and easy way to generate sales, compared to extracting higher productivity per rep. However, the resource-intensive sales force is now encountering its own challenges. First, wage rates have been increasing rapidly at more than 10 percent annually over the past decade. The average fully-loaded cost of a sales rep now exceeds $50,000 a year. On the other hand, the average productivity of a sales rep among the top ten companies grew only 4 percent from $250,000 in 2005 to $330,000. As MNCs move beyond the big hospitals in big cities to smaller and more geographically dispersed facilities, the economics make it increasingly difficult to justify the 1:1 sales force detailing model. Per-hospital output is much lower, and scattered hospitals require more time to reach. MNCs may consider hiring cheaper reps in lower-tier cities. However, the economic productivity gain may not be large, while the internal human resources management issues prove challenging.

Alternative Models among MNCs

Some companies have started experimenting with alternative commercial models. Innovations can be summarized along two dimensions: (1) technology-enabled communication channel innovation and (2) customer relationship innovation. On the technology front, the environment is highly conducive. China is on its way to becoming the largest digital country; by 2015, it will have more internet users than the United States and Japan combined. Over 70 percent of Chinese doctors (including those in rural areas) use mobile devices for communication; 86 percent of them spend at least one hour on the phone (mostly checking emails and searching for information on the internet). On the customer relationship innovation front, companies have realized that their relationships with current customers are evolving, and that relationships with new customers need to be changed and segmented. For example, as pharmaceutical firms expand their footprint into smaller cities, they recognize that decision making shifts from the *clinical customer* to the *economic customer*: i.e., from individual doctors and departmental heads in the larger hospitals and cities to the administrators of smaller and local hospitals. Among existing customers, payers and government decision makers have become more sophisticated in their efforts to manage drug spend. There is thus an increasing need to properly market and communicate the right information to them.

Given this market evolution and the internal pressures discussed above, pharmaceutical companies are experimenting with new commercial models. Merck Sharp and Dohme (MSD) is one of the first movers. They have brought the global Univadis marketing platform to China and tailored it to local needs by providing medical education and professional information to Chinese doctors. In the first two years following its 2010 entry, Univadis had registered more than 100,000 users. When MSD entered into smaller cities and county hospitals in China, it heavily leveraged marketing to generate demand and reduce 1:1 detailing effort. The sales reps make the first in-person contact with prescribers to obtain their contact information. MSD established a call center for subsequent customer contacts, as well as center check-ins to provide information and help to prescribers.

Alternative Models among Local Players

Chinese companies have likewise experimented with alternative commercial models. Jointown focuses on broad market distribution and contract sales for manufacturers. It balances customer reach with the economics of commercial investment by deploying different tools for different segments of its commercial activities. The "foot soldiers" provide customer services to hospitals and doctors; telephone reps take orders from providers; and a website provides B2B services for smaller accounts.

A closer examination reveals that the commercial models deployed by Chinese companies are associated with their product portfolios.

Most local companies outsource commercial activities to either distributors or contract sales organizations (CSOs) to sell non-differentiated generics. Hisun, for example, uses CSOs to conduct bidding, hospital listing, and sales promotion activities. Hisun employs roughly 100 people to manage the CSOs and distributors but has few staff devoted to product marketing.

Other pharmaceutical companies that have a few differentiated products which can obtain independent pricing and price premiums can justify having an in-house sales force that promotes their products directly to doctors. Hengrui, for example, has 2,000 sales reps; three-quarters of them are dedicated to selling products in the firm's oncology portfolio in large cities and hospitals using the single line detailing approach. Hengrui's primary products are Oxaliplatin and Paclitaxel, two popular oncology molecules. Hengrui organizes smaller scale marketing events such as local conferences and departmental seminars to educate physicians about how to treat disease using its products. This approach enables them to gain control of the end-customer relationship.

The third commercial approach uses a mixed model. Simcere, for example, initially leverages CSOs to get its priority products covered and listed on the hospital formulary. Once coverage and market access are reached, Simcere gradually builds its own sales force and takes the bidding and detailing

functions back in-house. Marketing of key products is also handled internally. Over time, the company has built up a sales force of 1,000–1,500 reps. For non-differentiated drugs and the majority of its portfolio, Simcere uses a large network of more than 1,300 distributors to penetrate the broader market.

Cost structures differ for each commercial model. Companies that deploy the agency model typically have a cost of goods sold (COGS) around 60 percent and a sales and marketing (S&M) spend of 10 percent of revenue. Companies using a sales force model typically have COGS of 10–15 percent of revenue and an S&M spend of 30–40 percent of revenue.

Corrupt Practices in Sales and Marketing: GlaxoSmithKline

On June 27, 2013, Chinese investigators raided the Shanghai headquarters of GlaxoSmithKline (GSK) alleging the company had paid bribes to hospital administrators, physicians, and local officials to increase the sales of its drugs. Such bribes could motivate providers to sell more expensive western brand drugs; they also reportedly increased the price of the drugs by one-third.[5] The head of the country's Ministry of Public Security asserted that bribes totaling $450 million were administered through a network of travel agencies and middlemen starting in 2009. Based on allegations of an internal whistle-blower, the company paid physicians between 7 percent and 10 percent of the proceeds from the drugs they ordered as an inducement.

A Chinese court subsequently fined GSK $492 million and sentenced five defendants to prison. GSK responded by terminating the contracts of over 100 employees, and by halting compensation of its sales representatives based on sales targets linked to the number of prescriptions that their physician customers wrote. Some industry observers were surprised that a multinational company was singled out in the country's cross-industry anti-corruption campaign, as this problem in the pharmaceutical industry has been deeply rooted and developing over many years.

Competitive Dynamics: Market Convergence

In the past few years, a great convergence has taken place as (a) MNCs move down to the "mid-market" (i.e., tier 3–7 cities and some top-tier counties) with lower-priced branded generics while (b) Chinese firms move up to the core market with more differentiated products. About 60–80 percent of the revenues among seven top MNCs have come from off-patent originator branded generics. The pricing premiums enjoyed by the originators on these off-patent products are declining, exposing their China business to a significant risk. At the same time, the MNCs have been unable to reach the vast majority of the Chinese market with their higher priced products due to lower purchasing power, affordability, and less advanced treatment practices outside the major cities.

Driven by these pressures, Merck, AstraZeneca, and Pfizer made moves to enter the mid-market by 2011–2012. Both Merck and Pfizer sought joint ventures (JVs) with leading local Chinese companies (e.g., Hisun); AstraZeneca pursued an acquisition strategy and formed a broad market business unit dedicated to commercializing branded generics. By contrast, Bayer pursued a complementary strategy by purchasing a generics company with specific products fitting onto the existing commercial platform in a given therapeutic area. The acquisition of Bioton's SciLin filled a portfolio gap in the treatment of diabetes and also provided a more affordable option to the higher-priced products sold by Novo and Lilly.

This wave of mid-market expansion and nonproprietary branded generics play now has a track record of a few years. The Pfizer–Hisun JV is showing early signs of success. According to the parent company's annual report, the JV business nearly doubled to reach 6.3 billion RMB (roughly $690 million) in 2013. A number of factors favor this JV. First and foremost, the portfolio consists of high-selling drugs and category leaders including Pfizer's Medrol and Tazocin and Hisun's Epirubicin. Medrol had 76 percent market share in 2012 in IV steroids, while Epirubicin was the top-selling brand in the antibiotic treatment of various cancers with 56 percent market share. Tazocin was

even still on patent. These drugs are expected to be in high demand clinically in the mid-market as well. Second, the relatively large product portfolio (60–80 molecules) enabled sales reps to detail multiple drugs to the same prescribers, lowering the cost of selling and providing selling synergies in the same therapeutic area.

By contrast, the lack of either critical mass in the portfolio or well-chosen molecules may imperil other companies' forays into the mid-market. AstraZeneca dismissed the broad market business unit in 2013, repurposed its $230 million manufacturing investment in Taizhou, and effectively exited its non-proprietary branded generics play in the broad Chinese market. The move partly reflected the company's selection of a new global CEO, who changed focus to innovative rather than generic products. The move also reflects the challenging time AstraZeneca has had with entry into the broad market in China. Due to difficulties in acquiring qualified local companies in China, AstraZeneca only managed to purchase Guangdong BeiKang (a maker of injectable antibiotics) to build up its non-proprietary branded generics portfolio. However, antibiotics suffered dearly in 2012 following the government's crackdown on the overuse of antibiotics in China (see Chapters 7 and 8). The acquisition alone could not enable AstraZeneca to establish a strong foundation. At the same time, the company was unsure how to bring its proprietary branded generics, such as Losec and Betaloc, into the broad market, since both the core business and the broad market business units competed to sell the same drugs. The commercial arrangement highlights the common challenges many MNCs face as they try to manage both the core market and broad market with the same products at the same prices.

JVs have either avoided such cannibalization or made the conflict a healthy competition between firms. This does not suggest that the road in front of Pfizer–Hisun or Merck–Simcere is a smooth one. Several key questions remain to be answered. Success will be highly dependent on careful navigation in the new market that neither JV party has much experience in. On average, top MNCs gain over 80 percent of their revenue from tier 1–2 cities; they have limited presence in mid-level cities or county hospitals. On the other hand, a leading local Chinese player often relies heavily on lower-level county hospitals. The mid-market can be quite new to the current players. How to assemble teams serving different markets with divergent capabilities into one integrated team backed by a common culture is a challenge. MNCs are used to resource-intensive selling to cultivate individual brands and physician brand loyalty in the top-tier market. Local companies are good at managing contract sales agents or distributors using relationships in selling. These different capabilities and experiences need to be integrated and well deployed in the mid-market. Further market segmentation is key, with allocation of the right portfolio to the right segment as a first step. Companies then need to design the right commercial model (from market access to marketing) and sell to medical providers in each segment. How to go beyond a strong generics portfolio and generate an ongoing supply of competitive products for the mid-market will be a long-term strategic concern. Companies require a dedicated R&D infrastructure to understand and address the unique needs of the mid-market while factoring in different provider practice patterns and affordability/reimbursement trends.

While some locals are working with MNCs to tackle the mid-market, others are gathering momentum to compete in the core market. Yangzijiang built the largest pharma business in China over the last several decades mainly through its differentiated selling model: a large in-house sales force that is managed centrally across different subsidiary companies. Realizing the importance of having a competitive portfolio and strong presence in the top-tier cities and large hospitals, Yangzijiang started to (a) build academic detailing capability in 2012, and (b) focus on sales and marketing of a handful of carefully selected differentiated molecules that are first-to-market generics, hard-to-copy generics, or molecules with limited competition. The local companies still have some distance to travel before they take majority share away from originator brands in top-tier cities and large hospitals. Government policy that equalizes the treatment of off-patent drugs will allow leading locals to gain a fair share in the core market.

The Race to Innovate

China has become an attractive destination for bio-pharmaceutical research and development (R&D). The government aims to transform China's economy from a manufacturing base to an innovation base. For the pharmaceutical sector, the Ministry of Science and Technology has set the goal to achieve world-leading R&D status by 2020.

The government is increasing funding, building infrastructure, and attracting talent to reach its innovation goals. R&D expenditure as a percentage of GDP will reach 2.2 percent by 2015, a level close to developed nations. Life science technology parks have been built around the country, including Shanghai Zhangjiang, Beijing Zhongguancun, and Suzhou BioBay. Tax exemptions and government subsidies are provided to pharmaceutical companies to incentivize innovation and R&D investment. Government funding of the pharmaceutical sector tripled from 2006 to 2010 to reach $3.5 billion. While this represents an impressive growth in scale, it is still dwarfed by what a global pharmaceutical company spends on R&D. National programs such as the "863 Plan" and the "Torch Plan" award dedicated grants to research projects that are deemed priority and of significant innovation. To stimulate the exchange of talent, the government developed people strategies such as the Thousand Talent plan where top Chinese scientists living overseas are given the recognition and rewards to return to China to conduct biopharma R&D activities. The overall life science talent pool is large and rapidly growing. Universities are turning out more graduates in relevant fields, and the rate of Chinese scientists returning from overseas educations has accelerated. Many of the western-educated and western-trained scientists are coming home with plans to apply their experience in drug discovery and development.

Banking on the dual promise of strategic commitment and burgeoning talent pool, MNCs have increasingly invested in captive R&D centers over the past decade. By 2012, all top ten pharmaceutical companies established some R&D infrastructure in China, with a publically announced investment commitment that exceeded $2.5 billion (see Table 14.3).

Table 14.3 MNCs with R&D bases in China

Company	Number of R&D Facilities in China
Bayer Healthcare	1- Beijing
Sanofi	2- R&D facilities in Shanghai Biometrics facility in Beijing and another R&D facility in Chengdu
Novartis	3- Shanghai (2) and Changshu
Roche	1- Shanghai
Novo Nordisk	1- Beijing
Merck & Co	2- Beijing (of which one is a R&D headquarter)
Merck Serono	1- Beijing
GSK	Over-the-counter R&D centre in Tianjin Global R&D centre in Shanghai
AstraZeneca	2- Shanghai
Pfizer	R&D facilities in Shanghai and Wuhan
Eli Lilly	2- Suzhou and Shanghai
Takeda	1- Shanghai

Source: BMI

Four different China R&D models emerged, although no one company approach is a "pure" model. The most common model is to have the internal team support global development projects with functional expertise such as analogue synthesis and compound generation. Others have internal teams that conduct research on unmet clinical needs in China or (more broadly) Asia, such as the high incidence of liver and gastrointestinal cancers. AstraZeneca and Novartis are two examples. A third model is characterized by highly externalized R&D: minimum internal resources with heavy scouting of external innovation conducted in academic institutions and local biotechnology companies. Sanofi's Asia R&D center used this model to in-license the development of a Phase II cancer compound from Shanghai Institute of Biologics Products. The most aggressive model is an integrated R&D center acting as a global therapeutic area center. A prominent example was the GlaxoSmithKline China R&D center dedicated to neuroscience research – the only dedicated research center in its global network. Pfizer almost decided to put its global anti-infectives research unit in China.

Going forward, global innovative firms need to recognize that their China R&D investment should not be driven by the flurry of activity or peer pressure exerted by the investments made by competitors. Rather, China R&D investment needs to be evaluated and managed by MNCs as rigorously as they would any other R&D project in the world.

In recent years, Chinese companies have been catching up to MNCs on R&D. Spurred by the government's goals for innovation, aggregate R&D spend as a percentage of revenue has grown (see Figure 14.18). Some firms reached as high as 10 percent (e.g., Hengrui's pursuit of category 1 innovation: see Figure 14.9). Perhaps as a result, the number of new drug applications has risen in recent years (Figure 14.19).

The challenge for Chinese companies is to balance long-term innovation goals with short-term returns on their R&D investment. Western management researchers label this the challenge of "ambidexterity." Recognizing the difficult road and significant investment required for novel drug discovery, industry leaders are embarking on a journey toward incremental innovation (仿创结合). Many are looking to develop differentiated generics, which are more difficult to copy than regular generics and are rewarded with price premiums. This means either first-to-market generics or existing molecules with a new formulation or dosage.

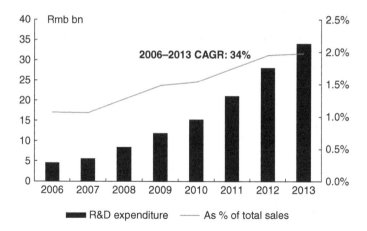

Figure 14.18 Trend in R&D spend
Source: Jessica Li & Lillian Wan 2015. *China Healthcare Primer – The Immense Structural Upside.* Bank of America Merrill Lynch (July 9).

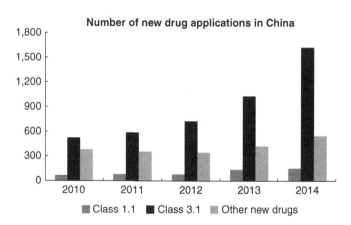

Figure 14.19 Innovation among domestic players
Source: Jessica Li & Lillian Wan 2015. *China Healthcare Primer – The Immense Structural Upside.* Bank of America Merrill Lynch (July 9).

Other companies are pursuing a frugal innovation path: i.e., develop a me-too or me-better drug but at a lower cost with faster than usual speed. This usually begins by working on a well-validated target, making sure not to complete all clinical trials alone but waiting for competitors' early study results. This enables them to move further along the drug development process with higher efficiency, which can save a couple of years' time.

The long-term investment can be daunting, but some are destined to succeed. Zhejiang Beta is a success story worth noting. The company spent ten years in R&D to develop an innovative compound (Icotinib, an EGFR-inhibitor) for the treatment of non-small-cell lung cancer. They made a key strategic bet on comparative effectiveness research (CER) by conducting a head-to-head clinical trial of their compound against AstraZeneca's leading drug, Iressa. The favorable CER results were celebrated by the Ministry of Health along with officials from several other ministries who attended the product's launch.

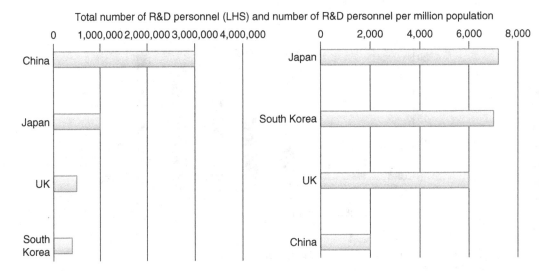

Figure 14.20 R&D personnel in China

The path to becoming a major innovation power-house will require Chinese companies to address a number of issues. The regulatory process is highly onerous. Companies need to strengthen their intellectual property (IP) rights protection as well as the quality of clinical trials. The investigational new drug (IND) application takes 12–18 months in China, compared to 30 days in the United States and three to six months in other developing countries such as India, Argentina, and Mexico. The CFDA is chronically understaffed, and yet both generics and innovative applications go through the same lengthy process and consume the same resources. As a result, the productivity of per-reviewer application processing is a serious issue.

China has made much progress in upgrading its legal framework for IP protection since the signing of the WTO; however, enforcement still lags behind. The current patent linkage mechanism requires drug registration applicants to provide information regarding any patent and patent ownership rights relating to the subject drug, to submit a certificate of non-infringement of patents, and agree to be liable for any consequences of possible patent infringement. However, the effort to gather the information and the burden of proof borne by the claimant are very high, which discourages innovator companies from pursuing litigation when their patents are infringed. In addition, litigation only makes available a small

amount of statutory damages. If various references are unavailable or unreasonable, damage awards can be as small as 5,000–300,000 RMB (and are capped at 500,000 RMB). In most cases, damage awards for lost profits, gained benefits, or royalty payments do not greatly exceed the maximum statutory damage. Another concern is trade secret leakage: it can be difficult to trace the "infringer" or "data leaker" due to the lack of documentation and the challenges in gathering evidence. Finally, on the quality front, despite a vast pool of raw talent, significant effort needs to be put into training, development, and retention of R&D personnel. China lags behind other leading pharma countries in R&D personnel (see Figure 14.20).

In summary, China is emerging as a major player on the global stage of R&D. Despite the myriad challenges noted above, China is making steady progress toward innovation in biopharmaceuticals. Companies who are planning to invest in R&D activities in China need a long-term view, well-calculated areas of investment, and a healthy dose of patience and commitment.

The Emergence of Therapeutic Biologics

Beyond chemically-based pharmaceutical products, China's life sciences sector also includes other product categories such as biologics, vaccines, and traditional Chinese medicines (TCMs). The distribution of sales across these categories is difficult to accurately represent, since available sales figures are based on a mix of retail prices and ex-factory prices.[6] This section discusses biologics; the following two sections consider the vaccine and OTC markets.

The Chinese government has designated biotechnology as one of the seven strategic emerging industries. The therapeutic biologics segment is a key pillar within the biotechnology sector.[7] In 2010, China's therapeutic biotech sector accounted for roughly 18 billion RMB, less than 2 percent of the global total; by comparison, the Chinese pharmaceutical sector accounted for 7 percent of the global total. By 2014, the biologics sector achieved $47 billion in ex-factory sales. China's biotech products are generally less complex molecules such as albumin and immunoglobulin; several innovative therapies are not yet marketed in China. Leading biologics worldwide such as monoclonal antibodies (mAbs) account for only a small share (10 percent). The country's biotech sector is also quite fragmented and underdeveloped. Except for mAb and insulin, there are a large number of Chinese players in the most commoditized product categories.

Nevertheless, the therapeutic biologics sector holds significant promise due to strong government backing, large unmet clinical need, and a rapidly evolving industry ecosystem. Compared to the small molecule sector, where some past policies have resulted in a largely fragmented and less competitive industry with no innovation, the therapeutic biologics sector is still embryonic. It has the potential to become world class if government policy can properly stimulate demand, reward and protect innovation, and set high standards for the quality of production. A number of challenges exist in today's policy environment for biologics innovators and manufacturers. These include market access, affordability, current regulatory framework, and IP protection.

Market access for therapeutic biologics takes much longer than for small molecules. Biologic drugs require an average 19–22 months to receive clinical trial approval in China, compared to only 10–18 months for small molecule drugs. Factors contributing to this delay include (1) a lack of reviewer resources within SFDA and CDE and (2) the biological sample test requirements necessary for a clinical trial at the National Institutes for Food and Drug Control (NIFDC). Such testing is unique to China among major markets like the United States, Europe, and South Korea.

The *high price* and thus the affordability of biologics products remain challenging. Most cutting-edge therapeutic biologics are still expensive with quite limited public insurance reimbursement. Adoption rates for innovative therapeutic biologics in China are low. In the case of rheumatoid arthritis, approximately 7 percent of eligible Chinese urban patients receive the biologics treatment of DMARDs (Disease-Modifying Anti-Rheumatic Drugs). By contrast, approximately 67 percent of US Medicare patients diagnosed with RA receive the biologics treatment. Companies are seeking creative solutions to enhance affordability and improve access. Roche formed a strategic partnership with Swiss Re to enroll oncology patients in an insurance program that covers oncology treatment. The government is also working on several solutions to improve the affordability of high-cost therapies. Some provinces have listed mAbs onto their PRDLs. There are also discussions on creating a new RDL list (RDL-C) in addition to the RDL-A and RDL-B lists to cover high-priced products.

The *current regulatory framework* does not require non-innovative biologics to prove similarity in efficacy, quality, and safety through systematic comparability exercises with the originator. Instead, it allows non-innovative biologics to be registered as new biologics products but with less stringent requirements. This could potentially pose risks to patients as the lower quality alternative could have unwanted immunogenicity and lower efficacy. Recognizing the importance of patient safety and quality, China is now considering the possibility of developing a biosimilar pathway to mitigate these risks.

Furthermore, to properly incentivize and protect innovation, China is looking to improve the *IP system* for biologics. Currently the scope of patent protection is narrower than global standards, making it easier for companies to obtain patents with only slight modification. For example, three similar molecule patents from different manufacturers coexist for Rituximab. In addition, there is no clear data exclusivity protection for biologics in China. Discussions are under way to broaden the scope of protection for biologics and to grant data exclusivity that is longer than chemical drugs. A more in-depth review of the China biologics industry can be found in Chapter 16 and online.[8]

Vaccines

China's vaccine industry is another strategic priority for the Chinese government. China is the largest manufacturer of vaccines in the world, producing 1 billion doses each year – roughly 20 percent of the global supply. However, China's immunization expenditure per capita is among the lowest in the world ($20 per person, 2009 currency). The vaccine sector has two distinct segments that operate very differently. The public segment continues a legacy system in China's Center for Disease Control (CDC) system that brings an adequate supply of mandatory immunizations to 16 million newborns each year. The private segment arose out of unexpected events rather than deliberate strategy; key industry policies have yet to be well defined. These two sectors are discussed below.

Public Vaccine Segment

The public segment contributes 70 percent of the volume but less than 30 percent of the total value of the market ($2 billion in 2011, $3 billion in 2014). The high level of growth in volume in the public sector reflects the inclusion of additional vaccines over time. From 1978 to 2002, China had four vaccines in its public program: BCG, Oral Polio, Measles, and whole cell DTP. From 2002 to 2008, Hepatitis B was added to curb the hepatitis B epidemic and the associated high incidence of liver cirrhosis and liver cancer. In 2008, the State Council announced a fourfold expansion and upgrade of the public program: (1) enlarge the inoculation population of HBV to 15 years old and under instead of only newborns; (2) upgrade two vaccines by changing Measles to MMR and whole cell DTP to acellular DTP which is the international

standard; (3) convert four Class II vaccines to Class I (Hepatitis A, Meningitis A and Meningitis A&C, Japanese Encephalitis); and (4) make three vaccines available as part of the public program to certain regions or when there is a disease outbreak (Endemic Hemorrhagic Fever F, Anthrax, Leptospirosis). The expansion boosted the public market by 34 percent in a single year from $365 million in 2007 to $492 million in 2008. By contrast, steady-state growth in the public sector had been a more modest 15 percent. The government kept prices low for the Class I mandatory pediatric vaccines. For example, the price of the DTP vaccine to the CDC was as low as $0.03 per dose, whereas the UNICEF/GAVI price was more than $0.15 per dose. The SOE China National Biologics Group (CNBG) accounted for 75 percent of the public market volume; other local companies made up 20 percent, with MNCs accounting for about 4 percent, mainly to answer calls to relieve local supply shortages.

Private Vaccine Segment

The private segment arose unexpectedly following the 2003 SARS outbreak that propelled the Chinese government to decentralize vaccine production and distribution in order to meet the needs of such pandemics. Coupled with the rise of a private equity industry and the inflow of foreign funds, the private sector mushroomed across China. By the end of 2012, there were 35 private Chinese vaccine companies, many of them established by former SOE employees (CNBG in particular). With a large number of players (more than any other country in the world), the industry competed on price; some companies inevitably cut corners on quality and safety. Flu vaccines account for over half of the volume in the private market. SOE manufacturers have 30–40 percent volume share, with the rest contributed by other local firms (40 percent) and MNCs (20 percent).

Issues with Vaccines

There are several issues and trends in China's vaccine industry. First, there is *evolving demand with a low rate of adoption*. Vaccine demand is maturing and aligning with developed countries, as more vaccines are included into the National Immunization Program (NIP) and combination products are developed. The adoption rate is still very low in the private segment. Consumers and parents are increasingly aware of the importance of Class II vaccines; however, there is no systematic education regarding Class II vaccines by providers. Affordability poses another barrier to adoption, especially when consumers do not understand the value and the benefit of the vaccines. For example, the flu vaccine adoption rate among the urban elderly remained below 1 percent for many years, compared to more than 60 percent of people 65+ years in the United States. Similarly, adoption rates for Hib (Hemophilia Influenza B) and Rotavirus are also quite low compared to developed countries. Adoption of the pediatric Pneumococcal vaccine (Prevenar) is a major challenge because the country lacks good epidemiological data on the disease burden. In the absence of demand generation by the government, companies must undertake significant market building efforts.

Second, *customers are changing as the point of vaccination (POV) integrates into CHCs.* Vaccine provision in China used to be separate from the hospital system. The country has 31 provincial CDCs, 390 municipal CDCs, 2,700 district CDCs, and 65,000 POVs that handle the distribution and administration of Class II vaccines. Since healthcare reform, CHCs have been strengthened to form a pseudo primary care system. The government is now moving vaccine POVs into CHCs so that primary care and preventive care can be managed together. However, implementation of such change varies geographically, as do CHC development and CDC operations. Most major cities where CHCs are up and running are integrating POVs; other provinces and cities are still in transition. During this transition, the financial and administrative responsibilities between the CHC/MOH system and CDC system remain to be streamlined.

Furthermore, vaccine *distribution channels and market access are complex.* When the government decentralized the vaccine distribution system in 2004 following SARS, responsibility for procurement cascaded down to city-level CDCs and POVs.

This contributed to significant variation in implementation at the local level. As of 2012, an estimated 30 percent of vaccines were sold directly to city-level CDCs without having to go through the provincial CDC (and thus perhaps centralized tenders). As a result, the overall channel markup for vaccines remains high, leading to higher retail prices for the consumers. For prescription drugs, total channel markup from manufacturers to end patients is about 25 percent; for Class II vaccines, the markup can range from 50 percent to 200 percent in most provinces.

Vaccine regulatory standards are in strong need of improvement. The year 2011 represented a milestone year for the Chinese vaccine industry. The country passed the World Health Organization (WHO) vaccine regulatory assessment, which allowed Chinese suppliers to qualify for UN procurement. Pharmacopeia quality standards were subsequently raised and new GMPs were issued. The government is now actively working to refine its Class II vaccine policy. The policy is expected to address the government's roles in demand generation (funding and reimbursement) and thereby formalize the process for NIP inclusion.

Local companies' capability is improving. Responding to the government's call to innovate in strategic industries such as vaccines and to foster globally competitive companies, leading local players are actively seeking to upgrade R&D and manufacturing quality improvement. Hualan and Sinovac are gearing up the Prequalification for WHO program. China National Biotec Group (CNBG) institutes with historical strengths in R&D are developing new vaccines. CNBG Lanzhou Institute successfully launched its monovalent Rotavirus vaccine. The rapid development of the H1N1 vaccines is another sign of indigenous vaccine R&D capability.

OTC and Consumer Health

China's consumer health market is a rare combination of size and growth. By 2010, the market size had already reached roughly $10 billion for OTC products and another $6 billion for vitamins, minerals, and supplements (VMS). By 2014, retail sales of OTC products reached $31 billion. Compared to the prescription drug market, the OTC and VMS markets are much smaller in absolute revenues. However, in terms of global penetration, China's OTC and VMS markets are much stronger: OTC and VMS represent 11 percent and 12 percent of the global market, respectively. By contrast, China's prescription medicines account for only 4 percent of the global total. The OTC/consumer health market has also slightly outpaced GDP growth (roughly 10 percent), driven by the increasing trend toward self-medication and improving regulations on the distribution, labeling, and advertising of OTC drugs.

A unique feature of the Chinese OTC market is that TCM products play a prominent role. Three-quarters of approved OTC drugs are TCM products. These products represent no less than 40 percent of the total OTC market by value. Chinese consumers are discrete in their OTC use of western medicines versus TCM medicines. Chinese resort to western medicines for acute and more severe conditions such as anti-fungal treatment and stomach discomfort. TCM products command more than 90 percent of the OTC market for milder conditions such as sore throat and cough. The appeal of TCM brands to the consumer lies in indications and claims that are deeply rooted in health beliefs. For example, to address constipation problems, an over-the-counter TCM product will assert on its label the following: "detoxifies the body, beautifies the skin." It is believed that if the body is not detoxified periodically, harmful substances will have multiple negative effects on the body, including slow bowel movement, dull skin, and acne.

Another unique aspect of the China's OTC market concerns uneven regional development. Unlike prescription medicine, the 50 largest cities among China's total of 350 cities comprise less than 40 percent of the total market. The remaining majority share is fairly dispersed across the country. The rise of lower-tier cities will serve as an important future growth driver for the OTC market.

To understand the consumer health market, it is important to understand the behavior of Chinese consumers. Several of their behaviors are unique and relevant to the OTC and consumer market. China is the only country where "trading up"

(consumers opt for more expensive goods rather than less expensive ones) still beats "trading down" in the purchase of consumer goods. Chinese consumers are increasingly investing in health and wellness. In recent years, in the face of several prominent food safety and environmental pollution scandals (see Chapter 3), citizens have taken extra care in selecting consumer products. Brand is also very important to the vast majority of the Chinese due to its association with quality and product integrity. The perception of higher quality is further associated with higher price. Finally, internet penetration has significantly increased to become an indispensable part of life – extending to online shopping for OTC drugs and consumer health products.

These trends have several implications for the consumer health and OTC business. First, companies can embrace the public health mantra of "from treatment to prevention" as a way to capture the public's rising awareness of the virtues of health and their greater willingness to spend on consumer products. Second, understanding different consumer behaviors and preferences will allow companies to cater to regional variations in the trade-up trend across provinces and city tiers. Third, companies can take advantage of opportunities to charge premium prices via branding as brand becomes critical to assure consumers about product quality and efficacy. Fourth, companies need to pursue new channels to reach and educate consumers about personal healthcare and medications.

To capitalize on market fundamentals, OTC/consumer health companies must be fully tuned into the complex and evolving dynamics in the retail channel. There are six types of retail channels at play: hospitals, retail pharmacies, modern trade (e.g., supermarkets), health and beauty specialty stores, internet shopping, and direct sale. The modern trade, health/beauty specialty stores, and online platform are growing quickly. They offer new sales platforms but also require new capabilities to manage these channels. The pharmacy channel is still the largest, however, and the retail pharmacy sector itself is undergoing continuous consolidation and upgrades in its management capability. Manufacturers who can collaborate with retail pharmacies to achieve common goals stand to reap long-term benefits. These collaborative goals can focus on pharmacist training/education, capability upgrades in specific therapeutic areas of interest to the manufacturer, and improved category management. The hospital channel should not be overlooked, as in some categories brand equity and provider-prescribing habits in the hospital carry over into the retail pharmacy setting. For the sale of VMS products, the modern trade and online pharmacy channels are gaining importance. Taobao cooperated with five State-approved B2C medicine companies to sell OTC and healthcare nutrition products in 2011. Direct sale could also become a powerful channel; however, the government is highly guarded about this channel and restrictive in granting licenses, particularly to foreign companies.

The China OTC and VMS markets are crowded and fiercely competitive. Of the 500 players, the top five possess less than 25 percent market share (and falling). While local companies have much higher aggregate share, the top three positions are held by MNCs in three out of the five largest categories (except cough & cold). Amway leads in VMS; Xi'an Janssen leads in dermatology (Daktarin for vaginal fungal infection and athlete's foot); and GSK leads in analgesics (Fenbid for pain relief). Companies employ three distinct businesses in this sector:

- Media-focused players have significantly increased "above-the-line" (ATL) spend to build brand and generate consumer pull;
- Balanced players rely on differentiated branding, product positioning, and a "balanced" marketing and sales approach; and
- Distribution-driven players focus on broad channel/geography coverage and strong in-store promotions/executions.

The front-runner in the Media category is Hayao – a short name for Ha'er bin Pharmaceuticals in the northern Heilongjiang Province. Hayao spends around 45–50 percent of its revenue on media advertising and branding. Their followers also spend a minimum of 30 percent of revenue on A&P expenditures. Competition is so strong that collectively the group members play leapfrog in spending, raising the bar against each other year

after year to generate demand via media such as the CCTV (national).

The prescription drug manufacturers "invented" the distribution pull model. Since their primary business is in prescription medicines, they lack the resources to compete against companies like Hayao on ATL spend. Instead they offer higher margins to distributors and retail pharmacies to gain business. Yangzijiang is an exemplar of this model: they spend a limited amount on marketing but provide large incentives to strong and capable distributors to push for coverage and penetration of their product. This model has been successfully used to sell their three leading TCM/OTC drugs. Yangzijiang is able to leverage the legacy brand and strong word of mouth in hospitals to negotiate better deals with distributors who cover both the hospital and retail channels.

Multinational companies such as Wyeth (now Pfizer), GSK, and Xi'an Janssen followed the balanced model. They are stronger than the others in strategic marketing. They also spend a large amount on A&P to build a strong brand equity that, traditionally, then creates leverage in the pharmacies and the distribution channel. At the same time, MNC OTC players extend the rigor of sales force effectiveness into the retail pharmacy channel as well. This holistic approach allows them to gain significant share in key categories.

Three critical elements are needed to achieve success to achieve a sustainable and profitable position in the OTC and VMS market. These include: (1) identify the right anchor platform (consumer segment and functional benefit) to enter; (2) achieve meaningful scale in a reasonable time frame; and (3) build strong competitive differentiation and leadership via product innovation and professional brand building. These are themselves based on deep consumer knowledge and strong channel and distribution management.

Conclusion

China's pharmaceutical sector is on its way to becoming the second largest in the world. However, prior success factors that have enabled its rise differ from factors necessary to win going forward. Companies need to commit to a better understanding of the nature of future market opportunities and the evolving operating environment, adopt flexible and adaptive approaches to actively shape the future environment, and create win–win solutions.

Notes

1. Lawton R. Burns. 2012. *The Business of Healthcare Innovation* (Cambridge, UK: Cambridge University Press).
2. Market value at ex-factory price.
3. MAC population refers to "middle and affluent consumers" with annual household disposable income of more than 75,000 RMB, in 2010 real renminbi.
4. "China Restructures Its Drug Pricing Regime." 2015. Covington (June 9). Available online at: www.cov.com./~/media/files/corporate/publica tions/2015/06/china_restructures_its_drug_pri cing_regime.pdf. Accessed on December 12, 2015.
5. John Quelch and Margaret Rodriguez. 2013. *GlaxoSmithKline in China (A)*. Case 9-514-049 (Boston, MA: Harvard Business School Publishers).
6. Retail price data suggest the total Chinese pharmaceutical market in 2014 was roughly $202 billion; of this, OTC accounts for $31 billion and vaccines another $3 billion. Ex-factory sales data suggest a market size of $100 billion for TCM products and $47 billion for biologics. Sources of these data include the CFDA Southern Medicine Economic Research Institute and McKinsey.
7. Therapeutic biologics includes substances that are produced by or extracted from a biological source and intended for therapeutic purposes. Recombinant DNA technology is often used. Examples include recombinant proteins, monoclonal antibodies, and advanced therapy medicinal products. Therapeutic biologics as used here excludes vaccines.
8. China Association of Enterprises with Foreign Investment R&D-based Pharmaceutical Association Committee (RDPAC). *Building a World-Class Innovative Therapeutics Biologics Industry in China*. Available online at: www .rdpac.org/UpLoad/UpLoadFileDir/201402/ 14/201402141611000652.pdf. Accessed on December 12, 2015.

China's Medical Technology Sector

JAMES DENG AND LAWTON ROBERT BURNS

Introduction

China will step into the "New Normal" in the next few years: undergoing economic restructuring while also maintaining reasonable and sustainable growth in GDP. Since 2012, the Chinese government has focused on regulating the healthcare industry through an anti-corruption campaign. At the same time, it is financing both supply-side and demand-side initiatives to spur growth in the industry. This presents short-term challenges of limited access to healthcare, but long-term opportunities of expansion, transparency, and competition. The growth of the medical device sector will likely slow down in the near future due to the changing regulatory environment, but will be buoyed by the country's ongoing healthcare reforms and favorable demographic trends (aging population and urbanization).

China's medical technology ("medtech") market size is now the fourth largest worldwide, and is following a development path similar to the country's pharmaceutical sector. This trajectory makes China attractive to medtech companies and the major growth engine for the global market. Nevertheless, despite its continuing promise, China's healthcare system differs markedly from that of the United States and of other western systems. Multinational medtechs are doing business in a very dynamic market that is influenced by government authorization at different levels. They are thus likely to encounter several headwinds in China, such as:

- Complicated market access
- Diversity across geography and customers

- Growing mid-market with requirements for multiple portfolio and alternate go-to-market models
- Fierce local competition
- Lack of capable talent (especially mid/high-level management)
- Challenging process for mergers and acquisitions

This chapter reviews the promise of China's medtech market and the challenges that need to be surmounted in the future. The chapter also integrates issues raised in prior chapters that impact the medtech sector.

What Are Medical Devices?

There are various definitions of "medical devices" or, more broadly, "medical equipment." Following the widely accepted definition advanced by the US Food and Drug Administration (USFDA), medical devices range from simple instruments such as tongue depressors and bedpans to more technologically complex pacemakers and implantable devices, but exclude pharmaceuticals. Medical devices also encompass in vitro diagnostic products, such as general-purpose lab equipment, reagents, and test kits, which may include monoclonal antibody technology. Specifically, the USFDA defines a medical device as:

> "an instrument, apparatus, implement, machine, contrivance, implant, in vitro reagent, or other similar or related article, including a component part, or accessory" that, in addition to other criteria, is "intended to affect the structure or any function of the body of man or other animals, and which does not achieve any of its primary intended purposes through chemical action within or on the body of man or other animals and which is not dependent upon being metabolized for the achievement of any of its primary intended purposes."[1]

The authors wish to thank Xi (Cecilia) Xie for her editorial work on this chapter.

For the purpose of this chapter, we use the above definition and the terms "medical devices" and "medical equipment" interchangeably. As noted, medical devices can span several functions and therapeutic areas. However, they can be classified into segments based on their intended use, as follows:[2]

- *Anesthetic and respiratory equipment*: oxygen masks, ventilators, anesthesia breathing circuits, and gas delivery units
- *Biotechnology products*: tissue engineered bone, cartilage, and skin
- *Consumables*: syringes, needles, staplers, wound care, hospital supplies
- *Dental devices*: tools and drills, alloys and resins, dental floss, etc.
- *Durable medical equipment*: wheelchairs
- *Imaging equipment*: X-ray machines, MRI and CT scanners
- *Implantable devices*: cardiac pacemakers, stents, hip implants, neuro-stimulators, and insulin pumps
- *In-vitro diagnostics*: auto analyzers, blood glucose monitors, blood test reagents
- *Information technology (IT)*: picture archival and communication systems (PACS)
- *Orthopedic equipment:* Knee prosthesis, shoes, spinal corsets
- *Ophthalmic equipment:* contact lenses, eyeglasses, ophthalmoscopes, etc.
- *Patient monitoring systems:* ICU monitors

Another way to segment the medical device and equipment market is to distinguish devices that do versus do not require an external energy source to be operational. The latter include obvious product categories such as consumables and commodity items. The former – including equipment, implants, and disposables – are collectively referred to as "medical electronics." Equipment, which may represent the largest and fastest growing of the three areas, is heavily represented by imported products. Subcategories include surgical equipment (e.g., robotics), imaging and diagnostics, and life-support technologies. Implants include cardiovascular and orthopedic products; disposables are products used in tandem with medical equipment.

Size and Diversity of Chinese Market to be Served

A major challenge facing all product firms operating in China – multinational corporations (MNCs) and local, medtech, and pharma – is the sheer size and diversity of the country. China has decentralized the governance of its 1.36 billion people (2013) and economic responsibility to the provincial government level and below. There are thus multiple economies at different stages of development (e.g., GDP per capita) from province to province. There are also 56 different ethnic groups, in which the Han dominate coastal and central China while the other groups occupy western China and several of the country's borders. The country's sheer geographic span makes it difficult (and often impossible) for companies to serve different regions as well as serve both urban and rural areas. As a result, there is no "one China" strategy that can be pursued.

Moreover, companies doing business in China must pay heed to *four* branches of government (executive, legislative, judicial, and Communist Party), *three* levels of government (central, provincial, local), and *multiple* stakeholders (insurance funds, hospitals, physicians, distributors, patients, and advocacy associations). Companies must therefore deal not only with 13 or more ministries at the central government level, but at provincial versions of these ministries across 32 provinces (13 times 32). This adds to the complexity of doing business in a country with a different culture and regulatory framework. Finally, the medtech sector itself is large, diverse, and fragmented. There are anywhere from 12,000 to 16,000 medtech firms, mostly selling lower-level products. There are also 165,000 device distributors as of 2010 (an increase over 145,000 in 2006); most of these are small, with average sales of 113,000 RMB.[3]

Growth Drivers of the Medical Device Market

Macroeconomic Trends

In contrast to the 9–10 percent growth in GDP in past decades, China is stepping into the "New

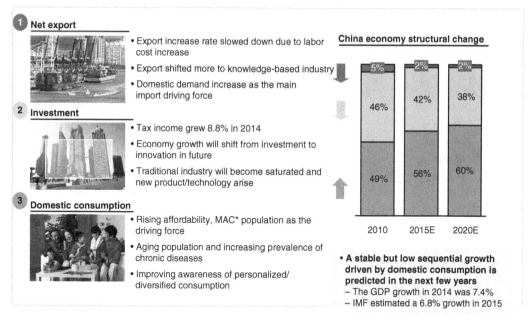

*refers to "middle and affluent class," defined as households with annual disposable incomes of at least 72,000 RMB(11,000 USD)

Figure 15.1 China's "New Normal"
Source: Goldman Sachs report; Team analysis.

Normal" (see Figure 15.1). Several key features illustrate the New Normal. China's GDP grew at 7.4 percent in 2014, with a 7.0 percent annual growth target for the 13th Five-Year Plan (FYP). In addition, the government is allocating resources to future-oriented industries to redirect economic development, using "small government" to shift growth from an investment to a consumption model, balancing the ratio of exports to imports, and promoting innovation via direct investment.

Between 2011 and 2015, the contribution of investment to GDP fell from 46 percent to 42 percent, while consumption's role grew from 49 percent to 56 percent. Domestic consumption is projected to reach 60 percent by 2020. The government has significantly increased its expenditures on social insurance, healthcare services, and education – with the aim of improving people's livelihoods, ensuring sustainable growth, and building a "harmonious society" and "healthy China." Harmony is important given the diversity in the country noted above; healthcare investment has become part of the government's solution to

maintaining harmony (see Chapter 2). Healthcare spending as a percentage of total GDP increased from 4.62 percent to 5.6 percent between 2010 and 2013, much higher than historical patterns; it is expected to rise to 7.0 percent according to the China Food and Drug Administration (CFDA) and National Health and Family Planning Commission (NHFPC). Such growth is driven by continuing urbanization, growth in China's smaller cities ("mid-market"), the rise in disposable income (17 percent rise in average income between 1999 and 2009), and the rising affordability of healthcare among the "mid and affluent class" (MAC).[4] China's intention to shift the basis of its economic growth away from exports and investment toward domestic consumption will ensure the growth of its medical device market.

The medical device sector accounts for only 15–16 percent of China's healthcare market, but is poised for growth. In 2014, China ranked as the world's fourth largest medical device market (behind the United States, Japan, and Germany); in 2020, its $33 billion market will be the third largest worldwide

World medical device market ranking by size

$ Billion

Rank	2014		2020E	
	Country	Market Size	Country	Market Size
1	US	133	US	215
2	Japan	32	Japan	71
3	Germany	27	China	33
4	China	17	Germany	31
5	France	15	France	18
6	UK	11	UK	14
7	Italy	10	Italy	10
8	Canada	7	Canada	5
9	Spain	5	Spain	5

World pharmaceutical market ranking by size

$ Billion

Rank	2014		2020E	
	Country	Market Size	Country	Market Size
1	US	371	US	421
2	China	156	China	245
3	Japan	106	Japan	116
4	Germany	54	Germany	53
5	France	44	France	46
6	UK	41	UK	45
7	Italy	28	Italy	26
8	Canada	23	Canada	25
9	Spain	23	Spain	20

- China is the major growth driver of the global market.
- China accounts for ~10% of the global increment from 2005 to 2013, while this number is expected to reach ~20% by 2017.

Figure 15.2 Growth in China's medical device and pharmaceutical markets
Source: BMI reports; Literature research; Team analysis.

and will serve as a growth engine for the global market (see Figure 15.2).[5] The Chinese medtech market accounted for roughly 10 percent of global medtech growth between 2005 and 2013 and is expected to reach ~20 percent by 2017. Its size and sustained momentum have increased China's prominence among multinational device manufacturers. Historically, medtech imports have outweighed medtech exports in volume and year-over-year (YOY) rate of growth: between 2010 and 2012, YOY growth ranged from 20 percent to 40 percent. Medtech imports have also exceeded the country's overall rate of growth in imports.[6]

Government Policies

Favorable government policies and underlying demographic trends are key drivers of the robust medical device market in China (see Figure 15.3). These policies and trends are described below.

Among all the domestic markets in China, healthcare remains a key growth area. China has wasted no effort in developing its medical device industry. On January 12, 2012, in accordance with the 12th

FYP issued by the State Council, the Ministry of Science and Technology (MoST) released its specific plan for the medical device and equipment industry and set a long list of broad goals to be accomplished by the end of 2015. Those goals range from discovering world-leading medical technology to establishing robust means of diagnosing and treating China's rural population, who live far from the country's high-tech urban hospitals. Specifically, these goals include:

Scientific goals: develop 200 core patents and 50–80 basic medical devices and new products; set up 10 new national engineering technology research centers and national key laboratories; establish 8–10 national scientific and technological industrial bases, and 20–30 technological R&D platforms.

Technological goals: focus on disease prevention through screening and warning programs to improve early diagnosis and cure rates; develop 50–80 disease diagnosis and treatment technologies, health promotion technologies, and innovative products suitable for rural areas.

Economic goals: increase export turnover to capture more than 5 percent of the global medical

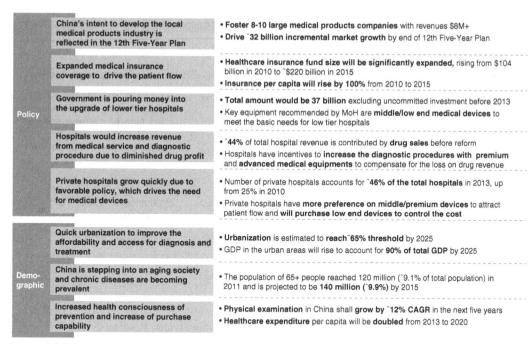

Policy	China's intent to develop the local medical products industry is reflected in the 12th Five-Year Plan	• **Foster 8-10 large medical products companies** with revenues $8M+ • **Drive ˜32 billion incremental market growth** by end of 12th Five-Year Plan
	Expanded medical insurance coverage to drive the patient flow	• **Healthcare insurance fund size will be significantly expanded,** rising from $104 billion in 2010 to ˜$220 billion in 2015 • **Insurance per capita will rise by 100%** from 2010 to 2015
	Government is pouring money into the upgrade of lower tier hospitals	• **Total amount would be 37 billion** excluding uncommitted investment before 2013 • Key equipment recommended by MoH are **middle/low end medical devices** to meet the basic needs for low tier hospitals
	Hospitals would increase revenue from medical service and diagnostic procedure due to diminished drug profit	• ˜**44%** of total hospital revenue is contributed by **drug sales** before reform • Hospitals have incentives to **increase the diagnostic procedures with premium** and **advanced medical equipments** to compensate for the loss on drug revenue
	Private hospitals grow quickly due to favorable policy, which drives the need for medical devices	• Number of private hospitals accounts for ˜**46% of the total hospitals** in 2013, up from 25% in 2010 • Private hospitals have **more preference on middle/premium devices** to attract patient flow and **will purchase low end devices to control the cost**
Demo-graphic	Quick urbanization to improve the affordability and access for diagnosis and treatment	• **Urbanization** is estimated to reach˜**65% threshold** by 2025 • GDP in the urban areas will rise to account for **90% of total GDP** by 2025
	China is stepping into an aging society and chronic diseases are becoming prevalent	• The population of 65+ people reached 120 million (˜9.1% of total population) in 2011 and is projected to be **140 million** (˜**9.9%**) by 2015
	Increased health consciousness of prevention and increase of purchase capability	• **Physical examination** in China shall **grow by** ˜**12% CAGR** in the next five years • **Healthcare expenditure** per capita will be **doubled** from 2013 to 2020

Figure 15.3 Government policies and demographic trends
Source: Lit. research; Team analysis.

devices market; and build 8–10 large medical device enterprises, each with revenue of over 5 billion RMB ($800 million).

In addition, as part of its "China Health Care 2020" plans, the government intends to invest 400 billion RMB in seven areas, including medtech. The goal is to spur domestic production of items now largely imported. Approximately 10 billion RMB will be invested in consumables (2 billion), large medical instruments (3 billion), and devices (5 billion). Investments will come in the form of grants and loans to local firms to spur R&D.

On the demand side, the government has achieved remarkable progress since the 2009 healthcare reform with a cumulative investment of 2,242 billion RMB. Basic medical insurance in China has achieved full coverage, although the financial burden of URBMI and NCMS has grown relative to UEBMI (see Figure 11.1). The UEBMI scheme, with its more comprehensive coverage, serves as a major financier of advanced medtech products and thus MNC revenues. In 2012, the government expanded NCMS insurance coverage

to include treatment of critical, catastrophic illnesses (including acute myocardial infarction, endstage renal disease, and several types of cancer) to prevent patient impoverishment from high out-ofpocket spending. As part of this effort, the government has asked commercial institutions to improve risk management and operational efficiency of the various urban medical insurance schemes.

The government has also encouraged commercial health insurance as a supplement to public insurance. While commercial health insurance accounted for only 3 percent of China's healthcare expenditures in 2012, this number is expected to reach 4.5 percent in 2020 (see Figure 11.5).

In addition to health insurance, the government is spending heavily to upgrade facilities outside the major cities. A chronic imbalance in resource allocation to urban and rural areas has plagued China's healthcare system. The largest Class III hospitals in big cities tend to have the highest quality physicians and equipment, as well as the lion's share of patient flows (see Figure 15.4). Class III hospitals accounted for 40 percent of

Government has emphasized the investment on infrastructure and equipment of lower-level hospitals since 2009					
	No. of hospitals		Investment of gov.		
Hospital	Unit, 2013	CAGR %, 2009–2013	Bn, 2013	CAGR %, 2009–2013	Recommended equipment
County hospital	• 2,692	5.9%	• 32.4	18.9%	• CT, color doppler, patient monitor, digital X-ray machine, hemodialysis machine, biochemical analyzer
County maternal and child health hospital	• 3,144	1.0%	• 9.5	41.3%	• Gynecological treatment instrument, fetal ECG
Township hospitals	• 37,015	−1.0%	• 74.9	40.6%	• Ultrasound, ECG, X-ray machine, anesthesia machine
CHC	• 33,965	5.6%	• 29.9	39.5%	• Ultrasound, ECG
Total	• 85,775	2.4%	• 146.7	33.9%	

Figure 15.4 Infrastructure upgrades in lower-tier hospitals
Source: China statistic yearbook of health (2010–2014); Expert interview; Team analysis.

patient visits in 2009 and 52 percent in 2014. By contrast, grassroots facilities, such as urban community health centers (CHCs) and county hospitals, tend to be underdeveloped, poorly funded, and disconnected from larger hospitals. This gap undercuts the strategic goal of broad and effective care, as well as equity and social harmony. Since 2009, the government has promoted a tiered medical system to rationalize patient flows across hospitals at different classes, but with limited success (see Figure 15.5).

To shrink the gap, the government plans to increase its funding of lower-level hospitals to $37 billion. The former Ministry of Health (MOH), which was dissolved in the reforms of 2013 and folded under the National Health and Family Planning Commission, recommended that lower-level hospitals offer key equipment (e.g., color doppler, digital X-ray machine, ECG) and middle/low medical devices to their patients to increase their volumes (see Figure 15.4). As a result, these hospitals are likely to increase revenues from diagnostic and medical services.

Public hospitals, which are the mainstay of healthcare provision in China, receive insufficient funding from the government to cover their operating costs. They have consequently relied on drug sales and price markups as their main revenue source. This has led to massive over-prescribing of expensive drugs and needless diagnostic testing (see Chapter 2). Prior to the 2009 healthcare reform, nearly half (44 percent) of total hospital revenues came from drug sales. The 2009 reform targeted, among other things, hospitals' extensive involvement with drug sales by cutting the prices charged for drugs. Hospitals have responded to the resulting price compression by increasing utilization of these services (including use of advanced medical equipment) as well as raising other fees (e.g., diagnostic and nursing) (see Figure 15.6). The medtech sector has been advantaged relative to the pharma sector by virtue of having less price regulation and fewer imposed price reductions in the past. However, there has been increased regulatory action in recent years covering most steps in market access such as registration, pricing, tendering, and hospital listing (covered below).

To enhance local level infrastructure, the government selected 500 county hospitals as pilot sites for capacity improvement with government support in 2015 (see Figure 15.7). The plan has two phases (2014–2017, 2018–2020) and two sets of

Healthcare service providers of China (2013)

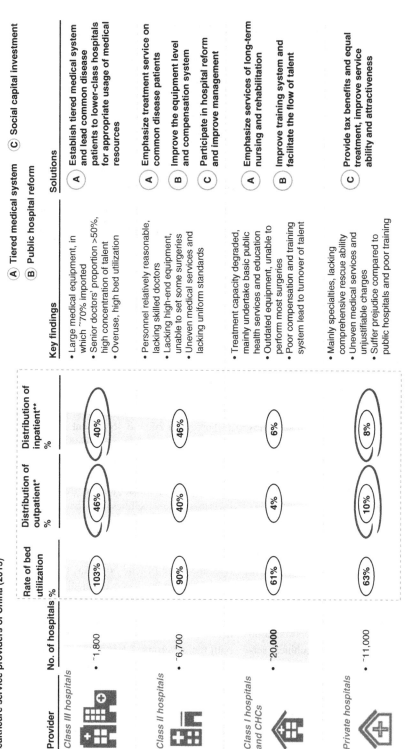

Provider	No. of hospitals	Rate of bed utilization %	Distribution of outpatient* %	Distribution of inpatient** %	Key findings	Solutions
Class III hospitals	~1,800	103%	46%	40%	• Large medical equipment, in which ~70% imported • Senior doctors' proportion >50%, high concentration of talent • Overuse, high bed utilization	**(A) Establish tiered medical system and lead common disease patients to lower-class hospitals for appropriate usage of medical resources**
Class II hospitals	~6,700	90%	40%	46%	• Personnel relatively reasonable, lacking skilled doctors • Lacking high-end equipment, unable to set some surgeries • Uneven medical services and lacking uniform standards	**(A) Emphasize treatment service on common disease patients** **(B) Improve the equipment level and compensation system** **(C) Participate in hospital reform and improve management**
Class I hospitals and CHCs	~20,000	61%	4%	6%	• Treatment capacity degraded, mainly undertake basic public health services and education • Outdated equipment, unable to perform most surgeries • Poor compensation and training system lead to turnover of talent	**(A) Emphasize services of long-term nursing and rehabilitation** **(B) Improve training system and facilitate the flow of talent**
Private hospitals	~11,000	63%	10%	8%	• Mainly specialties, lacking comprehensive rescue ability • Uneven medical services and unjustifiable charges • Suffer prejudice compared to public hospitals and poor training	**(C) Provide tax benefits and equal treatment, improve service ability and attractiveness**

(A) Tiered medical system (C) Social capital investment
(B) Public hospital reform

*The proportion of outpatient visits of various hospitals; **The proportion of inpatient visits of various hospitals

Figure 15.5 Tiered medical system, public hospital reform, and private hospitals
Source: Statistical Yearbook of NHFP (2009–2013).

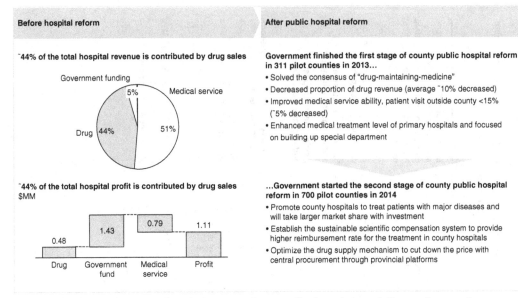

Figure 15.6 Reform impact on hospital revenue from medical services and diagnostic procedures
Source: Expert interview; Team analysis.

government targets for 2020: have 90 percent of pilot county hospitals meet basic operating requirements and 50 percent of pilot county hospitals meet recommended operating requirements (e.g., inpatient length of stay, bed usage rate, types of surgeries that can be performed). The government plans to supplement these reforms with multilevel plans, including: (a) increased subsidies of public health services from 35 RMB to 40 RMB per capita to pay rural physicians to provide basic public health services and thereby stabilize physician supply; (b) encourage physicians to practice in community clinics and grassroots hospitals by investing in those facilities; and (c) encourage the development of private hospitals.

Decentralization of hospital care will foster greater demand for equipment to staff hospitals outside of the major urban areas. Such decentralization will be abetted by decentralization of technical services beyond central departments (e.g., growth of ultrasound departments) and advances in point of care technology that enable adoption of ultrasound units in multiple departments (e.g., cardiology, emergency, anesthesiology, urology, obstetrics/gynecology).[7]

Private hospitals also have grown rapidly in response to supportive government policies and rising demand for hospitals and their medtech services. The proportion of private hospitals climbed from 31 percent in 2009 to 46 percent in 2013. Patients' willingness to pay for perceived superior quality, sophisticated medical devices, and cutting-edge technology has created an opportunity for private hospitals, especially those jointly owned by foreign investors. Such facilities may be better positioned than their public counterparts to provide these technology options (see Figure 15.8). To date, while private hospitals have grown in terms of both numbers and share of total hospitals, their bed capacity and utilization levels remain small.

In response to these favorable tailwinds, life science and medtech companies have ramped up investment in China and tapped into support from both the government and private sectors to finance technological upgrades in hospitals. While the government increased funding for innovation in the biomedical industry as part of the 12th FYP, funding for capital equipment and reagents/consumables has slowed since 2011 (see Figure 15.9). Multinational corporations have picked up some of

Working scheme on improving comprehensive capacity of county hospitals

Distribution of 500 county hospitals

Legend:
- Listed hospitals >40
- Listed hospitals 30~40
- Listed hospitals 20~30
- Listed hospitals 10~20
- Listed hospitals <10

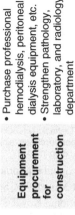

500

90%

50%

- **Phase I**
- 2014~2017
- Select 500 county hospitals in pilot counties

- **Phase II**
- 2018~2020
- 90% of county hospitals meet **basic requirements**
- 50% of county hospitals meet **recommended requirements by NHFPC**

Strengthen construction of clinical subjects
- Complete level I subjects
- Improve level II subjects

Equipment procurement for construction
- Purchase professional hemodialysis, peritoneal dialysis equipment, etc.
- Strengthen pathology, laboratory, and radiology department

Tier I: Eastern coastal provinces (incl. Zhejiang, Jiangsu, Shandong, Hebei, etc.)
- Have large medical market sizes and healthy growth
- Benefit from the development of county hospitals

Tier II: Central provinces (incl. Shaanxi, Shanxi, Hubei) and coastal provinces (incl. Guangdong, Fujian)
- Have good economic performance
- Medical resources are highly centralized in provincial capital cities
- Have sustainable drivers for development of county hospitals

Tier III: Henan, Anhui, Yunnan, etc.
- Rely on the central financial support for development of county hospitals

Leading position: Sichuan
- Fastest developing area of county hospitals
- Center of western economic development
- Center of western medical treatment

Figure 15.7 NHFPC pilot program with 500 county hospitals, January 2015
Source: 2014. Working scheme on improving the comprehensive capacity of county hospitals.

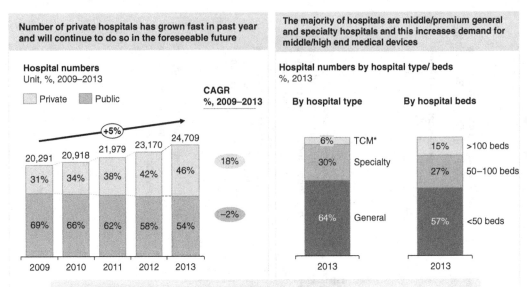

*Traditional Chinese medicine hospitals

Figure 15.8 Growth of private hospitals and demand for middle/high-end medical devices
Source: China statistic yearbook of health (2010–2014); Team analysis.

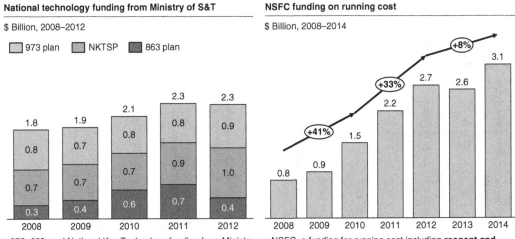

Figure 15.9 Growth of capital equipment and reagent/consumable funding
Source: Annual report of Ministry of Science and Technology of PRC, 2009–2013; NFSC annual report
2008–2013; NKTSP: National Key Technology support program.

the slack and shifted investment away from the United States (where NIH funding of biotech increased only 2 percent from 2009 to 2014) to set up or expand R&D centers and manufacturing sites in China. As one illustration, in 2012 Pfizer and Merck reduced their R&D investment in the US market by $1.5 billion and $0.5 billion, respectively, and built open research platforms in China by collaborating with local universities. At the same time, local players have scaled up their research and development (R&D) capabilities to take advantage of the "Major New Drug Development" initiative in the 12th FYP to promote the domestic biomedicine sector.

Expenditure Trends

The government's healthcare reforms have infused massive amounts of funding into the healthcare industry and its various sectors. This has had both positive consequences in the short term and negative consequences in the longer term. On the one hand, the 2009 reform called for 850 billion RMB in spending between 2009 and 2011; in reality, the government spent 1.241 trillion RMB – 46 percent higher than expected. Of this amount, 873 billion RMB came from provincial and local government, while the central government contributed 368 billion RMB. The destinations of central government funding favored investments in the insurance schemes (200 billion RMB or 54 percent of the total 368 billion RMB), with another 75 billion RMB (21 percent) going to public health and 63 billion RMB (15 percent) going to infrastructure.[8] Greater levels of government spending on insurance and infrastructure help to fuel the healthcare quadrilemma discussed in Chapter 1.

On the other hand, the rising cost of healthcare and the rising share of China's GDP consumed by healthcare have spurred greater efforts at cost containment by central and provincial governments. Such efforts have historically been undertaken with the philosophy that healthcare is more a cost than an investment (see Chapter 2). These efforts include group purchasing (provincial tenders), case payments, and ceilings on channel markups. These headwinds to medtech revenue generation are discussed below.

Demographic Trends

Over the past decade, China's urban population has increased annually by roughly 20 million and accounts for approximately 30 percent of the world's newborn population. In terms of sheer size, China has the largest urban population in the world; however, the urbanization rate only just surpassed 50 percent, still below the world's average. By 2025, China's urbanization rate is estimated to reach 65 percent, with GDP in urban areas accounting for 90 percent of total GDP. The country's rapid urbanization will thus increase the affordability of healthcare services and the population's access to more sophisticated diagnosis and treatment options.

Urbanization, industrialization, and car ownership have been accompanied by an increase in work-related injuries (1.3 million in 2009) and traffic-related injuries. Both trends have contributed to a growing need for orthopedic and trauma care, including specialized implants. Indeed, trauma products account for roughly twice the market share in China compared to the rest of the world.

China is an aging society with growing prevalence of chronic diseases (see Chapter 3). In 2005, the population of people aged 65 and over reached 120 million (about 9.1 percent of the population) and is projected to reach 140 million (~9.9 percent) by 2015. Chronic disease prevalence increases with age, and now accounts for roughly 80 percent of the country's 10.3 million deaths and 68.6 percent of total healthcare spending. This proportion will increase in the coming years. Growing levels of obesity, for example, are likely to spur demand for orthopedic surgery and implants.

As in other parts of the world, however, there are issues surrounding health awareness and health literacy among the Chinese population that serve as headwinds to demand. A nationwide survey conducted by the former Ministry of Health in 2008–2009 revealed that only 6.5 percent of the population aged 15–69 were equipped with "general health literacy" (basic health knowledge and concepts, healthy lifestyle and behaviors, and mastery of necessary health skills) – compared to 50 percent in the United States. An even lower percentage of the population (4.7 percent) were literate in the prevention of chronic disease. These are troubling

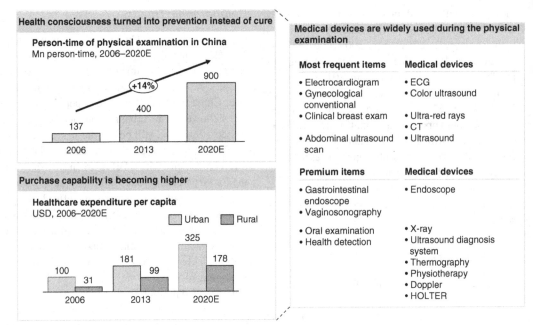

Figure 15.10 Drivers of sustainable development of medical device sector
Source: China statistic yearbook of health (2007–2014); Expert interview; Team analysis

statistics given China's demographic transition toward chronic illness.

Paradoxically, the demographic transition has been accompanied by a growing awareness of the importance of prevention. For example, physical exams are expected to grow at a compound annual growth rate (CAGR) of more than 10 percent over the next five years. Those medical devices widely used in physical examinations, such as ECG, color ultrasound, CT, endoscope, etc., will drive the growth of the medical device sector (see Figure 15.10). This growing "health consciousness" has been facilitated by the increased purchasing power of China's population: healthcare expenditures per capita are predicted to nearly double from 2013 to 2020.

Finally, the growing burden of chronic illness may or may not translate into higher demand for medtech products based on the care-seeking behavior of citizens. For example, research suggests there is a sizeable pool of 200 million Chinese who are candidates for hip, knee, and spinal implants due to osteoporosis, osteoarthritis, and avascular necrosis.[9] The lack of primary care physicians to diagnose and refer such patients to specialists, combined with a shortage of some specialists and/or patient tendencies to engage in self-management or use pain killers, may limit effective demand to just a fraction of the potential patient base.

Medical Device Market Segments

There are various ways to segment the medtech market in China. One method is to distinguish device segments based on their intended use (see above): for example, capital equipment, implantables, in vitro diagnostics, etc. As an example, Cowen decomposed the Chinese medtech sector according to diagnostic imaging (38 percent of market), consumables (20 percent), orthopedics (13 percent), dental (2 percent), and other (27 percent).[10] Another method is to distinguish segments based on disease categories and/or body parts (neuro, cardio, ortho, etc.). A third method is to distinguish segments based on the sizes of the (urban) markets served (e.g., premium market vs. mass market).

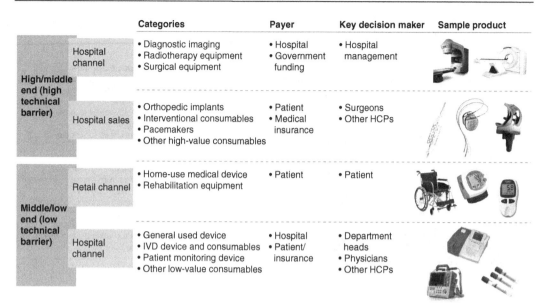

Categories	Payer	Key decision maker	Sample product

High/middle end (high technical barrier)

	Categories	Payer	Key decision maker
Hospital channel	• Diagnostic imaging • Radiotherapy equipment • Surgical equipment	• Hospital • Government funding	• Hospital management
Hospital sales	• Orthopedic implants • Interventional consumables • Pacemakers • Other high-value consumables	• Patient • Medical insurance	• Surgeons • Other HCPs

Middle/low end (low technical barrier)

	Categories	Payer	Key decision maker
Retail channel	• Home-use medical device • Rehabilitation equipment	• Patient	• Patient
Hospital channel	• General used device • IVD device and consumables • Patient monitoring device • Other low-value consumables	• Hospital • Patient/ insurance	• Department heads • Physicians • Other HCPs

Figure 15.11 Medical device segments
Source: Expert interview; Team analysis

Classification of Segments

This chapter combines several of these methods to classify the medical device market into high/middle end and middle/low end segments. These two groups are distinguished by the technical barriers of entry, distribution channels, payers, key decision makers, and end customers (see Figure 15.11).

High/Middle End Segment

This segment includes high-end equipment and physician preference items (PPIs). Equipment such as diagnostic imaging, radiotherapy, and surgical equipment is sold by manufacturers to hospital customers. Their large size, high price, and high-tech features require large buyers like hospitals. PPIs, on the other hand, are marketed by manufacturers to surgeons and interventional cardiologists but sold to (and purchased by) hospitals. Such products include orthopedic implants, interventional consumables, and pacemakers. Due to the sophistication of customers, the buying decision for these devices depends more on the preferences of specialist physicians than patients.

Middle/Low End Segment

This segment includes less sophisticated equipment and machines. Some are sold through retail channels to the home market (e.g., rehabilitation equipment). Since this equipment does not require high professional expertise, the purchase decision typically rests with patients and their families. Other equipment, such as in-vitro diagnostics (IVD), patient monitoring devices, and other low-value consumables, is sold through hospital channels. Some professional expertise is required in the purchasing decision, and the majority of the equipment is paid for by hospitals. Department heads, physicians, and other healthcare professionals are the key decision makers.

Growth Projections and Drivers

The leading market segments are diagnostic imaging, IVD, cardiovascular consumables, and orthopedic implants. The subsections describe their market growth projections and drivers.

Diagnostic Imaging

Diagnostic imaging comprises the biggest segment of the device market. Facility upgrades by

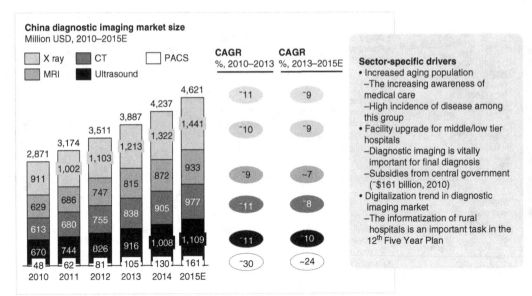

Figure 15.12 Diagnostic imaging market
Source: Millennium; Team analysis.

middle/low level hospitals are the key driver of this segment. Digitalization of rural hospitals is an important task set by the 12th FYP to improve patient diagnosis. In 2010, a $161 billion subsidy was allocated by the central government. Figure 15.12 depicts the estimated growth of this segment from 2010 to 2013 (roughly 11 percent CAGR) and from 2013 to 2015 (roughly 9 percent CAGR). X-ray equipment accounts for the largest share, while magnetic resonance imaging (MRI), computed tomography (CT), and ultrasound equipment exhibit smaller, similar shares of the market. PACS (picture archiving and communication system) exhibits the fastest rate of growth.

In-vitro Diagnostics (IVD)

The IVD segment is driven by soaring healthcare demand from expanded insurance, improved affordability, and increased health awareness. Facility upgrades to take advantage of new technology and standardized clinical pathways will ensure continuing demand. A good example is automatic and semiautomatic chemiluminescent assays, which

are replacing enzyme immunoassay products. Overall, the IVD market grew at 18 percent CAGR from 2010 to 2013 and will maintain roughly 14 percent CAGR from 2013 to 2015. Molecular diagnostic reagents exhibit the highest growth rate, while immunological reagents have the largest share of the market (see Figure 15.13).

Cardiovascular Consumables

China's aging population is associated with a rising prevalence of cardiovascular disease. This trend will fuel sustainable demand for cardiovascular consumables. Technological innovation in this segment will drive further growth. Advanced instruments like implantable cancer detectors have been introduced to China, while biodegradable, interventional stents are included in the promotion list of 12th FYP. Cardiovascular interventional surgical procedures have been rapidly adopted by clinicians, and the number of qualified surgeons is expected to surpass 1,000 in the near future. Figure 15.14 illustrates the market for coronary stents. This market increased from $1.16 billion in 2010 to $2.2 billion in 2013 and is projected to reach $3.2 billion by 2015.

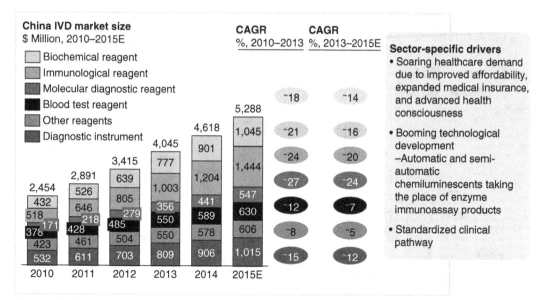

Figure 15.13 IVD market
Source: Expert interview; McEvoy and Farmer; Strategic policy dept. analysis; Team analysis.

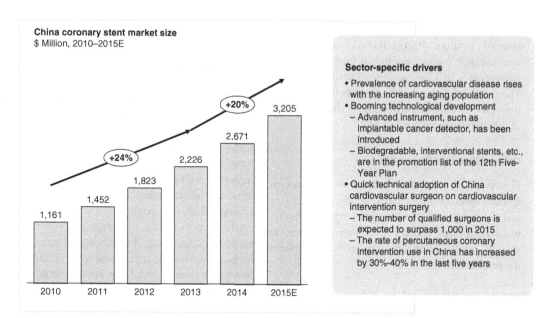

Figure 15.14 Cardiovascular consumables market
Source: MicroPort; Essence Securities; Team analysis.

Orthopedic Implants

Expanded insurance coverage and increased health awareness have also played important roles in the growth of orthopedic implants. Advanced therapy has been introduced and adopted, as evidenced by penetrating keratoplasty (PKP) becoming the main treatment for spine fracture. More surgeons have likewise accepted minimally invasive trauma

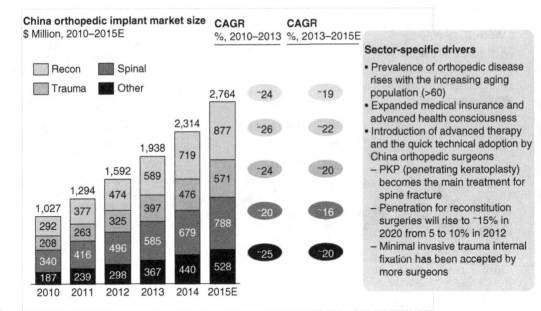

Figure 15.15 Orthopedic market
Source: Frost & Sullivan; Team analysis.

internal fixation. Reconstruction surgeries will increase their market penetration from 5 percent to 10 percent in 2012 to roughly 15 percent by 2020. The reconstruction market grew about 22 percent from 2013 to 2015 and now controls about one-third of the market (see Figure 15.15).

Other Attractive Segments

Figure 15.16 plots other attractive segments in China's medtech sector based on their market size and revenue growth. Cardio, endoscope, and family medical devices outpace the other segments in growth, while high-value consumables constitute the profit leaders.

Business Challenges Facing MNCs in China

Institutional differences in China's healthcare system can pose challenges for MNCs in the medtech sector. The nature and degree of those challenges may vary across device segments, as depicted in Figure 15.17.

Local Competition

MNCs still dominate some product categories due to high entry barriers stemming from technological sophistication. Nevertheless, MNCs face competition from 15,961 local manufacturers, including 4,587 companies making Class I devices and 8,649 companies making Class II devices.[11] Local firms enjoy several cost advantages over MNCs, including selling and promotion, R&D, and governance and administration (see Figure 15.18 for an example from orthopedics). Local players are also catching up to MNCs as a result of governmental support and financing of technological upgrades in hospitals, as well as recent procurement and reimbursement changes that favor lower-cost (and thus local) firms. According to the Boston Consulting Group, local firms dominate in healthcare information technology as well as in medical supplies and disposables, and have achieved parity with MNCs in such segments as orthopedics, patient monitoring, and wound care.[12] Moreover, Figure 15.19 suggests that local players will increasingly migrate from lower-end to higher-end markets. Additionally, as the mid-market outpaces other

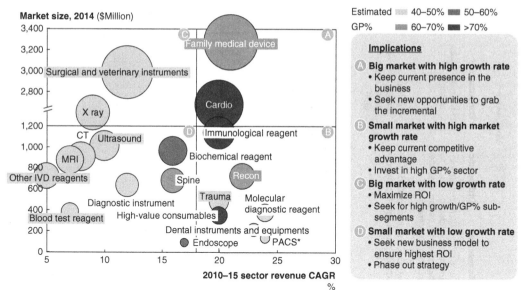

*Picture archiving and communications system

Figure 15.16 Other market segments
Source: Industry report; Expert interview; Team analysis.

segments, additional opportunities will open up for local players.

Local companies rapidly gain market share based on procurement mode and hospital type. As Figure 15.20 illustrates, hospitals below Class IIA and private hospitals favor local medical devices in purchases based on price. The government encourages domestic substitution through an evaluation of domestic equipment overseen by the Chinese Association of Medical Equipment authorized by the NHFPC. The association's mission is to select domestic medical equipment items with excellent quality, competitive advantage, and development potential that are added to a recommended catalogue for hospitals. The catalogue prioritizes hospital procurement of local brands, increases competition with imported equipment, increases local innovation, and lowers costs. The catalogue will expand to consumables in the future, further intensifying competition for MNCs.

Local firms have been steadily engaged in their own merger and acquisition (M&A) activity for the past seven years. In 2008, Kanghui acquired 100 percent interest in Beijing Libeier; in 2011,

Kanghui formed an exclusive partnership with Consensus Orthopedics to make joint implants; and that same year, Kanghui acquired a majority stake in Beijing Wei Rui Li Medical Device, which made knee and hip systems. Such local M&A is often undertaken to consolidate a very fragmented local market as well as broaden the acquiring firm's product line to itself become an attractive M&A target by an MNC. Indeed, Medtronic acquired Kanghui in 2012 for $816 million, increasing Medtronic's share of the Chinese orthopedic market to 7 percent.

Different Market Dynamics

China's healthcare system is dominated by four major players: government, service providers, payers, and product suppliers (pharmaceutical and medtech companies). These players and their channel relationships are portrayed in Figure 1.8. These four players differ from their counterparts in the United States in several important ways (see Figures 15.21; also see Tables 1.2 and 1.3). Public hospitals are major healthcare providers in China and dominate in numbers and

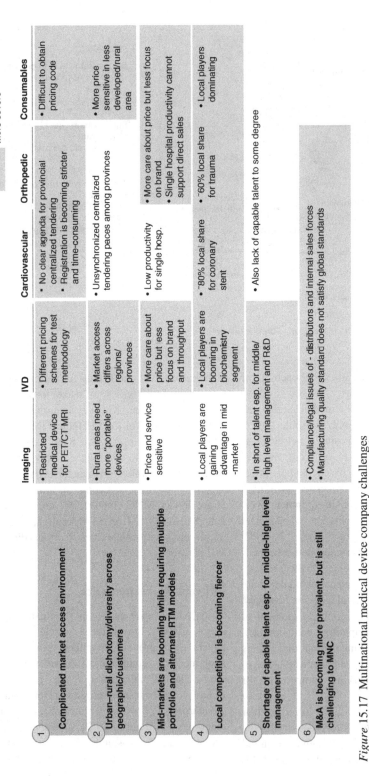

Figure 15.17 Multinational medical device company challenges

Source: Team analysis.

ORTHOPEDIC EXAMPLE

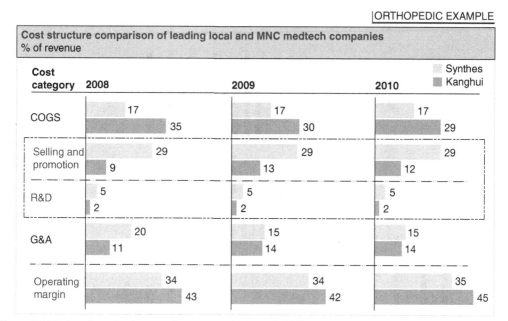

Figure 15.18 Local medtech cost advantages relative to MNCs

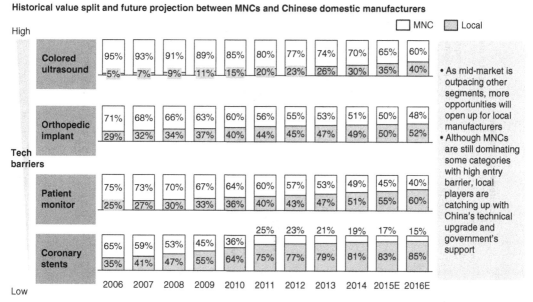

Figure 15.19 Multinational versus local manufacturer competition
Source: Literature research; Expert interviews; Team analysis.

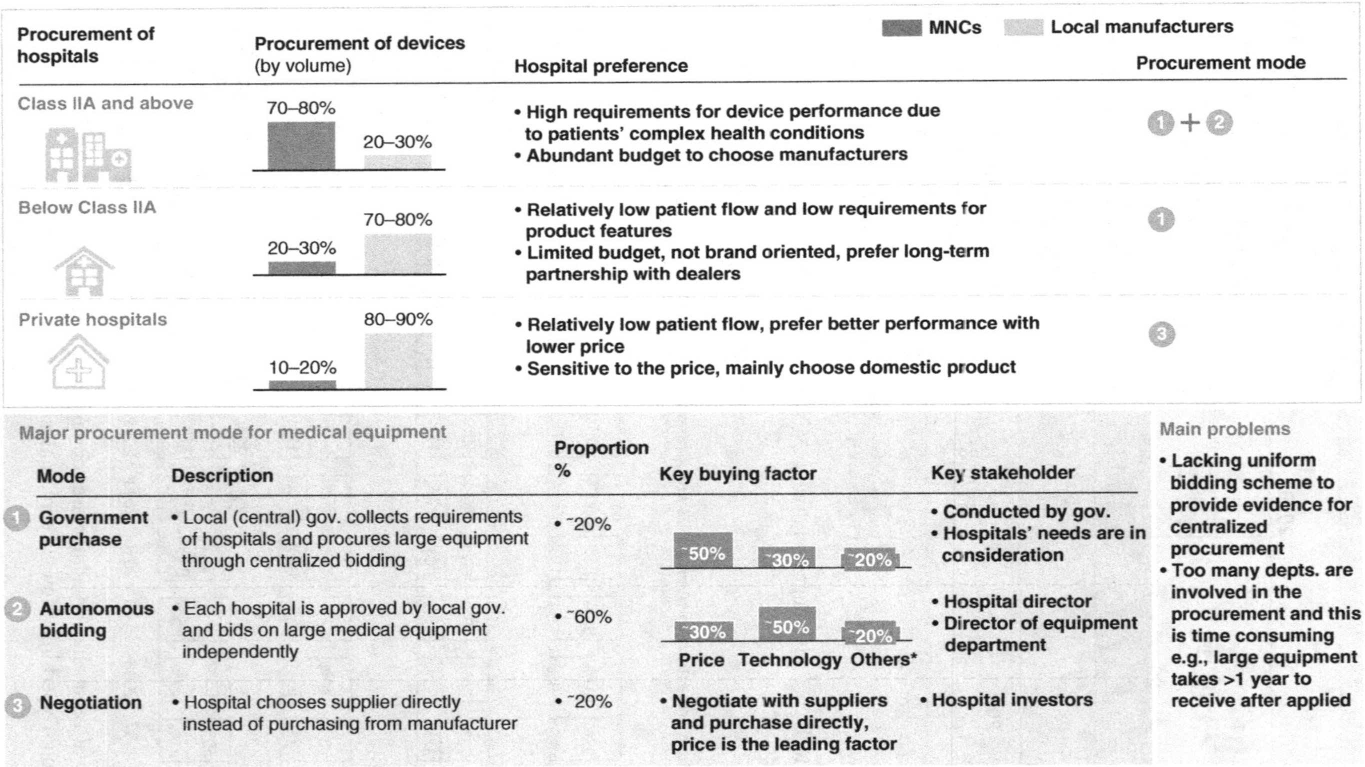

Legend: ▮ MNCs ▯ Local manufacturers

Procurement of hospitals	Procurement of devices (by volume)		Hospital preference	Procurement mode
Class IIA and above	70-80%	20-30%	• High requirements for device performance due to patients' complex health conditions • Abundant budget to choose manufacturers	①+②
Below Class IIA	70-80%	20-30%	• Relatively low patient flow and low requirements for product features • Limited budget, not brand oriented, prefer long-term partnership with dealers	①
Private hospitals	80-90%	10-20%	• Relatively low patient flow, prefer better performance with lower price • Sensitive to the price, mainly choose domestic product	③

Major procurement mode for medical equipment

Mode	Description	Proportion %	Key buying factor	Key stakeholder
① Government purchase	• Local (central) gov. collects requirements of hospitals and procures large equipment through centralized bidding	~20%	50% / 30% / 20%	• Conducted by gov. • Hospitals' needs are in consideration
② Autonomous bidding	• Each hospital is approved by local gov. and bids on large medical equipment independently	~60%	30% / 50% / 20%	• Hospital director • Director of equipment department
③ Negotiation	• Hospital chooses supplier directly instead of purchasing from manufacturer	~20%	• Negotiate with suppliers and purchase directly, price is the leading factor	• Hospital investors

Key buying factor: Price / Technology / Others*

Main problems
• Lacking uniform bidding scheme to provide evidence for centralized procurement
• Too many depts. are involved in the procurement and this is time consuming e.g., large equipment takes >1 year to receive after applied

*Including after-sales service, distributor capacity, etc.

Figure 15.20 Hospital preference and procurement
Source: Development of medical device industry blue book in 2013; Expert interview.

	China	US
Providers	• **Dominated by public hospitals** (non profit) which are the first choice of most patients • Patient flow from small cities to large cities is common • **Community health centers (CHCs)** will likely **improve** primary care patient flow	• Dominated **by nonprofit private hospitals** (~67% beds) • Number of hospitals and **hospital beds are declining** slowly and consistently
Payers	• Highly depend on **government-led insurance** • **Large increase in insurance coverage** (100% by 2015), driven by government initiatives • **Heavily funded by out-of-pocket payments** from patients (~30% in 2014)	• ~67% of the population and private insurance • ~26% have some **government-funded** coverage • **15% (~45 million) of people are uninsured** and have limited access to healthcare
Pricing	• Public hospitals **rely on drug/device sales** historically • **Government sets up service price** • Drug and device price under regulation of **price bureau**	• Hospitals less reliant on drug and device sales, which generate ~10–15% of total revenues for hospitals • Medicare price set up by federal government **based on DRG** (diagnosis related group) • Payers set up price based on **the negotiation with healthcare providers**
Govt roles	• **Central government sets up fundamental guidelines** (e.g., device reimbursement/exclusion list, development plan) • Provincial/municipal governments define regulations according to local economics	• **Government initiates public-funded insurance** to compensate for the vulnerability of the health care system, such as Medicare and Medicaid

Figure 15.21 Healthcare systems: China versus the United States

Source: Lit. research; Expert interview; Team analysis.

patient preference. Because of historical patterns of (unbalanced) resource allocation (see Chapter 2), patients have flowed from small cities to large cities seeking better treatment. Following the 2009 reform, the government hopes to redirect the flow of patients with primary care needs to CHCs and thereby alleviate the congestion in Class III hospitals.

Unlike the US insurance model which relies on private sector employer coverage supplemented by federal and state insurance programs, China relies on several government-sponsored insurance plans (see Chapters 2, 4, and 11). With the spread of coverage, the heavy burden of out-of-pocket spending is expected to fall from 35 percent to 30 percent between 2011 and 2015. Nevertheless, some insurance schemes (e.g., UEBMI) offer broader coverage than the others and thus are the more likely payers for medtech products.

In both the United States and China, product prices must be negotiated at the local level rather than the national level. Unlike the United States, where payers set prices based on negotiation with healthcare providers, China regulates the price of drugs and medical services using administered pricing at the provincial level through price bureaus. In general, the government plays a more central role in China's healthcare system, compared with the United States. The central government establishes general guidelines (e.g., the medical device industry 12th FYP), but then leaves the task of defining the regulations to provincial/municipal governments who tailor them to their local situation.

In both the United States and China, products reach hospitals and physicians through distributor intermediaries – which can either be contracted or owned by the manufacturer. In contrast to the United States, the Chinese market is entirely fragmented and enormous in size (165,000 distributors). Few if any distributors provide nationwide coverage. Moreover, with so many distributors, medtech firms have customarily relied on multiple channel partners (e.g., tier 1 and tier 2 distributors, or logistics firms working with a distributor) to get their products to providers. This arrangement adds complexity (multiple invoices) and cost (multiple channel markups).

Government Bureaucracy and Regulatory Oversight

A complex government bureaucracy also oversees China's medtech sector (see Figure 15.22; see also Figures 2.1 and 2.3). At least ten government bureaus set policy and issue regulations; multiple government agencies and departments strongly influence the market access of products, including registration, pricing, tendering, hospital listing, and reimbursement (see Figure 15.23). This complexity lengthens the decision-making process, not only for government but also for device manufacturers. This poses difficulties in market access for medtech companies.

Product/Price Registration Process

Registration of medical devices in China is governed by two main regulations: (1) "Regulations for the Supervision & Administration of Medical Devices," enacted in April 2000; and (2) "Measures for the Administration of Medical Device Registration," enacted in August 2004. The new "Regulations on Medical Device Supervision and Administration" went into effect in June 2014, accompanied by 20–30 supporting regulations. The government updated the regulations to standardize and streamline the approval process (e.g., eliminate 7 of 16 administrative clearances in the registration process; eliminate clinical trial approval for Class II devices, and now only need to file clinical trial with CFDA authorities), simplify registration procedures (e.g., no registration certificate required for Class I devices, whether local or imported; no longer need to obtain a production permit before you apply for a product registration certificate), and enhance supervision and product tracking. Such changes are intended to reduce bureaucracy, increase the path-to-market for low-risk Class I devices, and increase innovation.

The new regulations offer opportunities to MNCs, including reduced frequency of re-registration and re-labeling (if product changes are not substantial) and more time for supplementary document provision. They also pose several challenges such as registration fees, increased post-marketing surveillance, mandatory local clinical trials (e.g., for IVDs) as required of local products,

Government bureau	Roles related to medical device	Latest policies/regulations issued
State Council	▪ Overall guidance	▪ 13 FYP of healthcare service system (2015) ▪ The notice on the main tasks of healthcare in 2015
National Health and Family Planning Commission (NHFPC)	▪ RCMS insurance funding ▪ Centralized tendering product list	▪ Management of occupational health examination (2015)
National Food Quality Supervision and Inspection Center (CFDA)	▪ Product registration ▪ Medical device standardization ▪ Supervision over medical device manufacturing ▪ Medical device vigilance	▪ The law of food safety (2015) ▪ Supervision and administration of medical devices (2014)
National Development and Reform Commission (NDRC)	▪ Pricing management of medical devices ▪ Channel mark up management ▪ Drug list management	▪ Supervision and management of food and drugs online (2015) ▪ Low-cost drug list (2014)
Ministry of Human Resources and Social Security (MoHRSS)	▪ Medical insurance fund management ▪ Reimbursement list formulation	▪ Promotion of medical insurance fund surveillance (2015) ▪ Medical settlement in non-local treatment (2014)
Ministry of Commerce	▪ Medical device circulation management ▪ Antitrust investigation	▪ Pharmaceutical/medical device distribution management (2015)
State Intellectual Property Office (SIPO)	▪ IP registration ▪ IP management	▪ NA
Ministry of Science and Technology (MOST)	▪ Local technology/innovation support	▪ Promotion of local medical device manufacturer innovation

Figure 15.22 Government bureaus influencing medical device market access

Source: Literature research; Expert interviews; Team analysis.

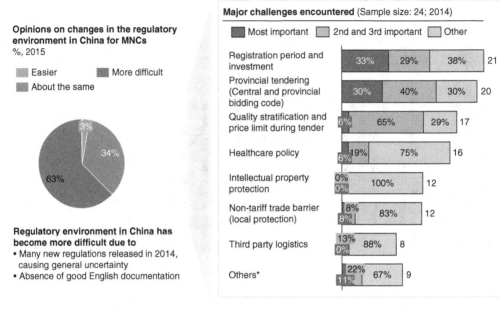

Opinions on changes in the regulatory environment in China for MNCs
%, 2015

Easier
More difficult
About the same

3%
34%
63%

Regulatory environment in China has become more difficult due to
• Many new regulations released in 2014, causing general uncertainty
• Absence of good English documentation

Major challenges encountered (Sample size: 24; 2014)

Most important   2nd and 3rd important   Other

Registration period and investment	33%	29%	38%	21
Provincial tendering (Central and provincial bidding code)	30%	40%	30%	20
Quality stratification and price limit during tender	6%	65%	29%	17
Healthcare policy	19% 6%	75%		16
Intellectual property protection	0% 0%	100%		12
Non-tariff trade barrier (local protection)	8% 8%	83%		12
Third party logistics	13% 0%	88%		8
Others*	22% 11%	67%		9

*include fair competition in local tenders as well, time for product registration is very long, code-related matters due to the current enforcement environment, etc.

Figure 15.23 Key concerns in regulatory environment for multinationals
Source: Emergo Global Medical Device Industry Outlook For 2015; AdvaMed Member Survey Report 2015.

and uncertainties due to the lack of clear CFDA guidelines.

Devices are categorized into three classes (Class I, II, and III) according to the CFDA. The class determines the set of procedures and requirements for obtaining relevant licenses and/or certificates for importation and investment. The overall timeline for the registration process varies from 12 months (for Class I medical devices) to 36 months (Class III devices). This process takes much longer compared with the United States (1 month for Class I devices, 4–10 months for Class II). The process for general medical device registration is depicted in Figure 15.24.

The price application process resembles the registration process. Providers can charge for medical devices either separately or together with specific services as part of a bundle. In the latter case, hospitals are careful about the price paid for the medical device by virtue of working under a price ceiling for the service. Both the service fee pricing and pricing application are conducted at the provincial level by meetings of organizing experts and related officials. In some cases, pricing applications can occur at the level of individual cities or even specific hospitals (see Figure 15.25).

In 2012, the NDRC (supported by the NHFPC) issued the "Green Book"[13] that defines the detailed items for 9,360 medical services. Implementation has been delayed at the provincial level due to the restructuring of the National Development and Reform Commission (NDRC) and drug price reform. The government has begun to move away from administered drug pricing to market-based pricing for five types of drugs and may apply this same approach to medical devices in the near future (see Figure 15.26).

The government is considering other efficiency measures to deal with rising healthcare costs and the threatened depletion of medical insurance funds. Several proposals target the prices of drugs and medical devices (see Figure 15.27). One measure, a manufacturer price cut, aims to reduce profit

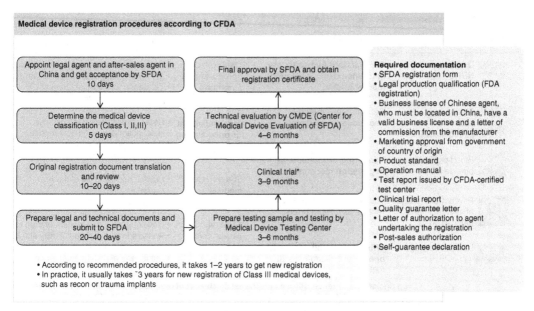

*Class II and III without clinical trial: (1) Marketed in country of origin (2) Manufacture is ISO 9000-certified (3) Product modification does not affect safety and efficiency (4) Non-implants, no radioactive sources (5) Would not cause serious injury or death to patient and operator

Figure 15.24 Product registration process
Source: SFDA; Team analysis.

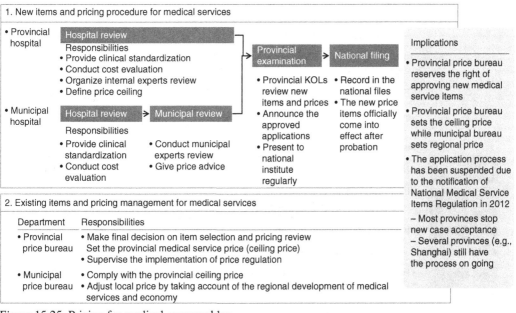

Figure 15.25 Pricing for medical consumables
Source: Literature research; Expert interviews; Team analysis.

Pricing mechanisms of five types of medicine		Four supervision measures after cancelling the pricing rights	
Medicine type	**Pricing mechanism**	**Measure**	**Description**
Drugs listed in NDRL	• **Set standard by healthcare insurance dept., leading to market pricing**	**Multiple drug procurement methods**	• Categorical/centralized procurement • Multilateral negotiation mechanism • Tendering for manufacturing of designated production
Patent drugs, exclusive Chinese patent medicines	• **Establish multilateral negotiation mechanism**	**Encouragement for price-cutting and cost control**	• Cost savings belong to hospitals • Help institutions to get lower price • Conduct mixed payments • Develop internal incentive system
Blood products outside NDRL	• **Tendering or multilateral negotiation mechanism**	**Supervision on medical behavior**	• Publish price and list of medical expenses • Publicize medical service and drug prices
Psychotropic drugs of category I and narcotic drugs	• **Management of highest ex-factory and retail price**	**Supervision on drugs' price**	• Develop monitoring system of drug prices • Analyze frequent price volatility and other abnormal phenomena • Punish illegal pricing and monopoly
Low-priced drugs	• **With current policies, daily upper control limit is still valid**		

Key insight
- **Drug pricing liberalization will promote the establishment of regulations of central tendering regulations**
- **The successful pilot of drug pricing reform will accelerate the pricing reform of consumables, etc.**
- **It is reimbursement and tendering that are supposed to control the price of drugs in the future**

Figure 15.26 Pricing liberalization and decentralization in drug procurement
Source: 2014 Plans on promoting drug pricing reform (Exposure Drafts); Expert interview.

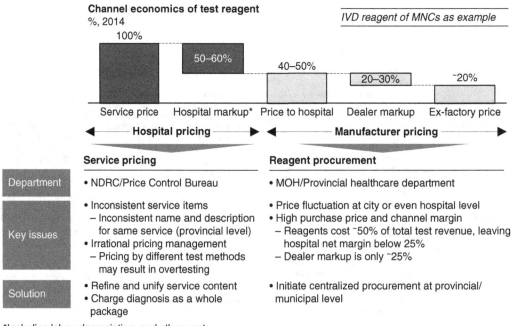

Channel economics of test reagent
%, 2014

IVD reagent of MNCs as example

100%

Service price	Hospital markup*	Price to hospital	Dealer markup	Ex-factory price
	50–60%	40–50%	20–30%	~20%

◀――― **Hospital pricing** ―――▶ ◀――― **Manufacturer pricing** ―――▶

	Service pricing	**Reagent procurement**
Department	• NDRC/Price Control Bureau	• MOH/Provincial healthcare department
Key issues	• Inconsistent service items – Inconsistent name and description for same service (provincial level) • Irrational pricing management – Pricing by different test methods may result in overtesting	• Price fluctuation at city or even hospital level • High purchase price and channel margin – Reagents cost ~50% of total test revenue, leaving hospital net margin below 25% – Dealer markup is only ~25%
Solution	• Refine and unify service content • Charge diagnosis as a whole package	• Initiate centralized procurement at provincial/ municipal level

*Including labor, depreciation, and other costs

Figure 15.27 Government pricing regulation and centralized procurement
Source: MoHRSS; Team analysis.

margins in the supply channel. A second measure aims to reduce hospital markups and service fees. Industry experts anticipate an average 6.5 percent price compression per year in some product categories. A third initiative undertaken by the NDRC in 2012 targeted channel mark-ups to a percentage (e.g., 60 percent) of port price (for imports) or manufacture price (local products), with both subject to a cap of 6,000 RMB. Provincial governments would issue the detailed rules, following the general principle of "high mark-up ceiling for low-value goods, low mark-up ceiling for high-value goods."[14] A fourth initiative dating from 2005 restricts hospitals from making large-scale equipment purchases over 5 million RMB. There will likely be more price-cutting policies in the future, including possible nationwide implementation of global budgets and per-case payments for hospital procedures. A final proposal deals with centralized procurement (covered below).

Tendering Process

At present, the majority of device purchases are conducted via hospital "tenders" (i.e., group purchasing using a bidding process). There are three major types of tendering, which vary according to funding source and product type: government tendering, mediated tendering, and direct tendering. These are briefly described below.

Government tendering, particularly for high-value consumables like orthopedic and cardiovascular implants, is usually administrated by the Bureau of Health at the provincial or municipal level. By contrast, tendering for restricted medical equipment (e.g., PET/CT) is conducted at the national level. As urban medical insurance scheme expenditures have grown, the Chinese government has placed cost containment measures at the top of its agenda. The government is centralizing medical equipment procurement, especially for large equipment, and has issued multiple policies over the past ten years. Once equipment procurement is fully centralized, consumables may be the next target. Price is very important at both national and provincial levels, since the government is involved in the funding.

Mediated tendering is initiated by hospitals and administered by third-party bidding companies.

This process covers products that are not listed in the centralized tendering list and entail large invoice prices. For such products, quality and technological considerations accompany price as important factors in the purchasing decision. Class I/II hospitals finance much of the cost of these products themselves; Class III hospitals can rely on the significant support from the government.

Direct tendering covers hospitals' purchases without a formal bidding process. This occurs when the product is not listed in the centralized tendering list and the purchasing amount falls below the levels observed in mediated tendering. Here the hospital provides most of the funding, but government may screen products and set price ceilings. Direct tendering is thus a price-sensitive process, which must also take into account the different decision makers of hospitals. Figure 15.28 illustrates a tendering process for in-vitro diagnostics.

The push to contain hospital costs generally (and medical device costs specifically) will gain momentum as more provinces adopt tendering. The NHFPC drafted a proposal requiring all 30 provinces to procure medical consumables via provincial tenders, a process that was rapidly progressing by 2012. Followed by low-value consumables, provinces began to start tenders for high-value consumables in 2013. The scope of provincial tendering varies from high/low value consumables to reagents, in which cardiovascular and orthopedic products remain a priority. Three provincial tendering efforts for high-value products can pose obstacles to MNCs: local products only, equal access criteria for local and imported products, and price caps (see Figure 15.29). After the tendering process, hospitals have entered secondary price negotiations with pharmaceutical manufacturers to optimize drug procurement by reducing prices 20 percent below the tendering price. Such a model may migrate to medical device procurement. To drive business growth, medtech companies need to build strong market access teams to address the issues posed by tendering.

Medical device tenders will exert several effects: they will reduce price; they will reduce supplier margins; and they will reduce contract length and

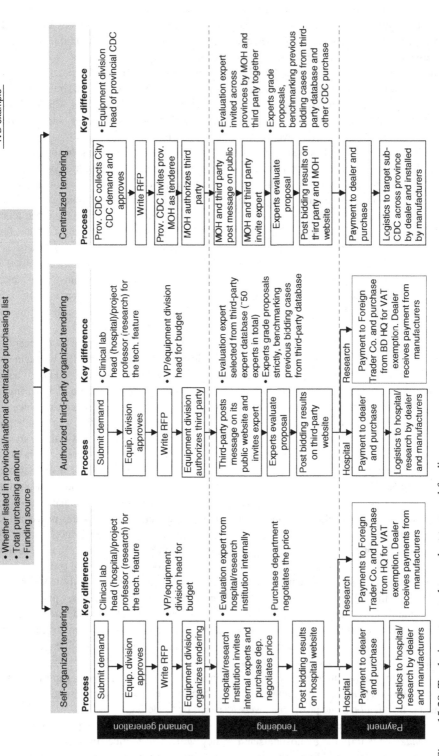

Figure 15.28 Tendering process by product type and funding source

Source: Literature research; Expert interviews; Team analysis.

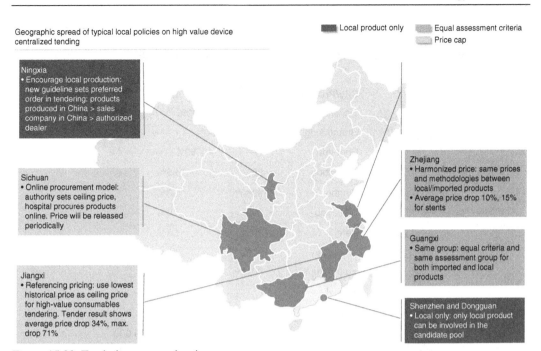

Geographic spread of typical local policies on high value device centralized tending

Local product only   Equal assessment criteria   Price cap

Ningxia
• Encourage local production: new guideline sets preferred order in tendering: products produced in China > sales company in China > authorized dealer

Sichuan
• Online procurement model: authority sets ceiling price, hospital procures products online. Price will be released periodically

Jiangxi
• Referencing pricing: use lowest historical price as ceiling price for high-value consumables tendering. Tender result shows average price drop 34%, max. drop 71%

Zhejiang
• Harmonized price: same prices and methodologies between local/imported products
• Average price drop 10%, 15% for stents

Guangxi
• Same group: equal criteria and same assessment group for both imported and local products

Shenzhen and Dongguan
• Local only: only local product can be involved in the candidate pool

Figure 15.29 Tendering process barriers
Source: Industry interview; Lit. research; Team analysis.

require more frequent contracting, further eroding prices. In addition, they may pressure small and mid-size manufacturers by creating higher administrative burdens for them.

Local Product Preference

Locally manufactured products have increased their market access due to several forms of government support. First, the government has made the product registration process easier for local products. For example, while all imported products are registered at the CFDA level, locally manufactured Class I and II medical products are approved at the provincial FDA level. Only Class III medical products (e.g., implantable devices) require SFDA registration. Second, government policies favor domestically developed innovations in the tendering process:

• All purchases funded by the government (central and local) must favor products on the list of domestic innovations;
• The key national projects funded by central and local governments have to devote more than

60 percent of overall purchases to domestically manufactured products;
• Products with "domestic innovation" status should be preferred in government tenders when other tender conditions are met; and
• If the price of a product with "domestic innovation" status is higher, it should nevertheless be preferred if the excess cost falls within a certain range depending on its technical and market merits.

Third, reimbursement policies have preferred local products in most areas. For example, many prefectural cities have set reimbursement rates that are 10–30 percent higher for local orthopedic implant products than imported ones (see also Figure 15.30). Such products are likely to be chosen by patients, especially those at middle- and low-income levels, as they will lower their out-of-pocket costs for surgical procedures.

Anti-corruption Campaign

To regulate industry behavior and strengthen the country's legal system, the government has

Recon example

Representative city/province with reimbursement policy for Recon implants

		City/Province	Imported	Local	Bias toward local products
Theme I: reimburse as % of total value, without ceiling	Same rate	Tianjin	← 70–85% →		
		Guangdong	← 50% →		
		Chengdu	← 40–80% →		
	Better rate for local products	Hangzhou	80%	95%	√
		Ningbo	90%	80%	√
		Wenzhou	80%	70%	√
		Hefei	80%	50%	√
		Shenzhen	90%	60%	√
		Huangshan	90%	70%	√
Theme II: set ceiling of total reimbursed value	Same term	Jiangxi		< 10,000	
		Beijing		< 9,000	
	Better term for local products	Shanghai	70%, <15,000	80%, <15,000	√
		Suzhou	60%, <30,000	80%, <30,000	√
		……	……	……	

Figure 15.30 Reimbursement policies favor local products
Source: Literature research; Expert interviews; Team analysis.

conducted an anti-corruption campaign since 2012. The campaign can be divided into two phases: "anti-Tigers" (i.e., target "big tigers" like Zhou Yongkang, former head of security services, and Xu Caihou, former general in the People's Liberation Army) and "anti-Flies" (i.e., government officials). By June 2015, more than 50 officials (provincial/ministerial level and higher) had been punished for bribery and corruption.

In addition, the NHFPC has issued a series of "circulars" since 2013 to tackle systemic bribery in the healthcare sector (see Chapter 2). These include nine prohibitions on revenue-generating activities by hospitals and doctors (Circular 49) and a blacklist of manufacturers and distributors engaged in bribery (Circular 50). The NHFPC also issued a work plan to inspect 41 hospitals in 2014 to strengthen its monitoring and surveillance of provider practices. The anti-corruption campaign poses several benefits and challenges to stakeholders in the healthcare sector: reduced provider autonomy in revenue generation and procurement, reduced effectiveness of provider marketing, etc.

The investigation of GlaxoSmithKline (GSK) illustrates government's determination to fight corruption and high prices. The NDRC initiated a special investigation of drug prices among 60 pharmaceutical companies. Several governmental departments have formed a joint task force to more closely regulate the pharmaceutical industry and make drug prices more reasonable. Although its immediate impact on the medical device market is minor, price cuts for medical devices will likely occur in the long run.

Customer Segments and Purchasing Behavior

Customer Segments

There are four major customer segments for medical devices: public hospitals, Center for Disease Control (CDC)/China Inspection and Quarantines

Flow cytometry example

Demographics			Using environment		Key buying factor
Customer type	**Example**	**Estimated #**	**Funding source**	**Chargeable to patients**	
Public hospital	• Shanghai Huashan Hosp. • Jishuitan Hosp.	• ¯13,000	• Government • Own revenue	• Chargeable to patients	• Valid clinical registration for both equipment and consumables • Profitable price versus test pricing • Suitable throughput
CDC/CIQ/ blood bank	• Beijing CDC • Shanghai CIQ	• ¯4,000	• Government • Annual funding	• Non-chargeable	• In compliance with government standards • Whole solutions • Price-insensitive
Research institute	• China Academy of Science	• ¯1,000	• Government • Research funding	• Non-chargeable	• Peer recommendation • After-sales service/support • Economic for consumables
Pharmaco/ CRO	• Wuxi AppTec • Roche China R&D center	• ¯7,600	• Private • Own revenue • R&D budget	• Non-chargeable	• High throughput • Economic for consumables

Figure 15.31 Needs and buying factors by customer type
Source: Literature research; Expert interviews; Team analysis.

(CIQs), research institutes, and pharmaceutical firms and contract research organizations (CROs). They exhibit different buying behaviors due to different user environments. Hospitals are interested in both price and quantity. For example, public hospitals can charge patients for medical consumables in the form of direct charges or service fees; thus profitability ("purchase price vs. test price") is a prerequisite for procurement. Sufficient patient volume and flow are also important to prestigious Class III hospitals. Purchasing by the CDC/CIQ is another story. Because the government provides annual funding for device procurement, CDC/CIQs are less price-sensitive and more interested in a "total solution" (e.g., after-sales service and support) (see Figure 15.31).

Product Procurement and Consumption

Medtech companies must understand product procurement, illustrated here by the example of high-value implants. Two processes typically separate the launch and purchase of an implant by a hospital. The first is the hospital listing process, which is required before the implant can be legally sold in a specific hospital. The second is the consumption process, which involves physician decision making and the flow of patients among hospital departments. Key decision makers in the listing process are hospital/department management teams and the head of procurement (e.g., materials management); physicians and patients are the major stakeholders in the consumption process.

Value Proposition

Class III hospitals (as well as their physicians) care more about product brand, advanced technological features, and adequate hospital revenues to afford premium-priced products. By contrast, the purchase decisions of Class II facilities focus more on product value due to budget constraints and smaller patient volumes. Class I hospitals and below are the most price-sensitive.

Hospital stakeholders can be further segmented by their product needs, buying behaviors, and trade-offs between product benefits (see Figure 15.32). As a result, a single value proposition is inadequate to address the whole market and maximize sales across heterogeneous stakeholders. Medtechs thus need to develop multiple portfolios, value propositions, go-to-market models, and marketing plans to

Hospitals are showing different buying behaviors...				Even in a single hospital, stakeholders can be further segmented based on their needs and attitudes	
				Consumable and diagnostic product case	
Hospital type	No.	Key buying factors for equipment	Key buying factors for consumable	Top benefits	Willing to trade off
Top hospitals (Class III)	• 1,787	• Well-known brand name • Advanced technology with premium parameters • Timely after-sales service	• High price consumables • Premium clinical outcome	• Accurate diagnostic testing • Accurate sample collection • Reputation improvement	• Efficient sample collection • Alternate purchasing arrangements • Safety-engineered products
				• More accurate diagnostic testing • Clinical decisions and outcomes improvement • Medical devices of superior quality	• Reduction in the incidence of MDROs • Effective reduction in antibiotics prescription • Improve emergency room turnaround
Middle-level hospitals (Class II)	• 6,709	• Well-known brand • Decent price	• Value products	• Shapes the local medical guidelines • More accurate sample collection • Best clinical outcomes	• Faster diagnostic turnaround • Applications support • Reduces medication delivery errors
Low-level hospitals (Class I and others)	• 16,213	• Value for money, products with decent performance • Easy to maintain	• Value products		
Private sector	• ~7,500	• Well-known brand name • Easy to maintain	• Based on patients' choice	• Patient satisfaction • Highest quality • Adopting the latest technologies	• More accurate diagnostic • More accurate sample collection • Increasing accuracy of lab results

Figure 15.32 Hospital behaviors and buying factors by tier
Source: Literature research; Expert interviews; Team analysis.

address customer heterogeneity in China's medical device market.

High-end versus Low-end Markets

As noted earlier, the high-end market is typically the entry point for MNCs because of their global value proposition, advanced technologies, and business models. Conversely, local competitors have concentrated on the low-end market and tailored their business models by offering a full range of lower-end products. Local players enjoy a systematic advantage in pricing, market coverage, and sales and service models to address this market (see Figure 15.33). Local players also have more flexibility in developing and maintaining government relationships, which are vital in customer decision making in middle/low tier markets. To compete, MNCs are investing to develop and maintain relationships with key opinion leaders.

In recent years, both MNCs and domestic manufacturers have adjusted their go-to-market strategy. Local players are stepping into the premium market, which is the historical domain of the MNCs, while MNCs are now stepping into the lower-level hospitals and cities to grab market share from the locals (see Figure 15.34). Both MNCs and local players now seek growth opportunities by penetrating the mid-market, which will foster an intense competitive battle (see Figure 15.35).

Mid-market Boom

China's mid-market mainly consists of Class II hospitals in smaller (tier 3/4/5) cities. Due to favorable governmental policies and rapid urbanization in these cities, China's mid-market has become one of the fastest growing markets for medtech (see Figure 15.36). At the same time, the mid-market displays more price sensitivity and focuses more on the specific value of expensive products. The mid-market thus possesses some unique market dynamics and poses a different set of challenges:

• Customers demand simpler, easy-to-use products at affordable prices
• Physicians are less sophisticated, requiring more product education and training

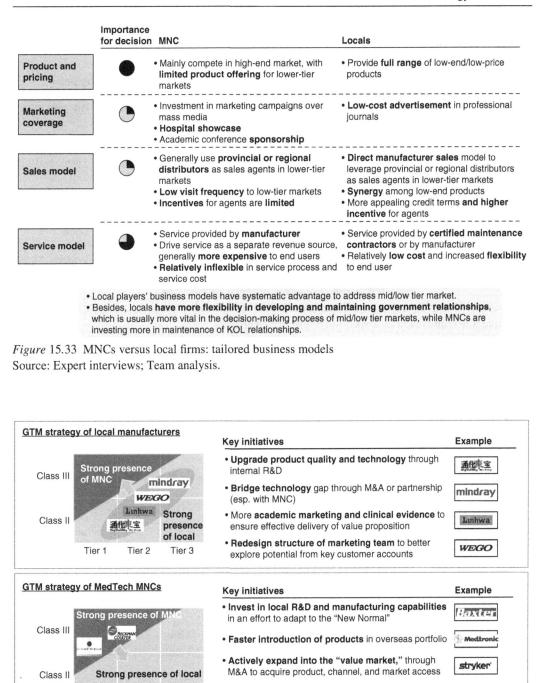

	Importance for decision	MNC	Locals
Product and pricing	●	• Mainly compete in high-end market, with **limited product offering** for lower-tier markets	• Provide **full range** of low-end/low-price products
Marketing coverage	◔	• Investment in marketing campaigns over mass media • **Hospital showcase** • Academic conference **sponsorship**	• **Low-cost advertisement** in professional journals
Sales model	◔	• Generally use **provincial or regional distributors** as sales agents in lower-tier markets • **Low visit frequency** to low-tier markets • **Incentives** for agents are **limited**	• **Direct manufacturer sales** model to leverage provincial or regional distributors as sales agents in lower-tier markets • **Synergy** among low-end products • More appealing credit terms **and higher incentive** for agents
Service model	◕	• Service provided by **manufacturer** • Drive service as a separate revenue source, generally **more expensive** to end users • **Relatively inflexible** in service process and service cost	• Service provided by **certified maintenance contractors** or by manufacturer • Relatively **low cost** and increased **flexibility** to end user

• Local players' business models have systematic advantage to address mid/low tier market.
• Besides, locals **have more flexibility in developing and maintaining government relationships**, which is usually more vital in the decision-making process of mid/low tier markets, while MNCs are investing more in maintenance of KOL relationships.

Figure 15.33 MNCs versus local firms: tailored business models
Source: Expert interviews; Team analysis.

GTM strategy of local manufacturers

Key initiatives	Example
• **Upgrade product quality and technology** through internal R&D	通化東宝
• **Bridge technology** gap through M&A or partnership (esp. with MNC)	mindray
• More **academic marketing and clinical evidence** to ensure effective delivery of value proposition	Linhwa
• **Redesign structure of marketing team** to better explore potential from key customer accounts	WEGO

GTM strategy of MedTech MNCs

Key initiatives	Example
• **Invest in local R&D and manufacturing capabilities** in an effort to adapt to the "New Normal"	Baxter
• **Faster introduction of products** in overseas portfolio	Medtronic
• **Actively expand into the "value market,"** through M&A to acquire product, channel, and market access	stryker

Figure 15.34 MNCs versus local firms: go-to-market strategy
Source: LEK report on competitive benchmarking; Team analysis.

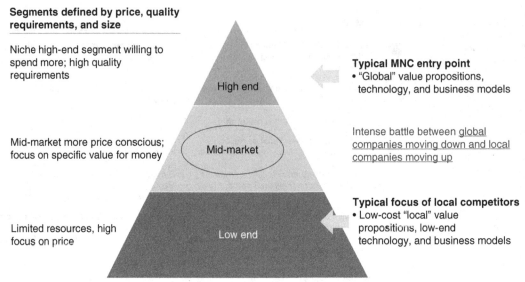

Figure 15.35 MNCs versus local firms: mid-market battleground
Source: Literature research; Expert interviews; Team analysis.

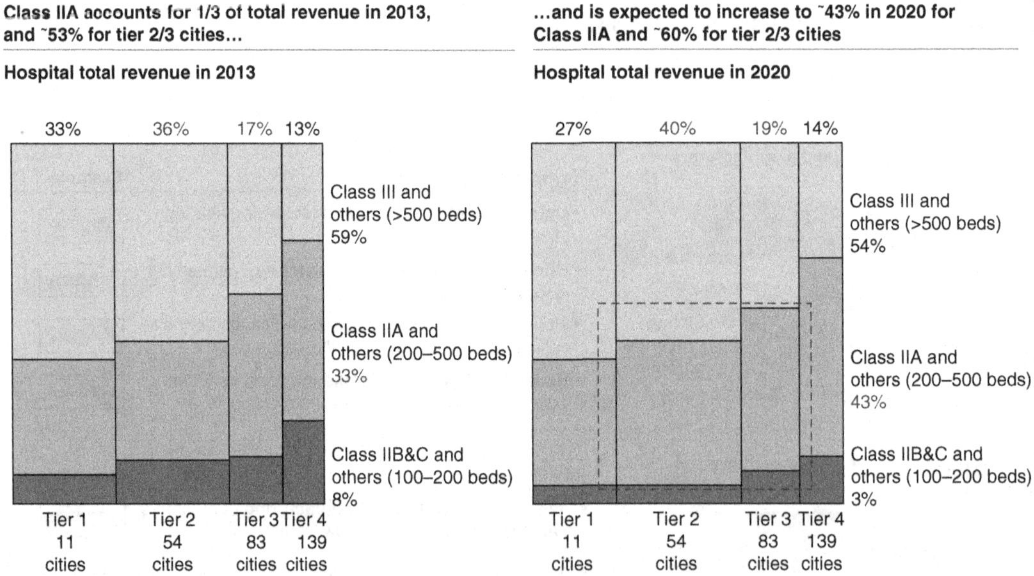

Class IIA accounts for 1/3 of total revenue in 2013, and ˜53% for tier 2/3 cities...

Hospital total revenue in 2013

33%   36%   17% 13%

Class III and others (>500 beds) 59%

Class IIA and others (200–500 beds) 33%

Class IIB&C and others (100–200 beds) 8%

Tier 1   Tier 2   Tier 3 Tier 4
11   54   83   139
cities   cities   cities cities

...and is expected to increase to ˜43% in 2020 for Class IIA and ˜60% for tier 2/3 cities

Hospital total revenue in 2020

27%   40%   19% 14%

Class III and others (>500 beds) 54%

Class IIA and others (200–500 beds) 43%

Class IIB&C and others (100–200 beds) 3%

Tier 1   Tier 2   Tier 3 Tier 4
11   54   83   139
cities   cities   cities cities

Figure 15.36 Growth of mid-market Class IIA hospitals in tier 2/3 cities
Source: Literature research; MOH; Team analysis.

- Purchasing decision criteria can be quite different from the high-end market
- Evolving distribution landscape creates challenges for balancing the use of distributors versus owned sales forces

MNC Strategies

Distribution

As noted above, the China market is too large and diverse to be serviced by a single firm. At a minimum, MNCs require a host of local distributors to get their products to hospital and physician providers. Distributors typically purchase the product from the manufacturer, and then handle the logistics and payment collection from hospitals. This is an important function in China, where the hospitals rely on their own cash flow to fund their operations (in the absence of government funding) and thus take 12–18 months to pay their bills to suppliers. Like distributors of other products, distributors hold cash reserves to buy the inventory, serve multiple manufacturers, maintain close ties with clinicians (both doctors and nurses) and hospital departments, provide technical support to doctors, and may even manage the purchasing and equipment departments of hospitals. In some cases, the distributors may assist in hospital tenders and physician education (see below). As provincial tenders become more widespread and institutionalized, and as government efforts to decentralize the provision of hospital care proceed, distributors may assume even more important roles in reaching procurement officials and tier 2 markets.

Distributor markups are common and enormous. Using orthopedic products as an illustration, the import manufacturer's price can be 1.5–3.0 times the price of a comparable domestic product; the distributor markup over this price can be a multiple as high as 7.0 times the domestic price; then the hospital marks up the product an additional 0.5 times the domestic price. For domestic products, the distributor markup is only 4.0 times, while the hospital markup is only 0.3 times.[15] Overall, distributor margins are reportedly in the range of 25–30 percent.

Why are these markups so high? One reason is the multiple channels through which the physician products flow to get to the hospital. Another reason is that, in some cases, distributors may serve as a vehicle by which manufacturers pay kickbacks to physicians for using their products. In this manner, manufacturers subsidize the salaries of Chinese physicians. Kickbacks are reportedly higher for orthopedic and cardiovascular disease products.[16] The size of the kickbacks may be related to shortages of specialists in these areas, which increase the physicians' bargaining power and leverage. The presence of these kickbacks may

depend on the manufacturer as well. MNCs have a code of conduct that prohibits the payment of such kickbacks.

Physician Marketing

As noted in Chapter 7, continuing medical education in China is rudimentary. By contrast, MNCs are a major source of physician training in China and a major avenue by which physicians upgrade their skill sets. This training is conducted in hospital settings (with perhaps some hospital funding). Hospitals can offer high-end surgical procedures (e.g., joint reconstruction) to attract patients, to fund the hospital's operating costs, and contribute to hospital profit margins – which are then used to reward the physicians.

The education and training function is more sorely needed outside of China's major cities. As noted in Chapter 7, the educational profile of Chinese physicians diminishes as you move from the urban centers to the local periphery. The lesser-trained physicians need more training and support, and have less experience due to the historically lower popularity and procedural volumes in those hospitals. As the government decentralizes the provision of hospital care to such areas, the training and support functions assume greater importance.

The government's aspiration to develop tiered hospital delivery and feeder-referral hospital networks may further mean that physician training must be multi-level and networked. That is, MNCs may need to assist hospitals and their physicians with identifying and classifying patients according to their severity-of-illness and helping to develop criteria for treatment and referral.

R&D Efforts

MNCs will increasingly focus on conducting a portion of their R&D activities in China. The cost of clinical trials in China is relatively low, and the country has patients with every clinical problem in the West (and then some). MNCs have increased their investment in building local R&D capabilities. Philips invested $54 million between 2009 and 2012 to establish its China R&D center with the goal of having 300 engineers by 2015;

Covidien (now part of Medtronic) invested $45 million in 2012 with the same goal.

M&A Efforts

Finally, MNCs are engaged in acquisitions of local firms for several reasons. One strategic intent is to acquire local distribution capabilities; for example, Medtronic's acquisition of Kanghui brought it a network of 237 distributors operating in most of China's provinces and covering over 1,800 hospitals by 2010. Another strategic intent is to develop local R&D capability and the ability to customize products to the local population. Medtronic acquired Kanghui in part to gain access to the latter's 54 experienced engineers at two R&D sites who were familiar with Asian patient sizes and bone anatomy. A third reason is to acquire the product lines of local firms and thereby develop a broad range of low-priced products to serve the middle/lower end market. A fourth reason is that local deals enable MNCs to achieve rapid market expansion.

Local Competitors

Local companies currently control approximately 60 percent of China's medical device market. While they have claimed leadership positions in many of the less advanced product groups, such as black & white ultrasound, they have been less successful than MNCs in penetrating the high-end market. They are now turning their attention to more cutting-edge products, such as orthopedic implants, pacemakers, and CT imaging. Until recently, a handful of MNCs such as Medtronic, St. Jude Medical, and Biotronik controlled two-thirds of the pacemaker market (see Figure 15.37).

Local companies are now developing market presences in the pacemaker, orthopedic implant, and stent segments, although it will likely take time before they gain serious traction. Qinming Medical, which is 30 percent owned by Lepu Medical, launched its first single-chamber pacemaker in 2009. Likewise, Trauson and KangHui have moved into the knee and spinal implant categories, while other Chinese players like Lepu and

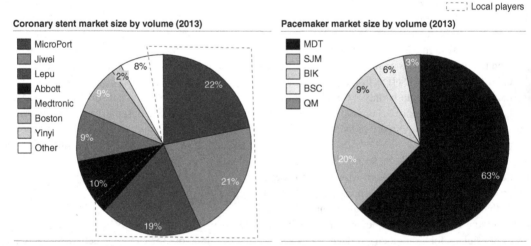

- MicroPort, Lepu, and Jiwei are major local players and share 62% of the market in 2013
- MNCs, such as J&J, Medtronic, and Boston, only take 33% of the market share
- Local companies provide products of the same quality as MNCs, with low prices, so that their market shares are increasing year by year

- MDT is the leading player with 63% market share, while facing increasing competition from followers especially SJM
- The only local player QM got SFDA certification in 2009
- Qinming 2312, independently made by a local manufacturer acquired the certification in 2015
- More local players are expected to share the market

Figure 15.37 Cardiovascular implant competitive landscape

Source: MOH report; MDT internal data; Literature research; Expert interviews; Team analysis.

MicroPort quickly built leadership positions in categories such as coronary stents. As they mature, many local companies are changing their strategy from imitating multinationals' products to developing their own and tailoring products to meet local needs and priorities. The evolution of China's medical device market will depend on the success of this transition.

Growth Strategies

Five themes underpin the growth strategies of leading Chinese medical products companies. These include organic growth, multiple innovation sources, acquisitions, global penetration, and business model adaptation.

Organic Growth

Chinese medical products companies have been able to achieve healthy bottom lines. Between 2008 and 2011, orthopedic product companies such as Trauson and KangHui reported operating margins of 40–50 percent. Over the same period, leading stent manufacturers such as Lepu and WEGO reported operating margins of 30–50 percent. A healthy profit & loss (P&L) statement has enabled many locals to fund the development of critical capabilities, such as R&D investment, hiring of more expensive returnee talent, expansion of sales forces, distribution for both domestic and international coverage, and channel management.

Locals have also enjoyed easy access to capital over the past few years. In 2011, six medical product companies went public, including (a) Grandhope Biotech, a biological mesh company; (b) Zhuhai Hokai Medical Instruments, a producer of minimally-invasive oncology treatment devices; and (c) Edan, a patient-monitor and ultrasound devices company. Private equity financing and venture capital investment increased from 1–2 deals per year in the 1996–2000 period, to an average of about 20 deals a year from 2007 to 2011. The release of the 12th FYP for the medical device industry by MoST has inspired further confidence in the local medical device industry and further stimulated the enthusiasm of the capital markets.

Multiple Sources of Innovation

In prior years, Chinese companies pursued an imitation strategy to replicate successful MNC products that enabled them to cash in on markets already developed. As they matured, however, local firms have become more ambitious. Innovation, rather than imitation, is now viewed as the basis of sustainable growth. Building their own innovation capabilities will require companies to combine internal development, external sourcing of technology/products, and collaboration with academic institutions. Investments in internal R&D are steadily increasing. MicroPort's 2011 R&D budget supported an R&D team of more than 180 scientists and engineers and accounted for roughly 18 percent of firm revenues (a 30 percent increase over 2010). MicroPort also launched an application for CE mark1 approval for Firehawk, its third-generation drug-eluting stent, and is awaiting SFDA approval for its new neurovascular stent. The company is now diversifying to develop products in new categories such as orthopedics, cardiac rhythm management, and insulin pumps.

Acquisitions

Leading Chinese medtech manufacturers have prioritized acquisitions. In 2011, at least 15 M&A deals expanded product portfolios, strengthened leadership positions in specialty areas, and/or developed overseas distribution channels. Mindray acquired shares of four local companies with a presence in IVD, infusion pumps, medical imaging software, and microbiological analyzers. MicroPort spent 110 million RMB to acquire local player Suzhou Best Orthopedics. Lepu expanded its cardiovascular portfolio by either acquiring or obtaining shares in four companies developing cardiac treatments: Beijing Weijinfan Medical Technology Development (angiography), Beijing Star Medical Devices (heart valves), Shanghai XingZhuang (occluders), and Shaanxi Qinming Medical Equipment (pacemakers). YuYue Medical, a leader in personal medical equipment, brought Kangli Medical Instruments (manufacturer of single-use syringes) and Huatuo (acupuncture instrument manufacturer) into its portfolio.

Global Penetration

Chinese companies have also started to expand their footprint overseas. Mindray, an early global pioneer, generated approximately 57 percent of its 2011 sales outside China. Mindray works with over 1,000 third-party distributors but is also selectively developing its own direct sales force to support globalization efforts. KangHui, the first Chinese company to enter the global orthopedic implant market, is further expanding its global presence. As of March 2011, KangHui had built a network of 38 distributors to sell the company's products in 28 countries across Asia, Europe, South America, and Africa. International sales accounted for 15–20 percent of KangHui's net revenues and increased 49 percent year-on-year (albeit from a small base) to reach 59 million RMB in 2011. Although a global newcomer, Lepu is also aggressively pursuing opportunities to capture sales outside China. By the end of 2011, the company had obtained regulatory approval for 16 of its products in 20 countries. It also acquired CE certification for 21 products, including percutaneous transluminal coronary angioplasty balloons and catheters, and established distribution networks in 40 countries.

Business Model Adaptation

China's medtech industry is becoming more regulated not only in terms of market access steps including product registration, pricing, reimbursement, and tendering, but also in terms of marketing and promotion. A more regulated market requires medtechs to adapt their business models at many levels.

Previously, medtech companies relied heavily on distributors to promote their products to hospital customers. As the mid-market becomes the battlefield of MNCs and domestic players, companies will switch to a direct selling model by deploying their own sales forces to gain better access to and influence over the end customers. Key account management will also need to become more effective to manage the key decision makers. Finally, marketing promotion will need to become more sophisticated and evidence-based, where personnel in Medical Affairs, Post Market Surveillance, and Health Economics & Outcomes Research will play an increasingly critical role.

Talent Management

A McKinsey survey showed that talent management, in particular recruiting and paying for talent, is a pressing concern in China (see Figure 15.38). The country is short on talent, especially for those with technical and educational backgrounds relevant to medical devices. Moreover, fierce competition among employers has bid up salaries, the cost of talent acquisition, and the associated costs of high turnover. These challenges can significantly constrain growth.

Undersupply and Uneven Distribution

Few Chinese universities have established training programs that prepare scientists and managers for the medtech sector. Capable talent will thus continue to be in short supply. In Guangdong, only 2 percent of medical device employees have relevant specialty training in biomedical engineering (BME) (see Figure 15.39). Among the 2 percent with BME degrees, more than half have at most college training, about one-third have bachelor level training, and only 7 percent have degrees beyond bachelor's level. Fewer than 50 universities have established BME specialty programs, including only 10 medical schools and 40 comprehensive universities. Less than 1,000 BME students graduate annually, a level of output too small to satisfy the roughly 14,000 medical device companies (as of 2012).

Moreover, talent is overly concentrated in tier 1 cities. The percentage of employees with master degrees or higher is 3.4 percent in Beijing and 6.0 percent in Guangzhou, compared to the national average of 0.3 percent. Consequently, medtechs must balance their direct coverage and dealer coverage models when promoting products to mid-market hospitals. The direct coverage model is not competitive in the mid-market compared to the dealer model due to the high overhead and turnover rates.

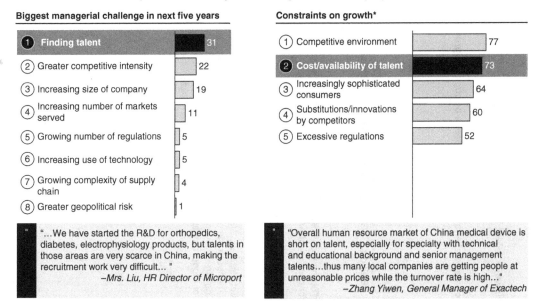

Survey of "biggest managerial challenge" and "growth constraints"
% of respondents indicating factor as "significant" or "very significant"

Biggest managerial challenge in next five years

1. Finding talent — 31
2. Greater competitive intensity — 22
3. Increasing size of company — 19
4. Increasing number of markets served — 11
5. Growing number of regulations — 5
6. Increasing use of technology — 5
7. Growing complexity of supply chain — 4
8. Greater geopolitical risk — 1

Constraints on growth*

1. Competitive environment — 77
2. Cost/availability of talent — 73
3. Increasingly sophisticated consumers — 64
4. Substitutions/innovations by competitors — 60
5. Excessive regulations — 52

"...We have started the R&D for orthopedics, diabetes, electrophysiology products, but talents in those areas are very scarce in China, making the recruitment work very difficult... "
– *Mrs. Liu, HR Director of Microport*

"Overall human resource market of China medical device is short on talent, especially for specialty with technical and educational background and senior management talents...thus many local companies are getting people at unreasonable prices while the turnover rate is high..."
– *Zhang Yiwen, General Manager of Exactech*

*All data weighted by GDP of constituent countries to adjust for differences in response rates from various regions

Figure 15.38 Talent management
Source: McKinsey Quarterly survey of 9,346 global business executives, March 2005.

Capability Gaps

China has a huge working-age population and a relatively large number of graduates, including those with PhD degrees in life sciences. Even so, much of the workforce is relatively inexperienced and poorly suited to working in multinational pharmaceutical companies. The McKinsey survey found that only 10 percent of scientists and engineers graduating from Chinese universities were ready for the MNC workplace – a proportion unlikely to have improved much in the last decade. As a result of the theoretical bent of the Chinese educational system, students spend less time on practical projects and teamwork development than their western counterparts. Chinese students thus graduate with little experience in the application of academic knowledge to industrial problems and settings, little or no managerial experience or business knowledge, and little familiarity with the product development process – in addition to a limited facility with the

English language. China also has few programs to train students for the field of healthcare administration. Graduates thus lack systematic knowledge of hospitals, physicians, and the healthcare supply chain. Local medtech firms in China thus operate at a comparative disadvantage with regard to international benchmark skills in multiple fields such as sales and marketing, key account management, medical affairs, R&D, and operations (see Figure 15.40).

Sales and Marketing

For example, the sales and marketing strategies and tactics of local companies are outdated. Client acquisition heavily leverages relationship-based sales without customer segmentation analysis. Local firms have limited skills in developing new clients and tailoring their products to customer needs. To be successful in marketing specialty products, firms now require an understanding of

Medical device industry lacks suitable talent in both quantity and quality

Guangdong medical device employees' specialty composition

- Electronic
- Mechanical
- Medical
- BME*
- Others

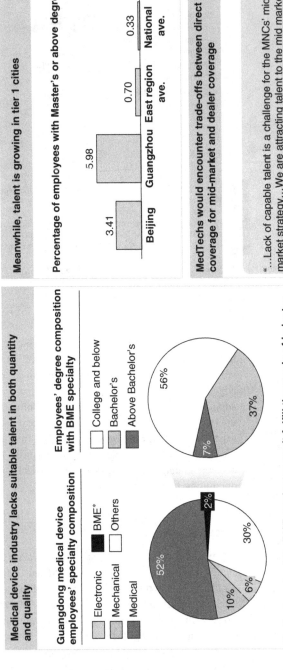

52%
10%
6%
30%
2%

Employees' degree composition with BME specialty

- College and below
- Bachelor's
- Above Bachelor's

56%
37%
7%

On the supply side, BME graduates can't fulfill the needs of industry
- Less than 50 universities have established BME specialty, including
  - ~10 medical colleges
  - ~40 general universities
- Less than 1,000 BME graduates annually versus ~14,000 medical device companies in 2012

Meanwhile, talent is growing in tier 1 cities

Percentage of employees with Master's or above degree

3.41   5.98   0.70   0.33

Beijing   Guangzhou   East region ave.   National ave.

MedTechs would encounter trade-offs between direct coverage for mid-market and dealer coverage

" ...Lack of capable talent is a challenge for the MNCs' mid market strategy...We are attracting talent to the mid market by better package and opportunities for career development, but the direct coverage model is not so competitive in ROI than dealer model due to high turnover rate and headcount cost..."
--Government Affairs Director of a MNC

*Biomedical engineering

Figure 15.39 Lack of medtech training programs in Chinese universities

Source: Literature research; expert interview; Team analysis.

	Current client capability	Capability requirement

Marketing and sales	• **Relationship-based sales**, heavily leveraging existing distributor network for sales; limited capability to develop new clients
	• **No customer segmentation analysis**, and therefore, cannot provide tailored products to meet customer demands
	
	"Many of our sales come from distributors. Their job is to sell through 'old relationships,' which is quite different from real sales"
		• Sales for commodity products
		  – **Pricing capability:** clever pricing strategy, give volume instead of price discount to lock in long-term and high-value contracts
		  – **Distributor network:** access to large number of distributors
		• Sales for specialty products
		  – **Customer segmentation:** segment markets and clients based on their preferences and develop different service models for each segment
		  – **Client relationship:** deeply understand healthcare environment, can forecast client needs, and come up with the right products

Medical affairs	• Only participate in the **design, implementation of clinical trial**	• Work closely with RA/marketing/market access to **gain KOL endorsement** at the early stage of product registration • Proactively **collect health economics data** by proper design of the experiments for the smooth market access process
R&D	• R&D projects are **poorly linked with core business and strategic directions;** cannot provide sufficient technology support to BUs • **No forward-looking product innovation**, product development centers are around replicating and doing small tweaks to existing formula • Some projects are around process innovation, but **not enough to continually improve** manufacturing process and cut cost	• Technical services: **strong medical/clinical background** and the ability to work with different teams, to provide timely support to manufacturing and sales teams • **Process improvement:** understand cutting-edge technology of production process, continually cut production cost through process improvement (e.g., catalyst reaction) • **Product innovation:** closely link medical device innovation with corporate strategy, market position, and client needs to develop attractive product features
Operation	• Start to promote the concept of "world-class manufacturing" and lean operation • **Lean operation talent** still to be trained	• **Production management:** familiar with tools and concepts of lean operation, capable of leading team to design and launch systematic and continual improvement plan • Supply chain: **Optimize supply chain** to lower cost

Figure 15.40 Capability gaps

Source: Literature research; Expert interviews; Team analysis.

pricing, distribution networks for commodity products, customer segmentation, and clinicians. Sophisticated pricing can lock in long-term and high-value contracts to increase volume; distribution networks can increase the number of sales representatives and points of call which can also increase volume; segmentation can help to develop different service models; and client understanding can apply future needs to deliver the right technologies.

Medical Affairs

Departments responsible for medical affairs also need enhanced capabilities that can foster efficiencies and growth. Current capabilities include the design and implementation of clinical trials. However, medical affairs can potentially work more closely with groups responsible for research assistance, marketing, and market access to gain the endorsement of key opinion leaders in the early stages of product registration. Medical affairs can employ properly designed quasi-experimental studies to collect health economics data that facilitate market access by giving providers information on the value and cost-effectiveness of their products.

Research & Development (R&D)

Current R&D in China is far from effective in achieving its objectives. R&D is poorly linked with core business needs and strategic directions, and is more focused on incremental rather than substantive innovation. Even among those projects that are innovative, they do not serve to improve the efficiency of the manufacturing process or reduce cost. R&D requires personnel with strong medical and clinical backgrounds, the ability to work in (often different) teams, and the ability to provide timely support to manufacturing and sales teams. With the right skills, R&D personnel should understand the cutting-edge technology to create product/ process improvements and product innovation. Progress here will be limited by the lack of education in BME. Current medtech operations have begun to adopt world-class manufacturing and lean techniques, but such skills still need to be taught in China's universities.

Employee Turnover

Employee turnover rates have increased in recent years. According to a survey of MBAs working for MNCs in China, four-fifths of the respondents did not intend to remain in their current jobs for more than two years. According to another report, the turnover rate of employees in China's medical device sector worsened between 2013 and 2014; better career opportunities and salary issues are now leading causes. For medtech firms, the higher turnover rate means higher costs of recruiting, training, and retaining talent. Competition among the thousands of medtech firms for scarce talent will continue to inflate the overhead costs of human resources.

Challenging M&A Process

M&A activity has picked up in China's medical device sector (see Figure 15.41), particularly in product segments such as orthopedics, cardiology, imaging, and IVD segments. The value of the top ten deals consummated between 2013 and 2014 exceeded $1.9 billion, led by the $764 million deal between Stryker and Trauson. By contrast, the value of the nine top deals consummated between 2008 and 2013 was only $100 million. Nevertheless, participants see many challenges throughout the M&A process, with several key lessons already learned.

During the pre-acquisition stage, potential acquirers have found it difficult to identify a viable shortlist of targets due to the lack of transparent and accurate information. There may also be a shortage of sizeable candidates. Growth potential and strategic match may be more important than target size, however.

During the acquisition stage, compliance and legal issues involving distributors and internal sales forces may surface. It is also possible that manufacturing quality standards do not satisfy global standards. MNCs may need to be realistic and patient about enforcing global quality standards in China. An additional issue germane to China is how to compensate the target firm's owners, especially for state-owned enterprises with a background of government sponsorship.

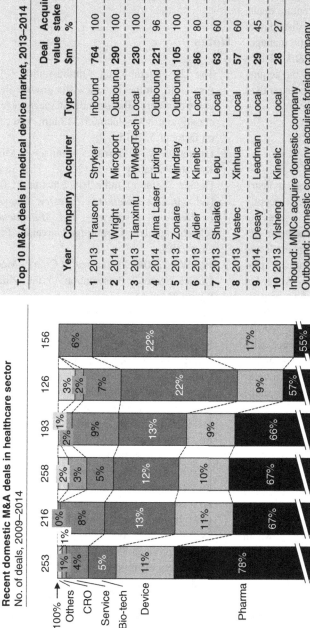

Recent domestic M&A deals in healthcare sector
No. of deals, 2009–2014

	253	216	258	193	126	156
Others	1%–1%	0%	2%	1%	3%	6%
CRO	4%	8%	3%	2%	2%	
Service	5%		5%	9%	7%	22%
Bio-tech	11%	13%	12%	13%	22%	
Device		11%	10%	9%	9%	17%
Pharma	78%	67%	67%	66%	57%	55%
	2009	2010	2011	2012	2013	2014

Top 10 M&A deals in medical device market, 2013–2014

	Year	Company	Acquirer	Type	Deal value $m	Acquired stake %	Sector
1	2013	Trauson	Stryker	Inbound	764	100	Ortho
2	2014	Wright	Microport	Outbound	290	100	Stent
3	2013	Tianxinfu	PWMedTech	Local	230	100	Ortho
4	2014	Alma Laser	Fuxing	Outbound	221	96	Cosmetic
5	2013	Zonare	Mindray	Outbound	105	100	Imaging
6	2013	Aidier	Kinetic	Local	86	80	Ortho
7	2013	Shuaike	Lepu	Local	63	60	Stent
8	2013	Vastec	Xinhua	Local	57	60	IVD
9	2014	Desay	Leadman	Local	29	45	IVD
10	2013	Yisheng	Kinetic	Local	28	27	Stent

Inbound: MNCs acquire domestic company
Outbound: Domestic company acquires foreign company
Local: Domestic M&A

Figure 15.41 M&A activity in medtech markets
Source: CV source; Literature research; Expert interviews; Team analysis.

Post M&A integration requires careful planning and professional management to realize synergies. The main difficulties here include tricky organizational integration issues stemming from differences in culture and management style, potential cannibalization resulting from poor brand management, intellectual property leakage in joint venture deals, potential patent lawsuits, loss of key distributors and core management team members, and management of unwanted assets. China's M&A history suggests that keeping the operations of the acquiring and target companies separate works better than forced integration.

Role for AdvaMed in China

AdvaMed, a well-recognized medtech industry association based in the United States, recently entered China's market. AdvaMed aspires to increase opportunities in the Chinese medtech sector by supporting the country's healthcare goals and improving patient access to life-enhancing products. Based on the discussion above, AdvaMed China might pursue several initiatives to help its members overcome the challenges of the Chinese market and achieve sustainable business growth. These include establishing a local presence with an office and staff, enhancing AdvaMed's reputation with key stakeholders including the government and industry players, and helping to shape a favorable market environment.

Summary and Conclusion

After years of rapid growth, China's medtech sector has entered a new phase of development under China's "New Normal." Though the growth of the industry will likely slow down in the near future due to the changing regulatory environment, it remains a promising growth market due to two factors: the government's continuing commitment to improve healthcare and the underlying demographic trends in China. Among the challenges that multinationals face in this very dynamic market, the most significant obstacles are local competitors, scarcity of capable

talent, market access hurdles, and other non-tariff barriers. AdvaMed can play a big role to facilitate a dialogue with the Chinese government to create fair and efficient regulations for the medtech sector that guarantee high safety standards, increased access, and equal treatment.

Notes

1. The US Federal Drug Administration (FDA). Available online at: www.fda.gov/medicalde vices/deviceregulationandguidance/overview/ classifyyourdevice/ucm051512.htm. Accessed on October 5, 2015.
2. Lawton R. Burns, Tanmay Mishra, Kalyan Pamarthy et al. 2014. "The Medical Device Sector in India," in Lawton R. Burns (Ed.), *India's Healthcare Industry: Innovation in Delivery, Financing, and Manufacturing* (Cambridge, UK: Cambridge University Press): chapter 15.
3. Jian Wang. 2013. "Overview of China's Medical Device Sector." Presentation to the Wharton School (March).
4. The mid and affluent class is defined as households with annual disposable incomes of at least $11,000.
5. Estimates of the size of the medtech share of the Chinese healthcare market vary considerably, usually depending on the definition of the medtech sector (what is included in the numerator) or the definition of the overall (what is included in the denominator). For 2011, McKinsey offered a much lower medtech share of 6 percent ($20 billion out of $334 billion); accounting for the remainder were services ($166 billion, or 50 percent), channel markups by distributors ($80 billion, or 24 percent), pharmaceuticals ($50–55 billion, or 16 percent), and over-the-counter products ($14–16 billion, or 4 percent). Regardless of the percentage share attributed to medtech, estimates of the absolute dollar spend of the sector are fairly close. For example, in 2013, the varying estimates of medtech volume range between $22 and 27 billion.
6. Katherine Lu. 2012. "In Search for Strategic Assets in the Global Healthcare Market."

Presentation to the Wharton School (January). Urs Mattes, Jingjing Cao, Stanley Chang et al. 2012. *The People's Republic of China Market for Medical Devices* (Bern, Switzerland: MedTech Switzerland).

7. Celia Deng, Wei Sun, Zhiyi Tong et al. 2012. "Tales of Three Medical Device Markets in China," *In Vivo* (November): 44–50.

8. Wang. 2013. "Overview of China's Medical Device Sector."

9. Xin Zhang. 2013. "Chinese Orthopedic Industry Overview: Opportunities and Challenges." Presentation to the Wharton School (March).

10. Lu. 2012. "In Search for Strategic Assets in the Global Healthcare Market."

11. Kristine Yang. 2014. "Asia in the Spotlight: Reform in China Creating More Challenges for Device Companies," *Medical Device Daily* (September 22).

12. Ying Luo, John Wong, and Magen Xia. 2014. *Winning in China's Changing Medtech Market* (Beijing: Boston Consulting Group, July 17).

13. The *National Green Book* defines the medical service items that Chinese public hospitals can charge to a patient. It does not set the price for those items, however.

14. Chuan Chen. 2012. "Overview of the Medical Device Sector." Presentation to the Wharton School (January).

15. Zhang. 2013. "Chinese Orthopedic Industry Overview."

16. Mattes et al. 2012. *The People's Republic of China Market for Medical Devices.*

Life Sciences Investment and Biotechnology in China

STEPHEN M. SAMMUT AND LAWTON ROBERT BURNS

Introduction

A prior chapter (Chapter 14) analyzed China's pharmaceutical sector; this chapter focuses on the country's biotechnology sector. There are important similarities between the two. The two sectors have benefited from increased investments in life sciences research. Biotechnology has actually grown faster, partially because it is now designated as a strategic priority by China's central government and partly because it is relatively new and smaller in size. They are also both heavily based on generic and bio-similar products, rather than on innovative therapies. There are also important differences between the pharmaceutical and biotechnology sectors, including their research methods and products. Both sectors will need to develop sources of intellectual and financial capital in order to grow.

This chapter addresses these issues and challenges. The first section reviews the historical, global investment in research and development (R&D) in the life sciences. The section compares not only public versus private sector investment, but also the level and change in investment in China versus western countries. The second section distinguishes biotechnology from pharmaceuticals. The third section analyzes some of the earlier important milestones and progress in the Chinese biotechnology sector. The fourth section briefly reviews selected Chinese biotechnology companies, many of which are publicly traded on the Hong Kong or US stock exchanges, to identify some of the important scientific, clinical, and commercial trends under way in this sector. The fifth section analyzes the deliberate efforts undertaken by China's national and local governments to promote the sector's development, as well as the obstacles to the sector's growth.

Public and Private Investment in Life Sciences Research

The growth in life sciences R&D over the last 70 years owes a lot to government funding of "basic research," particularly in the United States (with the establishment of the National Institutes of Health, or NIH, in 1948) and Europe. For example between 1995 and 2012, NIH funding rose from $10.8 billion to $30.9 billion. US government funding contributed to the development of 48 percent of all drugs approved by the US Food and Drug Administration (FDA) and 65 percent of drugs that received priority review between 1988 and 2005. Owing to cuts mandated by the Budget Control Act of 2011, the NIH budget for fiscal year 2013 was reduced by $1.7 billion to $29.2 billion, but regained some ground in 2014 ($30.0 billion).

The public research funding and output provided the impetus and foundation for unprecedented private investment in commercially oriented and "applied research" by private companies, including pharmaceutical and biotechnology firms (see Figure 16.1).[1] These companies invested $48.5 billion in 2012 to translate the applied findings into new medicines and diagnostics. However, between 2007 and 2012, the small increase in US public sector investment in research ($0.9 billion, or 2 percent rise) was more than offset by a large decline ($12.9 billion, or 15.5 percent) in private sector investment (see Table 16.1). Overall, the United States witnessed a 9.1 percent drop in life sciences investment of $12 billion. Industry's share of the tab fell from 63.4 percent in 2007 to 59.0 percent in 2012. A similar slowdown occurred in Europe.

Why did private investment slow down in the West? A major reason was the declining productivity and efficiency of these investments. The output of

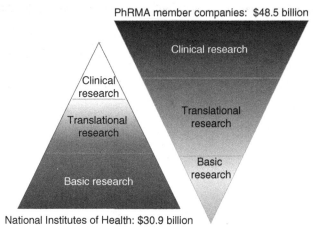

PhRMA member companies: $48.5 billion

Clinical research

Clinical research

Translational research

Translational research

Basic research

Basic research

National Institutes of Health: $30.9 billion

Figure 16.1 Government and industry roles in research and development
Sources: PhRMA Annual Membership Survey 2013; NIH Office of Budget https://officeofbudget.od.nih
.gov/pdfs/FY12/Approp.%20History%20by%20IC%292012.pdf; Adapted from E. Zerhouni,
"Transforming Health: NIH and the Promise of Research," Washington, DC, November 2007.

new drug approvals remained relatively flat between 2000 and 2013, while the expenditures that yielded this output skyrocketed (see Figure 16.2). This led to a drop in venture capital investment in the sector. The flat-lining productivity level observed in the United States was replicated globally (Figure 16.3).

China has been gaining ground on the West, in both absolute and relative terms, with respect to both levels of investment and intellectual output (e.g., scientific peer reviewed papers, patents, and products). To illustrate, researchers recently profiled China and other countries in Asia-Oceania in their levels of life sciences funding between 2007 and 2012. Compared to the $12 billion and 9 percent drop in total funding in the United States, China increased its level of investment in life sciences research by $6.4 billion, or 320 percent. The country enjoyed higher investment in both the public ($1.4 billion increase) and private sectors ($4.8 billion). Private sector investment as a percentage of the total remained constant at 75 percent. China's compound annual growth rate (CAGR) in biomedical R&D spending of 32.8 percent far outstripped all other countries (see Figure 16.4).

As a percentage of *total* global investment, the US share of biomedical R&D expenditures fell from 51.2 percent in 2007 to 45.4 percent in 2012. Europe's share remained essentially unchanged:

28.5 percent in 2007 versus 29.2 percent in 2012. By contrast, the proportion spent by Asia-Oceania increased from 18.1 percent to 23.8 percent. China's share grew from 0.9 percent to 3.1 percent. In terms of *public* investment, the United States has continued to contribute the largest share of total global public sector expenditures, but its share fell from 52.9 percent in 2007 to 50.8 percent in 2012; by contrast, Europe's share rose slightly from 26.7 percent in 2007 to 27.4 percent in 2012; Asia-Oceania increased its share from 16.6 percent to 19.1 percent. In terms of *private* investment, the US share of global industry R&D expenditures decreased from 50.4 percent in 2007 to 42.3 percent in 2012. European industry R&D expenditures decreased by $2.3 billion; its share remained unchanged (29.6 percent vs. 30.2 percent) because its purchasing power increased by 7 percent. In Asia-Oceania, an increase of $15.1 billion in industry's R&D expenditure (from 19.0 percent to 26.5 percent) was driven primarily by a $6.7 billion increase in Japan and a $4.8 billion increase in China.

One explanation for the shift in global R&D expenditures to Asia-Oceania may be its lower R&D costs: labor is cheaper and government subsidies are more available. This is especially so as the development costs per FDA drug approval have increased considerably. Thus, the decline in the

Table 16.1 Biomedical R&D expenditures by the public and private sectors, adjusted for inflation, 2007–2012

Region			2007	2008	2009	2010	2011	2012
						$billions		
United States			131.3	123.8	119.1	126.3	120.0	119.3
	Public		48.0	46.9	47.9	51.4	50.6	48.9
	Industry		83.3	76.9	71.2	74.9	69.4	70.4
Canada			6.0	6.1	5.6	5.6	5.6	5.3
	Public		4.0	4.1	3.8	3.5	3.4	3.3
	Industry		2.0	2.0	1.8	2.1	2.2	2.0
Europe			83.6	90.0	85.6	80.9	84.9	81.8
	Public		27.7	31.1	29.0	28.0	28.4	28.1
	Industry		55.9	58.8	56.7	52.9	56.5	53.6
	Asia-Oceania		41.1	45.6	49.3	52.9	59.8	62.0
	Total							
		Public	13.5	14.4	15.9	17.3	19.1	19.3
		Industry	27.6	31.3	33.4	35.6	40.7	42.7
	China		2.0	2.9	4.6	4.0	7.0	8.4
		Public	0.6	1.1	1.2	1.1	1.7	2.0
		Industry	1.5	1.8	3.4	2.9	5.4	6.3
	Japan		28.2	31.3	33.1	34.9	37.5	37.2
		Public	7.3	7.6	8.6	9.0	9.6	9.5
		Industry	20.9	23.7	24.5	26.0	27.9	27.6
	South Korea		3.5	3.6	3.4	4.3	4.9	6.0
		Public	0.9	0.9	0.8	1.0	1.0	1.1
		Industry	2.6	2.7	2.6	3.3	3.9	4.9
	India		1.4	1.7	1.7	1.8	1.8	2.0
		Public	0.4	0.4	0.4	0.4	0.4	0.4
		Industry	1.1	1.3	1.3	1.3	1.4	1.6
	Australia		4.4	4.3	4.6	5.8	6.3	6.1
		Public	3.3	3.1	3.6	4.4	4.9	4.7
		Industry	1.1	1.2	1.0	1.4	1.4	1.4
	Other Asia-Pacific		1.6	1.8	1.9	2.1	2.2	2.4
		Public	1.2	1.2	1.3	1.4	1.5	1.6
		Industry	0.5	0.5	0.6	0.7	0.7	0.8
Total			262.1	265.6	259.6	265.7	270.3	268.4
Total in nominal values			226.6	240.4	241.8	254.9	266.6	268.4

Note: Unless otherwise noted, all values are shown in billions of US dollars, adjusted for inflation to 2012, with the use of the National Institutes of Health Biomedical Research and Development Price Index according to the mean exchange rate for US dollars for each year (Chakma et al. 2014).

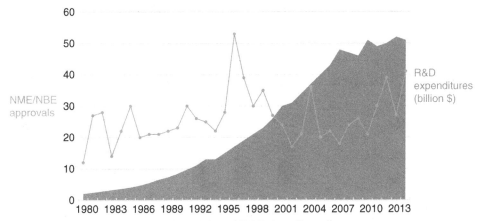

Figure 16.2 New drug and biologics approvals and R&D spending
Source: FDA; PhRMA, 2014 Industry Profile.

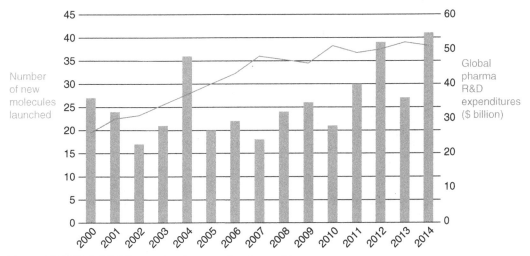

Figure 16.3 Global R&D spend and new molecular entities
Source: FDA; PhRMA, 2014 Industry Profile.

US share and the flattening of global private R&D investment (after adjustment for inflation) suggests that industry is simply reallocating R&D funding to Asia-Oceania. Another obvious explanation is the large potential Chinese market for pharmaceutical and biotechnology products. IMS estimates that between 2005 and 2015 the global market grew primarily due to the emerging markets such as China, the other BRIC countries, and South Korea (see Figure 16.5).

China's global share of life sciences R&D, both public and private, is increasing in absolute and relative terms. The country's advantage related to purchasing power parity (PPP) suggests that the country's growth may be even greater than the numbers indicate. In other words, $1 billion in available research funding in China can support an effort that might take $4 billion in the United States. Recent reports suggest that China has become Asia's top biopharma cluster in terms of several metrics: biomedical R&D spending ($165 billion in 2013, out of the total $243 billion), number of life sciences firms (7,500 in 2013), the total number of industry jobs (250,000+), and active venture capital investment.

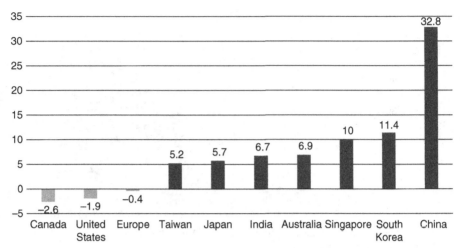

Figure 16.4 Compound annual growth rate of biomedical R&D expenditures by country, adjusted for inflation, 2007–2012
Note: The compound annual growth rate was calculated on the basis of total inflation-adjusted biomedical R&D expenditures in US dollars for 2007 and 2012.
Source: Chakma et al. (2014).

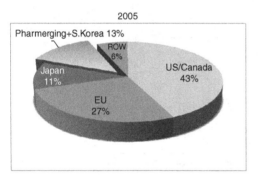
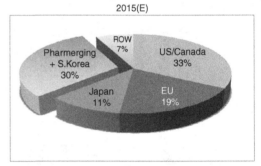

Figure 16.5 Growth mostly in emerging markets
Source: IMS Market Prognosis (April 2011).
Note: "Pharmerging" markets (China, Brazil, Mexico, South Korea, Turkey, India, and Russia): countries in the top 20 markets in 2008–2012, with higher 2006–2011 CAGR than the other top 20 markets.

China ranked second (only to Japan) in terms of initial public offerings (IPOs), with $2.1 billion raised since 2010. The country also ranked third in biotech/biopharma patents (9,302 since 1970).[2]

Life Sciences: Pharmaceuticals versus Biotechnology

This chapter focuses on life sciences companies that make products for human consumption, that are specifically developed to impact a disease, and (in the case of branded, non-generic drugs) that undergo a regulatory process designed to approve prescription medications for marketing to physicians and use in patients. This definition does not cover over-the-counter (OTC) medications, nutritional supplements, or herbal remedies such as traditional Chinese medicine (TCM). Two broad classes of life sciences products are "new chemical entities" (NCEs) and "new biologic entities" (NBEs: proteins, peptides, monoclonal antibodies, vaccines, etc.), which are collectively referred to in the West as "new molecular entities" (NMEs). These two classes of products roughly map onto the pharmaceutical and biotechnology sectors, although the distinction has broken down (see below).[3] They nevertheless serve to distinguish the products covered in this chapter from those analyzed in Chapter 14.

Small Molecule versus Large Molecule

A pharmaceutical company develops small molecular compounds that typically bind to a target and cause a biological process to start or stop. These products need to be quite small – 10–20 atoms with a relative molecular weight of less than 900 Daltons – in order to be taken orally, then survive the stomach and/or colon, pass into the blood, survive or be appropriately metabolized by the liver, and successfully reach their target in an organ or tissue. For a centrally-acting drug, such as an antidepressant or many pain medications, the NCE must also cross the blood-brain barrier and achieve concentration in the central nervous system. Small molecules thus have the advantage of convenience (oral administration), which can foster compliance with the medication regimen, as well as the advantage of low-cost production.

However, the body's natural chemistry is complex and involves many different types of molecules. The human body relies heavily on proteins that perform functions that small molecules cannot. Biological products such as insulin, growth hormone, and erythropoietin can supplement a needed molecule in the body that a small molecule cannot create. Some diseases require hitting more than one target or designing a complex inhibitor that decreases an enzyme's activity. Such areas are better treated using large molecule products made by biotechnology companies. The basis of biotechnology products are proteins, peptides, antibodies, etc., which are quite large – 000's of atoms and greater than 900 Daltons in weight. Because biotechnology products are larger and more complex molecules, they degrade when administered orally and are not easily transported across cell membranes. As a result, they tend to be injected or infused.

Other Differences

Thus, one major difference between the pharmaceutical and biotechnology sectors lies in their scientific base: pharmaceutical development is rooted in chemistry, while biotech development is rooted in biology (DNA, RNA, proteins). Another related difference is the method by which the drugs are produced: small molecules are manufactured through a series of chemical syntheses, while large molecules are manufactured in living organisms such as bacteria, yeast, and mammalian cells.

There are other important differences. *First*, the pharmaceutical sector dates back to the 1800s (e.g., the founding of Bayer and Johnson & Johnson); the biotechnology sector dates back more recently to the 1976 incorporation of Genentech. *Second*, pharmaceutical companies historically conducted extensive research in-house and relied on their own scientists for new products. By contrast, biotechnology companies started out as small entrepreneurial ventures often linked to university research programs. *Third*, the pharmaceutical companies are typically vertically integrated enterprises that span the entire value chain of research, discovery, manufacture, marketing, and sales; by contrast, biotechnology firms are smaller in size and centrally focused on the research side, with (until recently) little vertical integration. This is another way of saying that biotechnology firms are good at cutting-edge, basic research, while pharmaceutical firms are good at managing drug development and commercialization. *Fourth*, pharmaceutical firms focused on blockbuster products to treat large segments of the population, while biotechnology firms began their operation by focusing on niche-market products like orphan drugs. *Fifth*, the pharmaceutical sector has historically relied on internal capital generated in the core chemical business; by contrast, the biotechnology sector has typically relied on external capital, such as private equity and venture capital (PE/VC). *Sixth*, there has been virtually no new firm creation in the western pharmaceutical sector in the last several decades. The pharmaceutical sector in the United States consists of five large firms (Pfizer, Eli Lilly, Merck, Bristol-Myers Squibb, and Abbott) – a list that has not changed much over time. By contrast, the biotechnology sector has witnessed a lot of new firm creation (as many as 4,000 – 5,000 firms), as well as many firm failures. *Seventh,* there is a greater threat of generic competition in the pharmaceutical sector than in the biotechnology sector, due to their differences in product complexity and manufacturing.

Sector Boundaries Breaking Down

It is no longer easy to distinguish pharmaceutical from biotechnology companies in meaningful ways. First, pharmaceutical firms have acquired biotechnology firms (Roche's acquisition of Genentech, Sanofi's acquisition of Genzyme) or developed platforms in large molecule research; conversely, biotechnology companies have developed platforms in small molecule research. Second, a small number of biotechnology companies have begun to vertically integrate and occupy more of the value chain of drug development. Third, the top biotechnology company today in terms of sales is Gilead Sciences, but most of the company's products are synthetic chemistry drugs. Fourth, both sets of companies are largely interested in the same therapeutic areas; biotechnology companies are just more focused on the research side of the business. Fifth, as the twentieth century drew to a close, new drug discovery shifted at the major pharmaceutical companies from intramural discovery to collaborative discovery and development with universities and/or biotechnology companies that emerged from academia.

Rates of Innovation

Until recently, the major difference between the two sectors was that a pharmaceutical firm was a drug development company that made money, while a biotechnology firm was a drug development company that lost money. That is changing. Certainly in the past five years, and perhaps going back as far as the last 15 years, biotechnology stocks have outperformed pharmaceutical companies. Data from Cowen shows that between 2011 and 2015, the "Biotech Index" rose 258 percent compared to the "Pharma Index" (+84 percent) and the S&P 500 (+73 percent).[4] The productive base of the life

sciences sector in the West is shifting from a small number of large pharmaceutical firms ("Big Pharma") to a larger number of small- and mid-sized bio-pharmaceutical firms. The shift is abetted not only by the emergence of the biotechnology firms but also by Big Pharma's investment in their own venture capital funds or collaborative investments with venture partners in life sciences projects.

Why the change (and contrast) in performance? Biotechnology products now constitute a large and growing share of all new drug approvals (NDAs). In 2013, biologicals represented 22 percent of NDAs; in 2014, they accounted for 16 of the 44 (39 percent) NDAs. While big pharmaceutical companies still dominate the number of NDAs over the last five years, biotech firms such as Biogen and Gilead are fast followers.[5] While biotechnology companies still are much less profitable than large pharmaceutical firms, they have a much bigger pipeline of potential new products.

A historical review of "priority reviews" and "fast track designations" by FDA paints an even sharper picture.[6] Products that undergo priority reviews treat serious or life-threatening conditions and represent significant improvements in safety or effectiveness; products designated for fast-track address serious conditions with unmet clinical need. Both sets reflect more innovative therapies. Between 1998 and 2012, the FDA granted priority review to 162 products; 70 of these products received fast-track status. Among the 162 priority review products, 89 (55 percent) originated in a handful ($n = 53$) of biotechnology firms; among the 70 fast-track products, 49 (70 percent) originated in biotechnology firms. Not surprisingly, biotechnology firms dominated pharmaceutical firms in the priority review of NBEs (24 of 26); more surprisingly, biotechnology firms nearly equaled pharmaceutical firms in the priority review of NCEs (65 vs. 71).

A sizeable percentage (30 percent) of the new products developed by biotechnology firms was acquired by their pharmaceutical counterparts. By contrast, a much smaller percentage (12 percent) of innovative products originating in pharmaceutical firms was acquired by biotechnology companies. In terms of average global sales in the fifth year following FDA approval, the market profile of biotechnology products resembled that of pharmaceutical products ($534.6 million vs. $562.8 million).[7]

Finally, evidence suggests that biotechnology firms operate more efficiently. The top five biotechnology firms have invested 15–25 percent of sales in R&D, compared to 13–17 percent by large pharmaceutical firms. The higher costs of manufacturing complex biologics is offset by lower selling, general, and administrative (SG&A) costs compared to Big Pharma (20–25 percent vs. 25–30 percent), due to their targeted sales niches and need for fewer sales representatives.[8] Research suggests there is a fourfold difference between pharmaceutical firms and biotechnology firms in their aggregate R&D expense per product ($6.30 billion vs. $1.63 billion).[9]

Source of Innovation Advantage

This raises the question: why have biotechnology companies achieved such success in both NBEs and NCEs? One explanation is the technology. Biologics have greater specificity: they bind to the target and wrap themselves around the target using their larger mass. This means they have lower potential for off-target toxicity and side effects. This also means they have greater success in clinical trials in terms of product safety.

Another explanation is the target selection. Biotechnology companies have targeted "orphan diseases" where there is huge unmet clinical need (which leads to rapid adoption by clinicians and patients). Orphan diseases also require clinical trials with smaller patient sizes and may not need to undertake expensive Phase III trials. This reduces the amount of capital needed to develop them. Orphan products also have no competitors, which allows companies to charge a higher price for their products. Their complexity also minimizes the threat of generics, which makes them more immune to patent cliffs.

A third explanation is that biotechnology companies have always had to operate more efficiently than their pharmaceutical counterparts. Biotech firms are perpetually raising funds to stay in operation, and need to move their products forward as quickly and inexpensively as possible at every stage of development. By contrast, pharmaceutical companies enjoy financial slack that can be used to conduct additional testing at each stage of clinical development. Their financial slack has also been deployed to acquire biotechnology companies and their products, which may be reflected in their R&D costs.

A fourth, related explanation is their smaller scale and product scope. Biotechnology firms began as small start-up operations focused on discovery and then development of one or a small number of drugs. They thus did not suffer from the diseconomies of scale and scope often found in large pharmaceutical firms.[10]

A fifth explanation is that the research productivity of biotechnology firms has incentivized pharmaceutical firms to reorient their R&D from internal to external strategies, including the in-licensing of biotech products. Big Pharma's R&D efforts thus may have shifted to scrutinizing external compound candidates and business development activities.[11]

All of these advantages effectively confer higher rewards and lower risks on biotechnology companies. This may explain their productivity and cost advantage relative to pharmaceutical firms. This may also help to explain why China's government has prioritized the development of this sector.

Historical Growth of China's Biotechnology Sector

Benchmarking the progress of an industrial sector is usually measured in decades or even generations. While Chinese biotechnology is relatively new (approximately 20 years old), it has essentially leapfrogged many of the positive and negative experiences of the West. In a 2008 analysis, researchers examined a small sample of 22 homegrown healthcare biotechnology firms in China.[12] They sought out companies with innovative research, products, and business models. They analyzed their funding sources, business development efforts, and product portfolios by comparing them with their western counterparts.

In the new millennium, Chinese biotechnology firms faced a scarcity of risk capital, the vagaries of Chinese security rules for listing companies on public exchanges, and limitations on foreign capital flows. As a result, unlike their western counterparts, Chinese companies built portfolios of low-margin, lower risk products that they could bring to market over a shorter time horizon. In this manner, they could establish a level of credibility and a flow of revenue that would hopefully set the stage for more speculative research on products addressing significant, unmet health needs.

In the US experience, government funding is a substantial part of the sector's origination and growth, but it largely took the form of funding basic academic research that later laid the foundation for technology transferred to companies. At that juncture, PE/VC and other sources of risk capital funded the industry, supplemented ultimately by public trading of stock and alliances with established pharmaceutical companies. The Chinese experience was different, and still differs from the United States today. There has been a high dependence on government support at all levels, as well as some reliance on securing investment by state-owned enterprises.

In contrast to the United States and EU, Chinese biotechnology companies operated with modest amounts of capital, but were nevertheless productive based on cost advantages. They also benefited from the infrastructure developed in the country's life sciences clusters and high-tech parks by central and local government (see Figure 16.6). There are four main life sciences clusters in China, most of which are on China's east coast:

> *Yangtze River Delta cluster* (Shanghai, Suzhou, Wuxi: focus on pharmaceutical R&D, bioengineering, medical devices, biomedicine)
> *Beijing cluster* (Tianjin: focus on biopharmaceutical, medical devices)
> *Pearl River Delta (South) cluster* (Shenzhen, Guangdong, and Hong Kong: focus on medical devices and low cost manufacturing)
> *Central cluster* (Chengdu, Chongqing, and Xi'an: focus on TCM, medical devices, biomedicine)

In line with China's 12th Five-Year Plan (FYP), many provincial and local governments established life sciences and biotechnology parks. Government-backed "guidance funds" are heavily concentrated in these clusters. The parks and clusters – also known as high-tech development zones – provide companies with a full range of support services in legal, accounting, patenting, supply chain management, office and laboratory space – all of which would ordinarily represent significant costs. The parks and clusters have dedicated incubators to foster start-ups, provide free or subsidized rent, offer fiscal incentives (reduced taxes or tax refunds for specific investments/milestones), support human resources (talent grants, housing programs), provide subsidies for innovation, and assist with market access (consulting services).[13]

The main high-tech parks include Beijing Daxing District, Beijing Zhongguancun (ZGC) Life Science Park (ZLSP), Shanghai Zhangjiang Hi-Tech Park, Suzhou Industrial Park's BioBay, Chengdu's Tianfu Life Science Park (TLSP), and four life sciences parks in Guangdong Province. They are briefly profiled below:[14]

> Beijing Daxing District encompasses two life sciences parks: the Beijing Economic and Technological Development Zone (BDA) and the Daxing Biomedicine Industrial Base (CBP). BDA is one of three national biological pharmaceutical innovation incubator bases in China. CBP is a biotechnology industrialization base, founded in 2002.
>
> ZGC, which opened in 1988, is one of China's most dense and diverse innovation ecosystems, containing 40 colleges and universities (including Peking University and Tsinghua University). It is a rich industrial cluster featuring biomedical firms as well as venture capital firms. The life sciences park houses Chinese research institutes such as the National Institutes of Biological Science, the State Biological Chips Engineering Research Center, and six other biological research institutes as well as R&D centers for Novo Nordisk and Genzyme.
>
> Zhangjiang Hi-Tech Park was established in 1992. It is home to several western MNCs and biotechnology firms, with over 100 domestic players. The Zhangjiang Park was one of the first to attract many of the major pharmaceutical and biotech companies and now boasts R&D centers for the majority of the world's leading pharma companies. Indeed, according to a survey undertaken in 2009, there were 319 life sciences companies undertaking R&D in the park, employing 20,000 scientists with 42 research facilities, hospitals, and many supporting small and medium-sized businesses.

Guangdong Province
China Regional Innovation
Capability
2nd
2 National Life Sciences Parks
3 Life Sciences State Key
Laboratories
800+ Life Sciences
Companies
Total VC investment in
Shenzhen, 2013
12% by amount of capital
8% by amount of deals
Total R&D investment in
the region
2013: $24B (12.2%)

Beijing and Tianjin
China Regional Innovation
Capability
Beijing *3rd*
2 National Life Sciences Parks
19 Life Sciences State Key
Laboratories
Total VC investment in Beijing,
2013:
34% by amount of capital
32% by amount of deals
Total R&D investment, 2013:
Beijing $20B (10%)
Tianjin $7B (3.6%)

Yangtze River Delta -
Jiangsu/Shanghai
China Regional Innovation
Capability
Jiangsu *1st,* Shanghai *4th*
3 National Life Sciences Parks
9 Life Sciences State Key
Laboratories
3000+ Life Sciences Companies
Life Sciences Market Share 27%
Total VC investment in the region,
2013:
25% by amount of capital
33% by amount of deals
(Shanghai, Jiangsu, and Zhejiang
combined)
Total R&D investment, 2013:
Shanghai $13B (6.6%)
Jiangsu $25B (12.6%)
Zhejiang $14B (6.9%)

Figure 16.6 Life sciences clusters
Source: China Regional Innovation Capability Report, 2013.

BioBay, located in Jiangsu Province, opened in 2007 to help the country develop its biological sector. The park has developed capabilities in gene technology (including both diagnostics and therapeutics). TLSP opened in 2008 as the gateway to the life sciences sector in western China.

Guangdong Province is home to the National Bio-Industry Base, the Guangzhou International Biological Island, the Shenzhen Biomedicine Innovations Industry Park, and the Zhongshan National Health Technology Industry Base. Shenzhen is also home to the Beijing Genomics Institute (BGI), the largest genomics organization in the world.

During the first decade of its existence, the Chinese biotechnology sector also had to build credibility with its western counterparts, as well as with the academic community (e.g., through peer-reviewed publications). This is a time-consuming process that requires focus and patience. Chinese companies formed numerous partnerships with multinational pharmaceutical companies (MNCs), many of whom established research facilities in China (see Chapter 14).

Regulatory reforms were also undertaken to build the credibility of the R&D and manufacturing effort. Regulation provided confidence that clinical trials could be conducted professionally and that the data acquired would be usable in drug applications in other countries. Clinical research organizations (CROs) were also formed to facilitate clinical development and regulatory filing for both domestic and foreign players. Other reforms included the 2010 Good Manufacturing Practice (GMP) regulations issued by China's State Food and Drug Administration (SFDA) to raise quality production standards to align with international standards.

Researchers advanced several recommendations that (a) elaborated the shortcomings present at that time and (b) served as benchmarks to chart the sector's progress from then on.[15] These recommendations included:

- Reform the financial environment to facilitate exit mechanisms for entrepreneurs and investors in the healthcare biotechnology sector.
- Create and promote specialty programs in biotech entrepreneurship and management.

- Leverage the phenomenon of the repatriation of Chinese scientists and business people to promote transnational companies that will be attractive to western investors and strategic partners.
- Promote credibility of domestic firms to the international community by enforcing uniform financial reporting, a transparent regulatory regime, and fair business practices.
- Enact timely legislation and regulations to nurture scientific and economic development.
- Stimulate rapid development of the intellectual property infrastructure through academic and exchange programs.
- Strengthen health systems infrastructure and distribution mechanisms in concert with the development of the industry to ensure that innovative healthcare biotechnology products are available to the entire domestic population.

The Chinese government has addressed several of these recommendations. The following two sections suggest that the impact on the sector as a whole and on companies in particular has been measurable.

Overview of Selected Biotechnology Companies

The landscape of Chinese biotechnology firms is complex by any definition. The variety of companies runs the gamut of specialties. National statistics on the Chinese biotechnology sector as a whole are sketchy, partly due to the definitional challenges as well as to the vibrancy of the industry.[16] One must also validate their real progress versus what the companies themselves report on their websites. This task of characterizing the sector has become more difficult as some securities analysts have terminated coverage of the Chinese biotechnology sector, fearing that it might never take off. It has also become more difficult due to a recent trend to take companies private, which results in a lack of transparency of their financial performance. Many of the public companies were taken private a few years after their initial public offerings. Two reasons for this trend were operating performance volatility related to price restraints in China and a significant supply of private equity capital. Nevertheless, despite the opacity, a recent report on the Chinese biotechnology industry provides some useful insights.[17]

China has a number of publicly traded companies in biotechnology or related fields. The companies list on stock exchanges globally, with a number listed in Hong Kong or the exchanges in New York. Estimates of that number vary widely, ranging from as few as 200 to as many as 1,000. The list of companies include those engaged in TCM, generic small molecule pharmaceuticals, pharmaceutical services such as contract manufacturing and clinical trial management, bioinformatics, and other activities not directly representative of molecularly driven research.

While in a growth phase, the Chinese biotechnology industry still has a significant focus on the "modernizing" of TCM – i.e., improving quality control and GMPs in the production, cultivation, and manufacturing of the herbal drugs. Indeed, analysts estimate the biotechnology sector lags far behind the market size of the chemical and TCM sides of the life sciences (see Figure 16.7). While the scientific community has made breakthroughs in some priority areas such as genomics, bioinformatics, identification of genes related to major diseases, molecular biology and biochemistry, cell and developmental biology, neurobiology, systematics and coevolution of animals and plants, it is not yet clear how these capabilities and the related technologies have transferred to industrial innovation.

The subsections below provide thumbnail sketches of companies that seem to fit the biotechnology definition; nevertheless, some are also active in TCM and pharmaceutical services. The companies are profiled in alphabetical order.

Amoytop Biotech (privately held)

Amoytop (http://amoytop.com) has been active for over 20 years and focuses on recombinant protein drugs developed under national standards.[18] It has positioned itself as the main provider under China's National Institute for the Control of Pharmaceutical and Biological Products (NICPBP) inside China's SFDA. Its capabilities have allowed it to produce and market three recombinant protein drugs, with an additional five drugs in clinical studies. Moreover, several countries have approved its GMPs that will allow it to export its products.

Beijing Tri-Prime Genetic Engineering Co., Ltd. (privately held)

Tri-Prime (www.triprime.com), formed in 1992, is credited as being one of the first Chinese biotech companies. It has pursued a fully integrated business model and established capability across the value chain from product development to commercial sales. It has proven itself adept at managing the regulatory and legal systems, as well as participating in out-licensing arrangements with a broad array of Chinese companies. It has led in the production

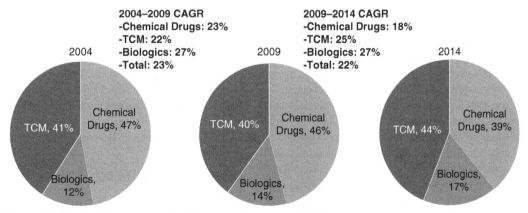

Figure 16.7 Biotech sector growth relative to pharma and TCM
Source: Jessica Li and Lillian Wan. China Healthcare Primer (Merrill Lynch, July 9, 2015).

and marketing of interferon, and its products are estimated to comprise half of total biologic sales in China. Its early activity established its leadership in establishing GMP standards.

Beijing Peking University WBL Biotech Co., Ltd (WPU)

WPU (www.wpu.com.cn/en/about/) could well be a global model for industrial/academic collaboration. While the focus has been on the modernization of TCM, its operational model has broader implications. It was created within ZLSP in 1994 and operates as a high-tech pharmaceutical joint venture with Luye Pharmaceutical Co., Ltd of Shandong and Peking University. It engages in research, development, manufacture, and marketing of medicines derived from natural sources and modern Chinese medicine. Its leading product – the Xuezhikang Capsule – is an advanced blood lipids regulator that melds modern biotechnology and TCM. The drug has been available in China for over 20 years, holds a pivotal place in patient care, and has become a standard of practice in the treatment of coronary disease. As the company extends sales into foreign markets, it has become a centerpiece of Chinese progress. The company is currently applying its model of drug discovery and development to depression.

BGI Shenzhen

BGI was founded in 1999 as a nonprofit research organization. Since then, it has grown into a multinational genomics company with significant global operations and a wide variety of next-generation sequencing (NGS) services – including whole genome sequencing, exome sequencing, and RNA sequencing. With more than 5,000 employees and R&D, manufacturing, and commercial operations around the world, BGI provides genomics solutions to address the research, pharmaceutical, and clinical markets. It also employs next-generation sequencing technology to improve human health and enable large-scale human, plant, and animal genomics research. The Gates Foundation and BGI signed a memorandum of understanding in September 2012 to join hands in global health and agricultural development, a partnership that has earned BGI many fans in the United States, including government officials who approved of BGI's acquisition of Complete Genomics for $180 million.[19] US competitors criticized the acquisition, stating that BGI would dominate the market.[20]

China National Biotec Group (HKSE: CNBG)

While not a new entity, CNBG (http://en.cnbg.com.cn/html/about/show_1.html) is a good example of a traditional pharmaceutical firm creating a subsidiary to focus on biotechnology. The China National Pharmaceutical Group Corporation (SinoPharm) formed CNBG as the first manufacturer of vaccines and blood products. CNBG includes six "Biological Products Institutes" that focus on R&D, production, and supply of vaccines for smallpox, polio, and other infectious diseases. Since its establishment nearly a century ago, it has produced billions of doses. The company is active in over 100 SFDA production facilities with current GMPs that produce over 200 types of biological products for disease prevention, diagnosis, and intervention. With operating revenue approaching US$ 1 billion, it is the largest biotechnology company in China.

China Shineway Pharmaceutical Group Limited (HKSE: 2877)

China Shineway (www.shineway.com.hk/eng/about/profile.php) engages in the development, manufacture, and sales of "modern Chinese medicines" – the application of contemporary quality control and production processes to the manufacture of TCM products. The company has 11 State Protected Chinese Medicines and has pursued quality control over its raw materials inputs by producing its herbs on dedicated farms. The company also has research programs in anti-virals.

Livzon Mabpharm (NSDQ: EPRS)

Livzon (www.livzon.com.cn/english/index.html) is five years old and operates as a subsidiary of Livzon Pharmaceutical Group Inc. Located in the center of

Zhuhai city, Guangdong Province, its research and process development center is equipped with advanced cell culture, fermentation, protein purification, formulation, and analytical facilities. The company enjoys support from the local government and expects to be one of the largest monoclonal antibody drug research and manufacturing centers in China. Livzon has developed an interesting business model to enable broad biotechnology research by other firms. It entered a joint venture with Zhuhai MAB Biological Technology Company Ltd. to develop monoclonal antibody and Fc-fusion protein therapeutics.

SciClone Pharmaceuticals, Inc (NASDAQ: SCLN)

SciClone Pharmaceuticals (www.sciclone.com/) is a US-based, publicly owned, and China-focused specialty pharmaceutical company based in Foster City, California. SciClone describes itself as a revenue-generating (~$150 million in annual sales as of this printing) specialty pharmaceutical company with a substantial commercial business in China and a product portfolio spanning major therapeutic markets including oncology, infectious diseases, and cardiovascular disorders. SciClone's proprietary lead product, ZADAXIN® (thymalfasin), is approved in over 30 countries and may be used for the treatment of hepatitis B (HBV), hepatitis C (HCV), certain cancers, and as a vaccine adjuvant, according to the local regulatory approvals. The company has successfully in-licensed and commercialized products to drive the company's long-term growth, including DC Bead®, a novel treatment for liver cancer. Through its promotion business with pharmaceutical partners, such as Baxter and Pfizer, SciClone also markets multiple branded products in China that are therapeutically differentiated.

Sinovac Biotech Ltd. (NASDAQ: SVA)

Sinovac Biotech Ltd. (www.sinovac.com/index.php) is a biopharmaceutical company that focuses on the research, development, manufacture, and commercialization of vaccines that protect against human infectious diseases. Sinovac's history dates back to its successful development of a hepatitis A vaccine in 1999 – the first inactivated hepatitis A vaccine developed in China. Over the past two decades, the company has developed and commercialized six human-used vaccines and one animal vaccine, advanced its R&D pipeline, and developed the first H1N1 vaccine in the world in 2009. Moreover, it has expanded its fully integrated platform with state-of-the-art research facilities, GMP-certified manufacturing facilities, and a sales force that reaches across China. The company is currently developing a novel vaccine against enterovirus 71, the cause of severe hand, foot, and mouth disease (HFMD) among children. The company's sales in 2014 were ~$63 million, but have been somewhat erratic over time. The company is not profitable but invests heavily (annual average of ~15 percent of sales) in R&D.

Shenzhen SiBiono Gene-Tech Co. Ltd. (SSGTCZ)

SiBiono Gene-Tech (http://en.sibiono.com/) is arguably the current centerpiece of Chinese biotechnology, due to its innovation and leadership in gene therapy globally. It opened at the Shenzhen High-Tech Industrial Park in March 1998. In 2003, the company's innovative product Gendicine®, an adenovirus-based recombinant human p53 for injection (rAd-p53, Inj), was approved by the SFDA, making it the world's first marketable gene therapy new drug. The company recently diversified away from its original research-centered enterprise to become a more fully integrated biopharmaceutical enterprise. As a private company it does not report its financial performance.

Shanghai ChemPartner (privately held)

Established in 2002, ChemPartner (www.shangpharma.com/) is the service division of the ShangPharma group and provides a range of services for the pharmaceutical and biotechnology industry. Services consist of discovery biologics, discovery chemistry, discovery biology and preclinical development, pharmaceutical development, and small molecule and biologics manufacturing services. The company was briefly listed on the

NASDAQ but was taken private in 2013 and, as such, does not report financials.

Simcere Pharmaceutical Group

Founded in 1995, Simcere (http://eng.simcere.com /index.asp) transformed itself from a distributor of pharmaceutical products to a manufacturer and supplier of medicines in China's rapidly growing pharmaceutical market. Simcere currently operates five GMP-certified manufacturing facilities, two nationwide sales and marketing subsidiaries, a research and development center, and manages over 4,000 employees. It was the first Chinese chemical and biological drug company to list on the New York Stock Exchange (NYSE). The company currently manufactures and sells over 45 pharmaceutical products that treat a range of medical conditions such as tumors, cardio-cerebral vascular diseases, and infections. Endu, an innovative anti-angiogenic drug used in the treatment of non-small-cell lung cancer, was the world's first listed recombinant human endostatin and has acquired patent protection in China and the United States. In 2009, Simcere acquired a 35 percent equity stake in Shanghai Celgen Bio-Pharmaceutical Co., Ltd., which marked its entry into the field of antibody development. In 2011, it received a new drug approval from SFDA for Iremod, a new drug in the category of disease modifying anti-rheumatic drugs. The company was listed on the NYSE but was taken private in 2013 in the wake of revenue volatility stemming, in part, from mandated price cuts by the government.

WuXi PharmaTech (NYSE: WX)

WuXi PharmaTech (http://ir.wuxipharmatech.com /phoenix.zhtml?c=212698&p=irol-IRHome)   is China's leading global contract R&D services provider serving the pharmaceutical, biotechnology, and medical device sectors. The company is headquartered in Shanghai and operates in both China and the United States. The company provides a broad, integrated portfolio of laboratory and manufacturing services that span the R&D process. The services are designed to help its global partners shorten the time and lower the cost of R&D. WuXi

PharmaTech is the product of the 2008 merger of WuXi PharmaTech Inc., a chemistry-based company, and AppTec Laboratory Services Inc., a US company with expertise in medical-device and biologics testing. WuXi PharmaTech Inc. expanded its services rapidly throughout the decade, offering discovery chemistry services (in 2001), process development (2003), research manufacturing (2004), bioanalytical chemistry (2005), discovery biology (2006), toxicology and formulation (2007), commercial manufacturing (2009), genomics, clinical trial management, and research reagents (2011), and biologics discovery, development, and manufacturing (2012). The company's client list includes most of the major pharmaceutical and biotechnology companies. Revenues for 2015 are projected to reach ~$800 million.

Biotechnology Expansion: Strategies and Obstacles

China designated the biotechnology industry as one of seven pillar industries in its 12th FYP. These are emerging industries that are expected to transform the economy and drive economic growth. Based on that decision, the Chinese government is dramatically expanding its resources for innovative biopharmaceutical R&D. The FYP called for an initial investment of 10 billion RMB in biotechnology between 2011 and 2015, with an additional infusion of 73 billion RMB between 2015 and 2020. Key investment areas in biologics in the 12th FYP included genetically-engineered proteins and peptides, nucleic acid drugs and gene therapies, vaccines, humanized monoclonal antibodies, stem cell therapies, and blood products (e.g., Factor VIII).[21] Key investment areas in China's 13th FYP include new antibody structures, biospecific antibodies, antibody-drug conjugates, proteins and peptide drugs with new structures, biosimilars, and vaccines with new formulations.[22]

The focus on biotechnology is evidenced by a dramatic undertaking of western-originated projects by Chinese firms. The increase is reflected in growing numbers of in-licenses, joint ventures, and mergers and acquisitions. China's research institutes and universities have fully recognized the potential impact of biotechnology and have oriented themselves to R&D activities and industrialization.[23]

Still, problems remain that limit the sustainable development of China's biotechnology sector. For example, despite the growing amount of public R&D funds invested in biotechnology, the accumulation of science and technology (S&T) innovation is relatively small. As an emerging market, China's biotechnology lacks commercial experience, original products, and suitable and effective ways to transform its S&T achievements into products. These limitations are discussed in greater detail in the subsections below.

R&D Investment

In 2010, analysts estimated that the Chinese biopharmaceutical sector would reach revenues of $9 billion by 2015. While the data are somewhat elusive and variable, given the private nature of the sector, the reality is probably closer to $3–4 billion (see Chapter 14 for comparable estimates). This is respectable performance, especially relative to India. However, R&D investment is generally a function of three elements: the percentage of sales invested, the use of venture capital, and the development of contractual agreements with MNCs. China reportedly has over 300 private equity and venture capital (PE/VC) investors that focus on the life sciences sector, with an aggregate investment of roughly $7 billion between 2009 and 2013. Life sciences must compete with other healthcare sectors such as medical devices, diagnostics, and healthcare services; in turn, healthcare must compete with other industrial sectors (e.g., internet, logistics, and telecommunications).[24] Other funding sources include venture arms established by large Chinese pharmaceutical firms (e.g., Sinopharm Capital) and government "guidance funds" to leverage PE/VC investments.

Venture capital as a means of funding the growth of the industry is still in scarce supply, especially for the formation and launch of new biotechnology companies. The Chinese government began to address this need when they modified the Guidance Fund Scheme to encourage the formation of early stage tech-oriented venture funds throughout the country. A pilot program of 20 venture funds

that launched with approximately $1 billion quickly proliferated to nearly 100 funds managing in excess of $5 billion.[25] These venture funds are directed at six strategic technology areas, one of which is biotechnology.

Perhaps 10 percent of drugs in various stages of development are ultimately destined to reach the market, and, of these, only one in five recovers the investment made. This is a risky business and the aggregate investment in medicinal development must necessarily be large to support an extensive pipeline and deliver a reasonable portfolio of products. It is difficult for a sector to start from a standstill in any circumstances; a sector as capital intensive as biotechnology must often rely on investment by governments to kick-start it. Even in the free-enterprise US market, the biotechnology sector was built on NIH investments in basic research over a 30-year period prior to the establishment of the first biotechnology companies in the mid-1970s.

National investment in basic life sciences research continues in parallel with private investment today. In China, many R&D investments in biotechnology originate with government funding. The FYPs include funding support for pre-commercialization pharmaceutical research from the National Major Scientific and Technological Special Project for Significant New Drugs Development (SNDD). SNDD funding amounted to $1.1 billion in the 11th FYP, $6.5 billion in the 12th FYP, and $12.5 billion in the 13th FYP. Funding is also available from National Nature Science and the National S&T Program; the latter encompasses China National Basic Research Program (Program 973) and China State High-Tech Development Plan (Program 863).[26] Within the industrial sector in China, the allocation of revenues toward R&D is still far below the normal level of counterpart biotechnology companies in the United States, Europe, Japan, and even India, an emerging market in its own right. For example, the percent of R&D investment in new medicines in the United States and Japan was 22 percent and 15 percent of revenues, respectively; by contrast, the most recent data in China suggest that such investment is in the low single digits, perhaps as low as 2 percent.[27]

Of course, as noted above, biotechnology research is no longer the sole province of the so-called biotechnology companies in the United States. The long-established MNCs began to shift their research approach from traditional medicinal chemistry to genetics and molecular biology in the 1980s. This shift was built on a platform of drug discovery and development that was already a century in the making. Arguably, China's modern pharmaceutical enterprises were generally established in the 1950s, but their emphasis from then until now has been largely on the production of generic medicines based on the innovative work of western companies. In recent years, the Chinese pharmaceutical industry has begun more discovery and innovation, and now is a key global provider of active pharmaceutical ingredients (APIs). By the same token, the emerging Chinese biotechnology enterprises have relatively short histories on which to build the fully integrated capability of rival companies outside China. This, of course, requires evolution, which may be accelerated by national policies that promote the industry and through educational priorities that promote the investment of financial and human resources in the sector.

Sector Fragmentation

Part of the innovation problem in China's biopharmaceutical sector lies in its fragmentation. The sector has anywhere from 5,000 to 7,500 companies, has developed no blockbuster products, and makes mostly low-profit, generic drugs. According to one analyst, many of the smaller pharmaceutical companies earn less than 1.5 cents per pill and struggle to survive.[28] Most companies thus lack the capital to develop their competitive capabilities, let alone manage start-up risks. The situation is also challenging the larger companies, who face patent expirations on 800–900 drugs in 2016.[29]

The irony here is striking. While western biopharmaceutical firms are moving from larger R&D enterprises to smaller and more agile operations, China's biopharmaceutical sector needs to move in the opposite direction to larger-scale enterprises. Such consolidation can help the country's biotechnology firms achieve some scale economies (at least in terms of land, construction, and production) as

well as handle the cost of meeting regulatory requirements. Larger size may also help in terms of human resource recruitment as well as firm survival.

Translation Chasm

Innovation systems in biotechnology are evolving. Research institutes and universities still play the dominant role. The good news is that universities and research institutes are producing a large and growing number of biotechnical R&D personnel as well as considerable technical capabilities and experience.[30] This training pipeline includes growing numbers of graduates from both bachelor's programs and doctoral programs.[31] This is an investment that will pay off and have a positive impact on the sector's future. Figure 16.8 describes the biotechnology innovation ecosystem in China. However, the sector requires translational capabilities that can turn academic research and R&D into products that meet market needs. To make that type of transition, China may need to develop innovation ecosystems like those found in the United States (see, for example, the life sciences cluster in Boston/Cambridge, Massachusetts – Figure 16.9).

A case in point is the celebrated increase in the number of peer-reviewed journal articles and filing of patents in China. There are two problems with the increased scholarly output, however. First, while China ranks second to the United States in terms of scientific publications issued between 2003 and 2011, it ranks quite low in the percentage of top-cited publications.[32] This low number is likely due to the fact that Chinese researchers have not undertaken many collaborative efforts with foreign researchers (see Figure 16.10).[33] Additionally, while more papers and patents are produced, S&T achievements often do not translate into commercial potential.

As an example, biotechnology patent applications from academic and research institutions have outnumbered those filed by commercial enterprises by approximately three to one. This in and of itself is not a problem. Similar ratios are found in the United States and Europe. The problem arises from a still-evolving technology transfer system. While the Chinese government has addressed the need for

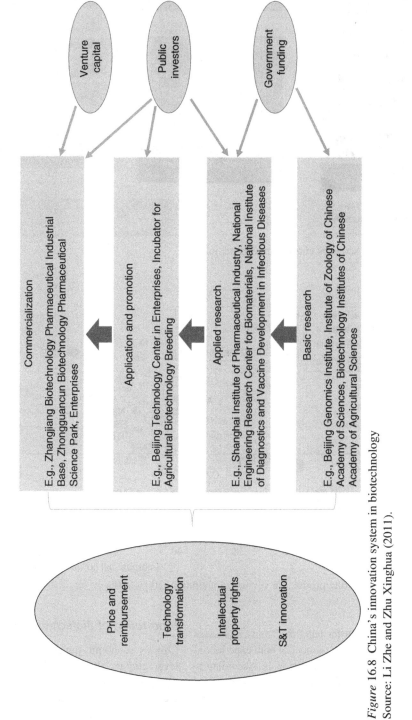

Figure 16.8 China's innovation system in biotechnology
Source: Li Zhe and Zhu Xinghua (2011).

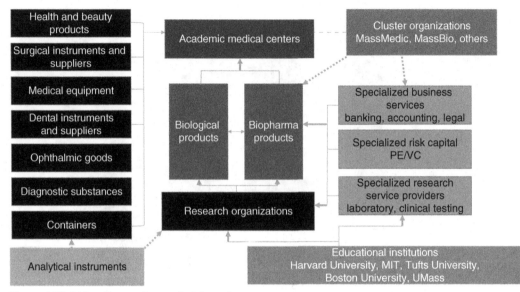

Figure 16.9 Life sciences clusters in Massachusetts

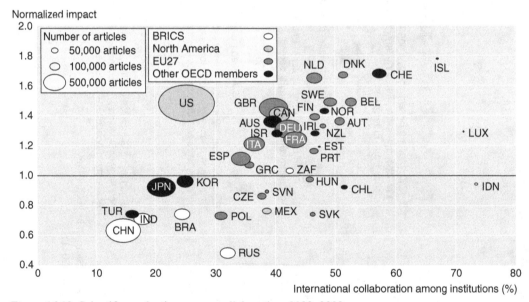

Figure 16.10 Scientific production versus collaboration, 2003–2009

new technology transfer legal mechanisms, success depends on an adequate number of both experienced academic and industrial professionals. According to the OECD, China's life sciences sector faces some of the highest barriers to entrepreneurship (e.g., administrative burdens on start-ups).[34]

Exportation of Biotechnology Products

China's economic juggernaut has been fueled by leveraging its labor cost advantages and extraordinary capability in industrial engineering and manufacturing. Its biotechnology sector has not yet demonstrated such capability. To be sure, the country has a potential market of 1.3 billion patients with enormous needs and the capacity to absorb the output of even global medical industries. There is thus enormous potential for Chinese biotechnology to grow simply by meeting potential domestic demand, especially if the sector focuses on diseases that affect the Chinese and East Asian populations (see Chapter 3).

Nevertheless, China measures the progress and performance of its domestic industries in terms of their contribution to the positive balance of payments that the Chinese economy has enjoyed for the last two decades. One metric to illustrate this perceived gap is that nearly 1,300 pharmaceutical enterprises in China have met the standards for domestic GMP certification, but as of this writing, fewer than 100 have been registered or certified under current GMPs by US and EU regulators. By contrast, over 1,000 facilities in India have been so approved and contribute some $30 billion to the Indian economy.

Another metric is the number of Patent Cooperation Treaty (PCT) applications filed through the World Intellectual Property Organization (WIPO). Such applications allow life sciences companies to seek simultaneous patent protection in member countries. Such applications can reduce the costs and barriers to both global trade and innovation, but are not a substitute for seeking patent protection at the national level. Global data reveal a 130 percent increase in pharmaceutical and biotechnology PCT applications by China between 2009 and 2012, and a 34.2 percent increase between 2011 and 2012.[35] Across all life sciences sectors (biopharma, medical equipment and instruments, crop and food sciences), Asia ranked third in PCT applications (26 percent) behind North America (41 percent) and Europe (31 percent). However, additional data show that China ranks low in terms of (a) the proportion of its PCT applications with at least one foreign inventor and (b) the percentage of foreign inventors among all inventors on these applications. Thus, the countries in Asia that are growing the fastest in terms of life sciences applications are the least collaborative.

Given the role of collaborative networks in R&D and economic clusters, this gap may inhibit China's growth as a global player in biopharma. China may be banking on domestic government funding of life sciences parks and the return of foreign-trained scientists to staff them in order to be self-sustaining. Research suggests that scientists who "go it alone" do so to gain credit and improve their reputations, but also do so at the expense of the quality, creativity, and external citation count of the work.[36]

Tracking of Progress

According to media reports, "China's big biotech bet [is] starting to pay off."[37] One illustration is the publication of research that used CRISPR-Cas9 gene editing technology to alter the DNA of human embryos.[38] There is growing patent portfolio activity in gene editing by Chinese research institutions. China and its BGI facility are also reportedly global leaders in gene sequencing.[39] Another illustration is the success of Chipscreen Biosciences in achieving its primary endpoint in a Phase II oncology clinical trial in 2014.[40] Moreover, there appears to be growing collaboration with western biotechnology firms (e.g., Cellular Biomedicine Group).[41] In recent years, life sciences and biotechnology research has made considerable progress in the post-genomics, proteomics, stem cell, transgenic plant, and other life sciences. A growing number of biological drugs with intellectual property rights have entered clinical trials.[42] The existence of pharmaceutical service businesses, such as WuXi and the overall rich and unique population available for clinical trials of diseases, provides an inviting setting for the application of new technology. The country is also taking steps to speed up the regulatory approval process for new drugs within the SFDA as well as approval for biosimilars.

Conclusion: Policy Innovation and the Road to Progress

China's government has developed a set of policies to accelerate the development of its biotechnology sector (see Table 16.2).[43] Policy objectives include: (1) focus technological, human capital, and financial capital resources on the biotechnology sector, (2) promote innovation and

Table 16.2 Relevant policy initiatives

Policy	Agencies Issued	Year
Decision on accelerating the fostering and development of new strategic industries	State Council	2010
Policies on promoting the development of biotechnology industry	State Council	2009
Eleventh Five-Year Plan for biotechnology industry development	State Council	2007
Eleventh Five-Year Plan for science and technology development	Ministry of Science and Technology	2006
The guidelines on national medium and long-term program for science and technology development (2006–2020)	State Council	2006

Source: Li Zhe and Zhu Xinghua (2011).

industrialization of biotechnology, (3) accelerate the scaling up, agglomeration, and international development of China's biotechnology sector, (4) enhance the innovation capability of biotech enterprises, and encourage them to develop new biological technologies, products, and standards with intellectual property rights, and (5) foster several large transnational biotechnology enterprises, as well as a large number of innovative small and medium-sized enterprises, to build a new biotechnology industrial base with marked specialization.

Notes

1. This section borrows heavily from the lead author's prior work. See Justin Chakma, Gordon Sun, Jeffrey Steinberg et al. 2014. "Asia's Ascent – Global Trends in Biomedical R&D Expenditures," *New England Journal of Medicine* 370(1): 3–6.
2. Richard Daverman. 2014. "China is Asia's Biggest Biotech Cluster," *ChinaBio Today.* Available online at: www.chinabiotoday.com/articles/20140405. Accessed on January 11, 2016.
3. For a more in-depth analysis and comparison of these two sectors, see Lawton R. Burns (Ed.). 2012. *The Business of Healthcare Innovation – Second Edition* (Cambridge, UK: Cambridge University Press): chapters 2 and 4.
4. Eric Schmidt. 2015. "Biotechnology Sector Overview." Presentation to the Wharton School, Novermber 17.
5. Bernard Munos. 2015. "2014 New Drug Approvals Hit 18-Year High," *Fortune* (January 2).
6. Donald Drakeman. 2014. "Benchmarking Biotech and Pharmaceutical Product Development," *Nature Biotechnology* 32(7): 621–625.
7. Drakeman. 2014. "Benchmarking Biotech and Pharmaceutical Product Development."
8. Schmidt. 2015. "Biotechnology Sector Overview."
9. Drakeman. 2014. "Benchmarking Biotech and Pharmaceutical Product Development."
10. Lawton R. Burns, Sean Nicholson, and Joanna Wolkowski. 2012. "Pharmaceutical Strategy and the Evolving Role of Merger and Acquisition," in Lawton R. Burns (Ed.), *The Business of Healthcare Innovation – Second Edition* (Cambridge, UK: Cambridge University Press): chapter 3.
11. Drakeman. 2014. "Benchmarking Biotech and Pharmaceutical Product Development."
12. Sarah Frew, Stephen Sammut, Alysha Sore et al J. 2008. "Chinese Health Biotech and the Billion-patient Market," *Nature Biotechnology* 25(1) (January): 37–53.
13. bioXclusters. 2012. *Country Report: China.* Available online at: https://bioxclusters.files.wordpress.com/2012/11/country-report-china.pdf. Accessed on January 12, 2016.
14. Roger Humphrey. 2014. *Life Sciences Cluster Report: Global 2014* (New York: JLL). Martyn Link. 2011. "China's Life Science Clusters," *The Foresighter* (April 11).

Available online at: https://theforesighter.word press.com/2011/04/18/chinas-life-science-clus ters/. Accessed on January 12, 2016.

15. Chakma et al. 2014. "Asia's Ascent."

16. The 2015 Chinese Statistical Yearbook can be found at www.stats.gov.cn/tjsj/ndsj/2015/ indexeh.htm, but the classification of industries is not broken down to a level of granularity where pharmaceutical, let alone biotechnology, companies can be identified. Many of the Chinese biotechnology companies – similar to their US counterparts – are no more than two scientists and a dog in the equivalent of a Chinese garage, or so the saying goes. The OECD website (at www.oecd.org /science/biotech/biotechnologystatistics-china .htm) offers a framework for a statistical compilation done in 2003, but the output is not widely available. The survey structure is a useful paradigm for gathering data in the future. Readers seeking to establish an international basis for benchmarking China are directed to www.oecd.org/sti/inno/keybiotechnologyindi cators.htm.

17. Acquisdata. 2015. "China Biotechnology: Industry Snapshots No 3335" (September 3). Available online at: www.acquisdata.com. Accessed on January 13, 2016.

18. These include rhGM-CSF, rhG-CSF, rh-IL-11, rhIFNα-2a, rhIFNα-2b.

19. Shu-Jing Chen. 2013. "How China's Biggest Biotech Company Cracked the U.S. Market," *Forbes Asia*. Available online at: www.forbes .com/sites/shuchingjeanchen/2013/09/13/how-chinas-biggest-biotech-company-cracked-the-u-s-market/#2715e4857a0b5a7ae3dc2b48. Accessed on January 13, 2016.

20. Michael Specter. 2014. "The Gene Factory," *The New Yorker* (January 6). Available online at: www.newyorker.com/magazine/2014/01/ 06/the-gene-factory. Accessed on January 12, 2016.

21. Jessica Li and Lillian Wan. 2015. *China Healthcare Primer* (Hong Kong: Bank of America/Merrill Lynch, July 9). Xuefei Mao. 2014. *Entering China's Emerging Life Sciences Markets: The Opportunity for Ontario Startups*

(Toronto, ON, Canada: MaRS Market Insights, December).

22. Mao. 2014. *Entering China's Emerging Life Sciences Markets*.

23. Li Zhe and Zhu Xinghua. 2011. "China's Biotechnology Industry: Barriers to Overcome and Opportunities to Exploit," *Tech Monitor* (March–April): 31–36.

24. Mao. 2014. *Entering China's Emerging Life Sciences Markets*.

25. Data are taken from an unpublished report that the lead author prepared for the Chinese NDRC, Ministry of Finance, and the World Bank.

26. Fangzhu Zhang, Philip Cooke, and Fulong Wu. 2011. "State-sponsored Research and Development: A Case Study of China's Biotechnology," *Regional Studies* 45(5) (May): 575–595.

27. Zhu Chen, Hong-Guang Wang, Zhao-Jun Wen et al. 2007. "Life Sciences and Biotechnology in China," *Philosophical Transactions of the Royal Society* 362: 947–957.

28. Mao. 2014. *Entering China's Emerging Life Sciences Markets*.

29. Ibid.

30. Grace Wong. 2008. "Developing China's Homegrown Biotechnology Workforce," *Nature Biotechnology* 26(3): 353–354.

31. Humphrey. 2014. *Life Sciences Cluster Report*.

32. Ibid.

33. OECD. 2011. *OECD Science, Technology and Industry Scoreboard 2011*. Available online at: www.oecd.org/science/sci-tech/48712591.pdf. Accessed on January 12, 2016.

34. OECD. 2013. *Science, Technology and Industry Scoreboard 2013*.

35. Humphrey. 2014. *Life Sciences Cluster Report*.

36. Michael Bikard, Fiona Murray, and Joshua Gans. 2015. "Exploring Trade-offs in the Organization of Scientific Work: Collaboration and Scientific Reward," *Management Science* 61(7): 1473–1495.

37. Alexandra Harney and Ben Hirschler. 2015. "China's Big Biotech Bet Starting to Pay Off," *Reuters* (June 9). Available online at:

www.reuters.com/article/us-china-biotech-idUSKBN0OP2EF20150609. Accessed on January 12, 2016.

38. Puping Liang, Yanwen Xu, Xiya Zhang et al. 2015. "CRISPR/Cas9-mediated Gene Editing in Human Triponuclear Zygotes," *Protein Cell* 6(5): 363–372.

39. Specter. 2014. "The Gene Factory."

40. E. J. Lane. 2015. "Biotech in China is Built Brick-by-Brick, But More Money Would Help, BeiGene's Oyler Says," *FiercePharmaAsia* (March 12). Available online at: www.fiercepharmaasia.com/story/biotech-china-getting-built-brick-brick-more-money-would-help-beigenes-oyle/2015-03-12. Accessed on January 12, 2016.

41. E. J. Lane. 2015. "CBMG says China and U.S. Growing Quickly Closer in Biotech Space," *FiercePharmaAsia* (May 25). Available online at: www.fiercepharmaasia.com/story/cbmg-says-china-and-us-growing-quickly-closer-biotech-space/2015-05-25. Accessed on January 12, 2016.

42. Ming Hu and Jiao Feng. 2014. "Legal Protection of China's Biotechnology Patents," *Biotechnology Law Report* 33(3): 103–107.

43. Zhe and Xinghua. 2011. "China's Biotechnology Industry."

Index

Printed in the United States
By Bookmasters